CHILTON COMPANY

REPAIR MANUAL

TOYOTA

DATE DUE

CELICA · SUPRA
1986-90

Covers all models of Toyota Celica and Toyota Supra

President GARY INGERSOLL

Senior Vice President, Book Publishing and Research RONALD A. HOXTER

Publisher KERRY A. FREEMAN, S.A.E.

Editor–in–Chief DEAN F. MORGANTINI, S.A.E.

Senior Editor RICHARD J. RIVELE, S.A.E.

Editor ANTHONY TORTORICI, S.A.E.

CHILTON BOOK COMPANY
Radnor, Pennsylvania
19089

CONTENTS

GENERAL INFORMATION and MAINTENANCE

1 How to use this book
2 Tools and Equipment
4 Safety
6 Vehicle Identification
10 Routine Maintenance
53 Trailer Towing

ENGINE PERFORMANCE and TUNE-UP

59 Tune-Up Procedures
60 Tune-Up Specifications
63 Firing Orders

ENGINE and ENGINE OVERHAUL

92 Engine Electrical System
122 Engine Service
109 Engine Specifications
189 Exhaust System

EMISSION CONTROLS

191 Emission Controls System and Service
195 Vacuum Diagrams

FUEL SYSTEM

203 Gasoline Fuel Injection System

CHASSIS ELECTRICAL

241 Heating and Air Conditioning
245 Instruments and Switches
245 Lighting
249 Circuit Protection

DRIVE TRAIN

265 Manual Transmission
298 Clutch
303 Automatic Transmission

SUSPENSION and STEERING

321 Front Suspension
336 Rear Suspension
344 Steering

BRAKES

368 Front Disc Brakes
375 Rear Disc Brakes
372 Rear Drum Brakes
377 Parking Brake

BODY

371 Exterior
383 Interior

MECHANIC'S DATA

388 Mechanic's Data
390 Glossary
396 Abbreviations

**221 Chilton's Fuel Economy
and Tune-Up Tips**

381 Chilton's Body Repair Tips

SAFETY NOTICE

Proper service and repair procedures are vital to the safe, reliable operation of all motor vehicles, as well as the safety of those performing repairs. This book outlines procedures for serviceing and repairing vehicles using safe effective methods. The procedures contain many NOTES, CAUTIONS and WARNINGS which should be followed along with standard safety procedures to eliminate the possibility of personal injury or improper service which could damage the vehicle or compromise its safety.

It is important to note that repair procedures and techniques, tools and parts for servicing motor vehicles, as well as the skill and experience of the individual performing the work vary widely. It is not possible to anticipate all of the conceivable ways or conditions under which vehicles may be serviced, or to provide cautions as to all of the possible hazards that may result. Standard and accepted safety precautions and equipment should be used during cutting, grinding, chiseling, prying,or any other process that can cause material removal or projectiles.

Some procedures require the use of tools specially designed for a specific purpose. Before substituting another tool or procedure, you ust be com-pletely satisfied that neither your personal safety, nor the performance of the vehicle will be endangered.

Although the information in this guide is based on industry sources and is as complete as possible at the time of publication, the possibility exists that the manufacturer made later changes which could not be included here. While striving for total accuracy, Chilton Book Company cannot assume responsibilty for any errors, changes, or omissions that may occur in the compilation of this data.

PART NUMBERS

Part numbers listed in the reference are not recommendations by Chilton for any product by brand name. They are references that can be used with interchange manuals and aftermarket supplier catalogs to locate each brand supplier's discrete part number.

SPECIAL TOOLS

Special tools are recommended by the vehicle manufacturer to perform their specific job. Use has been kept to a minimum, but where absolutely neccesary, they are referred to in the text by the part number of the tool manufacturer. These tools can be purchased, under the appropiate part number, from Toyota dealers or Toyota Motor Sales, U.S.A. (address below) or an equivalent tool can be purchased locally from a tool supplier or parts outlet. Before substituting any tool for the one recommended, read the SAFETY NOTICE at the top of this page.

ACKNOWLEDGEMENTS

The Chilton Book Company expresses appreciation to Toyota Motor Sales, U.S.A., Inc.. 2055 W. 190th Street, Torrance California 90504, for their generous assistance

Copyright© 1990 by Chilton Book Company
All Rights Reserved
Published in Radnor, Pennsylvania 19089 by Chilton Book Company

Manufactured in the United States of America
 34567890   765432109

Chilton's Repair Manual: Toyota Celica/Supra 1986–90
ISBN 0–8019–8058–5
Library of Congress Catalog Card No. 90–055425

General Information and Maintenance

HOW TO USE THIS BOOK

Chilton's Repair Manual for the Toyota Celica and Supra is intended to teach you more about the inner workings of your automobile and save you money on its upkeep. Chapters 1 and 2 will probably be most frequently used in the book. Chapter 1 contains all the information that may be required at a moment's notice. Aside from giving the location of various serial numbers and the proper towing instructions, it also contains all the information on basic day-to-day maintenance that you will need to insure good performance and long component life. Chapter 2 covers the necessary tune-up procedures which will assist you not only in keeping the engine running properly and at peak performance levels, but also in restoring some of the more delicate components to operating condition in the event of a failure. Chapters 3 through 10 cover repairs (rather than maintenance) for various portions of the car, with each chapter covering either one separate system or two related systems. The Mechanic's Data then lists general information which may be useful in rebuilding the engine or performing some other operation on any car.

When using the Table of Contents, refer to the bold listings for the subject of the chapter and the smaller listings (or the index) for information on a particular component.

In general, there are three things a proficient mechanic has which must be considered when a non-professional does work on a car. These are:

1. A sound knowledge of the construction of the parts he is working with, their order of assembly, etc. Much of this knowledge simply comes from past experience.

2. A knowledge of potentially hazardous situations, particularly how to prevent them. Common sense and thinking ahead are a large part of this knowledge.

3. Manual dexterity and simple knowledge of mechanical laws. When it comes to tightening things, there is generally a slim area between too loose to properly seal and too tight, risking damage or warping. When dealing with major engine parts, or with any aluminum component, it pays to buy a torque wrench and go by the recommended figures.

This book provides step-by-step instructions and illustrations whenever possible. Use them carefully and wisely—don't jump headlong into disassembly. When there is doubt about being able to readily reassemble something, make a careful drawing of the component before taking it apart. Assembly always looks simple when everything is still together.

Throughout the procedures in this book you will encounter assorted **CAUTIONS, WARNINGS** and **NOTES.**

• A **CAUTION** warns you of the risk of personal injury. Pay strict attention to all conditions marked with a caution.

• A **WARNING** alerts you to the possibility of physical damage to mechanical components. Warnings may indicate something that must be done or something that must not be done. Observing the warnings will save you additional effort and possibly great expense.

• A **NOTE** is additional helpful information or a reminder. Use the notes to make the job easier.

Consequently, you should always read through the entire procedure before beginning the work so as to familiarize yourself with any special problems which may occur during the procedure. Since no number of warnings could cover every possible situation, you should work slowly and try to envision what is going to happen in each operation ahead of time.

On many illustrations you will notice components tagged with a small black diamond. This indicates the part cannot be reused once removed. Make certain to study the diagrams as well as the procedure; have all the necessary replacement parts on hand before beginning disassembly. There is nothing more frustrating than walking to the bus stop Monday morning because you were one part short on Sunday afternoon. In general, cotter pins, spring clips, fiber or paper gaskets, oil seals, grease seals, O-rings and all self–locking nuts cannot be reused. Pushing your luck to save on minor parts will cost you much more in lost time and money later.

Many procedures in this book require you to "label and disconnect..." a group of lines, hoses or wires. Don't be lulled into thinking you can remember where everything goes—you won't. If you hook up vacuum or fuel lines incorrectly, the car will run poorly, if at all. If you hook up electrical wiring incorrectly, you may instantly learn a very expensive lesson.

You don't need to know the official or engineering name for each hose or line. A piece of masking tape on the hose and a piece on its fitting will allow you assign your own label such as the letter A or a short name. As long as you remember your own code, the lines can be reconnected by matching similar letters or names. Do remember that tape will dissolve in gasoline or other fluids; if a component is to be washed or cleaned, use another method of identification. A permanent felt tip marker can be very handy for marking metal parts. Remove any tape or paper labels after assembly.

It's necessary to mention the difference between maintenance and repair. Maintenance includes routine inspections, adjustments, and replacement of parts which show signs of wear. Maintenance compensates for wear or deterioration. Repair implies that something has broken or is not working. Need for repair is often caused by lack of maintenance. Example: Draining and refilling the automatic transmission fluid is maintenance recommended by the manufacturer at specific mileage intervals. Failure to do this will ruin the transmission, requiring very expensive repairs. While no maintenance program can prevent items from breaking or wearing out, a general rule can be stated: MAINTENANCE IS CHEAPER THAN REPAIR.

Some basic mechanic's rules must be learned. Whenever the left side of the car is mentioned it means the driver's side of the car; this rule does not change because you are under the car. Conversely, the right side of the car means the passenger's side. Most screws and bolts are removed by turning counterclockwise and tightened by turning clockwise.

Safety is the most important rule. Constantly be aware of the dangers involved in working on an automobile and take the proper precautions.Think ahead, work slowly, and anticipate problems before they occur. Use jackstands when working under a raised vehicle. Don't smoke or allow an exposed flame to come near the battery or any parts of the fuel system. If you are using a kerosene heater during the winter, always turn it off or put it well away from the car when charging the battery or performing any item that could release liquid gasoline or gasoline vapors. Use the proper tool and use it correctly. Bruised knuckles and skinned fingers aren't a mechanic's standard equipment. Always take your time and have patience; once you have some experience and gain confidence, working on your car will become an enjoyable hobby.

NOTE: *Special tools are occasionally necessary to perform a specific job or are recommended to make a job easier. Their use has been kept to a minimum. When a special tool is indicated, it will be referred to by the manufacturer's designation. Toyota designates these as SSTs—Special Shop Tools, followed by the part number. Where possible, an illustration will be provided. Some special tools are unique to the vehicle, others are the manufacturer's version of common repair tools. Please reread the safety notice and special tools notice at the very front of the book.*

TOOLS AND EQUIPMENT

The service procedures in this book pre–suppose a familiarity with hand tools and their proper use. However, it is possible that you may have a limited amount of experience with the sort of equipment needed to work on an automobile. This section is designed to help you assemble a basic set of tools that will handle most of the jobs you may undertake.

In addition to the normal assortment of screwdrivers and pliers, automotive service work requires an investment in wrenches, sockets (and the handles needed to drive them), and various measuring tools such as torque wrenches and feeler gauges.

You will find that virtually every nut and bolt on your Toyota is metric. Therefore, despite a few close size similarities, standard inch size tools will not fit and must not be used. You will need a set of metric wrenches as your most basic tool kit, ranging from about 6mm to 17mm in size. High quality forged wrenches are available in three styles: open end, box end, and combination open/box end. The combina-

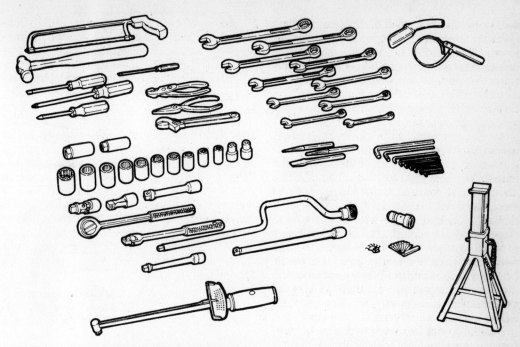

A basic collection of hand tools is necessary for automotive service

tion tools are generally the most desirable as a starter set; the wrenches shown in the accompanying illustration are of the combination type. If you plan to do any work on the hydraulic system, a set of line wrenches (sometimes called flare nut wrenches) is highly recommended.

The other set of tools inevitably required is a ratchet handle and socket set. This set should have the same size range as your wrench set. The ratchet, extension, and flex drives for the sockets are available in many sizes; it is advisable to choose a $^3/_8$ in. drive set initially. One break in the inch/metric sizing war is that metric sized sockets sold in the U.S. have inch sized drive ($^1/_4$ in., $^3/_8$ in., $^1/_2$ in., etc.). Thus, if you already have an inch sized socket set, you need only buy new metric sockets in the sizes needed. Sockets are available in six– and twelve–point versions; six–point types are stronger and are a good choice for a first set. The choice of a drive handle for the sockets should be made with some care.

If this is your first set, take the plunge and invest in a flex–head ratchet; it will get into many places otherwise accessible only through a long chain of universal joints, extensions, and adapters. An alternative is a flex handle, which lacks the ratcheting feature but has a head which pivots 180°; such a tool is shown below the ratchet handle in the illustration. In addition to the range of sockets mentioned, a rubber lined spark plug socket should be purchased with the set. Since spark plug size

varies, know (or ask) which size is appropriate for your car.

The most important thing to consider when purchasing hand tools is quality. Don't be

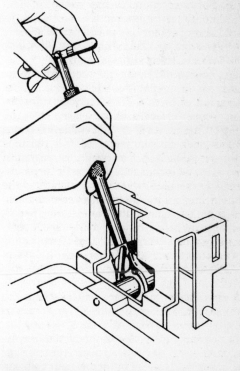

A new design speedwrench — for easy removal of retaining nuts

misled by the low cost of "bargain tools". Forged wrenches, tempered screwdriver blades, and fine tooth ratchets are much better investments than their less expensive counterparts. The skinned knuckles and frustration inflicted by poor quality tools make any job an unhappy chore. Another consideration is that quality hand tools come with an unbeatable replacement guarantee: if the tool breaks, you get a new one, no questions asked.

Most jobs can be accomplished using the tools on the accompanying lists. There will be an occasional need for a special tool, such as snap ring pliers; that need will be mentioned in the text. It would not be wise to buy a large assortment of tools on the theory that someday they will be needed. Instead, the tools should be acquired one or two at a time, each for a specific job. This will avoid unnecessary expense and help insure that you have the right tool for the job at hand.

The tools needed for basic maintenance jobs, in addition to the wrenches and sockets mentioned, include:

1. A floor jack, with a lifting capacity at least equal to the weight of the car. Capacity of $1\frac{1}{2}$ times the weight is better.
2. Jack stands, for support
3. Oil filter wrench
4. Oil filler spout or funnel
5. Grease gun
6. Battery post and clamp cleaner
7. Container for draining oil
8. Many rags for the inevitable spills
9. Oil dry or "kitty litter" for absorbing spilled fluids. Keep a broom handy.

In addition to these items there are several others which are not absolutely necessary, but handy to have around. These include a transmission funnel and filler tube, a drop (trouble) light on a long cord, an adjustable (crescent) wrench, and slip joint pliers. After performing a few projects on the car, you'll be amazed at the other tools and non–tools on your workbench. Some useful household items to have around are: a large turkey baster or siphon, empty coffee cans and ice trays (storing parts), ball of twine, assorted tape, markers and pens, whisk broom, tweezers, golf tees (for plugging vacuum lines), metal coat hangers or a roll of mechanics's wire (holding things out of the way), dental pick or similar long, pointed probe, a strong magnet, a small mirror (for seeing into recesses and under manifolds) and various small pieces of lumber.

A hydraulic floor jack is one of the best investments you can make if you are serious about repairing and maintaining your own car. The small jack that comes with the car is simply not safe enough to use when doing any-

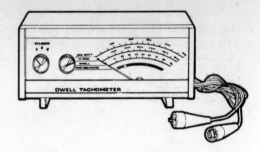

A dwell/tachometer is useful for tune-up work

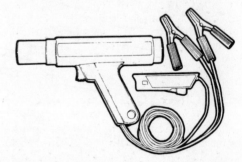

An inductive pickup simplifies timing light connection to the spark plug

thing more than changing a flat. The hydraulic floor jack ($1\frac{1}{2}$ ton is fine for the Toyota) will pay for itself quickly in convenience, utility and much greater safety. Watch the ads for your local department or automotive store. A good jack is always on special sale somewhere.

A more advanced list of tools, suitable for tune-up work, can be drawn up easily. While the tools are slightly more sophisticated, they need not be outrageously expensive. The key to these purchases is to make them with an eye towards adaptability and wide range. A basic list of tune-up tools could include:

1. Tachometer/dwell meter
2. Spark plug gauge and gapping tool
3. Feeler gauges for valve adjustment
4. Timing light.

You will need both wire type and flat type feeler gauges, the former for the spark plugs and the latter for the valves. The choice of a timing light should be made carefully. A light which works on the DC current supplied by the car battery is the best choice; it should have a xenon tube for brightness. Since many of the newer cars have electronic ignition, and since nearly all cars will have it in the future, the light should have an inductive pickup which clamps around the number one spark plug cable (the timing light illustrated has one of these pickups).

In addition to these basic tools, there are several other tools and gauges which you may find useful. These include:

1. A compression gauge. The screw-in type

is slower to use, but eliminates the possibility of a faulty reading due to escaping pressure.

2. A manifold vacuum gauge.

3. A test light.

4. A combination volt/ohmmeter.

5. An induction meter, used to determine whether or not there is current flowing in a wire; an extremely helpful tool for electrical troubleshooting.

Finally, you will find a torque wrench necessary for all but the most basic work. The beam-type models are perfectly adequate. The newer click–type (breakaway) torque wrenches are more accurate, but are much more expensive, and must be periodically recalibrated.

SERVICING YOUR CAR SAFELY

It is virtually impossible to anticipate all of the hazards involved with automotive maintenance and service, but care and common sense will prevent most accidents.

The rules of safety for mechanics range from "don't smoke around gasoline", to "use the proper tool for the job". The trick to avoiding injuries is to develop safe work habits and take every possible precaution.

Dos

• Do work neatly. A few minutes spent clearing a workbench or setting up a small table for tools is well worth the effort. Make yourself put tools back on the table when not in use; doing so means you won't have to grope around on the floor for that wrench you need right now. Protect your car while working on it with fender covers. If you don't wish to buy a fender cover, an old blanket makes a usable substitute.

• Do follow manufacturer's directions whenever working with potentially hazardous materials. Both brake fluid and antifreeze are poisonous if taken internally. House Pets and small animals are attracted to the odor and taste of engine coolant (antifreeze). It is a highly poisonous mixture of chemicals; special care must be taken to protect open containers and spillage. If a house pet drinks any amount of coolant, it is a "drop everything" emergency--seek immediate veterinary care.

• Do keep a fire extinguisher and first aid kit within easy reach. Know how to use both of them before the need arises.

• Do wear safety glasses or goggles when cutting, drilling, grinding or prying. If you wear glasses for the sake of vision, they should be made of hardened glass that can serve also as safety glass, or wear safety goggles over your regular glasses.

• Do shield your eyes whenever you work around the battery. Batteries contain sulphuric acid. In case of contact with the eyes or skin, flush the area with water or a mixture of water and baking soda; get medical attention immediately.

• Do use safety stands for any undercar service. Jacks are for raising vehicles; safety stands are for making sure the vehicle stays raised until you want it to come down. Every year, several people are killed or maimed when their car falls on them. Whenever the car is raised, block the wheels remaining on the ground and set the parking brake.

• Do use adequate ventilation when working with any chemicals or hazardous materials.

• Do disconnect the negative battery cable when working on the electrical system. The secondary ignition system can contain up to 40,000 volts. Although the current (amperage) is very low, this voltage can stun you or set off other reactions within the body.

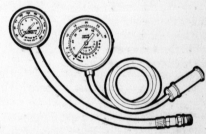

A compression gauge and a combination vacuum/fuel pressure gauge are handy for troubleshooting and tune-up work

• Do properly maintain your tools. Loose hammerheads, mushroomed punches and chisels, frayed or poorly grounded electrical cords, excessively worn screwdrivers, spread open–end wrenches, cracked sockets, slipping ratchets, or faulty drop light sockets can cause accidents.

• Do use the proper size and type of tool for the job being done.

• Do, when possible, pull on a wrench handle rather than push on it, and adjust your stance to prevent a fall.

• Do be sure that adjustable wrenches are tightly closed on the nut or bolt and pulled so that the face is on the side of the fixed jaw.

• Do select a wrench or socket that fits the nut or bolt. The wrench or socket should sit straight, not cocked.

• Do strike squarely with a hammer; avoid glancing blows.

• Do set the parking brake and block the

Always support the vehicle on jackstands when working under it

drive wheels if the work requires the engine running. Make yourself lower the car to the ground before starting the engine. There are very few test procedures which require the car to run while elevated.

Don'ts

• Don't run an engine in a garage or anywhere else without proper ventilation – EVER! Carbon monoxide is poisonous; it takes a long time to leave the human body and you can build up a deadly supply of it in your system by simply breathing in a little every day. You may not realize you are slowly poisoning yourself. Always use power vents, windows, fans or open the garage doors.

Carbon monoxide is odorless and colorless. Your senses cannot detect its presence. Early symptoms of monoxide poisoning include headache, irritability, improper vision (blurred or hard to focus) and/or drowsiness. When you notice any of these symptoms in yourself or your helpers, stop working immediately and get to fresh, outside air. Ventilate the work area thoroughly before returning to the car.

• Don't work around moving parts while wearing a necktie or other loose clothing. Short sleeves are much safer than long, loose sleeves; hard-toed shoes with neoprene soles protect your toes and give a better grip on slippery surfaces. Jewelry such as watches, fancy belt buckles, beads or body adornment of any kind is not safe working around a car. Long hair should be hidden under a hat or cap.

• Don't use pockets for tool boxes. A fall or bump can drive a screwdriver deep into your body. Even a wiping cloth hanging from the back pocket can wrap around a spinning shaft or fan.

• Don't use screwdrivers for anything other than driving screws! A screwdriver used as a prying tool or chisel can snap when least expected, causing bodily harm. Besides, you ruin a good tool when it is used for purposes other than those intended.

• Don't use an emergency jack (that little scis-

sors or pantograph jack that comes with the car) for anything other than changing a flat tire! If you are serious about repairing and maintaining your own car, one of the best investments you can make is a hydraulic floor jack of at least $1\frac{1}{2}$ ton capacity.

• Don't smoke when working around gasoline, cleaning solvent or other flammable material.

• Don't smoke when working around the battery. When the battery is being charged, it gives off explosive hydrogen gas.

• Don't use gasoline to wash your hands; there are excellent soaps available. Gasoline may contain lead, and lead can enter the body through a cut, accumulating in the body until you are very ill. Gasoline also removes all the natural oils from the skin so that bone dry hands will suck up oil and grease

• Don't service the air conditioning system unless you are equipped with the necessary tools and training. The refrigerant, R-12, is extremely cold when compressed, and when released into the air will instantly freeze any surface it contacts including your eyes. Although the refrigerant is normally non-toxic, R-12 becomes a deadly poisonous gas in the presence of an open flame. One good whiff of the vapors from burning refrigerant can be fatal. Additionally, it is being proven that the chemicals within air conditioning refrigerant are damaging to the upper atmosphere. Until a non-damaging substitute is in use, many local governments are considering requiring the use of scavenging equipment which would capture (and recycle) the refrigerant as it is released.

SERIAL NUMBER IDENTIFICATION

Vehicle

All models have the vehicle identification number (VIN) stamped on a plate which is attached to the left side of the instrument panel. This plate is visible through the windshield.

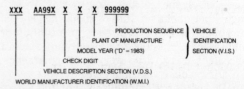

All manufacturers use the same format within the 17 digit VIN

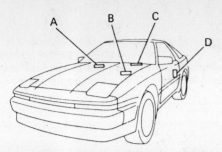

The VIN may be found in 4 locations. A and B are under the hood; C is viewed through the windshield and D is on the left door post

The VIN is also found on a plate mounted on the firewall in the engine compartment and on a plate mounted on the left doorpost.

The serial number on all 1981 and later models uses the 17 digit format. The first three digits are the World Manufacturer Identification, the next five digits are the Vehicle Description Section and the remaining nine numbers are the production–related numbers.

Engine

The engine serial number consists of an engine series identification number, followed by a 6-digit production number. Please find this number on your engine and write it down for easy reference. This book will refer to engines by their series or family group (example: 3S-FE), not by displacement or volume. When ordering parts for the engine – particularly internal or rebuild parts – the complete engine number should be provided to the supplier for ease of reference.

The location of this serial number varies from one engine type to another. Serial numbers may be found in the following locations:

1995cc (2S-E)

The serial number is stamped on the oil filter side of the engine block.

1998cc (3S-GE, 3S-GTE, 3S-FE and 5S-FE)

The serial number is stamped on the rear of the engine block.

2954cc (7M-GE and 7M-GTE)

The engine serial number is stamped on the right hand side of the cylinder block.

2800cc (5M-GE) Twin Cam

The engine serial number is stamped on the lower right hand side of the cylinder block, just above the oil pan.

1595cc (4A-FE)

The serial number is stamped on the left side of the engine block at the rear.

Engine I.D. number location, 2S–E

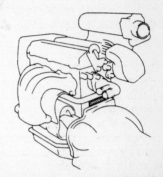

Engine I.D. number location, 3S–GE, 3S–FE

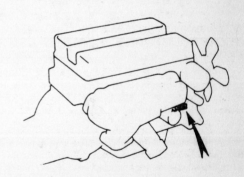

Engine I.D. number location, 7M–GE, 7M–GTE

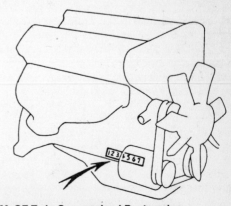

5M–GE Twin Cam engine I.D. stamping

ENGINE IDENTIFICATION CHART

Year	Model	Engine Family	Engine Displacement (cc)	Nominal Designation ①	No. of Cylinders	Type ②
1986	Celica	2S-E	1995	2.0L	4	SOHC, 2V, FWD
		3S-GE	1998	2.0L	4	DOHC, 4V, FWD
	Supra	5M-GE	2759	2.8L	6	DOHC, 2V, RWD
		7M-GE	2954	3.0L	6	DOHC, 4V, RWD
1987	Celica	3S-FE	1998	2.0L	4	DOHC, 4V, FWD
		3S-GE	1998	2.0L	4	DOHC, 4V, FWD
	Supra	7M-GE	2954	3.0L	6	DOHC, 2V, RWD
		7M-GTE	2954	3.0L	6	DOHC-T 4V, RWD
1988	Celica	3S-FE	1998	2.0	4	DOHC, 4V, FWD
		3S-GE	1998	2.0	4	DOHC, 4V, FWD
	Celica All-Trac	3S-GTE	1998	2.0	4	DOHC-T 4V, 4WD
	Supra	7M-GE	2954	3.0	6	DOHC, 4V, RWD
		7M-GTE	2954	3.0	6	DOHC-T 4V, RWD
1989	Celica	3S-FE	1998	2.0	4	DOHC, 4V, FWD
		3S-GE	1998	2.0	4	DOHC, 4V, FWD
	Celica All-Trac	3S-GTE	1998	2.0	4	DOHC-T 4V, 4WD
	Supra	7M-GE	2954	3.0	6	DOHC, 4V, RWD
		7M-GTE	2954	3.0	6	DOHC-T 4V, RWD
1990	Celica	4A-FE	1587	1.6L	4	DOHC, 4V, FWD
		5S-FE	2164	2.2L	4	DOHC, 4V, FWD
	All-Trac	3S-GTE	1998	2.0L	4	DOHC-T 4V, 4WD
	Supra	7M-GE	2954	3.0	6	DOHC, 2V, RWD
		7M-GTE	2954	3.0	6	DOHC-T 4V, RWD

① Be careful using this designation. There are 5 engines that may be referred to as ''2 liter.''
② SOHC—Single overhead camshaft
　DOHC—Double overhead camshaft
　V— Valves per cylinder
　FWD—Front wheel drive
　RWD—Rear wheel drive
　4WD—Four wheel drive
　T—Turbocharged

Transmission Identification

Like every other manufacturer, Toyota selects its transmissions and transaxles very carefully. Transmissions are selected to match the engine characteristics on the basis of gear ratios, power flow routing, durability, size, weight and economy of operation. Do not assume that similar body styles or similar engines will allow interchange of transmissions; drive ability and performance may suffer if the incorrect unit is installed.

TRANSMISSION AND TRANSAXLE IDENTIFICATION CHART

Year	Model	Engine Family	Transmission Type	
			Manual	Auto
1986	Celica	2S-E	S53	A140L
		3S-GE	S53	A140E
	Supra	5M-GE	W58	A43DE
		7M-GE	W58	A43DE
1987	Celica	3S-FE	S53	A140L
		3S-GE	S53	A140E
	Supra	7M-GE	W58	A340E
		7M-GTE	R154	A340E
1988	Celica	3S-FE	S53	A140L
		3S-GE	S53	A140E
	Celica All-Trac	3S-GTE	E50F2	—
	Supra	7M-GE	W58	A340E
		7M-GTE	R154	A340E
1989	Celica	3S-FE	S53	A140L
		3S-GE	S53	A140E
	Celica All-Trac	3S-GTE	E50F2	—
	Supra	7M-GE	W58	A340E
		7M-GTE	R154	A340E
1990	Celica	4A-FE	C52	A243L
		5S-GE	S53	A241L
				A241E
	All-Trac	3S-GTE	E150F	—
	Supra	7M-GE	W58	A340E
		7M-GTE	R154	A340E

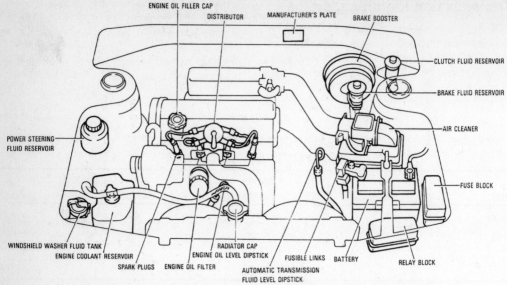

Maintenance related component location; 1986 Celica with 2S-E engine

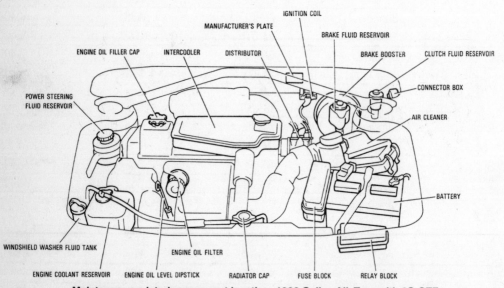

Maintenance related component location, 1988 Celica All–Trac with 3S-GTE

ROUTINE MAINTENANCE

Air Cleaner

REMOVAL AND INSTALLATION

All of the dust present in the air is kept out of the engine by means of the air cleaner filter element. Proper maintenance is vital, as a clogged element not only restricts the air flow and thus the power, but can also cause premature engine wear.

The filter element should be inspected and cleaned every 7,500 miles, or more often if the car is driven under dry, dusty conditions. Dusty or gritty conditions occur just as often in heavy urban or city traffic as in the country. Vehicles used mostly in city environments require frequent filter service.

Remove the filter element and use low pressure compressed air to blow the dirt out. Filters are the absolute cheapest form of insurance you can purchase for the engine; frequent changes are recommended.

NOTE: *The filter element used on Toyota vehicles is of the dry, disposable type. It should never be washed, soaked or oiled.*

The filter element must be replaced every 30,000 miles, or more often under dry, dusty

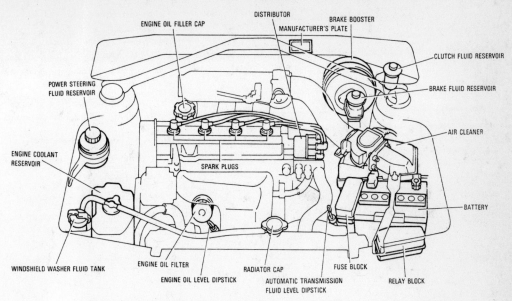

Maintenance related component location; 1987 Celica with 3S-FE engine

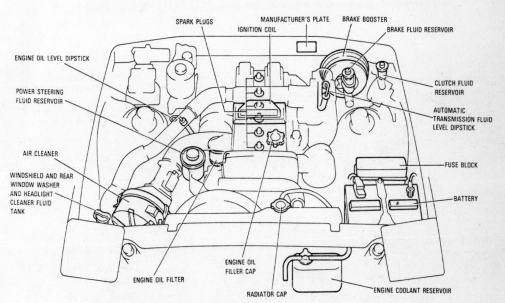

1987 Supra maintenance related component location for 7M-GTE engine

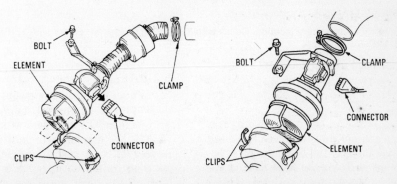

Changing the air filter element on the 7M-GE engine (left) and 7M-GTE

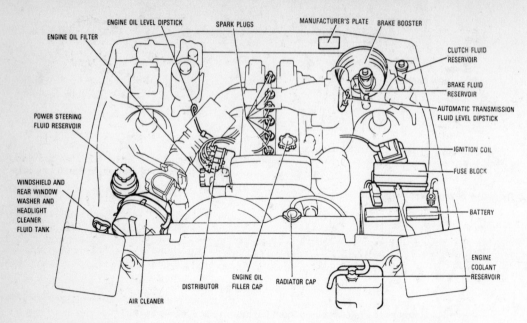

7M-GE maintenance related component location. 1987 Supra shown, others similar

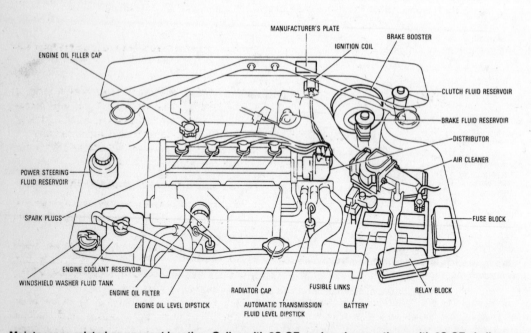

Maintenance related component location. Celica with 3S-GE engine shown; others with 3S-GE similar

conditions. Be sure to use the correct one; all Toyota elements are of the same type but they come in a variety of sizes and shapes. **To replace:**

1. Unfasten the clips or retaining screws on top of the air cleaner housing and lift off the top. Be careful; many of the housings have various components on top of the cover. Handle everything carefully. On Supras with the 7M-GE or 7M-GTE engine, it will be necessary to dis-

connect the wiring connector, remove the hose clamp and unbolt the brace.

2. Lift out the air filter element and clean it with compressed air or replace it.

3. Clean out the filter case with a rag.

4. Fit the filter element into the air box. Make certain it is not upside down. Double check that the element is properly seated; if it is crooked, the cover won't seat and air leaks will admit unfiltered air into the motor.

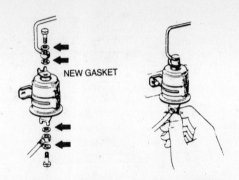

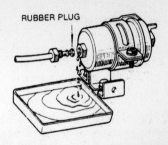

Always use new gaskets when installing fuel filters

When removing the fuel lines, it is always a good idea to place a pan underneath to catch any dripping fuel

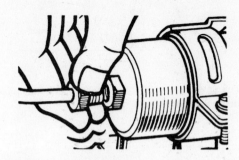

Hand tighten the fuel inlet line

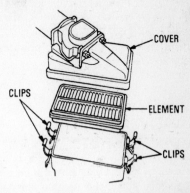

Carefully remove the cover to remove the filter element

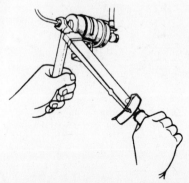

A torque wrench is essential when tightening the fuel lines to the Supra fuel filter

5. Install the cover and connect the retainers. Install the Supra brace and bolt, hose clamp and wiring connector.

Fuel Filter

Since any dirt is the absolute enemy of a fuel injection system, Celicas and Supras incorporate several fuel filters within the system. Most are not routinely replaced since they are extremely hard to reach (inside the fuel tank for example). The replaceable fuel filter is in the fuel line, either mounted on the firewall under the hood or located at the rear of the car near the tank.

The filter should be inspected for external damage and/or leakage at least once a year; it should be changed every 30,000 miles. Remember that even after removal the filter cartridge will retain some liquid fuel; drain it and allow it sit in the open for a period of time before discarding.

REMOVAL AND INSTALLATION

1. Unbolt the retaining screws and remove the protective shield (if equipped) for the fuel filter.

2. Place a pan under the delivery pipe (large connection) to catch the dripping fuel and SLOWLY loosen the union bolt to bleed off the fuel pressure.

CAUTION: *The fuel system is under pressure. Release pressure slowly and contain spillage. Observe no smoking/no open flame precautions. Have a Class B-C (dry powder) fire extinguisher within arm's reach at all times.*

3. Remove the union bolt and drain the remaining fuel.

4. Disconnect and plug the inlet line.

5. Unbolt and remove the fuel filter.

NOTE: *When tightening the fuel line bolts to the fuel filter, you must use a torque wrench. The tightening torque is very important, as under or over tightening may cause fuel leakage. Insure that there is no fuel line interfer-*

*ence and that there is sufficient clearance be-
tween it and any other parts.*

6. Coat the flare unit, union nut and bolt
threads lightly with engine oil.

7. Hand tighten the inlet line to the fuel
filter. Always use new gaskets.

8. Install the fuel filter and then tighten
the inlet line bolt to 38 Nm or 28 ft. lbs.

9. Reconnect the delivery pipe using new gaskets and then tighten the union bolt to 30 Nm
or 22 ft. lbs.

WARNING: *The fuel pump builds high pressure within the lines. If new gaskets are not
used, a high-pressure leak may spray fuel
onto the engine or other hot surface.*

10. Run the engine for a few minutes and
check for any fuel leaks.

11. Install the protective shield.

PCV Valve

REMOVAL AND INSTALLATION

The positive crankcase ventilation or PCV
valve regulates the release of crankcase vapors
during various engine operating conditions. As
the engine operates, some combustion gas will
escape from the cylinder by passing the piston
rings. These gasses accumulate in the oil pan.

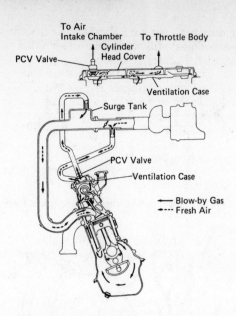

The 1986 Celica with 2S-E engine has a PCV valve
in the valve cover

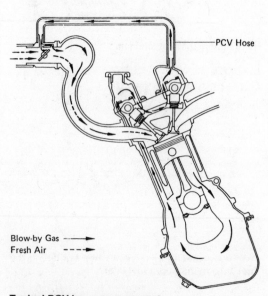

Typical PCV hose arrangement

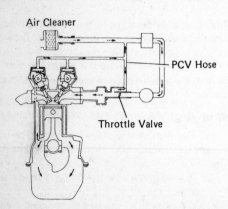

Some DOHC engines have a PCV hose on each
valve cover. Be careful not to break the plastic
"tee" fittings

Since a small amount of vapor is added on
every piston stroke, the pressure within the oil
pan quickly builds. If these vapors are not allowed to escape through a planned path they
will quickly find their own exit, usually by forcing a hole in an engine gasket.

Since the gasses contain hydrocarbons and
other pollutants, they cannot simply be vented
to the atmosphere. The PCV valve allows the
release of the vapors under controlled conditions back into the intake air stream. The
vapors are then mixed with the incoming air,
reintroduced to the combustion chamber and re-
burned. At high vacuum (idle speed and partial
load range) the PCV will open slightly and at
low vacuum (full throttle) it will open fully.
This causes vapor to be removed from the crankcase by the engine vacuum and then sucked
into the combustion chamber where it is dissipated.

Most of the cars covered in this book simply
use a hose from the valve cover to the air intake
to route the vapors into the engine; the computer controlled fuel injection deals with the
presence of the vapors automatically. If your

car does not have a PCV valve, the hose and passages must still be checked and cleaned periodically. To check or replace the valve:

1. Check the ventilation hoses for leaks or clogging. Clean or replace as necessary. Vapor passage in the ventilation lines is controlled by two orifices. Inspect the hoses for cracks, leaks or other damage. Blow through the orifices to make sure they are not blocked. Replace all components as necessary.

2. Locate the PCV valve in the valve cover. Remove it.

3. Blow into the crankcase end of the valve. There should be free passage of air through the valve.

4. Blow into the intake manifold end of the valve. There should be little or no passage of air through the valve.

WARNING: *Wrap the ends of the valve in a clean towel or paper. The vapors and deposits contain petrochemicals which can be harmful. Never inhale through the valve.*

5. If the PCV valve failed either of the preceding two checks, it will require replacement.

6. Install the valve, making sure it is not backwards. Connect the hoses and make certain they are not twisted or kinked.

Evaporative Emissions System Charcoal Canister

The gasoline used for automotive fuel is volatile; it evaporates at fairly low temperatures. The vapors released from the fuel tank become a major source of atmospheric pollution. For this reason, a vapor recovery system is included on all modern automobiles. The vapors within the tank (and other parts of the fuel system) are routed through lines to the charcoal canister.

The canister, filled with activated or expanded charcoal pellets, absorbs the most of the hydrocarbons and fumes. At proper times in the engine operation cycle, fresh air is drawn into the bottom of the canister. The hydrocarbons are mixed with the fresh air and introduced into the intake stream to be re-burned in the engine.

Check the evaporation control system every 15,000 miles or once a year. Check the fuel and vapor lines and the vacuum hoses for proper connections and correct routing, as well as condition. If any loose charcoal is seen coming out of the canister, it must be replaced. Replace clogged, damaged or deteriorated parts as necessary. If the charcoal canister is clogged, it may be cleaned using low pressure (no more than 43 psi) compressed air. Current design and manufacturing techniques allow the canister to be a "life of the car" component under

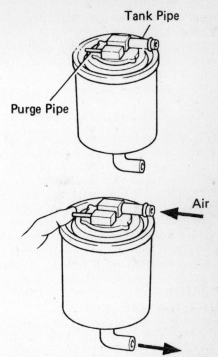

Checking the charcoal canister for blockage

normal circumstances. If there have been any unusual occurrances such as a flooded engine or a major fuel injection failure, the canister should be considered polluted. Any situation in which the canister is exposed to liquid fuel (instead of the normal vapor flow) requires the replacement of the canister. Once the charcoal is saturated, it cannot be cleaned or dried properly.

TESTING

NOTE: *This can be performed with the canister in place; you may find it easier to remove the canister for access to all the ports.*

1. The charcoal canisters on Celicas and Supras have three ports, 2 on top and 1 on the bottom. Label each hose and disconnect it from its port. The ports are plastic, and probably brittle; work carefully.

2. The purge pipe is either the smaller of the two ports on top of the canister or the one without the bulge at the end of it. Cover or block this port with your finger.

3. Use a straw or similar tube to blow gently into the tank port (the other top port); you should feel air coming out the bottom port.

4. A clogged or damaged canister will not allow all the air to come out. If you sense resistance while blowing, replace the canister.

5. Reinstall the canister if it was removed.

6. Reconnect the hoses to their proper ports.

Additionally, Toyota recommends that the

gasket on the fuel filler cap (gas cap) be inspected once per year and replaced at 60,000 mile intervals regardless of condition. The cap must seal tightly to prevent the escape of vapor through the filler neck.

Battery

INSPECTION AND SERVICE

NOTE: *When the battery is disconnected, various solid state accessories on the car may lose their memory. Be prepared to re-program the radio and reset the clock. 1989 and 1990 vehicles with anti–theft radios will require entry of the owner's identification number or the audio system will not work.*

Loose, dirty, or corroded battery terminals are a frequent cause of "no-start"conditions. Every 3 months or so, remove the battery terminals and clean them, giving them a light coating of petroleum jelly when you are finished. This will help to retard corrosion.

WARNING: *Never disconnect the battery with the engine running or with the ignition turned on. Severe and expensive damage to the on–board computers will result. With the ignition off and the key removed for safety, always disconnect the negative (–) cable first and connect it last.*

Check the battery cables for signs of wear or chafing and replace any cable or terminal that

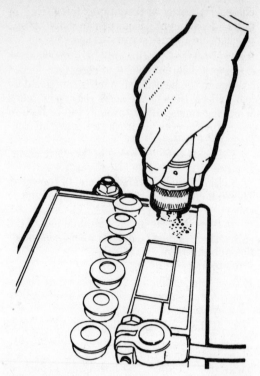

Clean the battery posts with a wire brush, or the special tool shown

looks marginal. Battery terminals can be easily cleaned; inexpensive cleaning tools are an excellent investment that will pay for themselves many times over. They can usually be pur-

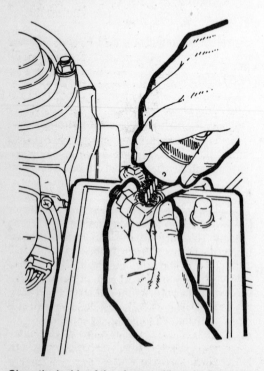

Clean the inside of the clamps with a wire brush, or the special tool

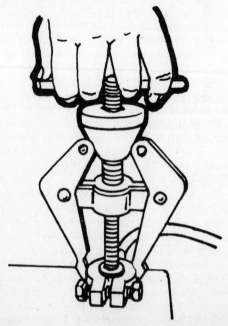

Special pullers are available to remove cable clamps

chased from any well-equipped auto store or parts department. The accumulated white powder and corrosion can be cleaned from the top of the battery with an old toothbrush and a solution of baking soda and water.

Unless you have a "maintenance-free" battery, check the electrolyte (fluid) level frequently. Be sure that the vent holes in each cell cap are not blocked by grease or dirt. The vent holes allow hydrogen gas, formed by the chemical reaction in the battery, to escape safely.

Check the battery electrolyte level at least once a month, more often in hot weather or during periods of extended operation. The level should be maintained between the upper and lower levels marked on the battery case, or to the split ring within the well in each cell. If the electrolyte level is low, distilled water should be added until the proper level is reached. Tap water is to be avoided if possible; the minerals it contains can shorten battery life by reacting with the metal plates inside the battery. Each cell is completely separate from the others, so each cell must be filled individually. It's a good idea to add the distilled water with a squeeze bulb to avoid having electrolyte (sulphuric acid) splash out.

NOTE: *Cars that are regularly driven at highway speeds over moderate to long distances may require battery service more frequently. Constant charging of the battery will cause some water to evaporate.*

At least once a year check the specific gravity of the battery electrolyte. It should be between 1.22 and 1.28 at room temperature. A reading of 1.00 or slightly above indicates nothing but water within the battery. The electrical. process has stopped and its time for a new battery. You cannot successfully add acid to a used battery. If water is added in freezing weather, the vehicle should be driven several miles to allow the water to mix with the electrolyte and prevent freezing.

If the battery becomes corroded, or if electrolyte should splash out during additions of water, a mixture of baking soda and water will neutralize the acid. This should be washed off with cold water after making sure that the cell caps are tight. Battery fluid is particularly nasty to painted surfaces; work carefully to avoid spillage on fenders and other painted bodywork.

If a charging is required while the battery is in the car, disconnect the battery cables, negative (ground) cable first. If you have removed the battery from the vehicle for charging, make sure the battery is not sitting on bare earth or concrete while being charged. A block of wood or a small stack of newspapers will prevent the

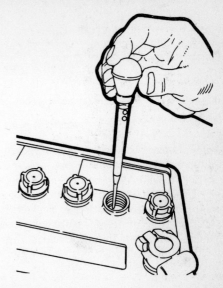

The specific gravity of the battery can be checked with a simple float-type hydrometer

battery from losing internal heat while charging.

When replacing a battery, it is important that the replacement have an output rating equal to or when greater than original equipment. Do not confuse physical size with electrical capacity. A stronger battery (capable of delivering more power) need not be much larger that the original. A physically larger battery may not fit in the car and may actually deliver less power than the original.

CAUTION: *If you get battery acid in your eyes or on your skin, rinse it off immediately with lots of water. Go to a doctor if it gets in your eyes. The gases formed inside the battery cells are highly explosive. Never check the level of the electrolyte in the presence of flame or when smoking. Never charge a battery in an unventilated area. Never smoke around a battery being charged.*

Drive Belts

INSPECTION

Check the condition of the drive belts and check and adjust the belt tension every 15,000 miles. Toyota has installed multi–ribbed belts for most of the belt driven accessories. Although these belts are quieter and longer lasting than traditional V–type belts, they are still prone to wear, cracking and separation.

1. Inspect the belts for signs of glazing or cracking. A glazed belt will be perfectly smooth from slippage, while a good belt will have a slight texture of fabric visible. Cracks will usually start at the inner edge of the belt and run

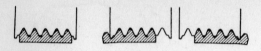

CORRECT   WRONG

If the belt is removed, it must be correctly reinstalled

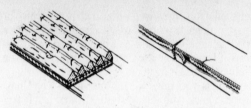

Check the belts for any sign of deterioration or cracking

outward. Replace the belt at the first sign of cracking or if the glazing is severe.

2. Belt tension does not refer to play or droop. Use a belt tension gauge to check the amount of force needed to deflect the belt. It is not possible to accurately measure belt tension by pushing with your thumb. Inadequate tension will result in slippage and wear, while excessive tension will damage bearings and cause belts to fray and crack.

3. Drive belts should be replaced as needed. If you are performing your maintenance inspections regularly, you should spot a wearing belt with plenty of time to replace it before it breaks.

DRIVE BELT TENSION CHART

Year	Model	Engine	Power Steering Pump lbs.	±	Alternator lbs.	±	A/C Compressor lbs.	±
1986	Celica	All	80	20	130 ①	10	—	
					95 ②	20	—	
	Supra	All	135 ③	20	135	20	—	
			80 ④	20	80	20	—	
1987	Celica	3S-FE	80	20	130 ①	10	—	
					95 ②	20	—	
		3S-GE	80	20	115 ①	20	—	
					130 ②	25	—	
	Supra	All	100	20	115	20	88	10
1988	Celica	3S-FE	80	20	130 ①	10	—	
					95 ②	20	—	
		3S-GTE & 3S-GE	80	20	115 ①	20	—	
					130 ②	25	—	
	Supra	All	100	20	115	20	105	10
1989	Celica	3S-FE	80	20	130 ①	10	—	
					95 ②	20	—	
		3S-GTE & 3S-GE	80	20	115 ①	20	—	
					130 ②	25	—	
	Supra	All	100	20	115	20	105	10
1990	Celica	4A-FE	80	20	130	20	100	20
		5S-FE	80	20	130 ①	10	—	
					95 ②	20	—	
	Supra	All	100	20	115	20	105	10

NOTE: All tensions are for used belts. Set new belts 10–20 lbs. tighter, then readjust after 200 miles.
① With A/C
② Without A/C
③ Ribbed belt
④ Conventional V-belt

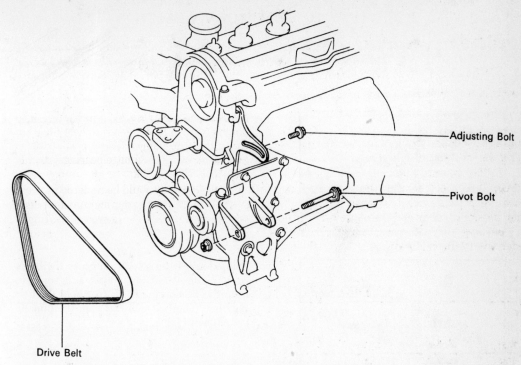

Adjusting Bolt

Pivot Bolt

Drive Belt

This alternator (not shown) is adjusted in the traditional fashion; loosen both bolts first

ADJUSTMENT

Before beginning any work, look carefully for any built–in adjuster in the system. These are generally small bolts which keep tension on either an idler pulley or the mounting bracket. It is much easier to adjust one bolt than to loosen and tighten two or three.

WARNING: *Do not use a screwdriver, pry bar or any other metal device as a lever. Do not exert force against manifolds, valve covers, or fuel injection components.*

Alternator

If no adjusting bolt is present, adjust the tension of the alternator drive belt by loosening the pivot and mounting bolts on the alternator. Using a wooden hammer handle, a broomstick or your hand, move the all alternator one way or the other until the proper tension is achieved.

Tighten the mounting bolts securely. If a new belt has been installed, recheck the tension after about 200 miles of driving.

Air Conditioning Compressor

Because of the great tension on the A/C compressor belt, belt tension can be adjusted by turning the adjuster bolt on all models. The bolt is located on the compressor tensioner bracket. Turn the bolt clockwise to tighten the belt and counterclockwise to loosen it. The belt should be just tight enough to turn without slipping; over tightening will damage the compressor.

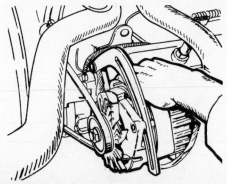

After loosening both bolts, move the unit outward to tighten the belt. Hold the unit in place and tighten the bolts

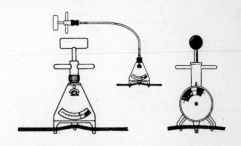

Several types of gauges for measuring belt tension. All of them measure belt deflection across a fixed distance

HOW TO SPOT WORN V-BELTS

V-Belts are vital to efficient engine operation—they drive the fan, water pump and other accessories. They require little maintenance (occasional tightening) but they will not last forever. Slipping or failure of the V-belt will lead to overheating. If your V-belt looks like any of these, it should be replaced.

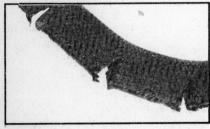

Cracking or weathering

This belt has deep cracks, which cause it to flex. Too much flexing leads to heat build-up and premature failure. These cracks can be caused by using the belt on a pulley that is too small. Notched belts are available for small diameter pulleys.

Softening (grease and oil)

Oil and grease on a belt can cause the belt's rubber compounds to soften and separate from the reinforcing cords that hold the belt together. The belt will first slip, then finally fail altogether.

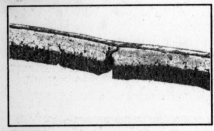

Glazing

Glazing is caused by a belt that is slipping. A slipping belt can cause a run-down battery, erratic power steering, overheating or poor accessory performance. The more the belt slips, the more glazing will be built up on the surface of the belt. The more the belt is glazed, the more it will slip. If the glazing is light, tighten the belt.

Worn cover

The cover of this belt is worn off and is peeling away. The reinforcing cords will begin to wear and the belt will shortly break. When the belt cover wears in spots or has a rough jagged appearance, check the pulley grooves for roughness.

Separation

This belt is on the verge of breaking and leaving you stranded. The layers of the belt are separating and the reinforcing cords are exposed. It's just a matter of time before it breaks completely.

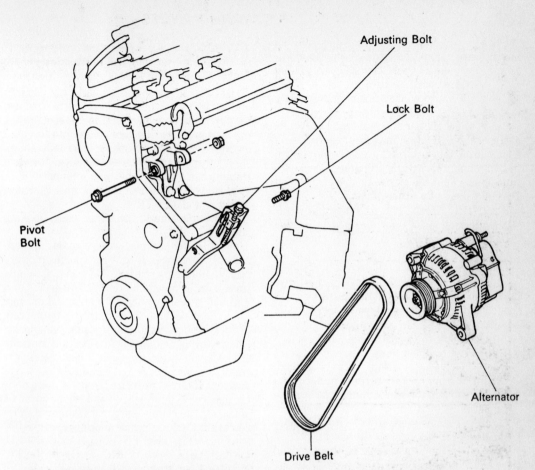

Adjusting Bolt

Lock Bolt

Pivot Bolt

Alternator

Drive Belt

This alternator can be adjusted with a single bolt. Always look for an adjuster before beginning

Power Steering Pump

Tension on the power steering belt is adjusted by means of an idler pulley. Turn the adjusting bolt on the idler pulley until the desired tension is felt and then retighten the lock bolt.

BELT REPLACEMENT

If a belt must be replaced, the driven unit must be loosened and moved to its extreme loosest position, generally by moving it toward the center of the motor. After removing the old belt, check the pulleys for dirt or built-up material which could affect belt contact. Carefully install the new belt, remembering that it is new and unused--it may appear to be just a little too small to fit over the pulley flanges. Fit the belt over the largest pulley (usually the crankshaft pulley at the bottom center of the motor) first, then work on the smaller one(s). Gentle pressure in the direction of rotation is helpful. Some belts run around a third or idler pulley, which acts as an additional pivot in the belt's path. It may be possible to loosen the idler

pulley as well as the main component, making your job much easier. Depending on which belt(s) you are changing, it may be necessary to loosen or remove other interfering belts to get at the one(s) you want.

When buying replacement belts, remember that the fit is critical according to the length of the belt ("diameter"), the width of the belt, the depth of the belt and the angle or profile of the V shape or the ribs. The belt shape should exactly match the shape of the pulley; belts that are not an exact match can cause noise, slippage and premature failure.

After the new belt is installed, draw tension on it by moving the driven unit away from the motor and tighten its mounting bolts. This is sometimes a three or four-handed job; you may find an assistant helpful. Make sure that all the bolts you loosened get retightened and that any other loosened belts also have the correct tension. A new belt can be expected to stretch a bit after installation so be prepared to re-adjust your new belt, if needed, within the first two hundred miles of use.

Hoses

Upper and lower radiator hoses and all heater hoses should be checked for deterioration, leaks and loose hose clamps every 15,000 miles or at least once a year.

Replacing hoses requires draining the cooling system. This potentially messy job involves working under the car and handling antifreeze, a slippery, smelly, stain-making chemical. Have a large drain pan or bucket available along with healthy supply of rags. Be prepared to deal with fluid spills immediately. See the previous list of Do's and Don'ts for other hints.

WARNING: *House Pets and small animals are attracted to the odor and taste of engine coolant (antifreeze). It is a highly poisonous mixture of chemicals; special care must be taken to protect open containers and spillage.*

1. Drain the cooling system. This is always done with the motor cold. Attempting to drain hot coolant is very foolish;you can be badly scalded.

　a. Remove the radiator cap.

　b. Position the drain pan under the point where the radiator drain cock is located. Open the drain cock by turning it; allow the fluid to run into the pan. A funnel can be helpful here.

　c. As soon as the system is drained, close the drain cock so you don't forget it.

2. Loosen the hose clamps on the damaged hose and slide the clamps in toward center.

3. Break the grip of the hose at both ends by prying it free with a suitable tool or by twisting it with your hand. Take great care not to twist or loosen the fitting under the hose.

4. Remove the hose.

5. Install a new hose. A small amount of soapy water on the inside of the hose end will ease installation.

NOTE: *The new hose should be in the same position as the original. If other than the exact hose is used, make sure it does not rub against either the engine or the frame while the engine is running, as this may wear a hole in the hose. Contact points may be insulated with a piece of sponge or foam; plastic wire ties are particularly handy for this job.*

6. Slide the hose clamps back into position and retighten. When tightening the clamps, tighten them enough to seal in the coolant but not so much that the clamp cuts into the hose or causes it internal damage. If a clamp shows signs of any damage (bent, too loose, hard to tighten, etc.) now is the time to replace it. A good rule of thumb is that a new hose is always worth new clamps.

7. Double check the drain cock, making sure it is closed.

8. Fill the system with coolant. Toyota strongly recommends that the coolant mixture be a 50-50 mix of antifreeze and water. This mixture gives best combination of anti-freeze and anti-boil characteristics for year-round driving.

9. Replace and tighten the radiator cap. Start the engine and check visually for leaks. Allow the engine to warm up fully and continue to check your work for signs of leakage. A very small leak may not be noticed until the system develops internal pressure. Leaks at hose ends are generally clamp related and can be cured by snugging the clamp. Larger leaks may require removing the hose again–to do this you MUST WAIT UNTIL THE ENGINE HAS COOLED, GENERALLY A PERIOD OF HOURS. NEVER UNCAP A HOT RADIATOR. After all leaks are cured, check the coolant level in the radiator (with the engine cold) and top up as necessary.

AIR CONDITIONING

SAFETY PRECAUTIONS

There are two particular hazards associated with air conditioning systems and they both relate to the refrigerant gas. The refrigerant (generic designation: R-12, trade name: Freon, a

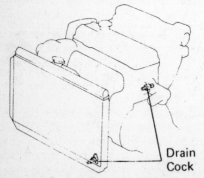

Use the radiator draincock to empty the system before replacing a hose. It is not usually necessary to drain the engine block

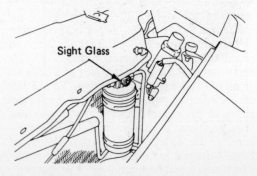

The sight glass is on the receiver–drier

HOW TO SPOT BAD HOSES

Both the upper and lower radiator hoses are called upon to perform difficult jobs in an inhospitable environment. They are subject to nearly 18 psi at under hood temperatures often over 280°F., and must circulate nearly 7500 gallons of coolant an hour—3 good reasons to have good hoses.

Swollen hose

A good test for any hose is to feel it for soft or spongy spots. Frequently these will appear as swollen areas of the hose. The most likely cause is oil soaking. This hose could burst at any time, when hot or under pressure.

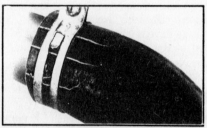

Cracked hose

Cracked hoses can usually be seen but feel the hoses to be sure they have not hardened; a prime cause of cracking. This hose has cracked down to the reinforcing cords and could split at any of the cracks.

Frayed hose end (due to weak clamp)

Weakened clamps frequently are the cause of hose and cooling system failure. The connection between the pipe and hose has deteriorated enough to allow coolant to escape when the engine is hot.

Debris in cooling system

Debris, rust and scale in the cooling system can cause the inside of a hose to weaken. This can usually be felt on the outside of the hose as soft or thinner areas.

Item	Symptom	Amount of refrigerant	Remedy
1	Bubbles present in sight glass	Insufficient	Check for leak with gas leak detector
2	No bubbles present in sight glass	Empty, proper or too much	Refer to items 3 and 4
3	No temperature difference between compressor inlet and outlet	Empty or nearly empty	Evacuate and charge system. Then check for leak with gas leak detector
4	Temperature between compressor inlet and outlet is noticeably different	Proper or too much	Refer to items 5 and 6
5	Immediately after the air conditioner is turned off, refrigerant in sight glass stays clear	Too much	Discharge the excess refrigerant to specified amount
6	When the air conditioner is turned off, refrigerant foams and then stays clear	Proper	—

Possible conditions found during the sight glass check

registered trademark of the Dupont Co.) is an extremely cold substance. When exposed to air, it will instantly freeze any surface it comes in contact with, including your eyes. The other hazard involves fire. Although normally non-toxic, refrigerant gas becomes highly poisonous in the presence of an open flame. One good whiff of the vapor formed by burning refrigerant can be fatal. Keep all forms of fire (including cigarettes) well clear of the air-conditioning system.

Further, it is being established that the chemicals in R-12 (dichlorodifluoromethane) contribute to the damage occurring in the upper atmosphere. The time may soon come when sophisticated recovery equipment will be necessary to prevent the release of this gas when working on an air conditioning system. Any repair work should be left to a professional. Do not, under any circumstances, attempt to loosen or tighten any fittings or perform any work other than that outlined here.

SYSTEM INSPECTION

A lot of A/C problems can be avoided by simply running the air conditioner at least once a week, regardless of the season. Let the system run for at least 5 minutes a week (even in the winter), and you'll keep the internal parts lubricated as well as preventing the hoses from hardening. If you're worried about cold air on a cold day, simply move the temperature selector to warm. The air conditioner will cool the air and the heater will re-warm it before it enters the car.

Refrigerant leaks show up as oily areas on the components because the compressor oil is transported around the entire system with the refrigerant. Look for oily spots on all the hoses

and lines, and especially on the hose and tubing connections. If there are oily deposits, the system may have a leak. A small area of oil on the front of the compressor is normal and no cause for alarm.

Factory installed Toyota air conditioners have a sight glass for checking the refrigerant charge. The sight glass is on top of the receiver/drier which is located in the front of the engine compartment, on the right or left side of the radiator depending upon the year of your car.

NOTE: *If your car is equipped with an after market air conditioner the following system check may not apply. Although almost every modern system has a sight glass, you should contact the manufacturer of the unit for instructions on system checks.*

NOTE: *This test works best if the outside air temperature is above 70°F (21°C).*

1. Place the automatic transmission in Park or the manual transmission in Neutral. Set the parking brake.

2. With the help of a friend, run the engine at a fast idle (about 2000 rpm).

3. Set the air conditioning controls for maximum cooling with the blower on high.

4. Look at the sight glass on the receiver/drier. If a steady stream of bubbles is present in the sight glass, the system is low on charge. It is very likely there is a leak in the system.

NOTE: *If it is determined that the system has a leak, it should be repaired as soon as possible. Leaks may allow moisture to enter the system, causing an expensive rust problem.*

5. If no bubbles are present, the system is either fully charged or completely empty. Feel the high and low pressure lines at the compres-

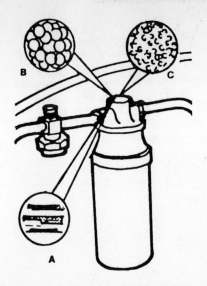

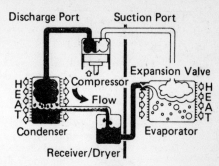

The air conditioning system transfers heat from the inside of the car to the outside air

Oil streaks (A), constant bubbles (B) or foam (C) indicate there is not enough refrigerant in the system. Occasional bubbles during initial operation is normal. A clear sight glass indicates a proper charge of refrigerant or no refrigerant at all, which can be determined by the presence of cold air at the outlets in the car

sor; if no appreciable temperature difference is felt, the system is empty, or nearly so.

6. If one hose is warm (high pressure) and the other is cold (low pressure), the system may be OK. However, you are probably making these tests because there is something wrong with the air conditioning, so proceed to the next step.

7. Either disconnect the compressor clutch

wire or have an assistant in the car turn the fan control On and Off. This will operate the compressor, turning it on and off. Watch the sight glass.

8. If bubbles appear when the clutch is disengaged (off) and disappear when it is engaged, the system is properly charged. You are seeing the refrigerant react to the changes in pressure within the system.

9. If the refrigerant takes more than 45 seconds to bubble when the clutch is disengaged, the system is most likely overcharged. This will usually result in poor cooling at low speeds and possible compressor damage.

SYSTEM OPERATION

Refrigerant Cycle

Once the system is fully charged and free of leaks, it is ready to operate on demand. When turned on, the compressor discharges high temperature and high pressure refrigerant. This re-

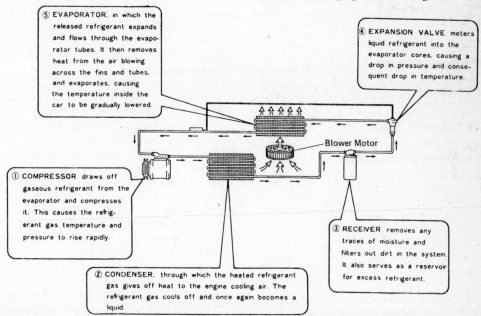

Schematic for the air conditioning system

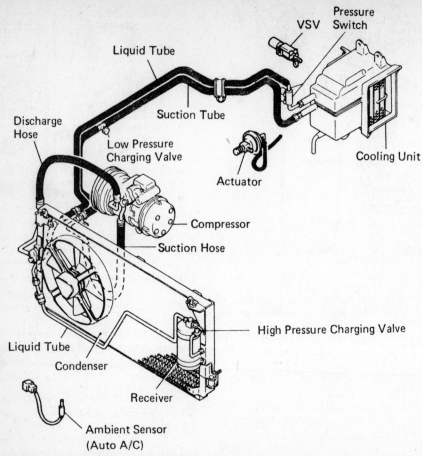

Typical air conditioning system (this one is on the 3S-FE engine). Component location and hose routing will vary from engine to engine but the theory of operation is always the same

frigerant contains heat transferred from inside the car plus the heat developed by the compressor on the discharge stroke.

This gaseous refrigerant flows into the condenser. Because of the airflow through the condenser (either from the motion of the car or the action of the fans), heat is removed from the gas. Now cooled, the gas condenses into a liquid and flows into the receiver–drier. The receiver–drier stores the liquid refrigerant and filters out small amounts of moisture which may be present.

Flowing from the receiver, the liquid refrigerant passes through an expansion valve which changes it into a low temperature, low pressure mixture of gas and liquid. This cold and foggy refrigerant flows to the evaporator.

Once in the evaporator (inside the cabin of the car) the refrigerant is exposed to the warmer air being moved by the blower fan. The refrigerant changes to a gas within the evaporator and absorbs heat from the air being circulated by the fan. After being fully vaporized within the evaporator, the heated refrigerant

gas is drawn out of the evaporator to the compressor where the cycle continues.

Keeping a picture or brief description of the system handy can greatly aid diagnosis and troubleshooting.

Gauge Sets

Before attempting any charge-related work, you will need a set of A/C gauges. These are easily available from good parts stores and automotive tool suppliers. Generally described, this tool is a set of two gauges and three hoses. By connecting the proper hoses to the car's system, the gauges can be used to "see" the air conditioning system at work. The gauge set is also used to discharge and recharge the system.

Additionally, if a component must be removed from the system, a vacuum pump will be needed to evacuate (draw vacuum within) the system and eliminate any moisture which has entered during repairs. These pumps can be purchased outright; many find it easier to rent one from a supplier on an as–needed basis. Small

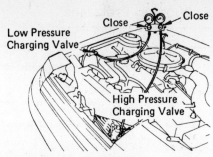

Connecting the gauges, all Celica

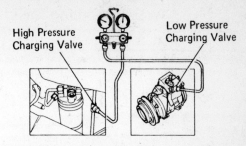

Gauge hook-up, 1987–90 Supra

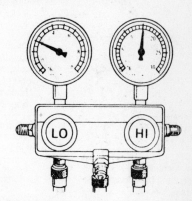

Typical manifold gauge set

cans of refrigerant will be needed; make sure you purchase enough meet the capacity of the system. Since the refrigerant is measured by weight (generally in ounces), you'll need a small spring scale (hanging scale) to weigh the refrigerant can(s) as the system is recharged.

CAUTION: *Wear protective goggles and gloves before proceeding with repairs!*

WARNING: *Hand tighten the fittings. Do not apply any oil or lubricant to the fittings.*

Connecting and disconnecting the gauges should always be done with the engine off to prevent injury from moving parts. To hook up the gauges, first make sure that the valves on the gauges are turned to the closed (off) position. The hose (generally blue) from the low-pressure gauge will attach to the low pressure or suction side of the system. The hose from the high pressure gauge (usually red) will attach to the high or discharge side.

With one exception, the high pressure port on all Celicas and Supras is located on or very near the receiver-drier at the front of the car. The 1986 Supra has this port on the compressor, adjacent to the low pressure fitting. Although these ports should be labeled on the compressor body, double check before connecting the gauges. The high pressure port will be at or near the hose running from the compressor to the condenser. It is NOT the hose running to the compressor from the firewall area.

Location of the low pressure port follows model designation. All Supras have this fitting on the compressor (at or near the hose running to the compressor from the firewall) and all Celicas have the fitting built into the line running along the right fender. The port is generally found towards the front of the car but the 1990 Celica has it at the shock tower.

DISCHARGING, EVACUATING, AND RECHARGING THE SYSTEM

Discharging

1. Connect the manifold gauge set as described previously.

2. The center hose will release the refrigerant charge. Place the end of the center hose in a towel or clean rag and place it out of the way. Do not attempt to hold the end of the hose (or the rag) during discharge of refrigerant.

3. Slowly open the high pressure hand valve to adjust the flow. Do not open the valve very much.

WARNING: *If the valve is opened too far, oil will be sucked out of the compressor.*

4. Check the towel or rag to make sure no oil is being released. If oil is present, partially close the hand valve.

5. After the manifold gauge drops below 50 psi or 343 kPa, slowly open the low pressure valve.

6. As the system pressure drops, slowly open both hand valves until both gauges read zero pressure.

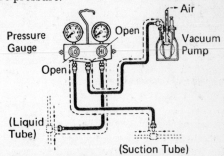

Schematic for evacuating the system

Troubleshooting Basic Air Conditioning Problems

Problem	Cause	Solution
There's little or no air coming from the vents (and you're sure it's on)	• The A/C fuse is blown • Broken or loose wires or connections • The on/off switch is defective	• Check and/or replace fuse • Check and/or repair connections • Replace switch
The air coming from the vents is not cool enough	• Windows and air vent wings open • The compressor belt is slipping • Heater is on • Condenser is clogged with debris • Refrigerant has escaped through a leak in the system • Receiver/drier is plugged	• Close windows and vent wings • Tighten or replace compressor belt • Shut heater off • Clean the condenser • Check system • Service system
The air has an odor	• Vacuum system is disrupted • Odor producing substances on the evaporator case • Condensation has collected in the bottom of the evaporator housing	• Have the system checked/repaired • Clean the evaporator case • Clean the evaporator housing drains
System is noisy or vibrating	• Compressor belt or mountings loose • Air in the system	• Tighten or replace belt; tighten mounting bolts • Have the system serviced
Sight glass condition Constant bubbles, foam or oil streaks Clear sight glass, but no cold air Clear sight glass, but air is cold Clouded with milky fluid	 • Undercharged system • No refrigerant at all • System is OK • Receiver drier is leaking dessicant	 • Charge the system • Check and charge the system • Have system checked
Large difference in temperature of lines	• System undercharged	• Charge and leak test the system
Compressor noise	• Broken valves • Overcharged • Incorrect oil level • Piston slap • Broken rings • Drive belt pulley bolts are loose	• Replace the valve plate • Discharge, evacuate and install the correct charge • Isolate the compressor and check the oil level. Correct as necessary. • Replace the compressor • Replace the compressor • Tighten with the correct torque specification
Excessive vibration	• Incorrect belt tension • Clutch loose • Overcharged • Pulley is misaligned	• Adjust the belt tension • Tighten the clutch • Discharge, evacuate and install the correct charge • Align the pulley
Condensation dripping in the passenger compartment	• Drain hose plugged or improperly positioned • Insulation removed or improperly installed	• Clean the drain hose and check for proper installation • Replace the insulation on the expansion valve and hoses
Frozen evaporator coil	• Faulty thermostat • Thermostat capillary tube improperly installed • Thermostat not adjusted properly	• Replace the thermostat • Install the capillary tube correctly • Adjust the thermostat
Low side low—high side low	• System refrigerant is low • Expansion valve is restricted	• Evacuate, leak test and charge the system • Replace the expansion valve
Low side high—high side low	• Internal leak in the compressor—worn	• Remove the compressor cylinder head and inspect the compressor. Replace the valve plate assembly if necessary. If the compressor pistons, rings or

Troubleshooting Basic Air Conditioning Problems (cont.)

Problem	Cause	Solution
Low side high—high side low (cont.)		cylinders are excessively worn or scored replace the compressor
	• Cylinder head gasket is leaking	• Install a replacement cylinder head gasket
	• Expansion valve is defective	• Replace the expansion valve
	• Drive belt slipping	• Adjust the belt tension
Low side high—high side high	• Condenser fins obstructed	• Clean the condenser fins
	• Air in the system	• Evacuate, leak test and charge the system
	• Expansion valve is defective	• Replace the expansion valve
	• Loose or worn fan belts	• Adjust or replace the belts as necessary
Low side low—high side high	• Expansion valve is defective	• Replace the expansion valve
	• Restriction in the refrigerant hose	• Check the hose for kinks—replace if necessary
	• Restriction in the receiver/drier	• Replace the receiver/drier
	• Restriction in the condenser	• Replace the condenser
Low side and high side normal (inadequate cooling)	• Air in the system	• Evacuate, leak test and charge the system
	• Moisture in the system	• Evacuate, leak test and charge the system

Evacuating

NOTE: *The system must be evacuated any time the system is exposed to the atmosphere. This includes line rupture, a system which has been empty for a period of time, or and disconnection of lines or components for repair.*

7. Confirm that high and low pressure hoses are correctly attached and secure on their fittings. Confirm that gauge valves are closed. Connect the center gauge hose to the vacuum pump.

8. Start the vacuum pump, allow it to run for a few seconds and then open both hand valves slowly and at the same time.

9. After the pump has run for about 10 minutes, check the low pressure gauge. It should read at least 23.62 in. Hg (80.0 kPa). If the reading does not meet or exceed this value, the system has a leak and the pump cannot develop proper vacuum. The leak must be found and repaired before continuing; close both valves and stop the vacuum pump.

10. If no leakage is indicated, continue with the evacuation. After the low pressure gauge indicates more than 27.56 in Hg. (93.3 kPa), note the time and continue the evacuation for 15 minutes.

11. When the pump has been run for the proper period of time, close both gauge valves and shut off the pump. Disconnect the hose from the vacuum pump. The air conditioning system has now been evacuated and sealed. A

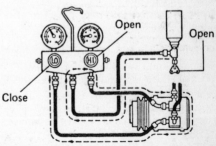

Charging hook-up for the 1986 Supra air conditioning system

system which is not leaking should hold this vacuum with the pump off.

Charging

WARNING: *Do not attempt to add refrigerant to a partially charged system. Over pressurizing the system will cause expensive damage. Do not perform this procedure with the engine running. do not open the low pressure valve during charging. Do not disconnect the gauge line(s) at the gauge set while the hoses are hooked to the car. This would result in rapid refrigerant loss from the system causing possible personal injury.*

12. Confirm that the high and low pressure hoses are correctly connected and secure on their fittings. Confirm that the hand valves are closed.

13. Attach the center hose to the R-12 refrig-

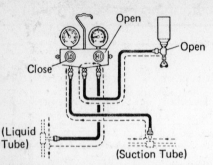

Open

Open

Close

(Liquid Tube)

(Suction Tube)

Recharging an empty system through the high pressure side. The refrigerant can must remain upside down throughout the procedure

erant source, usually a 16 ounce can. Make sure the control valve for the can is closed before connecting.

14. Hang or position the can on the scale so that it stays inverted or upside–down during the remaining procedures. DO NOT turn the can upright down or on its side during charging. Severe damage to the system can occur.

15. Open the high pressure hand valve and the refrigerant container valve. Check the chart to find the correct amount of refrigerant to admit into the system. All the systems will hold more than one pound (16 oz.) so an empty system will take at least one can.

16. When a can must be changed, close the valve on the can first, then close the high pressure valve. Exchange cans and open the high pressure valve and then the valve on the refrigerant container. Watch the scale; when the correct amount of weight is out of the can, it's in the system.

17. Close the high pressure gauge valve when the correct weight of refrigerant has been released into the system.

18. Close the valve on the container and disconnect the center hose from the can. Disconnect the hoses from the car; wear gloves and release the connectors rapidly to avoid refrigerant loss from the system.

19. Open the vehicle front doors, start the engine, and set the blower fan on top speed

with the air conditioning controls set for maximum cooling. Run the engine at 1500–2000 rpm.

20. Check the system operation by viewing the sight glass as explained earlier in this section. Check the flow of cold air within the car.

SYSTEM CAPACITIES

- 1986 Celica: 1.7–1.9 lbs.
- 1986 Supra: 1.4–1.7 lbs.
- 1987 Celica: 1.3–1.7 lbs.
- 1987 Supra: 1.3–1.7 lbs.
- 1988 Celica: 1.3–1.7 lbs.
- 1988 Supra: 1.3–1.7 lbs.
- 1989 Celica: 1.3–1.7 lbs.
- 1989 Supra: 1.4–1.7 lbs.
- 1990 Celica: 1.6–1.8 lbs.
- 1990 Supra: 1.4–1.7 lbs.

Windshield Wipers

REFILL (BLADE) REPLACEMENT

Intense heat and ultra-violet rays from the sun, snow, ice and frost, road oils, acid rain, and industrial pollution all combine quickly to deteriorate the rubber wiper refills. One pass on a frosty windshield can reduce a new set of refills to an unusable condition. The refills should be replaced about twice a year or whenever they begin to streak or chatter on wet glass. If the blades are found to be cracked, broken or torn, they should be replaced immediately and always in pairs.

Blade life can be prolonged by frequent clean-

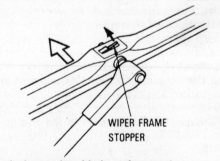

WIPER FRAME STOPPER

Typical rear wiper blade replacement

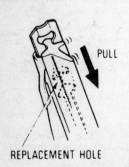

PULL

REPLACEMENT HOLE

PULL OUT

Most front wiper inserts can be easily changed

ings of the glass with a rag and a commercial glass cleaner. The use of a ammonia based cleaner will ease the removal of built-up road oils and grease from the glass. After cleaning the glass, use the damp rag to wipe the wiper blades.

Ammonia based cleaners are harmful to painted surfaces. Be careful when applying them and don't fill the washer jug with an ammonia based solvent; when used it will run onto the painted bodywork.

To replace the front wiper refills (blades or rubbers), pull the top end of the blade inward or away from the end of the arm. As it comes free from the end slot, you'll see the replacement hole. Pull the insert out of the replacement hole.

Install the new blade by inserting the end with the small protrusions into the replacement hole. Work the blade along the slot. Keep doing this until the entire blade is mounted in the slot. Release the tension on the rubber insert and allow it to expand into the end hole.

Double check the position of each blade and be sure that each end is secured in place. Check the sides of the insert, looking for any kinking or deformation. If necessary, remove the insert and start over, eliminating any distortion.

If the car is equipped with a rear wiper, the insert may be changed with little effort. To do this, remove the entire blade and holder assembly from the arm by releasing the stopper tab at the center of the holder; slide the holder off the arm. Pull the end of the blade outward until the cutout of the blade is free from the blade holder. Match the cutout of the blade with the small arms or side clamps and slide it out of the holder.

Install the new blade by sliding it into the side arms, making sure each is engaged on both sides. Once in place, fit the notch or cutout into place to lock the insert in the holder. Inspect the entire length of the blade for proper alignment and reinstall the holder on the arm.

Tires

Common sense and good driving habits will afford maximum tire life. Fast starts and stops or hard cornering are hard on tires and will shorten their useful life span. If you start at normal speeds, allow yourself sufficient time to stop, and take corners at a reasonable speed, the life of your tires will increase greatly. Also make sure that you don't overload your vehicle or run with incorrect pressure in the tires. Both of these practices increase tread wear.

Inspect your tires frequently. Be especially careful to watch for bubbles in the tread or side wall, deep cuts, or under inflation. Remove any

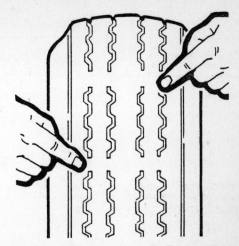

Tread wear indicators will appear when the tire is worn out

tires with bubbles. If the cuts are so deep that they penetrate to the cords, discard the tire. Any cut in the sidewall of a radial tire renders it unsafe. Also look for uneven tread wear patterns that indicate that the front end is out of alignment or that the tires are out of balance.

TIRE ROTATION

So that the tires wear more uniformly, it is recommended that the tires be rotated every 7,500 miles. This can be done when all four (or

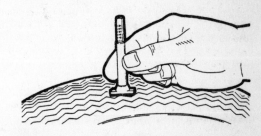

Tread depth can also be checked with an inexpensive gauge

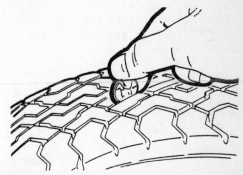

A penny works well as anything for checking tread depth; when the top of Lincoln's head is visible, it's time for new tires

Tire Size Comparison Chart

"Letter" sizes			Inch Sizes	Metric-inch Sizes		
"60 Series"	"70 Series"	"78 Series"	1965–77	"60 Series"	"70 Series"	"80 Series"
		Y78-12	5.50-12, 5.60-12 6.00-12	165/60-12	165/70-12	155-12
		W78-13	5.20-13	165/60-13	145/70-13	135-13
		Y78-13	5.60-13	175/60-13	155/70-13	145-13
			6.15-13	185/60-13	165/70-13	155-13, P155/80-13
A60-13	A70-13	A78-13	6.40-13	195/60-13	175/70-13	165-13
B60-13	B70-13	B78-13	6.70-13	205/60-13	185/70-13	175-13
			6.90-13			
C60-13	C70-13	C78-13	7.00-13	215/60-13	195/70-13	185-13
D60-13	D70-13	D78-13	7.25-13			
E60-13	E70-13	E78-13	7.75-13			195-13
			5.20-14	165/60-14	145/70-14	135-14
			5.60-14	175/60-14	155/70-14	145-14
			5.90-14			
A60-14	A70-14	A78-14	6.15-14	185/60-14	165/70-14	155-14
	B70-14	B78-14	6.45-14	195/60-14	175/70-14	165-14
	C70-14	C78-14	6.95-14	205/60-14	185/70-14	175-14
D60-14	D70-14	D78-14				
E60-14	E70-14	E78-14	7.35-14	215/60-14	195/70-14	185-14
F60-14	F70-14	F78-14, F83-14	7.75-14	225/60-14	200/70-14	195-14
G60-14	G70-14	G77-14, G78-14	8.25-14	235/60-14	205/70-14	205-14
H60-14	H70-14	H78-14	8.55-14	245/60-14	215/70-14	215-14
J60-14	J70-14	J78-14	8.85-14	255/60-14	225/70-14	225-14
L60-14	L70-14		9.15-14	265/60-14	235/70-14	
	A70-15	A78-15	5.60-15	185/60-15	165/70-15	155-15
B60-15	B70-15	B78-15	6.35-15	195/60-15	175/70-15	165-15
C60-15	C70-15	C78-15	6.85-15	205/60-15	185/70-15	175-15
	D70-15	D78-15				
E60-15	E70-15	E78-15	7.35-15	215/60-15	195/70-15	185-15
F60-15	F70-15	F78-15	7.75-15	225/60-15	205/70-15	195-15
G60-15	G70-15	G78-15	8.15-15/8.25-15	235/60-15	215/70-15	205-15
H60-15	H70-15	H78-15	8.45-15/8.55-15	245/60-15	225/70-15	215-15
J60-15	J70-15	J78-15	8.85-15/8.90-15	255/60-15	235/70-15	225-15
	K70-15		9.00-15	265/60-15	245/70-15	230-15
L60-15	L70-15	L78-15, L84-15	9.15-15			235-15
	M70-15	M78-15				255-15
		N78-15				

Note: Every size tire is not listed and many size comparisons are approximate, based on load ratings. Wider tires than those supplied new with the vehicle, should always be checked for clearance.

Troubleshooting Basic Tire Problems

Problem	Cause	Solution
The car's front end vibrates at high speeds and the steering wheel shakes	• Wheels out of balance • Front end needs aligning	• Have wheels balanced • Have front end alignment checked
The car pulls to one side while cruising	• Unequal tire pressure (car will usually pull to the low side) • Mismatched tires • Front end needs aligning	• Check/adjust tire pressure • Be sure tires are of the same type and size • Have front end alignment checked
Abnormal, excessive or uneven tire wear See "How to Read Tire Wear"	• Infrequent tire rotation • Improper tire pressure • Sudden stops/starts or high speed on curves	• Rotate tires more frequently to equalize wear • Check/adjust pressure • Correct driving habits
Tire squeals	• Improper tire pressure • Front end needs aligning	• Check/adjust tire pressure • Have front end alignment checked

Troubleshooting Basic Wheel Problems

Problem	Cause	Solution
The car's front end vibrates at high speed	• The wheels are out of balance • Wheels are out of alignment	• Have wheels balanced • Have wheel alignment checked/adjusted
Car pulls to either side	• Wheels are out of alignment • Unequal tire pressure • Different size tires or wheels	• Have wheel alignment checked/adjusted • Check/adjust tire pressure • Change tires or wheels to same size
The car's wheel(s) wobbles	• Loose wheel lug nuts • Wheels out of balance • Damaged wheel • Wheels are out of alignment • Worn or damaged ball joint • Excessive play in the steering linkage (usually due to worn parts) • Defective shock absorber	• Tighten wheel lug nuts • Have tires balanced • Raise car and spin the wheel. If the wheel is bent, it should be replaced • Have wheel alignment checked/adjusted • Check ball joints • Check steering linkage • Check shock absorbers
Tires wear unevenly or prematurely	• Incorrect wheel size • Wheels are out of balance • Wheels are out of alignment	• Check if wheel and tire size are compatible • Have wheels balanced • Have wheel alignment checked/adjusted

five) tires are of the same size and load rating capacity. Any abnormal wear should be investigated and the cause corrected.

Radial tires should not be cross-switched; they'll last longer if their direction of rotation is not changed. They will wear very rapidly if reversed. Studded snow tires will lose their studs if their direction of rotation is reversed.

NOTE: *Mark the wheel position or direction of rotation on radial tires or studded snow tires before removal.*

CAUTION: *Avoid over tightening the lug nuts; the brake disc or drum may become per-*

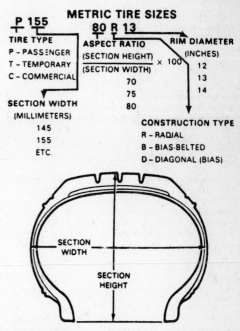

METRIC TIRE SIZES

Common tire coding. A performance code such as H or V may appear before the R; The designation 'M + S' may appear at the end of the code to indicate a snow or all–season tire

Two patterns for rotating radial tires

manently distorted. Alloy wheels can be cracked by over tightening. Generally, nut torque should not exceed 60 ft. lbs. Always tighten the nuts in a criss-cross pattern.

TIRE DESIGN

When buying new tires, you should keep the following points in mind, especially if you are switching to larger tires or a different profile series (50, 60, 70, 78):

1. All four tires should be of the same construction type. Radial, bias, or bias-belted tires should not be mixed. Radial tires are highly recommended for their excellent handling and fuel mileage characteristics. Most new vehicles from 1980 on were delivered with radial tires as standard equipment.

2. The wheels must be the correct width for the tire. Tire dealers have charts of tire and wheel compatibility. A mismatch can cause sloppy handling and rapid tread wear. The tread width should match the rim width (inside bead to inside bead) within an inch. For radial tires the rim width should be 80% or less of the tire (not tread) width.

3. The height (mounted diameter) of the new tires can change speedometer accuracy, engine speed per given road speed, fuel mileage, acceleration, and ground clearance. Tire manufacturers furnish full measurement specifications to their dealers.

4. The spare tire should be usable, at least for low speed operation, with the new tires. In the early 1980's, most manufacturers began using a space-saving spare tire mounted on a special wheel. This wheel and tire is for emergency use only. Never try to mount a regular tire on a special spare wheel.

5. There shouldn't be any body interference when the car is loaded, on bumps or in turning through maximum range.

TIRE INFLATION

The importance of proper tire inflation cannot be overemphasized. A tire employs air under pressure as part of its structure. It is designed around the supporting strength of air at a specified pressure. For this reason, improper inflation drastically reduces the tire's ability to perform as it was intended. Tire pressures should be checked regularly with a reliable pressure gauge. Too often the gauge on the end of the air hose at your corner garage is not accurate enough because it suffers too much abuse.

Always check tire pressure when the tires are cold, as pressure increases with temperature. If you must move the vehicle to check the tire inflation, do not drive more than a mile before checking. A cold tire is one that has not been driven for a period of about three hours.

 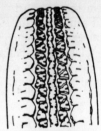

- DRIVE WHEEL HEAVY ACCELERATION
- OVERINFLATION

- HARD CORNERING
- UNDERINFLATION
- LACK OF ROTATION

Examples of inflation–related tire wear patterns. As little as two pounds under specification can induce premature wear

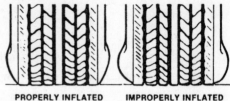

PROPERLY INFLATED   IMPROPERLY INFLATED
RADIAL TIRE

Radial tires have a characteristic sidewall bulge; don't try to measure the air pressure by looking at the tire. Always use a quality air gauge

CAUTION: *Never exceed the maximum tire pressure embossed on the tire. This maximum pressure is rarely the correct pressure for everyday driving. Consult your owners' manual for the proper tire pressures for your vehicle.*

CARE OF SPECIAL WHEELS

If you have invested money in magnesium, aluminum alloy or sport wheels, special precautions should be taken to make sure your investment is not wasted and that your special wheels look good for the lifetime of the car.

Special wheels are easily scratched and/or damaged. Occasionally check the rims for cracking, impact damage or air leaks. If any of these are found, replace the wheel. In order to prevent this type of damage, and the costly replacement of a special wheel, observe the following precautions:

• Use extra care not to damage the wheels during removal, installation, balancing, etc. After removal of the wheels from the car, place them on a mat or other protective surface.

• While driving, watch for sharp obstacles.

• When washing, use a mild detergent and water. Avoid cleansers with abrasives or the use of hard brushes. There are many cleaners and polishes for special wheels. Use them.

• If possible, remove your special wheels

from the car during the winter months. Salt and sand used for snow removal can severely damage the finish.

• Make sure that the recommended lug nut torque is never exceeded or the wheel may crack. Never use snow chains on special wheels; severe scratching will occur.

JACKING

There are certain safety precautions which should be observed when jacking the vehicle. They are as follows:
1. Always jack the car on a level surface.
2. Set the parking brake if the front wheels

 Front

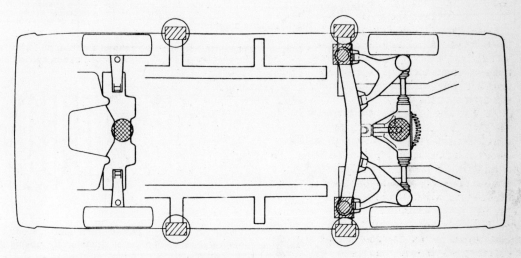

Jacking points, 1986–87 Supra

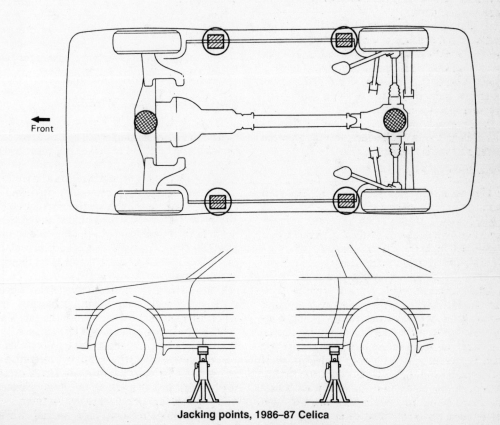

Jacking points, 1986–87 Celica

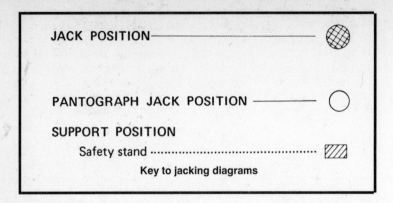

JACK POSITION ———————————

PANTOGRAPH JACK POSITION ———

SUPPORT POSITION
Safety stand ....

Key to jacking diagrams

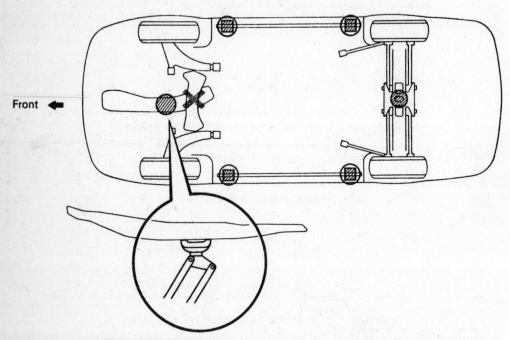

Front ◀

Jacking points, 1990 Celica; NEVER place the jack at the 'X'; the crossmember will be damaged

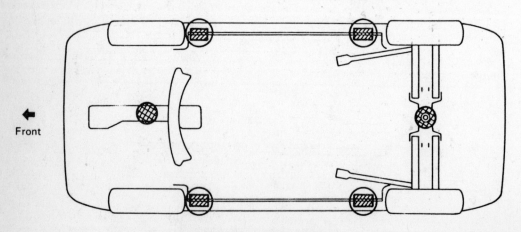

Front ◀

Jacking points, 1988 Celica FWD

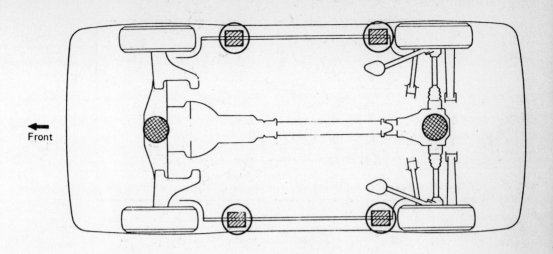

Jacking points, 1988 Supra

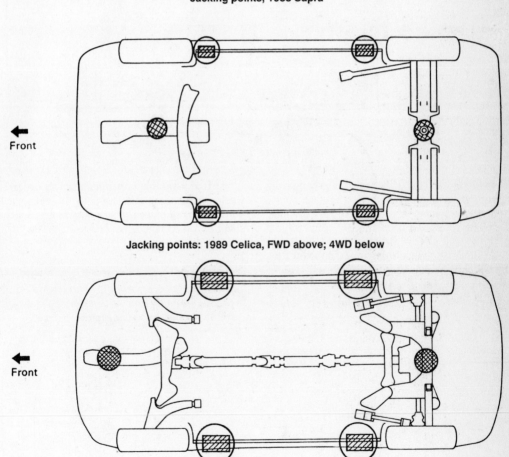

Jacking points: 1989 Celica, FWD above; 4WD below

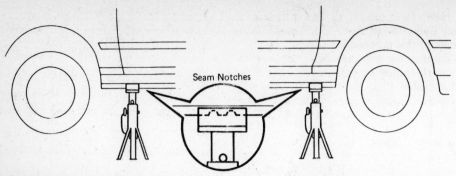

Seam Notches

Correct placement of the jackstands for all vehicles. Only certain portions of the lower panels are reinforced to carry the weight of the car

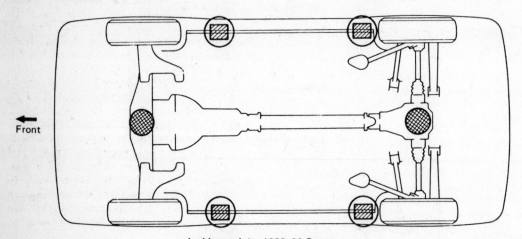

Front

Jacking points, 1989–90 Supra

are to be raised. This will keep the car from rolling backward off the jack.

3. If the rear wheels are to be raised, block the front wheels to keep the car from rolling forward.

4. Block the wheel diagonally opposite the one which is being raised.

NOTE: *The tool kit supplied with most Toyota passenger cars includes a wheel block.*

5. If the vehicle is being raised in order to work underneath it, support it with jack stands. Do not place the jack stands against the sheet metal panels beneath the car or they will become distorted.

CAUTION: *NEVER work under a car supported only by a jack. Jackstands MUST be placed correctly and fully support the weight of the car before beginning any work.*

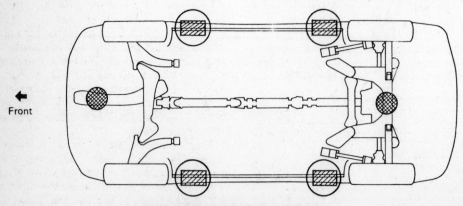

Front

Jacking points, 1988 Celica All-Trac

6. Never attempt to raise the car by placing the jack under the bumper; the jack is not designed for this purpose.

7. Jacking for non–emergency or maintenance work should be done with a hydraulic jack if available. Place the jack so it bears only on reinforced body points or structural frame members. Never place the jack under the radiator, oil pan, transmission, axles, drive shaft(s) or suspension pieces. Severe damage may result.

FLUIDS AND LUBRICANTS

Oil and Fuel Recommendations

Oil

The SAE (Society of Automotive Engineers) grade number indicates the viscosity of the engine oil; its resistance to flow at a given temperature. The lower the SAE grade number, the lighter the oil. For example, the monograde oils begin with SAE 5 weight, which is a thin light oil, and continue in viscosity up to SAE 80 or 90 weight, which are heavy gear lubricants. These oils are also known as "straight weight", meaning they are of a single viscosity, and do not vary with engine temperature.

Multi-viscosity oils offer the important advantage of being adaptable to temperature extremes. These oils have designations such as 10W–40, 20W–50, etc. The "10W–40" means that in winter (the "W" in the designation) the oil acts like a thin 10 weight oil, allowing the engine to spin easily when cold and offering rapid lubrication. Once the engine has warmed up, however, the oil behaves as a straight 40 weight, maintaining good lubrication and protection for the engine's internal components. A 20W–50 oil would therefore be slightly heavier than and not as ideal in cold weather as the 10W–40, but would offer better protection at higher rpm and temperatures because when warm it acts like a 50 weight oil. Whichever oil viscosity you choose when changing the oil, make sure you are anticipating the temperatures your engine will be operating in until the oil is changed again. Refer to the oil viscosity

Recommended Viscosity (SAE):

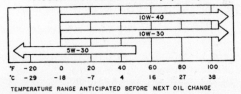

Oil viscosity chart for 1989 Celica and 1990 Supra

Recommended Viscosity (SAE):

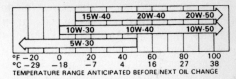

Oil viscosity chart for all except 1989 Celica and 1990 Supra

chart for oil recommendations according to temperature.

The API (American Petroleum Institute) designation indicates the classification of engine oil used under certain given operating conditions. For 1986 through 1989 vehicles, only oils designated "SF" or "SF/CC" should be used. 1990 vehicles require the designation "SG". SG oils may be used in earlier cars, but SF must not be substituted for for SG.

Oils of the SF and SG type perform a variety of functions inside the engine in addition to the basic function as a lubricant. Through a balanced system of metallic detergents and polymeric dispersants, the oil prevents the formation of high and low temperature deposits and also keeps sludge and particles of dirt in suspension. Acids, particularly sulfuric acid, as well as other by-products of combustion, are neutralized. Both the SAE grade number and the APE designation can be found on top of the oil can.

Straight weight oil or mineral oil must never be used in your Celica or Supra.

Toyota does not recommend the use of synthetic oils in their engines or gearboxes. Changing the oil and filter regularly (and frequently) is at least as important as choosing the correct oil to use.

Fuel

IMPORTANCE OF GASOLINE OCTANE RATINGS

Octane rating is based on the quantity of anti-knock compounds added to the gasoline and determines the speed at which the gas will burn; the lower the octane, the faster it burns. The higher the numerical octane rating, the slower the fuel will burn and the greater the percentage of compounds in the fuel to prevent pinging (knock), detonation, and pre-ignition. As the temperature of the engine increases, the air-fuel mixture shows a tendency to ignite before the spark plug is fired and the exhaust valve is opened.

This is especially critical in high compression engines (any engine with a compression ratio greater than 9.0:1) or turbocharged engines, where the use of low-octane gas will cause combustion to occur before the piston has completed its compression stroke. This pre–ignition attempts to force the piston down while it is still traveling up. Fuel of the proper octane rating for the compression ratio of your car will slow the combustion process sufficiently to allow the spark plug time to ignite the mixture completely and allow time for the exhaust valve to open. Spark ping, detonation, and pre-ignition may result in damage to the top of the pistons and burned exhaust valves.

All cars built in 1977 or later are designed to run on unleaded fuel. The use of leaded fuel in a car requiring unleaded fuel will plug the catalytic converter, rendering it inoperative and increasing exhaust backpressure to the point where engine output is severely reduced. In all cases, the minimum octane rating of the fuel used must be at least 91 RON. (The same fuel may be described as 87 octane using a different method of calculation. You may see the notation 'R + M/2' on the pump. This is the average of the research octane and the motor octane.) All unleaded fuels sold in the U.S. are required to meet this minimum research octane rating.

NOTE: *Your engine's fuel requirement can change with time due to carbon buildup which changes the compression ratio. If your engine pings, knocks, or runs on, switch to a higher grade of fuel. Sometimes just changing brands will cure the problem.*

With the exception of turbocharged engines, all Celica and Supra engines require 91 octane unleaded fuel. The turbocharged engines (denoted by the T in the engine designation—3S-GTE, for example) require fuel of 96 RON. Gasolines with a Research Octane Number as low as 91 may be used in these vehicles on a temporary basis or in emergencies. A steady diet of low octane fuel will impair or damage a turbocharged engine.

Engine

CAUTION: *Used motor oil may cause skin cancer if repeatedly left in contact with the skin for prolonged periods. Although this is unlikely unless you handle oil on a daily basis, it is wise to thoroughly wash your hands with soap and water immediately after handling used motor oil. Always follow simple precautions when handling used motor oil.*

• Avoid prolonged skin contact with used motor oil.
• Remove oil from skin by washing thoroughly with soap and water or waterless hand cleaner. Do not use gasoline, thinners or other solvents.
• Avoid prolonged skin contact with oil-soaked clothing.

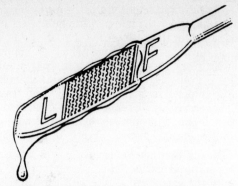

Oil level indicated on the dipstick should never be below the "LOW" line or above the "FULL" line

OIL LEVEL CHECK

Every time you stop for fuel, or at least once per week, check the engine oil as follows:

1. Park the car on level ground.
2. When checking the oil level it is best for the engine to be at operating temperature, although checking the oil immediately after a stopping will lead to a false reading. Wait a few minutes after turning off the engine to allow the oil to drain back into the crankcase.
3. Open the hood and locate the dipstick. On transverse (sideways) engines, it will be on the front side of the motor. Fore-and-aft engines locate the dipstick on the right side. Pull the dipstick from its tube, wipe it clean and reinsert it.
4. Pull the dipstick out again and, holding it horizontally, read the oil level. The oil should be between the "F" and "L" marks on the dipstick. If the oil is below the "L" mark, add oil of the proper viscosity through the capped opening on the top of the cylinder head cover. See the "Oil and Fuel Recommendations" chart in this chapter for the proper viscosity ad rating of oil to use.

NOTE: *It is not wise to attempt to add less than a full quart of oil. Overfilling is worse than being slightly under.*

5. Replace the dipstick and check the oil level again after adding any oil. Be careful not to overfill the crankcase. Approximately one quart of oil will raise the level from the "L" to the "F". Excess oil will generally be consumed at an accelerated rate.

OIL AND FILTER CHANGE

CAUTION: *Used motor oil may cause skin cancer if repeatedly left in contact with the skin for prolonged periods. Although this is unlikely unless you handle oil on a daily basis, it is wise to thoroughly wash your hands with soap and water immediately after handling used motor oil. Always follow simple precautions when handling used motor oil.*

• Avoid prolonged skin contract with used motor oil.

• Remove oil from skin by washing thoroughly with soap and water or waterless hand cleaner. Do not use gasoline, thinners or other solvents.

• Avoid prolonged skin contact with oil-soaked clothing.

The oil drain plug is located on the bottom, rear of the oil pan (bottom of the engine, underneath the car). The oil filter is located on the right side of the engine or on the front of transverse engines.

The mileage figures given in the chart are the Toyota recommended maximum intervals assuming normal driving conditions. If your car is being used under dusty, polluted or towing conditions, change the oil and filter more frequently than specified. The same goes for cars driven in stop-and-go traffic or only for short distances. The term "normal operating conditions" applies to vehicles whose average driving cycle is 20–30 minutes in duration and includes some open road driving at highway speeds. Cars not meeting this use pattern regularly should be considered in "severe duty" and receive more frequent maintenance.

In general, the oil filter should be changed every time the oil is changed. The combination of fresh oil and filter will go a long way to re-

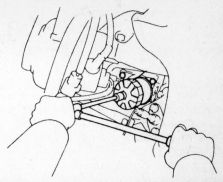

The cap or end wrench is available as a Toyota special service tool or from many local suppliers in the aftermarket

ducing friction related wear within the engine. Certain engines – notably turbos – require such frequent oil changes that a fresh filter every time could become a financial burden. The cost of frequent filters is far exceeded by the cost of engine repair, particularly on a modern turbocharged engine.

Always drain the oil after the engine has been running long enough to bring it to normal operating temperature. Hot oil will flow easier and more contaminants will be removed along with the oil than if it were drained cold.

CAUTION: *Be careful! Hot oil can exceed 200°F (93°C); you may be badly scalded!*

To change the oil and filter:

1. Run the engine until it reaches normal operating temperature, then shut it off.

2. Jack up the front of the car and support it on safety stands.

3. Slide a drain pan of at least 6 quarts capacity under the oil pan.

4. Loosen the drain plug with a wrench but turn the plug out by hand. By keeping an inward pressure on the plug as you unscrew it, oil won't escape past the threads and you can remove it without being burned by hot oil.

5. Allow the oil to drain completely. Before doing anything else, replace the drain plug. (If you forget, the fresh oil will run out the bottom of the engine as you pour it in the top. Almost everybody has embarrassed themselves this way at least once.) It is highly recommended that the gasket on the drain plug be replaced every time. It's worth the small extra cost to

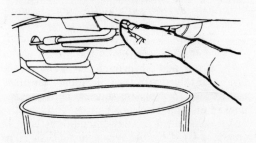

By keeping an inward pressure on the drain plug as you unscrew it, the oil won't escape past the threads

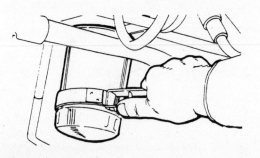

Remove the oil filter with a strap wrench

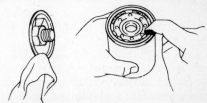

Wipe the block face with a clean rag. Use fresh engine oil to coat the gasket on the new filter

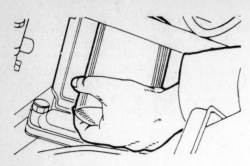

Install the new oil filter by hand

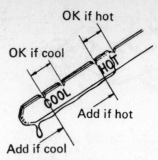

Automatic transmission dipstick

prevent leaks. Don't over tighten the plug, or you'll be buying a new oil pan or a replacement plug for stripped threads.

6. Using a strap wrench or a cap wrench (depending on model and access), remove the oil filter. Keep in mind that it's holding about one quart of dirty, hot oil.

NOTE: *Depending on model and engine family, certain components such as air ducts or wiring may need to be removed or repositioned for access to the filter. You can decide whether it's easier to reach a particular filter from above or below.*

7. Empty the old filter into the drain pan and dispose of the filter.

8. Using a clean rag, wipe off the filter adapter on the engine block. Be sure that the rag doesn't leave any lint which could clog an oil passage. Also make sure that the old gasket came off with the old filter; occasionally they stick to the engine. If you install the filter on top of the old gasket, you will have an oil leak of great magnitude upon starting the engine.

9. Coat the rubber gasket on the filter with fresh oil. Spin it onto the engine by hand; when the gasket touches the adapter surface give it another 1/2–3/4 turn. No more, or you'll squash the gasket and it will leak.

10. Refill the engine with the correct amount of fresh oil. See the Capacities Chart in this section.

11. Check the oil level on the dipstick. It is normal for the level to be a bit above the full mark. Start the engine and allow it to idle for a few minutes.

WARNING: *Do not run the engine above idle speed until it has built up oil pressure, indicated when the oil light on the dash goes out. The light should go out within 10–15 seconds; if the light does not go off quickly, shut the engine off immediately and look for causes of low oil pressure.*

12. Shut off the engine, allow the oil to drain within the engine for a minute, and recheck the oil level. Check around the filter and drain plug for any leaks and correct as necessary.

Transmission

FLUID LEVEL CHECK

Manual

The oil in the manual transmission should be checked at least every 10,000 miles (or once per year) and replaced every 20,000 miles.

1. With the car parked on a level surface, remove the filler plug from the side of the transmission housing. If the car is elevated, it must be level on its stands.

2. If the lubricant begins to trickle out of the hole, there is enough. Otherwise, carefully insert your finger (watch out for sharp threads) and check to see if the oil is up to the edge of the hole.

CAUTION: *Used motor oil may cause skin cancer if repeatedly left in contact with the skin for prolonged periods. Although this is unlikely unless you handle oil on a daily basis, it is wise to thoroughly wash your hands with soap and water immediately after handling used motor oil.*

3. If not, add oil through the hole until the level is at the edge of the hole. Most gear lubricants come in a plastic squeeze bottle with a nozzle, making additions simple. You can also use a common, everyday kitchen baster. Use standard GL-4 hypoid type gear oil-SAE 80 or SAE 80/90 for Celica models and all Supra models. Use Dexron® II ATF fluid for 1986–90

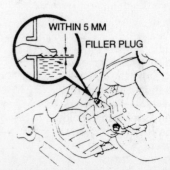

The manual transmission oil level should be up to the bottom of the filler (upper) plug

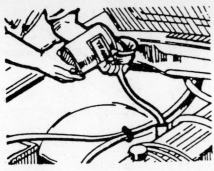

Add automatic transmission fluid through the dipstick tube

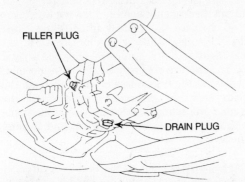

Typical rear wheel drive manual transmission drain and fill locations

Celica models with the S53 transmission. You read that correctly: use Automatic Transmission Fluid – Dexron® II in the S53 manual transmission.

4. Replace the filler plug (and its washer), run the engine and check for leaks.

Automatic Transmission

Check the automatic transmission fluid level at least every 5,000 miles (more if possible). The dipstick is on the right rear side of the engine compartment on fore–and–aft engines. On transverse engines, find the dipstick on the front left side of the engine.

The fluid level should be checked only when the transmission is hot (normal operating temperature); this temperature is usually achieved after about 20 miles of highway driving.

1. Park the car on a level surface with the engine idling. Shift the transmission into Neutral and set the parking brake.

2. Remove the dipstick, wipe it clean and re-insert if firmly. Be sure that it has been pushed all the way in. Remove the dipstick and check the fluid level while holding it horizontally. With the engine running, the fluid level should be between the second and third notches on the dipstick.

3. If the fluid level is below the second notch, add the necessary amount of Dexron® II

automatic transmission fluid. This is easily done with the aid of a funnel. Check the level often as you are filling the transmission. Be extremely careful not to overfill it. Overfilling will cause slippage, seal damage and overheating. Approximately one pint of ATF will raise the level from one notch to the other.

NOTE: *The fluid on the dipstick should always be a bright red color. It if is discolored (brown or black) or smells burnt, serious transmission troubles, probably due to overheating, should be suspected. The transmission should be inspected by a qualified service technician to locate the cause of the burnt fluid*

DRAIN AND REFILL

Manual

The manual transmission oil should be changed at least every 20,000 miles under normal conditions, or 10,000 miles under extreme duty conditions. To change the oil, proceed as follows:

1. The oil must be hot before it is drained. The car should be driven 10–20 miles before changing.

2. Depending on the your agility and arm length, this may be done with the car on the ground or elevated. Remove the filler plug to provide a vent. If the car is elevated and supported on jackstands, remember that oil may pour out the filler hole if the car is not level.

3. The drain plug is on the bottom of the transmission. Place a large container underneath the transmission and remove the plug.

CAUTION: *Work carefully and wear thick gloves. The hot oil can cause severe scalding.*

4. Allow the oil to drain completely. Clean off the plug and reinstall it. Tighten it until it is just snug.

5. Fill the transmission with SAE 80 or SAE 80/90 gear oil except for Celicas with the S53 transmissions; for these cars use Dexron® II ATF. The oil usually comes in a plastic squeeze bottle with a long nozzle; otherwise

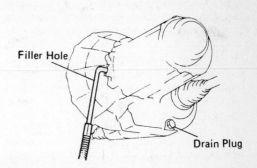

Typical drain and fill locations for FWD or 4WD manual transmissions

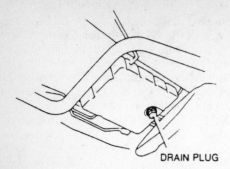

DRAIN PLUG

Typical drain plug location for automatic transmission

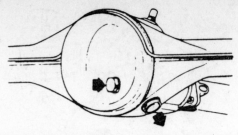

Filler (upper) plug and drain (lower) plug locations on the differential

you can use a squeeze bulb or a kitchen baster to squirt the oil in. Refer to the Capacities chart for the proper amount of oil to put in.

6. The oil level should come up to the top of the filler hole.

7. Replace the filler plug, drive the car for a few minutes, stop, and check for any leaks.

Automatic

The automatic transmission fluid should be changed every 20,000 miles. If the car is normally used in severe service, such as stop-and-go driving, trailer towing or the like, the interval should be reduced to every 10,000 miles. The fluid should be hot before it is drained; a 20 minute drive will accomplish this.

Toyota's automatic transmissions have a drain plug in them so that you can simply remove the plug, drain the fluid, replace the plug and then refill the transmission. If you keep the car in regular maintenance, removing the pan should not be necessary except for repair. Removing the pan is generally discouraged as unnecessary and a primary cause of leaks.

1. With the engine and transmission oil thoroughly warmed up, elevate and safely support the car on jackstands.

2. Remove the plug and drain the fluid into a large container.

CAUTION: *Work carefully and wear thick gloves. The hot oil can cause severe scalding!*

3. While the fluid is draining, clean the drain plug and replace the washer on it. The small metal washer is a non–reusable item; if you don't replace it, the plug may leak.

4. When the fluid stops coming out of the drain hole, install the drain plug and washer, tighten them to 20 Nm or 15 ft. lbs.

WARNING: *Do not over tighten the drain bolt!*

5. It is a good idea to measure the amount of fluid drained from the transmission to determine the correct amount of fresh fluid to add. This is because some parts of the transmission may not drain completely and using the dry

refill amount specified in the Capacities chart could lead to overfilling. Fluid is added only through the dipstick tube. Use only the proper automatic transmission fluid; do not overfill.

6. Replace the dipstick after filling. Start the engine and allow it to idle. DO NOT race the engine.

7. After the engine has idled for a few minutes, shift the transmission slowly through the gears and then return it to Park. With the engine still idling, check the fluid level on the dipstick. If necessary, add more fluid to raise the level.

Differential

FLUID LEVEL CHECK

The oil in the differential should be checked at least every 10,000 miles and replaced every 20,000 miles. Front wheel drive Celicas with automatic transaxles employ a separate differential (final drive) from the transmission. Draining the transaxle does NOT drain the differential. On FWD cars with manual transmissions, the lubricant is shared by the transaxle and final drive.

Rear wheel drive Supras have the differential at the rear of the car.

All-Trac 4wd Celicas have the front differential incorporated with the manual transaxle and also have a separate rear unit which must be included in the maintenance schedule. To inspect the oil level on the separate FWD Celica

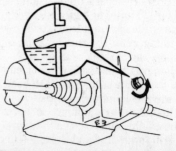

Front wheel drive automatic transmissions have a separate differential. It must be checked periodically

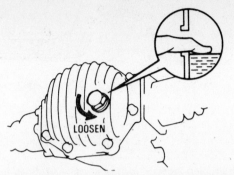

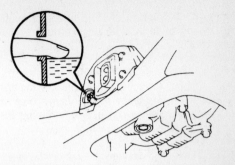

Check the fluid level in the rear axle with your finger

Checking the rear differential on 4WD All-Trac Celicas

with automatic or the rear differential on RWD or 4wd cars:

1. Elevate and safely support the car on jackstands. It must be level to obtain an accurate reading.

2. Remove the filler plug from the differential.

3. If the oil begins to trickle out of the hole, there is enough. Otherwise, carefully insert your finger (watch out for sharp threads) into the hole and check to see if the oil is up to the bottom edge of the filler hole.

4. If not, add oil through the hole until the level is at the edge of the hole. Most gear oils come in a plastic squeeze bottle with a nozzle, making additions simple. You can also use a common kitchen baster. Use standard GL-5 hypoid type gear oil; SAE 90 or SAE 80 if you live in a particularly cold area.

5. Replace the filler plug. Lower the car to the ground.

6. Drive the car for 5–10 miles. Inspect for leaks.

NOTE: *The car must be driven to warm the oil. Idling the engine will not warm the differential oil.*

DRAIN AND REFILL

The gear oil in the differential should be changed at least every 20,000 miles.

To drain and fill differential or final drive unit:

1. After driving the car 5–10 miles to warm the oil, elevate and safely support the vehicle on a level surface.

2. Remove the filler (upper) plug. Place a large container under the drain plug.

3. Remove the drain (lower) plug and gasket, if so equipped. Allow all of the oil to drain into the container.

4. Install the drain plug. Tighten it so that it will not leak, but do not over tighten.

5. Refill with the proper grade and viscosity of lubricant (see Recommended Lubricants chart). Be sure that the level reaches the bottom of the filler plug (or to within 5mm of

the plug on independent type differentials). DO NOT overfill.

6. Install the filler plug.

7. Lower the car to the ground and drive it 5–10 miles to warm the oil. Inspect for leakage.

Radiator Coolant

FLUID LEVEL CHECK

It's a good idea to check the coolant once or twice per month. If the engine is hot, let it cool for a few minutes and then check the level by

The freezing protection rating can be checked with an antifreeze tester

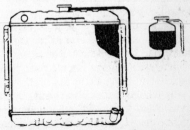

Always check the level in the expansion tank; do not remove the cap if there is any heat in the system

looking at the amount of fluid in the translucent expansion tank. The level should be between the "FULL" and "LOW" marks.

NOTE: *This level will change with engine
temperature. Try to check the level under the
same conditions every time (always cool or
always hot) to avoid confusion. following the
procedure given earlier in this chapter.*

CAUTION: *NEVER uncap a hot or warm radiator; you can be badly scalded by steam
and liquid. ALWAYS check the level in the
expansion tank without removing its cap.*

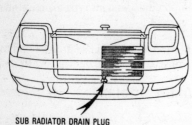

SUB RADIATOR DRAIN PLUG

**The 3S-GTE intercooler has its own radiator which
must be drained separately**

Check the antifreeze and anti-boil protection
rating at least once a year, preferably just
before the winter sets in. This can be done with
an antifreeze tester (most service stations have
one on hand and will probably check it for you.
This inexpensive tool is available at auto parts
stores.) The tester, shaped like a kitchen
baster, has a float or balls inside which (when
floating) indicate the strength of the coolant
and the protection it will give. Be sure to draw
the proper amount of coolant into the tester to
lift the float or balls. Most testers have a mark
or line on the case to show the correct level.
Once filled, tap the case once or twice to dis-
lodge any air bubbles in the fluid.

DRAIN SYSTEM, FLUSH AND REFILL

The cooling system should be drained, thoroughly flushed and refilled at least every
60,000 miles and then every 30,000 thereafter.
This is a minimum requirement; more frequent replacement may be needed due to driving conditions in your area.

In general, antifreeze does not "wear out". If
the system is free of leaks and the car receives
normal usage, the coolant is well capable of lasting several seasons. The main reason for changing the coolant periodically is to remove pollutants which have gotten into the system.

The coolant should always be changed with
the engine cold. Overnight or stone cold is best;
if this is not possible, allow the engine to cool at
least 3 full hours from last use. In very hot

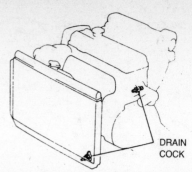

DRAIN
COCK

**Drain plug location for the 3S-GE and 3S-FE en-
gines**

weather this time period may need to be extended or even doubled.

CAUTION: *When draining the coolant, keep
in mind that cats and dogs are attracted by
the ethylene glycol antifreeze, and are quite
likely to drink any that is left in an uncovered container or in puddles on the ground.
This will prove fatal in sufficient quantity.
Always drain the coolant into a sealable container. Coolant should be reused unless it is
contaminated or several years old.*

1. Depending on agility and the length of
your arm, this procedure may be done on the
ground or with the front of the car elevated. If
you raise the front of the car, set the parking
brake and block the rear wheels. Always use
jackstands to safely support the vehicle.

2. Inside the car, set the heater temperature control to the hottest position; this will
allow the heater core to drain as well. Remove
the radiator cap and the expansion tank cap.

3. Open the drain cocks on the radiator and
the engine block. Drain the coolant into suitable large containers. The drain plugs on all four
cylinder engines are located on the bottom of
the radiator and on the firewall side of the
engine block. On the six cylinder engines, the
plugs are on the bottom of the radiator and on
the right side of the engine block (under the
manifold).

NOTE: *All-Trac Celicas with the 3S-GTE
engine have a separate cooling system for the
intercooler and turbocharger. The small sub-
radiator has its own drain cock and the
system has its own expansion tank. These are
drained and filled separately from the
engine cooling system.*

4. If desired, flush the cooling system after
it has drained.

a. Using a garden hose, fill the radiator
and allow the water to run out the engine
drain cocks. Continue until the water runs
clear. Be sure to clean the expansion tank as
needed.

b. If the system is badly contaminated
with rust or scale, use a commercial cleaner

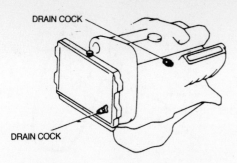

Drain plug locations for the 5M-GE engine

to clean it out. Follow the manufacturer's instructions.

c. Some common causes of extremely dirty systems are: engine damage (leaking oil into the coolant), air in the system, poor maintenance or failure to change coolant, leaks, use of excessively hard or soft water or failure to use the correct mixture of antifreeze and water.

4. Close the drain cocks without over tightening them.

5. Using fresh, ethylene glycol based antifreeze, prepare a container of coolant which is 50% water and 50% anti-freeze. Slightly more anti-freeze may be added for special conditions but must never exceed 70% of the solution. The

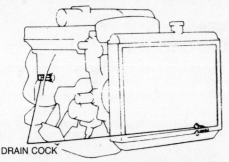

Drain plug locations for the 7M-GE and 7M-GTE engines

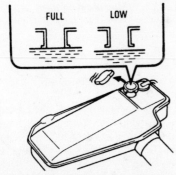

Don't forget the intercooler coolant system on 3S-GTE

use of de–mineralized or distilled water is recommended to eliminate corrosion and deposits in the system. Refer to the Capacities Chart for the correct amount to mix for your car.

WARNING: *Never use alcohol based coolant!*

6. Slowly pour this mixture into the radiator. Take your time; if air is trapped, you'll be there longer. If your first container does not fill the system, remix another batch and continue pouring. To refill the intercooler system on the 3S-GTE engine, follow the procedure below:

a. Pour the coolant mixture into the intercooler tank until it is full.

b. Turn the ignition key to the "ON" position, press the accelerator pedal and release it. This causes the intercooler water pump to operate and circulate the coolant within the system. Turn the ignition off and top up the fluid level.

c. Repeat the pattern of 'ignition on – pump the pedal – check the level' several times until the level no longer drops in the tank. Always turn the key off before checking the coolant level; the level will drop when the pump is running.

d. Make certain you have refilled the main cooling system. Install the intercooler cap and start the engine. After a minute of low rpm warm up, gun the engine to about 3000 rpm. Do this several times, then shut the engine off.

e. Carefully remove the cap from the intercooler tank and check the coolant level, topping it up as needed.

f. Wait 20 minutes (engine and ignition off) and repeat step b (above) once or twice. Top the coolant as needed and install the intercooler cap.

NOTE: *If the intercooler is not filled to capacity, its performance will suffer. Double check that all the air is removed. Additionally, if the fluid level drops too far within the intercooler, the pump will not operate due to a built-in safety system.*

7. When the radiator is full, simply wait a few minutes as some air will need to escape. Top off the radiator either with the pre-mixed coolant or fresh water.

8. Start the engine with the radiator cap off. After about a minute, top off the radiator fluid level (just to the bottom of the neck) and install the cap.

9. Fill the reservoir (expansion tank) about 1/2 full and install the cap.

10. Shut the engine off and check the drain cocks for leakage.

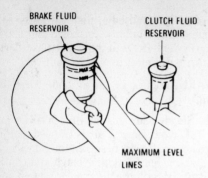

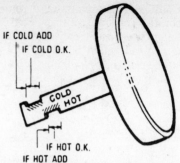

Power steering pump dipstick on newer models

Brake and clutch master cylinder locations-typical

Brake and Clutch Master Cylinders

FLUID LEVEL CHECK

The brake and clutch master cylinders are located under the hood, in the left rear section of the engine compartment on the firewall. They are made of translucent plastic so that the levels may be checked without removing the tops. The fluid level in both reservoirs should be checked at least every month.

The fluid level should be maintained at the upper most mark on the side of the reservoir. Any sudden decreases in the level indicates a possible leak in the system and should be checked immediately. A gradual lowering of the reservoir level will occur as the brakes wear over the life of the linings. This is not a cause for immediate concern; the fluid is not lost, but relocated into the system. If you add fluid to compensate for this effect, you will need to remove some when the brakes are replaced.

When it is necessary to remove the cap from a reservoir, first use a clean rag to wipe the cap and reservoir completely free of dust and dirt. These are the enemies of any hydraulic system and care must be used to keep the system clean.

Use only fresh, uncontaminated brake fluid meeting or exceeding DOT 3 standards. Be careful not to spill any brake fluid on the painted surfaces; it eats the paint. Do not allow the brake fluid container or the master cylinder reservoir to remain open any longer than necessary; brake fluid absorbs moisture from the air, reducing its effectiveness and causing corrosion in the lines.

Power Steering Pump

FLUID LEVEL CHECK

The fluid level in the power steering reservoir should be checked at least every month. The vehicle should be parked on level ground, with the engine warm and running at normal idle.

After wiping the lid and tank with a clean rag, remove the filler cap and check the level on the dipstick; it should be within the "HOT" area on the dipstick. If you check the level without warming the car up, use the "COLD" range to gauge the fluid level. If the level is low, add Dexron® type automatic transmission fluid until the proper level is achieved. Don't overfill the system.

Look down into the reservoir and check for evidence of foaming or emulsification which indicates the existence of air in the system. Air may also be indicated by a distinct growling from the system as the wheels are turned to full lock in either direction. The air may be present simply due to low fluid or because of a leak in the system.

Battery

FLUID LEVEL CHECK

Check the battery electrolyte level at least once a month, or more often in hot weather or during periods of extended open-road opera-

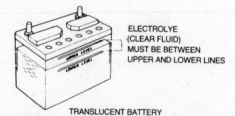

Some batteries have level indicator lines on their sides

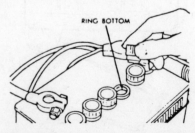

Fill each battery cell to the bottom of the split ring with water

tion. (Continuous charging causes some water to evaporate.) The level can be checked through the case on translucent polypropylene batteries; the cell caps must be removed on other models. The electrolyte level in each cell should be kept filled to the split ring inside, or the line marked on the outside of the case.

If the level is low, add only distilled water, or colorless, odorless drinking water. If you live in an area of hard or mineral water, the use of softened water is recommended. (The reason for using distilled water is to eliminate the internal mineral and chemical deposits which can shorten the life of the battery.)

Add water through the opening until the level is correct. Each cell is completely separate from the others, so each must be checked and filled individually.

If water is added in freezing weather, the car should be driven several miles to allow the water to mix with the electrolyte. Otherwise, the battery could freeze.

Chassis Greasing and Lubrication

Neither the Celica nor Supra require chassis lubrication in the classic sense. Due to the use of reliable, sealed suspension joints, there are no grease fittings under the car. This does not excuse you from lubricating everyday components like door hinges and the hood latch.

There is no set period recommended by Toyota for body lubrication. However, it is a good idea to lubricate the following body points at least once a year, especially before cold weather.

Lubricate with engine oil or light spray lubricant:
- Door latches
- Door rollers
- Door, hood, and hinge pivots Lubricate with Lubriplate®:
- Trunk lid latch and glove box door latch
- Front seat slides
- Hood latch and release Lubricate with silicone spray:
- All rubber weather stripping
- Hood stops Lubricate with graphite powder:
- Key locks in doors.
- Trunk or hatch lock

When finished lubricating a body part, be sure that all the excess lubricant has been wiped off, especially in the areas of the car which may come in contact with clothing.

Wheel Bearings

With one exception, the front and rear wheel bearings used on Celicas and Supras are permanently sealed and pressed into place. They are considered life-of-the-car components and require no maintenance. Replacement of these sealed bearings—a difficult job requiring special tools—is discussed in Chapter 8.

The front wheels of the 1986 Supra have open or serviceable bearings. They should be cleaned and repacked every 40,000 miles or every 4 years, whichever occurs first. These bearings should be inspected and serviced more

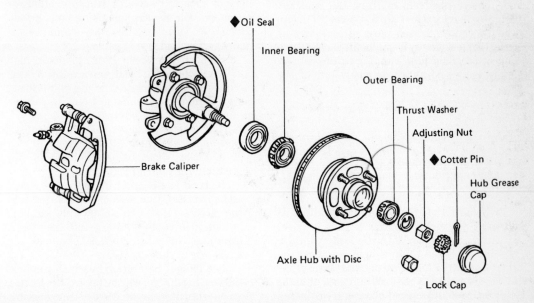

Front wheel bearing components, 1986 Supra

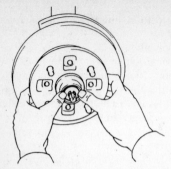

Slide the axle hub and disc off the wheel spindle

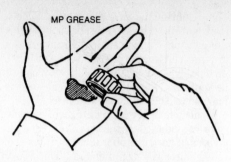

Packing the wheel bearing with grease

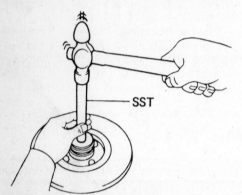

Installing a new grease seal. Always use a seal driver or the seal may be damaged

frequently in areas of heavy road salt use or extremely rainy areas. To service these bearings:

1. Loosen the lug nuts while the car is on the ground. Elevate the car and place jackstands at the correct support points. Remove the wheel.

2. Remove the brake caliper mounting bolts and remove the caliper from the knuckle. (Refer to Chapter 9 for help if you need it). Support the caliper from a piece of stiff wire or string tied to a nearby component. Do NOT disconnect the fluid hose running to the caliper; simply move the entire assembly out of the way.

CAUTION: *Some brake pads and shoes contain asbestos, which has been determined to be a cancer causing agent. Never clean the brake surfaces with compressed air! Avoid inhaling any dust from brake surfaces! When cleaning brakes, use commercially available brake cleaning fluids.*

3. Remove the grease cap (don't distort it) the cotter pin, lock cap and nut.

4. Hold the outside of the hub with your fingers and place the thumbs lightly against the inner edge of the hub. Pull outward gently; the whole assembly will slide off and your thumbs will keep the outer wheel bearing from falling to the ground. The inner bearing (on the other side of the hub) is held in by the grease seal.

5. Place the hub and disc assembly on the work bench. Remove the outer bearing and flat washer. Turn the assembly over and use a seal remover or similar suitable tool to pry out the inner grease seal. Remove the inner bearing.

NOTE: *Since this is a maintenance procedure, do NOT attempt to remove the bearing races from the inside of the hub and disc. The races should be removed only in the event of bearing replacement, discussed in Chapter 9.*

6. Clean all the components thoroughly, including the inside of the hub, both bearings and the stub axle on which everything mounts. All traces of the old grease must be removed.

CAUTION: *Use only proper commercial parts cleaners. Do not use gasoline or similar products for cleaning parts.*

NOTE: *A stiff–bristled parts cleaning brush or even an old, clean paint brush is very handy for cleaning bearings.*

7. After cleaning, allow all the parts to air dry. Never blow bearings dry with compressed air. Inspect all the parts. Look carefully for any signs of imperfect surfaces, cracking, bluing or looseness. Check the matching surface on which the bearing run; the races should be virtually perfect and free of damage.

8. Repack the wheel bearings using high quality multi–purpose (MP) grease. Each bearing must be fully packed. The use of a bearing packer is highly recommended but the job can be done by hand if care is taken.

NOTE: *This is a messy job. Have plenty of rags handy and some hand cleaner*

a. Place a golf ball–sized lump of MP grease in the palm of your hand.

b. Hold the bearing in your other hand and force the wide side of the bearing into the grease. Use a pushing and scraping motion to force the grease up into the rollers. Continue this until grease oozes out the small side of the bearing.

c. Change the position by which you hold the bearing and repeat the procedure, forcing grease into an untreated area of the bearing.

d. Continue around the bearing until all the rollers are packed solid with grease.

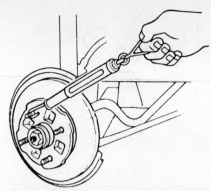

Use the spring scale to measure the preload

e. Place the bearing on a clean, lint–free rag or towel while greasing other components.

9. Coat the inside of the hub with a liberal layer of grease. Remember that the stub axle comes through here; don't pack it solid.

10. Fill the grease cup about 1/2 full of MP grease.

11. Install the inner bearing into the disc. Use a new grease seal and install it with a seal installer such as SST 09550-00050 or equivalent. Do not attempt to use a hammer or drift; the seal may be damaged. Coat the lip of the seal lightly with a bit of MP grease.

12. Fit the outer bearing loosely into place and put the large flat washer over it. Again holding the washer and bearing in place with your thumbs, fit the assembly onto the stub axle. Make sure the small tooth on the inside of the

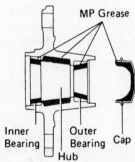

Correct locations and application of wheel bearing grease

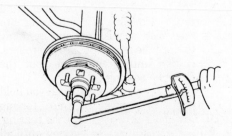

Preliminary tightening of the hub nut

bearing washer aligns with the groove in the stub axle.

13. Install the nut onto the axle. Use the torque wrench and set the nut to 29 Nm (22 ft. lbs).

NOTE: *After the nut is set, take a moment to thoroughly clean your hands and tools. If any grease got onto the brake disc, remove it with an aerosol cleaner.*

14. Turn the hub right and left two or three times each way; this will allow the bearings to seek their final positions.

15. Loosen the hub nut so that there is just a minimum amount of in-and-out free play. Correct axial free play at this point is 1.0mm or (0.039 in.) Check this by pulling on the hub as you did to remove it. You should feel a very slight motion but no more.

16. Use a spring tension gauge to measure the force needed to turn the hub. This is a measurement of the resistance of the grease seal without the resistance of the bearings. Write the measurement down.

17. Using just the socket in your hand, (remove the socket handle or ratchet), tighten the hub nut as tight as possible.

18. Again use the spring scale to measure rotational force of the hub. The measurement will now reflect the preload of the bearing. This number should be from 0–2.3 lbs. (0–10 N or 0–1050 g) MORE than the force measured with the nut loose.

19. If the preload is less than specification, tighten the nut slightly and remeasure. If the preload is excessive, loosen the nut and retighten it by holding the socket in your hand; remeasure.

WARNING: *Always perform the measuring procedure. A bearing either too loose or too tight will wear prematurely and possibly affect the behavior of the wheel.*

20. Install the lock cap, a new cotter pin (always!) and the grease cap. If the cotter pin hole does not line up, first try turning the lock cap to a different position. If this is ineffective, tighten the nut by the smallest possible amount.

21. Install the brake caliper. Tighten the mounting bolts to 91 Nm (67 ft. lbs).

22. Reinstall the wheel and lower the vehicle to the ground. Final tighten the lug nuts when the car is on the ground to 103 Nm or 76 ft. lbs.

PUSHING AND TOWING

Pushing

Push starting or "kick starting" Celicas and Supras is not recommended. If the engine should fail to start, the catalytic converter can be severely damaged by the build up of unburned fuel passing through the system. Additionally, if the battery is so low the car will not start, the fuel injection controls may be inoperative.

It is possible to push start a manual transmission Celica or Supra as an emergency, no–alternative measure. More than one car has received a dented fender or bumper from this operation. To push start the car; turn the ignition switch to the ON position, push in the clutch pedal, put the gear shift lever in second or third gear and depress the gas pedal just a bit. As the car begins to pick up momentum while being pushed, release the clutch pedal. Immediately as the engine catches, push the clutch pedal in and apply sufficient throttle to keep the engine running.

CAUTION: *NEVER attempt to push start the car while it is in reverse!*

Celicas and Supras equipped with an automatic transmission can NOT be push started no matter how far or how fast they are pushed.

Towing the Car

The absolute best way to have the car towed or transported is on a flat–bed or rollback transporter. These units are becoming more common and are very useful for moving disabled vehicles quickly. Both the Celica and Supra have lower bodywork and under trays which can be easily damaged by the sling of a conventional tow truck; an operator unfamiliar with your particular model can cause severe damage to the suspension or drive line by hooking up chains and J–hooks incorrectly.

If a flatbed is not available (your should specifically request one), the car may be towed by a hoist or conventional tow vehicle. Front wheel drive cars with automatic transmission must be towed with the drive wheels off the ground. FWD cars with a manual transmission can be towed with either end up in the air or with all four wheels on the ground. You need only remember that the transmission must be in Neutral, the parking brake must be off and the ignition switch must be in the **ACC** position. The steering column lock is not strong enough to hold the front wheels straight under towing.

Rear drive cars should also be towed with the drive wheels off the ground if possible. If the rear is elevated, the ignition should be in the **ACC** position to release the steering column. If a RWD car must be towed with the rear wheels on the ground, release the parking brake and put the transmission in **N** or neutral. Manual transmission RWD cars may be then be towed.

Alternative for towing the All–Trac. Note that all 4 wheels are off the ground

Automatic transmission RWD cars should not be towed faster than 30 mph or farther than 50 miles. (Although the car is in neutral, parts of the automatic transmission still turn with the wheels. Damage can result from towing farther or faster than recommended.) If the car must be towed farther or faster, the driveshaft must be disconnected at the differential to avoid damage.

The four wheel drive Celica All–Trac presents its own towing problems. Since the front and rear wheels are connected through the

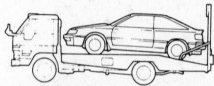

The preferred way to tow or transport your car

Alternate towing hook—ups for front wheel drive cars with automatic transaxles; Never tow the car backwards

TIE-DOWN TABS

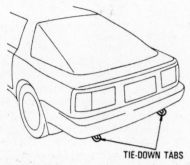

TIE-DOWN TABS

Exposed tabs front and rear allow quick connection of a rope or chain

drive system, all four wheels must be considered in the towing arrangement. If a flatbed is not available, the All–Trac should be towed with the front end elevated. As the rear wheels roll on ground, the front wheels will turn. They must be clear of the hoist and sling equipment. If the vehicle cannot be towed front–end–up, both ends must be elevated, using a set of dolly wheels. NEVER elevate the rear and tow the All–Trac; severe damage will result.

Celicas and Supras have conveniently located tie-down hooks at the front and rear of the vehicle. These make ideal locations to secure a rope or chain for flat–towing the car or extracting it from an off–road excursion. The vehicle may only be flat–towed on hard surfaced roads and only in a normal or forward direction.

A driver must be in the towed vehicle to control it. Before towing, the parking brake must be released and the transmission put in neutral. Do NOT flat tow the vehicle if the brakes, steering, axles, suspension or drive line is damaged.

CAUTION: *If the engine is not running, the power assists for the steering and brakes will not be operating. Steering and braking will require more time and much more effort without the assist.*

TOWING A TRAILER

WARNING: *Towing a trailer qualifies as severe duty for the tow vehicle. Maintenance must be performed more frequently!*

Recommendations

Your car was primarily designed to carry passengers and cargo. It is important to remember that towing a trailer will place additional loads on your vehicle's engine, drive train, steering, braking and other systems. However, if you find it necessary to tow a trailer, using the proper equipment is a must.

Local laws may require specific equipment such as trailer brakes or fender mounted mirrors. Check your local laws.

Trailer Weight

Toyota specifically limits total trailer weight to 2000 lbs. (trailer and load) for both Celica and Supra vehicles. Since these cars generally weigh 2400–3100 lbs, you can see that a fully loaded trailer can almost double the load. In addition to this maximum total weight, no more than 200 lbs. (or 10% of the total trailer load) should be supported by the hitch. This tongue weight limit is very important in maintaining control of the tow vehicle.

The trailer hitch should conform to all applicable laws and be sufficient for the maximum trailer load. Follow the directions supplied by the hitch manufacturer and bolt it securely to the rear bumper. do not use axle mounted hitches as they can cause damage to axles, wheels, tires and bearings. Never install a hitch which can interfere with the normal function of the energy absorbing bumper.

WARNING: *All—Trac vehicles require a hitch with a special protector. Please consult your local dealer for specific advice regarding this hitch.*

Almost all trailers now come equipped with a rear and side lighting. A wiring harness must be installed to connect the automotive lighting and brake light systems to the trailer. Any reputable hitch installer can perform this installation. You can also install the harnesses, but great care must be paid to matching the correct wires during the installation. Each circuit must be wired individually for taillights, brake lights,

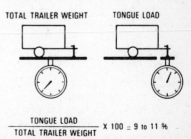

TOTAL TRAILER WEIGHT   TONGUE LOAD

$$\frac{\text{TONGUE LOAD}}{\text{TOTAL TRAILER WEIGHT}} \times 100 = 9 \text{ to } 11\%$$

Trailer weight and tongue load are both important when towing

right and left turn signals and in many cases, reverse lights. If the trailer is equipped with electric brakes, the wiring for this circuit should be installed at the same time as the lighting harness. Remember that the additional lighting may exceed the present fuse rating in the car's fuse box; upgrading the fuse may be necessary.

Cooling

One of the most common, if not THE most common, problems associated with trailer towing is engine overheating.

The cooling system should be checked frequently and maintained in top notch condition. If the engine temperature gauge indicates overheating, particularly on long grades, immediately turn off the air conditioner (if in use), pull off the road and stop in a safe location. Do not attempt to "limp in" with a hot motor—you'll cause severe damage.

Although most engines Celicas and Supras have some form of oil cooler, a larger after market engine oil cooler can be helpful for prolonging engine oil life and reducing overall engine temperatures. Both of these factors increase engine life.

Engine oil cooler systems consist of an adapter, screwed on in place of the oil filter, a remote filter mounting and a multi-tube, finned heat exchanger, which is mounted in front of the radiator or air conditioning condenser.

TRANSMISSION

An automatic transmission is usually recommended for trailer towing. Modern automatics have proven reliable and, of course, easy to operate, in trailer towing.

The increased load of a trailer causes an increase in the temperature of the automatic transmission fluid. Heat is the worst enemy of an automatic transmission. As the temperature of the fluid increases, the life of the fluid decreases.

It is essential, therefore, that you install an automatic transmission cooler or supplement the one already present.

The cooler, which consists of a multi-tube, finned heat exchanger, is usually installed in front of the radiator or air conditioning compressor, and hooked inline with the transmission cooler tank inlet line. Follow the cooler manufacturer's installation instructions.

Select a cooler of at least adequate capacity, based upon the combined gross weights of the car and trailer.

Cooler manufacturers recommend that you use an after market cooler in addition to he present cooling tank in your radiator.

NOTE: *A transmission cooler can sometimes cause slow or harsh shifting in the transmission during cold weather, until the fluid has a chance to come up to normal operating temperature. Some coolers can be purchased with or retrofitted with a temperature bypass valve which will allow fluid flow through the cooler only when the fluid has reached operating temperature or above.*

Handling A Trailer

Towing a trailer with ease and safety requires a certain amount of skill that can only be gained through experience. Many trailer accidents occur because the driver—however skilled—forgot some of the basics.

• When loading the trailer, keep about 60% of the weight forward of the axle. This will prevent the trailer from trying to pass the car during cornering.

• Always perform a walk–around check of all the lighting before pulling out.

• Check the tire pressure and condition on both the car and trailer frequently. Underinflated tires are a hazard.

• After connecting the trailer, observe the car for any extreme nose–up or nose–down attitudes. If the car is not approximately level with the trailer connected, rebalance the load in the trailer.

• Always connect the safety chains between the trailer and car. They should be crossed below the hitch to catch the tongue if the trailer separates from the car.

• Stopping distances are increased dramatically. Allow plenty of room and anticipate stops. Sudden braking may jackknife the trailer or throw the car into a skid.

• Accelerate slowly and smoothly. Jerky driving will cause increased wear on the drive line.

• Toyota recommends that you not exceed 45 mph when towing. Swaying and instability increase quickly above this speed.

• Avoid sharp turns. The trailer will always turn "inside" the car; allow plenty of room.

• Crosswinds and rough roads increase instability. Know when you're about to be passed by a large vehicle and prepare for it.

• If swaying begins, grip the steering wheel firmly and hold the vehicle straight ahead. Reduce speed gradually without using the brake. If you make NO extreme corrections in brakes, throttle or steering, the car and trailer will stabilize quickly.

• Passing requires much greater distances for acceleration. Plan ahead. Remember to allow for the length of the trailer when pulling back in.

• Use a lower gear to descend long grades.

Slow down before downshifting.

• Avoid riding the brake. This will overheat the brakes and reduce their efficiency.

• When parking the combination, always apply the parking brake and place blocks under the trailer wheels. A heavy trailer may literally drag the car down a grade. Don't forget to remove the chocks before leaving.

• Backing up with a trailer is a skill to be practiced before it is needed. Find a large open area (get permission if necessary) and spend at least an hour learning how to do it.

JUMP STARTING A DEAD BATTERY

The chemical reaction in a battery produces explosive hydrogen gas. This is the safe way to jump start a dead battery, reducing the chances of an accidental spark that could cause an explosion.

Jump Starting Precautions

1. Be sure both batteries are of the same voltage.

WARNING: *Some tow trucks or heavy-duty starting equipment provide 24 volts of electricity. This will absolutely destroy a 12 volt electrical system and the low voltage computers and sensors in the fuel injection system. If you're not sure of the voltage, don't hook up to it.*

2. Be sure both batteries are of the same polarity (have the same grounded terminal). Make certain you know which is which.

3. Be sure the vehicles are not touching.

4. Be sure the vent cap holes are not obstructed.

5. Do not smoke or allow electrolyte on your skin or clothing.

6. Be sure the electrolyte is not frozen. Never charge or jump a frozen battery.

Jump Starting Procedure

1. Determine voltages of the two batteries; they must be the same.

2. Bring the starting vehicle close (they must not touch) so that the batteries can be reached easily.

3. Turn off all accessories and both engines. Put both cars in Neutral or Park and set the handbrakes.

4. Cover the cell caps with a rag. Do not cover terminals.

5. If the terminals on the rundown battery are heavily corroded, clean them.

6. Identify the positive and negative posts on both batteries and connect the cables in the order shown.

7. Start the engine of the starting vehicle and run it at fast idle. Try to start the car with the dead battery. Crank it for no more than 10 seconds at a time and let it cool for 20 seconds in between tries.

NOTE: *A totally discharged battery may not be able to turn the starter even with the jumpers attached. Run the engine on the helper vehicle at 2000 rpm for 3–5 minutes; this will provide a minimal charge to the discharged battery.*

8. If it doesn't start in 3 tries, there is something else wrong.

9. Disconnect the cables in the exact reverse order of connection.

10. Replace the cell covers and dispose of the rags.

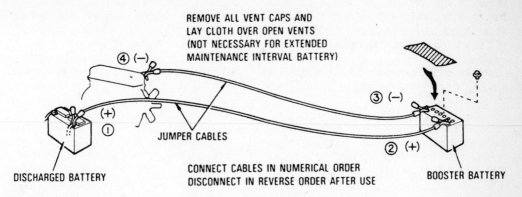

Using a booster battery to start a disabled car. Always observe the correct order of cable connection and removal

CAPACITIES CHART

Year	Model	Engine Series Identification	Engine Crankcase (qts.) with Filter	Manual Trans. (qts.)	Auto Trans. Drain & Refill (qts.)	Auto Trans. Dry Fill (qts.)	Differential (qts.)	Engine Coolant (qts.)
1986	Celica	2S-E	4.2	2.7 ①	2.5	6.3	1.7 ②	6.8
		3S-E	4.1	2.7 ①	2.5	6.3	1.7 ②	7.4
	Supra	5M-GE	5.4	2.5	2.5	6.9	1.3	7.8
		7M-GE	5.4	2.5	2.5	6.9	1.3	7.8
1987	Celica	3S-FE	4.3	2.7 ①	2.5	6.3	1.7 ②	6.8
		3S-GE	4.1	2.7 ①	2.5	6.3	1.7 ②	7.4
	Supra	7M-GE	4.7	2.5 ③	1.7	7.6	1.4	8.6
		7M-GTE	4.2	2.5 ③	1.7	7.6	1.4	8.6
1988	Celica	3S-FE	4.3	2.7 ①	2.6	6.3	1.7 ②	6.8
		3S-GE	4.1	2.7 ①	2.6	6.3	1.7 ③	7.4
	Celica All-Trac	3S-GTE	3.8	5.1 ④	—	—	—	8.5 ⑤
	Supra	7M-GE	4.4	2.5 ③	1.7	7.6	1.4	8.6
		7M-GTE	4.4	2.5 ③	1.7	7.6	1.4	8.7
1989	Celica	3S-FE	4.1	2.7 ①	2.6	6.3	1.7 ②	6.7
		3S-GE	4.1	2.7 ①	2.6	6.3	1.7 ②	6.6
	Celica All-Trac	3S-GTE	3.8	5.1 ④	—	—	—	6.8 ⑤
	Supra	7M-GE	4.7	2.5 ③	1.7	7.6	1.4	8.6
		7M-GTE	4.7	2.5 ③	1.7	7.6	1.4	8.6
1990	Celica	4A-FE	3.3	2.7	3.5	8.5 ⑦	2.7	5.6
		5S-FE	4.4 ⑥	2.7	3.5	8.5 ⑦	2.7	6.5
	Celica All-Trac	3S-GTE	4.3	2.7	3.5	8.5 ⑦	2.7	6.5
	Supra	7M-GE	4.7	2.5 ③	1.7	7.6	1.4	8.6
		7M-GTE	4.7	2.5 ③	1.7	7.6	1.4	8.7

① Includes differential fluid
② Auto Trans.
③ Type R154 Transmission 3.2 qts.
④ Includes differential and transfer case
⑤ 1.8 qts. for intercooler; drain and fill separately
⑥ Without oil cooler
⑦ Type A 243L Trans. 8.1 qts.

SEVERE CONDITION MAINTENANCE SCHEDULE

Any of the following are severe conditions:
- Towing a trailer or carrying heavy loads.
- Repeated short trips (under 5 miles) in below freezing weather
- Extended periods of idling
- Operation on dusty, rough or salted roads

	Months	6	12	18	24	30	36	42	48	54	60	66	72
	Miles × 1000	5	10	15	20	25	30	35	40	45	50	55	60
Timing Belt													R①
Valve clearance													A
Drive Belts						I							I
Engine Oil Filter②		R	R	R	R	R	R	R	R	R	R	R	R
Engine coolant⑤							I			R④			R
Exhaust pipes				I			I			I			I
Idle speed			A				A						A
Air filter		I	I	I	I	I	R	I	I	I	I	I	R
Fuel line & connections							I						I
Fuel filler cap gasket													R
Spark plugs 2S-E, 3S-FE							R						R
3S-GE, 3S-GTE, 5M-GE													R
7M-GE, 7M-GTE													R
4A-FE & 5S-FE							R						R
Charcoal canister													I
Brake linings & Drums			I		I		I		I		I		I
Brake pads & discs			I		I		I		I		I		I
Brake lines					I				I				I
Steering linkages			I		I		I		I		I		I
Drive shaft boots			I		I		I		I		I		I
Ball joints & dust covers			I		I		I		I		I		I
Trans. oil			R④		R		R④		R	R④			R
Differential oil and/or Transfer Case (4WD)					I				I/R③				I
Chassis & body bolts & nuts			I		I		I		I		I		I
Tire rotation		Every 7,500 miles or 6 months											

A—Check & adjust if nec.
R—Replace, change or lubricate
I—Inspect; replace or correct if nec.
① Vehicles which idle frequently and/or travel long distances @ low speeds.
② 7M-GTE & 3S-GTE: change oil every 2500 miles (or 3 months); change filter every 5000 miles or 6 months.
③ Replace oil in limited slip rear
④ 1990 vehicles only
⑤ After 1st change, change coolant every 30,000 miles (or 24 months).

NORMAL CONDITION MAINTENANCE SCHEDULE

	12	24	36	48	60	72
Months						
Miles × 1000	10	20	30	40	50	60
Valve clearance						A
Drive Belts						I
Engine Oil & Filter ①④	R	R	R	R	R	R
Engine coolant ③			I	R⑤		R
Exhaust pipes			I			I
Idle speed	A		A			A
Air filter			R			R
Fuel line & connections			I			I
Fuel filter cap gasket						R
Spark plugs 2S-E, 3S-FE			R			R
3S-GE, 2S-GTE						R
5M-GE, 7M-GE, 7M-GTE						R
4A-FE & 5S-FE			R			R
Charcoal canister						I
Brake linings & drums		I		I		I
Brake pads & discs		I		I		I
Brake lines		I		I		I
Steering linkage		I		I		I
Drive shaft boots		I		I		I
Ball joints & dust covers		I		I		I
Trans. oil		I		I		R
Differential oil		I		I/R②		I
Chassis & body bolts & nuts		I		I		I
Tire rotation	Every 7,500 miles or 6 months					

A—Check & adjust if nec.
R—Replace, change or lubricate
I—Inspect; replace or correct if nec.
① 7M-GTE & 3S-GTE: change oil every 2500 miles (or 3 months); change filter every 5000 miles or 6 months.
② Replace oil in limited slip rear
③ Includes liquid intercooler if so equipped.
④ For 1990 7M-GTE: change oil every 5000 miles (or 6 mos); change filter every 10,00 miles (or 1 year).
⑤ 1990 models (all): change coolant at 45,000 miles (or 36 months); then every 30,000 miles (or 24 months).

Engine Performance and Tune-Up

TUNE-UP PROCEDURES

In order to extract the best performance and economy from your engine it is essential that it be properly tuned at regular intervals. A regular tune-up will keep your Toyota's engine running smoothly and will prevent the annoying minor breakdowns and poor performance associated with an un-tuned engine.

A complete tune-up should be performed every 30,000 miles or twenty four months, whichever comes first. This interval should be halved if the car is operated under severe conditions, such as trailer towing, prolonged idling, continual stop and start driving, or if starting or running problems are noticed. It must be assumed that the routine maintenance described in Chapter 1 has been kept up, as this will have a decided effect on the results of a tune-up. All of the applicable steps of a tune-up should be followed in order, as the result is a cumulative one.

If the specifications on the tune-up sticker in the engine compartment of your Toyota disagree with the "Tune-Up Specifications" chart in this chapter, the figures on the sticker must be used. The sticker often reflects changes made during the production run.

Spark Plugs

Spark plugs ignite the air and fuel mixture in the cylinder as the piston reaches the top of the compression stroke. The controlled explosion that results forces the piston down, turning the crankshaft and the rest of the drive train.

Manufacturers are now required to certify that the spark plugs in their engines will meet emission specifications for 30,000 miles if other maintenance is performed properly. Certain types of plugs can be certified even beyond this point. The spark plugs should be removed periodically, inspected and perhaps cleaned; if they are in good condition there is no need to replace them. Condition of the plugs will vary over time, based on a number of factors: the mechanical condition of the engine; the type of fuel; the driving conditions; and the driver.

It is a good idea to remove the spark plugs every 10,000–15,000 miles to keep an eye on the mechanical state of the engine.

A small deposit of light tan or gray material (or rust red with unleaded fuel) on a spark plug that has been used for any period of time is to be considered normal. Any other color, or abnormal amounts of deposited material indicates that there is something amiss in the engine.

The gap between the center electrode and the side or ground electrode can be expected to increase not more than 0.001 in. (0.0254mm) every 1,000 miles under normal conditions.

When a plug fouls and begins to misfire, you will have to investigate, correct the cause of the fouling, and either clean or replace the plug.

Spark plugs suitable for use in your Toyota's engine are offered in a number of different heat ranges. The amount of heat which the plug absorbs is determined by the length of the lower insulator. The longer the insulator the hotter the plug will operate; the shorter the insulator, the cooler it will operate. A spark plug that absorbs (or retains) little heat and remains too cool will accumulate deposits of lead, oil, and carbon, because it is not hot enough to burn them off. This leads to fouling and consequent misfiring.

A spark plug that absorbs too much heat will have no deposits, but the electrodes will burn away quickly and, in some cases, pre–ignition may result. Pre–ignition occurs when the spark plug tips get so hot that they ignite the air/fuel mixture before the actual spark fires. This premature ignition will usually cause a pinging

TUNE-UP SPECIFICATIONS

Year	Model	Engine Displacement cu. in. (cc)	Spark Plugs Type	Gap (in.)	Ignition Timing (deg.) MT	AT	Com- pression Pressure (psi)	Fuel Pump (psi)	Idle Speed (rpm) MT	AT	Valve Clearance In.	Ex.
1986	Celica	121.7 (1995)	BPR5EY-11	0.043	10B	10B	171	35–38	700	700	Hyd.	Hyd.
		121.9 (1998)	BCPR5EP-11	0.043	10B	10B	171	35–38	750	750	0.008	0.012
	Supra	168.4 (2759)	BPR5EP-11	0.043	10B	10B	164	35–38	650	650	Hyd.	Hyd.
		180.3 (2954)	BCPR5EP-11	0.043	10B	10B	156	33–40	700	700	0.008	0.010
1987	Celica	3S-FE 121.9 (1998)	BCPR5EY-11	0.043	10B	10B	178	38–44	700	700	0.009	0.013
		3S-GE 121.9 (1998)	BCPR5EP-11	0.043	10B	10B	178	33–38	750	750	0.008	0.010
	Supra	7M-GE 180.3 (2954)	BCPR5EP-11	0.043	10B	10B	156	33–40	700	700	0.008	0.010
		7M-GTE 180.3 (2954)	BCPR6EP-N8	0.031	10B	10B	142	33–40	650	650	0.008	0.010
1988	Celica	3S-FE 121.9 (1998)	BCPR5EY-11	0.043	10B	10B	178	38–44	650	650	0.009	0.013
		3S-GE 121.9 (1998)	BCPR5EP-11	0.043	10B	10B	178	33–38	750	750	0.008	0.010
		3S-GTE 121.9 (1998)	BCPR5EP-8	0.031	10B	—	178	33–38	750	—	0.008	0.010
	Supra	7M-GE 180.3 (2954)	BCPR5EP-11	0.043	10B	10B	156	33–40	700	700	0.008	0.010
		7M-GTE 180.3 (2954)	BCPR6EP-N8	0.031	10B	10B	142	33–40	650	650	0.008	0.010
1989	Celica	3S-FE 121.9 (1998)	BCPR5EY-11	0.043	10B	10B	178	38–44	700	700	0.009	0.013
		3S-GE 121.9 (1998)	BCPR5EP-11	0.043	10B	10B	178	33–38	750	750	0.008	0.010
		3S-GTE 121.9 (1998)	BCPR5EP-8	0.031	10B	—	178	33–38	750	—	0.008	0.010
	Supra	7M-GE 180.3 (2954)	BCPR5EP-11	0.043	10B	10B	156	38–44	700	700	0.008	0.010
		7M-GTE 180.3 (2954)	BCPR6EP-N8	0.031	10B	10B	142	33–40	650	650	0.008	0.010
1990	Celica	4A-FE (1587)	BCPR5EY	0.031	10B	10B	191	38–44	700	700	0.008	0.010
		5S-FE (2164)	BKP5EYA-11	0.043	10B	10B	178	38–44	700	700	0.009	0.013
		3S-GTE 121.9 (1998)	BCPR5EP-8	0.031	10B	—	178	33–38	750	—	0.008	0.010
	Supra	7M-GE 180.3 (2954)	BCPR5EP-11	0.043	10B	10B	156	38–44	700	700	0.008	0.010
		7M-GTE 180.3 (2954)	BCPR6EP-N8	0.031	10B	10B	142	33–40	650	650	0.008	0.010

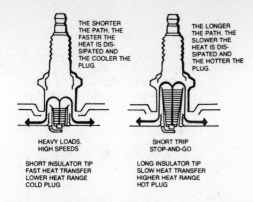

THE SHORTER THE PATH, THE FASTER THE HEAT IS DISSIPATED AND THE COOLER THE PLUG.

THE LONGER THE PATH, THE SLOWER THE HEAT IS DISSIPATED AND THE HOTTER THE PLUG.

HEAVY LOADS, HIGH SPEEDS

SHORT TRIP STOP-AND-GO

SHORT INSULATOR TIP
FAST HEAT TRANSFER
LOWER HEAT RANGE
COLD PLUG

LONG INSULATOR TIP
SLOW HEAT TRANSFER
HIGHER HEAT RANGE
HOT PLUG

Spark plug heat range

sound under conditions of low speed acceleration or heavy load. In severe cases, the heat may become high enough to start the air/fuel mixture burning throughout the combustion chamber rather than just to the Shorting the check connector—front of the plug. In this case, the resultant explosion will be strong enough to damage pistons, rings, and valves.

In most cases the factory recommended heat range is correct; it is chosen to perform well under a wide range of operating conditions. However, if most of your driving is long distance, high speed travel, you may want to install a spark plug one step colder than standard. If most of your driving is of the short trip variety, (when the engine may not always reach operating temperature) a hotter plug may help burn off the deposits normally accumulated under those conditions.

REMOVAL

NOTE: *The cylinder head is cast aluminum. Remove the spark plugs when the engine is cold, if possible, to prevent damage. If removal of the plugs is difficult, apply a few drops of penetrating oil or silicone spray to the area around the base of the plug, and allow it a few minutes to work.*

1. Number the wires so that you won't cross them when you replace them. Cylinder No. 1 is the one closest to the timing belt or pulley end of the engine.

2. Remove the wire from the end of the spark plug by grasping the rubber boot at the end of the wire. If the boot sticks to the plug, remove it by twisting and pulling at the same time. Do not pull wire itself or you will damage the core.

3. Use a $5/8$ in. or $13/16$ in. spark plug socket to loosen all of the plugs about two turns. Hold the socket and extension square to the plug while turning; do not allow the wrench to lean or move off center.

4. If compressed air is available, apply it to the area around the spark plug holes. Otherwise, use a rag or small brush to clean the area. Be careful not to allow any foreign material to drop into the spark plug holes.

5. Remove the plugs by unscrewing them the rest of the way from the engine.

INSPECTION

Check the plugs for deposits and wear. If they are not going to be replaced, clean the plugs thoroughly. Remember that any kind of deposit will decrease the efficiency of the plug. Plugs can be cleaned on a spark plug cleaning machine found in service stations, or you can do an acceptable job of cleaning with a stiff brush and a small file.

If the plugs are cleaned, the electrodes must be filed flat. Use an ignition or points file, not an emery board or the like, which will leave deposits. The electrodes must be filed perfectly flat with sharp edges; rounded edges reduce the spark plug voltage by as much as 50%.

Check the spark plug gap before installation. The ground electrode (the L-shaped one connected to the body of the plug) must be parallel to the center electrode and the specified size wire gauge (see "Tune-Up Specifications") must just pass the gap with slight resistance.

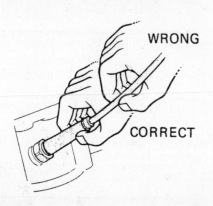

WRONG

CORRECT

WRONG

CORRECT

Use care when removing the spark plug wires

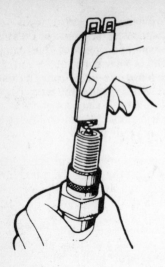

Bend the side electrode to adjust the gap

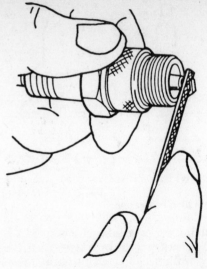

Plugs in good condition can be filed and re-used

WARNING: *NEVER adjust the gap on a used platinum tipped spark plug!*

Always check the gap on new plugs, too. Since one plug can fit many engines, the gap is unlikely to be exactly right out of the box. Do not use a flat feeler gauge when measuring the gap, because the reading will be inaccurate. Wire gapping tools usually have a bending tool attached.

Use the bending tool to adjust the side electrode until the proper distance is obtained. Absolutely never bend the center electrode. Be careful not to bend the side electrode too far or too often; it may weaken and break off within the engine. This rather spectacular occurrence will require major disassembly of both your engine and your checkbook.

INSTALLATION

1. Lubricate the threads of the spark plugs with a drop of oil. Install the plugs by hand and tighten them finger tight. Take care not to cross-thread them. You will be able to feel correct or incorrect threading almost immediately — never force the plug if resistance is felt. Remove it and start over.

2. Tighten the spark plugs with the socket. Do not apply the same amount of force you would use for a bolt; just snug them in. If a torque wrench is available, tighten to 11–15 ft. lbs.

3. Install the wires on their respective plugs. Make sure the wires are firmly connected. You will be able to feel them click into place.

WARNING: *Handle and route the wires carefully. Always replace them within any clips or holders.*

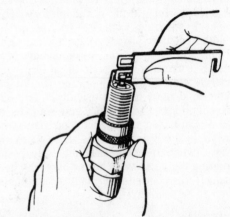

Check the spark plug gap with a wire feeler gauge

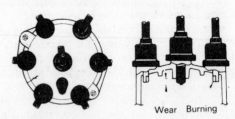

Wear   Burning

Check distributor cap for cracks and check cable ends for wear

INSPECTING SPARK PLUG CABLES

At every tune-up, visually inspect the spark plug cables for burns, cuts, or breaks in the insulation. Check the boots and the nipples on the distributor cap and coil. Replace any damaged wiring. It is always recommended to replace the wires as a complete set rather than one at a time.

Every 30,000 miles or three years, the resistance of the wires should be checked with an

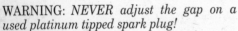

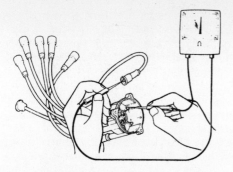

Checking plug wire resistance with ohmmeter

ohmmeter. Wires with excessive resistance will cause misfiring, and may make the engine difficult to start in damp weather.

To check resistance, remove the distributor cap with the wires attached and disconnect each wire at the spark plugs. Connect one lead of an ohmmeter to an electrode within the cap; connect the other lead to the corresponding spark plug terminal. Read the meter on the ohms x 1000 scale; any wire which shows a resistance over 25,000Ω is suspect and should be replaced. Although the wiring is usually at fault, don't overlook the distributor cap as a contributing factor to high resistance.

Test the high tension lead from the coil by connecting the ohmmeter between the center contact in the distributor cap and the coil end of the wire. Anything over 15,000Ω is cause for replacement. It should be remembered that resistance is also a function of length; the longer the cable, the greater the resistance. Thus, if the cables on your car are longer than the factory originals, resistance will be higher, quite possibly outside these limits. The correct length cables should be reinstalled.

The distributor cap should be checked for cracks (look carefully on the inside for hairline cracks in the plastic) or broken towers. The inside terminals should be checked for burning or severe etching. The terminals will show a bit of browning and scratching; this is normal and will increase with use. Any heavy damage or corrosion on the terminals is cause for replacement. The 7M-GTE Supra engine uses a distributor-less ignition; the plug wires connect directly to the ignition coils which are "fired" by a signal from the computer. Since it has no mechanical distributor, don't go looking for the cap.

When installing new cables or a new cap, replace them one at a time to avoid mix-ups. Start by replacing the longest one first. Install the boot firmly over the spark plug. Route the wire over the same path as the original. Insert the nipple firmly into the tower on the cap or the coil.

Always route the cables properly and engage them correctly in any clamps or holders. The cables should not touch or cross in direct contact. This is particularly important on 6 cylinder engines; damage may occur if two cylinders attempt to fire at the same time.

FIRING ORDERS

All 4-cylinder Celica and Supra engines fire the cylinders in the same order: 1–3–4–2. The rotor in the distributor turns in a clockwise direction when viewed from the top. Before completely removing the cap, check the rotor to see which terminal it points to; by following the wire to the appropriate plug, you can figure out which cylinder number is being pointed to. Once you have identified one cylinder's position on the cap, the others are easy to figure out. To avoid confusion, always replace the spark plug wires one at a time.

6-cylinder engines in Supras all fire in the order 1–5–3–6–2–4. These distributors also turn clockwise when viewed from above. Knowing what cylinder the rotor points to will allow you to figure out the other positions.

For the 7M-GTE, the computer (ECU) triggers the spark in the 1–5–3–6–2–4 pattern but the wires are arranged differently on the coils.

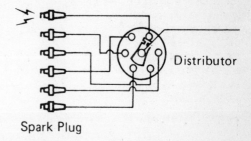

Spark Plug

Distributor

Six cylinder Supra firing schematic, except 7M-GTE. In the diagram, plug No. 6 is firing; No. 2 is next in the clockwise rotation

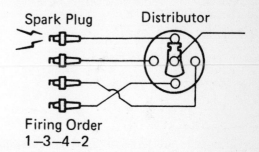

Spark Plug   Distributor

Firing Order
1–3–4–2

Firing schematic applies to all Celica and Supra 4-cylinder engines. The distributor rotates clockwise

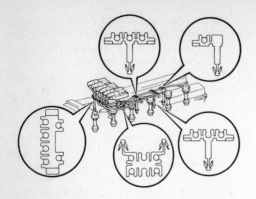

The wiring clips are very important on the 7M-GTE and all other engines

There are actually three coils, each controlling a pair of cylinders. If the spark plug wires are removed from the coils, both the wire and the coil should be labeled. The wires install on the coils in this order, beginning at the extreme left side coil: wire No. 5, wire No. 6, wire No. 3, wire No. 4, wire No. 1 and wire No.2. The presence and correct use of the wire clips and carriers is very important on this engine; make sure each wire is firmly held in its correct position.

Electronic Ignition

Electronic ignition systems offer many advantages over the older and less reliable breaker point system. By eliminating the points, maintenance requirements are greatly reduced. An electronic ignition system is capable of producing much higher voltage which in turn aids in starting, reduces spark plug fouling and provides better emission control.

With the exception of the 7M-GTE, the system Toyota uses consists of a distributor with a signal generator, an ignition coil and an electronic igniter. The signal generator is used to activate the electronic components of the igniter. It is located in the distributor and consists of three main components; the signal rotor, the pick-up coil and the permanent magnet.

The signal rotor (not to be confused with the distributor rotor) revolves with the distributor shaft, while the pick-up coil and the permanent magnet are stationary. As the signal rotor spins, the teeth on it pass a projection leading from the pick-up coil. When this happens, voltage is allowed to flow through the system, firing the spark plugs. There is no physical contact and no electrical arcing, hence no need to replace burnt or worn parts.

The 7M-GTE Supra motor has no distributor. Instead, a sensor on the camshaft signals the engine position to the fuel injection computer (ECU) which then signals the igniter. The igniter interprets the signal and discharges the correct coil (there are 6 coils) at the correct time.

Service on electronic distributor systems con-

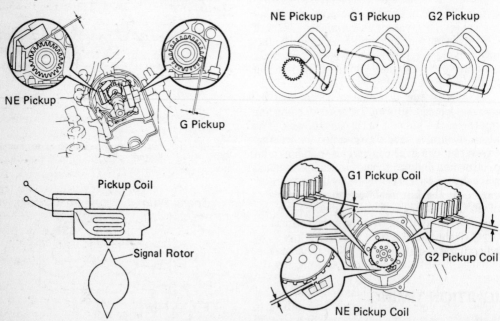

Examples of measuring the air gap on various distributors. Always use non-ferrous feeler gauges to perform this check

sists of inspection of the distributor cap, rotor and the ignition wires, replacing them as necessary. In addition, the air gap between the signal rotor and the projection on the pick-up coil should be checked periodically.

1. Remove the distributor cap. Inspect the cap for cracks, carbon tracks or a worn center contact. Replace it if necessary, transferring the wires one at a time from the old cap to the new one.

NOTE: *If working on the 7M-GTE, remove the protective dust cover from the front of the camshaft position sensor. There is no distributor.*

2. Except for the 7M-GTE, pull the ignition rotor (not the signal rotor) straight up and remove it. Replace it if the contact are worn, burned or pitted. Do not file the contacts.

3. Turn the engine over by hand (use a socket wrench on the front pulley bolt and ONLY turn in a clockwise direction. Clockwise should be determined as you face the motor.) until the projection on the pickup coil is directly opposite the signal rotor tooth.

4. Use a non-ferrous (not made of iron or steel – paper, brass, or plastic) feeler gauge of 0.30mm, (0.012 in.) and insert it into the pick-up air gap. The gauge should just touch either side of the gap. The permissible range is 0.20–0.40mm (0.008–0.016 in.)

WARNING: *Do NOT use an ordinary metal feeler gauge!*

NOTE: *The air gap on the 5M-GE, 7M-GE and 7M-GTE engines is NOT adjustable. If the gap is not within specifications, the pick-up coil (5M-GE), distributor (7M-GE or cam position sensor (7M-GTE) must be replaced.*

5. If the gap is either too wide or too narrow, loosen the two Phillips screws mounting the pick-up coil onto the distributor base plate. Wedge a small bladed screwdriver between the notch in the pick-up coil assembly and the two dimples on the base plate; turn the screwdriver back and forth until the pick-up gap is correct. You are dealing in thousandths of an inch; only small motions will be necessary.

6. Tighten the screws and recheck gap, readjusting if necessary.

IGNITION TIMING

Ignition timing is the measurement (in degrees) of crankshaft rotation at the instant the spark plug fires, in relation to the location of the piston on its compression stroke.

Ignition timing is adjusted by loosening the distributor locking device and turning the distributor in the engine.

Ideally, the air/fuel mixture in the cylinder will be ignited and just beginning its rapid expansion as the piston passes top dead center (TDC) on the compression stroke. If this happens, the piston will be beginning its downward power stroke just as the compressed air/fuel mixture starts to expand. The expansion of the air/fuel mixture will then force the piston down on the power stroke and turn the crankshaft.

It takes a fraction of a second for the spark from the plug to completely ignite the mixture in the cylinder. Because of this, the spark plug must fire before the piston reaches TDC if the mixture is to be completely ignited as the piston passes TDC. This measurement is given in degrees before the piston reaches top dead center (BTDC). If the ignition timing setting for your engine is seven (7°) BTDC, this means that the spark plug must fire as the piston for that cylinder is 7° before top dead center of its compression stroke. This setting only holds true while your engine is at idle speed.

As you accelerate from idle, the speed of your engine (revolutions per minute or rpm) increases. The increase in rpm means that the pistons are now traveling up and down much faster. Because of this, the spark plugs will have to fire even sooner if the mixture is to be completely ignited as the piston passes TDC. The change in spark timing is controlled by a microcomputer or ECU. The earliest computers were termed EFI units as they only controlled the electronic fuel injection and a few other functions. Modern computers control many different functions within the engine, including the spark advance. The black boxes are now termed Emission Control Units or Electronic Control Units – ECUs, since their main mission is to keep tight control of emissions through efficient engine operation.

The ECU is programmed with data for optimum ignition timing under any and all operating conditions. Using data provided by sensors which monitor various engine functions (rpm, intake air volume, engine temperature, etc.) the ECU triggers the spark at precisely the right instant. This system completely eliminates the vacuum leaks and rusted weights associated with the older mechanical advance systems.

If ignition timing is set too far advanced (BTDC), the ignition and expansion of the air/fuel mixture in the cylinder will try to force the piston down the cylinder while it is still traveling upward. This causes engine "ping", a sound which resembles marbles being dropped into an empty tin can. If the ignition timing is too far retarded (after, or ATDC), the piston

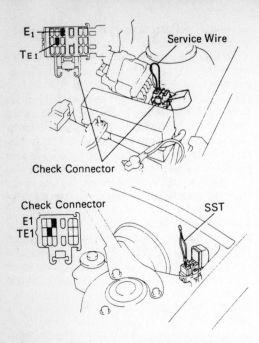

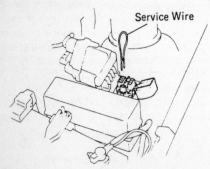

Typical locations of the service connector on Celicas and Supras after 1986. Where ever it's located, the relationship between the terminals E_1 and T, TE or TE_1 is always the same

will have already started down on the power stroke when the air/fuel mixture ignites and expands. This will cause the piston to be forced down only a portion of its travel. This will result in poor engine performance and lack of power.

Ignition timing adjustment is checked with a timing light. This instrument is connected to the number one (No. 1) spark plug of the engine as well as a power source — usually the battery terminals. The timing light flashes every time an electrical current is sent through the No. 1 spark plug wire, to the spark plug. The crankshaft pulley and the front cover of

You can easily make your own jumper wire if you purchase the correct terminals. Make certain the fit is secure but does not damage or bend the service connector

the engine are marked with a timing pointer and a timing scale. When the timing pointer is aligned with the **0** mark on the timing scale, the No. 1 piston is at TDC of its compression stroke. With the engine running, and the timing light aimed at the timing pointer and timing scale, the stroboscopic flashes from the timing light will allow you to check the ignition timing setting of the engine. The timing light flashes every time the spark plug in the No. 1 cylinder of the engine fires. Since the flash from the timing light makes the crankshaft pulley seem stationary for a moment you will be able to read the exact position of the piston in the No. 1 cylinder on the timing scale on the front of the engine.

There are three basic types of timing lights available. The first is a simple neon bulb with two wire connections (one for the spark plug and one for the plug wire, connecting the light in series). This type of light is quite dim, and must be held closely to the marks to be seen, but it is inexpensive. The second type of light operates from the car battery. Two alligator clips connect to the battery terminals, while a third wire connects to the spark plug with the clip–on inductive pickup. This type of light is more expensive, but the xenon bulb provides a bright flash which can seen in sunlight. The third type replaces the battery source with 110 volt house current. Some timing lights have other functions built into them, such as dwell meters, tachometers, or remote starting switches. These are convenient, but may duplicate the functions of tools you already have.

Since your Celica or Supra has electronic ignition, you should use a timing light with an inductive pickup. This pickup simply clamps onto the No. 1 plug wire. Most inductive pickups should only be installed in one direction on the plug wire; look for an arrow or other indicator showing how it connects. Read the specific directions for your light; each unit will be slightly different.

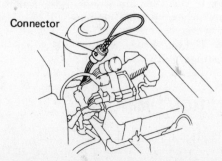

Location of service connector, 1986 Supra

CHECKING AND ADJUSTMENT

Before the timing can be checked or set, the electronic advance system must be disabled so that the base timing can be observed. Do this by first locating the service connector box. It is usually located on one of the shock towers or near the battery; it is easily mistaken for a relay because of its smooth cover. Remove the cover and find the terminal marked E_1. Locate the other terminal labeled T, TE or TE_1; this designation will vary by year and model.

NOTE: *For 1986 Supras, the check connector is at the end of a small harness near the igniter. The terminals are E_1 and T.*

After finding these two terminals, it is necessary to connect them with a jumper cable. A short loop of wire fitted with the correct terminals on each end is required; you can either make one yourself or obtain one from a Toyota dealer as a special tool. Install the jumper wire across the two terminals; this eliminates the electronic advance system.

1. Warm-up the engine. Check the engine idle speed to be sure that it is within the specification. Shut the engine off. Check the timing marks to make sure they are clean and visible. If not, clean the area or use a dab of paint to emphasize the marks.

2. Connect a timing light according to the manufacturer's instructions. Hook the inductive pick-up to No. 1 spark plug wire.

NOTE: *For 7M-GTE engines, connect pick-up to No. 6 spark plug wire.*

3. Be sure that the timing light wires are clear of the fan and start the engine.

CAUTION: *Keep fingers, clothes, tools, hair, and wiring clear of the spinning engine components and belts. Be sure that you are running the engine in a well ventilated area!*

4. Allow the engine to run at the specified idle speed with the gear shift in Neutral.

CAUTION: *Be sure that the parking brake is set and that the wheels are blocked to prevent the car from rolling.*

5. Point the timing light at the marks indicated in the chart and illustrations. With the engine at idle, timing should 10° BTDC for all Celicas and Supras covered by this book.

6. If the timing is not at specification, loosen the pinch bolt(s) or the holddown bolts at the base of the distributor (or camshaft position sensor on 7M-GTE) just enough so that the unit can be turned. Turn the distributor or cam sensor (7M-GTE) to advance or retard the timing as required. Once the marks align within the timing light, timing is correct.

CAUTION: *Avoid contact with the spark plug and coil wires while the engine is running. Accidental contact by a tool or a hand can result in electrical shock.*

7. Stop the engine and tighten the retaining bolt(s). Do not over tighten. Usually 13–20 Nm or 10–15 ft.lbs is enough.

8. Start the engine and remove the jumper wire from the service connector. Recheck the timing; you should notice a significant variation in timing as the engine runs. The timing will usually appear to be numerically higher than the 10°BTDC you set it to; this is due to the electronic system making corrections as the engine runs. The following normal readings may be expected with the jumper removed:

- 2S-E: Approximately 16° BTDC
- 3S-GE and -GTE except 1990: 14–19° BTDC
- 3S-GTE, 1990: 12–21° BTDC
- 5S-GE and 7M-GE through 1988: 10–13° BTDC

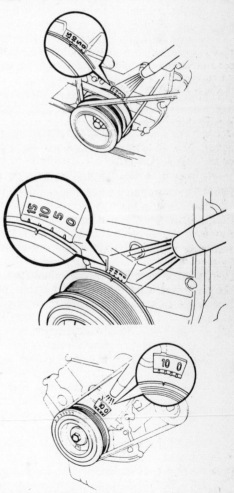

Examples of timing marks. Make sure both the notch and the scale are clean and readable before beginning work

- 7M-GE after 1988: 9–10° BTDC
- 3S-FE and 5S-FE: 13–22° BTDC
- 7M-GTE: more than 12° BTDC
- 4A-FE: 5–15° BTDC

9. Shut the engine off and remove the timing light. If no other work is needed, replace the cover on the service connector.

IDLE SPEED

To check idle speed, a tachometer must be connected into the engine electrical system. Having a meter visible under the hood while working is a large improvement over running back and forth checking the dashboard tach while working.

Not all tachometers are compatible with the Toyota electrical system. You are cautioned to check with the dealer and/or the tach manufacturer about suitability for your car. After a proper unit is selected, you may have to make or buy an adapter to connect the tachometer test lead to the Toyota terminal. This adapter is quite simple to make and should be kept handy with the tachometer.

The electrical system and computer(s) are easily damaged or destroyed through careless work habits. Since electricity travels at close to the speed of light, damage is instantaneous and expensive. Always observe these rules when connecting the tachometer:

- Do not leave the ignition switch ON for more than 5 minutes when the engine is not running.
- The tachometer lead must only be connected to the correct terminal; accidental contact with another terminal can cause great damage.
- Once connected to the terminal, the tachometer lead and connectors must be protected against grounding to any metal surface of the car. It is highly recommended that any adapter have fully insulated connectors or be wrapped in dry cloth or tape for protection.
- Never disconnect the battery cables while the engine is running.
- Make certain the engine and ignition wiring is correctly connected before connecting the tachometer. It is particularly important that ground circuits be clean and tight.

For the 2S-E and 3S-FE engines, the tachometer connector is found at the end of a small wire harness near the distributor. 1986 Supras (5M-GE and 7M-GE) have the connector near the coil and igniter. On all other models, the tachometer connects to the IG– terminal, located in the service connector; this is the same connector needed to check the timing (de-

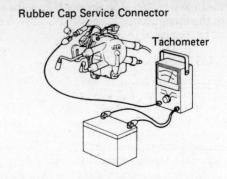

Rubber Cap Service Connector

Tachometer

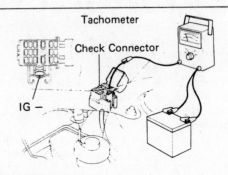

Tachometer

Check Connector

IG –

Tachometer connections 2S-E (above) and 3S-GE (below)

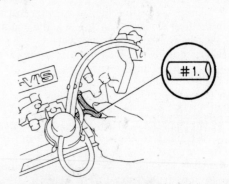

#1.

Disconnect the vacuum switching valve connector before adjusting the 2S-E idle

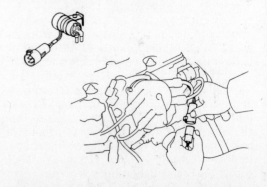

Disconnect the vacuum switching valve connector before adjusting the 2S-E idle

scribed earlier). The IG– terminal is separate from the other groups of connectors. The tach must be connected to this terminal only.

ADJUSTMENT

2S-E and 3S-GE Engines

1. Warm up the engine until it reaches normal operating temperature.

2. The air cleaner should be in place and all wires and vacuum hoses connected. All accessories should be off and transmission in neutral.

3. Connect a tachometer to the engine.

4. Run the engine at 2,500 rpm for 2 minutes. This insures that the oxygen sensor and other sensors are fully up to temperature and stabilized.

5. Let the engine return to idle. Pinch the No.1 air intake chamber vacuum hose on the

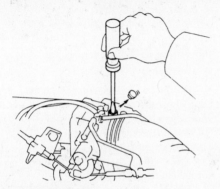

Adjusting the 3S-GE idle

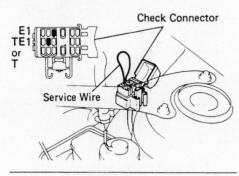

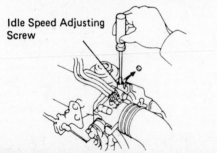

The jumper wire must be connected to check the idle on 3S-FE, 5S-FE and 3S-GTE engines

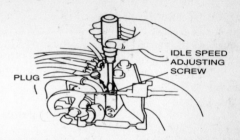

Adjusting the idle speed 2S-E engine

3S-GE. On the 2S-E, disconnect the vacuum switching valve (VSV) from the idle speed control (ISC) motor.

6. Set the idle speed by turning the idle adjusting screw to obtain the proper idle speed.

7. Remove the tachometer and reinstall any covers or caps which were removed from the service connector.

3S-FE, 5S-FE and 3S-GTE Engines

1. Make sure all these conditions are met before attempting to adjust the idle: all lines and hoses connected (including vacuum hoses), all fuel injection wiring correctly connected, air cleaner in place, all electrical accessories switched off, transmission in neutral (parking brake set and wheels blocked).

2. Warm the engine to normal operating temperature.

3. Connect the tachometer.

4. Use a jumper wire to connect terminal TE_1 or T and terminal E_1 of the check connector.

5. Hold the engine at 1000–1300 rpm for 5 seconds. Release the throttle and check the idle speed. With the jumper wire in place, the idle should be 650 ± 50 rpm.

6. If the idle is not at specification, remove the cap and adjust the idle speed adjusting screw on the throttle body.

7. Remove the jumper wire and check the idle speed again; it should now be 700 ± 50 rpm.

8. If the idle is not at the specified value, start the engine and idle it for 30 seconds. Turn it off, then repeat the entire pattern (start – idle – off) several times. This should store the correct idle value within the Idle Speed Control unit (ISC) and the idle rpm will be at the correct setting.

9. Disconnect the tachometer and replace any covers or plugs which were removed from the service connector.

4A-FE Engine

1. Make sure all these conditions are met before attempting to adjust the idle: all lines and hoses connected (including vacuum hoses),

all fuel injection wiring correctly connected, air cleaner in place, all electrical accessories switched off, transmission in neutral (parking brake set and wheels blocked).

2. Warm the engine to normal operating temperature.

3. Connect the tachometer.

4. Hold the engine at 2500 rpm for approximately 2 minutes.

5. Use a jumper wire to connect terminals TE_1 and E_1 of the check connector. The idle speed should be 800 ± 50 rpm with the cooling fan (radiator fan) off.

6. If the idle is not at specification, remove the cap and adjust the idle speed adjusting screw on the throttle body. Make the adjustment with the cooling fan off.

7. Remove the jumper wire and disconnect the tachometer. Replace any caps or covers removed from the service connector.

5M-GE, 7M-GE and 7M-GTE Engines

The idle speed on these engines is controlled by the Electronic Control Unit. The idle speed may be checked but is not externally adjustable. If there is a suspected idle speed problem, sub-systems such as the Idle Speed Control Valve and/or the Throttle Position Sensor will have to be tested. It should be noted the low idle or poor idle problems are most frequently caused by poor or corroded electrical connections, weak ground connections and/or vacuum leaks. Before undertaking a major diagnostic project, check the simple stuff.

VALVE LASH

All the Celica and Supra engines in this book except the 5M-GE and 2S-E are equipped with removable shims to adjust the valve clearance. Valves on these engines should be checked every 30,000 miles or 3 years. One of the advantages of a shim system is that clearances rarely change if proper maintenance and oil changes are performed.

The 5M-GE and 2S-E are equipped with hydraulic lash adjusters in the valve train. These adjusters maintain a zero clearance between the rocker arm and valve stem; no adjustment is possible or necessary.

Valve lash is one factor which determines how far the intake and exhaust valves will open into the cylinder.

If the valve clearance is too large, part of the camshaft motion will be used up removing the excessive clearance; the valves will not be opened far enough. This condition has two effects—the valve train components will emit a

tapping noise as they take up the excessive clearance and the engine will perform poorly due to restricted entrance of air and fuel. The less the exhaust valves open, the greater the back-pressure in the cylinder, preventing the proper mixture from entering the cylinder.

If the valve clearance is too small, the intake and exhaust valves will not fully seat on the cylinder head when they close. When a valve seats on the cylinder head, it seals the combustion chamber so none of the gases in the cylinder can escape and it cools itself by transferring some of the heat it absorbed through the cylinder head and into the engine cooling system. If the valve clearance is too small, the engine will run poorly (due to gases escaping from the combustion chamber), and the valves will overheat and warp.

NOTE: *While all valve adjustments must be as accurate as possible, it is better to have the valve adjustment slightly loose than slightly tight; burnt valves may result from overly tight adjustments.*

ADJUSTMENT

WARNING: *The use of the correct special tools or their equivalent is REQUIRED for this procedure. Tool set 09248–55010 or 09248–70012 (3S-GE), or its equivalent will be needed; additionally, a micrometer reading either to $^{10}/_{1000}$ in. (0.0001) or $^1/_{1000}$ mm (0.001) will be needed.*

WARNING: *Perform this operation on a cold motor. Overnight cold is best.*

3S-GE, 3S-GTE, 3S-FE, 4A-FE and 5S-FE Engines

1. Remove the valve cover (cylinder head cover).

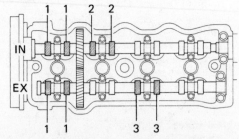

Adjust valves in these locations FIRST on 3S- and 5S- engines. 3S-FE shown, others similar

2. Use a wrench and turn the crankshaft clockwise until the notch in the pulley aligns with the timing mark 0 on the timing belt cover. This will insure that engine is at TDC/compression on No. 1 cylinder.

NOTE: *Check that the valve lifters on No. 1 cylinder are loose and those on No 4 cylinder*

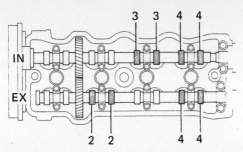

Adjust valves in these locations SECOND on 3S-
and 5S- engines. 3S-FE shown, others similar

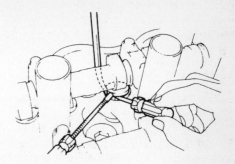

Removing the valve shim

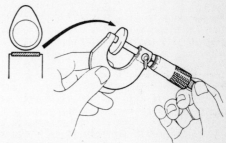

A micrometer must be used to measure the thickness of the shim

are tight. If not, turn the crankshaft one complete revolution (360°) and then realign the
marks.

3. Using a flat feeler gauge measure the
clearance between the camshaft lobe and the
valve lifter. This measurement should correspond to the one given in the "Tune-Up Specifications" chart. Check only the valves listed:
intake side, cylinders No.1 and 2. Exhaust side,
cylinders No. 1 and 3. Use the illustrations to
help you.

NOTE: If the measurement is within specifications, go on to the next step. If not, record
the measurement taken for each individual
valve.

4. Turn the crankshaft clockwise one complete revolution and realign the timing marks
at 0.

5. Measure the clearance of these valves:
intake side, cylinders No. 3 and 4; exhaust side,
cylinders No. 2 and 4.

NOTE: If the measurement for this set of
valves AND the previous set is within specifications, you need go no further; the checking
procedure is finished. If not, record the measurements and proceed.

6. Identify the valve(s) to be adjusted. Turn
the crankshaft to position the camshaft lobe of
the cylinder to be adjusted, upward.

7. Using a small tool, turn the valve lifter so
that the notch is easily accessible.

8. Use the special tool to press the shim and
lifter downward. Use the other tool from the

set to hold it in place; make sure the second tool
is not resting on the shim you're trying to
remove.

9. Using a small screwdriver and a magnetic arm or probe, lift the shim up and remove
it.

10. Measure the thickness of the old shim
with a micrometer. Locate that particular measurement in the "Installed Shim Thickness"
column of the shim charts, then locate the previously recorded measurement (from Step 3 or
5) for that valve in the "Measured Clearance "
column of the charts. Index the two columns to
arrive at the proper replacement shim thickness.

NOTE: Replacement shims are available in
many sizes, usually in increments of 0.05mm
(0.0020 in.), from 2.00mm (0.0787 in.) to
3.300mm (0.1299 in.).

11. Install the new shim, remove the special
tool and then recheck the valve clearance.

12. Repeat the procedure for each valve needing adjustment.

13. Reinstall the valve cover.

7M–GE and 7M-GTE Engines

NOTE: Both of these engines require substantial work simply to get the valve covers off.
Allow plenty of time to perform these opera-
tions.

1. For the 7M-GE engine, use the following
procedure to remove the valve covers. For 7M-
GTE, begin with Step 2.

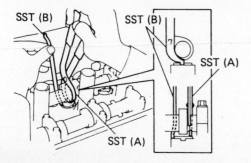

Using the special tools to depress the lifter

INTAKE

Installed shim thickness (mm) — column headers (left to right):
2.500, 2.550, 2.600, 2.620, 2.640, 2.650, 2.660, 2.680, 2.700, 2.720, 2.740, 2.750, 2.760, 2.780, 2.800, 2.820, 2.840, 2.850, 2.860, 2.880, 2.900, 2.920, 2.940, 2.950, 2.960, 2.980, 3.000, 3.020, 3.040, 3.050, 3.060, 3.080, 3.100, 3.120, 3.140, 3.150, 3.160, 3.180, 3.200, 3.250, 3.300

Measured clearance (mm)	Installed shim selection (shim numbers, in installed-thickness order)
0.000-0.025	02 02 02 02 02 04 04 04 06 06 06 08 08 08 10 10 10 12 12 12 14 14 14 16 16 16 18 18 18 20 20 20 22 24
0.026-0.050	02 02 02 02 02 04 04 04 06 06 06 08 08 08 10 10 10 12 12 12 14 14 14 16 16 16 18 18 18 20 20 20 22 22 24 26
0.051-0.075	02 02 02 02 02 04 04 04 06 06 06 08 08 08 10 10 10 12 12 12 14 14 14 16 16 16 18 18 18 20 20 20 22 22 24 26
0.076-0.100	02 02 02 02 02 04 04 04 06 06 06 08 08 08 10 10 10 12 12 12 14 14 14 16 16 16 18 18 18 20 20 20 22 22 22 24 24 26 28
0.101-0.125	02 02 02 02 04 04 04 06 06 06 08 08 08 10 10 10 12 12 12 14 14 14 16 16 16 18 18 18 20 20 20 22 22 22 24 24 26 28
0.126-0.150	02 02 02 04 04 04 06 06 06 08 08 08 10 10 10 12 12 12 14 14 14 16 16 16 18 18 18 20 20 20 22 22 22 24 24 24 26 26 28 30
0.151-0.175	02 02 04 04 04 06 06 06 08 08 08 10 10 10 12 12 12 14 14 14 16 16 16 18 18 18 20 20 20 22 22 22 24 24 24 26 26 26 28 30
0.176-0.189	02 04 04 06 06 06 08 08 10 10 10 12 12 14 14 14 16 16 18 18 18 20 20 22 22 22 24 24 26 26 26 28 30 32
0.190-0.290	
0.291-0.300	04 06 08 10 10 10 12 12 14 14 14 14 16 16 18 18 18 18 20 20 22 22 22 22 24 24 26 26 26 26 28 28 30 30 30 30 32 32 34
0.301-0.325	04 06 08 10 10 10 12 12 12 14 14 14 16 16 16 18 18 18 20 20 20 22 22 22 24 24 24 26 26 26 28 28 30 30 30 32 32 32 34
0.326-0.350	06 08 10 10 12 12 12 14 14 14 16 16 16 18 18 18 20 20 20 22 22 22 24 24 24 26 26 26 28 28 30 30 30 32 32 32 34 34
0.351-0.375	06 08 10 12 12 12 14 14 14 16 16 16 18 18 18 20 20 20 22 22 22 24 24 24 26 26 26 28 28 28 30 30 30 32 32 32 34 34 34
0.376-0.400	08 10 12 12 14 14 14 16 16 16 18 18 18 20 20 20 22 22 22 24 24 24 26 26 26 28 28 28 30 30 30 32 32 32 34 34 34
0.401-0.425	08 10 12 12 14 14 16 16 16 18 18 18 20 20 20 22 22 22 24 24 24 26 26 26 28 28 30 30 30 32 32 32 34 34 34 34
0.426-0.450	10 12 14 14 16 16 16 18 18 18 20 20 20 22 22 22 24 24 24 26 26 26 28 28 30 30 30 32 32 32 34 34 34 34
0.451-0.475	10 12 14 16 16 16 18 18 18 20 20 20 22 22 22 24 24 24 26 26 26 28 28 28 30 30 30 32 32 32 34 34 34
0.476-0.500	12 14 16 16 18 18 18 20 20 20 22 22 22 24 24 24 26 26 26 28 28 28 30 30 30 32 32 32 34 34 34 34
0.501-0.525	12 14 16 18 18 18 20 20 20 22 22 22 24 24 24 26 26 26 28 28 28 30 30 30 32 32 32 34 34 34 34
0.526-0.550	14 16 18 18 20 20 20 22 22 22 24 24 24 26 26 26 28 28 28 30 30 30 32 32 32 34 34 34 34
0.551-0.575	14 16 18 20 20 20 22 22 22 24 24 24 26 26 26 28 28 28 30 30 30 32 32 32 34 34 34
0.576-0.600	16 18 20 20 22 22 22 24 24 24 26 26 26 28 28 28 30 30 30 32 32 32 34 34 34 34
0.601-0.625	16 18 20 22 22 22 24 24 24 26 26 26 28 28 28 30 30 30 32 32 32 34 34 34 34
0.626-0.650	18 20 22 22 24 24 24 26 26 26 28 28 28 30 30 30 32 32 32 34 34 34 34
0.651-0.675	18 20 22 24 24 24 26 26 26 28 28 28 30 30 30 32 32 32 34 34 34
0.676-0.700	20 22 24 24 26 26 26 28 28 28 30 30 30 32 32 32 34 34 34 34
0.701-0.725	20 22 24 26 26 26 28 28 28 30 30 30 32 32 32 34 34 34 34
0.726-0.750	22 24 26 26 28 28 28 30 30 30 32 32 32 34 34 34 34
0.751-0.775	22 24 26 28 28 28 30 30 30 32 32 32 34 34 34 34
0.776-0.800	24 26 28 28 30 30 30 32 32 32 34 34 34 34
0.801-0.825	24 26 28 30 30 30 32 32 32 34 34 34 34
0.826-0.850	26 28 30 30 32 32 32 34 34 34 34
0.851-0.875	26 28 30 32 32 32 34 34 34 34
0.876-0.900	28 30 32 32 34 34 34 34
0.901-0.925	28 30 32 34 34 34 34
0.926-0.950	30 32 34 34 34
0.951-0.975	30 32 34
0.976-1.000	32 34
1.001-1.025	34 34
1.026-1.090	34

Shim thickness   mm (in.)

Shim No.	Thickness	Shim No.	Thickness
02	2.50 (0.0984)	20	2.95 (0.1161)
04	2.55 (0.1004)	22	3.00 (0.1181)
06	2.60 (0.1024)	24	3.05 (0.1201)
08	2.65 (0.1043)	26	3.10 (0.1220)
10	2.70 (0.1063)	28	3.15 (0.1240)
12	2.75 (0.1083)	30	3.20 (0.1260)
14	2.80 (0.1102)	32	3.25 (0.1280)
16	2.85 (0.1122)	34	3.30 (0.1299)
18	2.90 (0.1142)		

Valve adjustment selection chart: 3S-FE and 5S-FE intake valves

EXHAUST

Valve adjustment selection chart for installed shim thickness (mm) vs. measured clearance (mm). Shim numbers shown in body correspond to thicknesses in the reference table below.

Measured clearance (mm)	2.500	2.550	2.600	2.620	2.640	2.650	2.660	2.680	2.700	2.720	2.740	2.750	2.760	2.780	2.800	2.820	2.840	2.850	2.860	2.880	2.900	2.920	2.940	2.950	2.960	2.980	3.000	3.020	3.040	3.050	3.060	3.080	3.100	3.120	3.140	3.150	3.160	3.180	3.200	3.250	3.300
0.000–0.025																02	02	02	02	02	04	04	04		06	06	06	08	08		08	10	10	12	12		14	14	16	18	20 22
0.026–0.050														02	02	02	02	02	04	04	04	06	06		08	08	08	10	10		12	12	12	14	14		16	16	18	18	20 22
0.051–0.075													02	02	02	02	02	04	04	04	06	06	06		08	08	10	10	12		12	14	14	16	16		16	18	18	20	22 24
0.076–0.100										02	02	02	02	02	02	04	04	06	06	06	06	08	08		10	10	10	12	12		14	14	14	16	16		18	18	18	20	22 24
0.101–0.125									02	02	02	02	02	04	04	04	06	06	06	08	08	08	10		10	12	12	12	14		14	16	16	18	18		20	20	20	22	24 26
0.126–0.150								02	02	02	02	02	04	04	04	04	06	06	08	08	08	08	10		10	12	12	12	14		16	16	16	16	18		20	20	22	22	24 26
0.150–0.175						02	02	02	02	02	04	04	04	06	06	06	08	08	08	10	10	10	12		12	14	14	14	16		16	18	18	20	20		22	22	24	24	26 28
0.176–0.200					02	02	02	02	04	04	06	06	06	08	08	08	10	10	10	12	12	14	14		14	16	16	18	18		18	20	20	22	22		22	24	24	26	28
0.201–0.225				02	02	02	04	04	04	06	06	06	08	08	08	10	10	10	12	12	12	14	14		16	16	16	18	18		20	20	20	22	22		24	24	26	28	30
0.226–0.250		02	02	04	04	04	04	06	06	08	08	08	08	10	10	12	12	12	12	14	14	16	16		16	18	18	20	20		20	20	22	22	24		24	24	26	28	30
0.251–0.275		02	04	04	04	06	06	08	08	08	08	10	10	10	12	12	14	14	14	14	16	16	16		18	18	18	20	20		20	22	22	22	24		24	24	26	26	28 30 32
0.275–0.279		02	04	04	06	06	06	08	08	08	10	10	10	12	12	12	14	14	14	16	16	16	18		18	18	20	20	20		22	22	22	24	24		26	26	28	28	30 32
0.280–0.380																																									
0.381–0.400	04	06	08	10	10	10	12	12	14	14	14	14	16	16	18	18	18	18	20	20	22	22	22	22	24	26	26	26	26	28	28	30	30	30	30	32	32	34			
0.401–0.425	06	08	10	10	10	12	12	14	14	14	16	16	16	18	18	18	20	20	20	22	22	22	24	24	24	26	26	26	28	28	28	30	30	30	32	32	32	34	34		
0.426–0.450	06	08	10	12	12	12	14	14	16	16	16	16	18	18	20	20	20	20	22	22	24	24	24	24	26	26	28	28	28	30	30	30	32	32	32	34	34				
0.451–0.475	08	10	12	12	12	14	14	16	16	16	18	18	20	20	20	22	22	22	24	24	26	26	28	28	30	30	30	32	32	32	34	34	34	34							
0.476–0.500	08	10	12	14	14	14	16	16	18	18	18	20	20	22	22	22	24	24	26	26	26	28	30	30	30	32	32	34	34	34	34										
0.501–0.525	10	12	14	14	14	16	16	18	18	20	20	20	22	22	22	24	24	24	26	26	28	28	30	30	32	32	32	34	34	34	34										
0.526–0.550	10	12	14	16	16	16	18	18	20	20	20	20	22	22	24	24	24	24	26	26	28	28	28	30	30	32	32	32	34	34	34										
0.551–0.575	12	14	16	16	16	18	18	20	20	20	22	22	24	24	24	26	26	26	28	28	30	30	30	32	32	34	34	34													
0.576–0.600	12	14	16	18	18	18	20	20	22	22	22	22	24	24	26	26	26	28	28	30	30	30	32	32	34	34	34	34													
0.601–0.625	14	16	18	18	18	20	20	22	22	24	24	24	26	26	28	28	28	30	30	30	32	32	32	34	34	34															
0.626–0.650	14	16	18	20	20	20	22	22	24	24	24	26	26	28	28	28	30	30	32	32	32	34	34	34																	
0.651–0.675	16	18	20	20	20	22	22	24	24	24	26	26	26	28	28	30	30	30	32	32	34	34	34	34																	
0.676–0.700	16	18	20	22	22	22	24	24	26	26	26	28	28	30	30	30	32	32	34	34	34																				
0.701–0.725	18	20	22	22	22	24	24	26	26	26	28	28	30	30	30	32	32	32	34	34	34																				
0.726–0.750	18	20	22	24	24	24	26	26	28	28	28	30	30	32	32	32	34	34	34																						
0.751–0.775	20	22	24	24	24	26	26	28	28	30	30	30	32	32	34	34	34	34																							
0.776–0.800	20	22	24	26	26	26	28	28	30	30	30	32	32	34	34	34	34																								
0.801–0.825	22	24	26	26	26	28	28	30	30	30	32	32	32	34	34	34	34																								
0.826–0.850	22	24	26	28	28	28	30	30	32	32	32	32	34	34	34																										
0.851–0.875	24	26	28	28	28	30	30	30	32	32	32	34	34	34	34																										
0.876–0.900	24	26	28	30	30	30	30	32	32	34	34	34	34	34																											
0.901–0.925	26	28	30	30	30	32	32	32	34	34	34																														
0.926–0.950	26	28	30	32	32	32	32	34	34	34																															
0.951–0.975	28	30	32	32	32	34	34	34	34																																
0.976–1.000	28	30	32	34	34	34	34	34																																	
1.001–1.025	30	32	34	34	34	34																																			
1.026–1.050	30	32	34	34																																					
1.051–1.075	32	34	34																																						
1.076–1.100	32	34																																							
1.101–1.125	34	34																																							
1.126–1.180	34																																								

Shim thickness   mm (in.)

Shim No.	Thickness	Shim No.	Thickness
02	2.50 (0.0984)	20	2.95 (0.1161)
04	2.55 (0.1004)	22	3.00 (0.1181)
06	2.60 (0.1024)	24	3.05 (0.1201)
08	2.65 (0.1043)	26	3.10 (0.1220)
10	2.70 (0.1063)	28	3.15 (0.1240)
12	2.75 (0.1083)	30	3.20 (0.1260)
14	2.80 (0.1102)	32	3.25 (0.1280)
16	2.85 (0.1122)	34	3.30 (0.1299)
18	2.90 (0.1142)		

Valve adjustment selection chart: 3S-FE and 5S-FE exhaust valves

INTAKE

Measured clearance (mm)	Installed shim thickness (mm)
0.000-0.025	02 02 02 04 04 06 06 08 08 10 10 12 12 14 14 16 16 18 18 20 20 22 22 24 24 26 26 28 28 30 30 32 32 34 34 36 36 38 38 40 40 42 42 44 44 46 46
0.026-0.050	02 02 02 04 04 06 06 08 08 10 10 12 12 14 14 16 16 18 18 20 20 22 22 24 24 26 26 28 28 30 30 32 32 34 34 36 36 38 38 40 40 42 42 44 44 46 46 48
0.051-0.075	02 02 02 04 04 06 06 08 08 10 10 12 12 14 14 16 16 18 18 20 20 22 22 24 24 26 26 28 28 30 30 32 32 34 34 36 36 38 38 40 40 42 42 44 44 46 46 48 48 50
0.076-0.100	02 02 02 04 04 06 06 08 08 10 10 12 12 14 14 16 16 18 18 20 20 22 22 24 24 26 26 28 28 30 30 32 32 34 34 36 36 38 38 40 40 42 42 44 44 46 46 48 48 50
0.101-0.125	02 02 02 04 04 06 06 08 08 10 10 12 12 14 14 16 16 18 18 20 20 22 22 24 24 26 26 28 28 30 30 32 32 34 34 36 36 38 38 40 40 42 42 44 44 46 46 48 48 50 50
0.126-0.149	02 02 02 04 04 06 06 08 08 10 10 12 12 14 14 16 16 18 18 20 20 22 22 24 24 26 26 28 28 30 30 32 32 34 34 36 36 38 38 40 40 42 42 44 44 46 46 48 48 50 50 52
0.150-0.250	
0.251-0.275	04 06 06 08 08 10 10 12 12 14 14 16 16 18 18 20 20 22 22 24 24 26 26 28 28 30 30 32 32 34 34 36 36 38 38 40 40 42 42 44 44 46 46 48 48 50 50 52 52 54 54 54
0.276-0.300	06 06 08 08 10 10 12 12 14 14 16 16 18 18 20 20 22 22 24 24 26 26 28 28 30 30 32 32 34 34 36 36 38 38 40 40 42 42 44 44 46 46 48 48 50 50 52 52 54 54 54
0.301-0.325	06 08 08 10 10 12 12 14 14 16 16 18 18 20 20 22 22 24 24 26 26 28 28 30 30 32 32 34 34 36 36 38 38 40 40 42 42 44 44 46 46 48 48 50 50 52 52 54 54 54
0.326-0.350	08 08 10 10 12 12 14 14 16 16 18 18 20 20 22 22 24 24 26 26 28 28 30 30 32 32 34 34 36 36 38 38 40 40 42 42 44 44 46 46 48 48 50 50 52 52 54 54 54
0.351-0.375	08 10 10 12 12 14 14 16 16 18 18 20 20 22 22 24 24 26 26 28 28 30 30 32 32 34 34 36 36 38 38 40 40 42 42 44 44 46 46 48 48 50 50 52 52 54 54 54
0.376-0.400	10 10 12 12 14 14 16 16 18 18 20 20 22 22 24 24 26 26 28 28 30 30 32 32 34 34 36 36 38 38 40 40 42 42 44 44 46 46 48 48 50 50 52 52 54 54 54
0.401-0.425	10 12 12 14 14 16 16 18 18 20 20 22 22 24 24 26 26 28 28 30 30 32 32 34 34 36 36 38 38 40 40 42 42 44 44 46 46 48 48 50 50 52 52 54 54 54
0.426-0.450	12 12 14 14 16 16 18 18 20 20 22 22 24 24 26 26 28 28 30 30 32 32 34 34 36 36 38 38 40 40 42 42 44 44 46 46 48 48 50 50 52 52 54 54 54
0.451-0.475	12 14 14 16 16 18 18 20 20 22 22 24 24 26 26 28 28 30 30 32 32 34 34 36 36 38 38 40 40 42 42 44 44 46 46 48 48 50 50 52 52 54 54 54
0.476-0.500	14 14 16 16 18 18 20 20 22 22 24 24 26 26 28 28 30 30 32 32 34 34 36 36 38 38 40 40 42 42 44 44 46 46 48 48 50 50 52 52 54 54 54
0.501-0.525	14 16 16 18 18 20 20 22 22 24 24 26 26 28 28 30 30 32 32 34 34 36 36 38 38 40 40 42 42 44 44 46 46 48 48 50 50 52 52 54 54 54
0.526-0.550	16 16 18 18 20 20 22 22 24 24 26 26 28 28 30 30 32 32 34 34 36 36 38 38 40 40 42 42 44 44 46 46 48 48 50 50 52 52 54 54 54
0.551-0.575	16 18 18 20 20 22 22 24 24 26 26 28 28 30 30 32 32 34 34 36 36 38 38 40 40 42 42 44 44 46 46 48 48 50 50 52 52 54 54 54
0.576-0.600	18 18 20 20 22 22 24 24 26 26 28 28 30 30 32 32 34 34 36 36 38 38 40 40 42 42 44 44 46 46 48 48 50 50 52 52 54 54 54
0.601-0.625	18 20 20 22 22 24 24 26 26 28 28 30 30 32 32 34 34 36 36 38 38 40 40 42 42 44 44 46 46 48 48 50 50 52 52 54 54 54
0.626-0.650	20 20 22 22 24 24 26 26 28 28 30 30 32 32 34 34 36 36 38 38 40 40 42 42 44 44 46 46 48 48 50 50 52 52 54 54 54
0.651-0.675	20 22 22 24 24 26 26 28 28 30 30 32 32 34 34 36 36 38 38 40 40 42 42 44 44 46 46 48 48 50 50 52 52 54 54 54
0.676-0.700	22 22 24 24 26 26 28 28 30 30 32 32 34 34 36 36 38 38 40 40 42 42 44 44 46 46 48 48 50 50 52 52 54 54 54
0.701-0.725	22 24 24 26 26 28 28 30 30 32 32 34 34 36 36 38 38 40 40 42 42 44 44 46 46 48 48 50 50 52 52 54 54 54
0.726-0.750	24 24 26 26 28 28 30 30 32 32 34 34 36 36 38 38 40 40 42 42 44 44 46 46 48 48 50 50 52 52 54 54 54
0.751-0.775	24 26 26 28 28 30 30 32 32 34 34 36 36 38 38 40 40 42 42 44 44 46 46 48 48 50 50 52 52 54 54 54
0.776-0.800	26 26 28 28 30 30 32 32 34 34 36 36 38 38 40 40 42 42 44 44 46 46 48 48 50 50 52 52 54 54 54
0.801-0.825	26 28 28 30 30 32 32 34 34 36 36 38 38 40 40 42 42 44 44 46 46 48 48 50 50 52 52 54 54 54
0.826-0.850	28 28 30 30 32 32 34 34 36 36 38 38 40 40 42 42 44 44 46 46 48 48 50 50 52 52 54 54 54
0.851-0.875	28 30 30 32 32 34 34 36 36 38 38 40 40 42 42 44 44 46 46 48 48 50 50 52 52 54 54 54
0.876-0.900	30 30 32 32 34 34 36 36 38 38 40 40 42 42 44 44 46 46 48 48 50 50 52 52 54 54 54
0.901-0.925	30 32 32 34 34 36 36 38 38 40 40 42 42 44 44 46 46 48 48 50 50 52 52 54 54 54
0.926-0.950	32 32 34 34 36 36 38 38 40 40 42 42 44 44 46 46 48 48 50 50 52 52 54 54 54
0.951-0.975	32 34 34 36 36 38 38 40 40 42 42 44 44 46 46 48 48 50 50 52 52 54 54 54
0.976-1.000	34 34 36 36 38 38 40 40 42 42 44 44 46 46 48 48 50 50 52 52 54 54 54
1.001-1.025	34 36 36 38 38 40 40 42 42 44 44 46 46 48 48 50 50 52 52 54 54 54
1.026-1.050	36 36 38 38 40 40 42 42 44 44 46 46 48 48 50 50 52 52 54 54 54
1.051-1.075	36 38 38 40 40 42 42 44 44 46 46 48 48 50 50 52 52 54 54 54
1.076-1.100	38 38 40 40 42 42 44 44 46 46 48 48 50 50 52 52 54 54 54
1.101-1.125	38 40 40 42 42 44 44 46 46 48 48 50 50 52 52 54 54 54
1.126-1.150	40 40 42 42 44 44 46 46 48 48 50 50 52 52 54 54 54
1.151-1.175	40 42 42 44 44 46 46 48 48 50 50 52 52 54 54 54
1.176-1.200	42 42 44 44 46 46 48 48 50 50 52 52 54 54 54
1.201-1.225	42 44 44 46 46 48 48 50 50 52 52 54 54 54
1.226-1.250	44 44 46 46 48 48 50 50 52 52 54 54 54
1.251-1.275	44 46 46 48 48 50 50 52 52 54 54 54
1.276-1.300	46 46 48 48 50 50 52 52 54 54 54
1.301-1.325	46 48 48 50 50 52 52 54 54 54
1.326-1.350	48 48 50 50 52 52 54 54 54
1.351-1.375	48 50 50 52 52 54 54 54
1.376-1.400	50 50 52 52 54 54 54
1.401-1.425	50 52 52 54 54 54
1.426-1.450	52 52 54 54 54
1.451-1.475	52 54 54 54
1.476-1.500	54 54 54
1.501-1.525	54 54
1.526-1.550	54

Shim thickness mm (in.)

Shim No.	Thickness	Shim No.	Thickness
02	2.00 (0.0787)	30	2.70 (0.1063)
04	2.05 (0.0807)	32	2.75 (0.1083)
06	2.10 (0.0827)	34	2.80 (0.1102)
08	2.15 (0.0846)	36	2.85 (0.1122)
10	2.20 (0.0866)	38	2.90 (0.1142)
12	2.25 (0.0886)	40	2.95 (0.1161)
14	2.30 (0.0906)	42	3.00 (0.1181)
16	2.35 (0.0925)	44	3.05 (0.1201)
18	2.40 (0.0945)	46	3.10 (0.1220)
20	2.45 (0.0965)	48	3.15 (0.1240)
22	2.50 (0.0984)	50	3.20 (0.1260)
24	2.55 (0.1004)	52	3.25 (0.1280)
26	2.60 (0.1024)	54	3.30 (0.1299)
28	2.65 (0.1043)		

Valve adjustment selection chart: 3S-GE and 3S-GTE intake valves

EXHAUST

Valve adjustment selection chart. The column headers run across the top as **Installed shim thickness (mm)**, from 2.000 to 3.300 in 0.025 mm steps (2.000, 2.025, 2.050, 2.075, 2.100, 2.125, 2.150, 2.175, 2.200, 2.225, 2.250, 2.275, 2.300, 2.325, 2.350, 2.375, 2.400, 2.425, 2.450, 2.475, 2.500, 2.525, 2.550, 2.575, 2.600, 2.625, 2.650, 2.675, 2.700, 2.725, 2.750, 2.775, 2.800, 2.825, 2.850, 2.875, 2.900, 2.925, 2.950, 2.975, 3.000, 3.025, 3.050, 3.075, 3.100, 3.125, 3.150, 3.175, 3.200, 3.225, 3.250, 3.275, 3.300). For each measured clearance row the printed shim numbers (left-to-right, following the diagonal band) are:

Measured clearance (mm)	Installed shim thickness → shim numbers (left to right)
0.000-0.025	02 02 02 04 04 06 06 08 08 10 10 12 12 14 14 16 16 18 18 20 20 22 22 24 24 26 26 28 28 30 30 32 32 34 34 36 36 38 38 40 40 42 42 44 44
0.026-0.050	02 02 02 04 04 06 06 08 08 10 10 12 12 14 14 16 16 18 18 20 20 22 22 24 24 26 26 28 28 30 30 32 32 34 34 36 36 38 38 40 40 42 42 44 44 46
0.051-0.075	02 02 02 04 04 06 06 08 08 10 10 12 12 14 14 16 16 18 18 20 20 22 22 24 24 26 26 28 28 30 30 32 32 34 34 36 36 38 38 40 40 42 42 44 44 46 46
0.076-0.100	02 02 02 04 04 06 06 08 08 10 10 12 12 14 14 16 16 18 18 20 20 22 22 24 24 26 26 28 28 30 30 32 32 34 34 36 36 38 38 40 40 42 42 44 44 46 46 48
0.101-0.125	02 02 02 04 04 06 06 08 08 10 10 12 12 14 14 16 16 18 18 20 20 22 22 24 24 26 26 28 28 30 30 32 32 34 34 36 36 38 38 40 40 42 42 44 44 46 46 48 48
0.126-0.150	02 02 02 04 04 06 06 08 08 10 10 12 12 14 14 16 16 18 18 20 20 22 22 24 24 26 26 28 28 30 30 32 32 34 34 36 36 38 38 40 40 42 42 44 44 46 46 48 48 50
0.151-0.175	02 02 02 04 04 06 06 08 08 10 10 12 12 14 14 16 16 18 18 20 20 22 22 24 24 26 26 28 28 30 30 32 32 34 34 36 36 38 38 40 40 42 42 44 44 46 46 48 48 50 50
0.176-0.199	02 02 02 04 04 06 06 08 08 10 10 12 12 14 14 16 16 18 18 20 20 22 22 24 24 26 26 28 28 30 30 32 32 34 34 36 36 38 38 40 40 42 42 44 44 46 46 48 48 50 50 50
0.200-0.300	(blank — clearance within acceptable range, no adjustment)
0.301-0.325	04 06 06 08 08 10 10 12 12 14 14 16 16 18 18 20 20 22 22 24 24 26 26 28 28 30 30 32 32 34 34 36 36 38 38 40 40 42 42 44 44 46 46 48 48 50 50 52 52 54 54 54
0.326-0.350	06 06 08 08 10 10 12 12 14 14 16 16 18 18 20 20 22 22 24 24 26 26 28 28 30 30 32 32 34 34 36 36 38 38 40 40 42 42 44 44 46 46 48 48 50 50 52 52 54 54 54
0.351-0.375	06 08 08 10 10 12 12 14 14 16 16 18 18 20 20 22 22 24 24 26 26 28 28 30 30 32 32 34 34 36 36 38 38 40 40 42 42 44 44 46 46 48 48 50 50 52 52 54 54 54
0.376-0.400	08 08 10 10 12 12 14 14 16 16 18 18 20 20 22 22 24 24 26 26 28 28 30 30 32 32 34 34 36 36 38 38 40 40 42 42 44 44 46 46 48 48 50 50 52 52 54 54 54
0.401-0.425	08 10 10 12 12 14 14 16 16 18 18 20 20 22 22 24 24 26 26 28 28 30 30 32 32 34 34 36 36 38 38 40 40 42 42 44 44 46 46 48 48 50 50 52 52 54 54 54
0.426-0.450	10 10 12 12 14 14 16 16 18 18 20 20 22 22 24 24 26 26 28 28 30 30 32 32 34 34 36 36 38 38 40 40 42 42 44 44 46 46 48 48 50 50 52 52 54 54 54
0.451-0.475	10 12 12 14 14 16 16 18 18 20 20 22 22 24 24 26 26 28 28 30 30 32 32 34 34 36 36 38 38 40 40 42 42 44 44 46 46 48 48 50 50 52 52 54 54 54
0.476-0.500	12 12 14 14 16 16 18 18 20 20 22 22 24 24 26 26 28 28 30 30 32 32 34 34 36 36 38 38 40 40 42 42 44 44 46 46 48 48 50 50 52 52 54 54 54
0.501-0.525	12 14 14 16 16 18 18 20 20 22 22 24 24 26 26 28 28 30 30 32 32 34 34 36 36 38 38 40 40 42 42 44 44 46 46 48 48 50 50 52 52 54 54 54
0.526-0.550	14 14 16 16 18 18 20 20 22 22 24 24 26 26 28 28 30 30 32 32 34 34 36 36 38 38 40 40 42 42 44 44 46 46 48 48 50 50 52 52 54 54 54
0.551-0.575	14 16 16 18 18 20 20 22 22 24 24 26 26 28 28 30 30 32 32 34 34 36 36 38 38 40 40 42 42 44 44 46 46 48 48 50 50 52 52 54 54 54
0.576-0.600	16 16 18 18 20 20 22 22 24 24 26 26 28 28 30 30 32 32 34 34 36 36 38 38 40 40 42 42 44 44 46 46 48 48 50 50 52 52 54 54 54
0.601-0.625	16 18 18 20 20 22 22 24 24 26 26 28 28 30 30 32 32 34 34 36 36 38 38 40 40 42 42 44 44 46 46 48 48 50 50 52 52 54 54 54
0.626-0.650	18 18 20 20 22 22 24 24 26 26 28 28 30 30 32 32 34 34 36 36 38 38 40 40 42 42 44 44 46 46 48 48 50 50 52 52 54 54 54
0.651-0.675	18 20 20 22 22 24 24 26 26 28 28 30 30 32 32 34 34 36 36 38 38 40 40 42 42 44 44 46 46 48 48 50 50 52 52 54 54 54
0.676-0.700	20 20 22 22 24 24 26 26 28 28 30 30 32 32 34 34 36 36 38 38 40 40 42 42 44 44 46 46 48 48 50 50 52 52 54 54 54
0.701-0.725	20 22 22 24 24 26 26 28 28 30 30 32 32 34 34 36 36 38 38 40 40 42 42 44 44 46 46 48 48 50 50 52 52 54 54 54
0.726-0.750	22 22 24 24 26 26 28 28 30 30 32 32 34 34 36 36 38 38 40 40 42 42 44 44 46 46 48 48 50 50 52 52 54 54 54
0.751-0.775	22 24 24 26 26 28 28 30 30 32 32 34 34 36 36 38 38 40 40 42 42 44 44 46 46 48 48 50 50 52 52 54 54 54
0.776-0.800	24 24 26 26 28 28 30 30 32 32 34 34 36 36 38 38 40 40 42 42 44 44 46 46 48 48 50 50 52 52 54 54 54
0.801-0.825	24 26 26 28 28 30 30 32 32 34 34 36 36 38 38 40 40 42 42 44 44 46 46 48 48 50 50 52 52 54 54 54
0.826-0.850	26 26 28 28 30 30 32 32 34 34 36 36 38 38 40 40 42 42 44 44 46 46 48 48 50 50 52 52 54 54 54
0.851-0.875	26 28 28 30 30 32 32 34 34 36 36 38 38 40 40 42 42 44 44 46 46 48 48 50 50 52 52 54 54 54
0.876-0.900	28 28 30 30 32 32 34 34 36 36 38 38 40 40 42 42 44 44 46 46 48 48 50 50 52 52 54 54 54
0.901-0.925	28 30 30 32 32 34 34 36 36 38 38 40 40 42 42 44 44 46 46 48 48 50 50 52 52 54 54 54
0.926-0.950	30 30 32 32 34 34 36 36 38 38 40 40 42 42 44 44 46 46 48 48 50 50 52 52 54 54 54
0.951-0.975	30 32 32 34 34 36 36 38 38 40 40 42 42 44 44 46 46 48 48 50 50 52 52 54 54 54
0.976-1.000	32 32 34 34 36 36 38 38 40 40 42 42 44 44 46 46 48 48 50 50 52 52 54 54 54
1.001-1.025	32 34 34 36 36 38 38 40 40 42 42 44 44 46 46 48 48 50 50 52 52 54 54 54
1.026-1.050	34 34 36 36 38 38 40 40 42 42 44 44 46 46 48 48 50 50 52 52 54 54 54
1.051-1.075	34 36 36 38 38 40 40 42 42 44 44 46 46 48 48 50 50 52 52 54 54 54
1.076-1.100	36 36 38 38 40 40 42 42 44 44 46 46 48 48 50 50 52 52 54 54 54
1.101-1.125	36 38 38 40 40 42 42 44 44 46 46 48 48 50 50 52 52 54 54 54
1.126-1.150	38 38 40 40 42 42 44 44 46 46 48 48 50 50 52 52 54 54 54
1.151-1.175	38 40 40 42 42 44 44 46 46 48 48 50 50 52 52 54 54 54
1.176-1.200	40 40 42 42 44 44 46 46 48 48 50 50 52 52 54 54 54
1.201-1.225	40 42 42 44 44 46 46 48 48 50 50 52 52 54 54 54
1.226-1.250	42 42 44 44 46 46 48 48 50 50 52 52 54 54 54
1.251-1.275	42 44 44 46 46 48 48 50 50 52 52 54 54 54
1.276-1.300	44 44 46 46 48 48 50 50 52 52 54 54 54
1.301-1.325	44 46 46 48 48 50 50 52 52 54 54 54
1.326-1.350	46 46 48 48 50 50 52 52 54 54 54
1.351-1.375	46 48 48 50 50 52 52 54 54 54
1.376-1.400	48 48 50 50 52 52 54 54 54
1.401-1.425	48 50 50 52 52 54 54 54
1.426-1.450	50 50 52 52 54 54 54
1.451-1.475	50 52 52 54 54 54
1.476-1.500	52 52 54 54 54
1.501-1.525	52 54 54 54
1.526-1.550	54 54 54
1.551-1.575	54 54
1.576-1.600	54

Shim thickness mm (in.)

Shim No.	Thickness	Shim No.	Thickness
02	2.00 (0.0787)	30	2.70 (0.1063)
04	2.05 (0.0807)	32	2.75 (0.1083)
06	2.10 (0.0827)	34	2.80 (0.1102)
08	2.15 (0.0846)	36	2.85 (0.1122)
10	2.20 (0.0866)	38	2.90 (0.1142)
12	2.25 (0.0886)	40	2.95 (0.1161)
14	2.30 (0.0906)	42	3.00 (0.1181)
16	2.35 (0.0925)	44	3.05 (0.1201)
18	2.40 (0.0945)	46	3.10 (0.1220)
20	2.45 (0.0965)	48	3.15 (0.1240)
22	2.50 (0.0984)	50	3.20 (0.1260)
24	2.55 (0.1004)	52	3.25 (0.1280)
26	2.60 (0.1024)	54	3.30 (0.1299)
28	2.65 (0.1043)		

Valve adjustment selection chart: 3S-GE 3S-GTE exhaust valves

a. Drain the engine coolant, collecting it for re-use in a large container.

WARNING: *Housepets and small animals are attracted to the odor and taste of engine coolant (antifreeze). It is a highly poisonous mixture of chemicals; special care must be taken to protect open containers and spillage.*

b. Remove the air cleaner hose and connector pipe.

c. Disconnect the cruise control cable, the accelerator cable and, if equipped with automatic transmission, the throttle cable (throttle control cable).

d. Remove the PCV hose.

e. Disconnect the accelerator rod.

f. Disconnect the water by-pass hoses from the throttle body.

g. Label and disconnect these hoses: VSV for EGR, BVSV hose, EGR vacuum modulator hoses and No.7 air hose.

h. Disconnect the throttle position sensor electrical connector.

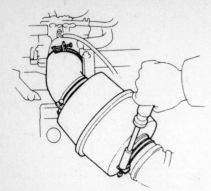

Removing the 7M-GE air cleaner hose

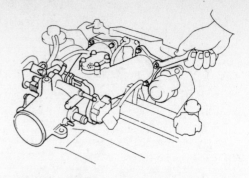

Removing the 7M-GE air intake connector

i. Remove the brackets holding the throttle body.

j. Remove the air intake connector bracket mounting bolts.

k. Remove the four bolts and two nuts holding the air intake connector. Remove the air intake connector and its gasket.

l. Remove the accelerator link.

m. Remove the heater hose clamp.

n. Remove the valve covers. Proceed to Step 3.

2. For the 7M-GTE, remove the valve covers as follows:

a. Remove the first or No.1 air cleaner hose.

b. Disconnect the accelerator link with the cable, the accelerator rod and, if equipped

with automatic transmission, the throttle (throttle control) cable.

c. Disconnect the six hoses from the Idle Speed Control (ISC) pipe. Remove the two bolts and remove the pipe.

d. Release the oxygen sensor wire from the two clamps along the PCV pipe.

e. Disconnect the No. 4 PCV hose from the PCV pipe. Remove the two bolts holding the pipe.

f. Disconnect the PCV pipe (with hoses attached) from the valve covers and the throttle body.

g. Disconnect the air valve hose from the intake air connector.

h. Loosen the clamp, remove the two bolts and remove the air intake connector.

i. Remove the oil filler cap.

j. Remove the 5 nuts holding the ignition coil cover and remove the cover.

k. Disconnect the harness and ground strap to the ignition coils.

l. Remove the nut.

m. Disconnect the Nos. 1 and 2 spark plug wires from the coil and the clamp(s).

n. Remove the coil with the bracket and other plug wires attached. Remove plug wires 1 and 2 from the spark plugs.

o. Remove the accelerator link and disconnect the No.3 PCV hose.

p. Remove the valve covers.

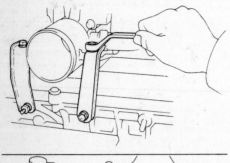

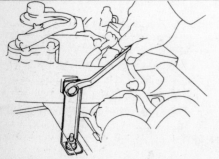

Both the throttle body bracket (above) and the intake air connector brackets must be removed from the 7M-GE

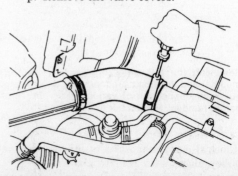

Removing the 7M-GTE air cleaner hose

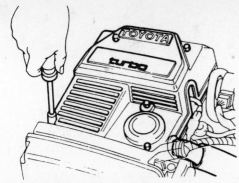

Removing the 7M-GTE coil cover

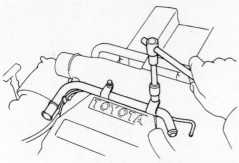

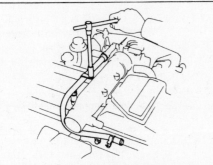

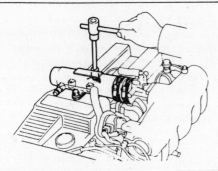

Removing the ISC pipe (upper), the PCV tube (middle) and the intake air connector. Each unit requires disconnection of various lines and hoses before removal. Remember to label everything

3. Use a wrench and turn the crankshaft (Clockwise as you face it) until the notch in the pulley aligns with the timing mark 0 of the timing belt cover. This will insure that engine is at TDC.

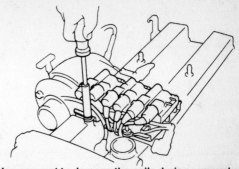

Use care not to damage the coils during removal or installation

NOTE: *Check that the valve lifters on the No 1 cylinder are loose and those on No 6 cylinder are tight. If not, turn the crankshaft one complete revolution (360°) and then realign the marks.*

4. Using a flat feeler gauge measure the clearance between the camshaft lobe and the valve lifter. This measurement should correspond to the one given in the "Tune-Up Specifications" chart. Check only the valves listed: intake side, cylinders No. 1 and 4; exhaust side, cylinders No. 1 and 5. Use the illustration to help you.

NOTE: *If the measurement is within specifications, go on to the next step. If not, record the measurement taken for each individual valve.*

5. Turn the crankshaft ⅔ revolution (240°). To help picture this rotation, make a small mark exactly straight up on the crank pulley. This represents 12 o'clock on a clock face; turn the crank pulley clockwise until this mark is at 8 o'clock. Check that the lifters on cylinder No.3 are loose.

6. Measure the clearance of the valves listed: Intake side, cylinders No. 3 and 5; exhaust side, cylinders No. 3 and 6. Use the illustration to help you.

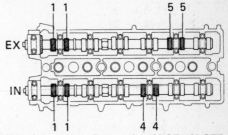

Adjust these valves first on the 7M-GE, 7M-GTE engines

NOTE: *If the measurement is within specifications, go on to the next step. If not, record the measurement taken for each individual valve.*

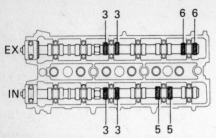

Adjust these valves second on the 7M-GE, 7M-GTE engines

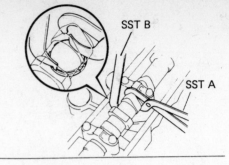

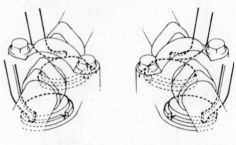

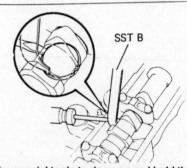

Using the special tools to depress and hold the lifters

7. Turn the crankshaft ⅔ revolution (240°). The reference mark made earlier ends up at 4 o'clock. Check that the valve lifters on cylinder No. 2 are loose.

8. Measure the clearance of these valves: intake side, cylinder No. 2 and 6; exhaust side, cylinders No. 2 and 4.

NOTE: *If the measurements for this set of valves and ALL the previous ones are within specifications, you need go no further, the inspection procedure is finished. If not, record the measurements and then proceed.*

9. Identify the valve(s) to be adjusted. Turn the crankshaft to position the camshaft lobe of the cylinder to be adjusted, upward.

10. Using a small tool, turn the valve lifter so that the notch is easily accessible.

11. Use the special tool to press the shim and lifter downward. Use the other tool from the set to hold it in place; make sure the second tool is not resting on the shim you're trying to remove.

12. Using a small screwdriver and a magnetic arm or probe, lift the shim up and remove it.

13. Measure the thickness of the old shim with a micrometer. Locate that particular measurement in the "Installed Shim Thickness"

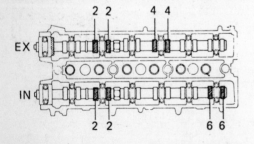

Adjust these valves third on the 7M-GE, 7M-GTE engines

column of the shim charts, then locate the previously recorded measurement for that valve in the "Measured Clearance " column of the charts. Index the two columns to arrive at the proper replacement shim thickness.

NOTE: *Replacement shims are available in many sizes, usually in increments of 0.05mm (0.0020 in.), from 2.500mm (0.0984 in.) to 3.300mm (0.1299 in.).*

14. Install the new shim, remove the special tool and then recheck the valve clearance.

15. Repeat the procedure for each valve needing adjustment.

16. Reinstall the valve covers. For the 7M-GE, proceed with the next step. For the 7M-GTE, skip the next step and proceed with Step 17.

17. Install the air intake connector with a new gasket. Tighten the bolts to 18 Nm or 13 ft.lbs.

  a. Install the air intake connector bracket. Install the throttle body support brackets.

  b. Connect the wiring to the throttle position sensor.

  c. Connect the disconnected vacuum hoses, making sure they are not twisted or kinked.

  d. Connect the water by-pass hose.

INTAKE

Measured Clearance (mm)	2.500	2.525	2.550	2.575	2.600	2.620	2.625	2.640	2.650	2.660	2.675	2.680	2.700	2.720	2.725	2.740	2.750	2.760	2.775	2.780	2.800	2.820	2.825	2.840	2.850	2.860	2.875	2.880	2.900	2.920	2.925	2.940	2.950	2.960	2.975	2.980	3.000	3.020	3.025	3.040	3.050	3.060	3.075	3.080	3.100	3.120	3.125	3.140	3.150	3.160	3.175	3.180	3.200	3.225	3.250	3.275	3.300

Installed Shim Thickness (mm)

Measured Clearance (mm)	values
0.000 – 0.009	02 02 02 04 04 04 06 06 06 08 08 08 10 10 10 12 12 12 14 14 14 16 16 16 18 18 18 20 20 20 22 22 24 24 26 26
0.010 – 0.025	02 02 02 02 04 04 04 06 06 06 08 08 10 10 10 12 12 12 14 14 16 16 16 18 18 18 20 20 20 22 22 22 24 24 26 26
0.026 – 0.029	02 02 02 04 04 04 06 06 06 08 08 08 10 10 10 12 12 12 14 14 14 16 16 16 18 18 18 20 20 20 22 22 22 24 24 26 26 28
0.030 – 0.040	02 02 02 02 04 04 04 06 06 06 08 08 08 10 10 10 12 12 12 14 14 14 16 16 16 18 18 18 20 20 20 22 22 22 24 24 26 26 28
0.041 – 0.050	02 02 02 02 04 04 04 06 06 06 08 08 08 10 10 10 12 12 12 14 14 14 16 16 16 18 18 18 20 20 20 22 22 22 24 24 26 26 28
0.051 – 0.070	02 02 02 02 02 04 04 04 06 06 06 08 08 08 10 10 10 12 12 12 14 14 14 16 16 16 18 18 18 20 20 20 22 22 22 24 24 26 26 28 28
0.071 – 0.075	02 02 02 02 04 04 04 06 06 06 08 08 08 10 10 10 12 12 12 14 14 14 16 16 16 18 18 18 20 20 20 22 22 22 24 24 26 26 28 28
0.076 – 0.090	02 02 02 02 04 04 04 06 06 06 08 08 08 10 10 10 12 12 12 14 14 14 16 16 16 18 18 18 20 20 20 22 22 22 24 24 26 26 28 28 30
0.091 – 0.100	02 02 02 04 04 04 06 06 06 08 08 08 10 10 10 12 12 12 14 14 14 16 16 16 18 18 18 20 20 20 22 22 22 24 24 24 26 26 28 28 30
0.101 – 0.120	02 02 04 04 04 06 06 06 08 08 08 10 10 10 12 12 12 14 14 14 16 16 16 18 18 18 20 20 20 22 22 22 24 24 24 26 26 28 28 30 30
0.121 – 0.125	02 02 02 04 04 04 06 06 06 08 08 08 10 10 10 12 12 12 14 14 14 16 16 16 18 18 18 20 20 20 22 22 22 24 24 24 26 26 26 28 28 30 30
0.126 – 0.140	02 02 04 04 04 06 06 06 08 08 08 10 10 10 12 12 12 14 14 14 16 16 16 18 18 18 20 20 20 22 22 22 24 24 24 26 26 28 28 30 30
0.141 – 0.149	02 02 04 04 04 06 06 06 08 08 08 10 10 10 12 12 12 14 14 14 16 16 16 18 18 18 20 20 20 22 22 22 24 24 24 26 26 26 28 28 30 30 32
0.150 – 0.250	
0.251 – 0.270	04 06 06 08 08 10 10 10 12 12 12 14 14 14 16 16 18 18 18 18 20 20 20 22 22 22 22 24 24 24 26 26 26 28 28 30 30 30 30 30 32 32 32 34 34
0.271 – 0.275	04 06 06 08 08 10 10 10 12 12 12 14 14 14 16 16 16 18 18 18 18 20 20 20 22 22 22 22 24 24 24 26 26 26 28 28 28 28 30 30 30 32 32 32 34 34
0.276 – 0.290	06 06 08 08 10 10 10 12 12 12 14 14 14 16 16 16 18 18 18 18 20 20 20 22 22 22 22 24 24 24 24 26 26 26 28 28 28 28 30 30 30 30 32 32 32 34 34
0.291 – 0.300	06 06 08 08 10 10 10 12 12 12 14 14 16 16 16 18 18 18 18 20 20 20 22 22 22 22 24 24 24 24 26 26 28 28 28 28 30 30 30 32 32 32 32 34 34 34
0.301 – 0.320	06 08 08 10 10 12 12 12 14 14 14 16 16 16 18 18 18 18 20 20 20 20 22 22 22 24 24 24 24 26 26 26 28 28 28 30 30 30 32 32 32 32 34 34 34 34
0.321 – 0.325	06 08 08 10 10 12 12 12 14 14 14 16 16 16 18 18 18 18 20 20 20 20 22 22 22 22 24 24 24 26 26 26 28 28 30 30 30 32 32 32 32 34 34 34 34
0.326 – 0.340	08 08 10 10 12 12 12 14 14 14 16 16 16 18 18 18 18 20 20 20 22 22 22 22 24 24 26 26 26 28 28 28 30 30 30 30 32 32 32 34 34 34 34
0.341 – 0.350	08 10 10 12 12 12 14 14 14 16 16 16 18 18 18 18 20 20 20 22 22 22 22 24 24 24 26 26 26 28 28 28 30 30 30 30 32 32 32 34 34 34 34
0.351 – 0.370	08 10 10 12 12 14 14 14 16 16 16 18 18 18 18 20 20 20 22 22 22 22 24 24 24 26 26 26 28 28 28 30 30 30 30 32 32 32 34 34 34 34 34
0.371 – 0.375	08 10 10 12 12 14 14 14 14 16 16 18 18 18 18 20 20 20 22 22 22 22 24 24 24 26 26 26 28 28 28 30 30 30 30 32 32 32 34 34 34 34 34
0.376 – 0.390	10 10 12 12 14 14 14 16 16 16 18 18 18 20 20 20 22 22 22 22 24 24 24 26 26 26 28 28 28 30 30 30 32 32 32 32 34 34 34 34
0.391 – 0.400	10 10 12 12 14 14 14 16 16 16 18 18 18 20 20 20 20 22 22 22 24 24 24 26 26 26 28 28 28 30 30 30 32 32 32 32 34 34 34 34
0.401 – 0.420	10 12 12 14 14 16 16 16 18 18 18 20 20 20 20 22 22 22 24 24 24 24 26 26 26 28 28 28 30 30 30 32 32 32 32 34 34 34 34
0.421 – 0.425	10 12 12 14 14 16 16 16 18 18 18 20 20 20 22 22 22 22 24 24 24 26 26 26 28 28 28 30 30 30 32 32 32 32 34 34 34 34
0.426 – 0.440	12 12 14 14 16 16 16 18 18 18 20 20 20 22 22 22 22 24 24 24 26 26 26 28 28 28 30 30 30 32 32 32 32 34 34 34 34
0.441 – 0.450	12 12 14 14 16 16 16 18 18 18 20 20 20 22 22 22 22 24 24 24 26 26 26 28 28 28 30 30 30 32 32 32 34 34 34 34 34
0.451 – 0.470	12 14 14 16 16 18 18 18 18 20 20 22 22 22 22 24 24 26 26 26 28 28 28 30 30 30 30 32 32 32 34 34 34 34
0.471 – 0.475	12 14 14 16 16 18 18 18 18 20 20 20 22 22 22 22 24 24 24 26 26 26 28 28 30 30 30 32 32 32 32 34 34 34 34
0.476 – 0.490	14 14 16 16 18 18 18 20 20 20 22 22 22 22 24 24 24 26 26 26 28 28 30 30 30 30 32 32 32 34 34 34
0.491 – 0.500	14 14 16 16 18 18 18 20 20 20 22 22 22 24 24 24 24 26 26 26 28 28 28 30 30 30 32 32 32 32 34 34 34
0.501 – 0.520	14 16 16 18 18 20 20 20 20 22 22 24 24 24 26 26 26 28 28 28 30 30 30 32 32 32 32 34 34 34
0.521 – 0.525	14 16 16 18 18 20 20 20 22 22 22 22 24 24 24 26 26 26 28 28 28 30 30 30 30 32 32 32 34 34 34
0.526 – 0.540	16 16 18 18 20 20 20 22 22 22 24 24 24 26 26 26 28 28 28 30 30 30 32 32 32 32 34 34 34
0.541 – 0.550	16 16 18 18 20 20 20 22 22 22 22 24 24 24 26 26 26 28 28 30 30 30 30 32 32 32 34 34 34 34
0.551 – 0.570	16 18 18 20 20 22 22 22 24 24 24 26 26 26 28 28 30 30 30 30 32 32 32 34 34 34 34
0.571 – 0.575	16 18 18 20 20 22 22 22 22 24 24 24 26 26 26 28 28 30 30 30 32 32 32 32 34 34 34
0.576 – 0.590	18 18 20 20 22 22 22 22 24 24 24 26 26 26 28 28 28 30 30 30 32 32 32 34 34 34 34
0.591 – 0.600	18 18 20 20 20 22 22 22 24 24 24 26 26 26 28 28 28 30 30 30 32 32 32 34 34 34 34
0.601 – 0.620	18 20 20 22 22 24 24 24 24 26 26 28 28 28 28 30 30 32 32 32 32 34 34 34 34
0.621 – 0.625	18 20 20 22 22 24 24 24 26 26 26 28 28 28 30 30 30 32 32 32 32 34 34 34 34
0.626 – 0.640	20 20 22 22 24 24 24 26 26 26 28 28 30 30 30 32 32 32 32 34 34 34 34
0.641 – 0.650	20 20 22 22 24 24 24 26 26 26 28 28 28 30 30 30 30 32 32 32 34 34 34 34 34
0.651 – 0.670	20 22 22 24 24 26 26 26 26 28 28 30 30 30 30 32 32 32 34 34 34 34
0.671 – 0.675	20 22 22 24 24 26 26 26 28 28 28 30 30 30 32 32 32 32 34 34 34
0.676 – 0.690	22 22 24 24 26 26 26 28 28 28 30 30 30 30 32 32 32 34 34 34 34
0.691 – 0.700	22 22 24 24 26 26 26 28 28 28 30 30 30 32 32 32 32 34 34 34
0.701 – 0.720	22 24 24 26 26 28 28 28 28 30 30 32 32 32 32 34 34 34
0.721 – 0.725	22 24 24 26 26 28 28 28 30 30 30 32 32 32 32 34 34 34
0.726 – 0.740	24 24 26 26 28 28 28 30 30 30 32 32 32 32 34 34 34 34
0.741 – 0.750	24 24 26 26 28 28 28 30 30 30 30 32 32 32 34 34 34 34
0.751 – 0.770	24 26 26 28 28 30 30 30 30 32 32 32 34 34 34 34 34
0.771 – 0.775	24 26 26 28 28 30 30 30 32 32 32 32 34 34 34 34 34
0.776 – 0.790	24 26 26 28 28 30 30 30 32 32 32 32 34 34 34 34
0.791 – 0.800	26 26 28 28 30 30 30 32 32 32 32 34 34 34 34
0.801 – 0.820	26 28 28 30 30 32 32 32 32 34 34 34 34
0.821 – 0.825	26 28 28 30 30 32 32 32 32 34 34 34 34
0.826 – 0.840	28 28 30 30 32 32 32 32 34 34 34 34
0.841 – 0.850	28 28 30 30 32 32 32 32 34 34 34 34
0.851 – 0.870	28 30 30 32 32 34 34 34 34 34
0.871 – 0.875	28 30 30 32 32 34 34 34 34 34
0.876 – 0.890	30 30 32 32 34 34 34 34
0.891 – 0.900	30 30 32 32 32 34 34 34
0.901 – 0.925	30 32 32 32 34 34
0.926 – 0.950	32 32 34 34
0.951 – 0.975	32 34 34
0.976 – 1.000	34 34
1.001 – 1.025	34

Shim thicknesses			mm (in.)
Shim No.	Thickness	Shim No.	Thickness
02	2.500 (0.0984)	20	2.950 (0.1161)
04	2.550 (0.1004)	22	3.000 (0.1181)
06	2.600 (0.1024)	24	3.050 (0.1201)
08	2.650 (0.1043)	26	3.100 (0.1220)
10	2.700 (0.1063)	28	3.150 (0.1240)
12	2.750 (0.1083)	30	3.200 (0.1260)
14	2.800 (0.1102)	32	3.250 (0.1280)
16	2.850 (0.1122)	34	3.300 (0.1299)
18	2.900 (0.1142)		

Valve adjustment selection chart: 7M-GE and -GTE intake valves

e. Install the accelerator connecting rod.

f. Install the PCV pipe.

g. Connect the throttle cable (auto. trans., the accelerator cable and the cruise control cable.

h. Install the air cleaner hose and connector pipe.

i. Refill the cooling system with coolant.

18. For 7M-GTE, attach the No. 1 and 2 spark plug wires to the spark plugs. Install the ignition coil with its brackets and connect the plug wires. Tighten the nut only to 5.4 Nm (48 INCH lbs or 4 ft. lbs). Do not over tighten this nut.

EXHAUST

Measured Clearance (mm)	Installed Shim Thickness (mm)																																																							
	2.500	2.525	2.550	2.575	2.600	2.620	2.625	2.640	2.650	2.660	2.675	2.680	2.700	2.720	2.725	2.740	2.750	2.760	2.775	2.780	2.800	2.820	2.825	2.840	2.850	2.860	2.875	2.880	2.900	2.920	2.925	2.940	2.950	2.960	2.975	2.980	3.000	3.020	3.025	3.040	3.050	3.060	3.075	3.080	3.100	3.120	3.125	3.140	3.150	3.160	3.175	3.180	3.200	3.225	3.250	3.275	3.300
0.000 - 0.009														02	02	02	02	02	04	04	04	06	06	06	06	06	08	08	08	10	10	10	10	10	12	12	12	14	14	14	14	14	16	16	16	18	18	18	18	18	20	20	20	22	22	24	24
0.010 - 0.025														02	02	02	02	04	04	04	06	06	06	06	06	08	08	08	10	10	10	10	10	12	12	12	14	14	14	14	14	16	16	16	18	18	18	18	18	20	20	20	22	22	22	24	26
0.026 - 0.040													02	02	02	02	04	04	04	04	06	06	06	06	08	08	08	08	10	10	10	10	12	12	12	12	14	14	14	14	16	16	16	16	18	18	18	18	20	20	20	20	22	22	24	24	26
0.041 - 0.050												02	02	02	02	04	04	04	04	06	06	06	06	08	08	08	08	10	10	10	10	12	12	12	12	14	14	14	14	16	16	16	16	18	18	18	18	20	20	20	20	22	22	22	24	24	26
0.051 - 0.070											02	02	02	04	04	04	04	04	06	06	06	08	08	08	08	08	10	10	10	12	12	12	12	12	14	14	14	16	16	16	16	16	18	18	18	20	20	20	20	20	22	22	22	24	24	26	26
0.071 - 0.090									02	02	02	02	04	04	04	04	06	06	06	06	08	08	08	08	10	10	10	10	12	12	12	12	14	14	14	14	16	16	16	16	18	18	18	18	20	20	20	20	22	22	22	22	24	24	26	26	28
0.091 - 0.100								02	02	02	02	04	04	04	04	06	06	06	06	08	08	08	08	10	10	10	10	12	12	12	12	14	14	14	14	16	16	16	16	18	18	18	18	20	20	20	20	22	22	22	22	24	24	24	26	26	28
0.101 - 0.120						02	02	02	02	02	04	04	04	06	06	06	06	06	08	08	08	10	10	10	10	10	12	12	12	14	14	14	14	14	16	16	16	18	18	18	18	18	20	20	20	22	22	22	22	22	24	24	24	26	26	28	28
0.121 - 0.140					02	02	02	02	04	04	04	04	06	06	06	06	08	08	08	08	10	10	10	10	12	12	12	12	14	14	14	14	16	16	16	16	18	18	18	18	20	20	20	20	22	22	22	22	24	24	24	24	26	26	28	28	30
0.141 - 0.150					02	02	02	04	04	04	04	06	06	06	06	08	08	08	08	10	10	10	10	12	12	12	12	14	14	14	14	16	16	16	16	18	18	18	18	20	20	20	20	22	22	22	22	24	24	24	24	26	26	26	28	28	30
0.151 - 0.170				02	02	04	04	04	04	04	06	06	06	08	08	08	08	08	10	10	10	12	12	12	12	12	14	14	14	16	16	16	16	16	18	18	18	20	20	20	20	20	22	22	22	24	24	24	24	24	26	26	26	28	28	30	30
0.171 - 0.190			02	02	04	04	04	04	06	06	06	06	08	08	08	08	10	10	10	10	12	12	12	12	14	14	14	14	16	16	16	16	18	18	18	18	20	20	20	20	22	22	22	22	24	24	24	24	26	26	26	26	28	28	30	30	32
0.191 - 0.199			02	02	04	04	04	06	06	06	06	08	08	08	08	10	10	10	10	12	12	12	12	14	14	14	14	16	16	16	16	18	18	18	18	20	20	20	20	22	22	22	22	24	24	24	24	26	26	26	26	28	28	28	30	30	32
0.200 - 0.300																																																									
0.301 - 0.320	04	06	06	08	08	10	10	10	10	10	12	12	12	14	14	14	14	14	16	16	16	18	18	18	18	18	20	20	20	22	22	22	22	22	24	24	24	26	26	26	26	26	28	28	28	30	30	30	30	30	32	32	32	34	34
0.321 - 0.325	04	06	06	08	08	10	10	10	10	12	12	12	12	14	14	14	14	16	16	16	16	18	18	18	18	20	20	20	20	22	22	22	22	24	24	24	24	26	26	26	26	28	28	28	28	30	30	30	30	32	32	32	32	34	34
0.326 - 0.340	06	06	08	08	10	10	10	10	12	12	12	12	14	14	14	14	16	16	16	16	18	18	18	18	20	20	20	20	22	22	22	22	24	24	24	24	26	26	26	26	28	28	28	28	30	30	30	30	32	32	32	32	34	34
0.341 - 0.350	06	06	08	08	10	10	10	12	12	12	12	12	14	14	14	16	16	16	16	16	18	18	18	20	20	20	20	20	22	22	22	24	24	24	24	24	26	26	26	28	28	28	28	28	30	30	30	32	32	32	32	32	34	34
0.351 - 0.370	06	08	08	10	10	12	12	12	12	12	14	14	14	16	16	16	16	16	18	18	18	20	20	20	20	20	22	22	22	24	24	24	24	24	26	26	26	28	28	28	28	28	30	30	30	32	32	32	32	32	34	34	34
0.371 - 0.375	06	08	08	10	10	12	12	12	12	14	14	14	14	16	16	16	16	18	18	18	18	20	20	20	20	22	22	22	22	24	24	24	24	26	26	26	26	28	28	28	28	30	30	30	30	32	32	32	32	34	34	34	34
0.376 - 0.390	08	08	10	10	12	12	12	12	14	14	14	14	16	16	16	16	18	18	18	18	20	20	20	20	22	22	22	22	24	24	24	24	26	26	26	26	28	28	28	28	30	30	30	30	32	32	32	32	34	34	34	34
0.391 - 0.400	08	08	10	10	12	12	12	14	14	14	14	14	16	16	16	18	18	18	18	18	20	20	20	22	22	22	22	22	24	24	24	26	26	26	26	26	28	28	28	30	30	30	30	30	32	32	32	34	34	34	34	34
0.401 - 0.420	08	10	10	12	12	14	14	14	14	14	16	16	16	18	18	18	18	18	20	20	20	22	22	22	22	22	24	24	24	26	26	26	26	26	28	28	28	30	30	30	30	30	32	32	32	34	34	34	34	34
0.421 - 0.425	08	10	10	12	12	14	14	14	14	16	16	16	16	18	18	18	18	20	20	20	20	22	22	22	22	24	24	24	24	26	26	26	26	28	28	28	28	30	30	30	30	32	32	32	32	34	34	34	34
0.426 - 0.440	10	10	12	12	14	14	14	14	16	16	16	16	18	18	18	18	20	20	20	20	22	22	22	22	24	24	24	24	26	26	26	26	28	28	28	28	30	30	30	30	32	32	32	32	34	34	34	34
0.441 - 0.450	10	10	12	12	14	14	14	16	16	16	16	16	18	18	18	20	20	20	20	20	22	22	22	24	24	24	24	24	26	26	26	28	28	28	28	28	30	30	30	32	32	32	32	32	34	34	34
0.451 - 0.470	10	12	12	14	14	16	16	16	16	16	18	18	18	20	20	20	20	20	22	22	22	24	24	24	24	24	26	26	26	28	28	28	28	28	30	30	30	32	32	32	32	32	34	34	34
0.471 - 0.475	10	12	12	14	14	16	16	16	16	18	18	18	18	20	20	20	20	22	22	22	22	24	24	24	24	26	26	26	26	28	28	28	28	30	30	30	30	32	32	32	32	34	34	34	34
0.476 - 0.490	12	12	14	14	16	16	16	16	18	18	18	18	20	20	20	20	22	22	22	22	24	24	24	24	26	26	26	26	28	28	28	28	30	30	30	30	32	32	32	32	34	34	34	34
0.491 - 0.500	12	12	14	14	16	16	16	18	18	18	18	18	20	20	20	22	22	22	22	22	24	24	24	26	26	26	26	26	28	28	28	30	30	30	30	30	32	32	32	34	34	34	34	34
0.501 - 0.520	12	14	14	16	16	18	18	18	18	18	20	20	20	22	22	22	22	22	24	24	24	26	26	26	26	26	28	28	28	30	30	30	30	30	32	32	32	34	34	34	34	34
0.521 - 0.525	12	14	14	16	16	18	18	18	18	20	20	20	20	22	22	22	22	24	24	24	24	26	26	26	26	28	28	28	28	30	30	30	30	32	32	32	32	34	34	34	34
0.526 - 0.540	14	14	16	16	18	18	18	18	20	20	20	20	22	22	22	22	24	24	24	24	26	26	26	26	28	28	28	28	30	30	30	30	32	32	32	32	34	34	34	34
0.541 - 0.550	14	14	16	16	18	18	18	20	20	20	20	20	22	22	22	24	24	24	24	24	26	26	26	28	28	28	28	28	30	30	30	32	32	32	32	32	34	34	34
0.551 - 0.570	14	16	16	18	18	20	20	20	20	20	22	22	22	24	24	24	24	24	26	26	26	28	28	28	28	28	30	30	30	32	32	32	32	32	34	34	34
0.571 - 0.575	14	16	16	18	18	20	20	20	20	22	22	22	22	24	24	24	24	26	26	26	26	28	28	28	28	30	30	30	30	32	32	32	32	34	34	34	34
0.576 - 0.590	16	16	18	18	20	20	20	20	22	22	22	22	24	24	24	24	26	26	26	26	28	28	28	28	30	30	30	30	32	32	32	32	34	34	34	34
0.591 - 0.600	16	16	18	18	20	20	20	22	22	22	22	22	24	24	24	26	26	26	26	26	28	28	28	30	30	30	30	30	32	32	32	34	34	34	34	34
0.601 - 0.620	16	18	18	20	20	22	22	22	22	22	24	24	24	26	26	26	26	26	28	28	28	30	30	30	30	30	32	32	32	34	34	34	34	34
0.621 - 0.625	16	18	18	20	20	22	22	22	22	24	24	24	24	26	26	26	26	28	28	28	28	30	30	30	30	32	32	32	32	34	34	34	34
0.626 - 0.640	18	18	20	20	22	22	22	22	24	24	24	24	26	26	26	26	28	28	28	28	30	30	30	30	32	32	32	32	34	34	34	34
0.641 - 0.650	18	18	20	20	22	22	22	24	24	24	24	24	26	26	26	28	28	28	28	28	30	30	30	32	32	32	32	32	34	34	34
0.651 - 0.670	18	20	20	22	22	24	24	24	24	24	26	26	26	28	28	28	28	28	30	30	30	32	32	32	32	32	34	34	34
0.671 - 0.675	18	20	20	22	22	24	24	24	24	26	26	26	26	28	28	28	28	30	30	30	30	32	32	32	32	34	34	34	34
0.676 - 0.690	20	20	22	22	24	24	24	24	26	26	26	26	28	28	28	28	30	30	30	30	32	32	32	32	34	34	34	34
0.691 - 0.700	20	20	22	22	24	24	24	26	26	26	26	26	28	28	28	30	30	30	30	30	32	32	32	34	34	34	34	34
0.701 - 0.720	20	22	22	24	24	26	26	26	26	26	28	28	28	30	30	30	30	30	32	32	32	34	34	34	34	34
0.721 - 0.725	20	22	22	24	24	26	26	26	26	28	28	28	28	30	30	30	30	32	32	32	32	34	34	34	34
0.726 - 0.740	22	22	24	24	26	26	26	26	28	28	28	28	30	30	30	30	32	32	32	32	34	34	34	34
0.741 - 0.750	22	22	24	24	26	26	26	28	28	28	28	28	30	30	30	32	32	32	32	32	34	34	34
0.751 - 0.770	22	24	24	26	26	28	28	28	28	28	30	30	30	32	32	32	32	32	34	34	34
0.771 - 0.775	22	24	24	26	26	28	28	28	28	30	30	30	30	32	32	32	32	34	34	34	34
0.776 - 0.790	24	24	26	26	28	28	28	28	30	30	30	30	32	32	32	32	34	34	34	34
0.791 - 0.800	24	24	26	26	28	28	28	30	30	30	30	30	32	32	32	34	34	34	34	34
0.801 - 0.820	24	26	26	28	28	30	30	30	30	30	32	32	32	34	34	34	34	34
0.821 - 0.825	24	26	26	28	28	30	30	30	30	32	32	32	32	34	34	34	34
0.826 - 0.840	26	26	28	28	30	30	30	30	32	32	32	32	34	34	34	34
0.841 - 0.850	26	26	28	28	30	30	30	32	32	32	32	32	34	34	34
0.851 - 0.870	26	28	28	30	30	32	32	32	32	32	34	34	34
0.871 - 0.875	26	28	28	30	30	32	32	32	32	34	34	34	34
0.876 - 0.890	28	28	30	30	32	32	32	32	34	34	34	34
0.891 - 0.900	28	28	30	30	32	32	32	34	34	34	34	34
0.901 - 0.925	28	30	30	32	32	34	34	34	34
0.926 - 0.950	30	30	32	32	34	34	34
0.951 - 0.975	30	32	32	34	34
0.976 - 1.000	32	32	34	34
1.001 - 1.025	32	34	34
1.026 - 1.050	34	34
1.051 - 1.075	34

Shim thicknesses mm (in.)

Shim No.	Thickness	Shim No.	Thickness
02	2.500 (0.0984)	20	2.950 (0.1161)
04	2.550 (0.1004)	22	3.000 (0.1181)
06	2.600 (0.1024)	24	3.050 (0.1201)
08	2.650 (0.1043)	26	3.100 (0.1220)
10	2.700 (0.1063)	28	3.150 (0.1240)
12	2.750 (0.1083)	30	3.200 (0.1260)
14	2.800 (0.1102)	32	3.250 (0.1280)
16	2.850 (0.1122)	34	3.300 (0.1299)
18	2.900 (0.1142)		

Valve adjustment selection chart: 7M-GE and -GTE exhaust valves

a. Connect the ground strap and connector.

b. Install the coil cover panel with five nuts and install the oil filler cap.

c. Install the intake air connector to the throttle body. Install and tighten the two bolts.

d. Tighten the clamp.

e. Connect the air valve hose to the intake air connector.

f. Install the PCV pipe with its hoses to the throttle body and valve covers. Tighten the two bolts holding the pipe.

g. Connect the No.4 hose to the PCV pipe; refit the oxygen sensor wire into the two clamps.

h. Install the ISC pipe and tighten its bolts. Connect the six hoses to the pipe.

i. Connect the throttle cable (auto. trans.), the accelerator rod and the accelerator link with the cable.

j. Install the air cleaner hose.

Engine and Engine Overhaul

3

ENGINE ELECTRICAL

UNDERSTANDING BASIC ELECTRICITY

Understanding the basic theory of electricity makes electrical troubleshooting much easier. Several meters and special tools are used in electrical troubleshooting to see inside the circuit being tested. Without a basic understanding, it will be difficult to understand testing procedures.

Electricity is the flow of electrons, particles thought to constitute the basic "stuff" of electricity. In a comparison with water flowing in a pipe, the electrons would be the water. As the flow of water can be measured, the flow of electricity can be measured. The unit of measurement is amperes, frequently abbreviated "amps". An ammeter will measure the actual amount of current flowing in the circuit.

Just as the water pressure is measured in units such as pounds per square inch, electrical pressure is measured in volts. When a voltmeter's two probes are placed on two "live" portions of an electrical circuit with different electrical pressures, current will flow through the voltmeter and produce a reading which indicates the difference in electrical pressure between the two parts of the circuit.

While increasing the voltage in a circuit will increase the flow of current, the actual flow depends not only on voltage, but on the resistance of the circuit. The standard unit for measuring circuit resistance is an ohm (Ω), measured by an ohmmeter. The ohmmeter is somewhat similar to an ammeter, but incorporates its own source of power so that a standard voltage is always present.

An actual electric circuit consists of four basic parts. These are: the power source such as a alternator or battery; a "hot" wire, which conducts the electricity under a relatively high voltage to the component in the circuit; the load (such as a lamp, motor, resistor, or relay coil) which uses the electricity; and the ground wire (or neutral), which carries the current back to the source under very low voltage. In such a circuit the bulk of the resistance exists between the point where the hot wire is connected to the load, and the point where the load is grounded.

In electrical testing, the voltmeter is connected in parallel with the circuit being tested (without disconnecting any wires) and measures the difference in voltage between the locations of the two probes. The ammeter is connected in series with the load (the circuit is separated at one point and the ammeter inserted so it becomes a part of the circuit).

For any electrical system to operate, it must make a complete circuit. This simply means that the power flow from the source — usually the battery — must make a complete circle. When an electrical component is operating, power flows from the battery to the component, passes through the component causing it to function (lighting a bulb for example) and then returns to the battery through the ground of the circuit. This ground is may be either the metal part of the car on which the electrical component is mounted or a separate ground wire. As more solid–state equipment is installed on cars, it becomes necessary to use discreet ground paths which will not interfere with other circuits.

Perhaps the easiest way to visualize this is to think of connecting a light bulb with two wires attached to it to your car battery. The battery in your car has two posts, termed negative and positive. If one of the two wires attached to the light bulb was attached to the negative post of the battery and the other attached to the positive post of the battery, you would have a complete circuit. Current from the battery would flow out one post, through the wire attached to it and then to the light bulb. It would pass through the bulb, causing it to light, then travel through the other wire and return to the opposite post of the battery.

The normal automotive circuit may differ from this simple example in two ways. First, instead of having a return wire from the bulb to the battery, the light bulb may return the current to the battery through the chassis of the vehicle. Since the negative battery cable is attached to the chassis and the chassis is made of electrically conductive metal, the chassis of the vehicle can serve as a ground wire to complete the circuit. Secondly, most automotive circuits contain switches to turn components on and off.

Some electrical components which require a large amount of current to operate also have a relay in their circuit. Since these circuits carry a large amount of current (amperage or amps), the thickness of the wire in the circuit (wire gauge) is also greater. If this large wire were connected from the load to the control switch on the dash, the switch would have to carry the high amperage load and the dash would be twice as large to accommodate wiring harnesses as thick as your wrist. To prevent these problems, a relay is used. The large wires in the circuit are connected from the battery to one side of the relay and from the opposite side of the relay to the load. The relay is normally open, preventing current from passing through the circuit. An additional, smaller wire is connected from the relay to the control switch for the circuit. When the control switch is turned on, it grounds the smaller wire to the relay and completes its circuit. The main switch inside the relay closes, sending power to the component without routing the main power through the inside of the car. Some common circuits which may use relays are the horn, headlights, starter and rear window defogger systems.

Every complete circuit must include a load--something to use the electricity coming from the source. If you were to connect a wire between the two terminals of the battery (DON'T do this) without the light bulb, the battery would attempt to deliver its entire power supply from one pole to another almost instantly. This is a short circuit. The electricity is taking a short-cut to get to ground and is not being used by any load in the circuit. This sudden and uncontrolled electrical flow can cause great damage to other components in the circuit and can develop a tremendous amount of heat. A short in an automotive wiring harness can develop sufficient heat to melt the insulation on all the surrounding wires and reduce a multi-wire cable to one sad lump of plastic and copper. Two common causes of shorts are broken insulation (thereby exposing the wire to contact with surrounding metal surfaces) or a failed switch (the pins inside the switch come out of place, touch each other and reroute the electricity).

It is possible for larger surges of current to pass through the electrical system of your car. If this surge of current were to reach the load in the circuit, it could burn it out or severely damage it. To prevent this, fuses and/or circuit breakers and/or fusible links are connected into the supply wires of the electrical system. These items are nothing more than a built-in weak spot in the system. It's much easier to go to a known location (the fuse box) to see why a circuit is inoperative than to dissect 15 feet of wiring under the dashboard, looking for what happened.

When an electrical current of excessive power passes through the fuse, the fuse blows and breaks the circuit, preventing the passage of current and protecting the components.

A circuit breaker is basically a self-repairing fuse. It will open the circuit in the same fashion as a fuse, but when either the short is removed or the surge subsides, the circuit breaker resets itself and does not need replacement.

A fuse link (fusible link or main link) is a wire that acts as a fuse. It is normally connected between the starter relay and the main wiring harness under the hood. Since the starter is the highest electrical draw on the car, an internal short during starter use could direct about 130 amps into the wrong places. Consider the damage potential of introducing this current into a system whose wiring is rated at 15 amps and you'll understand the need for protection. Since this link is very early in the electrical path, it's the first place to look if nothing on the car works but the battery seems to be charged and is properly connected.

Electrical problems generally fall into one of three areas:

1. The component that is not functioning is not receiving current.

2. The component itself is not functioning.

3. The component is not properly grounded.

Problems that fall into the first category are by far the most complicated. It is the current supply system to the component which contains all the switches, relays, fuses., etc.

The electrical system can be checked with a test light and a jumper wire. A test light is a device that looks like a pointed screwdriver with a wire attached to it. It has a light bulb in its handle. A jumper wire is a piece of insulated wire with an alligator clip attached to each end. You can either make or buy jumper wires; you should have an assortment of lengths. Different colors of wire make some jobs much easier.

If a light bulb is not working, you must follow a systematic plan to determine which of the three causes is the villain.

1. Turn on the switch that controls the inoperable bulb.

2. Disconnect the power supply wire from the bulb; this may mean disconnecting a plug a few inches away from the lamp.

3. Attach the ground wire on the test light to a good metal ground.

4. Touch the probe end of the test light to the end of the power supply wire that was disconnected form the bulb. If the bulb is receiving current, the test light will go on.

NOTE: *If the bulb is one which works only when the ignition is on (turn signal), make sure the key is turned on.*

If the test light does not go on, then the problem is in the circuit between the battery and the bulb. As mentioned before, this includes all the switches, fuses, and relays in the system. Follow the wire that runs back to the battery. The problem is an open circuit between the battery and the bulb. If the fuse is blown and, when replaced, immediately blows again, there is a short circuit in the system which must be located and repaired. If there is a switch in the system, bypass it with a jumper wire. This is done by connecting one end of the jumper wire to the power supply wire into the switch and the other end of the jumper wire to the wire coming out of the switch. If the test light lights with the jumper wire installed, the switch or whatever was bypassed is defective.

NOTE: *Never substitute the jumper wire for the bulb, as the bulb is the component required to use the power from the power source.*

5. If the bulb in the test light goes on, then the current is getting to the bulb that is not working in the car. This eliminates the first of the three possible causes. Connect the power supply wire and connect a jumper wire from the bulb to a good metal ground. Do this with the switch which controls the bulb turned on, and also the ignition switch turned on if it is required for the light to work. If the bulb works with jumper wire installed, then it has a bad ground. This is usually caused by the metal area on which the bulb mounts to the car being coated with some type of foreign matter.

6. If neither test located the source of the trouble, then the light bulb itself is defective.

It should be noted that generally the last place to look for an electrical problem is in the wiring itself. Unless the car has undergone unusual circumstances (major body work, flood damage, improper repairs, etc.) the wiring is not likely to change its condition. A systematic search through the fuse, the connectors and switches and the component itself will almost always yield an answer. Loose and/or corroded connectors—particularly in ground circuits—are becoming a larger problem in modern cars. The computers and on-board electronic (solid state) systems are highly sensitive to improper grounds and will change their function drastically if one occurs. Remember that for any electrical system to work, all connections must be clean and tight.

UNDERSTANDING THE ENGINE ELECTRICAL SYSTEM

The engine electrical system can be broken down into separate and distinct systems:

1. The starting system.
2. The charging system.
3. The ignition system.
4. The electronic fuel injection system.

Battery and Starting System

The battery is the first link in the chain of mechanisms which work together to provide cranking of the automobile engine. In most modern cars, the battery is a lead/acid electrochemical device consisting of six two-volt (2V) cells connected in series so the unit is capable of producing approximately 12 V of electrical pressure. Each cell consists of a series of positive and negative plates held a short distance apart in a solution of sulfuric acid and water. The two types of plates are of dissimilar metals. This causes a chemical reaction to be set up, and this reaction produces current flow from the battery when its positive and negative terminals are connected to an electrical appliance such as a lamp or a motor.

The continued transfer of electrons would eventually convert sulfuric acid in the electrolyte to water, and make the two plates identical in chemical composition. As electrical energy is removed from the battery, its voltage output tends to drop. Thus, measuring battery voltage and battery electrolyte composition are two ways of checking the ability of the unit to supply power. During the starting of the engine, electrical energy is removed from the battery. However, if the charging circuit is in good condition and the operating conditions are normal, the power removed from the battery will be replaced by the alternator which will force electrons back through the battery, (reversing the normal flow) restoring the battery to its original chemical state.

The battery and starting motor are linked by very heavy electrical cables designed to minimize resistance to the flow of current. Generally, the major power supply cable that leaves the battery goes directly to the starter, while other electrical needs are supplied by a smaller cable. During the starter operation, power flows from the battery to the starter and is grounded through the car's frame and the battery's negative ground strap.

The starting motor is a specially designed, direct current electric motor capable of producing a very great amount of power for its size. One thing that allows the motor to produce a great deal of power is its tremendous rotating speed. It drives the engine through a tiny pinion gear (attached to the starter's armature), which drives the very large flywheel ring gear at a greatly reduced speed. Another factor allowing it to produce so much power is that only intermittent operation is required of it. Thus, little allowance for air circulation is required, and the windings can be built into a very small space. For this reason, the starter should never be engaged for more than 10–15 seconds without a 20–30 second pause in between. This allows the starter to cool and work more efficiently.

The starter solenoid is a magnetic device which employs the small current supplied by the ignition switch circuit. The magnetic action moves a plunger which mechanically engages the starter and electrically closes the heavy switch which connects it to the battery. The starting switch circuit consists of the starting switch contained within the ignition switch, a transmission neutral safety switch or clutch pedal switch, and the wiring necessary to connect these with the starter solenoid or relay.

A small gear or pinion is mounted to a one-way drive clutch. This clutch is splined to the starter armature shaft. When the ignition switch is moved to the **START** position, the solenoid plunger slides the pinion toward the flywheel ring gear. If the teeth on the pinion and flywheel match properly, the pinion will engage the flywheel immediately. If the gear teeth butt one another, the spring will be compressed and will force the gears to mesh as soon as the starter turns far enough to allow them to do so. As the solenoid plunger reaches the end of its travel, it closes the contacts that connect the battery and starter and then the engine is cranked.

As soon as the engine starts, the flywheel ring gear begins turning fast enough to drive the pinion at an extremely high rate of speed. At this point, the one-way clutch begins allowing the pinion to spin faster than the starter shaft so that the starter will not operate at excessive speed. When the ignition switch is released from the starter position, the solenoid is de-energized, and a spring pulls the gear out of

mesh and interrupts the current flow to the starter.

Some starters employ a separate relay, mounted away from the starter, to switch the motor and solenoid current on and off. The relay thus replaces the solenoid electrical switch, but does not eliminate the need for a solenoid mounted on the starter used to mechanically engage the starter drive gears. The relay is used to reduce the amount of current the starting switch must carry.

The Charging System

The automobile charging system provides electrical power for operation of the vehicle's ignition and starting systems and all the electrical accessories. The battery serves as an electrical surge or storage tank, storing (in chemical form) the energy originally produced by the engine-driven alternator. The system also provides a means of regulating electrical output to protect the battery from being overcharged and to avoid excessive voltage to the components.

The alternator is driven mechanically, through belts by the engine crankshaft. It consists of two coils of fine wire, one stationary (the stator), and one movable (the rotor). The rotor may also be known as the armature, and consists of fine wire wrapped around an iron core mounted on the shaft. The electricity which flows through the two coils of wire (provided initially be the battery in some cases) creates an intense magnetic field around both the rotor and stator, and the interaction between the two fields creates voltage, allowing the generator to power the accessories and charge the battery.

The alternator must be provided with a small amount of power before it can make large amounts of electricity. It is possible to have a battery so discharged that it cannot provide sufficient amperage to the alternator. This may account for a car which was jump started not recharging its battery after extensive driving. Just because the engine is running does not guarantee that the battery will be charged. Since most alternators become electrically efficient above 1500–2000 rpm, the battery does not receive much of a charge at idle speeds.

Automobiles use alternating current generators (alternators) because they are more efficient, can be rotated at higher speeds, and have fewer brush problems. In an alternator, the field rotates while all the current produced passes only through the stator windings. The brushes bear against continuous slip rings rather than a commutator. This causes the current produced to periodically reverse the direction of its flow. Diodes (electrical one-way switches) block the flow of current from traveling in the wrong direction. A series of diodes is wired together to permit the alternating flow of the stator to be converted to a pulsating, but unidirectional flow at the alternator output. The alternator's field is wired in series with the voltage regulator.

All the Celicas and Supras covered in this book use an IC regulator built into the case of alternator. This integrated circuit (IC) device watches the output of the alternator and the state of charge of the battery. It serves as a solid state switch, controlling the flow of electricity to the battery.

SAFETY PRECAUTIONS

Observing these precautions will ensure safe handling of the electrical systems components and will avoid damage to the vehicle's electrical system. Remember that electricity travels through the system with extreme speed; you must be absolutely certain of what you are doing before you do it. There are no second chances to do it right.

• Be absolutely sure of the polarity of a booster battery before making connections. Connect the cables positive to positive, and negative to negative. Connect positive cables first and then make the last connection to a ground on the body of the booster vehicle so that arcing cannot ignite hydrogen gas that may have accumulated near the battery. Even momentary connection of a booster battery with the polarity reversed will damage alternator diodes.

• Disconnect both vehicle battery cables before attempting to charge a battery.

• Never ground the alternator output or battery terminal. Be cautious when using metal tools around a battery to avoid creating a short circuit between the terminals.

• Never disconnect the battery or alternator cables while the engine is running.

• Never attempt to polarize an alternator.

• Do not allow the ignition switch to be ON for more than ten minutes if the engine will not start.

SPECIAL WARNING 1990 VEHICLES WITH SRS (AIR BAGS)

The supplemental restraint system (SRS) found on 1990 Celicas and Supras requires some special precautions and knowledge when working on the car. This sophisticated system uses electrical, mechanical and solid state components to detect high deceleration situations and trigger the air bag in the steering wheel pad. Improper repair or diagnostic techniques may cause unintentional deployment during service, possibly leading to serious injury. Additionally, poor or incorrect work may disable the system, causing it not to work when it is needed.

• The SRS system is NOT repairable or serviceable by the owner/mechanic. This book will cover SRS only as it relates to other components or procedures such as steering wheel removal. Any SRS–related problem should be referred to either the dealer or other trained personnel.

• Most electrical repair procedures begin with disconnecting the negative battery terminal. (This guarantees a "cold" circuit during repair.) On SRS vehicles, you must wait AT LEAST 30 seconds after disconnecting the battery before doing any electrical work. The SRS has a built-in backup which will allow the system to remain energized for a period of time after the power is disconnected.

• Never remove the steering wheel without following the procedures and safety information. Never attempt to test the electrical circuitry of the air bag system.

• Although the SRS wiring is included in the under–dash wiring harnesses, it is identified by a corrugated yellow outer sheath. All the connectors for the system are a standard yellow color. If any of the wiring or connectors are damaged or broken, contact a dealer for specific repair instructions.

• If ANY electric welding—no matter how minor—is to be done on the car (minor body work, etc.) the air bag connector under the steering column (2 pin connector near the combination switch connector) MUST be disconnected. The current induced in the body by the welding equipment may trigger the air bag.

• The air bag system uses three sensors. There is one at approximately each front corner of the car under the hood and one center sensor inside the cabin of the car. On Celicas, the center sensor is mounted under the console, ahead of the shifter; Supras locate the center sensor under the console box, behind the parking brake lever assembly. Knowing where these units are should serve well to prevent damage or accidental impact.

• If the center sensor must be removed from its mounted position, the wiring must be disconnected while the unit is bolted in place. Conversely, the harness must be reconnected after the unit is reinstalled in position.

Ignition System

TROUBLESHOOTING

Troubleshooting this system is easy, but you must have an accurate ohmmeter and voltmeter. These two tools are quite frequently found combined into a volt–ohmmeter or VOM. This handy tool allows several tests to be performed with one instrument. The operator must remember to switch scales as tests are performed for voltage or resistance (ohms). Applying voltage to the resistance circuit can destroy the meter.

Check for spark at the spark plugs by hooking up a timing light in the usual manner. The inductive pickup may be connected to each plug wire in turn; as the charge passes through each wire, it should trigger the light. If the light flashes, it can be assumed that voltage is reaching the plugs, which should then be inspected along with the fuel system. If no flash is generated, the problem may be within the ignition system. Ignition Coil

PRIMARY RESISTANCE CHECK

The primary side of the ignition coil receives the power from the electrical system, about 12 volts. The resistance of the coil determines how efficiently it converts the low voltage received into the high voltage needed to fire the spark plugs.

In order to check the coil primary resistance, you must first disconnect all wires from the ignition coil terminals. On cars with the IIA system, the distributor cap and rotor must be removed to gain access to the terminals. On the 7M-GTE motor, the small harness to each coil must be carefully disconnected after removing the coil cover. This test is always performed with the ignition **OFF**

Using an ohmmeter, check the resistance between the positive and the negative terminals on the coil. The meter should be set to its lowest ($\Omega \times 1$) scale. You are anticipating readings of less than 1Ω except for the 1990 Celica with the 4A-FE engine. For that engine, set the scale to $\Omega \times 10$. Correct resistance is:

- 1986 Celica 2S-E: 0.3–0.5Ω primary; 7.7–$10.4\text{k}\Omega$ secondary
- 1986 Celica 3S-GE: 0.4–0.5Ω primary; 10.2–$13.8\text{k}\Omega$ secondary
- 1986 Supra 5M-GE: 0.4–0.5Ω primary; 8.5–$11.0\text{k}\Omega$ secondary
- 1986 Supra 7M-GE: 0.4–0.5Ω primary; 8.5–$11.0\text{k}\Omega$ secondary
- 1987 Celica 3S-FE: 0.38–0.46Ω primary; 7.7–$10.4\text{k}\Omega$ secondary
- 1987 Celica 3S-GE: 0.4–0.5Ω primary; 10.2–$13.8\text{k}\Omega$ secondary
- 1987 Supra 7M-GE: 0.2–0.3Ω primary; 9.2–$12.5\text{k}\Omega$ secondary
- 1987 Supra 7M-GTE: 0.3–0.6Ω primary; 9.2–$12.5\text{k}\Omega$ secondary
- 1988 Celica 3S-FE: 0.38–0.46Ω primary; 7.7–$10.4\text{k}\Omega$ secondary
- 1988 Celica 3S-GE: 0.4–0.5Ω primary; 10.2–$13.8\text{k}\Omega$ secondary
- 1988 Celica 3S-GTE: 0.4–0.5Ω primary; 10.2–$13.8\text{k}\Omega$ secondary
- 1988 Supra 7M-GE: 0.2–0.3Ω primary; 9.2–$12.5\text{k}\Omega$ secondary

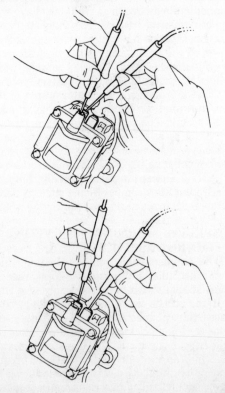

5M-GE, checking coil resistance

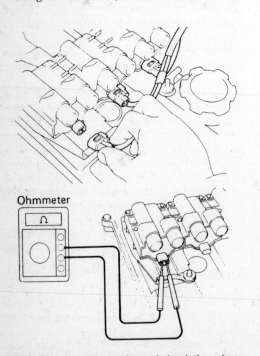

Ohmmeter

Disconnect the primary wire and check the primary circuit resistance on the 7M-GTE engine

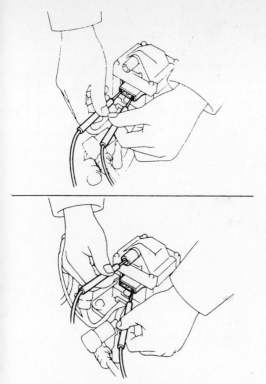

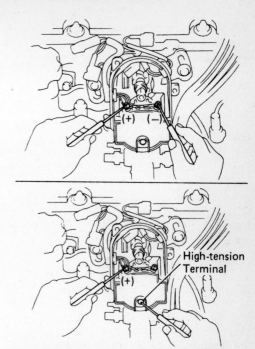

Checking the coil resistance, 2S-E and 3S-FE

Checking primary resistance (upper) and secondary resistance on 7M-GE

- 1988 Supra 7M-GTE: 0.3–0.5Ω primary; 9.2–12.5kΩ secondary
- 1989 Celica 3S-FE: 0.38–0.46Ω primary; 7.7–10.4kΩ secondary
- 1989 Celica 3S-GE: 0.4–0.5Ω primary; 10.2–13.8kΩ secondary
- 1989 Celica 3S-GTE: 0.4–0.5Ω primary; 10.2–13.8kΩ secondary
- 1989 Supra 7M-GE: 0.2–0.3Ω primary; 9.2–12.5kΩ secondary
- 1989 Supra 7M-GTE: 0.3–0.5Ω primary; 9.2–12.5kΩ secondary
- 1990 Celica 4A-FE: 1.28–1.56Ω primary; 10.4–14.0kΩ secondary
- 1990 Celica 5S-FE: 0.41–0.5Ω primary; 10.2–13.8kΩ secondary
- 1990 Celica 3S-GTE: 0.41–0.5Ω primary; 10.2–13.8kΩ secondary
- 1990 Supra 7M-GE: 0.24–0.30Ω primary; 9.2–12.4kΩ secondary
- 1990 Supra 7M-GTE: 0.3–0.5Ω primary; 9.2–12.5kΩ secondary

If the resistance is not within these tolerances, the coil will require replacement.

SECONDARY RESISTANCE CHECK

In order to check the coil secondary resistance, you must first disconnect all wires from the ignition coil terminals. Using an ohmmeter,

check the resistance between the positive terminal and the coil wire terminal. The resistance is measured in kilo–ohms (kΩ) so the meter should be set to the Ω × 1000 scale. Compare your reading to the chart. If the resistance is not within these tolerances, the coil will require replacement.

NOTE: *It is not possible to measure the secondary resistance on the 7M-GTE engine.*

Distributor

REMOVAL AND INSTALLATION

NOTE: *In all cases, the engine should be set to TDC/compression on No. 1 cylinder before removing the distributor. The reinstallation procedure assumes that the engine has not been moved while the distributor was out. If the engine was turned (during an overhaul, for example) refer to the item "Reinstallation—Timing Lost" at the end of the section.*

5M-GE Engine

1. Disconnect the battery ground, disconnect the electrical leads, vacuum hoses, and spark plug wires from the distributor.

2. Remove the pinch-bolt and lift the distributor straight out, away from the engine. The rotor and body are marked so that they can be returned to the position from which they were removed.

3. Do not turn or disturb the engine (unless absolutely necessary, such as for engine rebuilding), after the distributor has been removed.

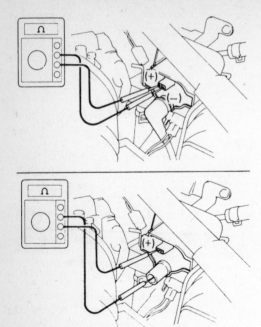

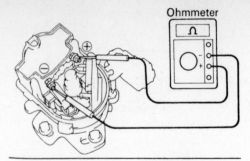

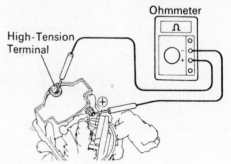

Checking coil resistance, 3S-GE and 5S-GE

Checking the coil, 4A-FE

4. Before reinstalling the distributor, remove the rubber O-ring on the distributor shaft and install a new one. This seal should be replaced any time the distributor is removed.

5. Align the matchmarks on the distributor before installation. The dot or drill mark on the spiral gear should be aligned with the scribe or line on the housing.

6. Carefully insert the distributor into the block. Align the center of the adjusting flange with the bolt hole.

7. Align the rotor tooth with the pickup coil; temporarily install the distributor hold–down bolt.

8. Install the rotor, cap and wires. Connect the external wiring to the distributor.

9. Adjust the timing and tighten the hold–down bolt.

2S-E and 4A-FE Engine

1. Disconnect the negative battery cable.

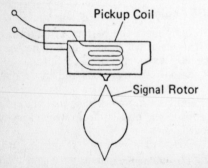

Align the pick-up coil and signal rotor on the 5M-GE

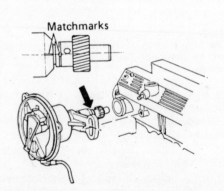

5M-GE — correct alignment before installing the distributor

2. Disconnect the wiring running to the Integrated Ignition Assembly (IIA) and disconnect the spark plug wires from the spark plugs.

3. Remove the mounting bolts and pull out the IIA from the block.

4. Before reinstalling, remove the rubber O-ring on the shaft and install a new one. This seal should be replaced any time the IIA is removed.

5. Align the matchmarks before installation. The dot or drill mark on the spiral gear should be aligned with the scribe or line on the housing.

6. Carefully insert the IIA into the block. Align the center of the adjusting flange with the bolt hole.

7. Temporarily install the hold–down bolts.

8. Connect the external wiring to the IIA unit.

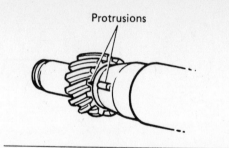

Protrusions

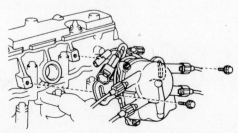

Alignment marks and installation of the IIA on the 2S-E

9. Adjust the timing and tighten the hold–down bolt.

3S-FE, 3S-GE, 7M-GE

1. Except on 7M-GE, remove the air cleaner hose.

2. Disconnect the negative battery cable. On 1990 vehicles, wait 30 seconds before performing any work.

3. Disconnect the distributor connector.

4. Remove the bolt holding the spark plug wire clamp.

5. Disconnect the spark plug and coil wires from the spark plug and coil. On 7M-GE engines, disconnect the wires at the cap and remove the cap and the gasket under the cap.

6. Remove the hold–down bolts and pull the distributor straight out of the engine.

7. Before reinstalling the distributor, remove the rubber O-ring on the distributor shaft and install a new one, coating it lightly with engine oil. This seal should be replaced any time the distributor is removed.

8. Align the matchmarks on the distributor before installation. The dot or drill mark on the spiral gear should be aligned with the scribe or line on the housing.

9. Carefully insert the distributor into the block. Align the center of the adjusting flange with the bolt hole.

10. Temporarily install the distributor hold–down bolt.

11. Install the wiring to the coil and spark plugs. Connect the external wiring harness to the distributor.

12. Reinstall the spark plug wiring clamp. In-stall the air cleaner hose and connect the battery.

13. Run the engine until it reaches normal operating temperature. Adjust the timing and tighten the hold–down bolt.

3S-GTE Engine

1. Disconnect the negative battery cable. On 1990 vehicles, wait 30 seconds before performing any other work.

2. Remove the intercooler. Refer to the instructions given in the Turbocharger and Intercooler Section later in this chapter.

3. Disconnect the distributor connector.

4. Remove the high tension from the spark plugs and ignition coil.

5. Remove the hold–down bolts and pull the distributor free of the engine.

6. Before reinstalling the distributor, remove the rubber O-ring on the distributor shaft and install a new one, coating it lightly with engine oil. This seal should be replaced any time the distributor is removed.

7. Align the matchmarks on the distributor before installation. The dot or drill mark on the spiral gear should be aligned with the scribe or line on the housing.

8. Carefully insert the distributor into the block. Align the center of the adjusting flange with the bolt hole.

9. Temporarily install the distributor hold–down bolt.

10. Install the wiring to the coil and spark

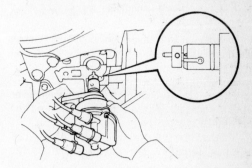

3S-GE distributor installation

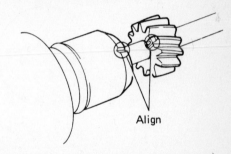

Align

7M-GE distributor matchmarks

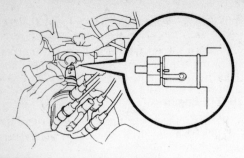

Distributor matchmarks, 3S-GTE

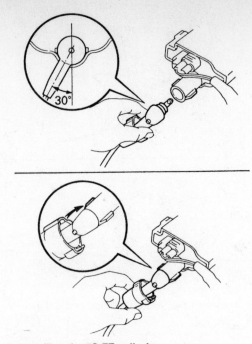

plugs. Connect the external wiring harness to the distributor.

11. Install the intercooler.

12. Run the engine until it reaches normal operating temperature. Adjust the timing and tighten the hold–down bolt.

5S-FE Engine

1. Disconnect the negative battery cable.

2. Wait at least 30 seconds before commencing any work. Refer to SRS warning at the beginning of this section.

3. Disconnect the distributor connector.

4. Use a small tool, lift up the lock claw and disconnect the holder over the ignition coil wire and terminal.

5. Disconnect the coil wire from the coil by holding the connector. Do NOT pull on or bend the wire.

6. Disconnect the spark plug wire holder(s) from the wires and remove the plug wires from the spark plugs.

7. Remove the hold-down bolt and remove the distributor. Remove the O-ring or gasket from the distributor housing.

8. Before reinstalling the distributor, install a new O-ring, coating it lightly with engine oil. This seal should be replaced any time the distributor is removed.

8. Align the matchmarks on the distributor before installation. The dot or notch on the

Reinstalling the 5S-FE coil wire

spiral gear should be aligned with the scribe or line on the housing.

9. Carefully insert the distributor into the block. Align the center of the adjusting flange with the bolt hole.

10. Temporarily install the distributor hold–down bolt.

11. Insert the coil wire into the coil. Note that it correctly installs at about a 30° angle from vertical. Expressed another way, position the cable at about 7 o'clock when installing.

12. Align the splines of the ignition coil with the splines of the cable holder (clip) and slide the clip onto the coil. Check that the holder is correctly installed over the wire.

13. Double check the retention of the wire by pulling gently on the coil wire. The key word is gently.

14. Install the wiring to the spark plugs and position the wires in the holders. Connect the external wiring harness to the distributor.

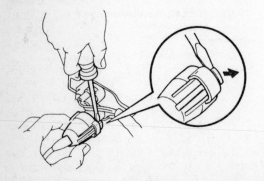

Carefully disconnect the 5S-FE coil wire holder

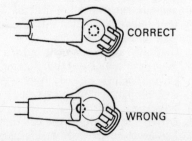

CORRECT

WRONG

Make certain the retainer is correctly placed on the 5S-FE coil wire

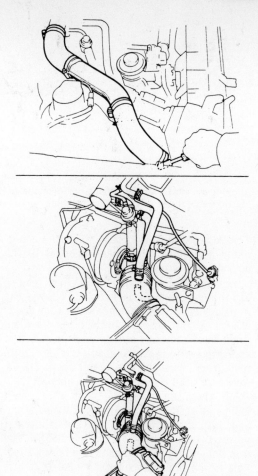

Many ducts and hoses must be removed for access to the 7M-GTE cam position sensor

15. Connect the battery cable. Run the engine until it reaches normal operating temperature. Adjust the timing and tighten the hold–down bolt.

7M-GTE Cam Position Sensor

1. Disconnect the negative battery cable. On 1990 vehicles, wait 30 seconds before performing any work.

2. Disconnect the wiring harness to the camshaft position sensor.

3. Remove the air cleaner pipe with the No. 1 and 2 air cleaner hoses.

4. Disconnect the three air hoses and PCV hose from the large air intake hose.

5. Disconnect the harness connector to the air flow meter.

6. Disconnect the power steering idle–up air hose.

7. Loosen the clamps and remove the bolt holding the air hose bracket.

8. Remove the air cleaner hose with the air flow meter and air cleaner cap. Handle this unit gently and place it in a protected location away from the work area.

9. Remove the two bolts and the nut holding the power steering reservoir tank. Leave the fluid hoses connected and simply move the tank out of the way.

10. Remove the hold–down bolt from the cam position sensor and remove the sensor. Remove the O-ring.

11. Install a new O-ring on the sensor before installation.

12. Align the drilled mark on the driven gear with the groove of the housing.

13. Install the sensor, aligning the center of the flange with the bolts hole on the cylinder head.

14. Tighten the hold–down bolt just snug.

15. Install the power steering reservoir and tighten the nuts and bolts.

16. Install the air cleaner hose with the air flow meter and the air cleaner cap.

17. Install the bracket and bolt; tighten the clamps on the air tube.

18. Connect the power steering idle–up air hose, the air flow meter harness connector and the PCV hose. Install the 3 vacuum hoses.

19. Install the remaining air cleaner piping and connect the No.1 and 2 air hoses.

20. Connect the wiring harness to the cam position sensor.

21. Start the engine and warm it to normal operating temperature.

22. Adjust the ignition timing and tighten the hold–down bolt.

INSTALLATION – TIMING LOST

If the engine has been turned, cranked or the timing position otherwise disturbed, the engine must be re-set to TDC/compression on No. 1 cylinder. This is necessary so that the distributor's position will agree with the engine's position. (When the distributor's matchmarks are aligned, it is set to fire cylinder 1.)

The engine must be turned clockwise until the timing marks align. Since this position occurs on both the compression and exhaust stroke of the piston, you have a 1–in–2 chance of being right; an additional check must be performed to guarantee the correct position.

On the 3S-FE, 3S-GE, 3S-GTE, and 5S-FE engines, observe the intake camshaft (look in the distributor hole as necessary) and position the slot vertically with the offset to the right as you view it. Note that the cam end is NOT symmetric but has a distinct offset. Once this position is achieved approximately, observe the timing marks and align them exactly at zero.

The 4A-FE follows the same steps as the 3S-FE except the slot aligns at 8 o'clock and 2

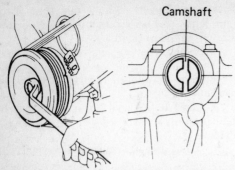

Camshaft

On 3S-GE and similar engines, align the intake camshaft slot vertically. Note that the offset is to the right as you view it

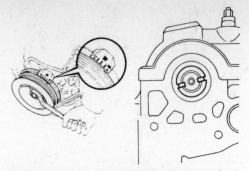

Aligning the intake cam and timing marks on the 4A-FE. Note that the slot is offset from center

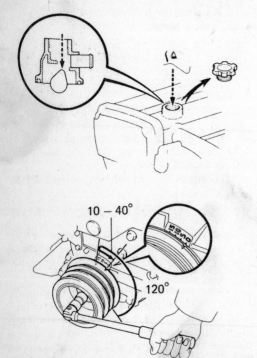

10 – 40°

120°

Two steps to aligning the 7M-GE and 7M-GTE motors to TDC

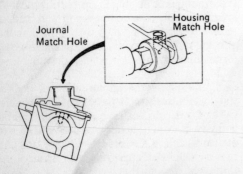

Housing Match Hole

Journal Match Hole

Aligning the 5M-GE to TDC/compression. The small hole in the camshaft journal must be visible

o'clock. Note that the slot is offset and is correctly positioned with the slot offset to the bottom or lower side.

The 7M-GE and 7M-GTE engines require you to remove the oil filler cap and observe the camshaft lobe. Turn the engine until the clockwise until the nose of the lobe can be seen. Turn the crankshaft counterclockwise (this is an exception to the rule) about 120° or 1/3 of a revolution. Turn the crankshaft about 10–40° clockwise until the timing marks align at zero.

For the 5M-GE engine, align the timing marks at zero. Remove the oil filler cap and look into the valve train (use a flashlight if needed). Look through the small hole in the cam holder and check that the matching small hole in the camshaft journal is visible. If it is not, turn the engine one full rotation clockwise; check the hole alignment again and check that the timing marks are at zero.

The 2S-E engine requires removal of the No.1 spark plug to confirm TDC. With the plug out, place a finger over the plug hole and rotate the engine clockwise. As the timing marks approach zero, you should feel compression (air pressure) against your finger; align the timing marks. If not, continue another full revolution and align the timing marks.

Any engine can be set to TDC/compression on No. 1 cylinder by checking for compression at the No. 1 spark plug hole as the timing marks approach zero. However, with many spark plugs found in deep wells within twin-cam heads, plugging the hole with a finger or tool handle becomes awkward and unreliable.

Alternator

All Celicas and Supras use a 12 volt alternator. Amperage ratings vary according to the year and model. All models have a transistorized, nonadjustable regulator, integral with the alternator.

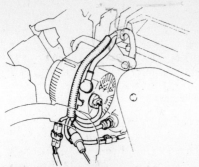

Unrelated wiring may need removal to allow access to the alternator. Work carefully

ALTERNATOR PRECAUTIONS

To prevent damage to the alternator and regulator, the following precautionary measures must be taken when working with the electrical system.

1. Never reverse the battery connections. Always check the battery polarity visually. This is to be done before any connections are made to ensure that all of the connections correspond to the battery ground polarity of the car.

2. Booster batteries must be connected properly. Make sure the positive cable of the booster battery is connected to the positive terminal of the battery which is getting the boost.

3. Disconnect the battery cables before using a fast charger; the charger has a tendency to force current through the diodes in the opposite direction for which they were designed.

4. Never use a fast charger as a booster for starting the car.

5. Never disconnect the alternator or battery while the engine is running.

6. Do not ground the alternator output terminal.

7. Do not operate the alternator on an open circuit with the field energized.

8. Do not attempt to polarize the alternator.

9. Disconnect the battery cables and remove the alternator before using an electric arc welder on the car.

10. Protect the alternator from excessive moisture. If the engine is to be steam cleaned, cover or remove the alternator.

REMOVAL AND INSTALLATION

1. Disconnect the negative battery cable. On 1990 vehicles, wait 30 seconds before performing any work.

2. Remove the alternator pivot bolt or loosen the belt adjustor bolt. Remove the drive belt.

3. Pull back the rubber boots and disconnect the wiring from the back of the alternator.

Some wiring may be held either by nuts and bolts or by connectors with locking tabs; disconnect them carefully.

WARNING: *Before removing the alternator, check for any wires or hoses which may interfere or be damaged as the alternator comes out. Move or disconnect lines before they become a problem.*

4. Remove the alternator mounting bolt(s) and then withdraw the alternator from its bracket. The alternator is heavier than it appears; use two hands.

5. Installation is in the reverse order of removal; place the alternator in position, install and secure the bolts and connect the wiring. Install and adjust the belt and final tighten the mounting hardware.

Voltage Regulator

The IC voltage regulator is contained within the alternator and is not adjustable. Should it fail, the alternator should be taken to a reputable automotive electric shop for disassembly and repair. It is not recommended that the home mechanic disassemble the alternator case.

Battery

Refer to Chapter 1 for details on battery maintenance.

REMOVAL AND INSTALLATION

1. Disconnect the negative battery cable from the terminal, then disconnect the positive cable. Special pullers are available to remove the clamps.

NOTE: *To avoid sparks, always disconnect the negative cable first and reconnect it last.*

2. Unscrew and remove the battery holddown clamp.

3. Remove the battery, being careful not to spill any of the acid.

NOTE: *Spilled acid can be neutralized with a baking soda and water solution. If you somehow get acid into your eyes, flush it out with lots of clean water and get to a doctor as quickly as possible.*

4. Clean the battery posts thoroughly before reinstalling or when installing a new one.

5. Clean the cable clamps using the special tools or a wire brush, both inside and out.

6. Install the battery, and the holddown clamp. Connect the positive and then the negative cable. Do not hammer them into place. The terminals should be coated with grease to prevent corrosion.

CAUTION: *Make absolutely sure that the battery is connected properly before you turn on*

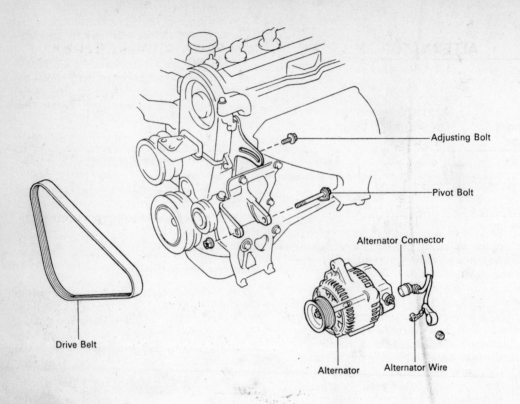

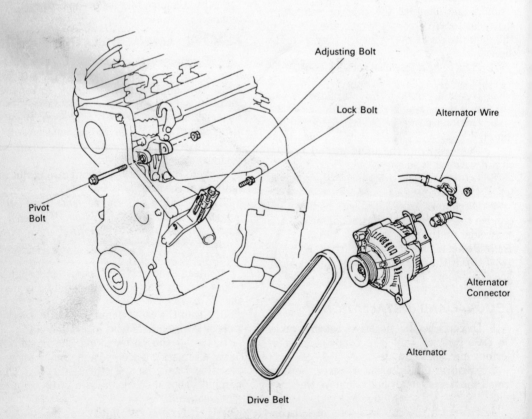

Typical alternator installations

ALTERNATOR AND REGULATOR SPECIFICATIONS CHART

Engine Type	Alternator Output (amps)	Regulator						
		Field Replay				Regulator		
		Contact Sprint Deflection (in.)	Point Gap (in.)	Volts to Close	Air Gap (in.)	Regulator Point Gap (in.)	Volts	
4M-E	55 ②	①	①	①	①	①	14.3– 14.9	
5M-E	60 ③	①	①	①	①	①	14.3– 14.9	
5M-GE	65 ④	①	①	①	①	①	13.8– 14.4 ⑤	
2S-E	70	①	①	①	①	①	13.5– 15.1	
3S-GE	60	①	①	①	①	①	13.5– 15.1	
3S-FE	70	①	①	①	①	①	13.5– 15.1	
7M-GE, 7M-GTE	70	①	①	①	①	①	13.5– 15.1	
3S-GTE	70	①	①	①	①	①	13.5– 14.3	
4A-FE	70	①	①	①	①	①	13.5– 14.3	
5S-FE	70	①	①	①	①	①	13.5– 14.3	

① Regulator not adjustable
② Optional 60 amp
③ Optional 65 amp
④ 1986—60A
⑤ 1985–86: 13.5–15.1
   1986: 13.5–15.1

the ignition switch. Reversed polarity can burn out our alternator and regulator in a matter of seconds.

Starter

REMOVAL AND INSTALLATION

2S-E, 3S-FE, 5M-GE, 7M-GE and 7M-GTE engines

For these engines, starter removal is straightforward.

1. Disconnect the negative battery cable. On 1990 cars, wait at least 30 seconds before performing any other work.

2. Label and disconnect all wiring leading from the starter.

3. Unscrew the two starter mounting bolts.

4. Using two hands if possible, remove the starter. It is a heavy unit.

5. Installation is in the reverse order of removal. Tighten the two mounting bolts to 29 ft. lbs.

3S-GE Engine

1. Disconnect the negative battery cable.

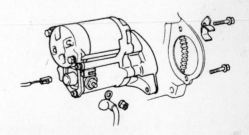

Starter installation

Troubleshooting Basic Charging System Problems

Problem	Cause	Solution
Noisy alternator	• Loose mountings • Loose drive pulley • Worn bearings • Brush noise • Internal circuits shorted (High pitched whine)	• Tighten mounting bolts • Tighten pulley • Replace alternator • Replace alternator • Replace alternator
Squeal when starting engine or accelerating	• Glazed or loose belt	• Replace or adjust belt
Indicator light remains on or ammeter indicates discharge (engine running)	• Broken fan belt • Broken or disconnected wires • Internal alternator problems • Defective voltage regulator	• Install belt • Repair or connect wiring • Replace alternator • Replace voltage regulator
Car light bulbs continually burn out— battery needs water continually	• Alternator/regulator overcharging	• Replace voltage regulator/alternator
Car lights flare on acceleration	• Battery low • Internal alternator/regulator problems	• Charge or replace battery • Replace alternator/regulator
Low voltage output (alternator light flickers continually or ammeter needle wanders)	• Loose or worn belt • Dirty or corroded connections • Internal alternator/regulator problems	• Replace or adjust belt • Clean or replace connections • Replace alternator or regulator

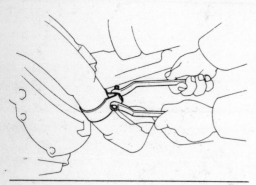

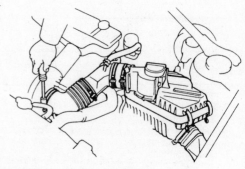

Removing the 3S-GE air cleaner

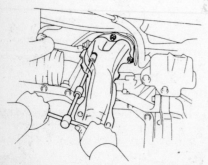

Remove the first exhaust pipe before removing the 3S-GE starter

2. Label and disconnect all wiring leading from the starter.

3. Disconnect the exhaust pipe. First, loosen the bolt and nut and disconnect the clamp from the bracket at the first exhaust joint under the car.

4. At the exhaust manifold, remove the three nuts holding the pipe and carefully remove the pipe.

5. Remove the two starter mounting bolts and remove the starter. It is a fairly heavy unit; be careful.

6. Remove the starter cover.

7. When reinstalling, the cover must be in place before installation. Place the starter into the engine and tighten the bolts to 29 ft. lbs.

8. Install a new gasket and connect the exhaust pipe to the manifold; tighten the nuts to 46 ft. lbs.

9. Install the exhaust pipe clamp and tighten the hardware.

10. Connect the starter wiring.

11. Connect the negative battery cable.

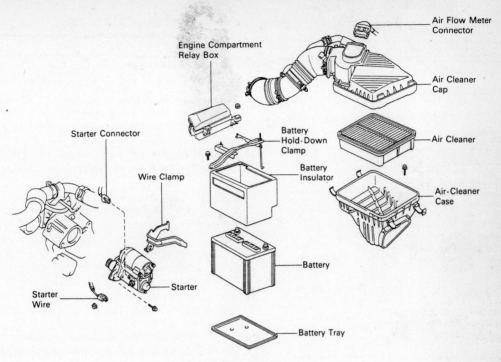

Starter removal; 1990 3S-GTE

3S-GTE except 1990

1. Disconnect the battery (negative terminal first) and remove the battery from the car.

2. Remove the air cleaner assembly:

a. Disconnect the air flow meter connector.

b. Disconnect the two air hoses. Release the 4 clamps holding the top of the air cleaner.

c. Loosen the hose clamps and disconnect the air cleaner hose from the turbocharger. Remove the air cleaner cap (top) together with the air cleaner hoses, connector pipe and air flow meter.

d. Remove the air cleaner element.

e. Remove the 3 bolts and remove the air cleaner case.

3. Disconnect and remove the connectors and wiring from the starter.

4. Remove the two starter mounting bolts and remove the starter. It is a fairly heavy unit; be careful.

5. Reinstall the starter and tighten the retaining bolts to 29 ft. lbs.

6. Connect the wiring to the starter terminals.

7. Install the air cleaner assembly. Start with the case and install the filter element. Install the top section, the air flow meter, connector pipe and air cleaner hoses. Connect the air flow meter harness connector.

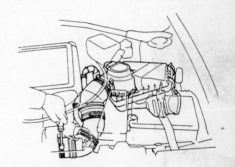

Removing 1990 3S-GTE air cleaner

8. Install the battery and connect the cables (negative cable last).

3S-GTE, 1990

1. Disconnect the battery, negative terminal first. Wait at least 30 seconds before performing any other work. Disconnect the positive cable.

2. Remove the air cleaner assembly:

a. Disconnect the air flow meter connector.

b. Disconnect the PCV hose from the valve cover and the air hose from the air tube. Release the 4 clamps holding the top of the air cleaner.

c. Loosen the hose clamps and disconnect the air cleaner hose from the turbocharger. Remove the air cleaner cap (top) together

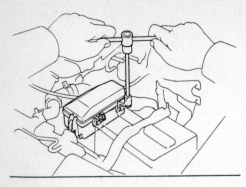

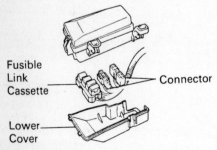

Fusible Link Cassette

Connector

Lower Cover

The relay box must be removed before removing the 1990 3S-GTE battery

with the air cleaner element and the air flow meter.

d. Remove the 3 bolts and remove the air cleaner case.

3. Remove the two nuts holding the relay box and remove the relay box from the battery.

4. Remove the lower cover from the relay box.

5. Disconnect the fusible link cassette (tray) and the two engine harness connectors from the relay box.

6. Remove the battery.

7. Disconnect and remove the connectors and wiring from the starter.

8. Remove the two starter mounting bolts and remove the starter. It is a fairly heavy unit; be careful.

9. Reinstall the starter and tighten the retaining bolts to 29 ft. lbs.

10. Connect the wiring to the starter terminals.

11. Install the battery.

12. Install the engine relay box. Remember to connect the engine harnesses and secure the cassette within the box. Install the lower cover and mount the box with the two nuts.

13. Install the air cleaner base and the filter element. Connect the air cleaner hose to the turbocharger, the PCV hose to the valve cover and the air hose to the air pipe. Install the air cleaner top and air flow meter; connect the wiring for the air flow meter.

14. Connect the battery cables to the battery, negative cable last.

4A-FE Engine

1. Disconnect the negative battery cable. Wait 30 seconds before performing any other work.

2. Elevate and safely support the car on jackstands.

3. Remove the 4 bolts and 2 nuts holding the lower crossmember. Remove the crossmember.

CAUTION: *Support the crossmember while removing the final hardware; do not allow it to fall free.*

4. Disconnect the intake air temperature sensor connector.

5. Disconnect the accelerator cable from the bracket on the top of the air cleaner.

6. Loosen the 4 clips holding the top of the air cleaner. Remove the air hose from the air pipe.

7. Disconnect the air cleaner hose from the throttle body and remove the air cleaner top and filter element.

NOTE: *The starter is removed from under the car.*

8. Loosen the two bolts holding the starter to the transaxle. Disconnect starter wiring connectors.

9. Remove the retaining bolts and remove the starter. Use two hands; it's heavy.

10. Reinstall the starter and tighten the retaining bolts to 29 ft. lbs.

11. Connect the starter wiring.

12. Install the air cleaner cap; connect the various lines and hoses.

13. Install the lower crossmember. Tighten the nuts and bolts to 152 ft. lbs.

14. Lower the car to the ground.

15. Connect the battery cables, negative cable last.

5S-FE Engine

1. Disconnect the negative battery cable. Wait 30 seconds before performing any other work.

2. Disconnect the intake air temperature sensor connector.

3. Disconnect the air cleaner hose from the throttle body and remove the air cleaner top and filter element.

4. Remove the 3 bolts and remove the air cleaner case.

5. Remove the two nuts holding the relay box and remove the relay box from the battery.

6. Remove the lower cover from the relay box.

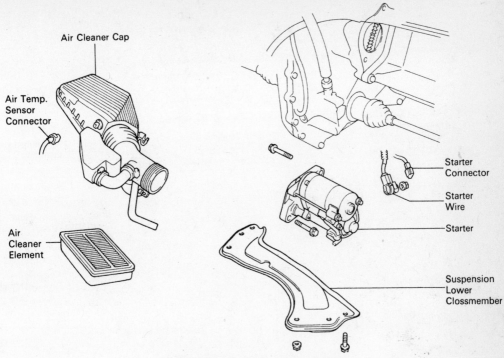

Components of 4A-FE starter removal

7. Disconnect the fusible link cassette (tray) and the two engine harness connectors from the relay box.

8. Remove the cruise control actuator. If the car is NOT equipped with Anti–lock Brake System (ABS), proceed as follows:

a. Remove the actuator cover.

b. Disconnect the actuator vacuum hose from the air intake chamber.

c. Disconnect the actuator connector.

d. Disconnect the cable from the actuator.

e. Remove the 3 retaining bolts and the actuator.

If the car is equipped with ABS, proceed as follows:

a. Disconnect the actuator connector.

b. Remove the 4 retaining bolts and remove the actuator.

9. Disconnect the starter connector and the starter wire. Remove the two bolts, wire clamp and the starter. The starter is heavy; be careful.

10. Reinstall the starter and tighten the bolts to 29 ft. lbs.

11. Connect the starter wiring and connectors.

12. Install the cruise control actuator by reversing the removal procedures.

13. Reinstall the relay box, remembering to connect the engine harnesses and secure the cassette in the box. Reinstall the lower cover and mount the relay box in position.

14. Install the air cleaner case, the filter element and top and the various hoses and ducts. Connect the wiring to the air flow sensor.

15. Connect the negative battery terminal.

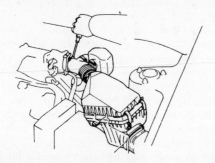

Removing the 4A-FE air cleaner top

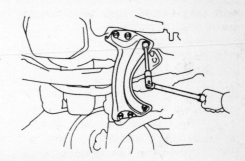

Removing the 4A-FE crossmember

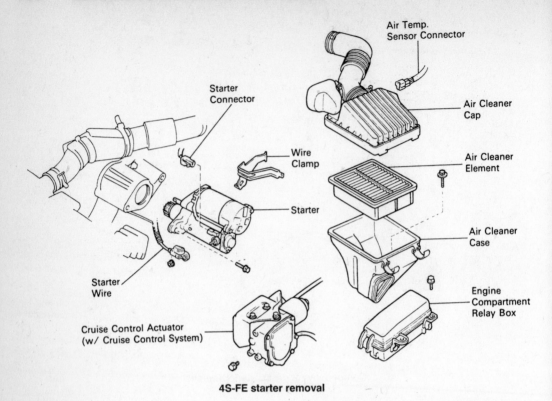

4S-FE starter removal

Labels in figure: Air Temp. Sensor Connector, Air Cleaner Cap, Air Cleaner Element, Air Cleaner Case, Engine Compartment Relay Box, Starter Connector, Wire Clamp, Starter, Starter Wire, Cruise Control Actuator (w/ Cruise Control System)

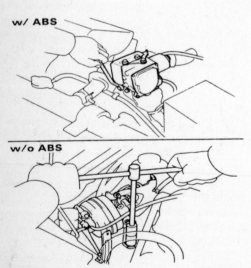

w/ ABS

w/o ABS

Removing the 5S-FE cruise control actuator. See text for detailed procedures.

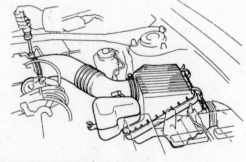

Removing the 5S-FE air cleaner

OVERHAUL

1. Position the removed starter in a suitable holding fixture. Do not damage the outer case of the starter.

2. Disconnect the lead from the solenoid (magnetic switch) terminal.

3. Unscrew the two mounting bolts and remove the field frame assembly from the solenoid housing.

4. Remove the O-ring and/or the felt seal if so equipped.

5. Unscrew the mounting screws and remove the starter housing (idler gear, bearing and clutch assembly) from the solenoid housing.

6. Pull out the clutch assembly and then remove the pinion and idler gears if necessary.

7. Using a magnetic tool or equivalent remove the steel ball from the clutch shaft hole.

8. Remove the end cover from the field frame. Remove the O-ring if so equipped.

9. Using a tool, separate the brush and brush spring and remove the brush from the brush holder.

10. Remove the armature from the field frame assembly.

11. To install use high-temperature grease

1.0 kW Type

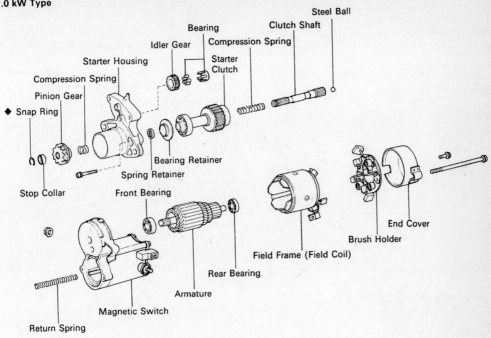

Steel Ball

Bearing

Clutch Shaft

Idler Gear

Compression Spring

Starter Housing

Starter Clutch

Compression Spring

Pinion Gear

◆ Snap Ring

Bearing Retainer

Spring Retainer

Stop Collar

Front Bearing

End Cover

Brush Holder

Field Frame (Field Coil)

Rear Bearing

Armature

Magnetic Switch

Return Spring

1.6 kW Type

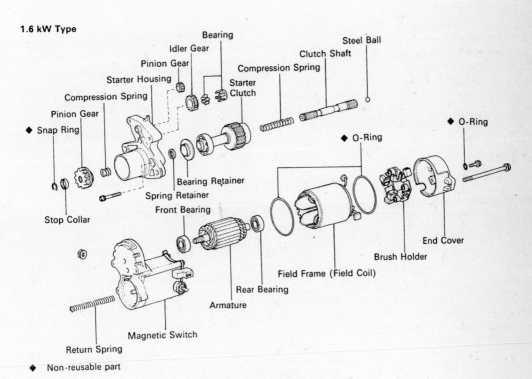

Bearing

Idler Gear

Steel Ball

Pinion Gear

Clutch Shaft

Starter Housing

Compression Spring

Starter Clutch

Compression Spring

Pinion Gear

◆ O-Ring

◆ Snap Ring

◆ O-Ring

Bearing Retainer

Spring Retainer

Stop Collar

Front Bearing

End Cover

Brush Holder

Field Frame (Field Coil)

Rear Bearing

Armature

Magnetic Switch

Return Spring

◆ Non-reusable part

Exploded view of starter

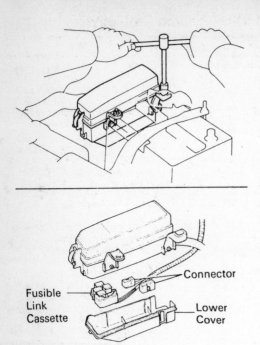

Fusible
Link
Cassette

Connector

Lower
Cover

The engine relay box must be removed before the 5S-FE starter will come out

to lubricate the bearing and gears when assembling the starter.

12. Apply grease to the armature bearings and insert the armature into the field frame.

13. Using a tool, hold the brush spring back and connect the brush onto the brush holder.

Connect the four brushes. Check that the positive lead wires are not grounded.

14. Place the O-ring on the field frame. Install the end cover to the field frame. Install the brush holder.

15. Apply grease to the steel ball. Insert the steel ball into the clutch shaft hole.

16. Apply grease to the gear and clutch assembly. Place the clutch assembly, idler gear, pinion gear (if so equipped) and bearing in the starter housing. Install the gears and clutch assembly.

17. Apply grease to the return spring. Insert the return spring into the magnetic hole. Place the starter housing on the magnetic switch and install the two screws. Install the starter housing.

18. Place the O-ring on the field frame. Align the protrusion of the field frame with the cutout of the magnetic switch. Install the two through bolts.

19. Connect the lead wire to the magnetic switch terminal C and install the nut. Install the field frame with armature to magnetic switch assembly.

ENGINE MECHANICAL

Engine Overhaul Tips

Most engine overhaul procedures are fairly standard. In addition to specific parts replacement procedures and complete specifications for your individual engine, this chapter also is

BATTERY AND STARTER SPECIFICATIONS CHART

All cars use 12 volt, negative ground electrical systems

Year	Model	Battery Amp Hour Capacity	Starter						Brush Spring Tension (oz.)	Min. Brush Length (in.)
			Lock Test			No Load Test				
			Amps	Volts	Torque (ft. lbs.)	Amps	Volts	RPM		
1986	5M-GE	①	Not Recommended			90	11.5	3,500	NA	0.39
	2S-E	①	Not Recommended			90	11.5	3,000	NA	②
1986–89	3S-FE, 3S-GE	①	Not Recommended			90	11.5	3,000	NA	②
1986–90	7M-GE, 7M-GTE	①	Not Recommended			90	11.5	3,500	NA	0.394
1988–90	3S-GTE	①	Not Recommended			90	11.5	3,000	NA	②
1990	4A-FE	①	Not Recommended			90	11.5	3,000	NA	②
	5S-FE	①	Not Recommended			90	11.5	3,000	NA	②

NA—Not available
① Replace w/battery of at least same capacity; consult application chart at battery dealer
② 1.0 KW: 0.335; 1.4 KW and 1.6 KW—limit 0.394

Troubleshooting Basic Starting System Problems

Problem	Cause	Solution
Starter motor rotates engine slowly	• Battery charge low or battery defective	• Charge or replace battery
	• Defective circuit between battery and starter motor	• Clean and tighten, or replace cables
	• Low load current	• Bench-test starter motor. Inspect for worn brushes and weak brush springs.
	• High load current	• Bench-test starter motor. Check engine for friction, drag or coolant in cylinders. Check ring gear-to-pinion gear clearance.
Starter motor will not rotate engine	• Battery charge low or battery defective	• Charge or replace battery
	• Faulty solenoid	• Check solenoid ground. Repair or replace as necessary.
	• Damage drive pinion gear or ring gear	• Replace damaged gear(s)
	• Starter motor engagement weak	• Bench-test starter motor
	• Starter motor rotates slowly with high load current	• Inspect drive yoke pull-down and point gap, check for worn end bushings, check ring gear clearance
	• Engine seized	• Repair engine
Starter motor drive will not engage (solenoid known to be good)	• Defective contact point assembly	• Repair or replace contact point assembly
	• Inadequate contact point assembly ground	• Repair connection at ground screw
	• Defective hold-in coil	• Replace field winding assembly
Starter motor drive will not disengage	• Starter motor loose on flywheel housing	• Tighten mounting bolts
	• Worn drive end busing	• Replace bushing
	• Damaged ring gear teeth	• Replace ring gear or driveplate
	• Drive yoke return spring broken or missing	• Replace spring
Starter motor drive disengages prematurely	• Weak drive assembly thrust spring	• Replace drive mechanism
	• Hold-in coil defective	• Replace field winding assembly
Low load current	• Worn brushes	• Replace brushes
	• Weak brush springs	• Replace springs

a guide to accept rebuilding procedures. Examples of standard rebuilding practice are shown and should be used along with specific details concerning your particular engine.

Competent and accurate machine shop services will ensure maximum performance, reliability and engine life.

In most instances it is more profitable for the do-it-yourself mechanic to remove, clean and inspect the component, buy the necessary parts and deliver these to a shop for actual machine work.

On the other hand, much of the rebuilding work (crankshaft, block, bearings, piston rods, and other components) is well within the scope of the do-it-yourself mechanic.

TOOLS

The tools required for an engine overhaul or parts replacement will depend on the depth of your involvement. With a few exceptions, they will be the tools found in a mechanic's tool kit (see Chapter 1). More in-depth work will require any or all of the following:

• a dial indicator (reading in thousandths) mounted on a universal base
• micrometers and telescope gauges
• jaw and screw-type pullers
• scraper
• valve spring compressor
• ring groove cleaner
• piston ring expander and compressor
• ridge reamer
• cylinder hone or glaze breaker
• Plastigage®
• engine stand

The use of most of these tools is illustrated in this chapter. Many can be rented for a one-time use from a local parts jobber or tool supply house specializing in automotive work.

Occasionally, the use of special tools is called for. See the information on Special Tools and Safety Notice in the front of this book before substituting another tool.

INSPECTION TECHNIQUES

Procedures and specifications are given in this chapter for inspecting, cleaning and assessing the wear limits of most major components. Other procedures such as Magnaflux® and Zyglo® can be used to locate material flaws and stress cracks. Magnaflux® is a magnetic process applicable only to ferrous materials. The Zyglo® process coats the material with a fluorescent dye penetrant and can be used on any material Check for suspected surface cracks can be more readily made using spot check dye. The dye is sprayed onto the suspected area, wiped off and the area sprayed with a developer. Cracks will show up brightly.

OVERHAUL TIPS

Aluminum has become extremely popular for use in engines, due to its low weight. Observe the following precautions when handling aluminum parts:

• Never hot tank aluminum parts (the caustic hot tank solution will eat the aluminum.

• Remove all aluminum parts (identification tag, etc.) from engine parts prior to the tanking.

• Always coat threads lightly with engine oil or anti-seize compounds before installation, to prevent seizure.

• Never over torque bolts or spark plugs especially in aluminum threads.

Stripped threads in any component can be repaired using any of several commercial repair kits (Heli-Coil®, Microdot®, Keenserts®, etc.).

When assembling the engine, any parts that will be frictional contact must be prelubed to provide lubrication at initial start-up. Any product specifically formulated for this purpose can be used, but engine oil is not recommended as a prelube.

When semi-permanent (locked, but removable) installation of bolts or nuts is desired, threads should be cleaned and coated with Loctite® or other similar, commercial non-hardening sealant.

REPAIRING DAMAGED THREADS

Several methods of repairing damaged threads are available. Heli-Coil® (shown here), Keenserts® and Microdot® are among the most widely used. All involve basically the same principle—drilling out stripped threads, tapping the hole and installing a prewound insert—making welding, plugging and oversize fasteners unnecessary.

Two types of thread repair inserts are usually supplied: a standard type for most Inch Coarse, Inch Fine, Metric Course and Metric Fine thread sizes and a spark lug type to fit most spark plug port sizes. Consult the individual manufacturer's catalog to determine exact applications. Typical thread repair kits will contain a selection of prewound threaded inserts, a tap (corresponding to the outside diameter threads of the insert) and an installation tool. Spark plug inserts usually differ because they require a tap equipped with pilot threads and a combined reamer/tap section. Most manufacturers also supply blister-packed thread repair inserts separately in addition to a master kit containing a variety of taps and inserts plus installation tools.

Before effecting a repair to a threaded hole, remove any snapped, broken or damaged bolts or studs. Penetrating oil can be used to free frozen threads. The offending item can be removed with locking pliers or with a screw or stud extractor. After the hole is clear, the thread can be repaired, as shown in the series of accompanying illustrations.

Checking Engine Compression

A noticeable lack of engine power, excessive oil consumption and/or poor fuel mileage measured over an extended period are all indications of internal engine wear. Worn pistons rings, scored and worn cylinder bores, blown head gaskets, sticking or burnt valves and worn valve seats are all possible culprits here. A check of each cylinder's compression will help you locate the problems.

As mentioned in the Tools and Equipment section of Chapter 1, a screw-in compression gauge is more accurate than the type you simply hold against the spark plug hole, although it takes slightly longer to use (it's worth it). To check compression:

1. Warm the engine up to operating temperature.

2. Remove all four or all six spark plugs.

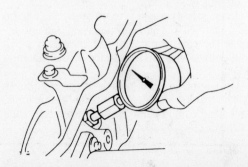

Checking compression all engines except 5M-GE

Standard Torque Specifications and Fastener Markings

In the absence of specific torques, the following chart can be used as a guide to the maximum safe torque of a particular size/grade of fastener.

- There is no torque difference for fine or coarse threads.
- Torque values are based on clean, dry threads. Reduce the value by 10% if threads are oiled prior to assembly.
- The torque required for aluminum components or fasteners is considerably less.

U.S. Bolts

SAE Grade Number	1 or 2			5			6 or 7		
Number of lines always 2 less than the grade number.									
Bolt Size (Inches)—(Thread)	**Maximum Torque**			**Maximum Torque**			**Maximum Torque**		
	Ft./Lbs.	Kgm	Nm	Ft./Lbs.	Kgm	Nm	Ft./Lbs.	Kgm	Nm
¼ — 20	5	0.7	6.8	8	1.1	10.8	10	1.4	13.5
— 28	6	0.8	8.1	10	1.4	13.6			
⁵⁄₁₆ — 18	11	1.5	14.9	17	2.3	23.0	19	2.6	25.8
— 24	13	1.8	17.6	19	2.6	25.7			
⅜ — 16	18	2.5	24.4	31	4.3	42.0	34	4.7	46.0
— 24	20	2.75	27.1	35	4.8	47.5			
⁷⁄₁₆ — 14	28	3.8	37.0	49	6.8	66.4	55	7.6	74.5
— 20	30	4.2	40.7	55	7.6	74.5			
½ — 13	39	5.4	52.8	75	10.4	101.7	85	11.75	115.2
— 20	41	5.7	55.6	85	11.7	115.2			
⁹⁄₁₆ — 12	51	7.0	69.2	110	15.2	149.1	120	16.6	162.7
— 18	55	7.6	74.5	120	16.6	162.7			
⅝ — 11	83	11.5	112.5	150	20.7	203.3	167	23.0	226.5
— 18	95	13.1	128.8	170	23.5	230.5			
¾ — 10	105	14.5	142.3	270	37.3	366.0	280	38.7	379.6
— 16	115	15.9	155.9	295	40.8	400.0			
⅞ — 9	160	22.1	216.9	395	54.6	535.5	440	60.9	596.5
— 14	175	24.2	237.2	435	60.1	589.7			
1 — 8	236	32.5	319.6	590	81.6	700.0	660	91.3	894.8
— 14	250	34.6	338.9	660	91.3	849.8			

Metric Bolts

Relative Strength Marking	4.6, 4.8			8.8		
Bolt Markings						
Bolt Size Thread Size x Pitch (mm)	**Maximum Torque**			**Maximum Torque**		
	Ft./Lbs.	Kgm	Nm	Ft./Lbs.	Kgm	Nm
6 x 1.0	2–3	.2–.4	3–4	3–6	.4–.8	5–8
8 x 1.25	6–8	.8–1	8–12	9–14	1.2–1.9	13–19
10 x 1.25	12–17	1.5–2.3	16–23	20–29	2.7–4.0	27–39
12 x 1.25	21–32	2.9–4.4	29–43	35–53	4.8–7.3	47–72
14 x 1.5	35–52	4.8–7.1	48–70	57–85	7.8–11.7	77–110
16 x 1.5	51–77	7.0–10.6	67–100	90–120	12.4–16.5	130–160
18 x 1.5	74–110	10.2–15.1	100–150	130–170	17.9–23.4	180–230
20 x 1.5	110–140	15.1–19.3	150–190	190–240	26.2–46.9	160–320
22 x 1.5	150–190	22.0–26.2	200–260	250–320	34.5–44.1	340–430
24 x 1.5	190–240	26.2–46.9	260–320	310–410	42.7–56.5	420–550

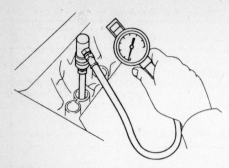

An adaptor may be needed to check compression on the 5M-GE engine

3. Disconnect the high tension wire from the ignition coil.

4. Screw the compression gauge into the No.1 spark plug hole until the fitting is snug. *Be very careful not to crossthread the hole, as the head is aluminum.*

5. Fully open the throttle on fuel injected cars.

6. As an assistant to crank the engine (remove coil wire so engine does not start) a few times using the ignition switch.

7. Record the highest reading on the gauge, and compare it to the compression specifications in the Tune-Up Specifications chart in Chapter 2. The specs listed are maximum, and a cylinder is usually acceptable if its compression is within about 20 pounds of maximum.compression. The difference between each cylinder should be no more than 14 pounds. If a cylinder is unusually low, pour a tablespoon of clean engine oil into the cylinder through the spark plug hole and repeat the compression test. If the compression comes up after adding the oil, it appears that the cylinder's piston rings or bore are damaged or worn. If the pressure remains low, the valves may not be seated properly (a valve job is needed) or the head gasket may be blown near that cylinder.

Engine

REMOVAL AND INSTALLATION

2S-E Engine (1986 Celica)

1. Disconnect the negative battery cable. Drain the engine coolant.

CAUTION: *When draining the coolant, keep in mind that cats and dogs are attracted by the ethylene glycol antifreeze, and are quite likely to drink any that is left in an uncovered container or in puddles on the ground. This will prove fatal in sufficient quantity. Always drain the coolant into a sealable container. Coolant should be reused unless it is contaminated or several years old.*

2. Mark hood hinges for correct installation and remove the hood.

3. Remove the battery holddown and battery.

4. Disconnect and tags all cables attached to various engine parts.

5. Disconnect and tag all electrical wires attached to various engine parts.

6. Disconnect and tag all vacuum lines connected to various engine parts.

7. Remove the cruise control actuator and bracket.

8. Disconnect the radiator and heater hoses.

9. Disconnect the automatic transaxle cooler lines if so equipped.

10. Unbolt the two radiator supports and lift out the radiator.

11. Remove the air cleaner assembly and air flow meter.

12. Disconnect all wiring and linkage at the transaxle.

13. Pull out the fuel injection system wiring harness and secure to the right side of fender apron.

14. Relieve the fuel pressure. Disconnect the fuel lines at the fuel filter and return pipes.

15. Disconnect the speedometer cable at the transaxle.

16. Remove the clutch release cylinder without disconnecting the fluid line.

17. Remove the drive belt, unbolt the air conditioning compressor and secure it out of the way.

18. Raise and support the car on jackstands.

19. Drain the transaxle fluid.

20. While someone holds the brake pedal depressed, unbolt both axle shafts. It's a good idea to wrap the boots with shop towels to prevent grease loss.

21. Remove the drive belt and unbolt the power steering pump and secure it out of the way.

22. Disconnect the exhaust pipe from the manifold.

23. Disconnect the front and rear engine mounts at the frame member.

24. Lower the vehicle.

25. Attach an engine crane at the lifting eyes.

26. Take up the engine weight with the crane and remove the right and left side engine mounts.

27. Slowly and carefully, remove the engine and transaxle assembly front the top of the vehicle.

28. With a suitable engine crane (always use lifting eyes for removal and installation procedures) install the removed engine/transaxle assembly in the vehicle. Install both engine

Troubleshooting Engine Mechanical Problems

Problem	Cause	Solution
External oil leaks	• Fuel pump gasket broken or improperly seated	• Replace gasket
	• Cylinder head cover RTV sealant broken or improperly seated	• Replace sealant; inspect cylinder head cover sealant flange and cylinder head sealant surface for distortion and cracks
	• Oil filler cap leaking or missing	• Replace cap
	• Oil filter gasket broken or improperly seated	• Replace oil filter
	• Oil pan side gasket broken, improperly seated or opening in RTV sealant	• Replace gasket or repair opening in sealant; inspect oil pan gasket flange for distortion
	• Oil pan front oil seal broken or improperly seated	• Replace seal; inspect timing case cover and oil pan seal flange for distortion
	• Oil pan rear oil seal broken or improperly seated	• Replace seal; inspect oil pan rear oil seal flange; inspect rear main bearing cap for cracks, plugged oil return channels, or distortion in seal groove
	• Timing case cover oil seal broken or improperly seated	• Replace seal
	• Excess oil pressure because of restricted PCV valve	• Replace PCV valve
	• Oil pan drain plug loose or has stripped threads	• Repair as necessary and tighten
	• Rear oil gallery plug loose	• Use appropriate sealant on gallery plug and tighten
	• Rear camshaft plug loose or improperly seated	• Seat camshaft plug or replace and seal, as necessary
	• Distributor base gasket damaged	• Replace gasket
Excessive oil consumption	• Oil level too high	• Drain oil to specified level
	• Oil with wrong viscosity being used	• Replace with specified oil
	• PCV valve stuck closed	• Replace PCV valve
	• Valve stem oil deflectors (or seals) are damaged, missing, or incorrect type	• Replace valve stem oil deflectors
	• Valve stems or valve guides worn	• Measure stem-to-guide clearance and repair as necessary
	• Poorly fitted or missing valve cover baffles	• Replace valve cover
	• Piston rings broken or missing	• Replace broken or missing rings
	• Scuffed piston	• Replace piston
	• Incorrect piston ring gap	• Measure ring gap, repair as necessary
	• Piston rings sticking or excessively loose in grooves	• Measure ring side clearance, repair as necessary
	• Compression rings installed upside down	• Repair as necessary
	• Cylinder walls worn, scored, or glazed	• Repair as necessary
	• Piston ring gaps not properly staggered	• Repair as necessary
	• Excessive main or connecting rod bearing clearance	• Measure bearing clearance, repair as necessary
No oil pressure	• Low oil level	• Add oil to correct level
	• Oil pressure gauge, warning lamp or sending unit inaccurate	• Replace oil pressure gauge or warning lamp
	• Oil pump malfunction	• Replace oil pump
	• Oil pressure relief valve sticking	• Remove and inspect oil pressure relief valve assembly
	• Oil passages on pressure side of pump obstructed	• Inspect oil passages for obstruction

Troubleshooting the Cooling System

Problem	Cause	Solution
High temperature gauge indication—overheating	• Coolant level low	• Replenish coolant
	• Fan belt loose	• Adjust fan belt tension
	• Radiator hose(s) collapsed	• Replace hose(s)
	• Radiator airflow blocked	• Remove restriction (bug screen, fog lamps, etc.)
	• Faulty radiator cap	• Replace radiator cap
	• Ignition timing incorrect	• Adjust ignition timing
	• Idle speed low	• Adjust idle speed
	• Air trapped in cooling system	• Purge air
	• Heavy traffic driving	• Operate at fast idle in neutral intermittently to cool engine
	• Incorrect cooling system component(s) installed	• Install proper component(s)
	• Faulty thermostat	• Replace thermostat
	• Water pump shaft broken or impeller loose	• Replace water pump
	• Radiator tubes clogged	• Flush radiator
	• Cooling system clogged	• Flush system
	• Casting flash in cooling passages	• Repair or replace as necessary. Flash may be visible by removing cooling system components or removing core plugs.
	• Brakes dragging	• Repair brakes
	• Excessive engine friction	• Repair engine
	• Antifreeze concentration over 68%	• Lower antifreeze concentration percentage
	• Missing air seals	• Replace air seals
	• Faulty gauge or sending unit	• Repair or replace faulty component
	• Loss of coolant flow caused by leakage or foaming	• Repair or replace leaking component, replace coolant
	• Viscous fan drive failed	• Replace unit
Low temperature indication—undercooling	• Thermostat stuck open	• Replace thermostat
	• Faulty gauge or sending unit	• Repair or replace faulty component
Coolant loss—boilover	• Overfilled cooling system	• Reduce coolant level to proper specification
	• Quick shutdown after hard (hot) run	• Allow engine to run at fast idle prior to shutdown
	• Air in system resulting in occasional "burping" of coolant	• Purge system
	• Insufficient antifreeze allowing coolant boiling point to be too low	• Add antifreeze to raise boiling point
	• Antifreeze deteriorated because of age or contamination	• Replace coolant
	• Leaks due to loose hose clamps, loose nuts, bolts, drain plugs, faulty hoses, or defective radiator	• Pressure test system to locate source of leak(s) then repair as necessary
	• Faulty head gasket	• Replace head gasket
	• Cracked head, manifold, or block	• Replace as necessary
	• Faulty radiator cap	• Replace cap
Coolant entry into crankcase or cylinder(s)	• Faulty head gasket	• Replace head gasket
	• Crack in head, manifold or block	• Replace as necessary
Coolant recovery system inoperative	• Coolant level low	• Replenish coolant to FULL mark
	• Leak in system	• Pressure test to isolate leak and repair as necessary
	• Pressure cap not tight or seal missing, or leaking	• Repair as necessary
	• Pressure cap defective	• Replace cap
	• Overflow tube clogged or leaking	• Repair as necessary
	• Recovery bottle vent restricted	• Remove restriction

Troubleshooting the Cooling System (cont.)

Problem	Cause	Solution
Noise	• Fan contacting shroud	• Reposition shroud and inspect engine mounts
	• Loose water pump impeller	• Replace pump
	• Glazed fan belt	• Apply silicone or replace belt
	• Loose fan belt	• Adjust fan belt tension
	• Rough surface on drive pulley	• Replace pulley
	• Water pump bearing worn	• Remove belt to isolate. Replace pump.
	• Belt alignment	• Check pulley alignment. Repair as necessary.
No coolant flow through heater core	• Restricted return inlet in water pump	• Remove restriction
	• Heater hose collapsed or restricted	• Remove restriction or replace hose
	• Restricted heater core	• Remove restriction or replace core
	• Restricted outlet in thermostat housing	• Remove flash or restriction
	• Intake manifold bypass hole in cylinder head restricted	• Remove restriction
	• Faulty heater control valve	• Replace valve
	• Intake manifold coolant passage restricted	• Remove restriction or replace intake manifold

NOTE: *Immediately after shutdown, the engine enters a condition known as heat soak. This is caused by the cooling system being inoperative while engine temperature is still high. If coolant temperature rises above boiling point, expansion and pressure may push some coolant out of the radiator overflow tube. If this does not occur frequently it is considered normal.*

GENERAL ENGINE SPECIFICATIONS

Year	Engine Type	Engine Displacement Cu. In. (cc)	Fuel System Type	Horsepower (@ rpm)▲	Torque @ rpm (ft. lbs.)▲	Bore × Stroke (in.)	Compression Ratio	Oil Pressure @ rpm (psi)
1986	5M-GE	168.4 (2759)	EFI	150 @ 5200 ①	159 @ 4400 ②	3.27×3.35	8.8:1	71.1 @ 3000
	2S-E	121.7 (1995)	EFI	97 @ 4400	118 @ 4000	3.31×3.54	8.7:1	4.3 ③
1986–89	3S-FE, 3S-GE	121.9 (1998)	EFI	135 @ 6000	125 @ 4800	3.39×3.39	9.2:1	4.3 ③
1986–90	7M-GE	180.3 (2954)	EFI	200 @ 6000	185 @ 4800	3.27×3.58	9.2:1	4.3 ③
1987–90	7M-GTE	180.3 (2954)	EFI (Turbo)	230 @ 5600	246 @ 4000	3.27×3.58	8.4:1	4.3 ③
1988–90	3S-GTE	121.9 (1998)	EFI (Turbo)	190 @ 6000	190 @ 3200	3.39×3.39	8.5:1	4.3 ③
1990	4A-FE	96.8 (1587)	EFI	103 @ 6000	130 @ 5400	3.19×3.03	9.5:1	④
	5S-FE	132.0 (2164)	EFI	130 @ 5400	140 @ 4400	3.43×3.58	9.5:1	④

▲ Horsepower and torque rating given in SAE net figures
EFI—Electronic fuel injection
① 1986—161 @ 5600
② 1986—169 @ 4400
③ At idle speed
④ 4.3 @ idle speed
   36–71 psi @ 3,000 rpm

CAMSHAFT SPECIFICATIONS

(All measurements in inches)

Year	Engine	Journal Diameter 1	2	3	4	5	6	7	Bearing Clearance	Lobe Life Intake	Exhaust	Camshaft End Play
1986	5M-GE	1.4944–1.4951	1.6913–1.6919	1.7110–1.7116	1.7307–1.7313	1.7504–1.7510	1.7700–1.7707	1.7897–1.7904	0.0010–0.0026	—	—	0.0028–0.0098
	2S-E	1.8291–1.8297	1.8192–1.8199	1.8094–1.8100	1.7996–1.8002	1.7897–1.7904	1.7799–1.7805	—	0.0010–0.0026	—	—	0.0031–0.0091
1986–89	3S-GE	1.0614–1.0620	1.0614–1.0620	1.0614–1.0620	1.0614–1.0620	—	—	—	0.0010–0.0024	—	—	0.0039–0.0094
1986–90	7M-GE 7M-GTE	1.0610–1.4951	1.0586–1.6919	1.0586–1.7116	1.0586–1.7313	1.0586–1.7510	1.0586–1.7707	1.0586–1.7904	0.0010–0.0037 ①	—	—	0.0031–0.0075
1987–89	3S-FE	1.0614–1.0620	1.0614–1.0620	1.0614–1.0620	1.0614–1.0620	—	—	—	0.0010–0.0024	—	—	0.0018–0.0039
1988–90	3S-GTE	1.0614–1.0620	1.0614–1.0620	1.0614–1.0620	1.0614–1.0620	—	—	—	0.0010–0.0024	—	—	0.0039–0.0094
1990	4A-FE	③	③	③	③	—	—	—	0.0014–0.0028	—	—	0.0043 ②
	5S-FE	1.0614–1.0620	1.0614–1.0620	1.0614–1.0620	1.0614–1.0620	—	—	—	0.0010–0.0024	—	—	④

—Not available
① No. 1: 0.0014–0.0028
② Maximum thrust clearance
③ Exhaust No. 1—0.9822–0.9829 in.
  Others 0.9035–0.9041 in.
④ Maximum thrust clearance
  0.0047 in. Intake
  0.0039 in. Exhaust

VALVE SPECIFICATIONS

Year	Engine Type	Seat Angle (deg.)	Face Angle (deg.)	Spring Test Pressure (lbs.) Inner	Outer	Spring Installed Height (in.) Inner	Outer	Stem to Guide Clearance (in.)▲ Intake	Exhaust	Stem Diameter (in.) Intake	Exhaust
1986	5M-GE	45	44.5	—	①	—	②	0.0010–0.0024	0.0012–0.0026	0.3138–0.3144	0.3136–0.3142
	2S-E	45.5	45.5	—	71.4	—	1.555	0.0010–0.0024	0.0012–0.0026	0.3138–0.3144	0.3136–0.3142
1986–89	3S-GE	45.5	44.5	—	38.6	—	1.366	0.0010–0.0023	0.0012–0.0025	0.2346–0.2352	0.2344–0.2350
1986–90	7M-GE, 7M-GTE	45.0	44.5	—	35.0	—	1.639	0.0010–0.0024	0.0012–0.0026	0.2350–0.2356	0.2348–0.2354
1987–89	3S-FE	45.5	44.5	—	39.6	—	1.366	0.0010–0.0024	0.0026–0.0030	0.2350–0.2356	0.2348–0.2354
1988–90	3S-GTE	45.5	44.5	—	44.1	—	1.366	0.0010–0.0023	0.0012–0.0025	0.2346–0.2352	0.2344–0.2350
1990	4A-FE	45	45	—	35	—	1.366	0.0010–0.0024	0.0012–0.0026	0.2350–0.2356	0.2348–0.2354
	5S-FE	45	45	—	40	—	1.366	0.0010–0.0024	0.0012–0.0026	0.2350–0.2356	0.2348–0.2354

▲ Valve guides are removable
① Intake springs 76.5–84.4 lbs.; exhaust 73.4–80.9 lbs.
② Intake 1.575 in.; exhaust 1.693 in.

TORQUE SPECIFICATIONS
(All readings in ft. lbs.)

Year	Engine Type	Cylinder Head Bolts	Rod Bearing Bolts	Main Bearing Bolts	Crankshaft Pulley Bolt	Flywheel to Crankshaft Bolts	Manifold Intake	Exhaust
1986	5M-GE	55–62.0	31.0–35.0	71.0–79.0	97.0–119.0 ⑤	50.0–58.0	15.0–17.0	25.0–33.0
	2S-E	45.0–50.0	33.0–38.0	40.0–45.0	78.0–82.0	70.0–75.0	30.0–33.0	30.0–33.0
	3S-GE	38.0–42.0	40.0–45.0	40.0–45.0	78.0–82.0	⑥	12.0–16.0	30.0–34.0
	7M-GE	55.0–61.0	45.0–49.0	72.0–78.0	185.0–205.0	51.0–57.0	11.0–15.0	26.0–32.0
1987	3S-GE	38.0–42.0	44.0–50.0	40.0–45.0	78.0–82.0	⑥	12.0–16.0	30.0–34.0
	3S-FE	45.0–50.0	33.0–38.0	40.0–45.0	78.0–82.0	70.0–75.0	11.0–17.0	27.0–33.0
	7M-GE, 7M-GTE	55.0–61.0	45.0–49.0	72.0–78.0	185.0–205.0	51.0–57.0	11.0–15.0	26.0–32.0
1988	3S-FE	45-50	33-38	40-45	78-82	70-75	11-17	27-33
	3S-GE	38-42	44-50	40-45	78-82	65	12-16	30-34
	3S-GTE	38-42	44-50	40-45	78-82	65	12-16	38
	7M-GE	55-61	45-49	72-78	185-205	51-57	11-15	26-32
	7M-GTE	55-61	45-49	72-78	185-205	51-57	11-15	26-32
1989	3S-FE	45-40	33-38	40-45	78-82	70-75	11-17	27-33
	3S-GE	38-42	44-50	40-45	78-82	65	12-16	30-34
	3S-GTE	38-42	44-50	40-45	78-82	65	12-16	38
	7M-GE	55-61	45-49	72-78	185-205	51-57	11-15	26-32
	7M-GTE	55-61	45-49	72-78	185-205	51-57	11-15	26-32
1990	4A-FE	47	36	44	87	47 ③	14	18
	5S-FE	47 ④	18 ④	43	80	61 ⑤	14	31
	3S-GTE	38-42	44-50	40-45	78-82	65	12-16	38
	7M-GE	55-61	45-49	72-78	185-205	51-57	11-15	26-32
	7M-GTE	55-61	45-49	72-78	185-205	51-57	11-15	26-32

① 1984—86—146—174
② New: 65; Used: 63
③ 58 ft. lbs. m/t
④ Torque to specification—then turn 90° additional
⑤ 72 ft. lbs. m/t

CRANKSHAFT AND CONNECTING ROD SPECIFICATIONS

(All measurements are given in inches)

| Year | Engine Type | Crankshaft | | | | Connecting Rod | | |
		Main Brg. Journal Dia.	Main Brg. Oil Clearance	Shaft End-Play	Thrust on No.	Journal Diameter	Oil Clearance	Side Clearance
1986	5M-GE	2.3617–2.3627	0.0013–0.0023	0.0020–0.0098	4	2.0463–2.0472	0.0008–0.0021	0.0063–0.0117
	2S-E	2.1648–2.1654	0.0008–0.0019 ①	0.0008–0.0087	3	1.8892–1.8898	0.0009–0.0022	0.0063–0.0083
	3S-GE	2.1648–2.1654	0.0008–0.0019 ①	0.0088–0.0087	3	1.8892–1.8898	0.0009–0.0022	0.0063–0.0124
1987–89	3S-GE, 3S-FE	2.1648–2.1653	0.0007–0.0015 ①	0.0008–0.0087	3	1.8892–1.8898	0.0009–0.0022	0.0063–0.0123
1986–90	7M-GE, 7M-GTE	2.3625–2.3625	0.0012–0.0022	0.0020–0.0098	4	2.1659–2.1663	0.0012–0.0019	0.0063–0.0117
1988–90	3S-GTE	2.1649–2.1655	②	0.0008–0.0087	3	1.8892–1.8898	0.0009–0.0022	0.0063–0.0123
1990	4A-FE	1.8891–1.8898	0.0006–0.0013	0.0008–0.0087	3	1.5742–1.5748 ④	0.0008–0.0020	0.0008–0.0020 ③
	5S-FE	2.1649–2.1655	0.0010–0.0017	0.0008–0.0087	3	1.8892–1.8898 ④	0.0009–0.0022	0.0009–0.0022 ③

① No. 3: 0.0012–0.0022
② No. 3: 0.0011–0.0019 (1988)
   No. 3: 0.0010–0.0017 (1989–90)
③ Rod oil clearance
④ Crank pin diameter

mounts in the correct location. Torque the engine mount bolts to 29 ft. lbs.

29. Raise and safely support the vehicle as necessary.

30. Connect the front and rear engine mounts at the frame member.

31. Install the exhaust pipe to the manifold. Always replace the exhaust manifold gaskets if so equipped.

32. Install the power steering pump in the correct location.

33. Reconnect the axle shafts to the transaxle assembly. Torque the axle shaft bolts to 27 ft. lbs.

34. Install the air conditioning compressor to the engine. Use caution when working near or around the air conditioning system.

35. Reconnect the clutch release cylinder and speedometer cable to the transaxle.

36. Connect the fuel lines at the fuel filter and return pipes. Torque the fuel line connectors to 22 ft. lbs.

37. Install and route the fuel injection system wiring harness in the correct manner.

38. Connect all wiring and linkage to the transaxle.

39. Install the air flow meter and air cleaner assembly to the vehicle.

40. Install the radiator and radiator supports to the vehicle.

41. Reconnect the automatic transaxle lines (if so equipped) and all water hoses.

42. Install the cruise control actuator and bracket.

43. Reconnect all marked vacuum lines, electrical wires, cables to the correct engine parts.

44. Install the battery and connect the battery cables. Install the engine hood in the correct location.

45. Refill all fluid levels with the correct fluid to the proper level. Bleed systems as necessary. Make all necessary adjustments. Start the engine. Check for any fluid leaks, road test the vehicle for proper operation.

3S-GE Engine (1986–89 Celica)

1. Disconnect the negative battery cable. Drain the engine coolant.

CAUTION: *When draining the coolant, keep in mind that cats and dogs are attracted by the ethylene glycol antifreeze, and are quite likely to drink any that is left in an uncov-*

PISTON AND RING SPECIFICATIONS

(All measurements in inches)

Year	Engine Type	Piston Clearance 68°F	Ring Gap			Ring Side Clearance		
			Top Compression	Bottom Compression	Oil Control	Top Compression	Bottom Compression	Oil Control
1986	5M-GE	0.0024–0.0031	0.0114–0.0185	0.0098–0.0217	0.0067–0.0335	0.0012–0.0028	0.0008–0.0024	Snug
	2S-E	0.0006–0.0014	0.0110–0.0209	0.0083–0.0189	0.0079–0.0323	0.0012–0.0028	0.0008–0.0024	Snug
	3S-GE	0.0012–0.0020	0.0130–0.0213	0.0079–0.0173	0.0079–0.0354	0.0008–0.0024	0.0006–0.0022	Snug
1986–89	7M-GE	0.0024–0.0031	0.0091–0.0150	0.0098–0.0209	0.0039–0.0201	0.0012–0.0028	0.0008–0.0024	Snug
1987–89	3S-GE	0.0012–0.0020	0.0130–0.0213	0.0079–0.0173	0.0079–0.0350	0.0012–0.0028	0.0008–0.0024	Snug
	3S-FE	0.0018–0.0026	0.0106–0.0193	0.0106–0.0197	0.0079–0.0311	0.0012–0.0028	0.0012–0.0028	Snug
1987–90	7M-GTE	0.0028–0.0035	0.0114–0.0173	0.0098–0.0209	0.0039–0.0220	0.0012–0.0028	0.0008–0.0024	Snug
1988–90	3S-GTE	0.0012–0.0020	0.0130–0.0217	0.0177–0.0264	0.0079–0.0236	0.0015–0.0031	0.0012–0.0028	Snug
1990	4A-FE	0.0024–0.0031	0.0098–0.0177	0.0059–0.0157	0.0039–0.0276	0.0016–0.0032	0.0012–0.0028	Snug
	5S-FE	0.0031–0.0039	0.0106–0.0197	0.0138–0.0234	0.0079–0.0217	0.0012–0.0028	0.0012–0.0028	Snug

ered container or in puddles on the ground. This will prove fatal in sufficient quantity. Always drain the coolant into a sealable container. Coolant should be reused unless it is contaminated or several years old.

2. Mark hood hinges for correct installation and remove the hood.

3. Remove the battery holddown and battery.

4. Tag and disconnect the connector high tension lead at the ignition coil. Remove the four nuts and two bolts securing the upper suspension brace and then remove the brace.

5. On models with automatic transaxles, disconnect the throttle cable and its bracket at the throttle body.

6. Disconnect the throttle cable from the throttle body on models with manual transaxles.

7. Remove the overflow tank.

8. Remove the cruise control actuator and its bracket.

9. Remove the oxygen sensor.

10. Tag and disconnect the cooling fan leads at the radiator. Disconnect the heater hoses and the automatic transaxle oil cooler lines (if so equipped). Remove the radiator and the two supports.

11. Remove the air cleaner assembly with the air flow meter and air cleaner hose attached.

12. Remove the air cleaner bracket.

13. Remove the igniter.

14. Relieve the fuel pressure. Tag and disconnect the fuel hoses at the filter and fuel return pipe.

15. Disconnect the speedometer cable.

16. Disconnect the transaxle control cable at the shift and selector levers on MT cars and then remove it from the bracket. On models with AT, disconnect the cable at the swivel and at the bracket and then remove it.

17. Remove the drive belt. Unbolt the air conditioning compressor (if so equipped) and then wire it out of the way with the refrigerant lines still attached.

18. Tag and disconnect any remaining wires or electrical leads.

19. Tag and disconnect any remaining vacuum hoses.

20. Raise and support the vehicle on safety stands.

21. Drain the engine oil.

CAUTION: *The EPA warns that prolonged contact with used engine oil may cause a number of skin disorders, including cancer!*

You should make every effort to minimize your exposure to used engine oil. Protective gloves should be worn when changing the oil. Wash your hands and any other exposed skin areas as soon as possible after exposure to used engine oil. Soap and water, or waterless hand cleaner should be used.

22. Remove the right side engine under cover. Remove the lower suspension crossmember.

23. With someone holding the brake pedal depressed, unbolt and remove both halfshafts. It's a good idea to wrap the boots with shop towels to prevent grease loss.

24. Unbolt the power steering pump. Disconnect the two vacuum hoses and remove the drive belt. Position the pump out of the way with the hydraulic lines still connected to it.

25. Disconnect the exhaust pipe at the manifold.

26. Remove the rear engine mount bolt. Lower the vehicle and then remove the front engine mount bolts.

27. Remove the power steering pump reservoir and position it out of the way.

28. Attach an engine hoist to the lifting hooks.

29. Take up the engine's weight with the hoist and remove the right and left engine mounts.

30. Slowly and carefully, remove the engine and transaxle assembly from the top of the vehicle. Be careful not to hit the power steering gear housing or the neutral safety switch.

31. With a suitable engine crane (always use lifting eyes for removal and installation procedures) install the removed engine/transaxle assembly in the vehicle. Install all engine mounts in the correct location. Torque the engine mount bolts to 29 ft. lbs.

32. Raise and safely support the vehicle as necessary.

33. Connect the front and rear engine mounts at the frame member.

34. Install the exhaust pipe to the manifold. Always replace the exhaust manifold gaskets if so equipped.

35. Install the power steering pump and reservoir in the correct location.

36. Reconnect the axle shafts to the transaxle assembly. Torque the axle shaft bolts to 27 ft. lbs.

37. Install lower suspension crossmember and engine undercover.

38. Reconnect all marked vacuum lines, electrical wires, cables to the correct engine parts.

39. Install the air conditioning compressor to the engine. Use caution when working near or around the air conditioning system.

40. Connect the transaxle control cable at the shift and selector levers on MT cars and install it to the bracket. On models with AT, connect the cable at the swivel and at the bracket.

41. Reconnect the speedometer cable to the transaxle.

42. Connect the fuel lines at the fuel filter and return pipes. Torque the fuel line connectors to 22 ft. lbs.

43. Install the igniter in the correct location.

44. Install the air cleaner bracket and air cleaner assembly with the air flow meter and hose.

45. Install the radiator (connect electrical leads for cooling fan) and radiator supports to the vehicle.

46. Reconnect the automatic transaxle lines (if so equipped) and all water hoses.

47. Install the oxygen sensor and reconnect the electrical lead.

48. Install the cruise control actuator and bracket. Install the overflow tank and hose.

49. On models with automatic transaxles, connect the throttle cable and its bracket at the throttle body.

50. Connect the throttle cable to the throttle body on models with manual transaxles.

51. Install the four nuts and two bolts securing the upper suspension brace and install the brace. Reconnect the connector high tension lead at the ignition coil.

52. Install the battery and connect the battery cables. Install the engine hood in the correct location.

53. Refill all fluid levels with the correct fluid to the proper level. Bleed systems as necessary. Make all necessary adjustments. Start the engine. Check for any fluid leaks, road test the vehicle for proper operation.

3S-FE Engine (1987–89 Celica)

1. Disconnect the battery cables. Remove the battery. Remove the hood. Drain the engine coolant. Tag and disconnect all vacuum hoses, electrical wires and cables that are necessary to remove the engine.

CAUTION: *When draining the coolant, keep in mind that cats and dogs are attracted by the ethylene glycol antifreeze, and are quite likely to drink any that is left in an uncovered container or in puddles on the ground. This will prove fatal in sufficient quantity. Always drain the coolant into a sealable container. Coolant should be reused unless it is contaminated or several years old.*

2. Disconnect the ignition coil connector and high tension wire from the coil. Remove the suspension upper brace.

3. Remove the radiator. Remove the reservoir tank. If the vehicle is equipped with auto-

matic transaxle, disconnect the throttle cable and bracket from the throttle body.

4. Disconnect the accelerator cable from the throttle body. Remove the cruise control actuator and bracket, if equipped. Remove the oxygen sensor.

5. Remove the air cleaner assembly, air flow meter and air cleaner hose. Remove the air cleaner bracket.

6. Remove the igniter. Remove the heater hoses. Relieve the fuel pressure. Disconnect and plug the fuel lines. Disconnect the speedometer cable.

7. If equipped with manual transaxle, remove the clutch release cylinder and tube bracket. Do not disconnect the tube from the bracket. Disconnect the transaxle control cable.

8. Remove the air condition compressor and position it to the side. Do not disconnect the lines.

9. Raise and support the vehicle safely. Drain the engine oil. Drain the transaxle fluid. Remove the right under cover.

CAUTION: *The EPA warns that prolonged contact with used engine oil may cause a number of skin disorders, including cancer! You should make every effort to minimize your exposure to used engine oil. Protective gloves should be worn when changing the oil. Wash your hands and any other exposed skin areas as soon as possible after exposure to used engine oil. Soap and water, or waterless hand cleaner should be used.*

10. Remove the power steering pump and position it to the side. Do not disconnect the lines. Remove the suspension lower crossmember. Remove the halfshafts.

11. Disconnect the exhaust pipe from the catalytic converter. Remove the engine rear mounting bolt. Lower the vehicle. Disconnect the TCCS and the ECU electrical connectors. Remove the power steering pump reservoir mounting bolts.

12. Properly attach the lifting device to the engine. Raise the engine slightly and remove the engine retaining brackets and bolts.

13. Carefully, start to lift and remove the engine/transaxle assembly from the vehicle.

14. Slowly and carefully, remove the engine and transaxle assembly from the top of the vehicle. Be careful not to hit the power steering gear housing or the neutral safety switch.

15. With a suitable engine crane (always use lifting eyes for removal and installation procedures) install the removed engine/transaxle assembly in the vehicle. Install all engine mounts in the correct location.

16. Raise and safely support the vehicle as necessary.

17. Connect the front and rear engine mounts at the frame member.

18. Install the exhaust system. Always replace the exhaust manifold gaskets if so equipped.

19. Install the power steering pump and reservoir in the correct location.

20. Reconnect all marked vacuum lines, electrical wires, cables to the correct engine parts.

21. Reconnect the axle shafts to the transaxle assembly. Torque the axle shaft bolts to 27 ft. lbs.

22. Install lower suspension crossmember and engine undercover.

23. Install the air conditioning compressor to the engine. Use caution when working near or around the air conditioning system.

24. Connect the transaxle control cable at the shift and selector levers on MT cars and install it to the bracket. On models with AT, connect the cable at the swivel and at the bracket.

25. Reconnect the speedometer cable to the transaxle. Connect the fuel lines at the fuel filter and return pipes.

26. Install the igniter in the correct location.

27. Install the air cleaner bracket and air cleaner assembly with the air flow meter and hose.

28. Install the radiator (connect electrical leads for cooling fan) and radiator supports to the vehicle.

29. Reconnect the automatic transaxle lines (if so equipped) and all water hoses.

30. Install the oxygen sensor and reconnect the electrical lead.

31. Install the cruise control actuator and bracket. Install the overflow tank and hose.

32. On models with automatic transaxles, connect the throttle cable and its bracket at the throttle body.

33. Connect the throttle cable to the throttle body on models with manual transaxles.

34. Reconnect the connector high tension lead at the ignition coil.

35. Install the suspension upper brace and all drive belts.

36. Install the battery and connect the battery cables. Install the engine hood in the correct location.

37. Refill all fluid levels with the correct fluid to the proper level. Bleed systems as necessary. Make all necessary adjustments. Start the engine. Check for any fluid leaks, road test the vehicle for proper operation.

3S-GTE Engine
1988–90 Celica All-Trac/4WD

1. Disconnect the negative battery cable and remove the battery. Drain all coolant from the engine and turbocharger intercooler.

CAUTION: *When draining the coolant, keep in mind that cats and dogs are attracted by the ethylene glycol antifreeze, and are quite likely to drink any that is left in an uncovered container or in puddles on the ground. This will prove fatal in sufficient quantity. Always drain the coolant into a sealable container. Coolant should be reused unless it is contaminated or several years old.*

NOTE: *On 1990 SRS vehicles, you must wait AT LEAST 30 seconds after disconnecting the battery before doing any work. The SRS has a built-in backup which will allow the system to remain energized for a period of time after the power is disconnected.*

2. Scribe matchmarks around the hinges and remove the hood.

3. Disconnect the accelerator cable at the throttle body. Remove the radiator, disconnect the transaxle cooling lines if so equipped. Disconnect the heater and intercooler hoses.

4. Relieve the fuel pressure. Disconnect the fuel inlet line at the fuel filter and the return line at the return pipe.

5. Remove the cruise control actuator and bracket. Remove the air cleaner assembly.

6. Remove the clutch release cylinder and bracket without disconnecting the hydraulic line. Wire it out of the way.

7. Disconnect the speedometer and transaxle control cables. Remove the alternator.

8. Remove the air conditioning compressor without disconnecting the refrigerant lines and position it out of the way.

9. Tag and disconnect any wires, connectors and vacuum lines which might interfere with engine removal.

10. Raise the vehicle and safely support it as necessary. Drain the engine oil and remove the undercovers.

CAUTION: *The EPA warns that prolonged contact with used engine oil may cause a number of skin disorders, including cancer! You should make every effort to minimize your exposure to used engine oil. Protective gloves should be worn when changing the oil. Wash your hands and any other exposed skin areas as soon as possible after exposure to used engine oil. Soap and water, or waterless hand cleaner should be used.*

11. Remove the lower suspension crossmember. Remove the front halfshafts and the (mark before removing) driveshaft.

12. Remove the power steering pump and bracket without disconnecting the hydraulic lines and position it out of the way.

13. Disconnect the front exhaust pipe at the manifold and tailpipe and remove it.

14. Remove the engine mounting center member and lower the vehicle.

15. Unplug the 3 TCCS ECU connectors, remove the 2 screws and pull the connectors out through the firewall. Remove the power steering pump reservoir tank.

16. Attach an engine hoist chain to the lifting brackets on the engine. Remove the 2 bolts holding the right engine mount insulator to the mounting bracket. Remove the 4 bolts holding the left engine mount insulator to the mounting bracket and then remove the engine out from the top of the vehicle.

17. Slowly and carefully, remove the engine and transaxle assembly for the top of the vehicle.

18. Install the removed engine/transaxle assembly in the vehicle. Install all engine mounts and brackets (mount isolator to mount bracket) in the correct locations. Tighten the right and left engine mount bracket bolts to 38 ft. lbs.

19. When installing the engine mounting center member, tighten the outer bolts to 29 ft. lbs., tighten the inner bolts to 38 ft. lbs.

20. Raise and safely support the vehicle as necessary.

21. Install the power steering pump reservoir tank. Plug the 3 TCCS ECU connectors, install (pull the connectors in through the firewall) the retaining screws.

22. Install the complete exhaust system. Use new exhaust manifold gaskets if necessary.

23. Install the power steering pump and bracket with hydraulic lines attached.

24. Install the front halfshafts and the driveshaft. Install the lower suspension crossmember. When installing the lower suspension crossmember, tighten the outer bolts to 154 ft. lbs., tighten the inner bolts to 29 ft. lbs.

25. Install the engine undercovers as necessary. Connect any wires, connectors or vacuum lines that were disconnected for engine removal procedure.

26. Install the air conditioning compressor to the engine. Use caution when working near or around the air conditioning system.

27. Reconnect the speedometer cable and transaxle control cables. Install the alternator assembly.

28. Install the clutch release cylinder and bracket in the proper position.

29. Install the cruise control bracket, control actuator and air cleaner assembly.

30. Reconnect the fuel lines and accelerator at the throttle body.

31. Install the radiator assembly reconnect transaxle cooling lines if so equipped and all water hoses.

32. Install the battery and connect the battery cables. Install the engine hood in the correct location.

33. Refill all fluid levels with the correct fluid to the proper level. Bleed systems as necessary. Make all necessary adjustments. Start the engine. Check for any fluid leaks, road test the vehicle for proper operation.

4A-FE Engine (1990 Celica)
5S-FE Engine (1990 Celica)

1. Disconnect the negative battery cable. Remove the battery.

NOTE: *On 1990 SRS vehicles, you must wait AT LEAST 30 seconds after disconnecting the battery before doing any work. The SRS has a built-in backup which will allow the system to remain energized for a period of time after the power is disconnected.*

2. Mark and remove the engine hood. Remove the engine under covers.

3. Raise and safely support the vehicle as necessary. Relieve the fuel pressure. Drain the engine oil and coolant. Remove the air cleaner assembly along with its hose and any attachments.

CAUTION: *When draining the coolant, keep in mind that cats and dogs are attracted by the ethylene glycol antifreeze, and are quite likely to drink any that is left in an uncovered container or in puddles on the ground. This will prove fatal in sufficient quantity. Always drain the coolant into a sealable container. Coolant should be reused unless it is contaminated or several years old.*

CAUTION: *The EPA warns that prolonged contact with used engine oil may cause a number of skin disorders, including cancer! You should make every effort to minimize your exposure to used engine oil. Protective gloves should be worn when changing the oil. Wash your hands and any other exposed skin areas as soon as possible after exposure to used engine oil. Soap and water, or waterless hand cleaner should be used.*

4. Disconnect the accelerator and throttle cables at the bracket.

5. Remove the lower cover from the relay box. Disconnect the fusible link cassette and connectors. Remove the engine relay box from the battery.

6. Remove the air conditioning relay box from the bracket. On the 5S-FE engine remove the cruise control actuator assembly.

7. Remove the coolant reservoir tank. Remove the radiator (transaxle cooling lines if so equipped) and cooling fan.

8. On the 5S-FE engine remove the two wiper arms and outside lower windshield molding. Remove the suspension upper brace.

9. On the 5S-FE engine remove the ignition coil assembly. Disconnect the check connector, igniter connector (5S-FE engine), vacuum sensor connector and ground strap from the left front fender apron. Remove the engine wiring bracket. Disconnect the noise filter assembly.

10. Mark and disconnect the vacuum hoses at the charcoal canister. Remove the charcoal canister.

11. Disconnect the heater hose from the water inlet and speedometer cable.

12. Disconnect the fuel hose. Recover all leaking fuel in a suitable container.

13. On models with a manual transaxle, remove the clutch release cylinder and position it out of the way with the hydraulic lines still attached.

14. Disconnect the shift control cables from the transaxle.

15. Mark and disconnect the following hoses: vacuum sensor hose from the gas filter on the air intake chamber, brake booster vacuum hose, air conditioning vacuum hoses on air intake chamber and air conditioning hose from air pipe (4A-FE engine).

16. Disconnect two cowl wire connectors and engine wire clamp from engine fender apron.

17. Mark and disconnect the following engine wiring from the cabin: engine ECU connector, cowl wire connectors, air conditioning amplifier connector and O/D diode connector (4A-FE engine).

18. Remove the suspension lower crossmember.

19. Disconnect the oxygen sensor connector. Remove all necessary brackets and retaining bolts. Remove the front exhaust pipe assembly.

20. On vehicles equipped with automatic transaxle disconnect control cable from engine mounting center member.

21. Remove the front halfshaft assemblies as required from the vehicle.

22. Remove the drive belt. Unbolt the air conditioning compressor (if so equipped) and then wire it out of the way with the refrigerant lines still attached.

23. Remove the drive belt and remove the power steering pump assembly without disconnecting the pressure and return hoses.

24. Remove the engine mounting center member.

25. Remove the front engine mounting insulator and bracket.

26. Remove the rear mounting insulator and bracket.

27. Disconnect the ground wire from the fender apron. Remove the ground strap from the transaxle.

28. Remove the right and left engine mounting stay.

29. Slowly and carefully, remove the engine and transaxle assembly from the top of the ve-

hicle. Be careful not to hit the power steering gear housing or the neutral safety switch if so equipped.

30. With a suitable engine crane (always use lifting eyes for removal and installation procedures) install the removed engine/transaxle assembly in the vehicle. Install all engine mounts (insulators) and brackets in the correct location.

31. Raise and safely support the vehicle as necessary.

32. Install the left and right engine mounting stay.

33. Connect the ground wire to the fender apron. Install the ground strap to the transaxle.

34. Install the engine mounting center member.

35. Install the power steering pump assembly. Install the air conditioning compressor assembly. Install drive belts in the correct position.

36. Install the front halfshaft assemblies as required to the vehicle.

37. On vehicles equipped with automatic transaxle connect the control cable to engine mounting center member.

38. Reconnect the front exhaust pipe assembly. Connect the oxygen senor electrical connector. Install all necessary brackets and retaining bolts.

39. Install the suspension lower crossmember.

40. Reconnect the following engine wiring to the cabin: engine ECU connector, cowl wire connectors, air conditioning amplifier connector and O/D diode connector (4A-FE engine).

41. Reconnect the two cowl wire connectors and engine wire clamp to the engine fender apron.

42. Reconnect the following hoses: vacuum sensor hose to the gas filter on the air intake chamber, brake booster vacuum hose, air conditioning vacuum hoses on air intake chamber and air conditioning hose to air pipe (4A-FE engine).

43. On models with a manual transaxle, install the clutch release cylinder with the hydraulic lines attached.

44. Reconnect the shift control cables to the transaxle.

45. Connect the fuel hose using new retaining clamps if necessary.

46. Connect the heater hose to the water inlet and reconnect the speedometer cable to the transaxle.

47. Install the charcoal canister and the vacuum hoses to the charcoal canister.

48. Install the engine wiring bracket. Connect the noise filter assembly.

49. On the 5S-FE engine install the ignition coil assembly. Reconnect the check connector, vacuum sensor connector, igniter connector (5S-FE engine) and ground strap to the left front fender apron.

50. On the 5S-FE engine install the two wiper arms and outside lower windshield molding. Install the suspension upper brace.

51. Install the radiator (transaxle cooling lines if so equipped) and cooling fan (connect electrical leads) assembly. Install the coolant reservoir tank in the correct location.

52. Install the air conditioning relay box to the bracket. Install the engine relay box to the battery. Reconnect the fusible link cassette and connectors. Install the lower cover to the relay box. On the 5S-FE engine install the cruise control actuator assembly.

53. Reconnect the accelerator and throttle cables at the correct bracket. Install the engine under covers.

54. Install the battery and connect the battery cables. Install the air cleaner assembly and attaching components and engine hood in the correct location.

55. Refill all fluid levels with the correct fluid to the proper level. Bleed systems as necessary. Make all necessary adjustments. Start the engine. Check for any fluid leaks, road test the vehicle for proper operation.

5M-GE Engine (1986 Supra)

1. Disconnect the battery cables and remove the battery.

2. Scribe aligning marks on the hood and hinges to aid in their assembly. Remove the hood.

3. Remove the fan shroud and drain the cooling system.

CAUTION: *When draining the coolant, keep in mind that cats and dogs are attracted by the ethylene glycol antifreeze, and are quite likely to drink any that is left in an uncovered container or in puddles on the ground. This will prove fatal in sufficient quantity. Always drain the coolant into a sealable container. Coolant should be reused unless it is contaminated or several years old.*

4. Disconnect both the upper and lower radiator hoses. Unfasten the oil lines from the oil cooler on cars with automatic transmissions.

5. Detach the hose which runs to the thermal expansion tank, at the tank. Remove the expansion tank from its mounting bracket.

6. Remove the radiator.

7. Remove the air cleaner assembly, including the air flow meter and air intake connector pipe.

8. On cars equipped with automatic transmissions, remove the throttle cable bracket

from the cylinder head. On all models, remove the accelerator and actuator cable bracket from the cylinder head.

9. Tag and disconnect the cylinder head ground cable, the oxygen sensor wire, oil pressure sending unit and alternator wires, the high tension coil wire, the water temperature sending unit and thermo-switch (AT) wires, and the starter wires.

10. Tag and disconnect the ECT connectors and the solenoid resistor wire connector.

11. Tag and disconnect the brake booster vacuum hose from the air intake chamber, along with the EGR valve vacuum hose and the actuator vacuum hose from the air intake chamber (if equipped with cruise control).

12. Disconnect the heater and by-pass hoses from the engine.

13. Remove the glove box, and remove the ECU computer module. Disconnect the three connectors, and pull out the EFI (fuel injection) wiring harness from the engine compartment side of the firewall.

14. Remove the four shroud and four fluid coupling screws, and the shroud and coupling as a unit.

15. Remove the engine undercover protector.

16. Disconnect the coolant reservoir hose and remove the radiator.

17. Remove the air conditioning compressor drive belt, and remove the compressor mounting bolts. Without disconnecting the refrigerant hoses, lay the compressor to one side and secure it.

CAUTION: *The air conditioning system is charged with the refrigerant R-12, which is dangerous when released. DO NOT disconnect the air conditioning hoses when removing the engine; if the hoses have to be disconnected at any time, the work should be done by a trained air conditioning mechanic.*

18. Disconnect the power steering pump drive belt and remove the pump stay. Unbolt the pump and lay it aside without disconnecting the fluid hoses.

19. Remove the engine mounting bolts from each side of the engine. Remove the engine ground cable.

20. On manual transmission cars, remove the shift lever from inside the car.

21. Jack up the car and safely support it with jackstands. Drain the engine oil.

CAUTION: *The EPA warns that prolonged contact with used engine oil may cause a number of skin disorders, including cancer! You should make every effort to minimize your exposure to used engine oil. Protective gloves should be worn when changing the oil. Wash your hands and any other exposed skin areas as soon as possible after exposure to used engine oil. Soap and water, or waterless hand cleaner should be used.*

22. Disconnect the exhaust pipe from the exhaust manifold. Remove the exhaust pipe clamp from the transmission housing.

23. On manual transmission cars, remove the clutch slave cylinder.

24. Disconnect the speedometer cable at the transmission.

25. On automatic transmission cars, disconnect the shift linkage from the shift lever. On manual transmission cars, disconnect the wire from the back-up light switch.

26. Remove the stiffener plate from the ground cable.

27. Relieve the fuel pressure. Disconnect the fuel line from the fuel filter and the return hose from the fuel hose support. Be sure to catch any leaking fuel. Plug the fuel line.

28. Remove the power steering gear housing brackets. With steering lines attached suspend the gear housing assembly.

29. Mark and remove the intermediate shaft from the driveshaft.

30. Position a hydraulic jack under the transmission, with a wooden block between the two to prevent damage to the transmission case. Place a wooden block between the cowl panel and cylinder head rear end to prevent damage to the heater hoses.

31. Unbolt the engine rear support member from the frame, along with the ground cable.

32. Make sure all wiring is disconnected (and tagged for later assembly), all hoses disconnected, and everything clear of the engine and transmission. Attach an engine lift hoist chain to the lift brackets on the engine, and carefully lift the engine and transmission up and out of the car. It is very helpful to have two or three helpers on this job. Place the engine on a work stand, and remove the transmission at this time.

33. Install the removed engine/transmission assembly in the vehicle. Install the engine mounting bolts on each side of the engine.

34. Raise and safely support the vehicle as necessary.

35. Install the engine rear support member with the ground strap to the body of the vehicle.

36. Install the intermediate shaft to the propeller shaft in the correct marked position.

37. Install the power steering gear housing assembly and brackets, with steering lines attached. Install tie rod ends with new cotter pins.

38. Connect the battery ground strap to engine mounting bracket. Install stiffener plate with ground strap.

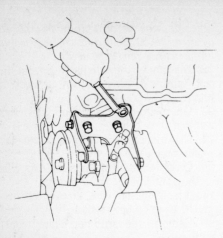

Power steering pump removal

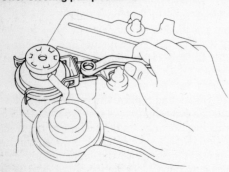

Removing the EGR vacuum module bracket

39. Reconnect all fuel lines with new retaining clamps as necessary.

40. Install coolant reservoir tank and radiator assembly. Connect all radiator hoses and transmission cooling lines if so equipped.

41. Install radiator cooling fan and fan shroud.

42. Install air cleaner case, air flow meter and air intake connector pipe.

43. Install the EFI wire harness to ECU module install the glove box and all removed components.

44. Reconnect all heater hoses using new retaining clamps if necessary.

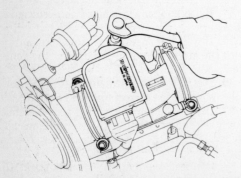

Removing the air flow meter

45. Reconnect all marked hoses, wires and cables to the correct engine location.

46. Install the accelerator and actuator cable bracket. Install throttle cable bracket for automatic transmission vehicles only.

47. On manual transmission vehicles, reconnect back-up light switch wiring and install clutch release cylinder and shifter assembly.

48. On automatic transmission vehicles, connect the shift linkage to shift lever.

49. Reconnect the speedometer cable to the transmission.

50. Install the exhaust pipe to the exhaust manifolds and all hangers. Use new exhaust manifold gaskets as required.

51. Install the power steering pump (drive belt) and pump stay.

52. Install air conditioning compressor (drive belt) with bracket to the engine block.

53. Install the engine undercovers and washer tank assembly.

54. Install the battery and connect the battery cables. Install the air cleaner assembly and attaching components and engine hood in the correct location.

55. Refill all fluid levels with the correct fluid to the proper level. Bleed systems as necessary. Make all necessary adjustments. Start

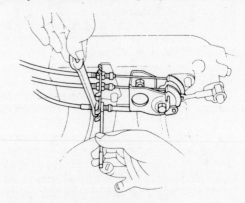

Disconnecting accelerator linkage

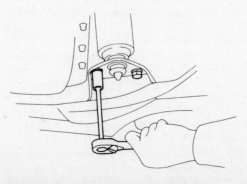

Disconnecting the engine shock absorber

the engine. Check for any fluid leaks, road test the vehicle for proper operation.

7M-GE Engine (1986–90 Supra) 7M-GTE Engine (1987–90 Supra)

1. Disconnect the negative battery cable. Remove the hood. Remove the engine under cover.

NOTE: *On 1990 SRS vehicles, you must wait AT LEAST 30 seconds after disconnecting the battery before doing any work. The SRS has a built-in backup which will allow the system to remain energized for a period of time after the power is disconnected.*

2. Drain the cooling system. Remove the radiator. Drain the engine oil. On 7M-GE remove the air cleaner assembly. On 7M-GTE remove the No. 4 air cleaner pipe along with the No. 1 and 2 air cleaner hose.

CAUTION: *When draining the coolant, keep in mind that cats and dogs are attracted by the ethylene glycol antifreeze, and are quite likely to drink any that is left in an uncovered container or in puddles on the ground. This will prove fatal in sufficient quantity. Always drain the coolant into a sealable container. Coolant should be reused unless it is contaminated or several years old.*

CAUTION: *The EPA warns that prolonged contact with used engine oil may cause a number of skin disorders, including cancer! You should make every effort to minimize your exposure to used engine oil. Protective gloves should be worn when changing the oil. Wash your hands and any other exposed skin areas as soon as possible after exposure to used engine oil. Soap and water, or waterless hand cleaner should be used.*

3. Remove the No. 7 air cleaner hose with the air flow meter and air cleaner cap.

4. Remove the air condition belt. Remove the alternator drive belt, water pump pulley and fan assembly. Remove the power steering belt.

5. Disconnect the brake booster hose, the heater valve hose, the cruise control hose and the charcoal canister hose. Remove the heater hoses.

6. Disconnect the engine ground strap, the noise filter connector, the theft deterrent horn connector, the check connector, the solenoid resistor connector, if equipped, the ignition coil connector on the 7M-GT, the igniter connectors on the 7M-GTE, the main relay connector, the alternator electrical connectors, the oxygen sensor connector on the 7M-GE, the heater valve connector, the ECU connector and the ECT connector.

7. Disconnect the cruise control cable, if equipped. Disconnect the accelerator cable. Disconnect the throttle cable, if equipped with automatic transmission.

8. Remove the air condition compressor. It may be possible to position the unit to the side without completely removing it from the vehicle.

9. On the 7M-GTE engine remove the No. 6 air cleaner hose and the upper radiator outlet hose.

10. Remove the power steering pump. It may be possible to position the unit to the side without completely removing it from the vehicle.

11. If equipped with manual transmission remove the shift lever. Disconnect the ground strap from the fuel hose clamp. On the 7M-GTE engine remove the engine mounting absorber.

12. Relieve the fuel pressure. Disconnect and plug the fuel lines.

13. Raise and support the vehicle safely as necessary. Remove the exhaust pipe. Mark and remove the driveshaft.

14. Disconnect the speedometer cable. If equipped with automatic transmission remove the shift linkage. If equipped with manual transmission remove the clutch release cylinder.

15. Properly support the engine and transmission assembly. Remove the No. 1 front crossmember. Remove the engine retaining mounts.

17. Position a piece of wood between the engine firewall and the rear of the cylinder head to prevent damage to the heater hose.

18. Make sure there are no remaining wires or hoses connected to the engine and then slowly and carefully remove the engine and transmission from the vehicle. Remove the engine and transaxle assembly from the top of the vehicle.

19. With a suitable engine crane (always use lifting eyes for removal and installation procedures) install the removed engine/transaxle assembly in the vehicle. Install all engine mounts (insulators) and brackets in the correct location.

20. Raise and safely support the vehicle as necessary.

21. Install the engine rear support member with ground strap to body.

22. Install the front crossmember.

23. On vehicles equipped with manual transmission, install the clutch release cylinder. On vehicles equipped with automatic transmission install the shift linkage in the correct location.

24. Reconnect the speedometer cable. Install the driveshaft in the correct position.

25. Install exhaust system use new exhaust gaskets if necessary. Reconnect all fuel hoses with new fuel retaining clamps.

26. Install engine mounting absorber on the

7M-GTE engine. Reconnect all ground straps.

27. Install the shift lever assembly on manual transmission vehicles.

28. Reconnect engine oil cooler hoses. Install the power steering pump assembly.

29. Install the No. 6 air cleaner hose on the 7M-GTE engine. Install the air conditioning compressor.

30. Reconnect all water hoses, vacuum hoses and engine wiring. Install water pump pulley and fan assembly. Install all drive belts.

31. Install the radiator assembly (connect transmission cooling lines if so equipped).

32. Install No. 7 air cleaner hose with air flow meter and air cleaner cap on 7M-GTE engine.

33. Install air cleaner case with attaching hoses on the 7M-GE engine.

34. Install No. 4 air cleaner pipe with No. 1 and No. 2 air cleaner hoses.

35. Install the battery and connect the battery cables. Install engine hood in the correct location.

36. Refill all fluid levels with the correct fluid to the proper level. Bleed systems as necessary. Make all necessary adjustments. Start the engine. Check for any fluid leaks, road test the vehicle for proper operation.

Camshaft Cover

REMOVAL AND INSTALLATION

2S-E, 3S-FE, 3S-GE, 3S-GTE, 4A-FE and 5S-FE Engines

1. Remove the air cleaner assembly. Disconnect and remove the air intake hose if so equipped.

2. Mark and disconnect all hose(s) from the cam cover for correct installation.

3. Remove the nuts and washers. Lift the cam cover off the cylinder head. Cover the oil return hole (make sure the return holes are not obstructed) in the head to prevent dirt or objects from falling in. Remove the cam cover gasket.

4. To install, replace the valve cover gasket. Tighten the nuts evenly, working from the center to the ends, reconnect the PCV hose and install the air cleaner assembly.

5M-GE Engine

1. Disconnect the air intake hose by loosening the clamps at either end. Remove the hose.

2. Tag and disconnect all PCV and other hoses which obstruct cam cover removal.

3. Remove the Phillips screws and lift off the cam covers and their gaskets.

4. Installation is the reverse of removal. Be sure to replace the cover gaskets. Tighten the

retaining screws evenly, working from the center to the ends.

7M-GE Engine

1. Drain the engine coolant, collecting it for re-use in a large container.

CAUTION: *When draining the coolant, keep in mind that cats and dogs are attracted by the ethylene glycol antifreeze, and are quite likely to drink any that is left in an uncovered container or in puddles on the ground. This will prove fatal in sufficient quantity. Always drain the coolant into a sealable container. Coolant should be reused unless it is contaminated or several years old.*

2. Remove the air cleaner hose and connector pipe.

3. Disconnect the cruise control cable, the accelerator cable and, if equipped with automatic transmission, the throttle cable (throttle control cable).

4. Remove the PCV hose. Disconnect the accelerator rod.

5. Disconnect the water by-pass hoses from the throttle body.

6. Label and disconnect these hoses: VSV for EGR, BVSV hose, EGR vacuum modulator hoses and No.7 air hose.

7. Disconnect the throttle position sensor electrical connector.

8. Remove the brackets holding the throttle body. Remove the air intake connector bracket mounting bolts.

9. Remove the four bolts and two nuts holding the air intake connector. Remove the air intake connector and its gasket. Remove the accelerator link.

10. Remove the heater hose clamp. Remove the valve covers.

11. To install, replace the valve cover gasket. Tighten the nuts evenly, working from the center to the ends, Install No. 3 cylinder head cover (center cover) torque the No. 3 cylinder head cover retaining bolts to 13 ft. lbs.

12. Apply seal packing to the cylinder head as necessary. Install the No. 1 and No. 2 cylinder head cover torque the retaining bolts to 22 in. lbs.

13. Install all brackets with necessary retaining bolts. Reconnect all cables, vacuum hoses, electrical connectors and water hoses.

14. Check oil level. Refill all necessary fluid levels. Start engine and check for oil leaks.

7M-GTE Engine

1. Remove the first or No.1 air cleaner hose.

2. Disconnect the accelerator link with the cable, the accelerator rod and, if equipped with

automatic transmission, the throttle (throttle control) cable.

3. Disconnect the six hoses from the Idle Speed Control (ISC) pipe. Remove the two bolts and remove the pipe.

4. Release the oxygen sensor wire from the two clamps along the PCV pipe.

5. Disconnect the No. 4 PCV hose from the PCV pipe. Remove the two bolts holding the pipe.

6. Disconnect the PCV pipe (with hoses attached) from the valve covers and the throttle body.

7. Disconnect the air valve hose from the intake air connector.

8. Loosen the clamp, remove the two bolts and remove the air intake connector. Remove the oil filler cap.

9. Remove the 5 nuts holding the ignition coil cover and remove the cover. Disconnect the harness and ground strap to the ignition coils. Remove the nut.

10. Disconnect the Nos. 1 and 2 spark plug wires from the coil and the clamp(s).

11. Remove the coil with the bracket and other plug wires attached. Remove plug wires 1 and 2 from the spark plugs.

12. Remove the accelerator link and disconnect the No.3 PCV hose. Remove the valve covers.

13. To install, replace the valve cover gasket. Tighten the nuts evenly, working from the center to the ends, Install No. 3 cylinder head cover (center cover) torque the No. 3 cylinder head cover retaining bolts to 13 ft. lbs.

14. Apply seal packing to the cylinder head as necessary. Install the No. 1 and No. 2 cylinder head cover torque the retaining bolts to 22 in. lbs.

15. Install all brackets with necessary retaining bolts. Reconnect all cables, vacuum hoses, electrical connectors and water hoses.

16. Check oil level. Refill all necessary fluid levels. Start engine and check for oil leaks.

Rocker Arms

REMOVAL AND INSTALLATION

5M-GE Engine

1. Remove the camshaft cover(s).
2. Remove the timing gears and timing belt assemblies.
3. Following the sequence shown, loosen the camshaft housing nuts and bolts in two passes. Remove the housings (with camshafts) from the cylinder head.
4. Remove the rocker arms, one at a time, from the head. As you remove each rocker, wipe it off and either tag it or mark it as to its

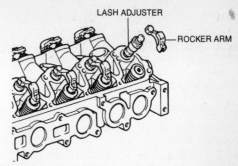

Removing lash adjuster and rocker arm — 5M-GE engine

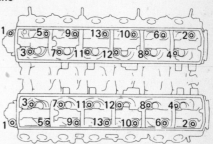

5M-GE engine camshaft housing bolt removal sequence. Loosen bolts gradually on three passes

proper location. It is critical that each rocker be re-installed in its correct location.

5. Remove each lash adjuster from the head (see Lash Adjusters Inspection below first), one at a time, and either mark or tag each one for correct installation later.

NOTE: *Remove and inspect oil pressure regulator before reassembly. Make sure that the match hole on each No. 2 cam journal is aligned with the hole on the respective camshafts.*

6. To install place each lash adjuster (bleed lash adjusters before installation or replace lash adjusters) and rocker arm in the correct position in the cylinder head. Check that the adjusters and rocker arms are installed in the correct order.

7. Install the camshaft housings (with camshafts) to the cylinder head using new gaskets.

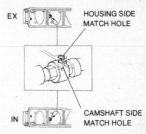

Before installing cam housings, align the match hole on each No. 2 cam journal with the hole in the housing

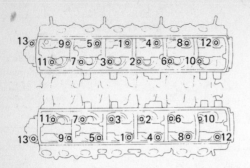

5M-GE engine camshaft housing torque sequence

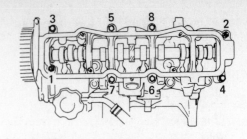

2S-E camshaft housing bolt removal sequence

8. Torque the retaining bolts uniformly and in 3 steps, in the correct sequence to 16 ft. lbs.

9. Install all necessary components that were removed to gain access to camshaft housing retaining bolts.

2S-E Engine

1. Remove the camshaft cover.

2. Remove the timing gears and timing belt assemblies.

3. Following the sequence shown, loosen the camshaft housing nuts and bolts in two passes. Remove the housings (with camshafts) from the cylinder head.

4. Remove the rocker arms, one at a time, from the head. As you remove each rocker, wipe it off and either tag it or mark it as to its proper location. It is critical that each rocker be re-installed in its correct location.

5. Remove each lash adjuster from the head (see Lash Adjusters Inspection below first), one at a time, and either mark or tag each one for correct installation later.

6. To install place each lash adjuster (bleed lash adjusters before installation or replace lash adjuster) and rocker arm in the correct position in the cylinder head. Check that the adjusters and rocker arms are installed in the correct order.

7. Install the camshaft housings (with camshafts) to the cylinder head. Apply seal packing to the cylinder head installation surface of the camshaft housing.

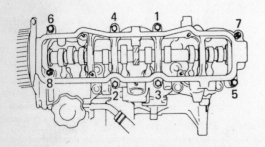

2S-E camshaft housing bolt installation sequence

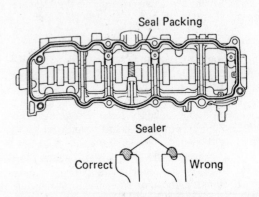

Cover the rod bolts with rubber tubing (arrow) before removing piston and rod assemblies

8. Torque the retaining bolts uniformly and in several steps, in the correct sequence to 11 ft. lbs.

9. Install all necessary components that were removed to gain access to camshaft housing retaining bolts.

INSPECTION

Inspect the all contact areas of each rocker arm for pitting and/or extreme or unusual wear: the cup end, which works against the ball of the lash adjuster; the valve stem end; and the pad on top of the rocker which works against the lobe of the camshaft. Replace the rocker arm(s) if there is evidence of such wear or surface cracks.

Hydraulic Lash Adjusters

BLEEDING

The hydraulic valve lash adjusters used on the twin cam six and the 2S-E must be bled and their leak down rate checked before they are re-assembled into the motor. Both of these procedures require special service equipment and should be performed by a professional mechanic at a quality machine shop. If you have the head disassembled for a valve job, cam replacement, etc., you will probably be taking the head to a machine shop anyway; the adjusters can be left in their recesses, removed and checked while the head is in the shop. If the lash adjusters are in doubt replace them before installing remaining components.

Oil Pressure Regulator

REMOVAL AND INSTALLATION

5M-GE Engine Twin Cam Only

NOTE: *The oil pressure regulator should be removed and checked whenever the lash adjusters have been removed and bled.*

1. Remove the No. 3 timing belt cover (see Timing Belt in this chapter). Remove the timing belt cover stay.
2. Unbolt and remove the oil pressure regulator and gasket.
3. Installation is in the reverse order of removal.

INSPECTION

Unscrew the relief valve plug and remove the spring and valve. Wipe all parts clean with a rag, and flush out the regulator body with solvent. Blow the body out with compressed air or let air dry; do not wipe out with a rag, as it may leave lint particles. Check the relief valve for scoring or wear; replace if wear is evident.

Reassembly the regulator in the reverse order of disassembly. Using a new gasket, install the regulator on the cylinder head. Install

Check condition of relief valve

the timing cover stay and timing belt cover. Check for leaks when the engine is first started.

Thermostat

REMOVAL AND INSTALLATION

All Engines

1. Disconnect the negative battery cable.
NOTE: *On 1990 SRS vehicles, you must wait AT LEAST 30 seconds after disconnecting the battery before doing any work. The SRS has a built-in backup which will allow the system to remain energized for a period of time after the power is disconnected.*
2. Drain the cooling system. Disconnect the water temperature switch connector if so equipped.
CAUTION: *When draining the coolant, keep in mind that cats and dogs are attracted by the ethylene glycol antifreeze, and are quite*

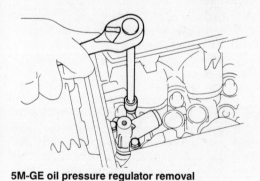

5M-GE oil pressure regulator removal

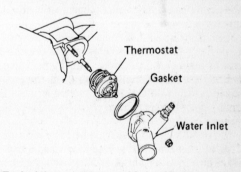

Typical thermostat assembly installation

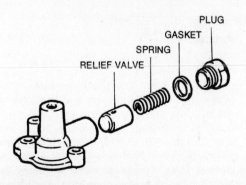

Oil pressure regulator, exploded view

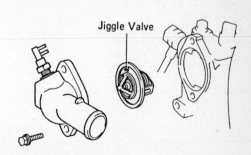

Typical thermostat assembly installation

Type A

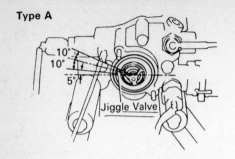

Type B

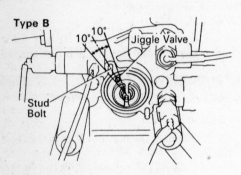

Installation of thermostat 4A-FE engine

likely to drink any that is left in an uncovered container or in puddles on the ground. This will prove fatal in sufficient quantity. Always drain the coolant into a sealable container. Coolant should be reused unless it is contaminated or several years old.

3. Unfasten the clamp and remove the radiator hose from the water outlet elbow. Unbolt and remove the water outlet (thermostat housing).

4. Withdraw the thermostat, but first note the position of the jiggle valve on the thermostat for correct installation. The jiggle valve may be set within 10° of either side of the prescribed position on the 4A-FE engine and 5° of either side of the prescribed position on the 5S-FE engine.

5. Installation is performed in the reverse order of the removal procedure. Use a new gasket on the water outlet. Make sure the ther-

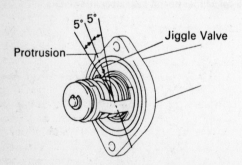

Installation of thermostat 5S-FE engine

mostat (jiggle valve on thermostat in correct location) is installed in the correct direction with a new thermostat gasket. Tighten water outlet bolts evenly (about 78 in. lbs.) in alternating steps. Refill cooling system, start engine and check for leaks.

Intake Manifold

REMOVAL AND INSTALLATION

NOTE: *Removal of the intake manifold assembly on fuel injected engines is a complicated and tedious procedure. Make sure all wire, hoses and vacuum lines are marked for simplify installation. It is advisable to have this work done by a professional (ASE certified) mechanic. If fuel lines must be disconnected for intake manifold removal ALWAYS relieve the fuel pressure.*

2S-E Engine

1. Disconnect the negative battery cable. Drain the coolant.

CAUTION: *When draining the coolant, keep in mind that cats and dogs are attracted by the ethylene glycol antifreeze, and are quite likely to drink any that is left in an uncovered container or in puddles on the ground. This will prove fatal in sufficient quantity. Always drain the coolant into a sealable container. Coolant should be reused unless it is contaminated or several years old.*

2. Disconnect and tag any wires, hoses or cable in the way of manifold removal. Remove the throttle body assembly.

3. Remove the intake manifold retaining bolts. Remove the intake manifold from the vehicle.

4. Installation is the reverse of the removal procedure. Use new gaskets, as required. Always torque all retaining bolts in progressive steps from the center to the ends to 30 ft. lbs. Refill the cooling system. Start the engine and check for leaks. Road test the vehicle for proper operation.

3S-GE and 3S-GTE Engines

1. Disconnect the negative battery cable. Drain the coolant. Remove the air cleaner assembly.

CAUTION: *When draining the coolant, keep in mind that cats and dogs are attracted by the ethylene glycol antifreeze, and are quite likely to drink any that is left in an uncovered container or in puddles on the ground. This will prove fatal in sufficient quantity. Always drain the coolant into a sealable container. Coolant should be reused unless it is contaminated or several years old.*

2. Disconnect and tag wires, hoses or cables in the way of manifold removal.

3. Remove the necessary components in order to gain access to the intake manifold retaining bolts.

4. Remove the intake manifold retaining bolts and intake manifold stays. Remove the intake manifold from the vehicle.

5. Installation is in the reverse of the removal procedure. Use new gaskets, as required.

6. Always torque manifold retaining bolts in progressive steps from the center to the ends to 14 ft. lbs. Install the intake manifold stays in the correct potion. Refill the cooling system. Start the engine and check for leaks. Road test the vehicle for proper operation.

3S-FE and 5S-FE Engines

1. Disconnect the negative battery cable. Drain the coolant. Remove the air cleaner assembly.

CAUTION: *When draining the coolant, keep in mind that cats and dogs are attracted by the ethylene glycol antifreeze, and are quite likely to drink any that is left in an uncovered container or in puddles on the ground. This will prove fatal in sufficient quantity. Always drain the coolant into a sealable container. Coolant should be reused unless it is contaminated or several years old.*

NOTE: *On 1990 SRS vehicles, you must wait AT LEAST 30 seconds after disconnecting the battery before doing any work. The SRS has a built-in backup which will allow the system to remain energized for a period of time after the power is disconnected.*

2. Disconnect and tag wires, hoses or cables in the way of manifold removal.

3. Remove the necessary components in order to gain access to the intake manifold retaining bolts.

4. Remove the throttle body assembly. Remove the cold start injector pipe.

5. Remove the air tube assembly. If equipped with power steering remove the hoses before removing the air tube assembly.

6. Remove the intake manifold retaining bolts. Remove the intake manifold from the vehicle.

7. Install intake manifold assembly using new gaskets, as required. Tighten the intake manifold mounting bolts to 14 ft. lbs. (always torque manifold retaining bolts in progressive steps from the center to the ends). Tighten the 12mm manifold stay bolt to 14 ft. lbs., tighten the 14mm bolts to 31 ft. lbs.

8. Install the air tube assembly. If equipped with power steering install the hoses to the air tube assembly.

9. Install the throttle body assembly. In-

stall the cold start injector pipe.

10. Install all the necessary components that were removed in order to gain access to the intake manifold retaining bolts.

11. Reconnect all wires, hoses or cables that were removed for manifold removal. Install the air cleaner assembly.

12. Connect the negative battery cable. Refill all fluid levels with the specified fluid to the correct level. Start the engine and check for leaks. Roadtest the vehicle for proper operation

4A-FE Engine

1. Disconnect the negative battery cable. Drain the coolant. Remove the air cleaner assembly.

CAUTION: *When draining the coolant, keep in mind that cats and dogs are attracted by the ethylene glycol antifreeze, and are quite likely to drink any that is left in an uncovered container or in puddles on the ground. This will prove fatal in sufficient quantity. Always drain the coolant into a sealable container. Coolant should be reused unless it is contaminated or several years old.*

NOTE: *On 1990 SRS vehicles, you must wait AT LEAST 30 seconds after disconnecting the battery before doing any work. The SRS has a built-in backup which will allow the system to remain energized for a period of time after the power is disconnected.*

2. Disconnect and tag wires, hoses or cables in the way of manifold removal.

3. Remove the necessary components in order to gain access to the intake manifold retaining bolts.

4. Remove the intake manifold retaining bolts and stays. Remove the intake manifold from the vehicle.

5. Installation is the reverse of the removal procedure. Use new gaskets, as required.

6. Always torque manifold retaining bolts in progressive steps from the center to the ends to 14 ft. lbs. Install the intake manifold stays in the correct position. Refill the cooling system. Start the engine and check for leaks. Roadtest the vehicle for proper operation.

5M-GE Engines

1. Disconnect the negative battery cable. Drain the engine coolant.

CAUTION: *When draining the coolant, keep in mind that cats and dogs are attracted by the ethylene glycol antifreeze, and are quite likely to drink any that is left in an uncovered container or in puddles on the ground. This will prove fatal in sufficient quantity. Always drain the coolant into a sealable container. Coolant should be reused unless it is contaminated or several years old.*

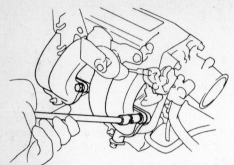

Removing air chamber and throttle body from intake manifold

2. Disconnect and tag wires, hoses or cables in the way of manifold removal.

3. Remove the air intake chamber. Disconnect and move the wiring away from the fuel delivery and injector pipe. Remove the fuel injector and delivery pipe.

4. Remove the fuel pressure regulator, which is mounted on the center of the intake manifold.

5. Remove the EGR valve from the rear of the manifold. Mark and disconnect the radiator hoses, heater hoses, and vacuum lines from the intake manifold.

6. Remove the distributor cap and position it out of the way.

7. Remove the intake manifold retaining bolts. Remove the intake manifold and gasket from the engine.

8. Install the intake manifold assembly to the engine. Use new gaskets, as required. Torque the manifold fasteners to 15 ft. lbs. Always torque manifold retaining bolts in progressive steps from the center to the ends. Install the intake manifold stays in the correct position if so equipped.

9. Install the distributor cap. Install the EGR valve to the rear of the manifold. Reconnect all the radiator hoses, heater hoses, and vacuum lines to the intake manifold.

10. Install the fuel pressure regulator, which

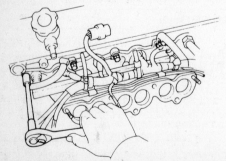

5M-GE engine intake manifold removal; when installing torque to specification

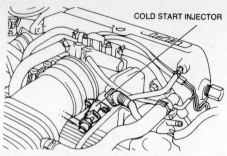

Cold start injector location 5M-GE engine

is mounted on the center of the intake manifold.

11. Install the air intake chamber. Reconnect the wiring for fuel delivery system. Install the fuel injector and delivery pipe as required.

12. Reconnect all wires, hoses or cables that were disconnected for manifold removal.

13. Refill the cooling system. Start the engine and check for leaks. Roadtest the vehicle for proper operation.

7M-GE and 7M-GTE Engines

1. Disconnect the negative battery cable. Drain the coolant. Remove the air cleaner assembly.

CAUTION: *When draining the coolant, keep in mind that cats and dogs are attracted by the ethylene glycol antifreeze, and are quite likely to drink any that is left in an uncovered container or in puddles on the ground. This will prove fatal in sufficient quantity. Always drain the coolant into a sealable container. Coolant should be reused unless it is contaminated or several years old.*

NOTE: *On 1990 SRS vehicles, you must wait AT LEAST 30 seconds after disconnecting the battery before doing any work. The SRS has a built-in backup which will allow the system to remain energized for a period of time after the power is disconnected.*

2. Disconnect and tag wires, hoses or cables in the way of manifold removal.

3. Remove the necessary components in order to gain access to the intake manifold retaining bolts.

4. Remove the air intake connector along with the air intake chamber assembly.

5. Remove the fuel delivery pipe with the injectors still attached.

NOTE: *Be careful that the injectors do not fall out of the delivery pipe.*

6. Remove the intake manifold retaining bolts. Remove the intake manifold from the vehicle.

7. Installation is the reverse of the removal procedure. Use new gaskets, as required.

Always torque manifold retaining bolts in progressive steps from the center to the ends to 15 ft. lbs. Install the intake manifold stays in the correct position. Refill the cooling system. Start the engine and check for leaks. Roadtest the vehicle for proper operation.

Exhaust Manifold

REMOVAL AND INSTALLATION

2S-E Engine

1. Disconnect the negative battery cable. Raise the vehicle and support it safely as necessary. Remove the right hand gravel shield from beneath the engine.

2. Remove the exhaust pipe support bracket. Unfasten the bolts (soak bolts with penetrating oil or equivalent) from the flange and detach the exhaust pipe from the manifold.

3. Remove the air cleaner stove hoses from the exhaust manifold, if so equipped. Remove the EGR valve, if so equipped.

4. Remove, or move aside, any of the air injection system components which may be in the way when removing the manifold.

5. Remove the exhaust manifold retaining bolts, in two or three stages, starting from the inside, working out. Remove the exhaust manifold from the vehicle.

6. Install the exhaust manifold to the engine block. Use a new gasket, as required. Tighten the exhaust manifold retaining bolts from the center to the ends in steps to 32 ft. lbs.

7. Install all air injection components. Install the EGR valve.

8. Install the air cleaner stove hoses to the exhaust manifold, if so equipped.

9. Install the exhaust pipe and brackets (stays) to the exhaust manifold (use new exhaust pipe gaskets as required).

10. Install gravel shield and reconnect the battery cable. Start engine and check for exhaust leaks.

3S-GE and 3S-GTE Engines

1. Disconnect the negative battery cable. Raise and support the vehicle safely as necessary. Remove the right hand gravel shield from underneath the car.

NOTE: *On 1990 SRS vehicles, you must wait AT LEAST 30 seconds after disconnecting the battery before doing any work. The SRS has a built-in backup which will allow the system to remain energized for a period of time after the power is disconnected.*

2. Remove the exhaust pipe support stay. Unbolt (soak bolts with penetrating oil or equivalent) the exhaust pipe from the exhaust manifold flange.

3. Disconnect the oxygen sensor connector.

On the 3S-GE engine, remove the upper heat insulator.

4. Remove the manifold retaining bolts. Remove the exhaust manifold from the vehicle.

5. Installation is the reverse of the removal procedure. Use a new gasket on exhaust manifold and exhaust pipe as required. Torque all retaining nuts and bolts evenly working from the center to the ends in steps to the specified torque. Reconnect the battery cable. Start engine and check for exhaust leaks.

3S-FE and 5S-FE Engines

1. Disconnect the negative battery cable. Remove the exhaust manifold heat insulator shield assembly.

NOTE: *On 1990 SRS vehicles, you must wait AT LEAST 30 seconds after disconnecting the battery before doing any work. The SRS has a built-in backup which will allow the system to remain energized for a period of time after the power is disconnected.*

2. Remove the necessary components in order to gain access to the exhaust manifold retaining bolts.

3. Disconnect the exhaust manifold bolts (soak bolts with penetrating oil or equivalent) at the exhaust pipe. It may be necessary to raise and support the vehicle safely before removing these bolts.

4. Remove the exhaust manifold retaining bolts. Remove the exhaust manifold from the vehicle.

5. Installation is the reverse of the removal procedure. Use a new gasket on exhaust manifold and exhaust pipe as required. Torque all retaining nuts and bolts evenly working from the center to the ends in steps to the specified torque. Reconnect the battery cable. Start engine and check for exhaust leaks.

4A-FE Engine

1. Disconnect the negative battery cable. Raise and support the vehicle safely as necessary. Remove the right hand gravel shield from underneath the car.

NOTE: *On 1990 SRS vehicles, you must wait AT LEAST 30 seconds after disconnecting the battery before doing any work. The SRS has a built-in backup which will allow the system to remain energized for a period of time after the power is disconnected.*

2. Remove the exhaust pipe support stay. Unbolt (soak bolts with penetrating oil or equivalent) the exhaust pipe from the exhaust manifold flange.

3. Disconnect the oxygen sensor connector. Remove the upper heat insulator.

4. Remove the manifold retaining bolts. Remove the exhaust manifold from the vehicle.

5. Installation is the reverse of the removal procedure. Use a new gasket on exhaust manifold and exhaust pipe as required. Torque all retaining nuts and bolts evenly working from the center to the ends in steps to 18 ft. lbs. Reconnect the battery cable. Start engine and check for exhaust leaks.

5M-GE Engine

1. Disconnect the negative battery cable. Raise and support the vehicle safely as necessary. Remove the right hand gravel shield from underneath the car.

NOTE: *The air intake hose may have to be removed to gain access to all the manifold retaining bolts.*

2. Remove the exhaust pipe support stay. Unbolt (soak bolts with penetrating oil or equivalent) the exhaust pipe from the exhaust manifold flange.

3. Disconnect the oxygen sensor connector.

4. Remove the manifold retaining bolts. Remove the exhaust manifold from the vehicle.

5. Installation is the reverse of the removal procedure. Use a new gasket on exhaust manifold and exhaust pipe as required. Torque all retaining nuts and bolts evenly working from the center to the ends in steps to 30 ft. lbs. Reconnect the battery cable. Start engine and check for exhaust leaks.

7M-GE and 7M-GTE Engines

1. Disconnect the negative battery cable. Remove the exhaust manifold heat insulator shield assembly, if so equipped.

NOTE: *On 1990 SRS vehicles, you must wait AT LEAST 30 seconds after disconnecting the battery before doing any work. The SRS has a built-in backup which will allow the system to remain energized for a period of time after the power is disconnected.*

2. Remove the necessary components in order to gain access to the exhaust manifold retaining bolts.

3. Disconnect the exhaust manifold bolts (soak bolts with penetrating oil or equivalent) at the exhaust pipe. It may be necessary to raise and support the vehicle safely before removing these bolts.

4. If equipped with turbocharger, remove the turbocharger assembly from the vehicle. Remove the exhaust manifold retaining bolts. Remove the exhaust manifold from the vehicle.

5. Installation is the reverse of the removal procedure. Use a new gasket on exhaust manifold and exhaust pipe as required. Torque all retaining nuts and bolts evenly working from the center to the ends in steps to 30 ft. lbs. Reconnect the battery cable. Start engine and check for exhaust leaks.

Turbocharger Assembly

REMOVAL AND INSTALLATION

3S-GTE Engine

1. Disconnect the negative battery cable. Raise and support the vehicle safely as necessary to complete this service operation.

NOTE: *On 1990 SRS vehicles, you must wait AT LEAST 30 seconds after disconnecting the battery before doing any work. The SRS has a built-in backup which will allow the system to remain energized for a period of time after the power is disconnected.*

2. Drain the engine coolant. Drain the intercooler coolant.

CAUTION: *When draining the coolant, keep in mind that cats and dogs are attracted by the ethylene glycol antifreeze, and are quite likely to drink any that is left in an uncovered container or in puddles on the ground. This will prove fatal in sufficient quantity. Always drain the coolant into a sealable container. Coolant should be reused unless it is contaminated or several years old.*

3. Remove the air cleaner assembly. Remove the catalytic converter and all necessary brackets.

4. Remove the oxygen sensor.

5. Remove the intercooler assembly as follows:

   a. Disconnect the intercooler radiator water hoses.

   b. Remove the reservoir tank water hose.

   c. Disconnect the intercooler coolant level warning sensor connector.

   e. Disconnect the intercooler air hoses. Remove the intercooler assembly retaining bolts.

6. Remove the alternator duct. Remove the No. 2 alternator mounting bracket.

7. Remove the turbocharger heat insulator.

8. Remove the heat insulator of turbine outlet elbow. Remove the turbine outlet elbow.

9. Remove the turbocharger retaining stay. Disconnect all water and oil pipe lines. Remove the turbocharger unit from the vehicle.

NOTE: *After replacing the turbocharger assembly, pour or squirt new oil into the oil (about 20cc new oil) inlet and turn the impeller wheel by hand to splash (circulate) oil on the bearing.*

10. To install the turbocharger unit, install the turbocharger water and oil pipe assemblies to the unit using new mounting gaskets.

11. Mount the turbocharger assembly, using new gaskets and temporarily tighten all nuts and bolts.

12. Torque the turbocharger to exhaust manifold mounting nuts to 47 ft. lbs. Connect all

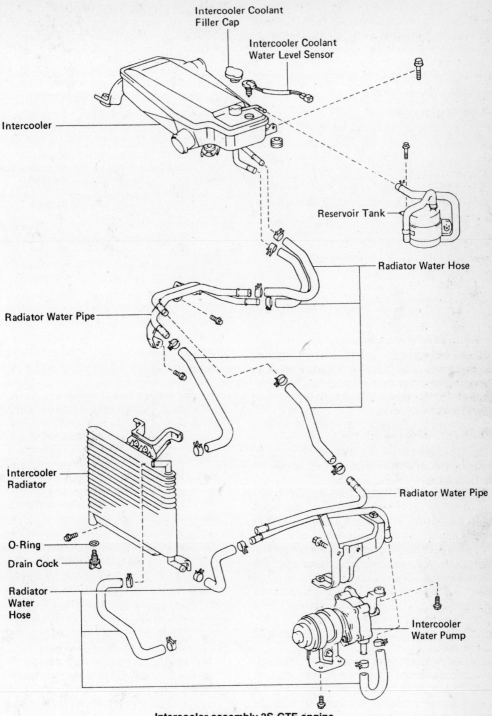

Intercooler Coolant
Filler Cap

Intercooler Coolant
Water Level Sensor

Intercooler

Reservoir Tank

Radiator Water Hose

Radiator Water Pipe

Intercooler
Radiator

Radiator Water Pipe

O-Ring

Drain Cock

Radiator
Water
Hose

Intercooler
Water Pump

Intercooler assembly 3S-GTE engine

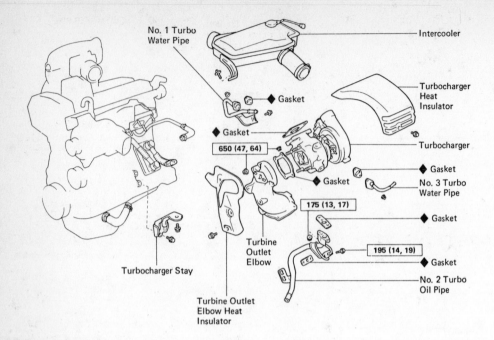

No. 1 Turbo Water Pipe

Intercooler

Gasket

Gasket

650 (47, 64)

Turbocharger Heat Insulator

Turbocharger

◆ Gasket

Gasket

No. 3 Turbo Water Pipe

175 (13, 17)

◆ Gasket

Turbine Outlet Elbow

195 (14, 19)

◆ Gasket

No. 2 Turbo Oil Pipe

Turbocharger Stay

Turbine Outlet Elbow Heat Insulator

| kg-cm (ft-lb, N·m) | : Specified torque
◆ Non-reusable part

Turbocharger assembly 3S-GTE engine

oil, water and vacuum hoses to the turbocharger assembly.

13. Install the turbocharger stay (mounting bracket) to the correct location.

14. Install the turbine outlet elbow.

15. Install heat insulator of turbine outlet elbow.

16. Install turbocharger heat insulator. Install the alternator bracket and alternator duct.

17. Install the intercooler assembly as follows:

a. Install the intercooler assembly retaining bolts. Connect the intercooler radiator water hoses.

b. Install the reservoir tank water hose.

c. Reconnect the intercooler coolant level warning sensor connector.

e. Reconnect the intercooler air hoses as necessary.

18. Install the oxygen sensor. Install the catalytic converter and all necessary brackets.

19. Install the air cleaner assembly.

20. Refill the engine and intercooler with the specified coolant to the correct level. Reconnect the battery cable and check oil level. Start engine check for any fluid leaks. Roadtest the vehicle for proper operation.

7M-GTE Engine

1. Disconnect the negative battery cable.

NOTE: *On 1990 SRS vehicles, you must wait AT LEAST 30 seconds after disconnecting the battery before doing any work. The SRS has a built-in backup which will allow the system to remain energized for a period of time after the power is disconnected.*

2. Drain the coolant.

CAUTION: *When draining the coolant, keep in mind that cats and dogs are attracted by the ethylene glycol antifreeze, and are quite likely to drink any that is left in an uncovered container or in puddles on the ground. This will prove fatal in sufficient quantity. Always drain the coolant into a sealable container. Coolant should be reused unless it is contaminated or several years old.*

3. Remove the air cleaner hoses and pipes, and also the air flow meter and air cleaner cap.

4. Disconnect the oxygen sensor connector and remove the turbo heat insulator.

5. Remove the oil dipstick guide.

6. Remove the three nuts and disconnect the front exhaust pipe.

7. Remove the oil outlet pipe mounting nuts.

8. Remove the oil inlet pipe mounting union bolt.

9. Remove the turbocharger stays (brackets).

10. Disconnect the turbo water hose from the outlet housing.

11. Disconnect the water by-pass pipe union.

12. Remove the turbocharger assembly.

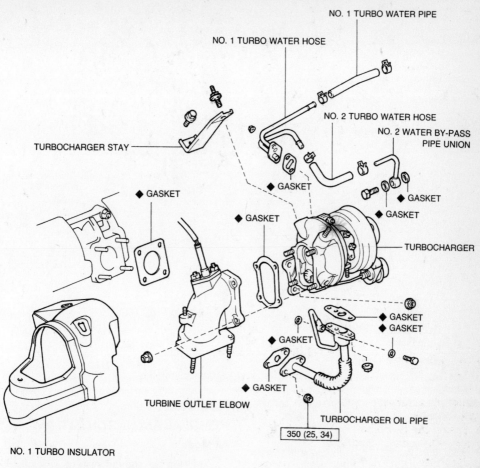

NO. 1 TURBO WATER PIPE

NO. 1 TURBO WATER HOSE

NO. 2 TURBO WATER HOSE

NO. 2 WATER BY-PASS
PIPE UNION

TURBOCHARGER STAY

◆ GASKET

◆ GASKET

◆ GASKET

◆ GASKET

◆ GASKET

TURBOCHARGER

◆ GASKET
◆ GASKET

◆ GASKET

◆ GASKET

TURBINE OUTLET ELBOW

TURBOCHARGER OIL PIPE

350 (25, 34)

NO. 1 TURBO INSULATOR

KG-CM (FT-LB, N·M) : SPECIFIED TORQUE
◆ NON-REUSABLE PART

Turbocharger assembly 7M-GTE engine

NOTE: *After replacing the turbocharger assembly, pour or squirt new oil into the oil inlet and turn the impeller wheel by hand to splash oil on the bearing.*

13. To install the turbocharger unit, install the turbine outlet elbow with a new gasket and torque the four nuts to 38 ft. lbs.

14. Install the oil pipe with a new gasket.

15. Install the water turbo pipe with a new gasket.

16. Mount the turbocharger assembly, using new gaskets and temporarily tighten all nuts and bolts.

17. Torque the turbocharger mounting nuts to 33 ft. lbs. and torque the oil pipe union bolt to 25 ft. lbs.; and flange nuts to 9 ft. lbs.

18. Connect the water by-pass pipe union with a new gasket.

19. Connect the water hose to the outlet housing.

20. Install the short turbocharger mounting stay (bracket).

21. Install the long turbocharger mounting

stay (bracket) and torque the turbocharger end to 59 ft. lbs. and the engine end to 43 ft. lbs.

22. Install the oil inlet pipe.

23. The remainder of the installation is the reverse of removal. Fill with coolant and check for leaks. Roadtest the vehicle for proper operation.

Air Conditioning Compressor

NOTE: *Refer to Chapter 1 for Charging and Discharging procedures as necessary.*

REMOVAL AND INSTALLATION

All Models

1. Run engine at idle speed with air conditioning on for 10 minutes. Stop engine.

2. Disconnect negative battery cable from battery. On 1990 SRS vehicles, you must wait AT LEAST 30 seconds after disconnecting the battery before doing any work. The SRS has a built-in backup which will allow the system to

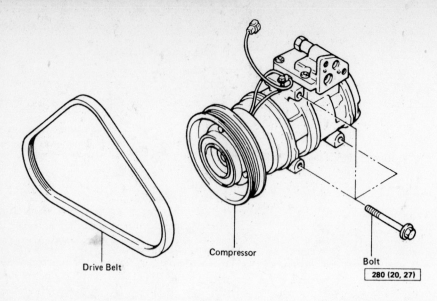

Drive Belt

Compressor

Bolt
280 (20, 27)

kg-cm (ft-lb, N·m) : Specified torque

Typical A/C compressor mounting

remain energized for a period of time after the power is disconnected.

3. Remove the battery from the vehicle.

4. Disconnect all electrical connections from the air conditioning compressor.

5. Discharge refrigerant from the refrigerant system as necessary.

6. Disconnect two hoses from compressor service valves. Cap or plug the open fitting to keep moisture out of the system.

7. Loosen the air conditioning drive belt. Remove the compressor mounting bolts and the compressor.

8. Install air conditioning compressor with the necessary mounting bolts. Torque the retaining bolts to 20 ft. lbs.

9. Install and adjust the AC compressor drive belt.

10. Reconnect air conditioning hoses to the compressor services valves. Always replace the O-rings or gaskets as required.

11. Connect all electrical connections to the air conditioning compressor.

12. Install the battery. Reconnect negative battery cable to battery.

13. Make sure the air conditioning compressor oil level is correct. Charge the system with the correct amount of refrigerant (usually stamped on label on compressor housing) and check for leaks.

Radiator
REMOVAL AND INSTALLATION
All Models

1. Drain the cooling system.

CAUTION: *When draining the coolant, keep in mind that cats and dogs are attracted by the ethylene glycol antifreeze, and are quite likely to drink any that is left in an uncovered container or in puddles on the ground. This will prove fatal in sufficient quantity. Always drain the coolant into a sealable container. Coolant should be reused unless it is contaminated or several years old.*

2. Unfasten the hose clamps and remove the radiator upper and lower hoses. If equipped with an automatic transmission, remove the oil cooler lines using suitable line wrenches.

3. Detach the hood lock cable and remove the hood lock from the radiator upper support if so equipped.

NOTE: *It may be necessary to remove the grille in order to gain access to the hood lock/radiator support assembly.*

4. Disconnect the condenser fan motor connection. Remove the fan shroud, if so equipped.

5. On models equipped with a coolant recovery system, disconnect the hose form the thermal expansion tank and remove the tank from its bracket.

6. Unbolt and remove the radiator upper support.

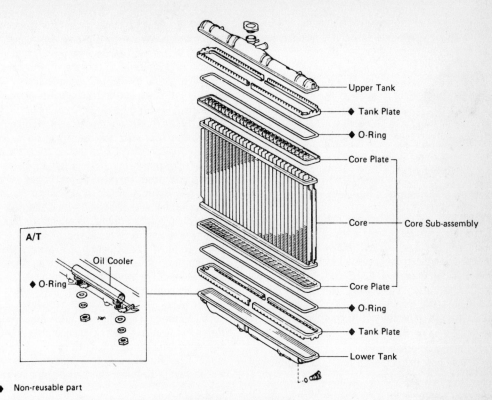

Upper Tank
◆ Tank Plate
◆ O-Ring
Core Plate
Core — Core Sub-assembly
Core Plate
◆ O-Ring
◆ Tank Plate
Lower Tank

A/T

Oil Cooler

◆ O-Ring

◆ Non-reusable part

Radiator components

7. Unfasten the bolts and remove the radiator. Use care not to damage the radiator fins or the cooling fan.

8. Installation is performed in the reverse order of removal. Remember to check the transmission fluid level on cars with automatic transmissions. (See Chapter 1).

9. Fill the radiator to the specified level as detailed under Fluid Level Checks, in Chapter 1.

Condenser

REMOVAL AND INSTALLATION

Celica

1. Disconnect negative battery cable from battery. On 1990 SRS vehicles, you must wait AT LEAST 30 seconds after disconnecting the battery before doing any work. The SRS has a built-in backup which will allow the system to remain energized for a period of time after the power is disconnected.

2. Discharge refrigerant from the refrigerant system as necessary.

3. Remove the front grille and front under cover.

4. Remove the center brace and hood lock brace assemblies as one unit. Disconnect the electrical connections from the horns and remove the horns.

5. Disconnect the electrical connections from the condenser fan and remove the condenser fan assembly.

6. Disconnect all refrigerant lines from the air conditioning condenser. Cap the open fittings to keep moisture out of the system.

7. Remove the air conditioning condenser retaining bolts and remove the condenser from the vehicle.

8. Install the air conditioning condenser with retaining bolts making sure the rubber cushions (washers) fit in the correct position.

9. Uncap and reconnect all refrigerant lines to the air conditioning condenser.

10. Install center brace, horns (all electrical connections as necessary), front grille and undercover.

11. If air conditioning condenser was replaced during this service operation add 1.5 fluid ounces to the air conditioning compressor.

12. Charge air conditioning system with the correct amount of refrigerant and check for leakage.

Supra

1. Disconnect negative battery cable from battery. On 1990 SRS vehicles, you must wait

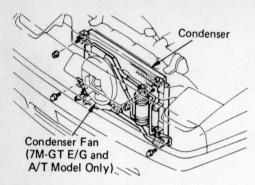

Condenser installation – Supra

AT LEAST 30 seconds after disconnecting the battery before doing any work. The SRS has a built-in backup which will allow the system to remain energized for a period of time after the power is disconnected.

2. Discharge refrigerant from the refrigerant system as necessary.

3. Remove the following components as required:

    a. Hood lock brace

    b. Center brace with horn (disconnect all electrical connections)

    c. Washer tank with the bracket attached

    d. On 7M-GTE engine, remove the engine undercover, intercooler and oil cooler assemblies.

    e. On 7M-GTE engine and automatic transmission vehicles remove the condenser fan (disconnect all electrical connections).

4. Disconnect all refrigerant lines from the air conditioning condenser. Cap the open fittings to keep moisture out of the system.

5. Remove the air conditioning condenser retaining bolts and remove the condenser from the vehicle.

6. To install the air conditioning condenser reverse the removal procedure. Install the air conditioning condenser with retaining bolts making sure the rubber cushions (washers) fit in the correct position.

7. If air conditioning condenser was replaced during this service operation add 1.5 fluid ounces to the air conditioning compressor.

8. Charge air conditioning system with the correct amount of refrigerant and check for leakage.

Water Pump

REMOVAL AND INSTALLATION

All Celica Engines Except 4A-FE Engine

1. Disconnect the negative battery cable. Disconnect the water temperature switch connector if so equipped.

NOTE: *On 1990 SRS vehicles, you must wait AT LEAST 30 seconds after disconnecting the battery before doing any work. The SRS has a built-in backup which will allow the system to remain energized for a period of time after the power is disconnected.*

2. Drain the cooling system in to suitable container if coolant is to be used again.

CAUTION: *When draining the coolant, keep in mind that cats and dogs are attracted by the ethylene glycol antifreeze, and are quite likely to drink any that is left in an uncovered container or in puddles on the ground. This will prove fatal in sufficient quantity. Always drain the coolant into a sealable container. Coolant should be reused unless it is contaminated or several years old.*

3. Remove the alternator, brackets (adjusting bar) and idler pulley bracket as necessary for clearance for water pump removal.

4. Disconnect the radiator water inlet hose (lower hose).

5. Remove the timing belt and pulleys. Refer to the correct service procedure BEFORE you start this service operation.

6. Disconnect water by-pass hose from water pump. Remove the heater pipe as necessary.

7. Remove the retaining nuts holding the water by-pass pipe to the water pump. Remove the water pump assembly. Remove the water pump, O-ring and gasket.

8. To install assemble the water pump and pump cover using a new gasket and O-rings. Torque the water pump cover retaining bolts to 7 ft. lbs.

9. Install the water pump assembly to engine using a new gasket. Torque the retaining bolts to 7 ft. lbs. using the following sequence top bolt, middle then bottom retaining bolt.

10. Install the heater pipe, connect water by-pass hose. Tighten nuts holding water by-pass pipe to water pump.

11. Install alternator adjusting bar (bracket).

12. Install pulleys and timing belt. Make sure that the timing belt assembly is installed in the correct manner.

13. Install idler pulley and alternator brackets. Connect radiator (lower) inlet hose. Install the alternator and electrical connections. Reconnect battery cable and water temperature switch connector if so equipped.

14. Refill the engine with the correct amount of the specified coolant. Start the engine and check for leaks.

Celica 4A-FE Engine

1. Disconnect the negative battery cable.

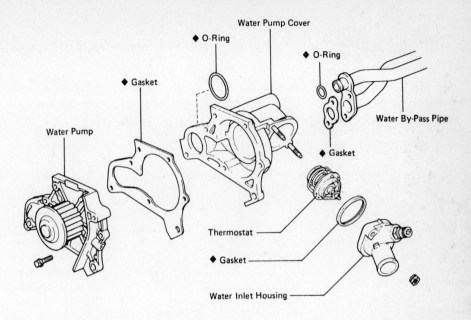

◆ Non-reusable part

Water pump installation − Celica

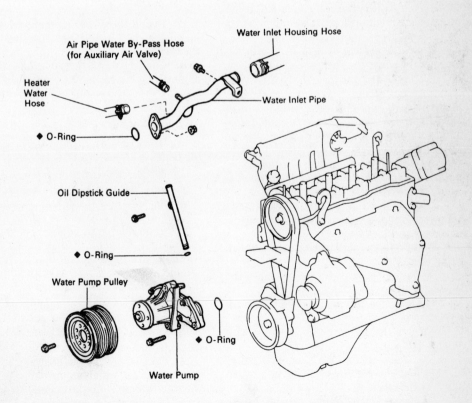

◆ Non-reusable part

Water pump installation − Celica 4A-FE engine

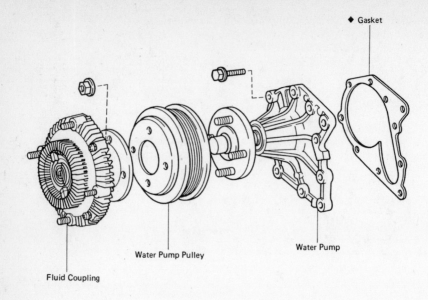

◆ Gasket

Water Pump

Water Pump Pulley

Fluid Coupling

◆ Non-reusable part

Water pump installation — Supra

NOTE: *On 1990 SRS vehicles, you must wait AT LEAST 30 seconds after disconnecting the battery before doing any work. The SRS has a built-in backup which will allow the system to remain energized for a period of time after the power is disconnected.*

2. Drain the cooling system in to suitable container if coolant is to be used again.

CAUTION: *When draining the coolant, keep in mind that cats and dogs are attracted by the ethylene glycol antifreeze, and are quite likely to drink any that is left in an uncovered container or in puddles on the ground. This will prove fatal in sufficient quantity. Always drain the coolant into a sealable container. Coolant should be reused unless it is contaminated or several years old.*

3. Remove the timing belt covers (upper and lower) to gain access to the water pump assembly.

4. Remove the power steering drive belt adjusting bracket.

5. Disconnect all water hoses. Remove the water inlet pipe.

6. Remove the oil dipstick and dipstick guide.

7. Remove the water pump (O-ring) with the drive pulley as an assembly.

8. To install water pump assembly (pulley must be on pump) place new O-ring in position on the engine block.

9. Torque the water pump retaining bolts to 11 ft. lbs. in steps.

10. Install oil dipstick guide with retaining bolt and dipstick.

11. Install water inlet pipe with new O-ring. Connect all water hoses using new water hose clamps if necessary to the water pump assembly.

12. Install the power steering drive belt adjusting bracket. Install the timing belt covers in the correct location.

13. Connect the battery cable. Refill the engine with the correct amount of the specified coolant. Start the engine and check for leaks.

All Supra Engines

1. Drain coolant. Remove the air conditioning belt.

CAUTION: *When draining the coolant, keep in mind that cats and dogs are attracted by the ethylene glycol antifreeze, and are quite likely to drink any that is left in an uncovered container or in puddles on the ground. This will prove fatal in sufficient quantity. Always drain the coolant into a sealable container. Coolant should be reused unless it is contaminated or several years old.*

2. Remove the fan assembly from the fluid coupling.

3. Remove the alternator drive belt, fluid coupling and water pump pulley.

4. Remove the power steering air pipe to gain access for water pump removal. Remove the water pump from the engine.

5. Installation is performed in the reverse order of removal. Always use a new gasket between the pump body and its mounting. Torque water pump retaining bolts to 7 ft. lbs.

and water pump nut and bolt assemblies to 14 ft lbs. Refill the engine with the correct amount of the specified coolant. Remember to check for leaks after installation is completed.

Cylinder Head

REMOVAL AND INSTALLATION

2S-E Engine (Celica)

1. Disconnect the battery ground.
2. Drain the coolant.

CAUTION: *When draining the coolant, keep in mind that cats and dogs are attracted by the ethylene glycol antifreeze, and are quite likely to drink any that is left in an uncovered container or in puddles on the ground. This will prove fatal in sufficient quantity. Always drain the coolant into a sealable container. Coolant should be reused unless it is contaminated or several years old.*

3. Disconnect the throttle cable.
4. Remove the air cleaner assembly.
5. Disconnect and tag all wires connected to or running across the head.
6. Disconnect and tag all vacuum hoses connected to or running across the head.
7. Remove the vacuum pipe from the head cover.
8. Disconnect and tag any remaining cables.
9. Remove the alternator.
10. Mark and remove the distributor.
11. Remove the upper radiator hose and bypass hose.
12. Unbolt and remove the water outlet housing.
13. Disconnect the heater hoses.
14. Disconnect the two air hoses from the fuel injection air valve.
15. Unbolt and remove the rear end housing.
16. Remove the heater pipe.
17. Disconnect the fuel line at the filter and the fuel return line at the return pipe.
18. Raise and support the car on jackstands.
19. Drain the oil.

CAUTION: *The EPA warns that prolonged contact with used engine oil may cause a number of skin disorders, including cancer! You should make every effort to minimize your exposure to used engine oil. Protective gloves should be worn when changing the oil. Wash your hands and any other exposed skin areas as soon as possible after exposure to used engine oil. Soap and water, or waterless hand cleaner should be used.*

20. Disconnect the exhaust pipe at the manifold.
21. Disconnect the power steering pump hoses.
22. Remove the intake manifold stay.

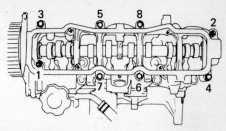

Remove camshaft housing bolts in this order Celica 2S-E engine

23. Lower the car.
24. Remove the timing belt.
25. Remove the No. 1 idler pulley and tension spring.
26. Remove the throttle body.
27. Remove the valve cover.
28. Unbolt and remove the camshaft housing. Loosen the bolts gradually in the order shown.
29. Remove the rocker arms and lash adjusters.
30. Loosen and remove the head bolts, in three passes in the order shown. Lift the head from the engine and place it on wood blocks in a clean work area.

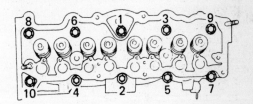

Install cylinder head bolts in this order Celica 2S-E engine

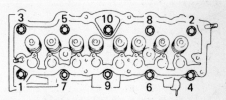

Remove cylinder head bolts in this order Celica 2S-E engine

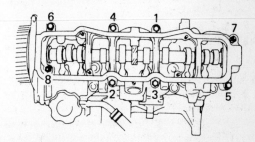

Install camshaft housing bolts in this order Celica 2S-E engine

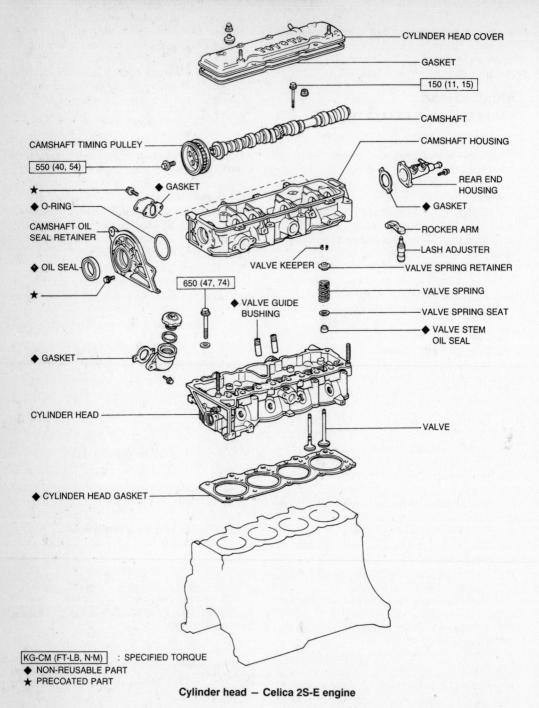

CYLINDER HEAD COVER
GASKET
150 (11, 15)
CAMSHAFT
CAMSHAFT HOUSING
CAMSHAFT TIMING PULLEY
550 (40, 54)
★
◆ GASKET
REAR END HOUSING
◆ O-RING
◆ GASKET
CAMSHAFT OIL SEAL RETAINER
ROCKER ARM
LASH ADJUSTER
◆ OIL SEAL
VALVE KEEPER
VALVE SPRING RETAINER
★
650 (47, 74)
VALVE SPRING
◆ VALVE GUIDE BUSHING
VALVE SPRING SEAT
◆ VALVE STEM OIL SEAL
◆ GASKET
CYLINDER HEAD
VALVE
◆ CYLINDER HEAD GASKET

KG-CM (FT-LB, N·M) : SPECIFIED TORQUE
◆ NON-REUSABLE PART
★ PRECOATED PART

Cylinder head — Celica 2S-E engine

31. Installation is the reverse of removal. Refer to the "Torque Specifications Chart" as required. Note the following points:

    a. Always use a new head gasket.
    b. Tighten the head bolts, in three passes, in the order shown, to 47 ft. lbs.
    c. When installing the camshaft housing, note that RTV silicone gasket compound is used in place of a gasket. Run a 2mm bead of compound around the sealing surface of the housing. Torque the housing bolts, in three passes, in the order shown, to 11 ft. lbs.
    d. Torque the fuel line connections to 22 ft. lbs.
    e. Road test the car.

3S-GE And 3S-GTE Engines (Celica)

1. Disconnect the cable at the negative terminal of the battery.

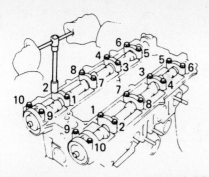

Install camshafts in this order — Celica 3S-GE and 3S-GTE engines

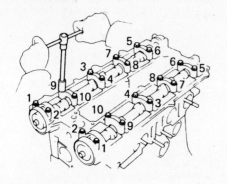

Remove camshafts in this order — Celica 3S-GE and 3S-GTE engines

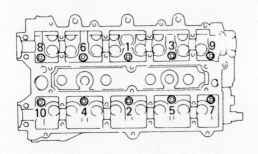

Install cylinder head bolt in this order — Celica 3S-GE and 3S-GTE engines

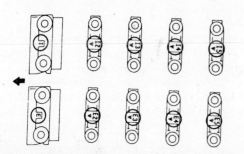

Install bearing caps in the proper location — Celica 3S-GE and 3S-GTE engines

NOTE: *On 1990 SRS vehicles, you must wait AT LEAST 30 seconds after disconnecting the battery before doing any work. The SRS has a built-in backup which will allow the system to remain energized for a period of time after the power is disconnected.*

2. Drain the engine coolant. On the 3S-GTE engine drain the intercooler coolant.

CAUTION: *When draining the coolant, keep in mind that cats and dogs are attracted by the ethylene glycol antifreeze, and are quite likely to drink any that is left in an uncovered container or in puddles on the ground. This will prove fatal in sufficient quantity. Always drain the coolant into a sealable container. Coolant should be reused unless it is contaminated or several years old.*

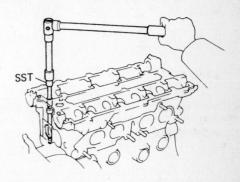

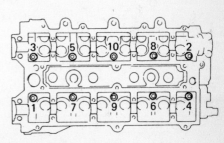

Remove cylinder head bolt in this order — Celica 3S-GE and 3S-GTE engines

3. Tag and disconnect the ignition coil connector and the spark plug wire at the ignition coil. Remove the four nuts and two bolts and lift out the upper suspension brace.

4. On models with AT, disconnect the throttle cable with its bracket from the throttle body.

5. Disconnect the accelerator cable from the throttle body.

6. Remove the radiator overflow tank.

7. Remove the cruise control actuator and its bracket.

8. Disconnect the air flow meter connector. Remove the air cleaner cap clips. Loosen the hose clamp and remove the air cleaner hose and

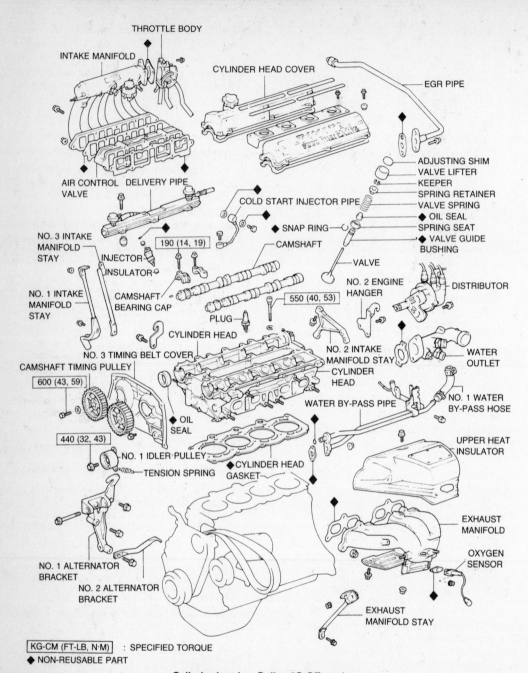

THROTTLE BODY

INTAKE MANIFOLD

CYLINDER HEAD COVER

EGR PIPE

ADJUSTING SHIM
VALVE LIFTER
KEEPER
SPRING RETAINER
VALVE SPRING
◆ OIL SEAL
SPRING SEAT
◆ VALVE GUIDE
BUSHING

AIR CONTROL VALVE   DELIVERY PIPE

COLD START INJECTOR PIPE

◆ SNAP RING

CAMSHAFT

VALVE

NO. 3 INTAKE MANIFOLD STAY

190 (14, 19)

INJECTOR INSULATOR

NO. 2 ENGINE HANGER

DISTRIBUTOR

NO. 1 INTAKE MANIFOLD STAY

CAMSHAFT BEARING CAP

550 (40, 53)

WATER OUTLET

PLUG

NO. 2 INTAKE MANIFOLD STAY

CYLINDER HEAD

NO. 3 TIMING BELT COVER

CAMSHAFT TIMING PULLEY

CYLINDER HEAD

600 (43, 59)

OIL SEAL

WATER BY-PASS PIPE

NO. 1 WATER BY-PASS HOSE

440 (32, 43)

NO. 1 IDLER PULLEY

TENSION SPRING

◆ CYLINDER HEAD GASKET

UPPER HEAT INSULATOR

NO. 1 ALTERNATOR BRACKET

NO. 2 ALTERNATOR BRACKET

EXHAUST MANIFOLD

OXYGEN SENSOR

EXHAUST MANIFOLD STAY

KG-CM (FT-LB, N·M) : SPECIFIED TORQUE
◆ NON-REUSABLE PART

Cylinder head — Celica 3S-GE engine

the air flow meter along with the air cleaner top. Lift out the filter element and then remove the air cleaner case.

9. Tag and disconnect the oxygen sensor lead. Remove the four mounting bolts and remove the exhaust manifold heat insulator.

10. Remove the alternator and its main bracket.

11. Raise the front of the vehicle and support it with safety stands. Remove the right front wheel.

12. Remove the right side engine under cover and remove the lower suspension crossmember.

13. On the 3S-GE engine disconnect the exhaust pipe at the manifold. On the 3S-GTE engine remove the turbocharger assembly and catalytic converter and attaching exhaust clamps.

14. Remove the exhaust manifold stay and the EGR pipe. Unbolt the manifold and remove it along with the lower heat insulator.

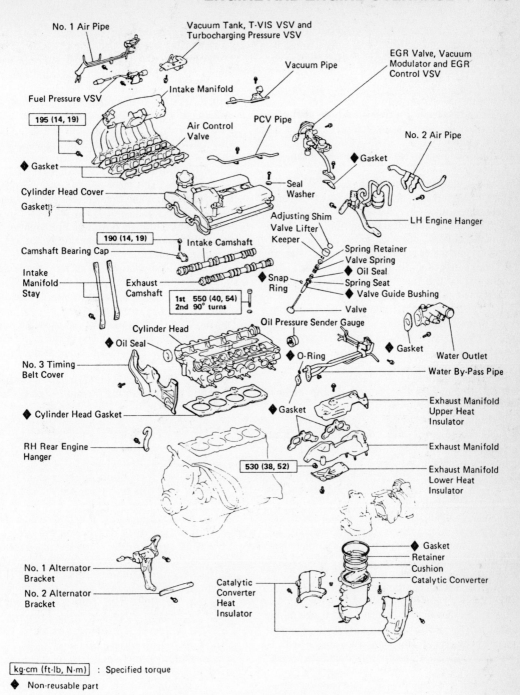

No. 1 Air Pipe

Vacuum Tank, T-VIS VSV and Turbocharging Pressure VSV

Vacuum Pipe

EGR Valve, Vacuum Modulator and EGR Control VSV

Fuel Pressure VSV

Intake Manifold

195 (14, 19)

Air Control Valve

PCV Pipe

No. 2 Air Pipe

◆ Gasket

◆ Gasket

Cylinder Head Cover

Seal Washer

Gasket

Adjusting Shim
Valve Lifter
Keeper

LH Engine Hanger

190 (14, 19)

Intake Camshaft

Spring Retainer
Valve Spring
◆ Oil Seal
Spring Seat
◆ Valve Guide Bushing

Camshaft Bearing Cap

Intake Manifold Stay

Exhaust Camshaft

◆ Snap Ring

1st 550 (40, 54)
2nd 90° turns

Valve

Cylinder Head

Oil Pressure Sender Gauge

◆ Oil Seal

◆ Gasket

Water Outlet

No. 3 Timing Belt Cover

◆ O-Ring

Water By-Pass Pipe

◆ Cylinder Head Gasket

◆ Gasket

Exhaust Manifold Upper Heat Insulator

RH Rear Engine Hanger

Exhaust Manifold

530 (38, 52)

Exhaust Manifold Lower Heat Insulator

No. 1 Alternator Bracket

No. 2 Alternator Bracket

Catalytic Converter Heat Insulator

◆ Gasket
Retainer
Cushion
Catalytic Converter

kg·cm (ft·lb, N·m) : Specified torque

◆ Non-reusable part

Cylinder head — Celica 3S-GTE engine

15. Remove the distributor.

16. Tag and disconnect the oil pressure switch connector.

17. Tag and disconnect all electrical leads and vacuum hoses at the water outlet. Remove the upper radiator hoses, the heater outlet hose and the water bypass hose. Remove the water outlet.

18. Disconnect the heater inlet hose and the water bypass hose and then remove the water bypass pipe.

19. Disconnect the throttle position sensor lead, the ventilation hose, the air valve hose and any emission control vacuum hoses at the throttle body. Remove the four bolts and lift out the throttle body.

20. Remove the forward engine hanger and the No. 2 intake manifold stay.

21. Remove the EGR vacuum modulator.

22. Tag and disconnect any remaining vacuum hoses which may interfere with cylinder head removal.

23. Tag and disconnect the fuel injector electrical leads at the injector.

24. Disconnect the fuel inlet hose at the fuel filter. Disconnect the fuel return hose at the return pipe.

25. Remove the No. 1 and No. 3 intake manifold stays.

26. Tag and disconnect the two VSV connectors. Disconnect the two power steering vacuum hoses.

27. Remove the intake manifold and the air control valve.

28. Remove the fuel delivery pipe with the injectors attached. Pull the four injector insulators out of the injector holes in the cylinder head.

29. Remove the cylinder head cover. Remove the spark plugs.

30. Remove the No. 1 engine hanger.

31. Remove the power steering reservoir and position it out of the way with the hydraulic lines still attached.

32. Remove the camshaft timing pulleys. Remove the No. 1 idler pulley and tension spring.

33. Remove the bolt holding the No. 2 and No. 3 timing covers. Remove the four mounting bolts and remove the No. 3 timing cover.

34. Loosen and remove the camshaft bearing caps, in several stages, in the order shown. Lift out the camshafts and the oil seal.

NOTE: *When removing the camshaft bearing caps, keep them in the proper order.*

35. Loosen and remove the cylinder head bolts, in several stages, in the order shown. Remove the cylinder head.

36. To install position the cylinder head onto the cylinder block with a new gasket. Lightly coat the cylinder head bolts with engine oil, install them into the head and tighten them in several passes, in the sequence shown, to 40 ft. lbs. Refer to the "Torque Specifications Chart" as required.

NOTE: *On the 3S-GTE turbocharged engine follow the same head bolt torque procedure as stated but after final torque (40 ft. lbs.) is reached tighten the head bolts an additional 90° degrees in sequence. If any head bolt does not meet the torque specification replace the bolt.*

37. Position the camshafts into the cylinder head so that the No. 1 cam lobes are facing outward.

38. Apply silicone sealant to the outer edge of the mating surface on the No. 1 bearing cap only. Position the bearing caps over each jour-

nal with the arrows pointing forward and in numerical order from the front to the rear.

39. Lightly coat the cap bolt threads with engine oil. Tighten them in several stages, in the sequence shown, to 14 ft. lbs.

40. Check the camshaft thrust clearance.

41. Coat the inside of a new oil seal with grease and carefully tap it onto the camshaft with a drift (SST No. 09223–50010) or equivalent.

42. Install the No. 3 timing belt cover.

43. Connect the idler pulley tension spring to the pulley and the pin on the cylinder head. Install the idler pulley onto the pivot pin, force it to the left as far as it will go and tighten it. Make sure that the tension spring is not out of groove in the pin.

44. Install the camshaft timing pulleys and the timing belt.

45. Installation of the remaining components is in the reverse order of removal. Tighten the lower suspension crossmember end bolts to 154 ft. lbs. and the center bolt to 29 ft. lbs. Tighten the upper suspension brace bolts to 15 ft. lbs. and the nuts to 47 ft. lbs. Refill the engine with coolant an check the idle speed and ignition timing. Road test the vehicle for proper operation.

3S-FE And 5S-FE Engines (Celica)

1. Disconnect the negative battery cable. Drain the coolant.

CAUTION: *When draining the coolant, keep in mind that cats and dogs are attracted by the ethylene glycol antifreeze, and are quite likely to drink any that is left in an uncovered container or in puddles on the ground. This will prove fatal in sufficient quantity. Always drain the coolant into a sealable container. Coolant should be reused unless it is contaminated or several years old.*

NOTE: *On 1990 SRS vehicles, you must wait AT LEAST 30 seconds after disconnecting the battery before doing any work. The SRS has a built-in backup which will allow the system to remain energized for a period of time after the power is disconnected.*

2. If equipped with automatic transmission, disconnect the throttle cable and bracket from the throttle body.

3. Disconnect the accelerator cable and bracket from the throttle body and intake chamber.

4. If equipped with cruise control, remove the actuator and bracket. Remove the air cleaner hose. Remove the alternator.

5. On the 5S-FE engine remove the air conditioning compressor as required. Remove the oil pressure gauge, engine hangers and alternator upper bracket.

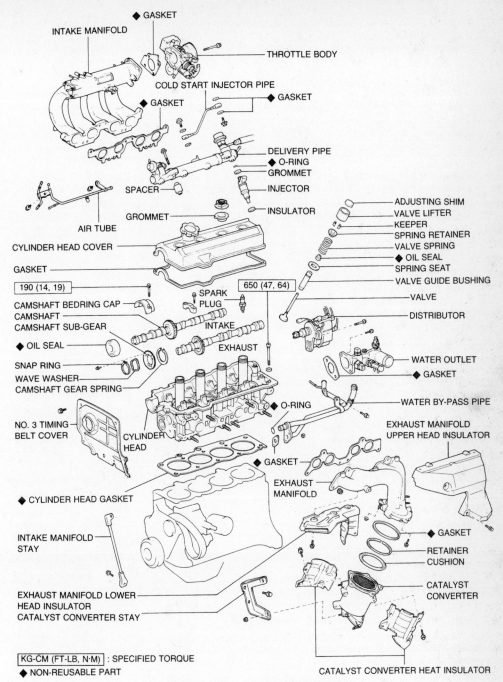

GASKET

INTAKE MANIFOLD

THROTTLE BODY

COLD START INJECTOR PIPE

◆ GASKET

◆ GASKET

DELIVERY PIPE
◆ O-RING
GROMMET

SPACER

INJECTOR

GROMMET

INSULATOR

AIR TUBE

ADJUSTING SHIM
VALVE LIFTER
KEEPER
SPRING RETAINER
VALVE SPRING
◆ OIL SEAL
SPRING SEAT
VALVE GUIDE BUSHING

CYLINDER HEAD COVER

GASKET

190 (14, 19)

650 (47, 64)

VALVE

CAMSHAFT BEDRING CAP
CAMSHAFT
CAMSHAFT SUB-GEAR

SPARK PLUG

INTAKE

DISTRIBUTOR

◆ OIL SEAL

EXHAUST

WATER OUTLET
◆ GASKET

SNAP RING
WAVE WASHER
CAMSHAFT GEAR SPRING

NO. 3 TIMING
BELT COVER

CYLINDER
HEAD

◆ O-RING

WATER BY-PASS PIPE

EXHAUST MANIFOLD
UPPER HEAD INSULATOR

◆ CYLINDER HEAD GASKET

◆ GASKET

EXHAUST
MANIFOLD

INTAKE MANIFOLD
STAY

◆ GASKET
RETAINER
CUSHION

EXHAUST MANIFOLD LOWER
HEAD INSULATOR
CATALYST CONVERTER STAY

CATALYST
CONVERTER

KG-CM (FT-LB, N·M) : SPECIFIED TORQUE
◆ NON-REUSABLE PART

CATALYST CONVERTER HEAT INSULATOR

Cylinder head — Celica 3S-FE engine

6. Raise and support the vehicle safely. Remove the right tire and wheel assembly.

7. Remove the right under cover. Remove the suspension lower crossmember. Disconnect the exhaust pipe from the catalytic converter. Separate the exhaust pipe from the catalytic converter.

8. Disconnect the water temperature sender gauge connector, water temperature sensor connector, cold start injector time switch connector, upper radiator hose, water hoses, and the emission control vacuum hoses.

9. Remove the water outlet and gaskets. Remove the distributor. Remove the water bypass pipe. Remove the EGR valve and modulator.

10. Remove the throttle body assembly. Remove the cold start injector pipe. Remove

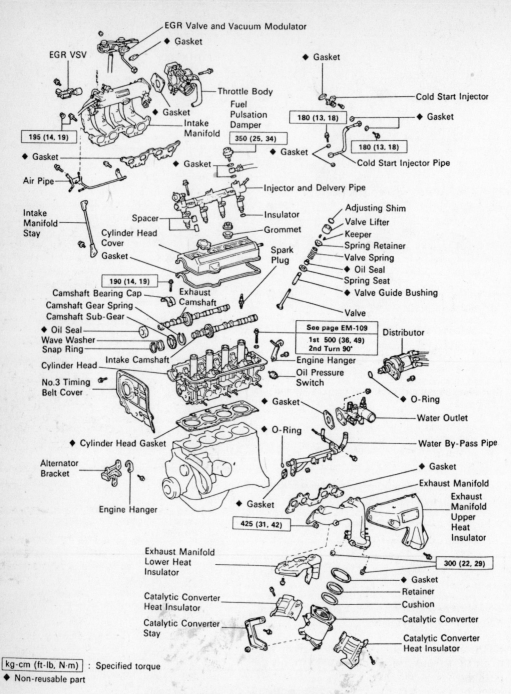

EGR Valve and Vacuum Modulator
◆ Gasket
EGR VSV
◆ Gasket
Throttle Body
Cold Start Injector
◆ Gasket
Fuel Pulsation Damper
◆ Gasket
Intake Manifold
180 (13, 18)
195 (14, 19)
350 (25, 34)
◆ Gasket
180 (13, 18)
◆ Gasket
Cold Start Injector Pipe
Air Pipe
◆ Gasket
Injector and Delvery Pipe
Intake Manifold Stay
Spacer
Insulator
Adjusting Shim
Valve Lifter
Cylinder Head Cover
Grommet
Keeper
Spring Retainer
Gasket
Spark Plug
Valve Spring
◆ Oil Seal
190 (14, 19)
Spring Seat
Camshaft Bearing Cap
Exhaust Camshaft
◆ Valve Guide Bushing
Camshaft Gear Spring
Camshaft Sub-Gear
Valve
◆ Oil Seal
See page EM-109
Wave Washer
1st 500 (36, 49)
Distributor
Snap Ring
2nd Turn 90°
Intake Camshaft
Engine Hanger
◆ O-Ring
Cylinder Head
Oil Pressure Switch
No.3 Timing Belt Cover
◆ Gasket
Water Outlet
◆ O-Ring
Water By-Pass Pipe
◆ Cylinder Head Gasket
◆ Gasket
Alternator Bracket
Exhaust Manifold
Engine Hanger
Exhaust Manifold Upper Heat Insulator
◆ Gasket
425 (31, 42)
300 (22, 29)
Exhaust Manifold Lower Heat Insulator
◆ Gasket
Retainer
Catalytic Converter Heat Insulator
Cushion
Catalytic Converter
Catalytic Converter Stay
Catalytic Converter Heat Insulator

kg-cm (ft-lb, N·m) : Specified torque
◆ Non-reusable part

Cylinder head — Celica 5S-FE engine

the air intake chamber air hose, the throttle body air hose, and the power steering pump hoses, if equipped. Remove the air tube.

11. Remove the intake manifold retaining bolts. Remove the intake manifold. Remove the fuel delivery pipe and the injectors. Remove the spark plugs.

12. Remove the camshaft timing pulley. Remove the No. 1 idler pulley and tension

spring. Remove the No. 3 timing belt cover. Properly support the timing belt so that meshing of the crankshaft timing pulley does not occur and the timing belt does not shift.

13. Remove the valve cover. Arrange the grommets in order so that they can be reinstalled in the correct order.

14. To remove the exhaust camshaft, set the knock pin of the exhaust camshaft at 10–45°

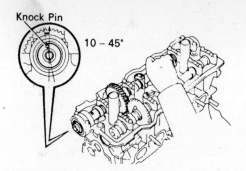

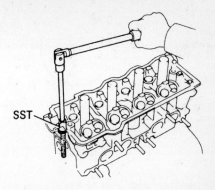

Removing exhaust camshaft — Celica 3S-FE and 5S-FE engines

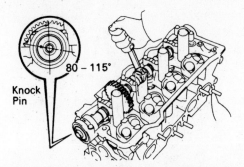

Removing intake camshaft — Celica 3S-FE and 5S-FE engines

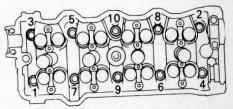

Remove cylinder head bolts in this order — Celica 3S-FE and 5S-FE engines

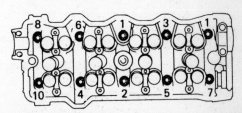

Install cylinder head bolts in this order — Celica 3S-FE and 5S-FE engines

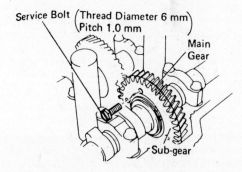

Secure the exhaust camshaft sub gear to main gear with a service bolt

BTDC of camshaft angle. This angle will help to lift the exhaust camshaft level and evenly by pushing No. 2 and No. 4 cylinder camshaft lobes of the exhaust camshaft toward their valve lifters.

15. Secure the exhaust camshaft sub gear to the main gear with a 16–20mm x 6mm x 1mm bolt. When removing the exhaust camshaft be sure that the torsional spring force of the sub gear has been eliminated.

16. Remove the No. 1 and No. 2 rear bearing cap bolts and remove the cap. Uniformly loosen and remove bearing cap bolts No. 3 to No. 8 in several phases and in the proper sequence. Do not remove bearing cap (No. 3) bolts No. 9 and

10 at this time. Remove No. 1, 2, and 4 bearing caps.

17. Alternately loosen and remove bearing cap (No. 3) bolts No. 9 and 10. As these bolts are loosened check to see that the camshaft is being lifted out straight and level.

NOTE: *If the camshaft is not lifting out straight and level retighten No. 9 and 10 bearing cap (No. 3) bolts. Reverse Steps 16 through 14, than start over from Step 14. Do not attempt to pry the camshaft from its mounting.*

18. Remove the exhaust camshaft from the engine.

19. To remove the intake camshaft, set the knock pin of the intake camshaft at 80–115° BTDC of camshaft angle. This angle will help to lift the intake camshaft level and evenly by pushing No. 1 and No. 3 cylinder camshaft lobes of the intake camshaft toward their valve lifters.

20. Remove the No. 1 and No. 2 rear bearing cap bolts and remove the front bearing cap and oil seal. If the cap will not come apart easily, leave it in place without the bolts.

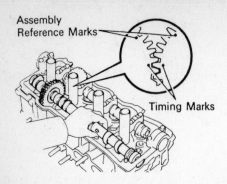

Install exhaust camshaft gear to intake camshaft gear by matching timing marks

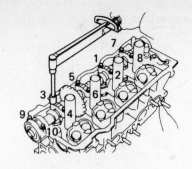

Intake camshaft bearing cap bolt torque sequence Celica 3S-FE and 5S-FE engines

21. Uniformly loosen and remove bearing cap bolts No. 3 to No. 8 in several phases and in the proper sequence. Do not remove bearing cap (No. 2) bolts No. 9 and 10 at this time. Remove No. 1, 3, and 4 bearing caps.

22. Alternately loosen and remove bearing cap (No. 2) bolts No. 9 and 10. As these bolts are loosened and after breaking the adhesion on the front bearing cap, check to see that the camshaft is being lifted out straight and level.

NOTE: *If the camshaft is not lifting out straight and level retighten No. 9 and 10 bearing cap bolts. Reverse Steps 22 through 19, than start over from Step 19. Do not attempt to pry the camshaft from its mounting.*

23. Remove the intake camshaft from the engine.

24. Loosen then remove the cylinder head bolts in three phases and in the proper sequence. Remove the cylinder head from the engine.

25. Install the cylinder head on the cylinder head block. Place the cylinder head in position on the cylinder head gasket.

26. Be sure to use a new head gasket. Apply a light coat of clean engine oil to the threads of the head bolts before installation. Torque the cylinder head bolts to specification and in three phases. Refer to the "Torque Specifications Chart".

27. Before installing the intake camshaft, apply multi purpose grease to the thrust portion of the camshaft. Position the camshaft at 80–115° BTDC of camshaft angle on the cylin-

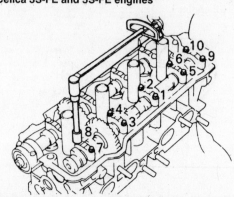

Exhaust camshaft bearing cap bolt torque sequence — Celica 3S-FE and 5S-FE engines

der head. Apply seal packing kit 08826–00080 or equivalent and apply it to the front bearing cap. Coat the bearing cap bolts with clean engine oil. Uniformly (bearing caps in the correct location) and in several phases tighten the camshaft bearing caps to 14 ft. lbs.

28. To install the exhaust camshaft, set the knock pin of the camshaft at 10–45° BTDC of camshaft angle. Apply multipurpose grease to the thrust portion of the camshaft. Position the exhaust camshaft gear with the intake camshaft gear so that the timing marks are in alignment with one another. Be sure to use the proper alignment marks on the gears. Do not use the assembly reference marks.

29. Turn the intake camshaft clockwise or counterclockwise little by little until the exhaust camshaft sits in the bearing journals evenly without rocking the camshaft on the bearing journals.

30. Coat the bearing cap bolts with clean engine oil. Uniformly (bearing caps in the correct location) and in several phases tighten the camshaft bearing caps to 14 ft. lbs. Remove the service bolt from the assembly.

31. Check and adjust the valve clearance as necessary.

32. Install the timing pulley, intake and exhaust manifold assemblies and all necessary

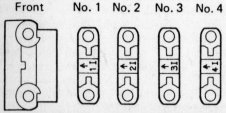

Install the bearing cap in proper location — Celica 3S-FE and 5S-FE engines

components that were removed during service procedure.

33. Install the cylinder head cover with new gasket and semi-circular plugs in the correct position.

34. Install or reconnect all vacuum hoses, lines, water hoses, electrical connections.

35. Fill engine the specified coolant to the correct level. Start the engine and check for leaks. Adjust ignition timing.

36. Check for abnormal noise, shock, slippage, correct shift points and smooth operation. Recheck all fluid levels.

4A-FE Engine (Celica)

1. Disconnect the negative battery cable. Drain the coolant.

CAUTION: *When draining the coolant, keep in mind that cats and dogs are attracted by the ethylene glycol antifreeze, and are quite likely to drink any that is left in an uncovered container or in puddles on the ground. This will prove fatal in sufficient quantity. Always drain the coolant into a sealable container. Coolant should be reused unless it is contaminated or several years old.*

NOTE: *On 1990 SRS vehicles, you must wait AT LEAST 30 seconds after disconnecting the battery before doing any work. The SRS has a built-in backup which will allow the system to remain energized for a period of time after the power is disconnected.*

2. If equipped with automatic transmission, disconnect the throttle cable and bracket from the throttle body.

3. Disconnect the accelerator cable and bracket from the throttle body.

4. Remove the air cleaner cap and hose.

5. Remove the engine under covers. Remove the suspension lower crossmember.

6. Disconnect the front exhaust pipe. Remove the distributor.

7. Remove the water outlet and gaskets. Remove the water inlet and inlet housing.

8. Disconnect the water temperature sender gauge connector, water temperature sensor connector, cold start injector time

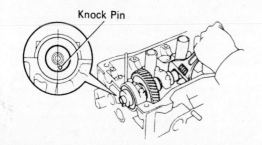

Remove exhaust camshaft – Celica 4A-FE engine

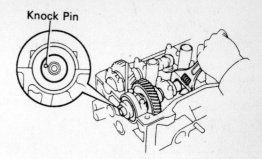

Remove intake camshaft – Celica 4A-FE Engine

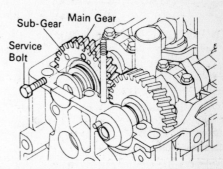

Secure the intake camshaft sub gear to main gear with a service bolt Celica 4A-FE engine

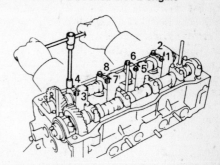

Remove camshaft bearing cap bolts in this order Celica 4A-FE engine

switch connector, radiator hose, water hoses, and the emission control vacuum hoses.

9. Disconnect all vacuum hoses. Remove the P/S pump without disconnecting hoses.

10. Remove the throttle body assembly. Remove the cold start injector pipe. Remove the cold start injector, delivery pipe and fuel injectors.

11. Remove the ACV assembly. Disconnect engine wiring from the timing belt cover and from the intake manifold.

12. Remove the vacuum pipe, EGR vacuum modulator and EGR VSV assembly.

13. Remove the EGR valve and gasket. Remove the water inlet pipe and fuel return hose from the fuel filter.

14. Remove the intake manifold assembly with retaining manifold stay (bracket).

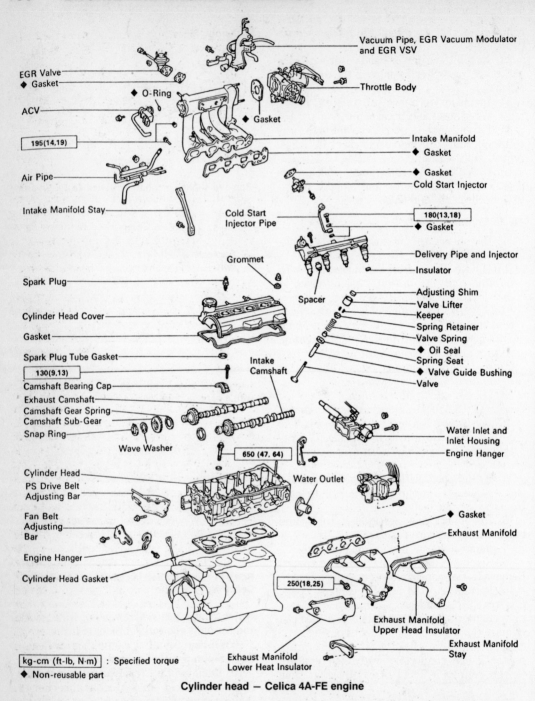

EGR Valve
◆ Gasket
ACV
◆ O-Ring
195(14,19)
Air Pipe
Intake Manifold Stay

Vacuum Pipe, EGR Vacuum Modulator and EGR VSV
Throttle Body
◆ Gasket
Intake Manifold
◆ Gasket
◆ Gasket
Cold Start Injector
Cold Start Injector Pipe
180(13,18)
◆ Gasket

Grommet
Spark Plug
Cylinder Head Cover
Gasket
Spark Plug Tube Gasket
130(9,13)
Camshaft Bearing Cap
Exhaust Camshaft
Camshaft Gear Spring
Camshaft Sub-Gear
Snap Ring
Wave Washer

Spacer
Intake Camshaft

Delivery Pipe and Injector
Insulator
Adjusting Shim
Valve Lifter
Keeper
Spring Retainer
Valve Spring
◆ Oil Seal
Spring Seat
◆ Valve Guide Bushing
Valve

650 (47, 64)

Water Inlet and Inlet Housing
Engine Hanger

Cylinder Head
PS Drive Belt Adjusting Bar
Fan Belt Adjusting Bar
Engine Hanger
Cylinder Head Gasket

Water Outlet

◆ Gasket
Exhaust Manifold

250(18,25)

Exhaust Manifold Upper Head Insulator

Exhaust Manifold Lower Heat Insulator

Exhaust Manifold Stay

kg-cm (ft-lb, N·m) : Specified torque
◆ Non-reusable part

Cylinder head — Celica 4A-FE engine

15. Remove the valve cover. Arrange the grommets in order so that they can be reinstalled in the correct order.

16. Remove the camshaft timing pulley. Remove the No. 1 idler pulley and tension spring. Remove the No. 3 timing belt cover. Properly support the timing belt so that meshing of the crankshaft timing pulley does not occur and the timing belt does not shift.

17. Remove the fan belt adjusting bar

(bracket), engine hangers and power steering drive belt adjusting strut or bracket.

18. Remove the intake camshaft, set the knock pin of the intake camshaft so it is slightly above the top of the cylinder head. This angle will help to lift the intake camshaft level and evenly by pushing No. 1 and No. 3 cylinder camshaft lobes of the camshaft toward their valve lifters.

19. Remove the bearing cap bolts and remove the front bearing cap.

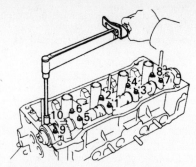

**Camshaft installation torque sequence
Celica 4A-FE engine**

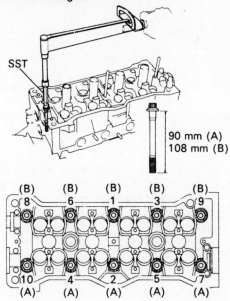

90 mm (A)
108 mm (B)

**Cylinder head bolt locations and torque sequence
Celica 4A-FE engine**

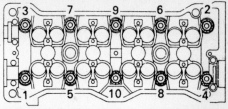

**Remove cylinder head bolts in this sequence
Celica 4A-FE engine**

20. Secure the intake camshaft sub gear to the main gear with a 16–20mm x 6mm x 1mm bolt. When removing the camshaft be sure that the torsional spring force of the sub gear has been eliminated.

21. Uniformly loosen and remove bearing cap bolts in several phases and in the proper sequence. Remove bearing caps and camshaft.

22. Remove the exhaust camshaft, set the knock pin of the exhaust camshaft so it is slightly counterclockwise from the vertical axis of the camshaft. This angle will help to lift the camshaft level and evenly by pushing No. 1 and No. 3 cylinder camshaft lobes of the camshaft toward their valve lifters.

23. Remove the bearing cap bolts and remove the front bearing cap and oil seal.

24. Uniformly loosen and remove bearing cap bolts in several phases and in the proper sequence. Remove bearing caps and camshaft.

25. Loosen then remove the cylinder head bolts in three phases and in the proper sequence. Remove the cylinder head from the engine (cylinder head mounted on dowel pins-head bolts are different sizes note location).

26. Install the cylinder head on the cylinder head block. Place the cylinder head in position on the cylinder head gasket.

27. Be sure to use a new head gasket. Apply a light coat of clean engine oil to the threads of the head bolts before installation. Torque the cylinder head bolts to specification (refer to the "Torque Specifications Chart" as required) and in three phases.

28. Before installing the exhaust camshaft, apply multi purpose grease to the thrust portion of the camshaft. Position the camshaft so the knock pin is located slightly counterclockwise from the vertical axis of the camshaft. Apply seal packing kit 08826–00080 or equivalent and apply it to the front bearing cap. Coat the bearing cap bolts with clean engine oil. Uniformly (bearing caps in the correct location) and in several phases tighten the camshaft bearing caps to 9 ft. lbs. Install camshaft oil seal

29. To install the intake camshaft, set the knock pin of the camshaft slightly above the top of the cylinder head. Apply multipurpose grease to the thrust portion of the camshaft. Position the intake camshaft gear with the exhaust camshaft gear so that the assembly or installation marks are in alignment (side by side) with one another. Be sure to use the proper alignment or installation marks on the gears. Do not use the timing marks.

30. Turn the camshaft clockwise or counterclockwise little by little until the camshaft sits in the bearing journals evenly. Coat the bearing cap bolts with clean engine oil. Uniformly (bearing caps in the correct location) and in several phases tighten the camshaft bearing caps to 9 ft. lbs. Remove the service bolt from the assembly.

31. Turn the exhaust camshaft clockwise and set it with knock pin facing upward. Check that the timing marks of the camshaft gears are aligned in the correct position. The assembly installation marks are straight up and the timing marks are side by side.

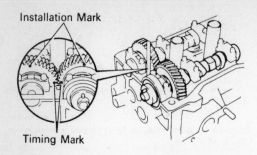

Installation Mark

Timing Mark

Check that the timing marks of camshaft gears are aligned before completing installation. — Celica 4A-FE engine

32. Check and adjust the valve clearance as necessary.

33. Install the timing pulley, timing belt, intake and exhaust manifold assemblies and all necessary components that were removed during service procedure.

34. Install the cylinder head cover with new gasket and semi-circular plugs in the correct position.

35. Install the fan belt adjusting bar (bracket), engine hangers and power steering drive belt adjusting strut or bracket.

36. Install or reconnect all vacuum hoses, lines, water hoses, electrical connections.

37. Fill engine the specified coolant to the correct level. Start the engine and check for leaks. Adjust ignition timing.

38. Check for abnormal noise, shock, slippage, correct shift points and smooth operation. Recheck all fluid levels.

5M-GE Engine (Supra)

1. Disconnect the battery cables.
2. Drain the cooling system.

CAUTION: *When draining the coolant, keep in mind that cats and dogs are attracted by the ethylene glycol antifreeze, and are quite likely to drink any that is left in an uncovered container or in puddles on the ground. This will prove fatal in sufficient quantity. Always drain the coolant into a sealable container. Coolant should be reused unless it is contaminated or several years old.*

3. Disconnect the exhaust pipe from the exhaust manifold.
4. Remove the throttle cable bracket from the cylinder head if equipped with automatic transmission, and remove the accelerator and actuator cable bracket.
5. Tag and disconnect the ground cable, oxygen sensor wire, high tension coil wire, distributor connector, solenoid resistor wire connector and thermo switch wire (AT).
6. Tag and disconnect the brake booster vacuum hose, EGR valve vacuum hose, fuel hose from the intake manifold and actuator vacuum hose (if equipped with cruise control).
7. Disconnect the radiator upper hose from the thermostat housing, and disconnect the two heater hoses.
8. Disconnect the No. 1 air hose from the air intake connector. Remove the two clamp bolts, loosen the throttle body hose clamp and remove the air intake connector and the connector pipe.
9. Tag and disconnect all emission control

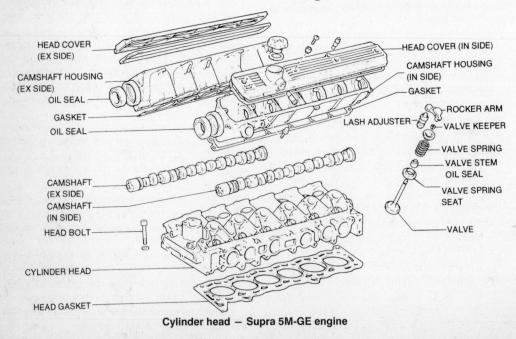

HEAD COVER (EX SIDE)

CAMSHAFT HOUSING (EX SIDE)

OIL SEAL

GASKET

OIL SEAL

CAMSHAFT (EX SIDE)

CAMSHAFT (IN SIDE)

HEAD BOLT

CYLINDER HEAD

HEAD GASKET

HEAD COVER (IN SIDE)

CAMSHAFT HOUSING (IN SIDE)

GASKET

ROCKER ARM

LASH ADJUSTER

VALVE KEEPER

VALVE SPRING

VALVE STEM OIL SEAL

VALVE SPRING SEAT

VALVE

Cylinder head — Supra 5M-GE engine

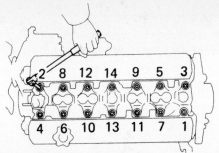

Remove cylinder head bolts in this order — Supra 5M-GE engine

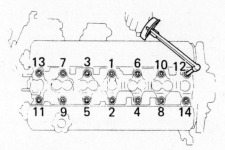

Tighten cylinder head bolts in this order — Supra 5M-GE engine

hoses from the throttle body and air intake chamber, the two PCV hoses from the cam cover and the fuel hose form the fuel hose support.

10. Remove the air intake chamber stay, the vacuum pipe and ground cable.

11. Remove the bolt that attaches the spark plug wire clip, leaving the wires attached to the clip. Remove the distributor from the cylinder head with the cap and wires attached, by removing the distributor holding bolt.

12. Tag and disconnect the cold start injector wire and disconnect the cold start injector fuel hose from the delivery pipe.

13. Loosen the nut of the EGR pipe, remove the five bolts and two nuts and remove the air intake chamber and gasket.

14. Remove the glove box and remove the ECU module. Disconnect the three connectors and pull the EFI (fuel injection) wire harness out through the engine side of the fire wall.

15. Remove the pulsation damper and the No. 1 fuel pipe.

16. Remove the water outlet housing by first loosening the clamp and disconnecting the water by-pass hose.

17. Remove the intake manifold.

18. Disconnect the power steering pump drive belt and remove the power steering pump without disconnecting the fluid hoses. Temporarily secure the pump out of the way.

19. Disconnect the oxygen sensor connector

and remove the exhaust manifold.

20. Remove the timing belt and camshaft timing gears.

21. Remove the timing belt cover stay, and remove the oil pressure regulator and gasket.

22. Remove the No. 2 timing belt cover and gasket.

23. Tag and disconnect any other wires, linkage and/or hoses still attached to the cylinder head.

24. Using a long extension on your ratchet handle (thin enough to get inside the head bolt recesses), remove the fourteen head bolts gradually in two or three passes in the numerical order shown.

NOTE: *Head warpage or cracking could result from removing the head bolts in incorrect order.*

25. Carefully lift the cylinder head from the dowels on the cylinder block, resting the mating surface on wooden blocks on the work bench. If the head is difficult to remove, tap around the mating surface gently with a rubber hammer. Keep in mind the head is aluminum and is easily damaged.

26. Install the cylinder head (clean all surfaces; always use new gasket) on the cylinder block. Place the cylinder head in position on the cylinder head gasket.

27. Be sure to use a new head gasket. Apply a light coat of clean engine oil to the threads of the head bolts before installation. Torque the cylinder head bolts to specifications (58 ft. lbs.) in three phases. Refer to the "Torque Specifications Chart" as required.

28. Install the No. 2 timing belt cover. Install oil pressure regulator with new gasket.

29. Install camshaft timing pulleys and timing belt.

30. Using new gasket install the exhaust manifold assembly to the cylinder head. Install exhaust pipe and related hangers or brackets.

31. Install the power steering pump onto the bracket. Install the pump pulley and drive belt. Adjust the belt as necessary.

32. Position a new gasket on the cylinder head and install the intake manifold assembly.

33. Reconnect the EFI wire harness to the ECU module and related components in the correct position.

34. Install water outlet housing and water hose.

35. Position a new gasket on the intake manifold and install air intake chamber assembly.

36. Connect the cold start injector fuel hose to the delivery pipe. Reconnect all electrical connections that were removed during this service procedure.

37. Install the distributor, spark plugs and ignition wires.

38. Install vacuum pipe subassembly and re-connect all emission control hoses to the correct location.

39. Install air intake connector pipe and air intake body hose. Tighten retaining clamp.

40. Install all water hoses using new hose clamps as necessary. Reconnect EGR vacuum hose, fuel hose, actuator vacuum hose and brake booster hose.

41. Install the throttle cable bracket to the cylinder head if equipped with automatic transmission, and install the accelerator and actuator cable bracket.

42. Fill the engine with the specified coolant to the correct level. Reconnect the negative battery cable and start engine. Perform all necessary engine adjustments then road test the vehicle. Recheck coolant and engine oil level.

7M-GE And 7M-GTE Engines (Supra)

1. Disconnect the negative battery cable. Drain the coolant.

CAUTION: *When draining the coolant, keep in mind that cats and dogs are attracted by the ethylene glycol antifreeze, and are quite likely to drink any that is left in an uncovered container or in puddles on the ground. This will prove fatal in sufficient quantity. Always drain the coolant into a sealable container. Coolant should be reused unless it is contaminated or several years old.*

NOTE: *On 1990 SRS vehicles, you must wait AT LEAST 30 seconds after disconnecting the battery before doing any work. The SRS has a built-in backup which will allow the system to remain energized for a period of time after the power is disconnected.*

2. Disconnect the exhaust pipe from the exhaust manifold. Disconnect the cruise control cable, if equipped.

3. Disconnect the accelerator cable. Disconnect the throttle cable, if equipped with automatic transmission. Disconnect the engine ground strap.

4. On the 7M-GE remove the No. 1 air cleaner hose along with the intake air pipe assembly. On the 7M-GTE remove the No. 4 air cleaner pipe along with the No. 1 and No. 2 air cleaner hose.

5. Disconnect the cruise control vacuum hose, the charcoal canister hose and the brake booster hose.

6. Remove the radiator inlet hose. Disconnect the heater inlet hose. Remove the alternator assembly.

7. On the 7M-GTE remove the power steering reservoir tank. On the 7M-GTE remove the cam position sensor.

8. Remove the air intake chamber with the connector. Remove the PCV pipe. Disconnect

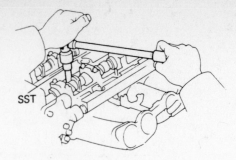

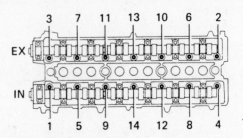

Remove cylinder head bolts in this order — Supra 7M-GE and 7M-GTE engines

and tag all required hoses and vacuum connections that are required to remove the cylinder head from the vehicle.

9. Remove the EGR pipe mounting bolts. Remove the manifold retaining bolts. On the 7M-GE remove the throttle body bracket. On the 7M-GTE remove the ISC pipe.

10. Remove the air intake connector mounting bolt. On the 7M-GE remove the cold start injector tube. On the 7M-GTE disconnect the cold start injector. Disconnect the EGR vacuum modulator from the bracket.

11. Disconnect the engine wire from the clamps of the intake chamber. Remove the nuts and bolts, vacuum pipes and intake chamber with the connector and gasket.

12. On the 7M-GTE remove the ignition coil and bracket. Disconnect all electrical connections that are required to remove the cylinder head from the engine.

13. Remove the pulsation damper, the VSV and the No. 1 fuel pipe. Remove the NO.3 fuel pipe. On the 7M-GTE remove the auxiliary air pipe.

14. On the 7M-GE remove the high tension wires and the distributor. Remove the oil dipstick. On the 7M-GTE remove the turbocharger assembly.

15. Remove the exhaust manifold. Remove the water outlet housing. Remove the valve covers. Remove the spark plugs.

16. Remove the timing belt and the camshaft timing pulleys. Remove the cylinder head retaining bolts gradually and in the proper se-

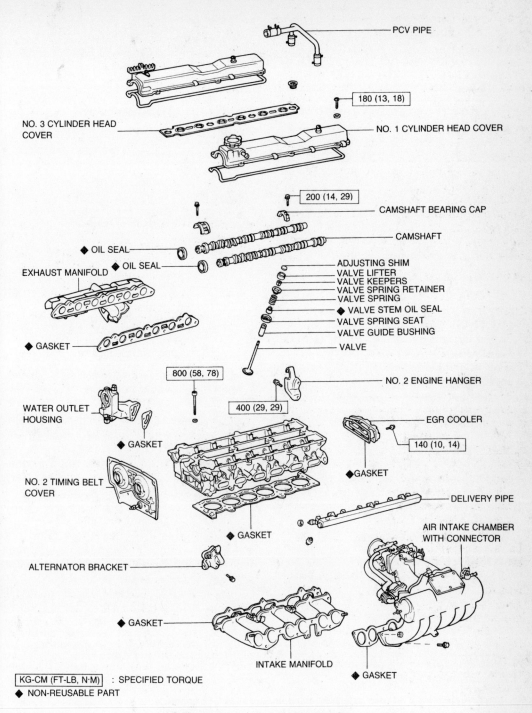

PCV PIPE

180 (13, 18)

NO. 3 CYLINDER HEAD COVER

NO. 1 CYLINDER HEAD COVER

200 (14, 29)

CAMSHAFT BEARING CAP

CAMSHAFT

◆ OIL SEAL

◆ OIL SEAL

EXHAUST MANIFOLD

ADJUSTING SHIM
VALVE LIFTER
VALVE KEEPERS
VALVE SPRING RETAINER
VALVE SPRING
◆ VALVE STEM OIL SEAL
VALVE SPRING SEAT
VALVE GUIDE BUSHING
VALVE

◆ GASKET

800 (58, 78)

NO. 2 ENGINE HANGER

400 (29, 29)

WATER OUTLET HOUSING

EGR COOLER

140 (10, 14)

◆ GASKET

◆ GASKET

NO. 2 TIMING BELT COVER

DELIVERY PIPE

AIR INTAKE CHAMBER WITH CONNECTOR

◆ GASKET

ALTERNATOR BRACKET

◆ GASKET

INTAKE MANIFOLD

◆ GASKET

KG-CM (FT-LB, N·M) : SPECIFIED TORQUE
◆ NON-REUSABLE PART

Cylinder head — Supra 7M-GE engine

quence. Carefully remove the cylinder head from the engine.

17. Install the cylinder head (clean all surfaces; always use new gasket) on the cylinder block. Place the cylinder head in position on the cylinder head gasket.

18. Be sure to use a new head gasket. Apply a light coat of clean engine oil to the threads of the head bolts before installation. Torque the cylinder head bolts to specifications in three phases. Refer to the "Torque Specifications Chart" as required.

19. Install camshaft timing pulleys and timing belt. Install spark plugs.

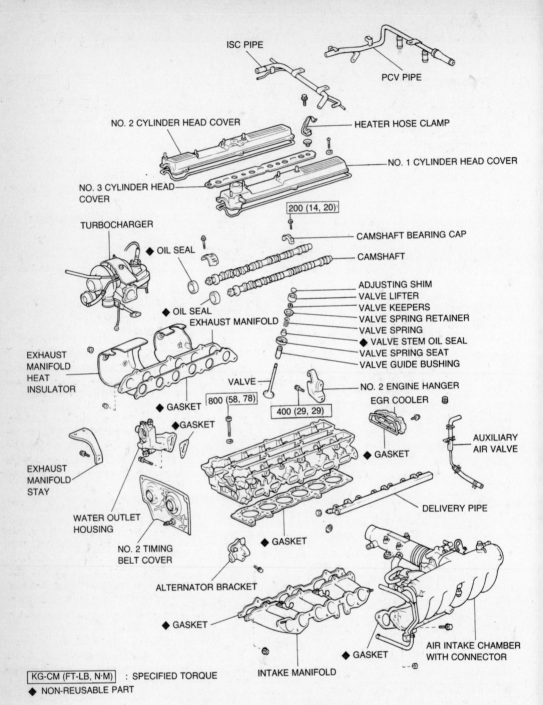

ISC PIPE

PCV PIPE

NO. 2 CYLINDER HEAD COVER

HEATER HOSE CLAMP

NO. 1 CYLINDER HEAD COVER

NO. 3 CYLINDER HEAD COVER

200 (14, 20)

TURBOCHARGER

CAMSHAFT BEARING CAP

◆ OIL SEAL

CAMSHAFT

◆ OIL SEAL
EXHAUST MANIFOLD

ADJUSTING SHIM
VALVE LIFTER
VALVE KEEPERS
VALVE SPRING RETAINER
VALVE SPRING
◆ VALVE STEM OIL SEAL
VALVE SPRING SEAT
VALVE GUIDE BUSHING

EXHAUST
MANIFOLD
HEAT
INSULATOR

VALVE

NO. 2 ENGINE HANGER
EGR COOLER

◆ GASKET

800 (58, 78)

400 (29, 29)

◆ GASKET

◆ GASKET

AUXILIARY
AIR VALVE

EXHAUST
MANIFOLD
STAY

WATER OUTLET
HOUSING

DELIVERY PIPE

NO. 2 TIMING
BELT COVER

◆ GASKET

ALTERNATOR BRACKET

◆ GASKET

AIR INTAKE CHAMBER
WITH CONNECTOR

◆ GASKET

INTAKE MANIFOLD

KG-CM (FT-LB, N·M) : SPECIFIED TORQUE

◆ NON-REUSABLE PART

Cylinder head — Supra 7M-GTE engine

20. Install cylinder head covers and water outlet housing using new gaskets.

21. Install the exhaust manifold assembly (with new exhaust manifold gasket) and exhaust manifold stay bracket and insulator if so equipped.

22. On the 7M-GTE engine install the turbocharger assembly and auxiliary air pipe.

23. Install oil dipstick and distributor with ignition wires.

24. Install fuel pipes and fuel pulsation damper. Reconnect all engine wiring to the correct location.

25. On the 7M-GTE engine install the ignition coil with bracket.

26. Install air intake chamber (using new

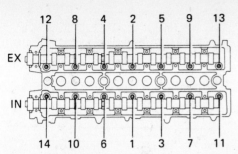

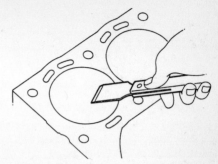

Install cylinder head bolts in this order — Supra 7M-GE and 7M-GTE engines

Removing carbon from the piston tops — do not scratch pistons

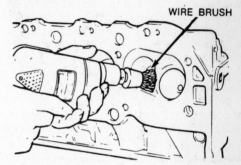

Removing combustion chamber carbon — make sure it is removed and not merely burnished

gasket) with connector and all related components.

27. On the 7M-GTE engine install the cam position sensor and power steering reservoir tank.

28. Install alternator, adjusting bar and drive belt. Adjust drive belt.

29. Reconnect all water hoses using new hose clamps as necessary.

30. Connect all emission hoses, cruise control vacuum hose brake booster hose.

31. Install air cleaner assembly and related hoses. Connect ground strap, throttle cable (automatic transmission only), accelerator rod, accelerator link with cable.

32. Reconnect exhaust pipe and related hangers and brackets to the exhaust manifold.

33. Fill the engine with the specified coolant to the correct level. Reconnect the negative battery cable and start engine. Perform all necessary engine adjustments then road test the vehicle. Recheck coolant and engine oil level.

CLEANING AND INSPECTION

When the valve train assembly has been removed from the cylinder head set the head on two wooden blocks or equivalent mounting fixture on the bench (always work in a clean area), combustion chamber side up. Using a scraper or putty knife, carefully scrape away any gasket

material that may have stuck to the head-to-block mating surface when the head was removed. Make sure you DO NOT gouge the mating surface with the tool. Using a wire brush chucked into your electric drill, remove the carbon in each combustion chamber. Make sure the brush is actually removing the carbon and not merely burnishing it.

Clean all the valve guides using a valve guide brush (available at most auto parts or auto tool shops) and solvent. A fine-bristled rifle bore cleaning brush also works here. Inspect the threads of each spark plug hole by screwing a plug into each, making sure it screws down completely. Heli-coil® or equivalent any plug hole this is damaged.

Finally, go over the entire head with a clean shop rag soaked in solvent to remove any grit, old gasket particles, etc. Blow out the bolt holes, coolant galleys, intake and exhaust ports, valve guides and plug holes with compressed air.

Inspect cylinder head for cracks using dye penetrant. Check the combustion chamber intake and exhaust ports, head surface and the top of the cylinder head for cracks. If the cylinder head is found to be cracked replace the cylinder as repair is not possible.

RESURFACING

While the head is removed, check the head-to-block mating surface for straightness. If the

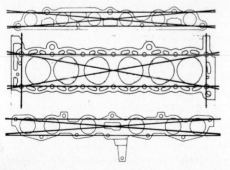

Check the mating surface widthwise, lengthwise and diagonally

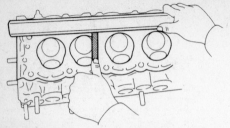

Check head mating surface straightness with a precision straight edge and feeler gauge

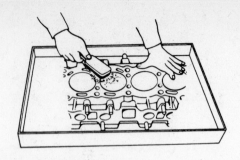

Wire brush the top of the block

engine has overheated and blown a head gasket, this must be done as a matter of course. A warped mating surface must be resurfaced (milled); this is done on a milling machine and is quite similar to planing a piece of wood.

Using a precision steel straightedge and a blade-type feeler gauge, check the surface of the head across its length, width and diagonal length as shown in the illustrations. Also check the intake and exhaust manifold mating surfaces, and the camshaft housing and cam cover (all) mating surfaces. If warpage exceed 0.003 in. in a 6 in. span, or 0.006 in. over the total length, the head must be milled. If warpage is highly excessive, the head must be replaced. Always, consult the machine shop operator on head milling limitations. It is far better to replace the cylinder head assembly if in doubt than trying to have head milled (machined).

CYLINDER BLOCK CLEANING

While the cylinder head is removed, the top

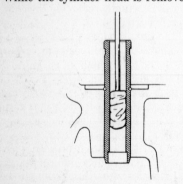

Cleaning the valve guides

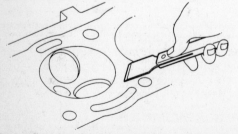

Do not scratch the head mating surface when removing old gasket material

of the cylinder block and pistons should also be cleaned. Before you begin, rotate the crankshaft until one or more pistons are flush with the top of the block (on the four cylinder engines, you will either have Nos. 1 and 4 up, or Nos. 2 and 3 up). Carefully stuff clean rags into the cylinders in which the pistons are down. This will help keep grit and carbon chips out during cleaning. Using care not to gouge or scratch the block-to-head mating surface and the piston top(s), clean away any old gasket material with a wire brush and/or scraper. On the piston tops, make sure you are actually removing the carbon and not merely burnishing it.

Remove the rags from the down cylinders after you have wiped the top of the block with a solvent soaked rag. Rotate the crankshaft until the other pistons come up flush with the top of the block, and clean those pistons.

NOTE: *Because you have rotated the crankshaft, you will have to re-time the engine following the procedure listed under the Timing Chain/Timing Belt removal. Make sure you wipe out each cylinder thoroughly with a solvent-soaked rag, to remove all traces of grit, before the head is reassembled to the block.*

Valves

REMOVAL AND INSTALLATION

A valve spring compressor is needed to remove the valves and springs; these are available at most auto parts and auto tool shops. A small magnet is very helpful for removing the keepers and spring seats.

Set the head on its side on the bench. Install the spring compressor so that the fixed side of the tool is flat against the valve head in the combustion chamber, and the screw side is against the retainer. Slowly turn the screw in towards the head, compressing the spring. As the spring compresses, the keepers will be revealed; pick them off of the valve stem with the magnet as they are easily fumbled and lost. When the keepers are removed, back the screw out and

Carefully scrape carbon from the valve head

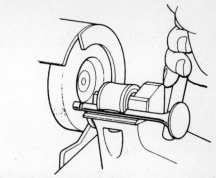

Grinding the valve stem tip

remove the retainers and springs. Remove the compressor and pull the valves out of the head from the other side. Remove the valve seals by hand and remove the spring seats with the magnet.

Since it is very important that each valve and its spring, retainer, spring seat and keepers is reassembled in its original location, you must keep these parts in order. The best way to do this to cut either eight (four cylinder) or twelve (six cylinder) holes in a piece of heavy cardboard or wood. Label each hole with the cylinder number and either **IN** or **EX**, corresponding to the location of each valve in the head. As you remove each valve, insert it into the holder, and assemble the seats, springs, keepers and retainers to the stem on the labeled side of the holder. This way each valve and its attending parts are kept together, and can be put back into the head in their proper locations.

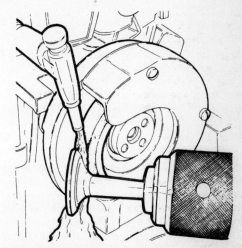

Valve refacing should be handled by a reputable machine shop

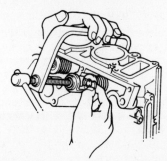

After compressing the valve spring, be careful removing the keepers — they are easily fumbled

After lapping each valve into its seat (see Valve Lapping below), oil each valve stem, and install each valve into the head in the reverse order of removal, so that all parts except the keepers are assembled on the stem. Always use new valve stem seals. Install the spring compressor, and compress the retainer and spring until the keeper groove on the valve stem is fully revealed. Coat the groove with a wipe of grease (to hold the keepers until the retainer is released) and install both keepers, wide end up.

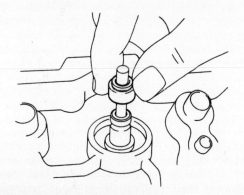

Always install new valve stem seals

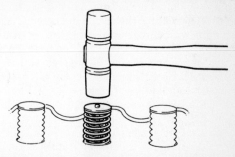

Lightly tap each assembled valve stem to ensure correct fit of the keepers, retainers and seals

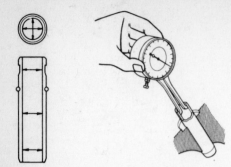

Check valve guide inside diameter with a dial gauge

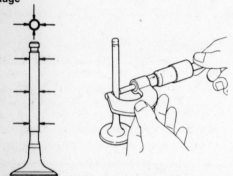

Mike up the valve stem at the indicated locations

Slowly back the screw of the compressor out until the spring retainer covers the keepers. Remove the tool. Lightly tap the end of each valve stem with a rubber hammer to ensure proper fit of the retainers and keepers.

INSPECTION

Before the valves can be properly inspected, the stem, lower end of the stem and the entire valve face and head must be cleaned. An old valve works well for chipping carbon from the valve head, and a wire brush, gasket scraper or putty knife can be used for cleaning the valve face and the area between the face and lower stem. Do not scratch the valve face during cleaning. Clean the entire stem with a rag soaked in thinners to remove all varnish and gum.

Thorough inspection of the valves requires the use of a micrometer, and a dial indicator is needed to measure the inside diameter of the valve guides. If there instruments are not available to you, the valves and head can be taken to a reputable machine ship for inspection. Refer to the Valve Specifications chart for valve stem and stem-to-guide specifications.

If the above instruments are at your disposal, measure the diameter of each valve stem at the locations illustrated. Jot these measurements down. Using the dial indicator, measure the inside diameter of the valve guides at their bottom, top and midpoint 90° apart. Jot these measurements down also. Subtract the valve

stem measurement from the valve guide inside measurement; if the clearance exceed that listed in the specifications chart under Stem-to-Guide Clearance, replace the valve(s). Stem-to-guide clearance can also be checked at a machine shop, where a dial indicator would be used.

Check the top of each valve stem for pitting and unusual wear due to improper rocker adjustment, etc. The stem tip can be ground flat if it is worn, but no more than 0.020 in. can be removed; if this limit must be exceeded to make the tip flat and square, then the valve must be replaced. If the valve stem tips are ground, make sure you fix the valve securely into a jig designed for this purpose, so the tip contacts the grinding wheel squarely at exactly 90°. Most machine shops that handle automotive work are equipped for this job.

REFACING

Valve refacing should only be handled by a reputable machine shop, as the experience and equipment needed to do the job are beyond that of the average owner/mechanic. During the course of a normal valve job, refacing is necessary when simply lapping the valves into their seats will not correct the seat and face wear. When the valves are reground (resurfaced), the valve seats must also be recut, again requiring special equipment and experience.

VALVE LAPPING

The valves must be lapped into their seats after resurfacing, to ensure proper sealing. Even if the valves have not been refaced, they should be lapped into the head before reassembly.

Set the cylinder head on the workbench, combustion chamber side up. Rest the head on wooden blocks on either end, so there are two or three inches between the tops of the valve guides and the bench.

1. Lightly lube the valve stem with clean engine oil. Coat the valve seat completely with valve grinding compound. Use just enough compound that the full width and circumference of the seat are covered.

2. Install the valve in its proper location in the head. Attach the suction cup end of the valve lapping tool to the valve head. It usually helps to put a small amount of saliva into the suction cup to aid it sticking to the valve.

3. Rotate the tool between the palms, changing position and lifting the tool often to prevent grooving. Lap the valve in until a smooth, evenly polished seat and valve face are evident.

4. Remove the valve from the head. Wipe away all traces of grinding compound from the valve face and seat. Wipe out the port with a

solvent soaked rag, and swab out the valve guide with a piece of solvent soaked rag to make sure there are no traces of compound grit inside the guide. This cleaning is important.

5. Proceed through the remaining valves, one at a time. Make sure the valve faces, seats, cylinder ports and valve guides are clean before reassembling the valve train.

Valve Springs

INSPECTION

Valve spring squareness, length and tension should be checked while the valve train is disassembled. Place each valve spring on a flat surface next to a steel square. Measure the length of the spring, and rotate it against the edge of the square to measure distortion. If spring length varies (by comparison) by more than $\frac{1}{16}$ in. or if distortion exceeds $\frac{1}{16}$ in., replace the spring.

Spring tension must be checked on a spring tester. Springs used on the Celica engines should be within one pound of each other when tested at their specified installed heights.

Lapping a valve in by hand

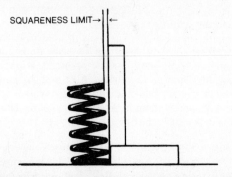

SQUARENESS LIMIT→

Check spring length and squareness with a steel square

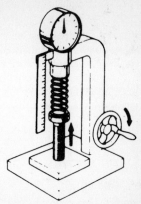

Have spring tension checked at a machine shop

Valve Seats

The valve seats in the engines covered in this guide are all non-replaceable, and must be recut when service is required. Seat recutting requires a special tool and experience, and should be handled at a reputable machine shop. Seat concentricity should also be checked by a machinist.

Valve Guides

INSPECTION

Valve guides should be cleaned as outlined earlier, and checked when valve stem diameter and stem-to-guide clearance is checked. Generally, if the engine is using oil through the guides (assuming the valve seals are OK) and the valve stem diameter is within specification, it is the guides that are worn and need replacing.

Valve guides which are not excessively worn or distorted may, in some cases, be knurled rather than replaced. Knurling is a process in which metal inside the valve guide bore is displaced and raised (forming a very fine cross-hatch pattern), thereby reducing clearance. Knurling also provides for excellent oil control. The possibility of knurling rather than replacing the guides should be discussed with a machinist.

REMOVAL AND INSTALLATION

Valve guide replacement on all Celica/Supra engines requires breaking off the top end of the

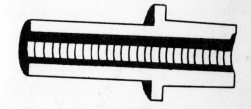

Cross-section of a knurled valve guide

guides, heating the cylinder head to almost 200°F, then driving the rest of the guide out of the head with a hammer and drift. Unless you and your family don't mind baking an oily cylinder head in the oven (and probably smelling it in the house for months), take the head to a machine shop and have a machinist replace the guides.

Oil Pan

REMOVAL AND INSTALLATION

Celica — All Engines

1. Disconnect the negative battery cable. Raise the front of the vehicle and support it with jackstands or equivalent.

NOTE: *On 1990 SRS vehicles, you must wait AT LEAST 30 seconds after disconnecting the battery before doing any work. The SRS has a built-in backup which will allow the system to remain energized for a period of time after the power is disconnected.*

2. Drain the engine oil.

3. Remove the engine undercovers.

CAUTION: *The EPA warns that prolonged contact with used engine oil may cause a number of skin disorders, including cancer! You should make every effort to minimize your exposure to used engine oil. Protective gloves should be worn when changing the oil. Wash your hands and any other exposed skin areas as soon as possible after exposure to used engine oil. Soap and water, or waterless hand cleaner should be used.*

4. Disconnect the exhaust pipe from the exhaust manifold and related exhaust hangers as necessary.

5. Remove the lower suspension crossmember. Remove the center engine mount.

6. Remove the engine stiffener plate and the oil level gauge. Remove the oil pan retaining bolts and oil pan.

7. Installation is in the reverse order of removal. Apply a 5mm bead of RTV gasket material to the groove around the pan flange. Apply the oil within 3 minutes of application and tighten the mounting bolts and nuts to 4–6 ft. lbs. working from the center to the ends in progressive steps.

Supra 5M-GE Engine

1. Disconnect the battery cables at the battery.

2. Raise the front of the vehicle and support it safely with jackstands.

3. Drain the engine oil and cooling system.

CAUTION: *The EPA warns that prolonged contact with used engine oil may cause a number of skin disorders, including cancer! You should make every effort to minimize*

your exposure to used engine oil. Protective gloves should be worn when changing the oil. Wash your hands and any other exposed skin areas as soon as possible after exposure to used engine oil. Soap and water, or waterless hand cleaner should be used.

4. Remove the air cleaner assembly. Mark any disconnected lines and/or hoses for easy reassembly.

5. Remove the oil level gauge. Disconnect the upper radiator hose at the radiator.

6. Loosen all of the drive belts for the crankshaft-driven accessories (alternator, power steering pump, etc.). Remove the four fan shroud bolts.

7. Remove the four fluid coupling flange attaching nuts, then remove the fluid coupling along with the fan and the fan shroud.

8. Remove the engine undercover. Remove the exhaust pipe clamp bolt from the exhaust pipe stay (bracket).

9. Remove the two stiffener plates from the exhaust pipe. Remove the clutch housing undercover.

10. Remove the four engine mount bolts from each side of the engine.

11. Place a jack under the transmission and raise the engine about 1^3/4 in. Remove the oil pan mounting bolts and remove the oil pan from the engine.

NOTE: *If difficulty is encountered while removing the pan, rotate the crankshaft a small amount to gain extra clearance.*

12. Clean all old gasket material from the engine block and oil pan. Install the oil pan to the engine with new gasket. Apply a small amount of sealer to the oil pan to hold gasket onto the oil pan while installation is being done.

13. Torque the oil pan fasteners to 5–7 ft. lbs. in progressive steps working from the center to the end of the oil pan.

14. Lower the engine to the proper position and install engine mount bolts.

15. Install engine and clutch housing covers, exhaust components, fan/shroud assembly, drive belts and all water hoses (with new retaining clamps as necessary) and electrical wiring.

16. Install oil level gauge and air cleaner (and vacuum hoses in the correct location) assembly. Adjust the drive belts and replenish the engine with oil and the cooling system with the proper type and quantity of coolant. Check for leaks after the engine is started.

Supra 7M-GE and 7M-GTE Engines

1. Disconnect the negative battery cable. Raise and support the vehicle safely. Remove the engine under cover. Drain the engine oil.

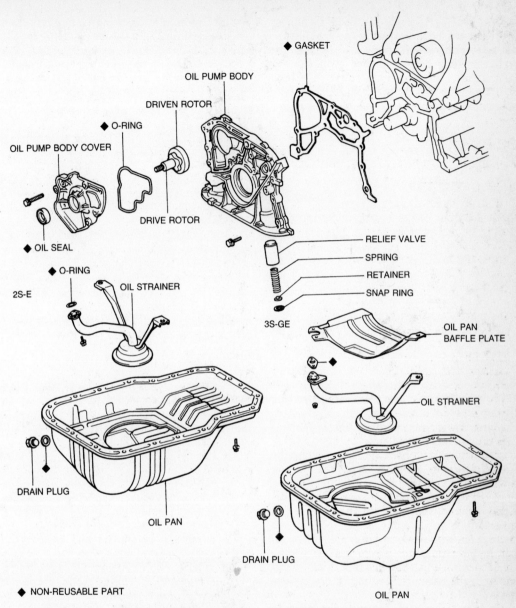

♦ NON-REUSABLE PART

Oil pan and pump assembly — Celica 2S-E and 3S-GE engines

CAUTION: *The EPA warns that prolonged contact with used engine oil may cause a number of skin disorders, including cancer! You should make every effort to minimize your exposure to used engine oil. Protective gloves should be worn when changing the oil. Wash your hands and any other exposed skin areas as soon as possible after exposure to used engine oil. Soap and water, or waterless hand cleaner should be used.*

NOTE: *On 1990 SRS vehicles, you must wait AT LEAST 30 seconds after disconnecting the battery before doing any work. The SRS has a built-in backup which will allow the system to remain energized for a period of time after the power is disconnected.*

2. If equipped with automatic transmission, remove the fluid cooler hose clamp.

3. Remove the No. 1 front suspension crossmember. Remove the front exhaust pipe bracket and stiffener plates.

4. On the 7M-GTE disconnect the engine oil cooler hose from the engine oil pan.

5. Remove the brake hose brackets and clips. Disconnect the intermediate shaft. Disconnect the stabilizer bar links from the lower control arms.

6. Properly support the engine assembly.

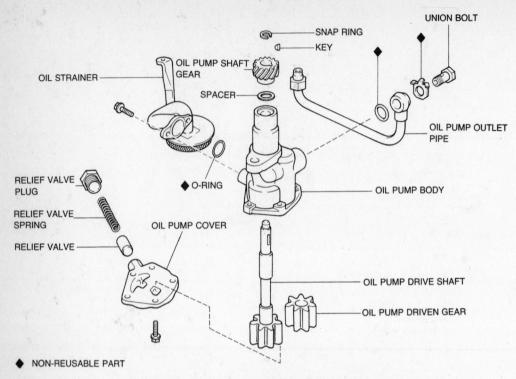

Oil pump assembly — Supra 7M-GE and 7M-GTE engines

Remove the engine mounting bolts. Remove the actuator assembly.

7. Remove the shock absorbers from the body. Disconnect the front suspension member.

8. Remove the oil pan retaining bolts. Remove the oil pan from the engine.

9. Thoroughly clean all components to remove all old gasket material. Install the oil pan to the engine with a new gasket. Torque the oil pan retaining oil bolts to 9 ft. lbs. working from the center to the ends in progressive steps.

10. Install the front suspension member to the body. Install engine mounting nuts.

11. Install shock absorbers, stabilizer bar links to lower arms, intermediate shaft, exhaust components (all necessary brackets) and front suspension crossmember.

12. Install engine under covers and connect the negative battery cable. Refill the engine with the correct amount of engine oil. Start the engine and check for leaks. Check/adjust the front wheel alignment as necessary.

Oil Pump

REMOVAL AND INSTALLATION

Celica — All Engines

1. Disconnect the negative battery cable.

Raise the front of the vehicle and support it with jackstands or equivalent.

NOTE: *On 1990 SRS vehicles, you must wait AT LEAST 30 seconds after disconnecting the battery before doing any work. The SRS has a built-in backup which will allow the system to remain energized for a period of time after the power is disconnected.*

2. Drain the engine oil and remove the engine oil pan as outlined.

CAUTION: *The EPA warns that prolonged contact with used engine oil may cause a number of skin disorders, including cancer! You should make every effort to minimize your exposure to used engine oil. Protective gloves should be worn when changing the oil. Wash your hands and any other exposed skin areas as soon as possible after exposure to used engine oil. Soap and water, or waterless hand cleaner should be used.*

3. Remove oil strainer. Using a suitable engine hoist support engine (remove engine hood if necessary).

4. Remove the engine timing belt, idler pulley, crankshaft timing pulley dipstick guide tube.

5. Remove the oil pump retaining bolts (note location of retaining bolts as the bolts are different sizes). Remove the oil pump assembly.

6. Installation is the reverse of the removal procedure. Place a new gasket in position on

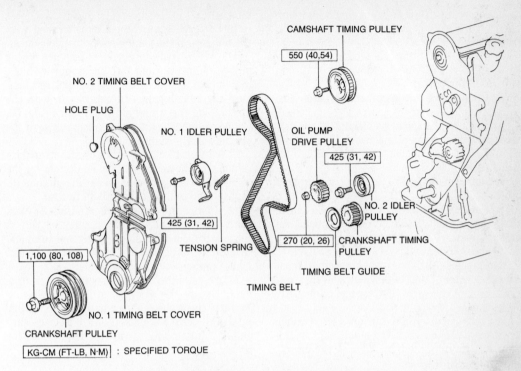

NO. 2 TIMING BELT COVER

HOLE PLUG

NO. 1 IDLER PULLEY

CAMSHAFT TIMING PULLEY

550 (40,54)

OIL PUMP DRIVE PULLEY

425 (31, 42)

NO. 2 IDLER PULLEY

425 (31, 42)

TENSION SPRING

270 (20, 26)

CRANKSHAFT TIMING PULLEY

1,100 (80, 108)

TIMING BELT GUIDE

TIMING BELT

NO. 1 TIMING BELT COVER

CRANKSHAFT PULLEY

KG-CM (FT-LB, N·M) : SPECIFIED TORQUE

Timing belt and cover — Celica 2S-E engine

the cylinder block. Engage the spline teeth of the oil pump drive rotor with the large teeth of the crankshaft and slide the oil pump on. Torque oil pump retaining bolts evenly.

Supra — All Engines

1. Disconnect the negative battery cable. Raise the front of the vehicle and support it with jackstands or equivalent.

NOTE: *On 1990 SRS vehicles, you must wait AT LEAST 30 seconds after disconnecting the battery before doing any work. The SRS has a built-in backup which will allow the system to remain energized for a period of time after the power is disconnected.*

2. Drain the engine oil and remove the engine oil pan as outlined.

CAUTION: *The EPA warns that prolonged contact with used engine oil may cause a number of skin disorders, including cancer! You should make every effort to minimize your exposure to used engine oil. Protective gloves should be worn when changing the oil. Wash your hands and any other exposed skin areas as soon as possible after exposure to used engine oil. Soap and water, or waterless hand cleaner should be used.*

3. Remove the oil pump outlet pipe. Remove the oil pump retaining bolts and remove it as assembly.

4. Installation is the reverse of the removal

procedure. Always prime oil pump with clean engine oil before installation.

Timing Belt Cover

REMOVAL AND INSTALLATION

For front cover removal procedures, please refer to the Timing Belt Removal and Installation procedure for your specific engine.

Timing Belt

REMOVAL AND INSTALLATION

2S-E Engine Celica

1. Disconnect the negative battery cable at the battery.

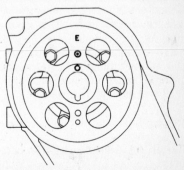

Aligning the knock pin with the camshaft timing pulley — Celica 2S-E engine

2. Raise the front of the vehicle and support it with safety stands. Remove the right front tire.

3. Remove the right side fender liner.

4. Remove the windshield washer and radiator reservoir tanks.

5. Remove the cruise control actuator if so equipped.

6. Remove the power steering drive belt and then remove the pump itself. Position the pump out of the way with the hydraulic lines still attached.

7. Remove the alternator and its support bracket.

8. Remove the spark plugs (do not remove spark plugs if just timing belt cover is being replaced). Remove the upper timing belt cover. Set No. 1 cylinder to TDC/COMPRESSION.

USA models: Align the oil seal retainer mark with the center of the small **E** mark on the camshaft timing pulley by turning the crankshaft pulley clockwise.

Canada models: Align the oil seal retainer mark with the center of the small hole on the camshaft timing pulley by turning the crankshaft pulley clockwise.

9. If the timing belt is to be reused, place a directional arrow on the belt and matchmark the camshaft timing pulley to the belt. Loosen the No. 1 idler pulley set bolt and shift the pulley to the left as far as it will go. Tighten the set bolt. Remove the timing belt from the camshaft pulley.

10. Remove the camshaft timing pulley. Remove the camshaft pulley.

11. Remove the lower timing belt cover.

12. Remove the timing belt and guide. If the belt is to be reused, matchmark it to the remaining pulleys as you did in Step 3. 13. Remove the No. 1 idler pulley. Remove the No. 2 idler pulley. Remove the crankshaft timing pulley and the oil pump pulley.

14. Install the oil pump pulley and tighten to 20 ft. lbs.

15. Install the crankshaft timing pulley by sliding it over the crankshaft key.

16. Install the No. 2 idler pulley and tighten it to 31 ft. lbs. Install the No. 1 idler pulley and tension spring. Pry the pulley to the left as far as it will go and tighten the set bolt.

17. Install the timing belt cover over all but the camshaft timing pulley. If reusing the old belt, be sure to align all the matchmarks made earlier.

18. Install the timing belt guide with the cup side facing outward.

19. Install the lower timing belt cover and then install the crankshaft pulley. Tighten the set bolt to 80 ft. lbs.

20. Check that the No. 1 cylinder is at TDC

by turning the crankshaft pulley clockwise until the groove on the pulley is aligned with the 0 mark on the timing cover.

21. When installing the camshaft timing pulley, align the camshaft knock pin with the matchmark on the camshaft oil seal retainer. On USA models, align the knock pin with the pin hole on the timing pulley **E** mark side. On Canadian models, align the knock pin with the pin hole on the timing pulley.

Check that the matchmark on the oil seal retainer and the center of the small hole on the camshaft timing pulley are in alignment. Tighten the pulley set bolt to 40 ft. lbs.

22. Install the timing belt around the camshaft pulley. Loosen the idler pulley set bolt 1/2 turn. Turn the crankshaft pulley two complete revolutions clockwise and then tighten the No. 1 idler pulley set bolt to 31 ft. lbs.

23. Installation of the remaining components is in the reverse order of removal. Tighten the right engine mount to 38 ft. lbs. Adjust all drive belts and perform all necessary engine adjustments. Road test the vehicle for proper operation.

3S-GE And 3S-GTE Engines Celica

1. Follow Steps 1–8 of the 2S-E procedure.

2. Set the No. 1 cylinder to TDC of the compression stroke by aligning the groove on the crankshaft pulley with the 0 mark on the lower timing belt cover. Check that the matchmarks on the two camshaft timing pulleys and the rear timing belt cover are aligned; if not, turn

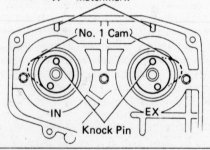

Two Hole Type

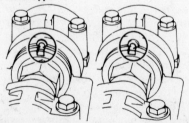

Five Hole Type

Installing camshaft timing pulleys — Celica 3S-GE and 3S-GTE engines

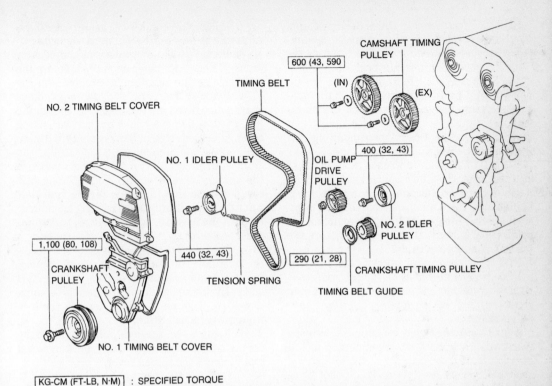

CAMSHAFT TIMING PULLEY

TIMING BELT

600 (43, 590)

(IN)   (EX)

NO. 2 TIMING BELT COVER

NO. 1 IDLER PULLEY

400 (32, 43)

OIL PUMP DRIVE PULLEY

NO. 2 IDLER PULLEY

1,100 (80, 108)

CRANKSHAFT PULLEY

440 (32, 43)

TENSION SPRING

290 (21, 28)

CRANKSHAFT TIMING PULLEY

TIMING BELT GUIDE

NO. 1 TIMING BELT COVER

KG-CM (FT-LB, N·M) : SPECIFIED TORQUE

Timing belt and cover — Celica 3S-GE and 3S-GTE engines

the crankshaft one complete revolution clockwise.

3. If the timing belt is to be reused, draw a directional arrow on it and matchmark the belt to the two camshaft pulleys. Loosen the No. 1 idler pulley bolt and shift the pulley as far left as possible; tighten the set bolt. Remove the timing belt from the two camshaft pulleys. Support the belt so that the meshing of the belt with the remaining pulleys does not shift.

4. Carefully hold the camshafts with an adjustable wrench and remove the camshaft pulley set bolts. Remove the pulleys and their set pins.

5. Remove the crankshaft pulley.

6. Remove the lower timing belt.

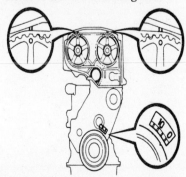

Valve timing marks after timing belt installation — Celica 3S-GE and 3S-GTE engines

7. Remove the timing belt guide and then remove the timing belt from the remaining pulleys. Be sure to matchmark the belt to the pulleys if it is to be reused.

8. Remove the No. 1 idler pulley and the tension spring. Remove the No. 2 idler pulley, the crankshaft timing pulley and the oil pump pulley.

9. Install the oil pump pulley and tighten it to 21 ft. lbs. Install the crankshaft timing pulley by sliding it onto the crankshaft over the woodruff key. Install the No. 2 idler pulley and tighten it to 32 ft. lbs.

10. Install the No. 1 idler pulley and the tension spring. Move the pulley as far to the left as it will go and then tighten it.

11. Install the timing belt on all pulleys except the two camshaft pulleys. Make sure the matchmarks made earlier are in alignment.

12. Install the timing belt guide with the cup side out.

13. Install the lower timing belt cover and then install the crankshaft pulley. Tighten it to 80 ft. lbs.

14. Check that the No. 1 cylinder is at TDC of the compression stroke for the crankshaft. The crankshaft pulley groove should be aligned with the 0 mark on the lower timing belt cover.

15. Check that the No. 1 cylinder is at TDC of the compression stroke for the camshaft.

NOTE: *There are two types of camshafts, one with two holes on the timing pulley contact surface and one with five holes on the timing pulley contact surface. All replacement camshaft have five holes.*

TWO HOLE: Using a wrench, turn the camshafts so that the camshaft knock pin aligns with the matchmark on the rear timing belt cover. And the No. 1 cam lobe is pointing outward as shown.

FIVE HOLE: Using a wrench, turn the camshaft so that the knock pin aligns with the notch in the No. 1 camshaft bearing cap.

16. Hang the timing belt on the two camshaft timing pulleys. Align all matchmarks made during removal. The **S** mark on the pulley should face outward.

NOTE: *There are two types of camshaft pulleys. One has five holes on the camshaft contact surface and one has one hole on the contact surface. All replacement pulleys have five holes.*

Align the timing pulley matchmark with the rear timing belt cover matchmark and install the pulleys with the belt.

NOTE: *On one hole pulleys, match the camshaft knock pin with the camshaft pulley hole. On five hole pulleys, insert the knock pin into whichever pulley and camshaft holes are aligned.*

Hold the camshaft with an adjustable wrench and tighten the pulley set bolt to 43 ft. lbs.

17. Loosen the No. 1 idler pulley set bolt just enough to move the pulley so it tensions the timing belt. Turn the crankshaft two complete revolutions clockwise and then tighten the idler pulley set bolt to 32 ft. lbs.

18. Check for proper timing belt tension.

19. Installation of the remaining components is in the reverse order of removal. Tighten the engine mount bracket bolts to 38 ft. lbs. Tighten the engine mount bolts to 58 ft. lbs. and the nuts to 38 ft. lbs.

20. Check all fluid levels. Adjust all drive belts. Perform all necessary engine adjustments. Road test the vehicle for proper operation.

3S-FE And 5S-FE Engines Celica

1. Disconnect the negative battery cable. Raise and support the vehicle safely. Remove the right tire and wheel assembly.

NOTE: *On 1990 SRS vehicles, you must wait AT LEAST 30 seconds after disconnecting the battery before doing any work. The SRS has a built-in backup which will allow the system to remain energized for a period of time after the power is disconnected.*

2. If equipped remove the cruise control actuator and bracket. Remove the drive belts.

3. Remove the alternator and alternator bracket. Raise the engine enough to remove the right side engine mounting assembly.

4. Remove the spark plugs (do not remove spark plugs if you are just replacing the timing belt cover). Remove the number two timing cover. Position the number one cylinder to TDC on the compression stroke by turning the crankshaft pulley and aligning its groove with the timing mark **0** of the No. 1 timing belt cover. Check that the hole of the camshaft timing pulley is aligned with the alignment mark of the bearing cap. If not, turn the crankshaft one revolution 360°.

5. If reusing the belt place matchmarks on the timing belt and the camshaft pulley. Loosen the mount bolt of the NO. 1 idler pulley and position the pulley toward the left as far as it will go. Tighten the bolt. Remove the belt from the camshaft pulley.

6. Remove the camshaft pulley. Remove the crankshaft pulley using the proper removal tool. Remove the timing cover.

7. Remove the timing belt and the belt guide. If reusing the belt mark the belt and the crankshaft pulley in the direction of engine rotation and matchmark for correct installation.

8. Remove the No. 1 idler pulley and the tension spring. Remove the No. 2 idler pulley. Remove the crankshaft timing pulley. Remove the oil pump pulley.

9. Inspect the belt for defects. Replace as required. Inspect the idler pulleys and springs. Replace defective components as required.

10. Align the cutouts of the oil pump pulley and shaft. Install the oil pump pulley and torque the retaining nut to 21 ft. lbs.

11. To install the crankshaft timing pulley, align the pulley set key with the key groove of the pulley and slide it in position. Install the No. 2 idler pulley and torque the bolt to 31 ft. lbs. Be sure that the pulley moves freely.

12. Temporarily install the No. 1 idler pulley

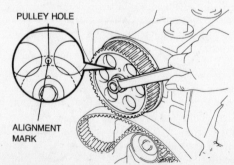

PULLEY HOLE

ALIGNMENT MARK

Aligning the hole of the camshaft timing pulley with the alignment mark of the bearing cap — Celica 3S-FE and 5S-FE engines

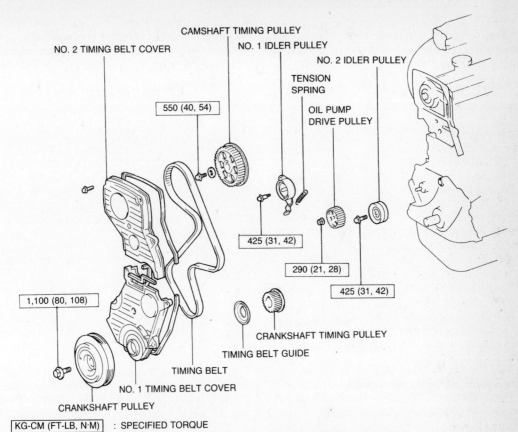

CAMSHAFT TIMING PULLEY

NO. 2 TIMING BELT COVER

NO. 1 IDLER PULLEY

NO. 2 IDLER PULLEY

TENSION SPRING

OIL PUMP DRIVE PULLEY

550 (40, 54)

425 (31, 42)

290 (21, 28)

425 (31, 42)

1,100 (80, 108)

CRANKSHAFT TIMING PULLEY

TIMING BELT GUIDE

TIMING BELT

NO. 1 TIMING BELT COVER

CRANKSHAFT PULLEY

KG-CM (FT-LB, N·M) : SPECIFIED TORQUE

Timing belt and cover — Celica 3S-E and 5S-FE engines

and tension spring. Pry the pulley toward the left as far as it will go. Tighten the bolt.

13. Temporarily install the timing belt. If reusing the old belt align the marks made during removal. Install the timing belt guide.

14. Install the No. 1 timing belt cover. Install the crankshaft pulley and torque the bolt to 80 ft. lbs.

15. Install the camshaft pulley by aligning the camshaft knock pin with the knock pin groove. Install the washer and torque the retaining bolt to 40 ft. lbs.

16. With the engine set at TDC on the compression stroke install the timing belt (all timing marks aligned). If reusing the belt align with the marks made during the removal procedure.

17. Once the belt is installed be sure that there is tension between the crankshaft pulley, water pump pulley and camshaft pulley. Loosen the NO. 1 idler pulley mount bolt $^{1}/_{2}$ turn. Turn the crankshaft pulley two revolutions from TDC in the clockwise direction. Check that all timing marks are in the correct location. Torque the No. 1 idler pulley mount bolt to 31 ft. lbs.

18. Continue the installation in the reverse order of the removal procedure. Check all fluid

levels and adjust all drive belts. Perform all necessary engine adjustments. Road test the vehicle for proper operation.

4A-FE Engine Celica

1. Disconnect the negative battery cable.
NOTE: *On 1990 SRS vehicles, you must wait AT LEAST 30 seconds after disconnecting the battery before doing any work. The SRS has a built-in backup which will allow the system to remain energized for a period of time after the power is disconnected.*

2. Raise and safely support the vehicle as necessary. Remove the right front wheel assembly.

3. Remove the alternator drive belt, air conditioning belt and air conditioning idler pulley.

4. Remove the power steering pump drive belt. Disconnect water pump pulley from the water pump.

5. Slightly raise engine to the right side to remove the weight from the motor mount.

6. Disconnect ground strap from right side fender apron. Remove the right side engine mounting stay and mount (insulator).

7. Remove the spark plugs (do not remove spark plugs if you are just replacing the timing belt cover). Remove the cylinder head cover.

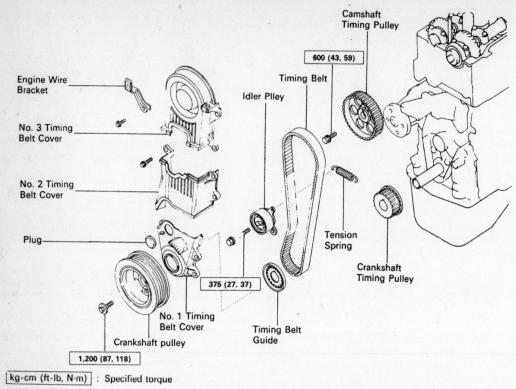

Engine Wire Bracket

No. 3 Timing Belt Cover

No. 2 Timing Belt Cover

Plug

Camshaft Timing Pulley

600 (43, 59)

Timing Belt

Idler Plley

Tension Spring

Crankshaft Timing Pulley

375 (27, 37)

No. 1 Timing Belt Cover

Timing Belt Guide

Crankshaft pulley

1,200 (87, 118)

kg-cm (ft-lb, N·m) : Specified torque

Timing belt and cover — Celica 4A-FE engine

8. Remove the upper and middle timing belt covers.

9. Position the number one cylinder to TDC on the compression stroke by turning the crankshaft pulley and aligning its groove with the timing mark **0** of the No. 1 (lower) timing belt cover. Check that the hole of the camshaft timing pulley is aligned with the alignment mark of the bearing cap. If not, turn the crankshaft one revolution 360°.

10. If reusing the belt place matchmarks on the timing belt and the camshaft pulley. Loosen the mount bolt of idler pulley and position the pulley toward the left as far as it will go. Tighten the bolt. Remove the belt from the camshaft pulley.

11. Remove the camshaft timing pulley. Remove the crankshaft pulley using the proper removal tool. Remove the No. 1 (lower) timing cover.

12. Remove the timing belt and the belt guide. If reusing the belt mark the belt and the crankshaft (also matchmark for correct installation) pulley in the direction of engine rotation.

13. Remove the idler pulley and the tension spring. Remove the crankshaft timing pulley.

14. Inspect the belt for defects. Replace as required. Inspect the idler pulley and spring. Replace defective components as required.

15. Install the crankshaft timing (flange side

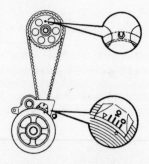

Timing marks — Celica 4A-FE engine

inward) pulley. Align the pulley set key with the key groove of the pulley and slide it in position.

16. Temporarily install the idler pulley and tension spring. Pry the pulley toward the left as far as it will go. Tighten the bolt.

17. Using the crankshaft pulley bolt, turn the crankshaft and align the timing marks of the crankshaft pulley and oil pump body.

18. Temporarily install the timing belt. If reusing the old belt align the marks made during removal. Install the timing belt guide.

19. Install the No. 1 timing belt cover. Install the crankshaft pulley and torque the bolt to 87 ft. lbs.

20. Install the camshaft pulley by aligning the camshaft knock pin with the knock pin

Belt deflection — Celica 4A-FE engine

groove. Install the washer and torque the retaining bolt to 43 ft. lbs.

21. With the engine set at TDC on the compression stroke install the timing belt (all timing marks aligned).

22. Once the belt is installed be sure that there is tension between the crankshaft pulley and camshaft pulley. Loosen the idler pulley mount bolt ½ turn. Turn the crankshaft pulley two revolutions from TDC in the clockwise direction. Check that all timing marks are in the correct location. Torque the idler pulley mount bolt to 27 ft. lbs.

23. At this point of the service procedure, check timing belt deflection at the center of the belt. The correct deflection should be 0.20 inch at 4.5 pounds of force. If the deflection specification is not correct adjust with the idler pulley.

24. Continue the installation in the reverse order of the removal procedure. Check all fluid levels. Perform all necessary engine adjustments. Road test the vehicle for proper operation.

5M-GE Engine Supra

1. Disconnect the battery cables at the battery.

2. Loosen the mounting bolts of each of the crankshaft-driven components at the front of the engine and remove the drive belts.

3. Rotate the crankshaft in order to set the No. 1 cylinder to TDC of its compression stroke (both valves of the No. 1 cylinder closed, and TDC marks aligned).

4. Remove the upper, front (No. 3) timing belt cover and gasket (five bolts).

5. Loosen the idler pulley bolt and lever the idler pulley toward the alternator side of the engine in order to relieve the tension on the timing belt. Hand tighten the idler pulley bolt.

6. Remove the timing belt from the camshaft pulleys.

7. Remove the camshaft timing pulleys as follows:

a. Hold the pulleys stationary with a spanner wrench.

b. Remove the center pulley bolt.

NOTE: *DO NOT attempt to use timing belt tension as a tool to remove the center pulley bolts, as the belt could become damaged. Do not interchange the intake and exhaust timing pulleys, as they differ for use with each camshaft.*

8. Remove the center crankshaft pulley bolt. Using a puller, remove the crankshaft pulley.

9. Using chalk or crayon, mark the timing belt to indicate its direction of rotation. This mark must face the same direction during installation of the belt.

10. Remove the lower timing belt cover, then the belt.

11. If damaged, the crankshaft pulley can be removed using a puller; the oil pump drive shaft pulley can be removed in the same manner as the camshaft pulleys.

12. Inspect the timing belt for damage, such as cuts, cracks, missing teeth, abrasions, nicks, etc.

a. If the belt teeth are damaged, check that the camshafts rotate freely and correct as necessary.

b. Should damage be evident on the belt face, check the idler pulley belt surface for damage.

c. If damage is present on one side of the belt only, check the belt guide and the alignment of each pulley.

d. If the belt teeth are excessively worn, check the timing belt cover gasket for damage and/or proper installation.

13. Check the idler pulley for damage and smoothness of rotation. Also check the free length of the tension spring, which should be 2.776 in., measured between the inside of each end clip. Replace the spring if the length exceeds this limit.

Install the timing belt as follows:

1. Install the crankshaft and oil pump drive shaft if these items were removed previously. Torque the oil pump drive shaft center pulley bolt to 14–18 ft. lbs. The crankshaft pulley must be evenly driven into place.

2. Install the idler pulley and the tension spring. Lever the pulley towards the alternator side of the engine and tighten the bolt.

3. Check the mark made during Step 9 of removal and temporarily install the timing belt on the crankshaft pulley. The mark must face in the same direction as it did originally.

4. Install the lower timing belt cover.

5. Install the crankshaft pulley and torque the center pulley bolt to 98–119 ft. lbs.

6. Remove the oil filter cap of the intake

camshaft cover, and the complete camshaft cover on the exhaust side.

7. Check that the match holes of both No. 2 camshaft journals are visible through the camshaft housing match holes. If necessary, temporarily install the camshaft pulley and guide pin, and rotate the camshaft(s) until the holes are aligned.

8. Install the timing pulleys. Note that the belt guide of the exhaust camshaft pulley should be positioned towards the engine; the belt guide of the intake camshaft pulley should be positioned away from the engine. DO NOT yet install the pulley retaining bolts.

9. Align the following marks:

a. Each camshaft pulley mark must be aligned with its respective mark on the rear, upper (No. 2) timing belt cover.

b. Align the crankshaft pulley notch on with the TDC (0) mark of the timing tab. NOTE: *The No. 1 cylinder MUST be positioned at TDC on its compression stroke.*

10. Install the timing belt.

11. Loosen the idler pulley bolt and tension the timing belt. The timing belt tension must be the same between the exhaust camshaft pulley and the crankshaft pulley, as it is between the intake camshaft pulley and the oil pump drive shaft pulley.

12. There are five pin holes on each camshaft and each timing pulley. On the exhaust side: Install the match pin into the one hole of the pulley which is aligned one of the camshaft pin holes. Repeat this on the intake side. Only one of the holes of each side should be aligned to allow insertion of the match pins.

13. Using a spanner wrench to hold the camshaft pulleys, install and tighten the camshaft pulley bolts. These bolts should be torqued to 48–54 ft. lbs.

14. Install the exhaust camshaft cover, using a new gasket. Install the oil filler cap.

15. Install the timing belt cover and gasket.

16. Install and adjust the drive belts at the front of the engine. Reconnect the battery cables.

17. Check all fluid levels. Perform all necessary engine adjustments. Road test the vehicle for proper operation.

7M-GE And 7M-GTE Engines Supra

1. Disconnect the negative battery cable. Drain the cooling system. Remove the radiator. Remove the water outlet.

CAUTION: *When draining the coolant, keep in mind that cats and dogs are attracted by the ethylene glycol antifreeze, and are quite likely to drink any that is left in an uncovered container or in puddles on the ground. This will prove fatal in sufficient quantity.*

Always drain the coolant into a sealable container. Coolant should be reused unless it is contaminated or several years old.

NOTE: *On 1990 SRS vehicles, you must wait AT LEAST 30 seconds after disconnecting the battery before doing any work. The SRS has a built-in backup which will allow the system to remain energized for a period of time after the power is disconnected.*

2. Remove the spark plugs (do not remove the spark plus if you are just replacing the timing belt cover). Remove the drive belts. Remove the No. 3 timing belt cover.

3. Position the engine at TDC on the compression stroke. Remove the timing belt from the camshaft sprockets. If reusing the belt matchmark the belt and the sprockets in the direction of engine rotation.

4. Remove the camshaft pulleys. Remove the crankshaft pulley using the proper removal tools. Remove the power steering air pipe, if equipped.

5. If equipped with air condition remove the compressor and position it out of the way. Do not disconnect the refrigerant lines.

6. Remove the No. 1 timing belt cover. Remove the timing belt. Remove the idler pulley and the tension spring. Remove the oil pump drive pulley.

7. Inspect the belt for defects. Replace as required. Inspect the idler pulleys and springs. Replace defective components as required.

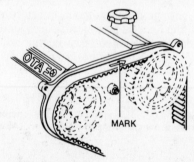

Mark the rotation direction on the timing belt with an arrow before removal — Supra

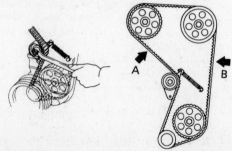

Timing belt tension should be equal at these two points following adjustment — Supra 5M-GE and 7M-GE engines

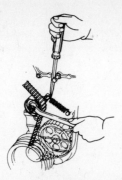

Loosen the idler pulley and push it out of the way — Supra

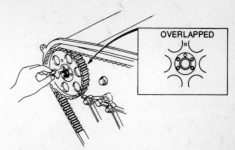

Aligning the cam pulley match hole with that of the camshaft — Supra

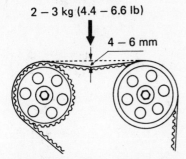

2 — 3 kg (4.4 — 6.6 lb)

4 — 6 mm

Check belt deflection here — Supra

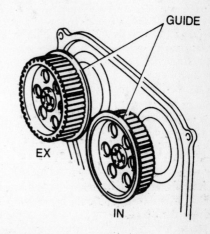

GUIDE

EX

IN

5M-GE engine cam pulley installation. Note guide position difference

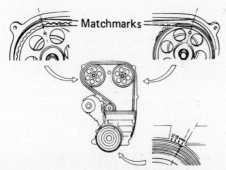

Matchmarks

Set the crankshaft pulley to TDC on the compression and align the cam pulley matchmarks — Supra 5M-GE engine

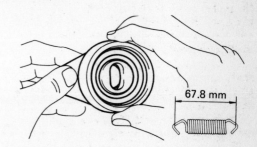

67.8 mm

The idler pulley should spin smoothly — Supra

8. Install the oil pump drive pulley and retaining bolt. Torque the bolt to 16 ft. lbs.

9. Install the crankshaft timing pulley. Temporarily install the idler pulley and tension spring. Torque the assembly to 36 ft. lbs. Pry the idler pulley toward the left as far as it will go and temporarily tighten the bolt.

10. Temporarily install the timing belt. If reusing the old belt install it using the marks made during the removal procedure. Install the No. 1 timing belt cover.

11. If equipped with air condition, install the compressor assembly. If equipped, install the power steering air pipe.

12. Align the set key with the key groove and

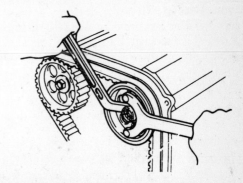

Removing the cam pulley set bolt — Supra

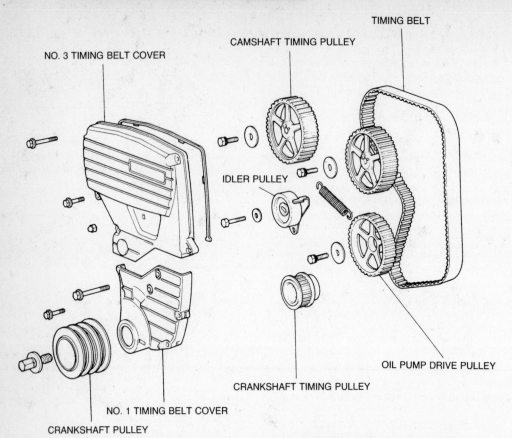

NO. 3 TIMING BELT COVER

CAMSHAFT TIMING PULLEY

TIMING BELT

IDLER PULLEY

OIL PUMP DRIVE PULLEY

CRANKSHAFT TIMING PULLEY

NO. 1 TIMING BELT COVER

CRANKSHAFT PULLEY

Timing belt and cover — Supra 7M-GE and 7M-GTE engines (5M-GE engine similar)

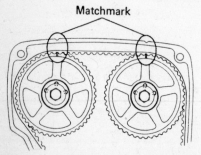

Matchmark

Timing marks — Supra 7M-GE and 7M-GTE engines

install the crankshaft pulley and torque the retaining bolt to 195 ft. lbs.

13. Set No. 1 cylinder to TDC/COMPRESSION of crankshaft. Install the camshaft timing pulleys. Torque the retaining bolts to 36 ft. lbs.

14. Loosen the idler pulley bolt. Install the timing belt to the INTAKE side and the EXHAUST side. Torque the idler pulley bolt to 36 ft. lbs.

15. Make sure that the timing belt tension A is equal to the timing belt tension B. If not adjust the idler pulley. Turn the engine two complete revolutions in the clockwise direction and check to see that everything is aligned properly (all timing marks aligned).

16. Turn both the intake and exhaust camshaft pulleys inward at the same time to slacken the timing belt between the two sprockets. Belt deflection should be 4.4–6.6 lbs. If not adjust the idler pulley.

17. Continue the installation in the reverse order of the removal

18. Check all fluid levels. Perform all necessary engine adjustments. Road test the vehicle for proper operation.

Camshaft Sprocket/Timing Pulley

REMOVAL AND INSTALLATION

To remove the sprockets/pulleys on all engines, first follow the timing belt removal procedures, then follow below.

1. Remove the retaining bolt(s) and positioning pins if so equipped for the drive sprocket/pulley you wish to remove. Do not use the timing belt as a means of holding the sprocket; use a spanner wrench that is made for the job.

2. Gently pry the sprocket/pulley off the shaft. If the sprocket/pulley is stubborn, use a gear puller. Never hammer on the sprocket/pulley or the camshaft.

3. Remove the sprocket/pulley and be careful not to lose the key if equipped.

4. Installation is the reverse of removal. On the engines with timing positioning pins, make sure the pins are properly aligned.

Camshaft and Bearings

REMOVAL AND INSTALLATION

2S-E Engine Celica

1. Remove the timing belt as previously detailed in service procedure.

2. Remove the camshaft housing as described in Cylinder Head Removal procedure.

3. Remove the camshaft pulley.

4. Remove the camshaft bearing caps.

5. Turning the camshaft slowly, slide it from the housing.

6. Installation is the reverse of removal. Always use new oil seals.

7. Installation is the reverse of removal. See Cylinder Head Installation procedure.

5M-GE Supra

1. Follow Steps 1-3 of the 5M-GE Rocker Arm Removal procedure, removing the camshaft housing (with cams) from the cylinder head.

2. Before removing the camshafts check camshaft end-play using a dial indicator set on the bench at one end of the front end of the camshaft. If this instrument is not available to you, take the housings to a reputable machine ship. Standard clearance is 0.0020–0.0098 in. If clearance is greater than this specification, the camshaft and/or cam housing must be replaced.

3. Remove the camshaft housing rear covers. Squirt clean oil down around the cam journals in the housing, to lubricate the lobes, oil seals and bearing as the cam is removed. Begin to pull the camshaft out of the back of the housing slowly, turning it as you pull. Remove the cam completely.

4. To install, lubricate the entire camshaft with clean oil. Insert the cam into the housing from the back, and slowly turn it as you push it into the housing. Install new O-rings in the housing end covers.

All Other Engines

The procedure for removing the camshaft(s) is given as part of the cylinder head removal procedure. Refer to the necessary service repair procedure as required. It will not be necessary to completely remove the cylinder head in order to remove the camshaft. Therefore, proceed only as far as necessary, to remove the camshaft, with the cylinder head removal procedure.

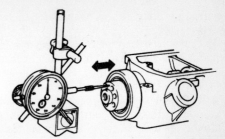

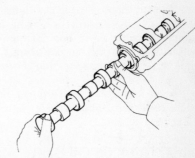

Measure camshaft end play with a dial indicator

Slowly turn the cam as you remove it from the back of the housing

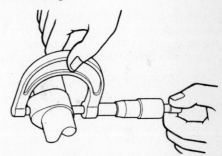

Measure lobe height and journal diameter with a micrometer

INSPECTION

A dial indicator, micrometer and inside micrometer are all needed to properly measure the camshaft and camshaft housing. If these instruments are available to you, proceed; if they are not available, have the parts checked at a reputable machine shop. Refer to the Camshaft

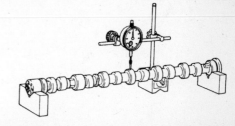

Camshaft run out must be measured with a dial indicator

Specification Chart in this chapter for the correct specification.

1. Using the micrometer, measure the height of each cam lobe. If a lobe height is less than the minimum specified, the lobe is worn and the cam must be replaced.

2. Place the cam in V-blocks and measure its run-out at the center journal with a dial indicator (refer to local machine shop or dealership parts for correct specification).

3. Using the micrometer, measure journal diameter, jot down the readings and compare the readings with those listed in the Camshaft Specifications Chart. Measure the housing bore inside diameter with the inside micrometer, and jot the measurements down. Subtract the journal diameter measurement from the housing bore measurement. If the clearance is greater than the maximum listed under Bearing Clearance in the chart, replace the camshaft and/or the housing.

Camshaft Housing Oil Seal

REMOVAL AND INSTALLATION

1. Using a small pry bar, carefully pry out the oil seals. If necessary carefully cut the oil seal lip using a utility knife. The lip is the inner diameter portion of the seal, closest to the camshaft.

2. Tape the blade end of a small pry bar so as not to damage the camshaft. Pry out the remaining part of the oil seals.

3. Coat the new seals with multi-purpose grease. Using an old socket or oil seal tool, gently tap the new seals into place.

Use an inside micro meter to measure camshaft housing bore diameter

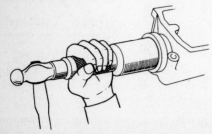

Installing an oil seal using and oil seal tool — an old socket also works

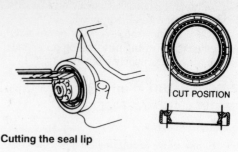

Cutting the seal lip

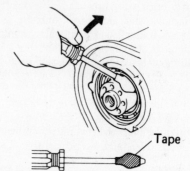

Pry the seal from the housing — do not scratch the camshaft

Pistons and Connecting Rods

REMOVAL AND INSTALLATION

All Engines

NOTE: *Before removing the piston assemblies, connecting rod bearing clearance and side clearance should be checked. Refer to the Connecting Rod Inspection procedure in this chapter.*

1. Remove the cylinder head as outlined in the appropriate preceding section.

2. Remove the oil pan and pump.

3. Position a cylinder ridge reamer into the top of the cylinder bore. Keeping the tool square, ream the ridges from the top of the bore. Clean out the ridge material with a sol-

Cover the rod bolts with rubber tubing (arrow) before removing piston and rod assemblies

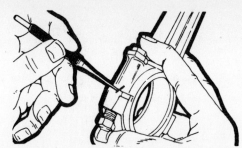

Matchmark each rod cap to its connecting rod

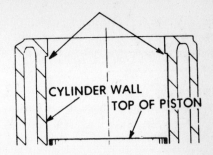

Ridge caused by cylinder wear

vent-soaked rag, or blow it out with compressed air.

4. Remove the oil strainer if it is in the way. Unbolt the connecting rod caps, after match marking each cap to its connecting rod.

5. Place pieces of rubber hose over the rod bolts, to protect the cylinder walls and crank journals from scratches. Push the connecting rod and piston up and out of the cylinder from the bottom using a wooden hammer handle.

NOTE: *Use care not to scratch the crank journals or the cylinder walls.*

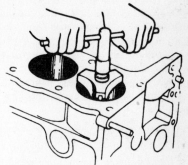

Removing the ridge with a ridge reamer

6. Mark each connecting rod with the number of the cylinder from which it was removed. Number stamps are available at most hardware or auto supply stores.

Installation is performed in the following order:

1. Apply a light coating of engine oil to the pistons, rings, and outer ends of the wrist pins.

2. Examine the piston to ensure that it has been assembled with its parts positioned correctly. (See the illustrations.) Be sure that the

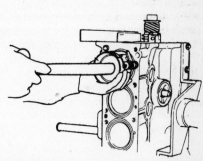

Install the piston and connecting rod into the cylinder with a ring compressor

ring gaps are not pointed toward the thrust face of the piston and that they do not overlap.

3. Place pieces of rubber hose over the connecting rod bolts, to keep the threads from damaging the crank journal and cylinder bore. Install the pistons, using a ring compressor, into the cylinder bore. Be sure that the appropriate marks on the piston are facing the front of the cylinder.

NOTE: *It is important that the pistons, rods, bearing, etc., be returned to the same cylinder bore from which they were removed.*

4. Install the connecting rod bearing caps and tighten them to the torque figures given in the Torque Specifications chart.

NOTE: *Be sure that the mating marks on the connecting rods and rod bearing caps are aligned.*

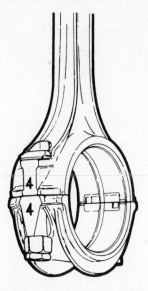

Number each rod and cap with its cylinder number for correct assembly

5. The rest of the removal procedure is performed in the reverse order of installation.

PISTON AND CONNECTING ROD IDENTIFICATION

The pistons are marked with a notch in the piston head. When installed in the engine, the notch markings must be facing towards the front of the engine.

The connecting rods should be installed in the engine with the forged marks on the bearing caps and on the bottom of the rod facing toward the front of the engine also.

NOTE: *It is advisable to number the pistons, connecting rods and bearing caps in some manner so that they can be reinstalled in the same cylinder, facing the same direction, from which they were removed.*

The piston rings must be installed with their gaps in the same position as shown in the illustrations below.

PISTON RING REPLACEMENT

NOTE: *The cylinder walls must be deglazed (honed) when the piston rings are replaced. De-glazing ensures proper ring seating and oil retention.*

Using a piston ring expander, remove the rings one by one. Always remove and replace the rings of each piston before going on to the next. This helps avoid mixing up the rings. When the rings have been removed from each

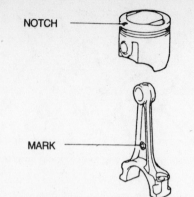

Piston and connecting rod identification — all engines

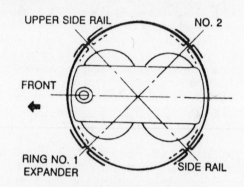

Piston ring gap positioning — 4A-FE engine

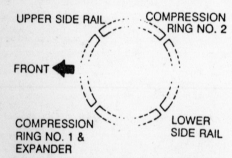

Piston ring gap positioning — 5M-GE engine

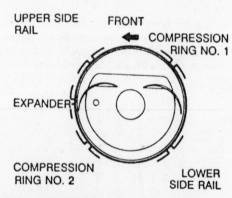

Piston ring gap positioning — 2S-E engine

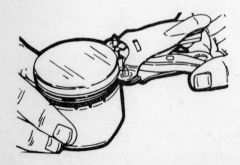

Remove and install the rings with a ring expander

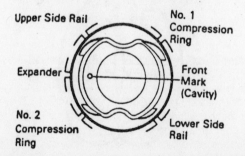

Piston ring gap positioning — 3S-FE and 5S-FE engines

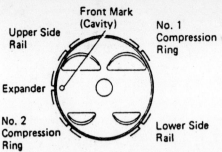

Piston ring gap positioning — 3S-GE and 3S-GTE engines

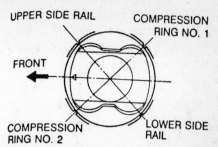

Piston ring gap positioning — 7M-GE and 7M-GTE engines

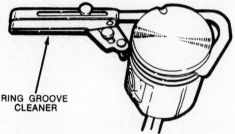

Clean the ring grooves with this tool or the edge of an old ring

Use needle-nose or snapring pliers to remove the piston pin snaprings

Rock the piston at a right angle to the wrist pin to check pin and small end bushing wear

When fully heated, the wrist pin should be able to be pushed into place by hand

piston, perform the end gap and piston inspection and cleaning procedure below. The rings are marked on one side, the mark denoting the up side for installation.

Install the rings using the ring expander, starting with the top compression ring and working down. Make sure the marks are facing up on each ring. Position the rings so that the ring and gaps are set as in the illustrations. Never align the end gaps!

WRIST PIN REMOVAL AND INSTALLATION

Wrist pin and/or connecting rod small-end bushing wear can be checked by rocking the piston at a right angle to the wrist pin by hand. If more than very slight movement is felt, the pin and/or rod busing must be replaced.

The pistons on the engines covered here must be heated in hot water to expand them before the wrist pins can be removed and installed. The four cylinder pistons must be heated to 176°F (80°C), and all six cylinder pistons must be heated to 140°F (60°C). This job can be performed at a machine shop if the idea of boiling pistons in the kitchen doesn't appeal to you. If you decide to do it, however, remember that each piston, pin and connecting rod assembly is a matched set and must be kept together until reassembly.

1. Using needle nose or snaping pliers, remove the snaprings from the piston.

2. Heat the piston(s) in hot water (as noted above depending on engine).

3. Using a plastic-faced hammer and driver, lightly tap the wrist pin out of the piston. Remove the piston from the connecting rod.

4. Assembly is in the opposite order of disassembly. The piston must again be heated to install the wrist pin and rod; it should be able to be pushed into place with your thumb when heated. When assembling, make sure the marks on the piston and connecting rod are aligned on the same side as shown.

CLEANING AND INSPECTION

Clean the piston after removing the rings, by first scraping any carbon from the piston top. Do not scratch the piston in any way during cleaning. Use a broken piston ring or ring cleaning tool to clean out the ring grooves. Clean the entire piston with solvent and a brush (NOT a wire brush).

Once the piston is thoroughly cleaned, insert the side of a good piston ring (both No. 1 and No. 2 compression on each piston) into its respective groove. Using a feeler gauge, measure the clearance between the ring and its groove. If clearance is greater than the maximum listed under Ring Side Clearance in the Piston and Ring chart, replace the ring(s) and if necessary, the piston.

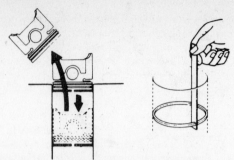

To check ring end gap, push the ring to the bottom of its travel — check gap with feeler gauge

To check ring end-gap, insert a compression ring into the cylinder. Lightly oil the cylinder bore and push the ring down into the cylinder with a piston, to the bottom of its travel. Measure the ring end-gap with a feeler gauge. If the gap is not within specification, replace the ring; DO NOT file the ring ends.

CYLINDER BORE INSPECTION

Place a rag over the crankshaft journals. Wipe out each cylinder with a clean, solvent-soaked rag. Visually inspect the cylinder bores for roughness, scoring or scuffing; also check the bores by feel. Measure the cylinder bore diameter with an inside micrometer, or a telescope gauge and micrometer. Measure the bore at points parallel and perpendicular to the engine centerline at the top (below the ridge) and bottom of the bore. Subtract the bottom measurements from the top to determine cylinder taper.

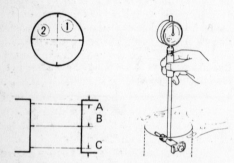

Use a dial gauge to check cylinder bore and piston clearance

Measure the piston diameter with a micrometer; since this micrometer may not be part of your tool kit as it is necessarily large, you have to have the pistons miked at a machine shop. Take the measurements at right angles to the wrist pin center line, about an inch down the piston skirt from the top. Compare this measurement to the bore diameter of each cylinder. The difference is the piston clearance. If the clearance is greater than that specified in the Piston and Ring Specifications chart, have the cylinders honed or rebored and replace the pistons with an oversize set. Piston clearance can also be checked by inverting a piston into a oiled cylinder, and sliding in a feeler gauge between the two.

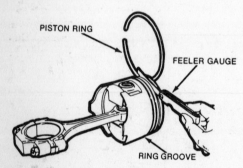

Checking ring side clearance

CONNECTING ROD INSPECTION AND BEARING REPLACEMENT

Connecting rod side clearance and big-end bearing inspection and replacement should be performed while the rods are still installed in the engine. Determine the clearance between the connecting rod sides and the crankshaft

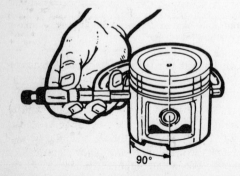

Check piston diameter at these points

using a feeler gauge. If clearance is below the minimum tolerance, check with a machinist about machining the rod to provide adequate clearance. If clearance is excessive, substitute an unworn rod and recheck; if clearance is still outside specifications, the crankshaft must be welded and reground, or replaced.

To check connecting rod big-end bearing clearances, remove the rod bearing caps one at a time. Using a clean, dry shop rag, thoroughly clean all oil from the crank journal and bearing insert in the cap.

NOTE: *The Plastigage® gaging material you will be using to check clearances which is soluble in oil; therefore any oil on the journal or bearing could result in an incorrect reading.*

Lay a strip of Plastigage® along the full length of the bearing insert (along the crank journal if the engine is out of the car and inverted). Reinstall the cap and torque to specifications listed in the Torque Specifications chart.

Remove the rod cap and determine the bearing clearance by comparing the width of the now flattened Plastigage® to the scale on the Plastigage® envelope. Journal taper is determined by comparing the width of the Plastigage® strip near its ends. Rotate the crankshaft 90° and retest, to determine journal eccentricity.

NOTE: *Do not rotate the crankshaft with the Plastigage® installed.*

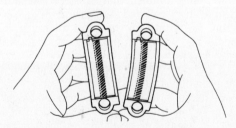

Inspect the rod bearings for scuffing and other wear — also check the crankshaft journal

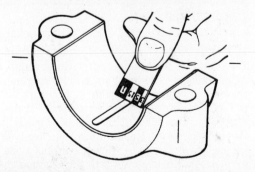

Measure Plastigage® width by using the scale on the envelope

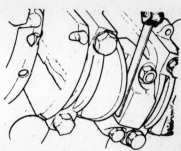

Checking connecting rod side clearance. Make sure feeler gauge is between shoulder of crank journal and side of rod

If the bearing insert and crank journal appear intact and are within tolerances, no further service is required and the bearing caps can be reinstalled (remove Plastigage® before installation). If clearances are not within tolerances, the bearing inserts in both the connecting rod and rod cap must be replaced with undersize inserts, and/or the crankshaft must be reground. To install the bearing insert halves, press them into the bearing caps and connecting rods. Make sure the tab in each insert fits into the notch in each rod and cap. Lube the face of each insert with engine oil prior to installing each rod into the engine.

The connecting rods can be further inspected when they are removed form the engine and separated from their pistons. Rod alignment (straightness and squareness) must be checked by a machinist, as the rod must be set in a special fixture. Many machine shops also perform a Magnafluxing service, which is a process that shows up any tiny cracks that you may be unable to see.

Rear Main Oil Seal

REMOVAL AND INSTALLATION

All Engines

1. Remove the transmission as detailed in service procedure.
2. Remove the clutch cover assembly and flywheel if so equipped or flex plate (refer to the necessary service procedure).

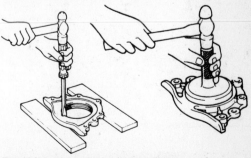

Rear oil seal removal and installation

3. Remove the oil seal retaining plate, complete with the oil seal.

4. Use a small pry bar to pry the old seal from the retaining plate. Be careful not to damage the plate.

5. Install the new seal, carefully, by using a block of wood to tap it into place.

NOTE: *Do not damage the seal; a leak will result.*

6. Lubricate the lips of the seal with multi-purpose grease.

7. Installation is performed in the reverse order from removal.

Crankshaft and Main Bearings

REMOVAL AND INSTALLATION

NOTE: *Before removing the crankshaft, check main bearing clearances as described under Main Bearing Clearance Check below.*

1. Remove the piston and connecting rod assemblies following the procedure in this chapter.

2. Check crankshaft thrust clearance (end play) before removing the crank from the block. Using a pry bar, pry the crankshaft the extent of its travel forward, and measure thrust clearance at the center main bearing (No. 4 bearing on 6 cylinder engines, No. 3 on

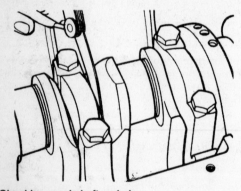

Checking crankshaft end play

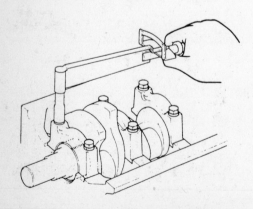

Torque all main bearing caps to specification

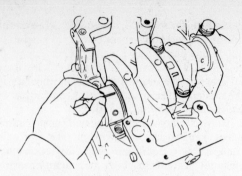

Use Plastigage® to check main bearing clearance

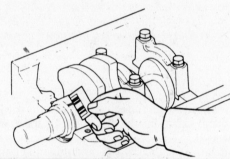

Compare width of now-flattened Plastigage® with scale on Plastigage® envelope

4 cylinder engines) with a feeler gauge. Pry the crankshaft the extent of its rearward travel, and measure the other side of the bearing. If clearance is greater than that specified, the thrust washers must be replaced (see main bearing installation, below).

3. Using a punch, mark the corresponding main bearing caps and saddles according to position: one punch on the front main cap and saddle, two on the second, three on the third, etc. This ensures correct reassembly.

4. Remove the main bearing caps after they have been marked.

5. Remove the crankshaft form the block.

6. Follow the crankshaft inspection, main bearing clearance checking and replacement procedures below before reinstalling the crankshaft.

INSPECTION

Crankshaft inspection and servicing should be handled exclusively by a reputable machinist, as most of the necessary procedures require a dial indicator and fixing jig, a large micrometer, and machine tools such as a crankshaft grinder. While at the machine shop, the crankshaft should be thoroughly cleaned (especially the oil passages). Magnafluxed (to check for minute cracks) and the following checks made: main journal diameter, crank pin (connecting rod journal) diameter, taper and out-of-round, and run-out. Wear, beyond specification limits, in any of these areas means the crankshaft must be reground or replaced.

MAIN BEARING CLEARANCE CHECK

Checking main bearing clearances is done in the same manner as checking connecting rod big-end clearances.

1. With the crankshaft installed, remove the main bearing cap. Clean all oil form the bearing insert in the cap and from the crankshaft journal, as the Plastigage® material is oil-soluble.

2. Lay a strip of Plastigage® along the full width of the bearing cap (or along the width of the crank journal if the engine is out of the car and inverted).

3. Install the bearing cap and torque to specification.

NOTE: *Do not rotate the crankshaft with the Plastigage® installed.*

4. Remove the bearing cap and determine bearing clearance by comparing the width of the now-flattened Plastigage® with the scale on the Plastigage® envelope. Journal taper is determined by comparing the width of the Plastigage® strip near its ends. Rotate the crankshaft 90° and retest, to determine journal eccentricity.

5. Repeat the above for the remaining bearings. If the bearing journal and insert appear in good shape (with not unusual wear visible) and are within tolerances, no further main bearing service is required. If unusual wear is evident and/or the clearances are outside specifications, the bearings must be replaced and the cause of their wear found.

MAIN BEARING REPLACEMENT

Main bearings can be replaced with the crankshaft both in the engine (with the engine still in the car) and out of the engine (with the engine on a work stand or bench). Both procedures are covered here. The main bearings must be replaced if the crankshaft has been reground; the replacement bearing being available in various undersize increments from most auto parts jobbers or your local Toyota dealer.

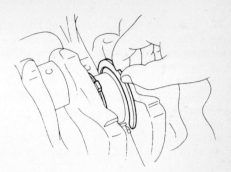

Install thrust washers with oil grooves facing out

Engine Out of Car

1. Remove the crankshaft from the engine block.

2. Remove the main bearing inserts from the bearing caps and from the main bearing saddles. Remove the thrust washers from the No. 3 (4-cylinder) or No. 4 (6-cylinder) crank journal.

3. Thoroughly clean the saddles, bearing caps, and crankshaft.

4. Make sure the crankshaft has been fully checked and is ready for reassembly. Place the upper main bearings in the block saddles so that the oil grooves and/or oil holes are correctly aligned with their corresponding grooves or holes in the saddles.

5. Install the thrust washers on the center main bearing, with the oil grooves facing out.

6. Lubricate the faces of all bearings with clean engine oil, and place the crankshaft in the block.

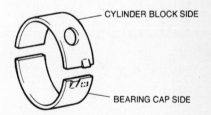

Bearing insert halves must be installed with oil notches and holes properly positioned

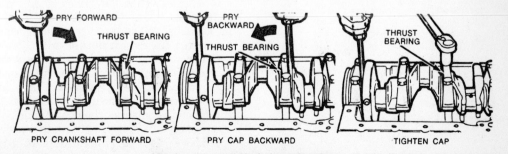

Aligning the crankshaft thrust bearing

7. Install the main bearing caps in numbered order with the arrows or any other orientation marks facing forward. Torque all bolts except the center cap bolts in sequence in two or three passes to the specified torque. Rotate the crankshaft after each pass to ensure even tightness.

8. Align the thrust bearing by prying the crankshaft the extent of its axial travel several times with a pry bar. On last movement hold the crankshaft toward the front of the engine and torque the thrust bearing cap to specifications. Measure the crankshaft thrust clearance (end play) as previously described in this chapter. If clearance is outside specifications (too sloppy), install a new set of oversize thrust washers and check clearance again.

Engine And Crankshaft Installed

1. Remove the main bearing caps and keep them in order.

2. Make a bearing roll-out pin from a cotter pin as shown.

3. Carefully roll out the old inserts from the upper side of the crankshaft journal, noting the positions of the oil grooves and/or oil holes so the new inserts can be correctly installed.

4. Roll each new insert into its saddle after lightly oiling the crankshaft-side face of each. Make sure the notches and/or oil holes are correctly positioned.

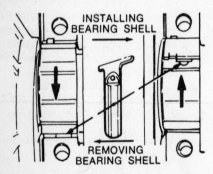

Upper bearing insert installation and removal

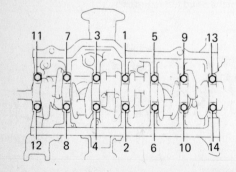

6-cylinder main bearing cap bolt torque sequence

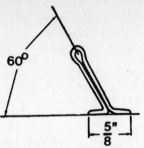

Home-made bearing roll out pin

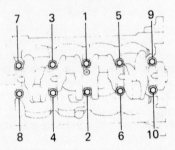

4-cylinder main bearing cap bolt torque sequence

5. Replace the bearing inserts in the caps with new inserts. Oil the face of each, and install the caps in numbered order with the arrows or other orientation marks facing forward. Torque the bolts to the specified torque in two or three passes in the sequence shown.

Cylinder Block

Most inspection and service work on the cylinder block should be handled by a machinist or professional engine rebuilding shop. Included in this work are bearing alignment checks, line boring, deck resurfacing, hot-tanking and cylinder honing or boring. A block that has been checked and properly serviced will last much longer than one which has not had the proper attention when the opportunity was there for it.

Cylinder de-glazing (honing) can, however, be performed by the owner/mechanic who is careful and takes his or her time. The cylinder bores become glazed during normal operation as the rings continually ride up and down against them. This shiny glaze must be removed in order for a new set of piston rings to be able to properly seat themselves.

Cylinder hones are available at most auto tool stores and parts jobbers. With the piston and rod assemblies removed from the block, cover the crankshaft completely with a rag or cover to keep grit from the hone and cylinder material off of it. Chuck a hone into a variable speed power drill (preferable here to a constant speed drill), and insert it into the cylinder.

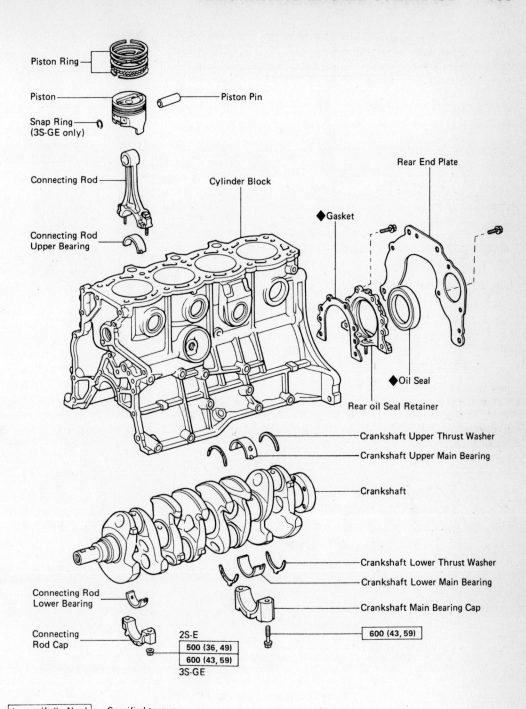

Piston Ring

Piston — — Piston Pin

Snap Ring
(3S-GE only)

Connecting Rod

Cylinder Block

Rear End Plate

◆Gasket

Connecting Rod
Upper Bearing

◆Oil Seal

Rear oil Seal Retainer

Crankshaft Upper Thrust Washer

Crankshaft Upper Main Bearing

Crankshaft

Crankshaft Lower Thrust Washer

Crankshaft Lower Main Bearing

Connecting Rod
Lower Bearing

Crankshaft Main Bearing Cap

Connecting
Rod Cap

2S-E

600 (43, 59)

500 (36, 49)

600 (43, 59)

3S-GE

kg·cm (ft·lb, N·m) : Specified torque

◆ Non-reusable part

Cylinder block — Celica 2S-E and 3S-GE engines

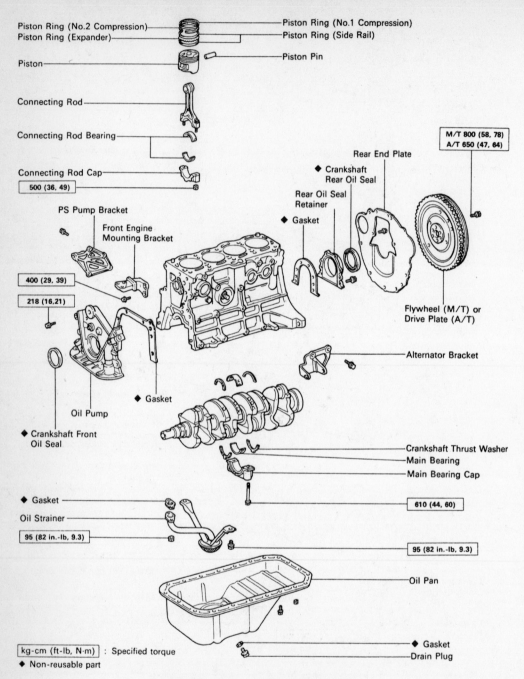

Piston Ring (No.2 Compression)
Piston Ring (Expander)
Piston Ring (No.1 Compression)
Piston Ring (Side Rail)
Piston
Piston Pin
Connecting Rod
Connecting Rod Bearing
Connecting Rod Cap
500 (36, 49)

M/T 800 (58, 78)
A/T 650 (47, 64)

PS Pump Bracket
Front Engine
Mounting Bracket
Rear End Plate
◆ Crankshaft
Rear Oil Seal
Rear Oil Seal
Retainer
◆ Gasket

400 (29, 39)
218 (16,21)

Alternator Bracket

Flywheel (M/T) or
Drive Plate (A/T)

◆ Gasket
Oil Pump
◆ Crankshaft Front
Oil Seal

Crankshaft Thrust Washer
Main Bearing
Main Bearing Cap

610 (44, 60)

◆ Gasket
Oil Strainer
95 (82 in.-lb, 9.3)
95 (82 in.-lb, 9.3)

Oil Pan

kg-cm (ft-lb, N·m) : Specified torque
◆ Non-reusable part

◆ Gasket
Drain Plug

Cylinder block — Celica 4A-FE engine

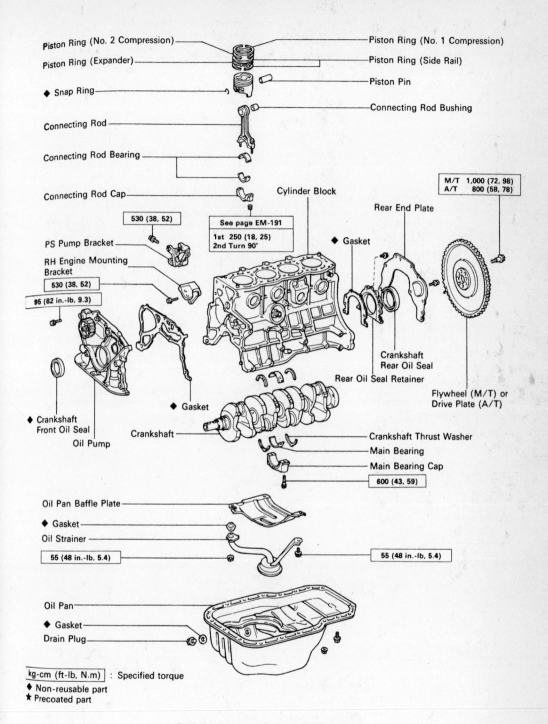

Piston Ring (No. 2 Compression)

Piston Ring (Expander)

◆ Snap Ring

Connecting Rod

Connecting Rod Bearing

Connecting Rod Cap

530 (38, 52)

PS Pump Bracket

RH Engine Mounting Bracket

530 (38, 52)

95 (82 in.-lb, 9.3)

◆ Crankshaft Front Oil Seal

Oil Pump

Piston Ring (No. 1 Compression)

Piston Ring (Side Rail)

Piston Pin

Connecting Rod Bushing

Cylinder Block

M/T 1,000 (72, 98)
A/T 800 (58, 78)

Rear End Plate

See page EM-191

1st 250 (18, 25)
2nd Turn 90°

◆ Gasket

◆ Gasket

Crankshaft Rear Oil Seal

Rear Oil Seal Retainer

Flywheel (M/T) or Drive Plate (A/T)

Crankshaft

Crankshaft Thrust Washer

Main Bearing

Main Bearing Cap

600 (43, 59)

Oil Pan Baffle Plate

◆ Gasket

Oil Strainer

55 (48 in.-lb, 5.4)

55 (48 in.-lb, 5.4)

Oil Pan

◆ Gasket

Drain Plug

kg-cm (ft-lb, N.m) : Specified torque
◆ Non-reusable part
★ Precoated part

Cylinder block – Celica 5S-FE engine

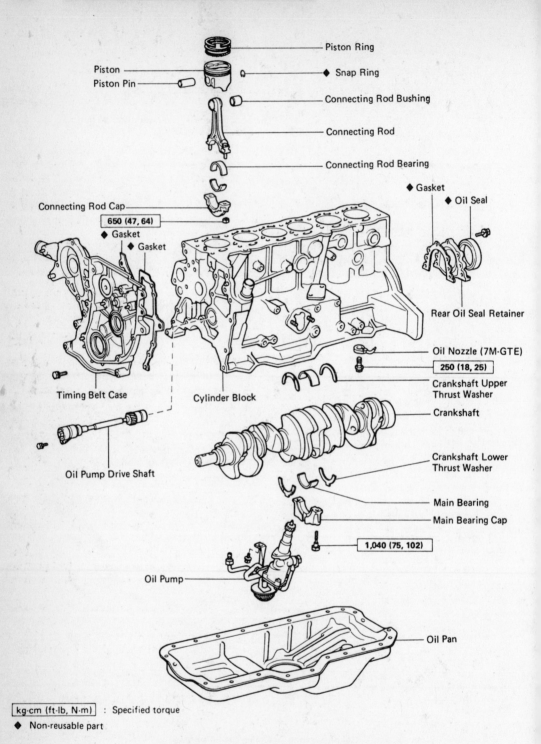

Piston Ring

Piston

Piston Pin

Snap Ring

Connecting Rod Bushing

Connecting Rod

Connecting Rod Bearing

Gasket

Oil Seal

Connecting Rod Cap

650 (47, 64)

Gasket

Gasket

Rear Oil Seal Retainer

Oil Nozzle (7M-GTE)

250 (18, 25)

Crankshaft Upper Thrust Washer

Timing Belt Case

Cylinder Block

Crankshaft

Crankshaft Lower Thrust Washer

Oil Pump Drive Shaft

Main Bearing

Main Bearing Cap

1,040 (75, 102)

Oil Pump

Oil Pan

kg-cm (ft-lb, N·m) : Specified torque

◆ Non-reusable part

Cylinder block — Supra 7M-GE and 7M-GTE engines

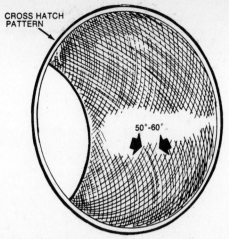

CROSS HATCH PATTERN

50°-60°

Cylinders should be honed to look like this

NOTE: *Make sure the drill and hone are kept square to the cylinder bore throughout the entire honing operation.*

Start the hone and move it up and down in the cylinder at a rate which will produce approximately a 60° cross-hatch pattern. DO NOT extend the hone below the cylinder bore! After developing the pattern, remove the hone and recheck piston fit. Wash the cylinders with a detergent and water solution to remove the hone and cylinder grit. Wipe the bores out several times with a clean rag soaked in clean engine oil. Remove the cover from the crankshaft, and check closely to see that no grit has found its way onto the crankshaft.

Flywheel/Flex Plate

REMOVAL AND INSTALLATION

All Engines

1. Remove the transmission, if the engine is installed in the car.
2. Remove the clutch assembly, if so equipped.
3. Remove the flywheel/flex plate.
4. To install, use new flywheel/flex plate bolts. Torque the bolts in a criss-cross pattern to the torque specified in the chart in this chapter.

EXHAUST SYSTEM

Safety Precautions

For a number of reasons, exhaust system work can be dangerous. Always observe the following precautions:

1. Support the vehicle securely by using jackstands or equivalent under the frame of the vehicle.

2. Wear safety goggles to protect your eyes from metal chips that may fly free while working on the exhaust system.
3. If you are using a torch be careful not to come close to any fuel lines.
4. Always use the proper tool for the job.

Special Tools

A number of special exhaust tools can be rented or bought from a local auto parts store. It may also be quite helpful to use solvents designed to loosen rusted nuts or bolts. Remember that these products are often flammable, apply only to parts after they are cool.

Front Pipe

REMOVAL AND INSTALLATION

1. Support the vehicle securely by using jackstands or equivalent under the frame of the vehicle.
2. Remove the exhaust pipe clamps and any front exhaust pipe shield.
3. Soak the exhaust manifold front pipe mounting studs with penetrating oil. Remove attaching nuts and gasket from the manifold.

NOTE: *If these studs snap off, while removing the front pipe the manifold will have to be removed and the stud will have to be drill out and the hole tapped.*

4. Remove any exhaust pipe mounting hanger or bracket.
5. Remove front pipe from the catalytic converter.
6. Install the front pipe on the manifold with seal if so equipped.
7. Install the pipe on the catalytic converter. Assemble all parts loosely and position pipe to insure proper clearance from body of vehicle.
8. Tighten mounting studs, bracket bolts on exhaust clamps.
9. Install exhaust pipe shield.
10. Start engine and check for exhaust leaks.

Catalytic Converter

REMOVAL AND INSTALLATION

1. Remove the converter lower shield.
2. Disconnect converter from front pipe.
3. Disconnect converter from center pipe.

NOTE: *Assemble all parts loosely and position converter before tightening the exhaust clamps.*

4. Remove catalytic converter.
5. To install reverse the removal procedures. Always use new clamps and exhaust seals, start engine and check for leaks.

Tailpipe And Muffler

REMOVAL AND INSTALLATION

1. Remove tailpipe connection at center pipe.

2. Remove all brackets and exhaust clamps.

3. Remove tailpipe from muffler. On some models the tailpipe and muffler are one piece.

4. To install reverse the removal procedures. Always use new clamps and exhaust seals, start engine and check for leaks.

EMISSION CONTROLS

There are three sources of automotive pollutants; crankcase fumes, exhaust gases, and gasoline evaporation. The pollutants formed from these substances fall into three categories: unburnt hydrocarbons (HC), carbon monoxide (C), and oxides of nitrogen (NOx). The equipment used to limit these pollutants is called emission control equipment.

Due to varying state, federal, and provincial regulations, specific emission control equipment have been devised for each. The U.S. emission equipment is divided into two categories: California and 49 State. In this section, the term "California" applies only to cars originally built to be sold in California. California emissions equipment is generally not shared with equipment installed on cars built to be sold in the other 49 States. Models built to be sold in Canada also have specific emissions equipment, although in most years 49 State and Canadian equipment is the same.

The following abbreviations are used in this section:
- PCV: Positive Crankcase Ventilation
- EVAP Fuel Evaporative Emission Control
- EGR: Exhaust Gas Recirculation
- TWC: Three-Way Catalyst
- EFI: Electronic Fuel Injection
- DP: Dash Pot
- BVSV: Bimetal Vacuum Switching Valve

Positive Crankcase Ventilation (PCV) System

OPERATION

To reduce emission, crankcase blow-by gas (HC) is routed through the PCV valve to the intake manifold for combustion in the cylinders.

SYSTEM SERVICE

Check the PCV system hoses and connections, to ensure that there are no leaks; then replace or tighten, as necessary.

To check the valve, remove it and blow through both of its ends. When blowing form the side which goes toward the intake manifold, very little air should pass through it. When blowing from the crankcase (valve cover/cylinder head side) side, air should pass through freely.

Replace the valve with a new one, if the valve fails to function as outlined. Do not attempt to clean or adjust the valve; replace it with a new one.

Remove the PCV valve from the cylinder head cover. Remove the hose (and retaining clamp if so equipped) from the valve as necessary. Installation is the reverse of removal.

Fuel Evaporative Emissions Control (EVAP) System

OPERATION

To reduce HC emission, evaporated fuel from the fuel tank is routed through the charcoal canister to the intake manifold for combustion in the cylinders. The system components are: fuel vapor lines, fuel tank, filler cap, char-

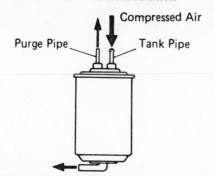

Typical charcoal canister

Compressed Air

Purge Pipe   Tank Pipe

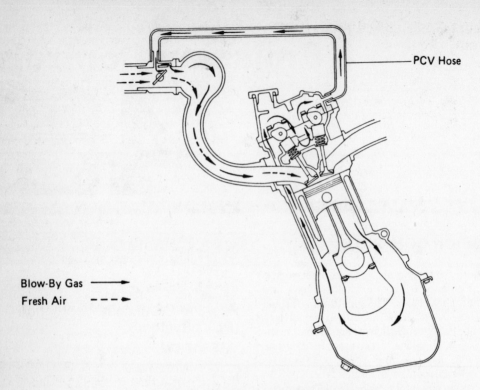

PCV Hose

Blow-By Gas ———→

Fresh Air - - - ➤

Typical PCV valve — Celica and Supra

coal canister, BVSV valve and a jet valve on manual transaxle vehicles.

SYSTEM SERVICE

Visually inspect fuel vapor lines, fuel tank and filler cap. Look for loose connections, sharp bends and or damage of these components. Check that the filler cap seals effectively. Replace the filler cap if the seal is damaged.

Remove the charcoal canister from the engine compartment and visually inspect it for cracks or other damage. Check for clogged filter or stuck check valves.

1. Using low pressure compressed air, blow into the tank pipe. The air should flow from the other pipes without resistance.

2. Blow into the purge pipe and check that air does not flow from other pipes.

3. If the air flow is incorrect, replace the charcoal canister.

4. Before installing the canister or during service procedures, clean the filter. Blow compressed air into the purge pipe while keeping the other blocked with your fingers. Do not attempt to wash the charcoal canister. While cleaning the canister, under no circumstances should any activated charcoal be removed. Check the jet valve if so equipped by blowing air from each side. Check for stoppage.

To check the BVSV valve on this system follow the service procedure below:

1. Drain the engine coolant and remove the BVSV from the water outlet on the engine block.

2. Place the end of the BVSV in cool water and blow into the top connection. The valve should be closed.

3. Heat the water to a temperature above 129°F (54°C) and again blow into the top connection. This time, the valve should be open.

4. If the valve is not operating properly it will require replacement.

5. Apply liquid sealer to the threads and reinstall the BVSV.

6. Refill the engine with coolant.

FILTER

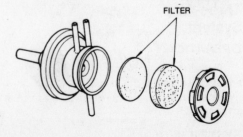

Unscrew the end cap to remove the vacuum modulator

Exhaust Gas Recirculation (EGR) System

OPERATION

To reduce NOx emission, part of the exhaust gases are recirculated through the EGR valve to the intake manifold to lower the maximum combustion temperature.

SYSTEM SERVICE

Inspect the EGR vacuum modulator for cracks or damage. Check and clean filters in the EGR vacuum modulator using the following service procedure:

1. Tag and disconnect all hoses leading form the vacuum modulator.

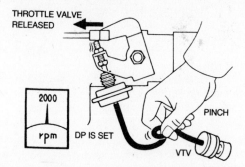

THROTTLE VALVE RELEASED

2000 rpm

DP IS SET

PINCH

VTV

Run the engine to 2500 rpm and pinch the vacuum hose

2. Remove the vacuum modulator.
3. Unscrew the vented top plate and remove the filter.
4. Check the filter for any contamination or other damage.
5. Clean the filter using compressed air.
6. Installation is in the reverse order of removal.

Inspection of the EGR valve is preformed by removing the EGR from the engine. Check the valve for sticking and heavy carbon deposits. If a problem is found replace the EGR valve. When replacing or reinstalling the EGR valve to the engine always use a new mounting gasket.

Three-Way Catalyst (TWC) System

OPERATION

To reduce HC, CO and NOx emissions, they are oxidized, reduced and converted to nitrogen (N_2), carbon dioxide (CO_2) and water by the catalyst agent.

SYSTEM SERVICE

Inspect the exhaust pipe assembly for loose connections or damage. Check exhaust clamps for cracks or damage. If any part of the catalyst converter protector/heat insulator is damaged or dented that it contacts the catalyst converter repair or replace it. Check for adequate clearance between catalytic converter and protector/heat insulator. Repair or replace system component parts as necessary.

NOTE: *California vehicles use a sub-catalytic converter in addition to the main catalytic converter system service is the same.*

Dash Pot (DP) System

OPERATION

To reduce HC and CO emissions, when decelerating the dash pot opens the throttle valve slightly more than idle. This causes a more efficient burn of the air/fuel mixture.

SYSTEM SERVICE

1. Run the engine until it reaches normal operating temperature.
2. Check the idle speed mixture and ignition timing. Adjust if necessary.
3. Run the engine at 2500 rpm (3000 rpm on the Supra) and pinch the vacuum hose between the dash pot and the VTV.
4. Release the throttle and check that the dash pot holds the engine speed at 2000 rpm.
5. Adjust the dash pot to the proper speed if necessary.
6. Release the pinched vacuum hose and check that the engine returns to idle speed within 1 second.

Service Lights

RESETTING

The Electronic Control Unit contains a self-diagnosis system. Troubles within the engine emission control and fuel control system signal network are detected causing a "CHECK ENGINE" warning light on the dash to illuminate. The light will illuminate briefly with the ignition key in the ON position and the engine not running and will normally go out when the engine is started. However, if the light comes on when the engine is running, the computer has detected a fault (trouble code) or malfunction within the system.

In the event you do get a "CHECK ENGINE" warning light, the only way to reset the light is to diagnose/repair the system and determine the component or components that are causing the malfunction.

After repair of the trouble area, the diagnostic code(s) are retained in the computer memory. Cancellation of the "CHECK ENGINE" warning light can be done by removing the EFI fuse for 10 seconds or more, depending

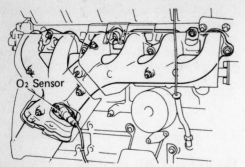

Remove the oxygen sensor carefully through the heat shield

codes that we are not able to address in this book. THESE SERVICE PROCEDURES REQUIRE PROPER EXPERIENCE, TRAINING (ASE CERTIFICATION) and SPECIAL DIAGNOSIS EQUIPMENT. However, if you wish to learn more about emission control related troubleshooting and diagnosis refer to "Chilton Electronic Engine Control Manual" for import cars.

Oxygen Sensor

REMOVAL AND INSTALLATION

NOTE: *Do not drop the oxygen sensor during removal or installation as this will damage the sensor.*

1. Disconnect the negative battery cable.
2. Unplug the electrical wiring connector leading from the O_2 sensor.
3. Unscrew the two nuts and carefully pull out the sensor.
4. Installation is in the reverse order of removal procedure. Always use a new mounting gasket. Tighten the nuts to 13–16 ft. lbs.

on the ambient temperature (the lower the temperature the longer the fuse must be left out) with the ignition switch in the OFF position.

Cancellation can also be done by removing the negative battery cable, but in this case, other memory systems will also be canceled out.

Identifying a malfunction involves complicated diagnosis procedures and fault (trouble)

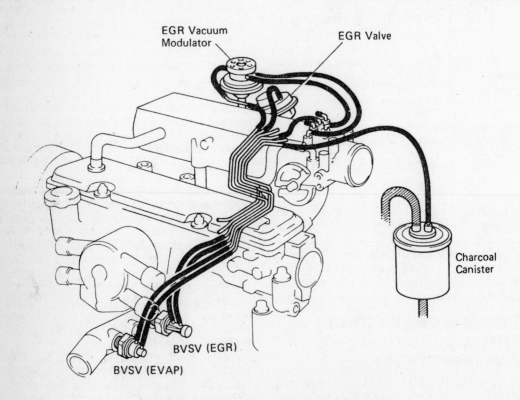

Emission component layout — Celica 2S-E engine

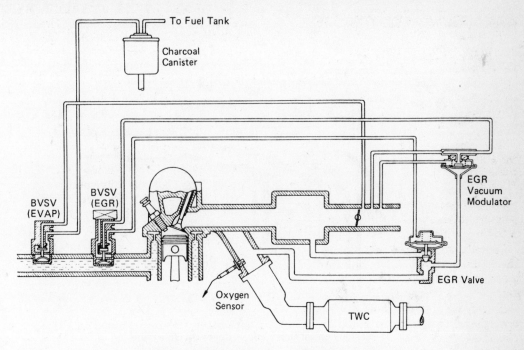

Emission control schematic — Celica 2S-E engine

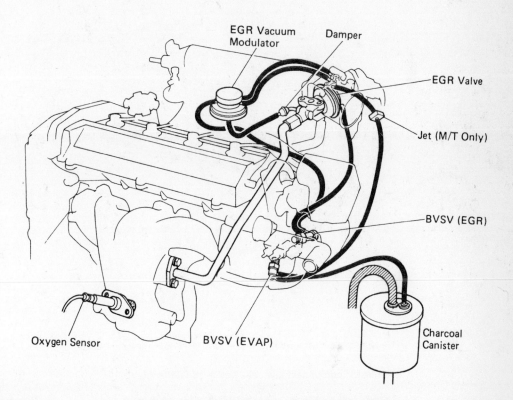

Emission component layout — Celica 3S-GE engine

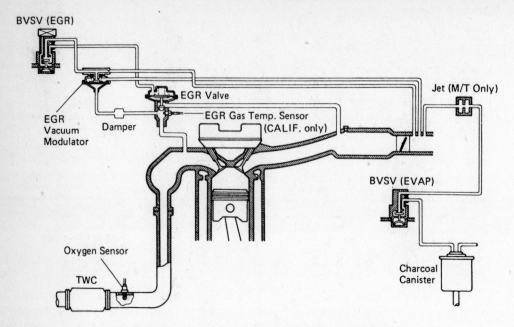

BVSV (EGR)

EGR Valve

EGR Vacuum Modulator

Damper

EGR Gas Temp. Sensor (CALIF. only)

Jet (M/T Only)

BVSV (EVAP)

Oxygen Sensor

TWC

Charcoal Canister

Emission control schematic — Celica 3S-GE engine

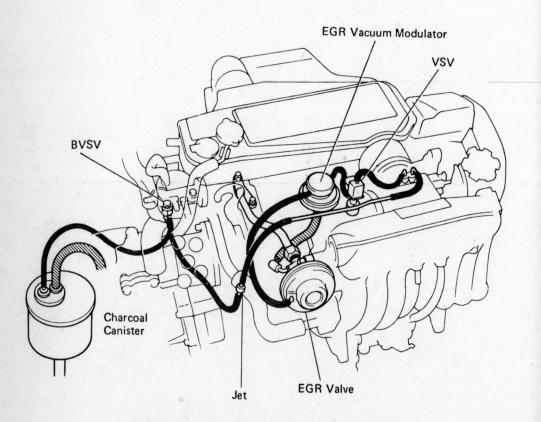

EGR Vacuum Modulator

VSV

BVSV

Charcoal Canister

Jet

EGR Valve

Emission component layout — Celica 3S-GTE engine

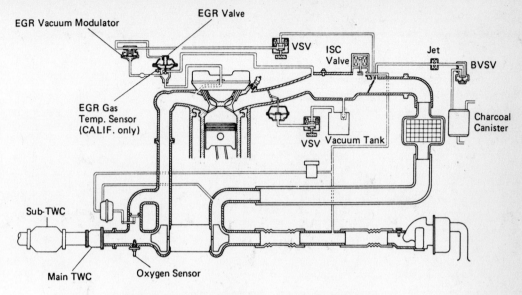

Emission control schematic — Celica 3S-GTE engine

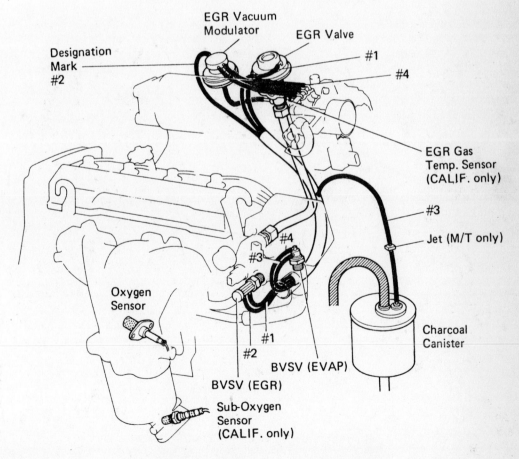

Emission component layout — Celica 3S-FE engine

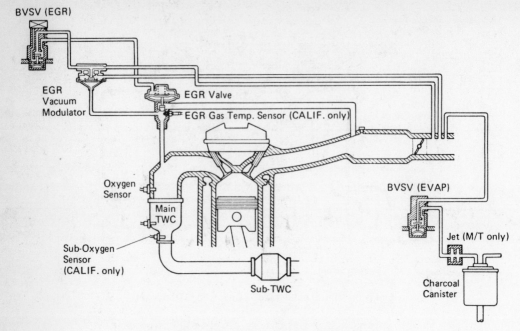

BVSV (EGR)

EGR Vacuum Modulator

EGR Valve

EGR Gas Temp. Sensor (CALIF. only)

Oxygen Sensor

Main TWC

Sub-Oxygen Sensor (CALIF. only)

Sub-TWC

BVSV (EVAP)

Jet (M/T only)

Charcoal Canister

Emission control schematic — Celica 3S-FE engine

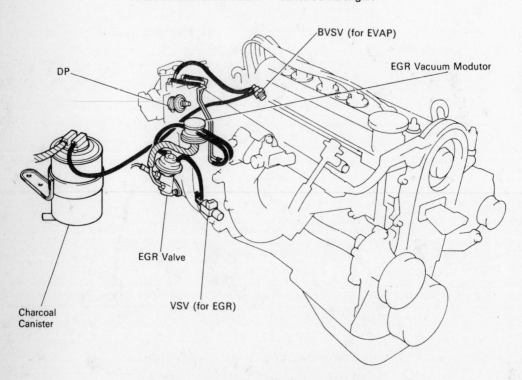

DP

BVSV (for EVAP)

EGR Vacuum Modutor

EGR Valve

VSV (for EGR)

Charcoal Canister

Emission component layout — Celica 4A-FE engine

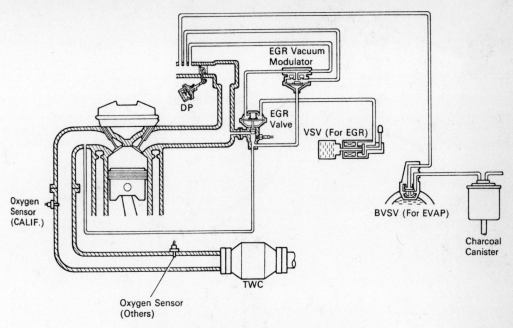

Emission control schematic — Celica 4A-FE engine

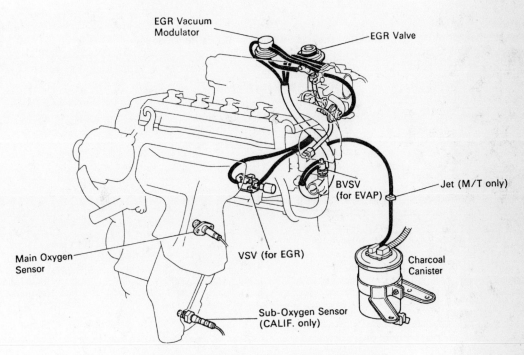

Emission component layout — Celica 5S-FE engine

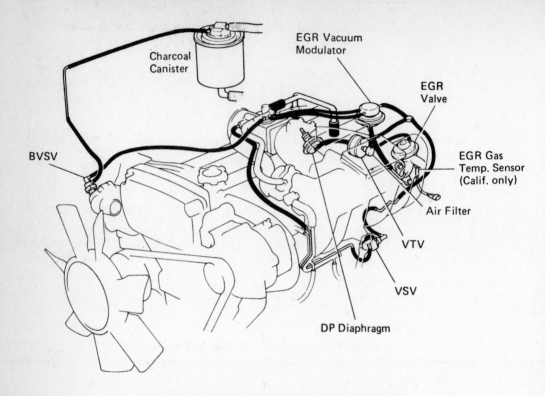

Charcoal Canister

EGR Vacuum Modulator

EGR Valve

BVSV

EGR Gas Temp. Sensor (Calif. only)

Air Filter

VTV

VSV

DP Diaphragm

Emission component layout — Supra 7M-GE engine

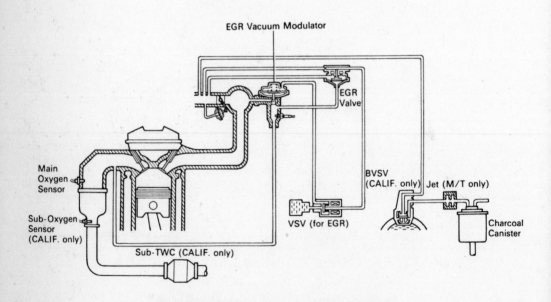

EGR Vacuum Modulator

EGR Valve

Main Oxygen Sensor

BVSV (CALIF. only)

Jet (M/T only)

Sub-Oxygen Sensor (CALIF. only)

VSV (for EGR)

Charcoal Canister

Sub-TWC (CALIF. only)

Emission control schematic — Celica 5S-FE engine

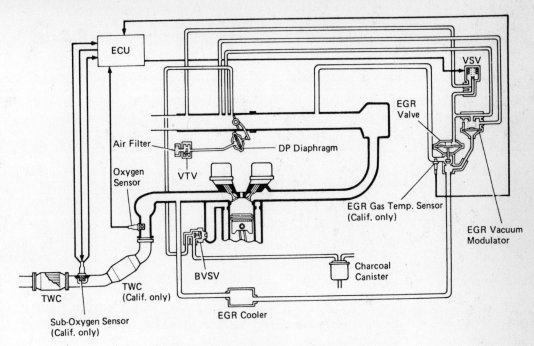

Emission control schematic — Supra 7M-GE engine

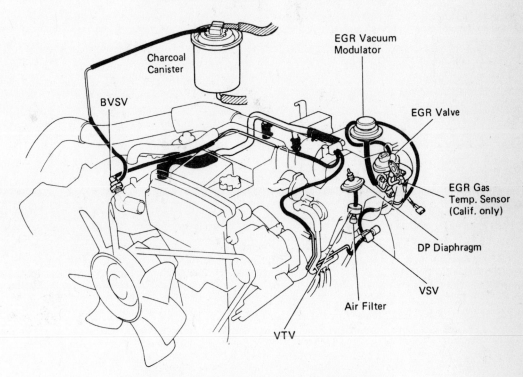

Emission component layout — Supra 7M-GTE engine

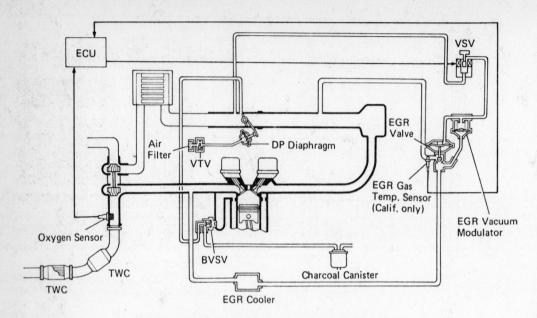

Emission control schematic — Supra 7M-GTE engine

Fuel System

5

GASOLINE FUEL INJECTION SYSTEM

Understanding the Fuel System

Fuel is supplied under constant pressure to the EFI injectors by an electric fuel pump. The injectors inject a metered quantity of fuel into the intake manifold in accordance with signals from the ECU (electronic control unit). The air induction system provides sufficient air for engine operation.

Use care any time a fuel pressure line is disconnected; a large amount of gasoline will spill out. Always slowly loosen the connection and place a container under it. Plug the connection afterwards.

General troubleshooting

Engine troubles are not usually caused by the EFI system. When troubleshooting, always check first the condition of all other related systems.

Many times the most frequent cause of problems is a bad contact in a wiring connector, so always make sure that the connections are secure. When inspecting the connector, pay particular attention to the following

1. Check to see that the terminals are not bent.

2. Check to see that the connector is pushed in all the way and locked.

3. Check that there is no change in signal when the connector is tapped or wiggled.

Actual troubleshooting of the EFI system and the EFI computer is a complex process which requires the use of a few expensive and hard to find tools. Other than checking the operation of the main components (to adjust the TPS sensor refer to throttle body removal and installation) individually, we suggest that you leave any further troubleshooting to an authorized service facility.

The worst enemy of any fuel injection system is water or moisture. The best (i.e., cheapest and simplest) insurance for your car's injection system is to change the fuel filter as frequently as the maintenance schedule recommends. When you follow the filter change interval strictly, many possible expensive injection system problems are eliminated.

Fuel System Service Precautions

Safety is very important when preforming fuel system maintenance. Failure to conduct fuel system maintenance and repairs in a safe manner may result in serious personal injury. Maintenance and testing of the vehicle's fuel system components can be accomplished safely and effectively by following a few rules and precautions.

• To avoid the possibility of fire and personal injury, always disconnect the negative battery cable unless the repair or test procedure specifically requires that battery voltage be applied.

• Always relieve the fuel system pressure prior to disconnecting any fuel system component (injector, fuel rail, pressure regulator, etc.), fitting or fuel line connection. Exercise extreme caution whenever relieving fuel system pressure to avoid exposing skin, face and eyes to fuel spray. Please be advised that fuel under pressure may penetrate the skin or any part of the body that it comes in contact with.

• Always place a shop towel or cloth around the fitting or connection prior to loosening to absorb any excess fuel due to spillage. Ensure that all fuel spillage (should it occur) is quickly removed from engine surfaces. Ensure that all fuel soaked cloths or towels are deposited into a suitable waste container.

• Always have a properly charged Class "B" fire extinguisher in the vicinity of the work

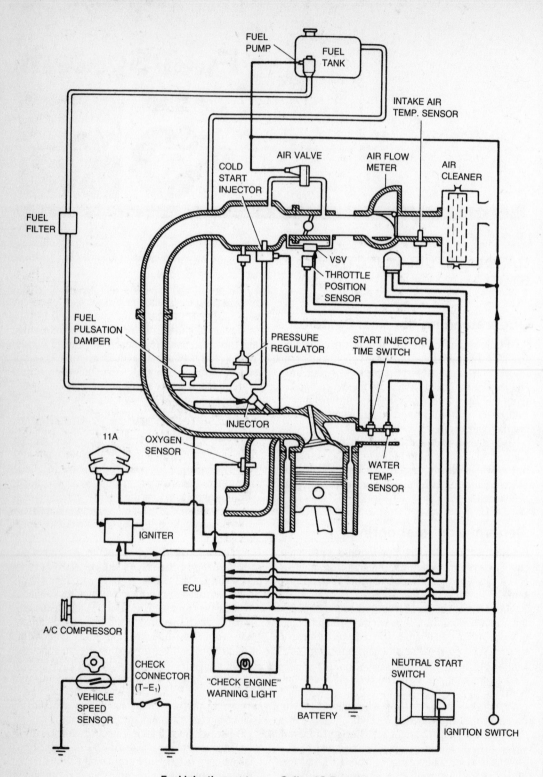

Fuel injection system — Celica 2S-E engine

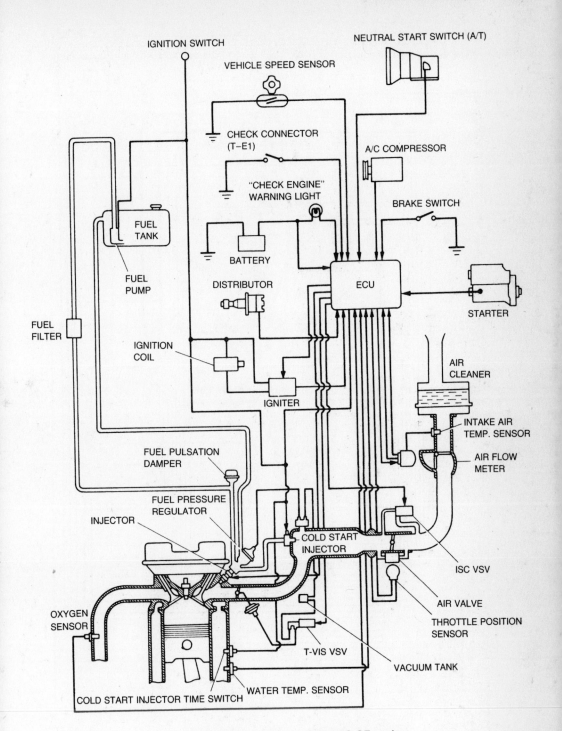

Fuel injection system — Celica 3S-GE engine

*CALIF. only

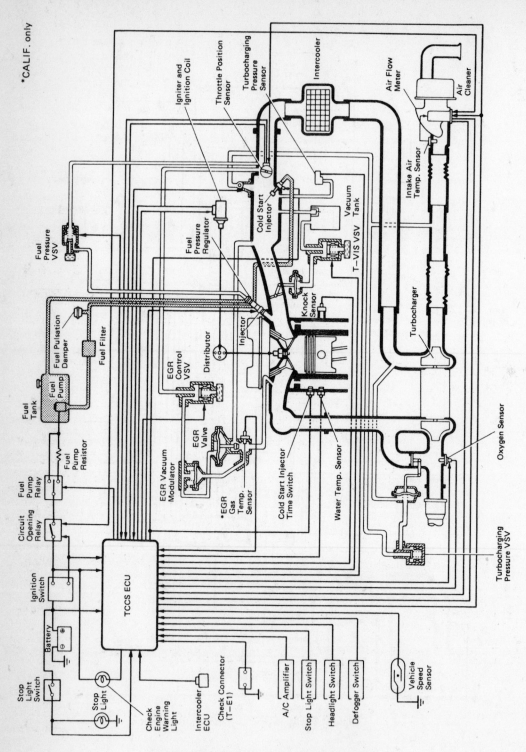

Fuel injection system — Celica 3S-GTE engine

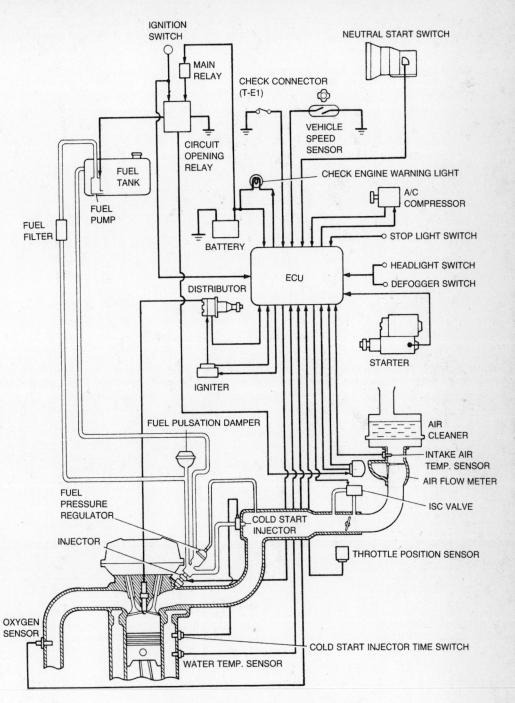

Fuel injection system — Celica 3S-FE engine

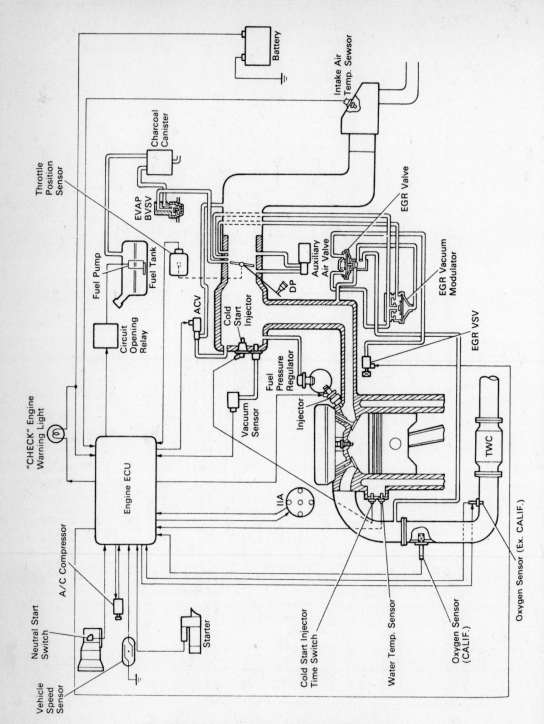

Fuel injection system — Celica 4A-FE engine

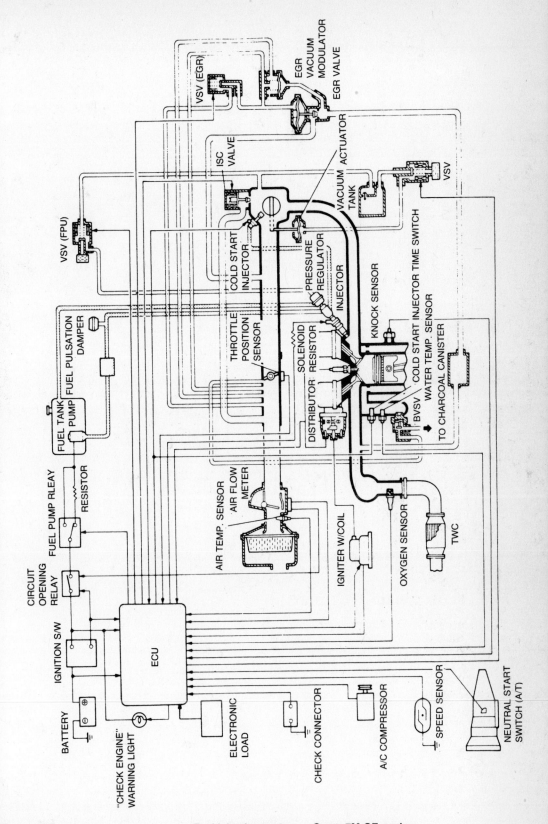

Fuel injection system — Supra 7M-GE engine

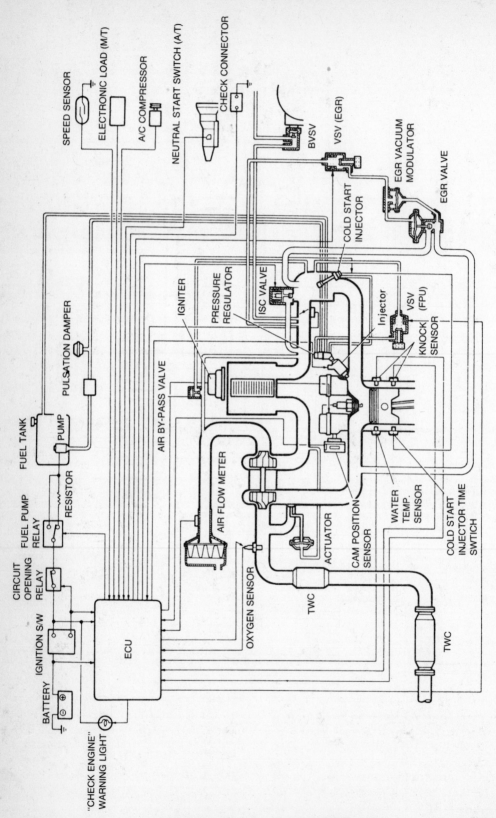

Fuel injection system — Supra 7M-GTE engine

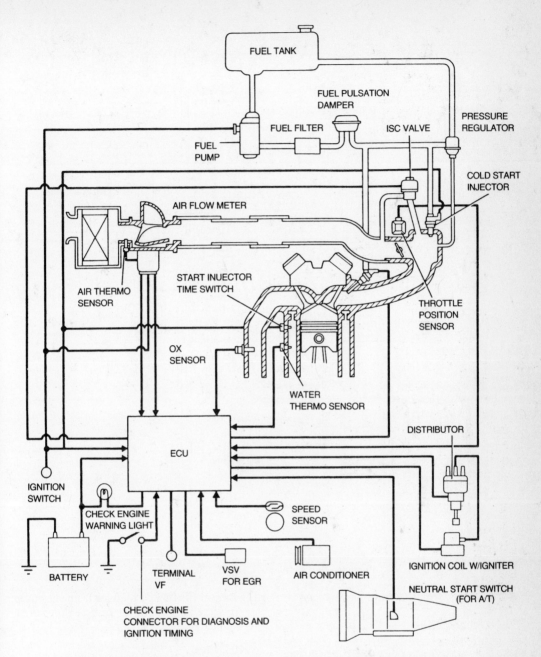

FUEL TANK

FUEL PULSATION DAMPER

PRESSURE REGULATOR

FUEL FILTER   ISC VALVE

FUEL PUMP

COLD START INJECTOR

AIR FLOW METER

START INUECTOR TIME SWITCH

AIR THERMO SENSOR

THROTTLE POSITION SENSOR

OX SENSOR

WATER THERMO SENSOR

DISTRIBUTOR

ECU

IGNITION SWITCH

CHECK ENGINE WARNING LIGHT

SPEED SENSOR

BATTERY

TERMINAL VF

VSV FOR EGR

AIR CONDITIONER

IGNITION COIL W/IGNITER

NEUTRAL START SWITCH (FOR A/T)

CHECK ENGINE CONNECTOR FOR DIAGNOSIS AND IGNITION TIMING

The fuel spray pattern should be even, V-shape one — typical cold start injector

area and always ensure work areas are adequately ventilated.

• Never allow fuel spray or fuel vapors to come in contact with spark or open flame.

• Always use a backup wrench when loosening and tightening fuel line connection fittings. This will prevent unnecessary stress and torsion to fuel line piping. Always follow the proper torque specifications.

• Always replace worn fuel fitting O-rings

with new. Do not substitute fuel hose or equivalent where fuel pipe is installed.

• Always use common sense. It is your best defense against personal injury.

Electric Fuel Pump

REMOVAL AND INSTALLATION

1986–89 Celica 1986–90 Supra

CAUTION: *Do not smoke or work near an open flame when working on the fuel pump assembly. Do not let fuel come in contact with*

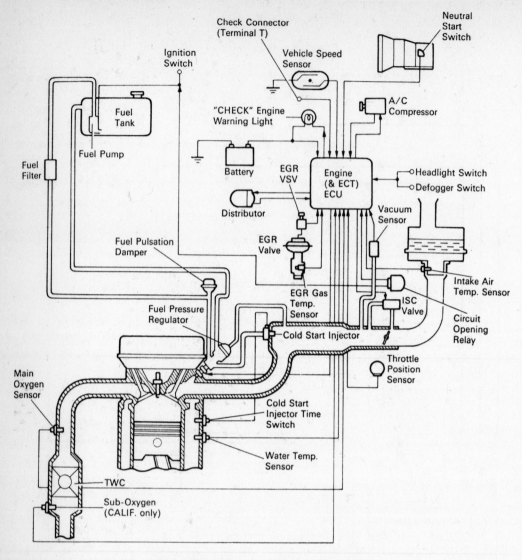

Fuel injection system — Celica 5S-FE engine

work light when performing service procedures.

1. Disconnect the negative battery cable. On 1990 SRS vehicles, you must wait AT LEAST 30 seconds after disconnecting the battery before doing any work. The SRS has a built-in backup which will allow the system to remain energized for a period of time after the power is disconnected.

2. Drain the fuel from the tank and then remove the fuel tank.

3. Remove the seven bolts and then pull the fuel pump bracket up and out of the fuel tank.

4. Remove the two nuts and then tag and disconnect the wires at the fuel pump.

5. Pull the fuel pump out of the lower side of the bracket. Disconnect the pump from the fuel hose.

6. Remove the rubber cushion and the clip.

Disconnect the fuel pump filter from the pump.

7. Installation is in the reverse order of removal procedure.

1990 Celica

CAUTION: *Do not smoke or work near an open flame when working on the fuel pump assembly. Do not let fuel come in contact with work light when performing service procedures.*

1. Disconnect the negative battery cable. On 1990 SRS vehicles, you must wait AT LEAST 30 seconds after disconnecting the battery before doing any work. The SRS has a built-in backup which will allow the system to remain energized for a period of time after the power is disconnected.

2. Remove the rear seat cushion.

3. Remove the 5 retaining screws and floor

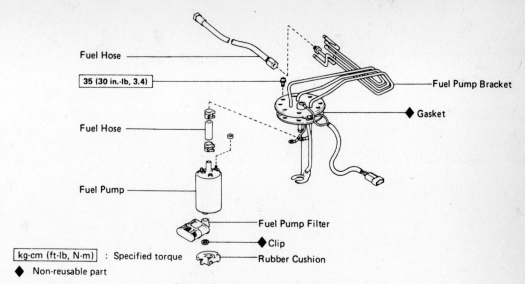

Fuel Hose

35 (30 in.-lb, 3.4)

Fuel Pump Bracket

Gasket

Fuel Hose

Fuel Pump

Fuel Pump Filter

♦ **Clip**

kg-cm (ft-lb, N-m) : Specified torque

Rubber Cushion

♦ **Non-reusable part**

Typical fuel pump — Celica/Supra

service hole cover. Disconnect all the electrical fuel pump connections at the fuel pump assembly.

4. Disconnect the fuel pipe and hose from the fuel pump bracket. Remove the fuel pump bracket assembly from the fuel tank. Remove the fuel pump from the fuel bracket.

5. Installation is the reverse of the removal procedures.

TESTING

Fuel Pump Operation

1. Turn the ignition switch to the ON position, but don't start the engine.

2. Using a service jumper wire, connect terminals **+B** and **FP** of the check connector.

3. Check that there is pressure in the hose from the fuel filter. At this time you should be able to hear the fuel return noise.

4. Remove the service wire. Turn ignition switch to the **OFF** position. If no pressure can be felt in the line, check the fuses and all other related electrical connections.

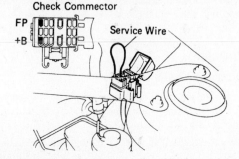

Check connector — Celica

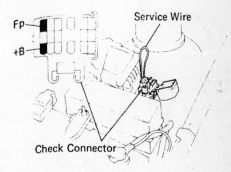

Check connector — Supra

Fuel Pressure Regulator

REMOVAL AND INSTALLATION

All Engines Except Celica 3S-GTE Engine

1. Disconnect vacuum sensing hose on all engines. On the Supra engines disconnect the PCV valve hose to gain access to the fuel pressure regulator assembly.

2. Place a suitable container or shop towel under the pressure regulator assembly. Slowly loosen the fuel return pipe union bolt. Disconnect the fuel return pipe from the pressure regulator.

3. Remove the two bolts and pull out the pressure regulator from the delivery pipe on most engines. On other engines loosen the pressure regulator lock nut and remove the pressure regulator.

4. Installation is the reverse of the removal procedures. After service procedures are completed start engine check for fuel leakage.

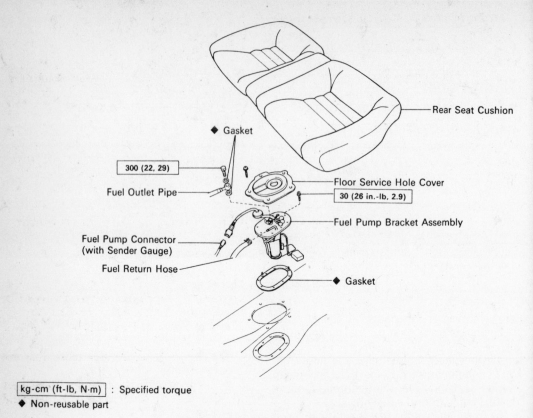

kg-cm (ft-lb, N·m) : Specified torque
◆ Non-reusable part

Fuel pump installation — 1990 Celica

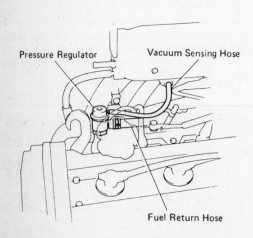

Fuel pressure regulator — Celica 3S-GE engine — others similar

Celica 3S-GTE Engine

1. Remove the throttle body assembly.
2. Disconnect the cold start injector pipe.
3. Disconnect vacuum sensing hose.
4. Place a suitable container or shop towel under the pressure regulator assembly. Slowly loosen the fuel return pipe union bolt. Discon-

nect the fuel return pipe from the pressure regulator.
5. Loosen the pressure regulator lock nut and remove the pressure regulator.
6. Installation is the reverse of the removal procedures. After service procedures are completed start engine check for fuel leakage.

Air Flow Meter

REMOVAL AND INSTALLATION

All Celica Engines

1. Disconnect the negative battery cable.
2. Disconnect air flow meter electrical connector and air cleaner hose/air cleaner cap.
3. Remove the retaining nuts and bolt and remove the air flow meter and gasket if so equipped.
4. Installation is the reverse of the removal procedures.

All Supra Engines

1. Disconnect the negative battery cable.
2. Disconnect air flow meter electrical connector and air cleaner hose. On the 7M-GTE engine remove air cleaner pipe and hose.
3. Remove the air cleaner cap (2 retaining bolts). On the 7M-GTE engine remove the air flow meter brace/bracket.

4. Pry off the lock plates and remove the air flow meter.

5. Installation is the reverse of the removal procedures.

Throttle Body

REMOVAL AND INSTALLATION

Celica 2S-FE And 3S-GE Engines

1. Drain the engine coolant. Disconnect the negative battery cable.

CAUTION: *When draining the coolant, keep in mind that cats and dogs are attracted by the ethylene glycol antifreeze, and are quite likely to drink any that is left in an uncovered container or in puddles on the ground. This will prove fatal in sufficient quantity. Always drain the coolant into a sealable container. Coolant should be reused unless it is contaminated or several years old.*

2. Disconnect throttle cable from the throttle linkage.

3. Remove the accelerator cable return spring. Remove cable bracket from the throttle body.

4. Disconnect air cleaner hose. Disconnect throttle position sensor electrical connector.

5. Label and disconnect all hoses (water and vacuum) from throttle body.

6. Remove the 4 bolts and throttle body with gasket.

7. Installation is the reverse of the removal procedures. Place a new gasket and torque the retaining bolts to 9 ft. lbs. (14 ft. lbs. on 3S-GE engine). Fill with coolant.

8. If necessary, adjust throttle position sensor as follows:

a. Loosen the 2 throttle position sensor retaining screws.

b. Insert a feeler gauge 0.70mm 2S-E engine or 0.60mm 3S-GE engine between the throttle stop screw and lever.

c. Connect a ohmmeter to terminals **IDL** and E_1 on 2S-E engine or **IDL** and E_2 on 3S-GE engine. Gradually turn the sensor counterclockwise on 2S-GE engine or clockwise on the 3S-GE engine until the ohmmeter deflects and secure the sensor with 2 screws.

Celica 3S-FE Engine

1. Drain the engine coolant. Disconnect the negative battery cable.

CAUTION: *When draining the coolant, keep in mind that cats and dogs are attracted by the ethylene glycol antifreeze, and are quite likely to drink any that is left in an uncovered container or in puddles on the ground. This will prove fatal in sufficient quantity. Always drain the coolant into a sealable con-*

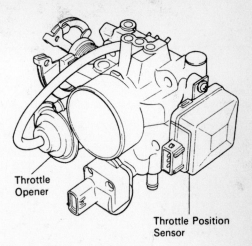

Throttle Opener

Throttle Position Sensor

Typical throttle body assembly

tainer. Coolant should be reused unless it is contaminated or several years old.

2. Disconnect throttle cable from the throttle linkage.

3. Remove the accelerator cable from the throttle linkage.

4. Disconnect air cleaner hose. Disconnect throttle position sensor and ISC valve electrical connector.

5. Label and disconnect all hoses (water and vacuum) from throttle body. Remove the 4 bolts and throttle body with gasket.

6. Installation is the reverse of the removal procedures. Place a new gasket and torque the retaining bolts to 14 ft. lbs. Fill with coolant.

7. If necessary, adjust throttle position sensor as follows:

a. Loosen the 2 throttle position sensor retaining screws.

b. Insert a feeler gauge 0.70mm 3S-FE engine between the throttle stop screw and stop lever.

c. Connect a ohmmeter to terminals **IDL** and E_1 on 3S-FE engine. Gradually turn clockwise on the 3S-FE engine until the ohmmeter deflects and secure the sensor with 2 screws.

Celica 3S-GTE Engine

1. Drain the engine coolant. Disconnect the negative battery cable.

NOTE: *On 1990 SRS vehicles, you must wait AT LEAST 30 seconds after disconnecting the battery before doing any work. The SRS has a built-in backup which will allow the system to remain energized for a period of time after the power is disconnected.*

2. Drain intercooler coolant. Disconnect accelerator cable from throttle linkage.

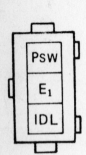 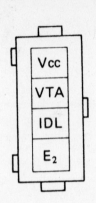 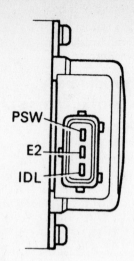

Throttle position sensor (TPS) terminal identification

CAUTION: *When draining the coolant, keep in mind that cats and dogs are attracted by the ethylene glycol antifreeze, and are quite likely to drink any that is left in an uncovered container or in puddles on the ground. This will prove fatal in sufficient quantity. Always drain the coolant into a sealable container. Coolant should be reused unless it is contaminated or several years old.*

3. Remove the intercooler assembly.

4. Remove the air connector and air connector stay.

5. Disconnect throttle position sensor and ISC valve electrical connector.

6. Label and disconnect all hoses (water and vacuum) from throttle body. Remove the 4 bolts and throttle body with gasket.

7. Installation is the reverse of the removal procedures. Place a new gasket and torque the retaining bolts to 14 ft. lbs. Fill with coolant.

8. If necessary, adjust throttle position sensor as follows:

a. Loosen the 2 throttle position sensor retaining screws.

b. Insert a feeler gauge 0.60mm 3S-GTE engine between the throttle stop screw and stop lever.

c. Connect a ohmmeter to terminals **IDL** and E_2 on 3S-GTE engine. Gradually turn clockwise on the 3S-GTE engine until the ohmmeter deflects and secure the sensor with 2 screws.

Celica 4A-FE Engine

1. Drain the engine coolant. Disconnect the negative battery cable.

NOTE: *On 1990 SRS vehicles, you must wait AT LEAST 30 seconds after disconnecting the battery before doing any work. The SRS has a built-in backup which will allow* the system to remain energized for a period of time after the power is disconnected.

CAUTION: *When draining the coolant, keep in mind that cats and dogs are attracted by the ethylene glycol antifreeze, and are quite likely to drink any that is left in an uncovered container or in puddles on the ground. This will prove fatal in sufficient quantity. Always drain the coolant into a sealable container. Coolant should be reused unless it is contaminated or several years old.*

2. Disconnect throttle cable from the throttle linkage.

3. Remove the accelerator cable from the throttle linkage.

4. Disconnect air cleaner hose. Remove air cleaner cap. Disconnect throttle position sensor electrical connector.

5. Remove the accelerator bracket from the throttle body.

6. Label and disconnect all hoses (water and vacuum) from throttle body. Remove the 2 bolts/2 nuts and throttle body with gasket.

7. Installation is the reverse of the removal procedures. Place a new gasket and torque the retaining bolts to 16 ft. lbs. Fill with coolant.

8. If necessary, adjust throttle position sensor as follows:

a. Loosen the 2 throttle position sensor retaining screws.

b. Insert a feeler gauge 0.70mm 4A-FE engine between the throttle stop screw and stop lever.

c. Connect a ohmmeter to terminals **IDL** and E_2 on 4A-FE engine. Gradually turn clockwise on the 4A-FE engine until the ohmmeter deflects and secure the sensor with 2 screws.

Celica 5S-FE Engine

1. Drain the engine coolant. Disconnect the negative battery cable.

NOTE: *On 1990 SRS vehicles, you must wait AT LEAST 30 seconds after disconnecting the battery before doing any work. The SRS has a built-in backup which will allow the system to remain energized for a period of time after the power is disconnected.*

CAUTION: *When draining the coolant, keep in mind that cats and dogs are attracted by the ethylene glycol antifreeze, and are quite likely to drink any that is left in an uncovered container or in puddles on the ground. This will prove fatal in sufficient quantity. Always drain the coolant into a sealable container. Coolant should be reused unless it is contaminated or several years old.*

2. Disconnect throttle cable from the throttle linkage.

3. Remove the accelerator cable from the throttle linkage.

4. Disconnect air cleaner hose and air cleaner cap. Disconnect throttle position sensor and ISC valve electrical connector.

5. Label and disconnect all hoses (water and vacuum) from throttle body. Remove the 4 bolts (note the locations of the bolts; they are different lengths) and throttle body with gasket.

6. Installation is the reverse of the removal procedures. Place a new gasket and torque the retaining bolts to 14 ft. lbs. Fill with coolant.

7. If necessary, adjust throttle position sensor as follows:

    a. Loosen the 2 throttle position sensor retaining screws.

    b. Apply vacuum to the throttle opener.

    c. Insert a feeler gauge 0.70mm 5S-FE engine between the throttle stop screw and stop lever. If vehicle is equipped with ECT (electronic controlled transaxle) insert a feeler gauge 0.60mm between the throttle stop screw and stop lever.

    d. Connect a ohmmeter to terminals **IDL** and E_2 on 5S-FE engine. Gradually turn clockwise on the 5S-FE engine until the ohmmeter deflects and secure the sensor with 2 screws.

Supra 5M-GE Engine

1. Disconnect the negative battery cable.

2. Drain the engine coolant.

CAUTION: *When draining the coolant, keep in mind that cats and dogs are attracted by the ethylene glycol antifreeze, and are quite likely to drink any that is left in an uncovered container or in puddles on the ground. This will prove fatal in sufficient quantity.*

Always drain the coolant into a sealable container. Coolant should be reused unless it is contaminated or several years old.

3. Tag and disconnect all lines, hoses or wires that lead from the throttle body. Position them out of the way. Remove the air intake connector.

4. Unscrew the mounting bolts and remove the throttle body and gasket.

5. Installation is in the reverse order of removal.

6. If necessary, adjust throttle position sensor as follows:

    a. Loosen the 2 throttle position sensor retaining screws.

    b. Insert a feeler gauge 0.50mm 5M-GE engine between the throttle stop screw and lever.

    c. Connect a ohmmeter to terminals **IDL** and E_2 on 5M-GE engine. Gradually turn the sensor clockwise on the 5M-GE engine until the ohmmeter deflects and secure the sensor with 2 screws.

Supra 7M-GE And 7M-GTE Engines

1. Drain the engine coolant. Disconnect the negative battery cable.

NOTE: *On 1990 SRS vehicles, you must wait AT LEAST 30 seconds after disconnecting the battery before doing any work. The SRS has a built-in backup which will allow the system to remain energized for a period of time after the power is disconnected.*

CAUTION: *When draining the coolant, keep in mind that cats and dogs are attracted by the ethylene glycol antifreeze, and are quite likely to drink any that is left in an uncovered container or in puddles on the ground. This will prove fatal in sufficient quantity. Always drain the coolant into a sealable container. Coolant should be reused unless it is contaminated or several years old.*

2. Disconnect the accelerator connecting rod.

3. Disconnect air cleaner hose. Disconnect throttle position sensor electrical connector.

4. Remove the throttle body bracket.

5. Label and disconnect all hoses (water and vacuum) from throttle body. Remove the 4 bolts and throttle body with gasket.

6. Installation is the reverse of the removal procedures. Place a new gasket and torque the retaining bolts to 9 ft. lbs. Fill with coolant.

7. If necessary, adjust throttle position sensor as follows:

    a. Loosen the 2 throttle position sensor retaining screws.

    b. Insert a feeler gauge 0.58mm 7M-GE engine or 0.70mm 7M-GTE engine between the throttle stop screw and lever.

c. Connect a ohmmeter to terminals **IDL** and **E$_2$**. Gradually turn the sensor clockwise on the until the ohmmeter deflects and secure the sensor with 2 screws.

Air Valve/Idle Speed Control/ Auxiliary Air Valve

REMOVAL AND INSTALLATION

All Engines

1. Disconnect the negative battery cable.
2. Remove the throttle body assembly as outlined only if access is necessary for removal/installation of specific component. On Supra engines (ISC valve) drain the engine coolant. Remove the water by-pass hose.

   CAUTION: *When draining the coolant, keep in mind that cats and dogs are attracted by the ethylene glycol antifreeze, and are quite likely to drink any that is left in an uncovered container or in puddles on the ground. This will prove fatal in sufficient quantity. Always drain the coolant into a sealable container. Coolant should be reused unless it is contaminated or several years old.*

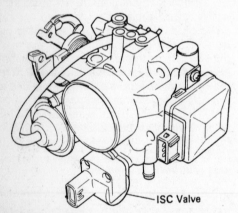

ISC valve — Celica

3. Remove the retaining screws, air hoses, idle speed control/air valve, gasket and O-ring if so equipped. Remove the idle speed control/air valve from the throttle body.
4. Install is the reverse of the removal procedures. Check fluid levels as necessary, road test the vehicle for proper operation.

Cold Start Injector

OPERATION

During cold engine starting, the cold start injector is used to supply additional fuel to the intake manifold to aid in initial start-up. The opening and closing of the injector is determined by the Start Injector Time Switch. when the engine coolant temperature falls below a cer-

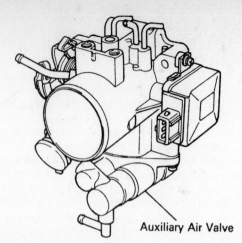

Auxiliary Air Valve

Auxiliary air valve — Celica

tain point, the switch is tripped and then opens the cold start injector. As the engine coolant warms up, the switch will eventually close the injector.

REMOVAL AND INSTALLATION

All Celica Engines Except 3S-GTE Engine

1. Disconnect the negative battery cable.
2. Disconnect the wiring connector at the cold start injector.
3. Remove the cold start injector union bolt(s) on the delivery pipe. Remove the cold start injector pipe as necessary.

   NOTE: *Before removing the union bolt, place a suitable container under it to catch any escaping fuel.*

4. Unscrew the two mounting bolts and then remove the cold start injector from the air intake chamber.
5. Installation is in the reverse order of removal. Torque the cold start injector retaining bolts to 48 inch lbs. on 2S-E engine, 52 inch lbs. on 3S-GE engine, 82 inch lbs. on all other engine. Always use a new gasket when reinstalling the injector. Start the engine and check for any leaks.

Celica 3S-GTE Engine

1. Disconnect the negative battery cable.
2. Remove the throttle body assembly as outlined.
3. Disconnect the wiring connector at the injector.
4. Remove the cold start injector union bolt(s) on the delivery pipe.

   NOTE: *Before removing the union bolt, place a suitable container under it to catch any escaping fuel*

5. Remove the 2 cold start injector retaining bolts. Remove the cold start injector.
6. Installation is in the reverse order of re-

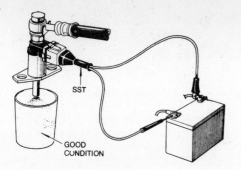

The fuel spray pattern should be even, V-shape one — typical cold start injector

moval. Torque the cold start injector retaining bolts to 52 inch lbs. Always use a new gasket when reinstalling the injector. Start the engine and check for any leaks.

Supra 5M-GE Engine

1. Drain the cooling system.

CAUTION: *When draining the coolant, keep in mind that cats and dogs are attracted by the ethylene glycol antifreeze, and are quite likely to drink any that is left in an uncovered container or in puddles on the ground. This will prove fatal in sufficient quantity. Always drain the coolant into a sealable container. Coolant should be reused unless it is contaminated or several years old.*

2. Remove the air intake connector at the throttle body.

3. Tag and disconnect all hoses from the air intake chamber, and all hoses from the throttle body which may interfere in intake chamber removal.

4. Tag and disconnect the accelerator linkage and cable from the throttle body.

5. Tag and disconnect the cold start injector wire, throttle position sensor wire, and the two wiring connectors near the distributor.

6. Remove the air intake chamber stay and the vacuum pipe sub-assembly.

7. Loosen the EGR pipe connecting nut. Disconnect the cold start fuel hose from the delivery pipe.

8. Remove the air intake chamber from the cylinder head, and remove the cold start injector from the intake chamber.

9. Installation is in the reverse order of removal. Always use new gaskets under the cold start injector.

10. Start the engine and check for leaks.

Supra 7M-GE And 7M-GTE ENGINES

1. Disconnect the negative battery cable.

2. Disconnect the wiring connector at the cold start injector.

3. Remove the cold start injector union

bolt(s) on the delivery pipe. Remove the cold start injector pipe as necessary.

NOTE: *Before removing the union bolt, place a suitable container under it to catch any escaping fuel.*

4. Unscrew the two mounting bolts and then remove the cold start injector from the air intake chamber.

5. Installation is in the reverse order of removal. Torque the cold start injector retaining bolts to 48 inch lbs. on both engines. Always use a new gasket when reinstalling the injector. Start the engine and check for any leaks.

TESTING

1. Unplug the wiring connector and remove the cold start injector from the air intake chamber. Do not disconnect the fuel line.

2. Using Special Tool 09843–30011 or equivalent, connect one end to the injector and the other to the battery.

3. Using a service jumper wire, connect terminals +**B** and **FP** of the check connector.

4. Hold the injector over a suitable container and then turn the ignition switch to the **ON** position. Do not start the engine.

5. Check that the fuel splash pattern is even and V-shaped.

6. Disconnect the test probes from the battery and check that the fuel does not leak from the injector tip any more than one drop or less per minute.

7. Remove the Special Tool and reinstall the cold start injector as outlined.

Fuel Injectors

OPERATION

There is one fuel injector for each cylinder. They spray fuel into the intake port, in front of the intake valve. When the injector is energized, the coil pulls the plunger up, opening the needle valve and allowing the fuel to pass through the injector. Opening of the injectors is controlled by the EFI computer. The injectors operate at low pressure and are open for only a fraction of a second at a time.

REMOVAL AND INSTALLATION

Celica 2S-E Engine

1. Disconnect the negative battery cable.

2. Drain the coolant.

CAUTION: *When draining the coolant, keep in mind that cats and dogs are attracted by the ethylene glycol antifreeze, and are quite likely to drink any that is left in an uncovered container or in puddles on the ground. This will prove fatal in sufficient quantity. Always drain the coolant into a sealable con-*

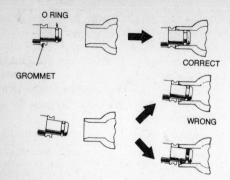

Make sure that you insert the injector into the fuel delivery pipe properly

tainer. Coolant should be reused unless it is contaminated or several years old.

3. Disconnect the throttle cable and the accelerator cable from the throttle linkage.
4. Tag and disconnect all hoses and wires which interfere with injector removal.
5. Remove the air intake chamber with the throttle body.
6. Remove the four bolts and the delivery pipe with the injectors.
7. Pull the injectors with the delivery pipe.
8. Before installing, insert four new insulators into the injector holes on the intake manifold.
9. Install the grommet and a new O-ring to the delivery pipe end of each injector.
10. Apply a thin coat of gasoline to the O-ring on each injector and then press them into the delivery pipe.
11. Install the injectors together with the delivery pipe in the intake manifold. Tighten the mounting bolts to 11–15 ft. lbs.
12. Installation of the remaining components is in the reverse order of removal.
13. Start the engine and check for any fuel leaks.

Celica 3S-GE Engine

1. Disconnect the negative battery cable.
2. Drain the coolant.

CAUTION: *When draining the coolant, keep in mind that cats and dogs are attracted by the ethylene glycol antifreeze, and are quite likely to drink any that is left in an uncovered container or in puddles on the ground. This will prove fatal in sufficient quantity. Always drain the coolant into a sealable container. Coolant should be reused unless it is contaminated or several years old.*

3. Disconnect the throttle cable and the accelerator cable from the throttle linkage.
4. Disconnect the ignition coil connector and the high tension cord, then remove the four nuts, two bolts and the suspension upper brace.
5. Disconnect the air cleaner hose.
6. Remove the ignitor.
7. Remove the throttle body.
8. Remove the No. 2 engine hanger and the No. 2 intake manifold stay.
9. Loosen the union nut of the EGR pipe.
10. Remove the cold start injector pipe.
11. Remove the EGR modulator.
12. Tag and disconnect all hoses and wires which interfere with injector removal.
13. Raise and properly support the vehicle.
14. Remove the suspension lower cross member.
15. Disconnect the exhaust pipe.
16. Remove the No. 1 and the No. 3 intake manifold stays.
17. Disconnect the ground strap.
18. Remove the intake manifold.
19. Remove the three bolts and the delivery pipe with the injectors.
20. Pull the injectors with the delivery pipe.
21. Before installing, insert four new insula-

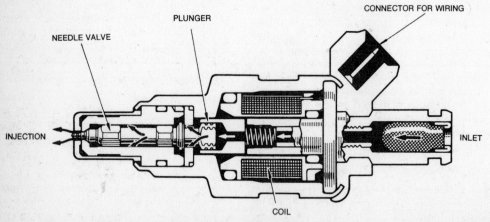

Cut-away view of fuel injector

CHILTON'S
FUEL ECONOMY & TUNE-UP TIPS

55 WAYS TO IMPROVE FUEL ECONOMY

Tune-up • Spark Plug Diagnosis • Emission Controls

Fuel System • Cooling System • Tires and Wheels

General Maintenance

CHILTON'S FUEL ECONOMY & TUNE-UP TIPS

Fuel economy is important to everyone, no matter what kind of vehicle you drive. The maintenance-minded motorist can save both money and fuel using these tips and the periodic maintenance and tune-up procedures in this Repair and Tune-Up Guide.

There are more than 130,000,000 cars and trucks registered for private use in the United States. Each travels an average of 10-12,000 miles per year, and, and in total they consume close to 70 billion gallons of fuel each year. This represents nearly ⅔ of the oil imported by the United States each year. The Federal government's goal is to reduce consumption 10% by 1985. A variety of methods are either already in use or under serious consideration, and they all affect you driving and the cars you will drive. In addition to "down-sizing", the auto industry is using or investigating the use of electronic fuel delivery, electronic engine controls and alternative engines for use in smaller and lighter vehicles, among other alternatives to meet the federally mandated Corporate Average Fuel Economy (CAFE) of 27.5 mpg by 1985. The government, for its part, is considering rationing, mandatory driving curtailments and tax increases on motor vehicle fuel in an effort to reduce consumption. The government's goal of a 10% reduction could be realized — and further government regulation avoided — if every private vehicle could use just 1 less gallon of fuel per week.

How Much Can You Save?

Tests have proven that almost anyone can make at least a 10% reduction in fuel consumption through regular maintenance and tune-ups. When a major manufacturer of spark plugs sur-

TUNE-UP

1. Check the cylinder compression to be sure the engine will really benefit from a tune-up and that it is capable of producing good fuel economy. A tune-up will be wasted on an engine in poor mechanical condition.

2. Replace spark plugs regularly. New spark plugs alone can increase fuel economy 3%.

3. Be sure the spark plugs are the correct type (heat range) for your vehicle. See the Tune-Up Specifications.

Heat range refers to the spark plug's ability to conduct heat away from the firing end. It must conduct the heat away in an even pattern to avoid becoming a source of pre-ignition, yet it must also operate hot enough to burn off conductive deposits that could cause misfiring.

The heat range is usually indicated by a number on the spark plug, part of the manufacturer's designation for each individual spark plug. The numbers in bold-face indicate the heat range in each manufacturer's identification system.

Periodically, check the spark plugs to be sure they are firing efficiently. They are excellent indicators of the internal condition of your engine.

Manufacturer	Typical Designation
AC	R **45** TS
Bosch (old)	WA **145** T30
Bosch (new)	HR **8** Y
Champion	RBL **15** Y
Fram/Autolite	41**5**
Mopar	P-**62** PR
Motorcraft	BRF-**42**
NGK	BP **5** ES-15
Nippondenso	W **16** EP
Prestolite	14GR **5** 2A

On AC, Bosch (new), Champion, Fram/Autolite, Mopar, Motorcraft and Prestolite, a higher number indicates a hotter plug. On Bosch (old), NGK and Nippondenso, a higher number indicates a colder plug.

4. Make sure the spark plugs are properly gapped. See the Tune-Up Specifications in this book.

5. Be sure the spark plugs are firing efficiently. The illustrations on the next 2 pages show you how to "read" the firing end of the spark plug.

6. Check the ignition timing and set it to specifications. Tests show that almost all cars have incorrect ignition timing by more than 2°.

veyed over 6,000 cars nationwide, they found that a tune-up, on cars that needed one, increased fuel economy over 11%. Replacing worn plugs alone, accounted for a 3% increase. The same test also revealed that 8 out of every 10 vehicles will have some maintenance deficiency that will directly affect fuel economy, emissions or performance. Most of this mileage-robbing neglect could be prevented with regular maintenance.

Modern engines require that all of the functioning systems operate properly for maximum efficiency. A malfunction anywhere wastes fuel. You can keep your vehicle running as efficiently and economically as possible, by being aware of your vehicle's operating and performance characteristics. If your vehicle suddenly develops performance or fuel economy problems it could be due to one or more of the following:

PROBLEM	POSSIBLE CAUSE
Engine Idles Rough	Ignition timing, idle mixture, vacuum leak or something amiss in the emission control system.
Hesitates on Acceleration	Dirty carburetor or fuel filter, improper accelerator pump setting, ignition timing or fouled spark plugs.
Starts Hard or Fails to Start	Worn spark plugs, improperly set automatic choke, ice (or water) in fuel system.
Stalls Frequently	Automatic choke improperly adjusted and possible dirty air filter or fuel filter.
Performs Sluggishly	Worn spark plugs, dirty fuel or air filter, ignition timing or automatic choke out of adjustment.

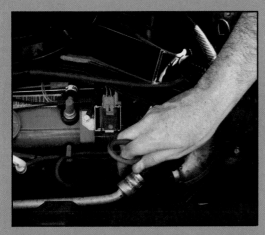

Check spark plug wires on conventional point type ignition for cracks by bending them in a loop around your finger.

Be sure that spark plug wires leading to adjacent cylinders do not run too close together. (Photo courtesy Champion Spark Plug Co.)

7. If your vehicle does not have electronic ignition, check the points, rotor and cap as specified.

8. Check the spark plug wires (used with conventional point-type ignitions) for cracks and burned or broken insulation by bending them in a loop around your finger. Cracked wires decrease fuel efficiency by failing to deliver full voltage to the spark plugs. One misfiring spark plug can cost you as much as 2 mpg.

9. Check the routing of the plug wires. Misfiring can be the result of spark plug leads to adjacent cylinders running parallel to each other and too close together. One wire tends to pick up voltage from the other causing it to fire "out of time".

10. Check all electrical and ignition circuits for voltage drop and resistance.

11. Check the distributor mechanical and/or vacuum advance mechanisms for proper functioning. The vacuum advance can be checked by twisting the distributor plate in the opposite direction of rotation. It should spring back when released.

12. Check and adjust the valve clearance on engines with mechanical lifters. The clearance should be slightly loose rather than too tight.

SPARK PLUG DIAGNOSIS

Normal

APPEARANCE: This plug is typical of one operating normally. The insulator nose varies from a light tan to grayish color with slight electrode wear. The presence of slight deposits is normal on used plugs and will have no adverse effect on engine performance. The spark plug heat range is correct for the engine and the engine is running normally.

CAUSE: Properly running engine.

RECOMMENDATION: Before reinstalling this plug, the electrodes should be cleaned and filed square. Set the gap to specifications. If the plug has been in service for more than 10-12,000 miles, the entire set should probably be replaced with a fresh set of the same heat range.

Oil Deposits

APPEARANCE: The firing end of the plug is covered with a wet, oily coating.

CAUSE: The problem is poor oil control. On high mileage engines, oil is leaking past the rings or valve guides into the combustion chamber. A common cause is also a plugged PCV valve, and a ruptured fuel pump diaphragm can also cause this condition. Oil fouled plugs such as these are often found in new or recently overhauled engines, before normal oil control is achieved, and can be cleaned and reinstalled.

RECOMMENDATION: A hotter spark plug may temporarily relieve the problem, but the engine is probably in need of work.

Incorrect Heat Range

APPEARANCE: The effects of high temperature on a spark plug are indicated by clean white, often blistered insulator. This can also be accompanied by excessive wear of the electrode, and the absence of deposits.

CAUSE: Check for the correct spark plug heat range. A plug which is too hot for the engine can result in overheating. A car operated mostly at high speeds can require a colder plug. Also check ignition timing, cooling system level, fuel mixture and leaking intake manifold.

RECOMMENDATION: If all ignition and engine adjustments are known to be correct, and no other malfunction exists, install spark plugs one heat range colder.

Carbon Deposits

APPEARANCE: Carbon fouling is easily identified by the presence of dry, soft, black, sooty deposits.

CAUSE: Changing the heat range can often lead to carbon fouling, as can prolonged slow, stop-and-start driving. If the heat range is correct, carbon fouling can be attributed to a rich fuel mixture, sticking choke, clogged air cleaner, worn breaker points, retarded timing or low compression. If only one or two plugs are carbon fouled, check for corroded or cracked wires on the affected plugs. Also look for cracks in the distributor cap between the towers of affected cylinders.

RECOMMENDATION: After the problem is corrected, these plugs can be cleaned and reinstalled if not worn severely.

Photos Courtesy Fram Corporation

MMT Fouled

APPEARANCE: Spark plugs fouled by MMT (Methycyclopentadienyl Maganese Tricarbonyl) have reddish, rusty appearance on the insulator and side electrode.

CAUSE: MMT is an anti-knock additive in gasoline used to replace lead. During the combustion process, the MMT leaves a reddish deposit on the insulator and side electrode.

RECOMMENDATION: No engine malfunction is indicated and the deposits will not affect plug performance any more than lead deposits (see Ash Deposits). MMT fouled plugs can be cleaned, regapped and reinstalled.

High Speed Glazing

APPEARANCE: Glazing appears as shiny coating on the plug, either yellow or tan in color.

CAUSE: During hard, fast acceleration, plug temperatures rise suddenly. Deposits from normal combustion have no chance to fluff-off; instead, they melt on the insulator forming an electrically conductive coating which causes misfiring.

RECOMMENDATION: Glazed plugs are not easily cleaned. They should be replaced with a fresh set of plugs of the correct heat range. If the condition recurs, using plugs with a heat range one step colder may cure the problem.

Ash (Lead) Deposits

APPEARANCE: Ash deposits are characterized by light brown or white colored deposits crusted on the side or center electrodes. In some cases it may give the plug a rusty appearance.

CAUSE: Ash deposits are normally derived from oil or fuel additives burned during normal combustion. Normally they are harmless, though excessive amounts can cause misfiring. If deposits are excessive in short mileage, the valve guides may be worn.

RECOMMENDATION: Ash-fouled plugs can be cleaned, gapped and reinstalled.

Detonation

APPEARANCE: Detonation is usually characterized by a broken plug insulator.

CAUSE: A portion of the fuel charge will begin to burn spontaneously, from the increased heat following ignition. The explosion that results applies extreme pressure to engine components, frequently damaging spark plugs and pistons.

Detonation can result by over-advanced ignition timing, inferior gasoline (low octane) lean air/fuel mixture, poor carburetion, engine lugging or an increase in compression ratio due to combustion chamber deposits or engine modification.

RECOMMENDATION: Replace the plugs after correcting the problem.

Photos Courtesy Champion Spark Plug Co.

Be aware of the general condition of the emission control system. It contributes to reduced pollution and should be serviced regularly to maintain efficient engine operation.

14. Check all vacuum lines for dried, cracked or brittle conditions. Something as simple as a leaking vacuum hose can cause poor performance and loss of economy.

15. Avoid tampering with the emission control system. Attempting to improve fuel econ-

FUEL SYSTEM

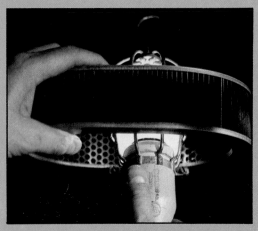

Check the air filter with a light behind it. If you can see light through the filter it can be reused.

Extremely clogged filters should be discarded and replaced with a new one.

18. Replace the air filter regularly. A dirty air filter richens the air/fuel mixture and can increase fuel consumption as much as 10%. Tests show that ⅓ of all vehicles have air filters in need of replacement.

19. Replace the fuel filter at least as often as recommended.

20. Set the idle speed and carburetor mixture to specifications.

21. Check the automatic choke. A sticking or malfunctioning choke wastes gas.

22. During the summer months, adjust the automatic choke for a leaner mixture which will produce faster engine warm-ups.

COOLING SYSTEM

29. Be sure all accessory drive belts are in good condition. Check for cracks or wear.

30. Adjust all accessory drive belts to proper tension.

31. Check all hoses for swollen areas, worn spots, or loose clamps.

32. Check coolant level in the radiator or expansion tank.

33. Be sure the thermostat is operating properly. A stuck thermostat delays engine warm-up and a cold engine uses nearly twice as much fuel as a warm engine.

34. Drain and replace the engine coolant at least as often as recommended. Rust and scale

TIRES & WHEELS

38. Check the tire pressure often with a pencil type gauge. Tests by a major tire manufacturer show that 90% of all vehicles have at least 1 tire improperly inflated. Better mileage can be achieved by over-inflating tires, but never exceed the maximum inflation pressure on the side of the tire.

39. If possible, install radial tires. Radial tires deliver as much as ½ mpg more than bias belted tires.

40. Avoid installing super-wide tires. They only create extra rolling resistance and decrease fuel mileage. Stick to the manufacturer's recommendations.

41. Have the wheels properly balanced.

omy by tampering with emission controls is more likely to worsen fuel economy than improve it. Emission control changes on modern engines are not readily reversible.

16. Clean (or replace) the EGR valve and lines as recommended.

17. Be sure that all vacuum lines and hoses are reconnected properly after working under the hood. An unconnected or misrouted vacuum line can wreak havoc with engine performance.

23. Check for fuel leaks at the carburetor, fuel pump, fuel lines and fuel tank. Be sure all lines and connections are tight.

24. Periodically check the tightness of the carburetor and intake manifold attaching nuts and bolts. These are a common place for vacuum leaks to occur.

25. Clean the carburetor periodically and lubricate the linkage.

26. The condition of the tailpipe can be an excellent indicator of proper engine combustion. After a long drive at highway speeds, the inside of the tailpipe should be a light grey in color. Black or soot on the insides indicates an overly rich mixture.

27. Check the fuel pump pressure. The fuel pump may be supplying more fuel than the engine needs.

28. Use the proper grade of gasoline for your engine. Don't try to compensate for knocking or "pinging" by advancing the ignition timing. This practice will only increase plug temperature and the chances of detonation or pre-ignition with relatively little performance gain.

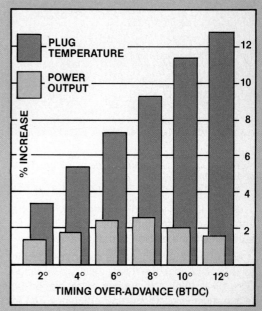

Increasing ignition timing past the specified setting results in a drastic increase in spark plug temperature with increased chance of detonation or preignition. Performance increase is considerably less. (Photo courtesy Champion Spark Plug Co.)

that form in the engine should be flushed out to allow the engine to operate at peak efficiency.

35. Clean the radiator of debris that can decrease cooling efficiency.

36. Install a flex-type or electric cooling fan, if you don't have a clutch type fan. Flex fans use curved plastic blades to push more air at low speeds when more cooling is needed; at high speeds the blades flatten out for less resistance. Electric fans only run when the engine temperature reaches a predetermined level.

37. Check the radiator cap for a worn or cracked gasket. If the cap does not seal properly, the cooling system will not function properly.

42. Be sure the front end is correctly aligned. A misaligned front end actually has wheels going in differed directions. The increased drag can reduce fuel economy by .3 mpg.

43. Correctly adjust the wheel bearings. Wheel bearings that are adjusted too tight increase rolling resistance.

Check tire pressures regularly with a reliable pocket type gauge. Be sure to check the pressure on a cold tire.

GENERAL MAINTENANCE

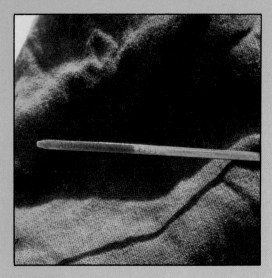

Check the fluid levels (particularly engine oil) on a regular basis. Be sure to check the oil for grit, water or other contamination.

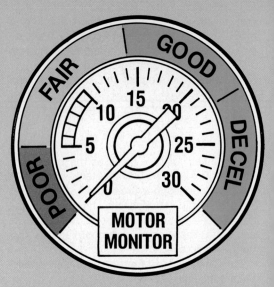

A vacuum gauge is another excellent indicator of internal engine condition and can also be installed in the dash as a mileage indicator.

44. Periodically check the fluid levels in the engine, power steering pump, master cylinder, automatic transmission and drive axle.

45. Change the oil at the recommended interval and change the filter at every oil change. Dirty oil is thick and causes extra friction between moving parts, cutting efficiency and increasing wear. A worn engine requires more frequent tune-ups and gets progressively worse fuel economy. In general, use the lightest viscosity oil for the driving conditions you will encounter.

46. Use the recommended viscosity fluids in the transmission and axle.

47. Be sure the battery is fully charged for fast starts. A slow starting engine wastes fuel.

48. Be sure battery terminals are clean and tight.

49. Check the battery electrolyte level and add distilled water if necessary.

50. Check the exhaust system for crushed pipes, blockages and leaks.

51. Adjust the brakes. Dragging brakes or brakes that are not releasing create increased drag on the engine.

52. Install a vacuum gauge or miles-per-gallon gauge. These gauges visually indicate engine vacuum in the intake manifold. High vacuum = good mileage and low vacuum = poorer mileage. The gauge can also be an excellent indicator of internal engine conditions.

53. Be sure the clutch is properly adjusted. A slipping clutch wastes fuel.

54. Check and periodically lubricate the heat control valve in the exhaust manifold. A sticking or inoperative valve prevents engine warm-up and wastes gas.

55. Keep accurate records to check fuel economy over a period of time. A sudden drop in fuel economy may signal a need for tune-up or other maintenance.

tors into the injector holes on the intake manifold.

22. Install the grommet and a new O-ring to the delivery pipe end of each injector.

23. Apply a thin coat of gasoline to the O-ring on each injector and then press them into the delivery pipe.

24. Install the injectors together with the delivery pipe in the intake manifold. Tighten the three mounting bolts to 14 ft. lbs.

25. Installation of the remaining components is in the reverse order of removal.

26. Start the engine and check for any fuel leaks.

Celica 3S-GTE Engine

1. Disconnect the negative battery cable.
2. Remove the throttle body assembly as outlined.
3. Remove the fuel pressure regulator.
4. Remove the EGR vacuum modulator
5. Disconnect the electrical connections from fuel injectors.
6. Remove the pulsation damper. Disconnect fuel inlet hose from the delivery pipe.
7. Disconnect the fuel return hose from the return pipe.
8. Remove the delivery pipe and fuel injectors and related components (insulators, spacers, O-ring and grommet). Remove injectors from the delivery pipe.
9. Apply a thin coat of gasoline to the O-ring on each injector and then press them into the delivery pipe.
10. Install the injectors, together with the delivery pipe, in the intake manifold. Tighten the three mounting bolts to 14 ft. lbs. Installation of the remaining components is in the reverse order of removal.
11. Start the engine and check for any fuel leaks.

Celica 3S-FE Engine

1. Disconnect the negative battery cable.
2. Remove the cold start injector pipe.
3. Disconnect the vacuum sensing hose from the fuel pressure regulator.

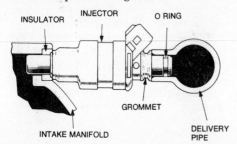

A cut away view of how it should look upon reinstallation — typical fuel injector

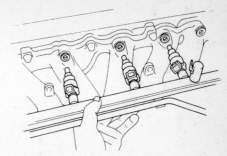

Installing injectors with delivery pipe

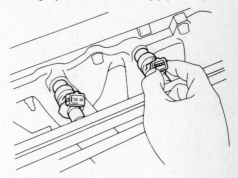

When installing, make sure injectors rotate smoothly; if not check O-ring

4. Disconnect the injector connectors.
5. Disconnect the hose from fuel return pipe.
6. Remove the fuel pressure pulsation damper.
7. Remove the two bolts and the delivery pipe together with the four injectors.
8. Remove the four insulators and the two spacers from the cylinder head, then pull out the four injectors from the delivery pipe.
9. Before installing, insert four new insulators and two spacers into the injector holes in the cylinder head.
10. Install the grommet and a new O-ring to the delivery pipe end of each injector.
11. Apply a thin coat of gasoline to the O-ring on each injector and then press them into the delivery pipe.
12. Install the injectors together with the delivery pipe into the cylinder head. Tighten the two mounting bolts to 9 ft. lbs.
13. Installation of the remaining components is in the reverse order of removal.

Celica 4A-FE Engine

1. Disconnect the negative battery cable.
2. Remove the cold start injector pipe.
3. Disconnect the vacuum sensing hose from the fuel pressure regulator.
4. Disconnect fuel return hose from fuel pressure regulator.

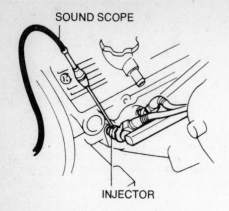

SOUND SCOPE

INJECTOR

Injectors should emit a buzzing sound

5. Disconnect electrical connections from fuel injectors.

6. Disconnect fuel inlet hose from delivery pipe.

7. Remove the delivery pipe (2 retaining bolts) and fuel injectors and related components (insulators, spacers, O-ring and grommet). Remove injectors from the delivery pipe.

8. Apply a thin coat of gasoline to the O-ring on each injector and then press them into the delivery pipe.

9. Install the injectors together with the delivery pipe in the intake manifold. Tighten the 2 mounting bolts to 11 ft. lbs. Installation of the remaining components is in the reverse order of removal. Start the engine and check for any fuel leaks.

Celica 5S-FE Engine

1. Disconnect the negative battery cable.

2. Remove the throttle body assembly as outlined.

3. Remove the cold start injector pipe.

4. Remove the fuel pressure regulator.

5. Disconnect necessary engine wiring and remove the left and right accelerator brackets.

6. Disconnect the electrical connections from fuel injectors.

7. Disconnect wire retaining clamps from the No. 2 timing belt cover and intake manifold as necessary to gain access for removal/installation of fuel injectors.

8. Disconnect the fuel return hose from the return pipe.

9. Remove the delivery pipe and fuel injectors and related components (insulators, spacers, O-ring and grommet). Remove injectors from the delivery pipe.

10. Apply a thin coat of gasoline to the O-ring on each injector and then press them into the delivery pipe.

11. Install the injectors together with the de-livery pipe in the intake manifold. Tighten the 2 mounting bolts to 9 ft. lbs. Installation of the remaining components is in the reverse order of removal.

12. Start the engine and check for any fuel leaks.

Supra 5M-GE Engine

1. Disconnect the negative battery cable.

2. Remove the air intake chamber. Refer to the "Cylinder Head Removal and Installation" section in Chapter 3.

3. Mark and remove the distributor.

4. Remove the fuel pipe.

5. Unplug the wiring connectors from the tops of the fuel injectors and remove the two plastic clamps that hold the wiring harness to the fuel delivery pipe.

6. Unscrew the four mounting bolts and remove the delivery pipe with the injectors attached. Do not remove the injector cover. Pull the injectors out of the delivery pipe.

7. Insert six new insulators into the injector holes on the intake manifold.

8. Install the grommet and a new O-ring to the delivery pipe end of each injector.

9. Apply a thin coat of gasoline to the O-ring on each injector and then press them into the delivery pipe.

10. Install the injectors together with the delivery pipe in the intake manifold. Tighten the mounting bolts to 11–15 ft. lbs.

11. Installation of the remaining components is in the reverse order of removal. Start the engine (check engine timing as necessary) and check for any fuel leaks.

Supra 7M-GE and 7M-GTE Engines

1. Disconnect the negative battery cable.

2. Drain the coolant.

CAUTION: *When draining the coolant, keep in mind that cats and dogs are attracted by the ethylene glycol antifreeze, and are quite likely to drink any that is left in an uncovered container or in puddles on the ground. This will prove fatal in sufficient quantity. Always drain the coolant into a sealable container. Coolant should be reused unless it is contaminated or several years old.*

3. Disconnect accelerator connecting rod.

4. Tag and disconnect all hoses and wires which interfere with injector removal.

5. Remove the air intake connector brackets and the throttle body.

6. Remove the ISC valve and gasket.

7. Disconnect the injector connectors.

8. Disconnect the cold start injector tube from the delivery pipe.

9. Remove the pulsation damper and the two gaskets.

10. Remove the union bolts and two gaskets from the fuel return pipe support.

11. Remove the clamp bolts from the No. 1 fuel pipe and VSV.

12. Remove the union bolts and two gaskets from the pressure regulator.

13. Disconnect the fuel hose from the No. 2 fuel pipe.

14. Remove the clamp bolt and the return fuel pipe.

15. Loosen the lock nut and remove the pressure regulator.

16. Remove the three bolts, and then remove the delivery pipe with the injectors.

17. Remove the 6 insulators and the 3 spacers from the cylinder head, then pull out the injectors from the delivery pipe.

18. Before installing, apply a thin coat of gasoline to the O-ring on each injector and then press them into the delivery pipe.

19. Insert 6 new insulators into the injector hole of the cylinder head.

20. Install the black rings on the upper portion of each of the 3 spacers, then install the spacers on the delivery pipe mounting hole of the cylinder head.

21. Install the three spacers and bolts and torque to 13 ft. lbs.

22. Fully loosen the locknut of the pressure regulator. Thrust the pressure regulator completely into the delivery pipe by hand, then turn the regulator counterclockwise until the outlet faces outward in the correct position. Torque the locknut to 18 ft. lbs.

23. Install the No. 2 fuel pipe and clamp bolt.

24. Connect the fuel hose.

25. Install the union bolt and two new gaskets to the pressure regulator and torque the union bolt to 18 ft. lbs.

26. Install the No. 1 fuel pipe, VSV and clamp bolt.

27. Install the union bolt and two new gaskets to the support pipe and torque the union bolts to 22 ft. lbs.

28. Install the pulsation damper and two new gaskets and torque to 29 ft. lbs.

29. Connect the injector connectors.

30. Install the ISC valve with a new gasket and torque to 9 ft. lbs.

31. Install the throttle body and the air intake connector.

32. Installation of the remaining components is in the reverse order of removal.

TESTING

We recommend that any checking or testing of the injectors, other than that included below, be left to an authorized service facility.

Injector operation can be checked with the injectors installed in the engine. A sound scope is needed here (a stethoscope-like device you can usually rent from tool rental shops; they are also available new from most auto tool and parts jobbers).

With the engine running or cranking, check each injector for normal operating noise (a buzzing or humming), which changes in proportion to engine rpm. If a sound scope is not available to you, check injector operation by touching each injector with your finger. It should be buzzing. If no sound or an unusual sound is heard, check the wiring connector, or have the injector checked professionally.

Fuel Tank

REMOVAL AND INSTALLATION

1. Disconnect the negative battery cable.

2. Remove the fuel tank drain plug. Drain fuel tank as required.

3. Disconnect and mark all electrical connections and fuel lines.

4. Remove fuel tank protector(s) and tank brackets if so equipped.

5. Support the fuel tank and slowly loosen the fuel tank band retaining nuts.

6. Installation is the reverse of the removal procedures. Always position the fuel tank cushions in the correct location (fuel tank will vibrate if not). Use new fuel line hose clamps as necessary, torque fuel tank band retaining nuts evenly to about 20 ft. lbs.

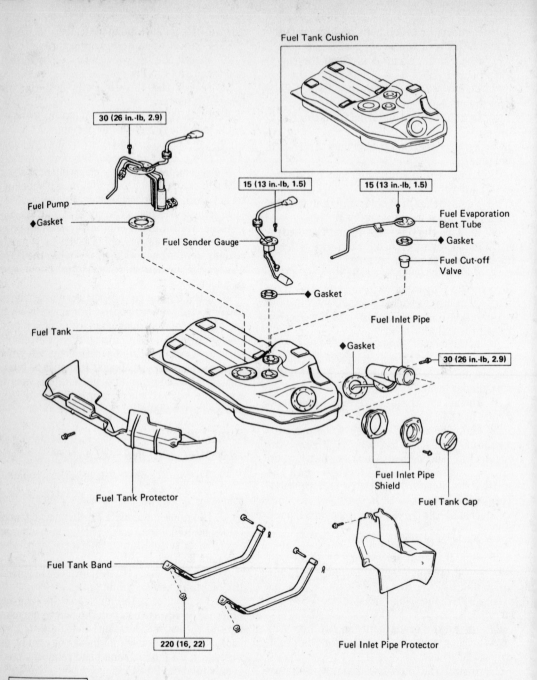

Fuel Tank Cushion

30 (26 in.-lb, 2.9)

15 (13 in.-lb, 1.5)

15 (13 in.-lb, 1.5)

Fuel Pump

◆Gasket

Fuel Sender Gauge

Fuel Evaporation
Bent Tube

◆Gasket

Fuel Cut-off
Valve

◆ Gasket

Fuel Tank

Fuel Inlet Pipe

◆Gasket

30 (26 in.-lb, 2.9)

Fuel Tank Protector

Fuel Inlet Pipe
Shield

Fuel Tank Cap

Fuel Tank Band

Fuel Inlet Pipe Protector

220 (16, 22)

kg-cm (ft-lb, N·m) : Specified torque

◆ Non-reusable part

Fuel tank assembly — Celica 4WD

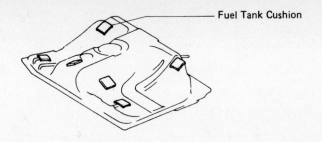

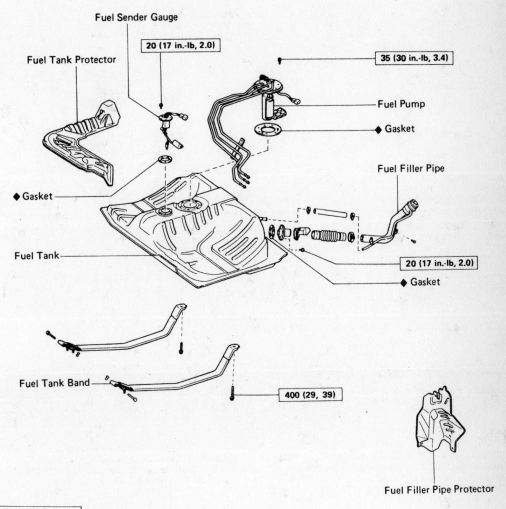

Fuel Tank Cushion

Fuel Sender Gauge

20 (17 in.-lb, 2.0)

35 (30 in.-lb, 3.4)

Fuel Tank Protector

Fuel Pump

◆ Gasket

Fuel Filler Pipe

◆ Gasket

Fuel Tank

20 (17 in.-lb, 2.0)

◆ Gasket

Fuel Tank Band

400 (29, 39)

Fuel Filler Pipe Protector

kg·cm (ft·lb, N·m) : Specified torque

◆ Non-reusable part

Fuel tank assembly — Celica 2WD

2S-E

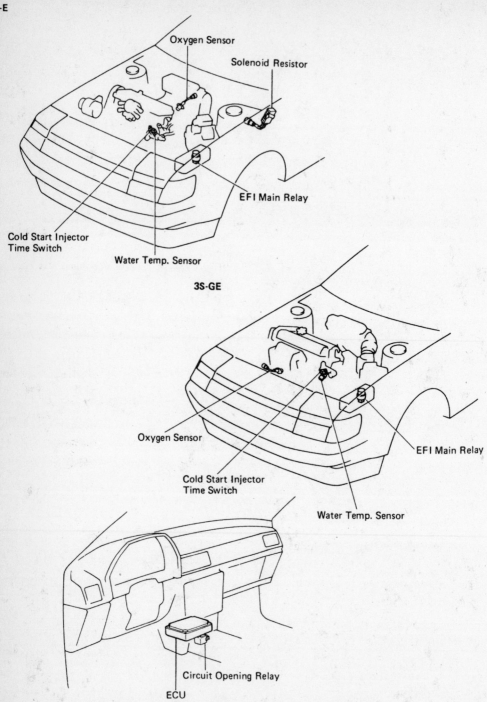

Oxygen Sensor

Solenoid Resistor

EFI Main Relay

Cold Start Injector
Time Switch

Water Temp. Sensor

3S-GE

Oxygen Sensor

EFI Main Relay

Cold Start Injector
Time Switch

Water Temp. Sensor

Circuit Opening Relay

ECU

Location of electronic control parts — Celica 2S-E and 3S-GE engines

7M–GE

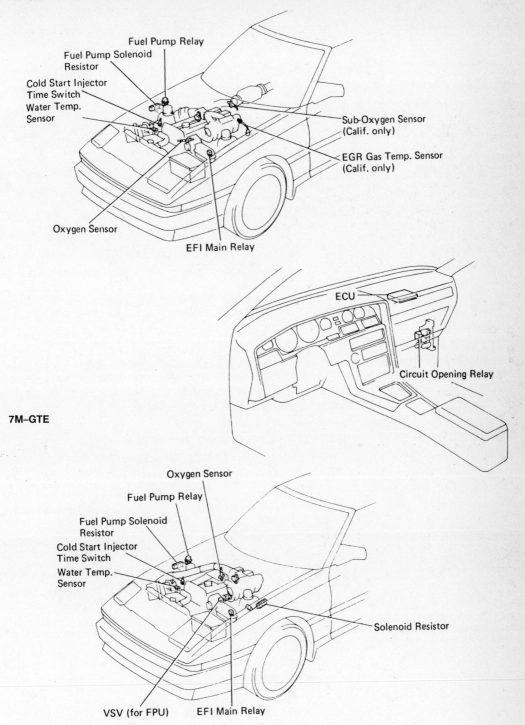

Fuel Pump Relay

Fuel Pump Solenoid Resistor

Cold Start Injector Time Switch

Water Temp. Sensor

Sub-Oxygen Sensor (Calif. only)

EGR Gas Temp. Sensor (Calif. only)

Oxygen Sensor

EFI Main Relay

ECU

Circuit Opening Relay

7M–GTE

Oxygen Sensor

Fuel Pump Relay

Fuel Pump Solenoid Resistor

Cold Start Injector Time Switch

Water Temp. Sensor

Solenoid Resistor

VSV (for FPU)

EFI Main Relay

Location of electronic control parts — Supra 7M-GE and 7M-GTE engines

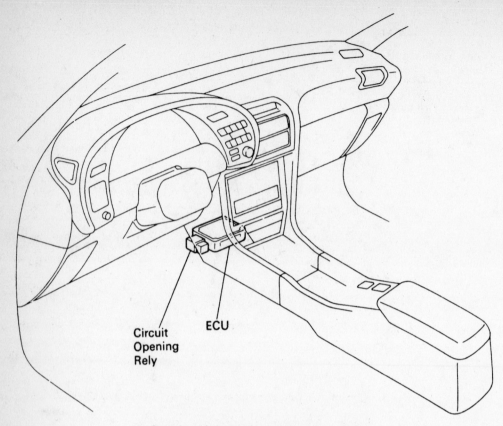

Location of electronic control parts — Celica

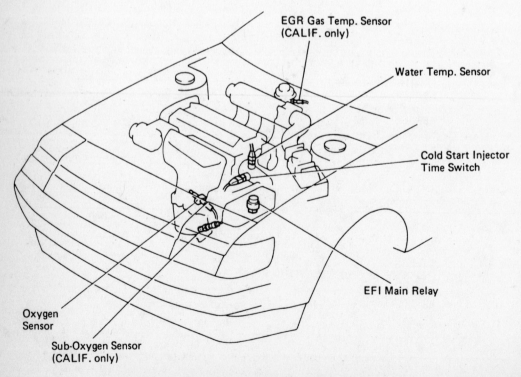

Location of electronic control parts — Celica 3S-FE engine

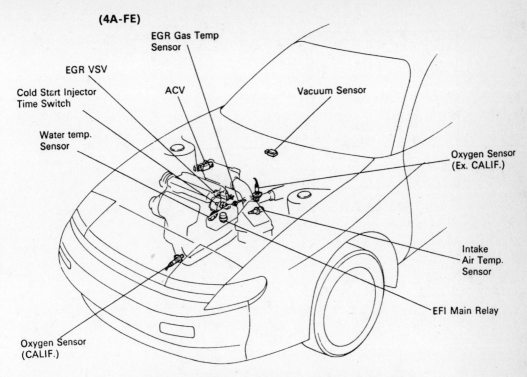

(4A-FE)

EGR Gas Temp Sensor

EGR VSV

ACV

Cold Start Injector Time Switch

Water temp. Sensor

Vacuum Sensor

Oxygen Sensor (Ex. CALIF.)

Intake Air Temp. Sensor

EFI Main Relay

Oxygen Sensor (CALIF.)

Location of electronic control parts — Celica 4A-FE engine

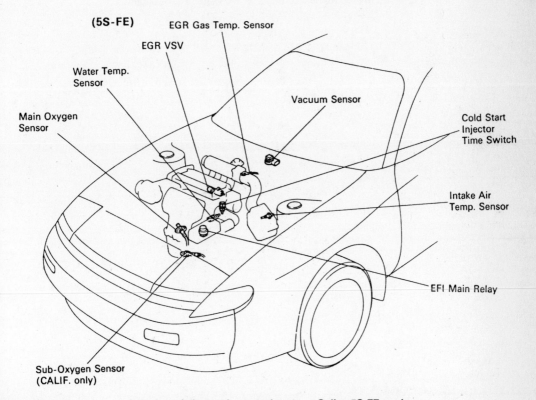

(5S-FE)

EGR Gas Temp. Sensor

EGR VSV

Water Temp. Sensor

Main Oxygen Sensor

Vacuum Sensor

Cold Start Injector Time Switch

Intake Air Temp. Sensor

EFI Main Relay

Sub-Oxygen Sensor (CALIF. only)

Location of electronic control parts — Celica 5S-FE engine

3S-GTE

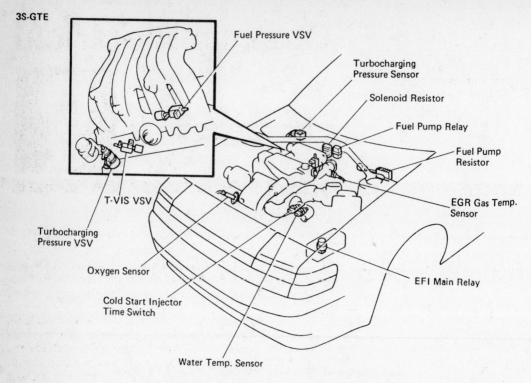

Fuel Pressure VSV

Turbocharging
Pressure Sensor

Solenoid Resistor

Fuel Pump Relay

Fuel Pump
Resistor

T-VIS VSV

Turbocharging
Pressure VSV

EGR Gas Temp.
Sensor

Oxygen Sensor

Cold Start Injector
Time Switch

EFI Main Relay

Water Temp. Sensor

Location of electronic control parts — Celica 3S-GTE engine

Chassis Electrical

6

UNDERSTANDING AND TROUBLESHOOTING ELECTRICAL SYSTEMS

At the rate which both import and domestic manufacturers are incorporating electronic control systems into their production lines, it won't be long before every new vehicle is equipped with one or more on-board computer. These electronic components (with no moving parts) should theoretically last the life of the vehicle, provided nothing external happens to damage the circuits or memory chips.

While it is true that electronic components should never wear out, in the real world malfunctions do occur. It is also true that any computer-based system is extremely sensitive to electrical voltages and cannot tolerate careless or haphazard testing or service procedures. An inexperienced individual can literally do major damage looking for a minor problem by using the wrong kind of test equipment or connecting test leads or connectors with the ignition switch **ON**. When selecting test equipment, make sure the manufacturers instructions state that the tester is compatible with whatever type of electronic control system is being serviced. Read all instructions carefully and double check all test points before installing probes or making any test connections.

The following section outlines basic diagnosis techniques for dealing with computerized automotive control systems. Along with a general explanation of the various types of test equipment available to aid in servicing modern electronic automotive systems, basic repair techniques for wiring harnesses and connectors is given. Read the basic information before attempting any repairs or testing on any computerized system, to provide the background of information necessary to avoid the most common and obvious mistakes that can cost both time and money. Although the replacement and testing procedures are simple in themselves, the systems are not, and unless one has a thorough understanding of all components and their function within a particular computerized control system, the logical test sequence these systems demand cannot be followed. Minor malfunctions can make a big difference, so it is important to know how each component affects the operation of the overall electronic system to find the ultimate cause of a problem without replacing good components unnecessarily. It is not enough to use the correct test equipment; the test equipment must be used correctly.

Safety Precautions

CAUTION: *Whenever working on or around any computer based microprocessor control system, always observe these general precautions to prevent the possibility of personal injury or damage to electronic components.*

• Never install or remove battery cables with the key ON or the engine running. Jumper cables should be connected with the key OFF to avoid power surges that can damage electronic control units. Engines equipped with computer controlled systems should avoid both giving and getting jump starts due to the possibility of serious damage to components from arcing in the engine compartment when connections are made with the ignition ON.

• Always remove the battery cables before charging the battery. Never use a high output charger on an installed battery or attempt to use any type of "hot shot" (24 volt) starting aid.

• Exercise care when inserting test probes into connectors to insure good connections without damaging the connector or spreading the pins. Always probe connectors from the rear (wire) side, NOT the pin side, to avoid accidental shorting of terminals during test procedures.

• Never remove or attach wiring harness connectors with the ignition switch ON, especially to an electronic control unit.

• Do not drop any components during service procedures and never apply 12 volts directly to any component (like a solenoid or relay) unless instructed specifically to do so. Some component electrical windings are designed to safely handle only 4 or 5 volts and can be destroyed in seconds if 12 volts are applied directly to the connector.

• Remove the electronic control unit if the vehicle is to be placed in an environment where temperatures exceed approximately 176°F (80°C), such as a paint spray booth or when arc or gas welding near the control unit location in the car.

ORGANIZED TROUBLESHOOTING

When diagnosing a specific problem, organized troubleshooting is a must. The complexity of a modern automobile demands that you approach any problem in a logical, organized manner. There are certain troubleshooting techniques that are standard:

1. Establish when the problem occurs. Does the problem appear only under certain conditions? Were there any noises, odors, or other unusual symptoms?

2. Isolate the problem area. To do this, make some simple tests and observations; then eliminate the systems that are working properly. Check for obvious problems such as broken wires, dirty connections or split or disconnected vacuum hoses. Always check the obvious before assuming something complicated is the cause.

3. Test for problems systematically to determine the cause once the problem area is isolated. Are all the components functioning properly? Is there power going to electrical switches and motors? Is there vacuum at vacuum switches and/or actuators? Is there a mechanical problem such as bent linkage or loose mounting screws? Doing careful, systematic checks will often turn up most causes on the first inspection without wasting time checking components that have little or no relationship to the problem.

4. Test all repairs after the work is done to make sure that the problem is fixed. Some causes can be traced to more than one component, so a careful verification of repair work is important to pick up additional malfunctions that may cause a problem to reappear or a different problem to arise. A blown fuse, for example, is a simple problem that may require more than another fuse to repair. If you don't look for a problem that caused a fuse to blow, for example, a shorted wire may go undetected.

Experience has shown that most problems tend to be the result of a fairly simple and obvious cause, such as loose or corroded connectors or air leaks in the intake system; making careful inspection of components during testing essential to quick and accurate troubleshooting. Special, hand held computerized testers designed specifically for diagnosing the system are available from a variety of aftermarket sources, as well as from the vehicle manufacturer, but care should be taken that any test equipment being used is designed to diagnose that particular computer controlled system accurately without damaging the control unit (ECM) or components being tested.

NOTE: *Pinpointing the exact cause of trouble in an electrical system can sometimes only be accomplished by the use of special test equipment. The following describes commonly used test equipment and explains how to put it to best use in diagnosis. In addition to the information covered below, the manufacturer's instructions booklet provided with the tester should be read and clearly understood before attempting any test procedures.*

TEST EQUIPMENT

Jumper Wires

Jumper wires are simple, yet extremely valuable, pieces of test equipment. Jumper wires are merely wires that are used to bypass sections of a circuit. The simplest type of jumper wire is merely a length of multi-strand wire with an alligator clip at each end. Jumper wires are usually fabricated from lengths of standard automotive wire and whatever type of connector (alligator clip, spade connector or pin connector) that is required for the particular vehicle being tested. The well equipped tool box will have several different styles of jumper wires in several different lengths. Some jumper wires are made with three or more terminals coming from a common splice for special purpose testing. In cramped, hard-to-reach areas it is advisable to have insulated boots over the jumper wire terminals in order to prevent accidental grounding, sparks, and possible fire, especially when testing fuel system components.

Jumper wires are used primarily to locate open electrical circuits, on either the ground (–) side of the circuit or on the hot (+) side. If an electrical component fails to operate, connect the jumper wire between the component and a good ground. If the component operates only with the jumper installed, the ground circuit is open. If the ground circuit is good, but the component does not operate, the circuit between the power feed and component is open. You can sometimes connect the jumper wire directly from the battery to the hot terminal of the component, but first make sure the component uses 12 volts in operation. Some electrical components, such as fuel injectors, are designed to operate on about 4 volts and running 12 volts directly to the injector terminals can burn out the wiring. By inserting an in-line fuse holder between a set of test leads, a fused jumper wire can be used for bypassing open circuits. Use a 5 amp fuse to provide protection against voltage spikes. When in doubt, use a voltmeter to check the voltage input to the component and measure how much voltage is being applied normally. By moving the jumper wire successively back from the lamp toward the power source, you can isolate the area of the circuit where the open is located. When the component stops functioning, or the power is cut off, the open is in the segment of wire between the jumper and the point previously tested.

CAUTION: *Never use jumpers made from wire that is of lighter gauge than used in the circuit under test. If the jumper wire is of too small gauge, it may overheat and possibly melt. Never use jumpers to bypass high resistance loads in a circuit. Bypassing resistances, in effect, creates a short circuit which may, in turn, cause damage and fire. Never use a jumper for anything other than temporary bypassing of components in a circuit.*

12 Volt Test Light

The 12 volt test light is used to check circuits and components while electrical current is flowing through them. It is used for voltage and ground tests. Twelve volt test lights come in different styles but all have three main parts; a ground clip, a probe, and a light. The most commonly used 12 volt test lights have pick-type probes. To use a 12 volt test light, connect the ground clip to a good ground and probe wherever necessary with the pick. The pick should be sharp so that it can penetrate wire insulation to make contact with the wire, without making a large hole in the insulation. The wraparound light is handy in hard to reach areas or where it is difficult to support a wire to push a probe pick into it. To use the wrap around light, hook the wire to probed with the hook and pull the trigger. A small pick will be forced through the wire insulation into the wire core.

CAUTION: *Do not use a test light to probe electronic ignition spark plug or coil wires. Never use a pick-type test light to probe wiring on computer controlled systems unless specifically instructed to do so. Any wire insulation that is pierced by the test light probe should be taped and sealed with silicone after testing.*

Like the jumper wire, the 12 volt test light is used to isolate opens in circuits. But, whereas the jumper wire is used to bypass the open to operate the load, the 12 volt test light is used to locate the presence of voltage in a circuit. If the test light glows, you know that there is power up to that point; if the 12 volt test light does not glow when its probe is inserted into the wire or connector, you know that there is an open circuit (no power). Move the test light in successive steps back toward the power source until the light in the handle does glow. When it does glow, the open is between the probe and point previously probed.

NOTE: *The test light does not detect that 12 volts (or any particular amount of voltage) is present; it only detects that some voltage is present. It is advisable before using the test light to touch its terminals across the battery posts to make sure the light is operating properly.*

Self-Powered Test Light

The self-powered test light usually contains a 1.5 volt penlight battery. One type of self-powered test light is similar in design to the 12 volt test light. This type has both the battery and the light in the handle and pick-type probe tip. The second type has the light toward the open tip, so that the light illuminates the contact point. The self-powered test light is dual purpose piece of test equipment. It can be used to test for either open or short circuits when power is isolated from the circuit (continuity test). A powered test light should not be used on any computer controlled system or component unless specifically instructed to do so. Many engine sensors can be destroyed by even this small amount of voltage applied directly to the terminals.

Open Circuit Testing

To use the self-powered test light to check for open circuits, first isolate the circuit from the vehicle's 12 volt power source by disconnecting the battery or wiring harness connector. Connect the test light ground clip to a good ground and probe sections of the circuit sequentially with the test light. (start from either end of the circuit). If the light is out, the open is between the probe and the circuit ground. If the light is on, the open is between the probe and end of the circuit toward the power source.

Short Circuit Testing

By isolating the circuit both from power and from ground, and using a self-powered test light, you can check for shorts to ground in the circuit. Isolate the circuit from power and ground. Connect the test light ground clip to a good ground and probe any easy-to-reach test point in the circuit. If the light comes on, there is a short somewhere in the circuit. To isolate the short, probe a test point at either end of the isolated circuit (the light should be on). Leave the test light probe connected and open connectors, switches, remove parts, etc., sequentially, until the light goes out. When the light goes out, the short is between the last circuit component opened and the previous circuit opened.

NOTE: *The 1.5 volt battery in the test light does not provide much current. A weak battery may not provide enough power to illuminate the test light even when a complete circuit is made (especially if there are high resistances in the circuit). Always make sure that the test battery is strong. To check the battery, briefly touch the ground clip to the probe; if the light glows brightly the battery is strong enough for testing. Never use a self-powered test light to perform checks for opens or shorts when power is applied to the electrical system under test. The 12 volt vehicle power will quickly burn out the 1.5 volt light bulb in the test light.*

Voltmeter

A voltmeter is used to measure voltage at any point in a circuit, or to measure the voltage drop across any part of a circuit. It can also be used to check continuity in a wire or circuit by indicating current flow from one end to the other. Voltmeters usually have various scales on the meter dial and a selector switch to allow the selection of different voltages. The voltmeter has a positive and a negative lead. To avoid damage to the meter, always connect the negative lead to the negative (–) side of circuit (to ground or nearest the ground side of the circuit) and connect the positive lead to the positive (+) side of the circuit (to the power source or the nearest power source). Note that the negative voltmeter lead will always be black and that the positive voltmeter will always be some color other than black (usually red). Depending on how the voltmeter is connected into the circuit, it has several uses.

A voltmeter can be connected either in parallel or in series with a circuit and it has a very high resistance to current flow. When connected in parallel, only a small amount of current will flow through the voltmeter current path; the rest will flow through the normal circuit current path and the circuit will work normally. When the voltmeter is connected in series with a circuit, only a small amount of current can flow through the circuit. The circuit

will not work properly, but the voltmeter reading will show if the circuit is complete or not.

Available Voltage Measurement

Set the voltmeter selector switch to the 20V position and connect the meter negative lead to the negative post of the battery. Connect the positive meter lead to the positive post of the battery and turn the ignition switch ON to provide a load. Read the voltage on the meter or digital display. A well charged battery should register over 12 volts. If the meter reads below 11.5 volts, the battery power may be insufficient to operate the electrical system properly. This test determines voltage available from the battery and should be the first step in any electrical trouble diagnosis procedure. Many electrical problems, especially on computer controlled systems, can be caused by a low state of charge in the battery. Excessive corrosion at the battery cable terminals can cause a poor contact that will prevent proper charging and full battery current flow.

Normal battery voltage is 12 volts when fully charged. When the battery is supplying current to one or more circuits it is said to be "under load". When everything is off the electrical system is under a "no-load" condition. A fully charged battery may show about 12.5 volts at no load; will drop to 12 volts under medium load; and will drop even lower under heavy load. If the battery is partially discharged the voltage decrease under heavy load may be excessive, even though the battery shows 12 volts or more at no load. When allowed to discharge further, the battery's available voltage under load will decrease more severely. For this reason, it is important that the battery be fully charged during all testing procedures to avoid errors in diagnosis and incorrect test results.

Voltage Drop

When current flows through a resistance, the voltage beyond the resistance is reduced (the larger the current, the greater the reduction in voltage). When no current is flowing, there is no voltage drop because there is no current flow. All points in the circuit which are connected to the power source are at the same voltage as the power source. The total voltage drop always equals the total source voltage. In a long circuit with many connectors, a series of small, unwanted voltage drops due to corrosion at the connectors can add up to a total loss of voltage which impairs the operation of the normal loads in the circuit.

INDIRECT COMPUTATION OF VOLTAGE DROPS

1. Set the voltmeter selector switch to the 20 volt position.

2. Connect the meter negative lead to a good ground.

3. Probe all resistances in the circuit with the positive meter lead.

4. Operate the circuit in all modes and observe the voltage readings.

DIRECT MEASUREMENT OF VOLTAGE DROPS

1. Set the voltmeter switch to the 20 volt position.

2. Connect the voltmeter negative lead to the ground side of the resistance load to be measured.

3. Connect the positive lead to the positive side of the resistance or load to be measured.

4. Read the voltage drop directly on the 20 volt scale.

Too high a voltage indicates too high a resistance. If, for example, a blower motor runs too slowly, you can determine if there is too high a resistance in the resistor pack. By taking voltage drop readings in all parts of the circuit, you can isolate the problem. Too low a voltage drop indicates too low a resistance. If, for example, a blower motor runs too fast in the MED and/or LOW position, the problem can be isolated in the resistor pack by taking voltage drop readings in all parts of the circuit to locate a possibly shorted resistor. The maximum allowable voltage drop under load is critical, especially if there is more than one high resistance problem in a circuit because all voltage drops are cumulative. A small drop is normal due to the resistance of the conductors.

HIGH RESISTANCE TESTING

1. Set the voltmeter selector switch to the 4 volt position.

2. Connect the voltmeter positive lead to the positive post of the battery.

3. Turn on the headlights and heater blower to provide a load.

4. Probe various points in the circuit with the negative voltmeter lead.

5. Read the voltage drop on the 4 volt scale. Some average maximum allowable voltage drops are:

FUSE PANEL: 7 volts
IGNITION SWITCH: 5 volts
HEADLIGHT SWITCH: 7 volts
IGNITION COIL (+): 5 volts
ANY OTHER LOAD: 1.3 volts

NOTE: *Voltage drops are all measured while a load is operating; without current flow, there will be no voltage drop.*

Ohmmeter

The ohmmeter is designed to read resistance in ohms () in a circuit or component. Although there are several different styles of ohmmeters,

all will usually have a selector switch which permits the measurement of different ranges of resistance (usually the selector switch allows the multiplication of the meter reading by 10, 100, 1,000, and 10,000). A calibration knob allows the meter to be set at zero for accurate measurement. Since all ohmmeters are powered by an internal battery (usually 9 volts), the ohmmeter can be used as a self-powered test light. When the ohmmeter is connected, current from the ohmmeter flows through the circuit or component being tested. Since the ohmmeter's internal resistance and voltage are known values, the amount of current flow through the meter depends on the resistance of the circuit or component being tested.

The ohmmeter can be used to perform continuity test for opens or shorts (either by observation of the meter needle or as a self-powered test light), and to read actual resistance in a circuit. It should be noted that the ohmmeter is used to check the resistance of a component or wire while there is no voltage applied to the circuit. Current flow from an outside voltage source (such as the vehicle battery) can damage the ohmmeter, so the circuit or component should be isolated from the vehicle electrical system before any testing is done. Since the ohmmeter uses its own voltage source, either lead can be connected to any test point.

NOTE: *When checking diodes or other solid state components, the ohmmeter leads can only be connected one way in order to measure current flow in a single direction. Make sure the positive (+) and negative (–) terminal connections are as described in the test procedures to verify the one-way diode operation.*

In using the meter for making continuity checks, do not be concerned with the actual resistance readings. Zero resistance, or any resistance readings, indicate continuity in the circuit. Infinite resistance indicates an open in the circuit. A high resistance reading where there should be none indicates a problem in the circuit. Checks for short circuits are made in the same manner as checks for open circuits except that the circuit must be isolated from both power and normal ground. Infinite resistance indicates no continuity to ground, while zero resistance indicates a dead short to ground.

RESISTANCE MEASUREMENT

The batteries in an ohmmeter will weaken with age and temperature, so the ohmmeter must be calibrated or "zeroed" before taking measurements. To zero the meter, place the selector switch in its lowest range and touch the two ohmmeter leads together. Turn the calibration knob until the meter needle is exactly on zero.

NOTE: *All analog (needle) type ohmmeters must be zeroed before use, but some digital ohmmeter models are automatically calibrated when the switch is turned on. Self-calibrating digital ohmmeters do not have an adjusting knob, but its a good idea to check for a zero readout before use by touching the leads together. All computer controlled systems require the use of a digital ohmmeter with at least 10M (megohms) impedance for testing. Before any test procedures are attempted, make sure the ohmmeter used is compatible with the electrical system or damage to the on-board computer could result.*

To measure resistance, first isolate the circuit from the vehicle power source by disconnecting the battery cables or the harness connector. Make sure the key is OFF when disconnecting any components or the battery. Where necessary, also isolate at least one side of the circuit to be checked to avoid reading parallel resistances. Parallel circuit resistances will always give a lower reading than the actual resistance of either of the branches. When measuring the resistance of parallel circuits, the total resistance will always be lower than the smallest resistance in the circuit. Connect the meter leads to both sides of the circuit (wire or component) and read the actual measured ohms on the meter scale. Make sure the selector switch is set to the proper ohm scale for the circuit being tested to avoid misreading the ohmmeter test value.

WARNING: *Never use an ohmmeter with power applied to the circuit. Like the self-powered test light, the ohmmeter is designed to operate on its own power supply. The normal 12 volt automotive electrical system current could damage the meter!*

Ammeters

An ammeter measures the amount of current flowing through a circuit in units called amperes or amps. Amperes are units of electron flow which indicate how fast the electrons are flowing through the circuit. Since Ohms Law dictates that current flow in a circuit is equal to the circuit voltage divided by the total circuit resistance, increasing voltage also increases the current level (amps). Likewise, any decrease in resistance will increase the amount of amps in a circuit. At normal operating voltage, most circuits have a characteristic amount of amperes, called "current draw" which can be measured using an ammeter. By referring to a specified current draw rating, measuring the amperes, and comparing the two values, one can determine what is happening within the circuit to aid in diagnosis. An open circuit, for example, will not allow any current to flow so the ammeter reading will be zero. More current flows through a heavily loaded circuit or when the charging system is operating.

An ammeter is always connected in series with the circuit being tested. All of the current that normally flows through the circuit must also flow through the ammeter; if there is any other path for the current to follow, the ammeter reading will not be accurate. The ammeter itself has very little resistance to current flow and therefore will not affect the circuit, but it will measure current draw only when the circuit is closed and electricity is flowing. Excessive current draw can blow fuses and drain the battery, while a reduced current draw can cause motors to run slowly, lights to dim and other components to not operate properly. The ammeter can help diagnose these conditions by locating the cause of the high or low reading.

Multimeters

Different combinations of test meters can be built into a single unit designed for specific tests. Some of the more common combination test devices are known as Volt/Amp testers, Tach/Dwell meters, or Digital Multimeters. The Volt/Amp tester is used for charging system, starting system or battery tests and consists of a voltmeter, an ammeter and a variable resistance carbon pile. The voltmeter will usually have at least two ranges for use with 6, 12 and 24 volt systems. The ammeter also has more than one range for testing various levels of battery loads and starter current draw and the carbon pile can be adjusted to offer different amounts of resistance. The Volt/Amp tester has heavy leads to carry large amounts of current and many later models have an inductive ammeter pickup that clamps around the wire to simplify test connections. On some models, the ammeter also has a zero-center scale to allow testing of charging and starting systems without switching leads or polarity. A digital multimeter is a voltmeter, ammeter and ohmmeter combined in an instrument which gives a digital readout. These are often used when testing solid state circuits because of their high input impedance (usually 10 megohms or more).

The tach/dwell meter combines a tachometer and a dwell (cam angle) meter and is a specialized kind of voltmeter. The tachometer scale is marked to show engine speed in rpm and the dwell scale is marked to show degrees of distributor shaft rotation. In most electronic ignition systems, dwell is determined by the control unit, but the dwell meter can also be used to check the duty cycle (operation) of some electronic engine control systems. Some tach/dwell meters are powered by an internal battery, while others take their power from the car battery in use. The battery powered testers usually require calibration much like an ohmmeter before testing.

Special Test Equipment

A variety of diagnostic tools are available to help troubleshoot and repair computerized engine control systems. The most sophisticated of these devices are the console type engine analyzers that usually occupy a garage service bay, but there are several types of aftermarket electronic testers available that will allow quick circuit tests of the engine control system by plugging directly into a special connector located in the engine compartment or under the dashboard. Several tool and equipment manufacturers offer simple, hand held testers that measure various circuit voltage levels on command to check all system components for proper operation. Although these testers usually cost about $300–500, consider that the average computer control unit (or ECM) can cost just as much and the money saved by not replacing perfectly good sensors or components in an attempt to correct a problem could justify the purchase price of a special diagnostic tester the first time it's used.

These computerized testers can allow quick and easy test measurements while the engine is operating or while the car is being driven. In addition, the on-board computer memory can be read to access any stored trouble codes; in effect allowing the computer to tell you where it hurts and aid trouble diagnosis by pinpointing exactly which circuit or component is malfunctioning. In the same manner, repairs can be tested to make sure the problem has been corrected. The biggest advantage these special testers have is their relatively easy hookups that minimize or eliminate the chances of making the wrong connections and getting false voltage readings or damaging the computer accidentally.

NOTE: *It should be remembered that these testers check voltage levels in circuits; they don't detect mechanical problems or failed components if the circuit voltage falls within the preprogrammed limits stored in the tester PROM unit. Also, most of the hand held testers are designed to work only on one or two systems made by a specific manufacturer.*

A variety of aftermarket testers are available to help diagnose different computerized control systems. Owatonna Tool Company (OTC), for example, markets a device called the OTC Monitor which plugs directly into the assembly line diagnostic link (ALDL). The OTC tester makes diagnosis a simple matter of pressing the correct buttons and, by changing the internal PROM or inserting a different diagnosis cartridge, it will work on any model from full size to subcompact, over a wide range of years. An adapter is supplied with the tester to allow connection to all types of ALDL links, regardless of the number of pin terminals used. By inserting an updated PROM into the OTC tester, it can be easily updated to diagnose any new modifications of computerized control systems.

Wiring Harnesses

The average automobile contains about $1/2$ mile of wiring, with hundreds of individual connections. To protect the many wires from damage and to keep them from becoming a confusing tangle, they are organized into bundles, enclosed in plastic or taped together and called wire harnesses. Different wiring harnesses serve different parts of the vehicle. Individual wires are color coded to help trace them through a harness where sections are hidden from view.

A loose or corroded connection or a replacement wire that is too small for the circuit will add extra resistance and an additional voltage drop to the circuit. A ten percent voltage drop can result in slow or erratic motor operation, for example, even though the circuit is complete. Automotive wiring or circuit conductors can be in any one of three forms:

1. Single strand wire
2. Multi-strand wire
3. Printed circuitry

Single strand wire has a solid metal core and is usually used inside such components as alternators, motors, relays and other devices. Multi-strand wire has a core made of many small strands of wire twisted together into a single conductor. Most of the wiring in an automotive electrical system is made up of multi-strand wire, either as a single conductor or grouped together in a harness. All wiring is color coded on the insulator, either as a solid color or as a colored wire with an identification stripe. A printed circuit is a thin film of copper or other conductor that is printed on an insulator backing. Occasionally, a printed circuit is sandwiched between two sheets of plastic for more protection and flexibility. A complete printed circuit, consisting of conductors, insulating material and connectors for lamps or other components is called a printed circuit board. Printed circuitry is used in place of individual wires or harnesses in places where space is limited, such as behind instrument panels.

Wire Gauge

Since computer controlled automotive electrical systems are very sensitive to changes in resistance, the selection of properly sized wires is critical when systems are repaired. The wire gauge number is an expression of the cross section area of the conductor. The most common system for expressing wire size is the American Wire Gauge (AWG) system.

Wire cross section area is measured in circular mils. A mil is $\frac{1}{1000}$ in. (0.001 in.); a circular mil is the area of a circle one mil in diameter. For example, a conductor $\frac{1}{4}$ in. in diameter is 0.250 in. or 250 mils. The circular mil cross section area of the wire is 250 squared (250²)or 62,500 circular mils. Imported car models usually use metric wire gauge designations, which is simply the cross section area of the conductor in square millimeters (mm^2).

Gauge numbers are assigned to conductors of various cross section areas. As gauge number increases, area decreases and the conductor becomes smaller. A 5 gauge conductor is smaller than a 1 gauge conductor and a 10 gauge is smaller than a 5 gauge. As the cross section area of a conductor decreases, resistance increases and so does the gauge number. A conductor with a higher gauge number will carry less current than a conductor with a lower gauge number.

NOTE: *Gauge wire size refers to the size of the conductor, not the size of the complete wire. It is possible to have two wires of the same gauge with different diameters because one may have thicker insulation than the other.*

12 volt automotive electrical systems generally use 10, 12, 14, 16 and 18 gauge wire. Main power distribution circuits and larger accessories usually use 10 and 12 gauge wire. Battery cables are usually 4 or 6 gauge, although 1 and 2 gauge wires are occasionally used. Wire length must also be considered when making repairs to a circuit. As conductor length increases, so does resistance. An 18 gauge wire, for example, can carry a 10 amp load for 10 feet without excessive voltage drop; however if a 15 foot wire is required for the same 10 amp load, it must be a 16 gauge wire.

An electrical schematic shows the electrical current paths when a circuit is operating properly. It is essential to understand how a circuit works before trying to figure out why it does not. Schematics break the entire electrical system down into individual circuits and show only one particular circuit. In a schematic, no attempt is made to represent wiring and components as they physically appear on the vehicle; switches and other components are shown as simply as possible. Face views of harness connectors show the cavity or terminal locations in all multi-pin connectors to help locate test points.

If you need to back probe a connector while it is on the component, the order of the terminals must be mentally reversed. The wire color code can help in this situation, as well as a keyway, lock tab or other reference mark.

NOTE: *Wiring diagrams are not included in this book. As trucks have become more complex and available with longer option lists, wiring diagrams have grown in size and complexity. It has become almost impossible to provide a readable reproduction of a wiring diagram in a book this size. Information on ordering wiring diagrams from the vehicle manufacturer can be found in the owner's manual.*

WIRING REPAIR

Soldering is a quick, efficient method of joining metals permanently. Everyone who has the occasion to make wiring repairs should know how to solder. Electrical connections that are soldered are far less likely to come apart and will conduct electricity much better than connections that are only "pig-tailed" together. The most popular (and preferred) method of soldering is with an electrical soldering gun. Soldering irons are available in many sizes and wattage ratings. Irons with higher wattage ratings deliver higher temperatures and recover lost heat faster. A small soldering iron rated for no more than 50 watts is recommended, especially on electrical systems where excess heat can damage the components being soldered.

There are three ingredients necessary for successful soldering; proper flux, good solder and sufficient heat. A soldering flux is necessary to clean the metal of tarnish, prepare it for soldering and to enable the solder to spread into tiny crevices. When soldering, always use a resin flux or resin core solder which is non-corrosive and will not attract moisture once the job is finished. Other types of flux (acid core) will leave a residue that will attract moisture and cause the wires to corrode. Tin is a unique metal with a low melting point. In a molten state, it dissolves and alloys easily with many metals. Solder is made by mixing tin with lead. The most common proportions are 40/60, 50/50 and 60/40, with the percentage of tin listed first. Low priced solders usually contain less tin, making them very difficult for a beginner to use because more heat is required to melt the solder. A common solder is 40/60 which is well suited for all-around general use, but 60/40 melts easier, has more tin for a better joint and is preferred for electrical work.

Soldering Techniques

Successful soldering requires that the metals to be joined be heated to a temperature that will melt the solder, usually 360–460°F (182–238°C). Contrary to popular belief, the purpose of the soldering iron is not to melt the solder itself, but to heat the parts being soldered to a temperature high enough to melt the solder when it is touched to the work. Melting flux-cored solder on the soldering iron will usually destroy the effectiveness of the flux.

NOTE: *Soldering tips are made of copper for good heat conductivity, but must be "tinned" regularly for quick transference of heat to the project and to prevent the solder from sticking to the iron. To "tin" the iron, simply heat it and touch the flux-cored solder to the tip; the solder will flow over the hot tip. Wipe the excess off with a clean rag, but be careful as the iron will be hot.*

After some use, the tip may become pitted. If so, simply dress the tip smooth with a smooth file and "tin" the tip again. An old saying holds that "metals well cleaned are half soldered." Flux-cored solder will remove oxides but rust, bits of insulation and oil or grease must be removed with a wire brush or emery cloth. For maximum strength in soldered parts, the joint must start off clean and tight. Weak joints will result in gaps too wide for the solder to bridge.

If a separate soldering flux is used, it should be brushed or swabbed on only those areas that are to be soldered. Most solders contain a core of flux and separate fluxing is unnecessary. Hold the work to be soldered firmly. It is best to solder on a wooden board, because a metal vise will only rob the piece to be soldered of heat and make it difficult to melt the solder. Hold the soldering tip with the broadest face against the work to be soldered. Apply solder under the tip close to the work, using enough solder to give a heavy film between the iron and the piece being soldered, while moving slowly and making sure the solder melts properly. Keep the work level or the solder will run to the lowest part and favor the thicker parts, because these require more heat to melt the solder. If the soldering tip overheats (the solder coating on the face of the tip burns up), it should be retinned. Once the soldering is completed, let the soldered joint stand until cool. Tape and seal all soldered wire splices after the repair has cooled.

Wire Harness and Connectors

The on-board computer (ECM) wire harness electrically connects the control unit to the various solenoids, switches and sensors used by the control system. Most connectors in the engine compartment or otherwise exposed to the elements are protected against moisture and dirt which could create oxidation and deposits on the terminals. This protection is important because of the very low voltage and current levels used by the computer and sensors. All connectors have a lock which secures the male and female terminals together, with a secondary lock holding the seal and terminal into the connector. Both terminal locks must be released when disconnecting ECM connectors.

These special connectors are weather-proof and all repairs require the use of a special terminal and the tool required to service it. This tool is used to remove the pin and sleeve terminals. If removal is attempted with an ordinary pick, there is a good chance that the terminal will be bent or deformed. Unlike standard blade type terminals, these terminals cannot be straightened once they are bent. Make certain that the connectors are properly seated and all of the sealing rings in place when connecting leads. On some models, a hinge-type flap provides a backup or secondary locking feature for the terminals. Most secondary locks are used to improve the connector reliability by retaining the terminals if the small terminal lock tangs are not positioned properly.

Molded-on connectors require complete replacement of the connection. This means splicing a new connector assembly into the harness. All splices in on-board computer systems should be soldered to insure proper contact. Use care when probing the connections or replacing terminals in them as it is possible to short between opposite terminals. If this happens to the wrong terminal pair, it is possible to damage certain components. Always use jumper wires between connectors for circuit checking and never probe through weather-proof seals.

Open circuits are often difficult to locate by sight because corrosion or terminal misalignment are hidden by the connectors. Merely wiggling a connector on a sensor or in the wiring harness may correct the open circuit condition. This should always be considered when an open circuit or a failed sensor is indicated. Intermittent problems may also be caused by oxidized or loose connections. When using a circuit tester for diagnosis, always probe connections from the wire side. Be careful not to damage sealed connectors with test probes.

All wiring harnesses should be replaced with identical parts, using the same gauge wire and connectors. When signal wires are spliced into a harness, use wire with high temperature insulation only. With the low voltage and current levels found in the system, it is important that the best possible connection at all wire splices be made by soldering the splices together. It is seldom necessary to replace a complete harness. If replacement is necessary, pay close attention to insure proper harness routing. Secure the harness with suitable plastic wire clamps to prevent vibrations from causing the harness to wear in spots or contact any hot components.

NOTE: *Weatherproof connectors cannot be replaced with standard connectors. Instructions are provided with replacement connector and terminal packages. Some wire harnesses have mounting indicators (usually pieces of colored tape) to mark where the harness is to be secured.*

In making wiring repairs, it's important that you always replace damaged wires with wires that are the same gauge as the wire being replaced. The heavier the wire, the smaller the gauge number. Wires are color-coded to aid in identification and whenever possible the same color coded wire should be used for replacement. A wire stripping and crimping tool is necessary to install solderless terminal connectors. Test all crimps by pulling on the wires; it should not be possible to pull the wires out of a good crimp.

Wires which are open, exposed or otherwise damaged are repaired by simple splicing. Where possible, if the wiring harness is accessible and the damaged place in the wire can be located, it is best to open the harness and check for all possible damage. In an inaccessible harness, the wire must be bypassed with a new insert, usually taped to the outside of the old harness.

When replacing fusible links, be sure to use fusible link wire, NOT ordinary automotive wire. Make sure the fusible segment is of the same gauge and construction as the one being replaced and double the stripped end when crimping the terminal connector for a good contact. The melted (open) fusible link segment of the wiring harness should be cut off as close to the harness as possible, then a new segment spliced in as described. In the case of a damaged fusible link that feeds two harness wires, the harness connections should be replaced with two fusible link wires so that each circuit will have its own separate protection.

NOTE: *Most of the problems caused in the wiring harness are due to bad ground connections. Always check all vehicle ground connections for corrosion or looseness before performing any power feed checks to eliminate the chance of a bad ground affecting the circuit.*

Repairing Hard Shell Connectors

Unlike molded connectors, the terminal contacts in hard shell connectors can be replaced.

Weatherproof hard-shell connectors with the leads molded into the shell have non-replaceable terminal ends. Replacement usually involves the use of a special terminal removal tool that depress the locking tangs (barbs) on the connector terminal and allow the connector to be removed from the rear of the shell. The connector shell should be replaced if it shows any evidence of burning, melting, cracks, or breaks. Replace individual terminals that are burnt, corroded, distorted or loose.

NOTE: *The insulation crimp must be tight to prevent the insulation from sliding back on the wire when the wire is pulled. The insulation must be visibly compressed under the crimp tabs, and the ends of the crimp should be turned in for a firm grip on the insulation.*

The wire crimp must be made with all wire strands inside the crimp. The terminal must be fully compressed on the wire strands with the ends of the crimp tabs turned in to make a firm grip on the wire. Check all connections with an ohmmeter to insure a good contact. There should be no measurable resistance between the wire and the terminal when connected.

Mechanical Test Equipment

Vacuum Gauge

Most gauges are graduated in inches of mercury (in.Hg), although a device called a manometer reads vacuum in inches of water (in. H_2O). The normal vacuum reading usually varies between 18 and 22 in.Hg at sea level. To test engine vacuum, the vacuum gauge must be connected to a source of manifold vacuum. Many engines have a plug in the intake manifold which can be removed and replaced with an adapter fitting. Connect the vacuum gauge to the fitting with a suitable rubber hose or, if no manifold plug is available, connect the vacuum gauge to any device using manifold vacuum, such as EGR valves, etc. The vacuum gauge can be used to determine if enough vacuum is reaching a component to allow its actuation.

Hand Vacuum Pump

Small, hand-held vacuum pumps come in a variety of designs. Most have a built-in vacuum gauge and allow the component to be tested without removing it from the vehicle. Operate the pump lever or plunger to apply the correct amount of vacuum required for the test specified in the diagnosis routines. The level of vacuum in inches of Mercury (in.Hg) is indicated on the pump gauge. For some testing, an additional vacuum gauge may be necessary.

Intake manifold vacuum is used to operate various systems and devices on late model vehicles. To correctly diagnose and solve problems in vacuum control systems, a vacuum source is necessary for testing. In some cases, vacuum can be taken from the intake manifold when the engine is running, but vacuum is normally provided by a hand vacuum pump. These hand vacuum pumps have a built-in vacuum gauge that allow testing while the device is still attached to the component. For some tests, an additional vacuum gauge may be necessary.

HEATER AND AIR CONDITIONING

Refer to Chapter 1 for discharging and charging service procedures for air condition system.

Heater/Air Conditioner Blower Motor

REMOVAL AND INSTALLATION

NOTE: *The air condition assembly is integral with the heater assembly (including the blower motor) and therefore the blower motor removal may differ from the procedures detailed below. In some case it may be necessary to remove the Air Conditioner/Heater housing assembly (Cooling Unit) or package tray to remove the blower motor. Due to the lack of information (no factory service procedure) available at the time of this publication, a general blower motor removal and installation procedure is outlined. The removal steps can be altered as necessary.*

Celica and Supra

1. Disconnect the negative battery cable.

NOTE: *On 1990 SRS vehicles, you must wait AT LEAST 30 seconds after disconnecting the battery before doing any work. The SRS has a built-in backup which will allow the system to remain energized for a period of time after the power is disconnected.*

2. Working from under the instrument panel, unfasten the defroster hoses from the heater box as necessary.

3. Remove all related components to gain access for blower motor assembly. Unplug the multi-connector.

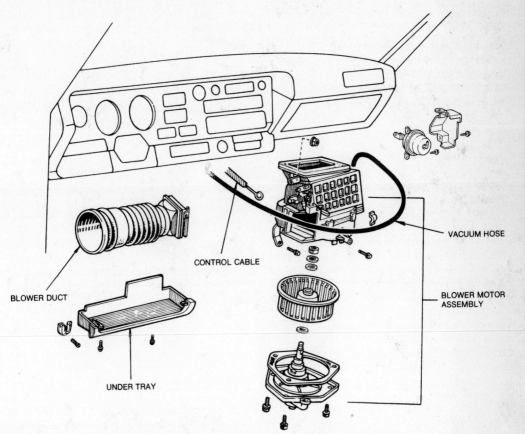

Typical blower motor installation without air conditioning

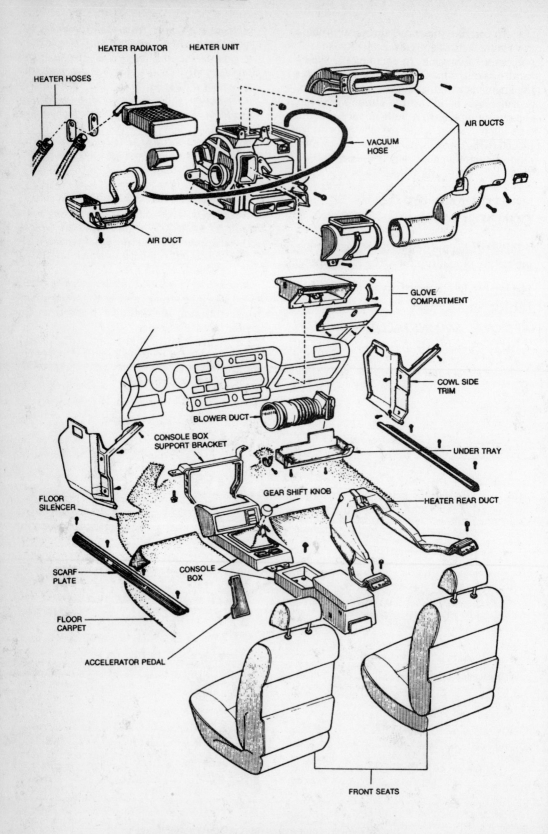

Typical heater core installation without air conditioning

4. Loosen the mounting screws and withdraw the blower assembly.

5. Installation is the reverse order of the removal procedure. Make sure to clean blower motor housing of all dirt, leaves etc. before installation. Check the blower motor for proper operation at all speeds after installation.

Heater Core

REMOVAL AND INSTALLATION

NOTE: *The air conditioner assembly is integral with the heater assembly (including the heater core) and therefore the heater core removal may differ from the procedures detailed below. In some case it may be necessary to remove the Air Conditioner/Heater housing assembly (Cooling Unit) or package tray to remove the heater core. Due to the variety of installations, a general heater core removal and installation procedure is outlined. The removal steps can be altered as necessary.*

Celica and Supra

1. Disconnect the negative battery cable. Drain the cooling system.

CAUTION: *When draining the coolant, keep in mind that cats and dogs are attracted by the ethylene glycol antifreeze, and are quite likely to drink any that is left in an uncovered container or in puddles on the ground. This will prove fatal in sufficient quantity. Always drain the coolant into a sealable container. Coolant should be reused unless it is contaminated or several years old.*

NOTE: *On 1990 SRS vehicles, you must wait AT LEAST 30 seconds after disconnecting the battery before doing any work. The SRS has a built-in backup which will allow the system to remain energized for a period of time after the power is disconnected.*

2. Remove the gear shift knob as necessary.

3. Unscrew the mounting bolts and lift the console box up and over the shift lever.

4. Remove the mounting bolts and remove the center console. Unplug any electrical connector if so equipped before removing the center console.

5. Remove and (mark for correct installation) all vacuum hoses form heater housing assembly.

6. Remove the under tray or package tray from the right side of the vehicle. Remove any necessary component for heater core removal.

7. Release the two clamps and remove the blower duct from the right side of the heater housing.

8. Remove all remaining air ducts.

9. Disconnect the 2 water (heater) hoses from the rear of the heater housing.

10. Tag and disconnect all wires and cables leading from the heater housing and position them out of the way.

11. Remove all mounting bolts and then remove the heater housing carefully toward the rear of the vehicle.

12. Remove the heater housing assembly from the vehicle. Remove any retaining brackets or hardware that may retain the heater core to the heater housing. Grasp the heater core by the end plate and carefully pull it out of the heater housing.

13. Install the heater core into the heater housing, make sure to clean heater housing of all dirt, leaves etc. before heater core installation.

14. Install the heater housing to the vehicle. Reconnect heater hoses, vacuum lines, electrical connections and control cables in the correct location.

15. Install all necessary (package tray, trim panels etc.) components that were remove for heater core removal. Connect battery and refill the cooling system. Check the heater system for proper operation.

Heater/Air Conditioner Control Unit

REMOVAL AND INSTALLATION

Celica and Supra

Refer to Instrument Panel/Safety Pad removal and installation for the necessary service procedures. Use service procedure as a guide to gain access to the heater control head, remove retaining screws, electrical connections and attaching control cables (with retaining clips if so equipped). Note length and position of heater control cables. Installation is the reverse of the removal procedures.

Evaporator Core/Cooling Unit

REMOVAL AND INSTALLATION

Celica and Supra

1. Disconnect the negative battery cable.

NOTE: *On 1990 SRS vehicles, you must wait AT LEAST 30 seconds after disconnecting the battery before doing any work. The SRS has a built-in backup which will allow the system to remain energized for a period of time after the power is disconnected.*

2. Discharge the air conditioning system. Refer to Chapter 1 for service procedures if necessary. Remove the charcoal canister with bracket on the Supra models.

3. Disconnect all air conditioning refrigera-

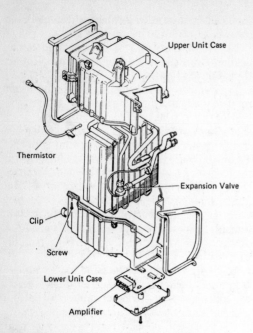

Thermistor

Upper Unit Case

Expansion Valve

Clip

Screw

Lower Unit Case

Amplifier

Cooling unit assembly — Celica and Supra

tion lines from the cooling unit. Plug or cap the open lines to keep moisture out of the system.

4. Remove the grommets from the air conditioning refrigeration lines to the cooling unit.

5. Remove the glove box assembly and reinforcement. Remove any trim panel if necessary.

6. Disconnect all connectors (electrical, vacuum, control cables etc.). On Supra models, remove the EFI and ABS computers.

7. Remove the cooling unit retaining bolts. Remove the cooling unit from the vehicle.

8. To disassemble the cooling unit follow the service procedure below:

a. Remove the 3 retaining clips and 5 screws.

b. Remove the thermistor from the evaporator assembly.

c. Remove the upper and lower case (and packing) from the evaporator assembly.

d. Remove all other components from the evaporator assembly.

9. Repair or replace the evaporator core as necessary. Check evaporator fins for blockage.

10. Install all necessary components to the evaporator assembly. Use all new O-rings for all service connections.

11. Install packing to the evaporator core. Install the upper and lower case to the evaporator assembly. Install the thermistor to the evaporator assembly and case retaining screws/clips.

12. Install the assembled cooling unit to the vehicle.

13. Install all connectors (electrical, vacuum,

control cables etc.). On Supra models, install the EFI and ABS computers.

14. Install grommets and reconnect the air conditioning refrigeration lines to the cooling unit, always use new O-rings as necessary.

15. Complete the remainder of the installation by following the reverse of the removal procedure. If the evaporator was replaced add compressor oil to the air conditioning compressor about 2 oz., connect the negative battery cable. Evacuate, charge and test refrigeration system for leaks.

RADIO

REMOVAL AND INSTALLATION

Celica and Supra

1. Disconnect the negative battery.

NOTE: *On 1990 SRS vehicles, you must wait AT LEAST 30 seconds after disconnecting the battery before doing any work. The SRS has a built-in backup which will allow the system to remain energized for a period of time after the power is disconnected.*

2. Remove the ash tray assembly. Remove the instrument center cluster finish panel assembly (remove the shifter knob if necessary).

3. Remove the 4 radio retaining screws. Disconnect all electrical connections and radio antenna cable.

4. Remove the radio from the vehicle.

5. Installation is the reverse of the removal procedures. Refer to Safety Pad/Instrument Panel exploded view as necessary.

WINDSHIELD WIPERS

Blade And Arm

REMOVAL AND INSTALLATION

Celica and Supra

To replace the wiper blade arms on both the front and rear windshields, remove the retaining nut that attaches the wiper arm to the wiper motor shaft. Note the position of the wiper arm (for correct installation). Remove the wiper arm. Install the replacement arm and tighten the retaining nut. After installation is complete, check the operation of the wiper blades.

NOTE: *The wiper blade element service replacement procedures are covered in Chapter 1. Do not operate the wipers if the windshield is dry. It may scratch the glass.*

Front Windshield Wiper Motor and Linkage

REMOVAL AND INSTALLATION

Celica and Supra

1. Remove the wiper arms/blades assemblies.
2. Remove the access hole covers and the ventilator louver as necessary.
3. Insert a tool between the linkage and the wiper motor crank arm (do not loose retaining clip if so equipped) and pry the link from the arm.
4. Unplug the electrical connector from the wiper motor.
5. Unscrew the mounting bolts and remove the wiper motor.
6. Insert a tool between the link and the pivot arm (do not loose retaining clip if so equipped) and pry the link from the arm.
7. Remove the screws holding the pivot arms and then remove the wiper linkage.
8. Install the wiper linkage and connect the link to the pivot arm.
9. Plug the electrical connector into the wiper motor.
10. Install the wiper motor.
11. Press the link on to the wiper motor crank arm and secure with retaining clip if so equipped.
12. Installation of the remaining components is in the reverse order of removal. Make sure that the front windshield wipers park in the correct position.

Rear Windshield Wiper Motor and Linkage

REMOVAL AND INSTALLATION

Celica and Supra

1. Remove the wiper arm/blade assembly.
2. Unscrew the mounting screws on the inside of the rear door and remove the trim panel.
3. Insert a tool between the link and the wiper motor crank arm and pry it off (do not loose the retaining clip if so equipped).
4. Unplug the electrical connector.
5. Unscrew the mounting bolts and remove the wiper motor.
6. Remove the link and support.
7. Install the support and the link.
8. Plug the electrical connector into the wiper motor.
9. Install the wiper motor.
10. Grease the end of the wiper link and then connect it to the crank arm.
11. Installation of the remaining components is in the reverse order of removal. Make

sure that the rear windshield wipers park in the correct position.

INSTRUMENTS AND SWITCHES

Instrument Cluster

REMOVAL AND INSTALLATION

Celica and Supra

Refer to Instrument Panel/Safety Pad removal and installation for the necessary service procedures. Use service procedure as a guide-preform only the necessary steps to gain access to the instrument cluster assembly.

Instrument Panel/Safety Pad

REMOVAL AND INSTALLATION

Celica

1. Disconnect the negative battery cable.
NOTE: *On 1990 SRS vehicles, you must wait AT LEAST 30 seconds after disconnecting the battery before doing any work. The SRS has a built-in backup which will allow the system to remain energized for a period of time after the power is disconnected.*
2. Remove the steering wheel (refer to the necessary safety procedures on vehicles equipped with SRS). On models without tilt steering remove the column cover.
3. Remove the shift lever knob if necessary. Remove 8 retaining screws and console box hole cover. Disconnect all connectors and remove the console box.
4. Remove the glove box door and door reinforcement.
5. Remove the left/right instrument panel speaker panel and speaker mounting bracket.
6. Remove the engine hood release lever.
7. Remove the instrument panel finish lower panel. Remove the heater to register duct work.
8. Remove the ash tray assembly. Remove the instrument center cluster finish panel assembly (remove the shifter knob if necessary).
9. Remove the 4 radio retaining screws. Disconnect all electrical connections and radio antenna cable.
10. Remove the radio from the vehicle.
11. Remove rear window defogger switch and hazard switch.
12. Remove the instrument cluster finish panel.
13. Disconnect the speedometer cable and all connections to the combination meter. Remove the 4 retaining screws and remove meter.
14. Remove the speedometer cable assembly from the instrument panel/safety pad.

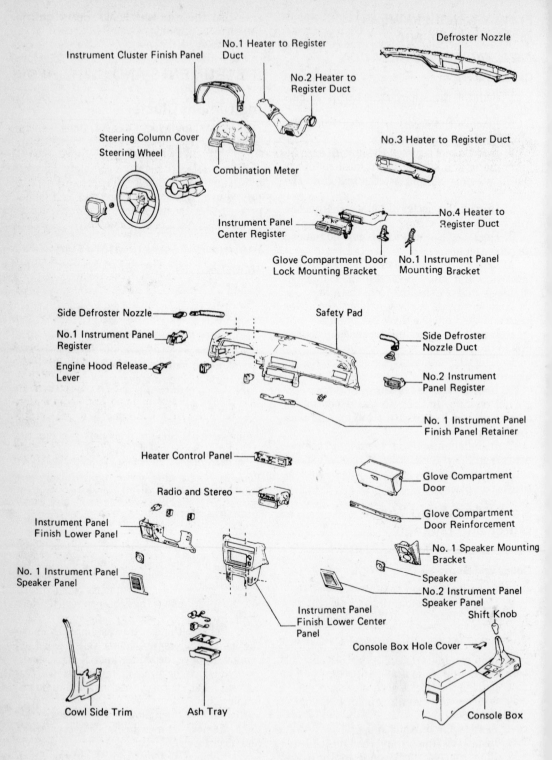

Instrument Cluster Finish Panel

No.1 Heater to Register Duct

No.2 Heater to Register Duct

Defroster Nozzle

Steering Column Cover
Steering Wheel

Combination Meter

No.3 Heater to Register Duct

Instrument Panel Center Register

No.4 Heater to Register Duct

Glove Compartment Door Lock Mounting Bracket

No.1 Instrument Panel Mounting Bracket

Side Defroster Nozzle

Safety Pad

No.1 Instrument Panel Register

Side Defroster Nozzle Duct

Engine Hood Release Lever

No.2 Instrument Panel Register

No. 1 Instrument Panel Finish Panel Retainer

Heater Control Panel

Glove Compartment Door

Radio and Stereo

Glove Compartment Door Reinforcement

Instrument Panel Finish Lower Panel

No. 1 Speaker Mounting Bracket

No. 1 Instrument Panel Speaker Panel

Speaker

No.2 Instrument Panel Speaker Panel

Shift Knob

Instrument Panel Finish Lower Center Panel

Console Box Hole Cover

Cowl Side Trim

Ash Tray

Console Box

Junction block and relay block on the driver's side kick panel — 1988 Supra

15. Remove the heater control panel mounting screws and cowl side trim. Disconnect any electrical connection or heater nozzles. Remove the safety pad from the vehicle.

NOTE: *The instrument panel/safety pad has a boss on the reverse side for clamping onto the clip on the body side. When removing the instrument panel/safety pad, pull upward at an angle.*

16. Install the instrument panel/safety pad in the correct position in the vehicle.

17. Reconnect all electrical connections. Install heater nozzles.

18. Install the heater control panel mounting screws and cowl side trim.

19. Install the speedometer cable assembly to the instrument panel/safety pad.

20. Install the combination meter. Reconnect the speedometer cable and all connections to the combination meter.

21. Install the instrument cluster finish panel.

22. Install rear window defogger switch, hazard warning and radio assembly.

23. Install the instrument panel finish lower panel. Install the heater to register duct work.

24. Install the glove box door and door reinforcement, left/right instrument panel speaker panel, speaker mounting bracket and engine hood release lever.

25. Install the console assembly and steering wheel assembly.

26. Reconnect the negative battery cable. Start the vehicle, road test and check operation of all accessories and components.

Supra

1. Disconnect the negative battery cable.

NOTE: *On 1990 SRS vehicles, you must wait AT LEAST 30 seconds after disconnecting the battery before doing any work. The SRS has a built-in backup which will allow the system to remain energized for a period of time after the power is disconnected.*

2. Remove the steering wheel (refer to the necessary safety procedures on vehicles equipped with SRS). Remove the steering column cover.

3. Remove the instrument panel undercover and lower instrument panel pad. Remove the engine hood release lever.

4. Remove the instrument lower finish panel.

5. Remove instrument center cluster finish panel.

6. Remove instrument cluster finish panel.

7. Remove the (disconnect the speedometer cable) combination meter.

8. Remove the console box, heater control, instrument undercover panel and radio.

9. Remove the glove box door, compartment panel and glove compartment door reinforcement (remove glove box door courtesy switch).

10. Remove the cowl left and right side trim panels and driver's foot rest.

11. Disconnect the electrical connectors and remove the EFI and ESC computer modules.

12. Remove the instrument panel/safety pad from the vehicle.

NOTE: *The instrument panel/safety pad has a boss on the reverse side for clamping onto the clip on the body side. When removing the instrument panel/safety pad, pull upward at an angle.*

13. Install the instrument panel/safety pad in the correct position in the vehicle.

14. Install the EFI and ESC computer modules and electrical connections.

15. Install the cowl left and right side trim panels and driver's foot rest.

16. Install the glove box door, compartment panel and glove compartment door reinforcement (install glove box door courtesy switch).

17. Install the console box, heater control, instrument undercover panel and radio (reconnect all electrical connections to all components).

18. Install combination meter (reconnect the speedometer cable and all necessary connections).

19. Install all necessary trim panels that were removed during removal service procedure. Install engine hood release lever.

20. Install the steering wheel assembly.

21. Reconnect the negative battery cable. Start the vehicle, road test and check operation of all accessories and components.

Console

REMOVAL AND INSTALLATION

Celica and Supra

1. Disconnect the negative battery cable.

NOTE: *On 1990 SRS vehicles, you must wait AT LEAST 30 seconds after disconnecting the battery before doing any work. The SRS has a built-in backup which will allow the system to remain energized for a period of time after the power is disconnected.*

2. Remove the shift lever knob if necessary.

3. Remove all console box retaining screws and console box hole cover. Disconnect all connectors and remove the console box.

4. Installation is the reverse of the removal procedures.

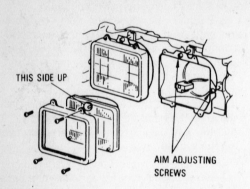

THIS SIDE UP

AIM ADJUSTING
SCREWS

Sealed beam headlight replacement. Do not loosen the aiming screws

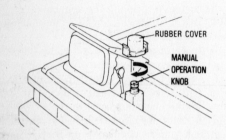

RUBBER COVER

MANUAL
OPERATION
KNOB

Manual operation of headlight doors — Celica and Supra

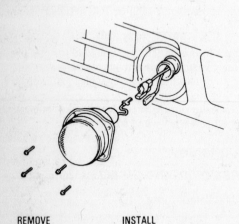

REMOVE   INSTALL

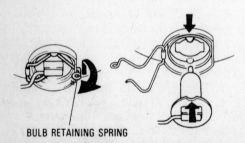

BULB RETAINING SPRING

Replacing front fog light bulb

Front And Rear Windshield Wiper Switches

REMOVAL AND INSTALLATION

Celica and Supra

The front and rear windshield wiper switches are incorporated with the combination switch, therefore it is necessary to refer to the combination switch removal procedure in order to remove the front or rear windshield wiper switch. Once the combination switch is removed, simply unscrew the front or rear wiper switch from the combination switch assembly. For the necessary service procedures see "Combination Switch Removal And Installation" in Chapter 8.

Headlight Switch

REMOVAL AND INSTALLATION

Celica and Supra

The headlight switch is incorporated in the combination switch. For the necessary service procedures see "Combination Switch Removal And Installation" in Chapter 8.

Back-Up Light Switch

REMOVAL AND INSTALLATION

Celica and Supra

For the necessary service procedures see Chapter 7.

Ignition Switch

REMOVAL AND INSTALLATION

Celica and Supra

Information on removing and installing ignition switches can be found in Chapter 8.

Speedometer Cable

REMOVAL AND INSTALLATION

Celica and Supra

Depending on the particular model, there are two types of methods for attaching the cable to the speedometer. One is the conventional screw-in type, while the other employs a locking lever to secure the cable.

1. Remove the instrument cluster and disconnect the cable from the speedometer.

NOTE: *On some models, cable disconnection can be accomplished by simply reaching under the dash. If possible, this method is much easier than removing the entire instrument cluster.*

2. Feed the cable through its hole in the fire wall and then trace it down to where it connects to the transmission/transaxle.

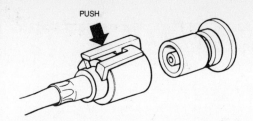

PUSH

Some models use a locking lever to secure the speedometer cable

3. Unscrew the cable from the transmission/transaxle end.

4. Installation is in the reverse order of removal procedure.

LIGHTING

Headlights
REMOVAL AND INSTALLATION

1. Raise the headlights.

NOTE: *Do not mistake the adjusting screws for the retaining ring screws. There are only two adjusting screws for each headlight. Turning these screws will result in improper headlight adjustment.*

2. Disconnect the negative battery cable or remove the RTR 30A fuse from the fuse and relay box under the hood near the battery.

CAUTION: *Unless power is disconnected, the headlights could suddenly retract and cause person injury.*

3. Remove the ornament and the beam unit retaining screws, ring and partially remove the sealed beam unit.

4. Compress the lock releases and disconnect the wire connector behind the beam unit. Remove the beam unit completely. If the wire connector is tight, wiggle it while holding in the lock releases and pulling out.

5. Installation is in the reverse order of removal. Install the beam unit with the single protrusion (TOP mark) on the glass face-upward. Use only a beam unit with the same number and wattage-regular sealed beam units are 65/55 watt, and halogen units are 65/35 watt. Check headlight aim.

Retractable Headlights Manual Operation

The retractable headlights can be manually operated if their electrical mechanism fails. To raise or lower the lights, remove the rubber cover from the manual operation knob (under the hood next to the headlight unit) and turn the knob clockwise. Manual operation should only be used if the system has failed; be sure to check the electrical operation of the lights as soon as possible.

Fog Lights
REMOVAL AND INSTALLATION

1. Loosen the retaining screws and remove the beam unit assembly.

2. Remove the rubber cover and disconnect the electrical connections.

3. Release the bulb retaining spring and remove the bulb. do not touch the glass part of the bulb. If you do , clean the glass with alcohol and clean rag.

4. To install a bulb, align the cutouts of the bulb with the protrusions of the mounting hole. use only a bulb with the same wattage.

5. Reconnect electrical connections and install the beam unit assembly to the vehicle.

Signal And Marker Lights
REMOVAL AND INSTALLATION
Front Turn Signal And Parking Lights

1. Remove turn signal/parking light lens.

2. Slightly depress the bulb and turn it counterclockwise to release it.

3. To install the bulb carefully push down and turn bulb clockwise at the same time.

4. Install the turn signal/parking light lens.

Side Marker Lights

1. Remove side marker light lens.

2. Pull bulb straight out.

3. To install bulb carefully push straight in.

4. Install side marker light lens with retaining screws.

Rear Turn Signal, Brake And Parking Lights

1. Remove rear trim panel in rear of vehicle if necessary to gain access to the bulb socket.

2. Slightly depress the bulb and turn it counterclockwise to release it.

3. To install the bulb carefully push down and turn bulb clockwise at the same time.

4. Install trim panel if necessary.

CIRCUIT PROTECTION

Fuses
REMOVAL AND INSTALLATION

The fuses can be easily inspected to see if they are blown. Simply pull the fuse from the block, inspect it and replace it with a new one, if necessary.

NOTE: *When replacing a blown fuse, be certain to replace it with one of the correct amperage.*

Fusible Links

A fusible link(s) is a protective device used in an electrical circuit. When current increases beyond a certain amperage, the fusible metal wire of the link melts, thus breaking the electrical circuit and preventing further damage to the other components and wiring. Whenever a fusible link is melted because of a short circuit, correct the cause before installing a new link. All fusible links are the plug in kind. To replace them, simply unplug the bad link and insert the new one.

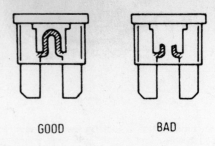

GOOD   BAD

Always replace a bad fuse with one of equal amperage

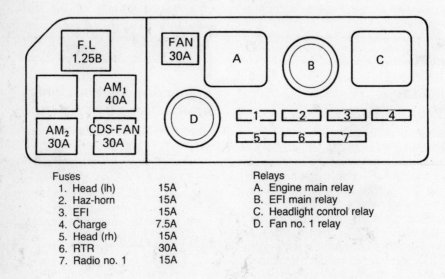

Fuses			Relays	
1. Head (lh)	15A		A.	Engine main relay
2. Haz-horn	15A		B.	EFI main relay
3. EFI	15A		C.	Headlight control relay
4. Charge	7.5A		D.	Fan no. 1 relay
5. Head (rh)	15A			
6. RTR	30A			
7. Radio no. 1	15A			

Fuse and relay block on the driver's side of engine compartment

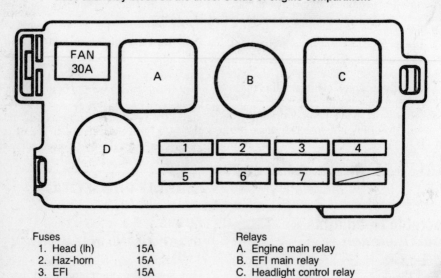

Fuses			Relays	
1. Head (lh)	15A		A.	Engine main relay
2. Haz-horn	15A		B.	EFI main relay
3. EFI	15A		C.	Headlight control relay
4. Charge	7.5A		D.	Fan no. 1 relay
5. Head (rh)	15A			
6. RTR	30A			
7. Radio no. 1	15A			

Fuse and relay block on the driver's side of engine compartment

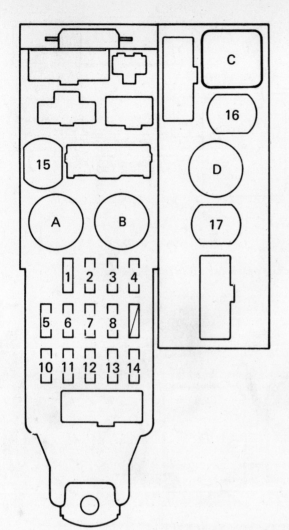

Fuses		
1.	Gauge	15A
2.	Dome	7.5A
3.	Stop	15A
4.	Tail	15A
5.	Cig	15A
6.	Radio	7.5A
7.	Turn	7.5A
8.	Mir-htr	10A
10.	Engine	10A
11.	Wiper	20A
12.	Ecu-ig	15A
13.	Inj	10A
14.	Ign	7.5A
15.	Circuit breaker (defogger)	
16.	Circuit breaker (door lock)	
17.	Circuit breaker (power window)	

Relays
A. Defogger relay
B. Taillight control relay
C. Turn signal flasher
D. Clutch start relay

Fuse and relay block on the driver's side kick panel

Circuit Breakers

Circuit breakers are also located in the fuse block. A circuit breaker is an electrical switch which breaks the circuit during an electrical overload. The circuit breaker will remain open until the short or overload condition in the circuit is corrected.

Flashers

To replace the flasher carefully pull it from the electrical connector. If necessary remove any component that restricts removal.

Fusible links can be found by the positive battery terminal

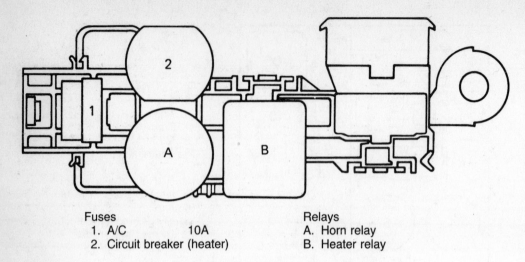

Fuses
1. A/C   10A
2. Circuit breaker (heater)

Relays
A. Horn relay
B. Heater relay

Fuse and relay block on passenger's side kick panel

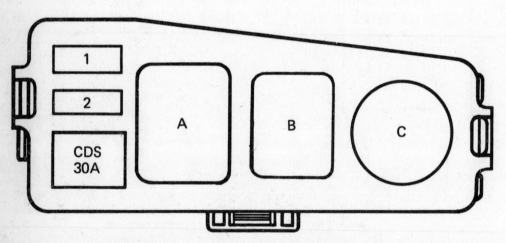

Relays
A. A·C fan no. 2 relay
B. A·C magnetic clutch relay
C. A·C fan no. 3 relay

Fuse and relay block on the passenger's side of engine compartment

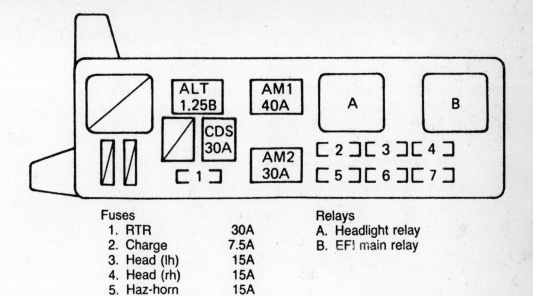

Fuses
1. RTR   30A
2. Charge   7.5A
3. Head (lh)   15A
4. Head (rh)   15A
5. Haz-horn   15A
6. Radio no. 1 15A
7. EFI   15A

Relays
A. Headlight relay
B. EFI main relay

Junction block in engine compartment — 1987 Supra

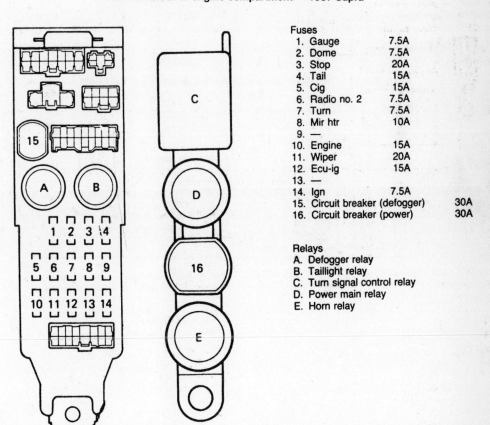

Fuses
1. Gauge   7.5A
2. Dome   7.5A
3. Stop   20A
4. Tail   15A
5. Cig   15A
6. Radio no. 2 7.5A
7. Turn   7.5A
8. Mir htr   10A
9. —
10. Engine   15A
11. Wiper   20A
12. Ecu-ig   15A
13. —
14. Ign   7.5A
15. Circuit breaker (defogger)   30A
16. Circuit breaker (power)   30A

Relays
A. Defogger relay
B. Taillight relay
C. Turn signal control relay
D. Power main relay
E. Horn relay

Junction block and relay block on the driver's side kick panel — 1987 Supra

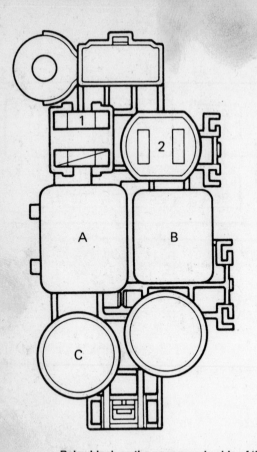

Fuses
1. A/C   10A
2. Circuit breaker (heater)   30A

Relays
A. Circuit opening relay
B. Heater relay
C. Clutch starter relay

Relay block on the passenger's side of the kick panel — 1987 Supra

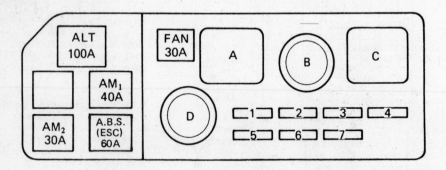

Fuses			Relays
1.	HEAD (LH)	15 A	A. Engine Main Relay
2.	HAZ-HORN	15 A	B. EFI Main Relay
3.	EFI	15 A	C. Headlight Control Relay
4.	CHARGE	7.5 A	D. Fan No. 1 Relay
5.	HEAD (RH)	15 A	
6.	RTR	30 A	
7.	DOME	20 A	

Fuse and relay block in engine compartment

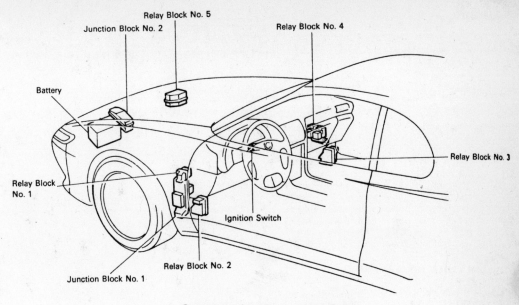

Component locations — 1990 Celica

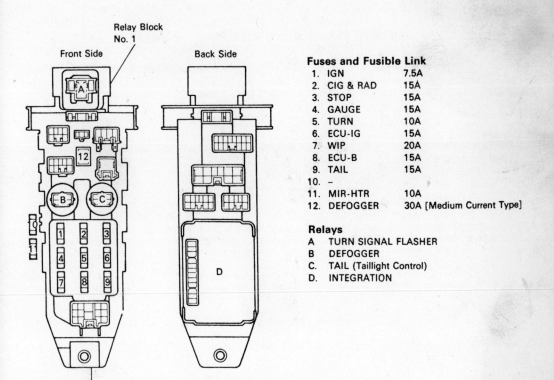

Relay Block No. 1

Front Side | Back Side

Fuses and Fusible Link
1. IGN   7.5A
2. CIG & RAD   15A
3. STOP   15A
4. GAUGE   15A
5. TURN   10A
6. ECU-IG   15A
7. WIP   20A
8. ECU-B   15A
9. TAIL   15A
10. –
11. MIR-HTR   10A
12. DEFOGGER   30A [Medium Current Type]

Relays
A   TURN SIGNAL FLASHER
B   DEFOGGER
C   TAIL (Taillight Control)
D   INTEGRATION

Junction Block No. 1

Fuse and relay block — 1990 Celica

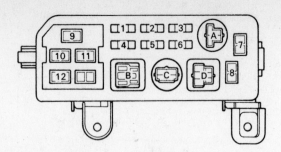

Fuses and Fusible Links

1.	HEAD (LH)	15A	7.	FAN	30A FL
2.	RTR	30A	8.	CDS	30A FL
3.	HEAD (RH)	15A	9.	ALT	100A FL
4.	EFI	15A	10.	AM2	40A FL
5.	DOME	20A	11.	AM1	30A FL
6.	HAZ-HORN	15A	12.	ABS	60A FL

Relays

A. FAN No. 1
B. HEAD (Headlight Control)
C. EFI
D. ENGINE MAIN

RELAY BLOCK NO. 2 and NO. 3

Relay Block No. 2

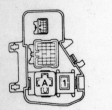

Relay Block No. 3

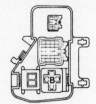

Fuse

1. Power   30A [Medium Current]

Relays

A. Power Main
B. Front Fog Light Control

RELAY BLOCK NO.4

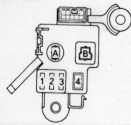

Fuses

1. –
2. FOG   20A
3. A·C   10A
4. HEATER   40A [Medium Current Type]

Relays

A. STARTER
B. HEATER MAIN

RELAY BLOCK NO. 5

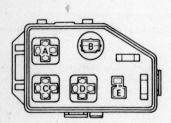

Relays

A. A·C FAN No. 2
B. SUB FAN
C. A·C FAN No. 3
D. A·C MG
E. HORN

Fuse and relay block — 1990 Celica

(No. 1)

(No. 5)

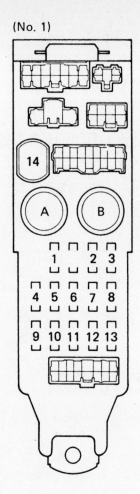

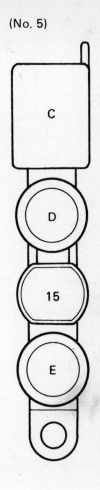

Fuses

1.	GAUGE	7.5A
2.	STOP	20A
3.	TAIL	15A
4.	CIG	15A
5.	RADIO No. 2	7.5A
6.	TURN	7.5A
7.	MIR HTR	10A
8.	–	
9.	ENGINE	15A
10.	WIPER	20A
11.	ECU-IG	15A
12.	–	
13.	IGN	7.5A
14.	Circuit Breaker (Defogger)	30A
15.	Circuit Breaker (Power)	30A

Relays

A. Defogger Relay
B. Taillight Relay
C. Turn Signal Control Relay
D. Power Main Relay
E. Horn Relay

Junction block and relay block on the driver's side kick panel — 1988 Supra

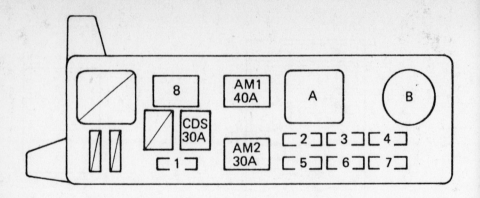

Fuses
1. RTR   30A
2. CHARGE   7.5A
3. HEAD (LH)   15A
4. HEAD (RH)   15A
5. HAZ-HORN   15A
6. RADIO No. 1   20A
7. EFI   15A
8. ALT   1.25B (7M-GE E/G)
   ALT   100A (7M-GTE E/G)

Relays
A. Headlight Relay
B. EFI Main Relay

Junction block in engine compartment — 1988 Supra

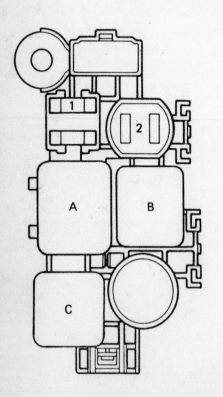

Fuses
1. A/C   10A
2. Circuit Breaker (Heater) 30A

Relays
A. Circuit Opening Relay
B. Heater Relay
C. Clutch Starter Relay

Relay block on the passenger's side of the kick panel — 1988 Supra

(No. 1)

(No. 5)

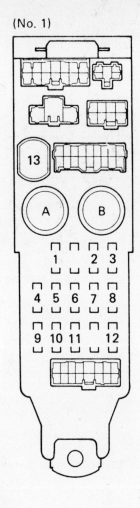

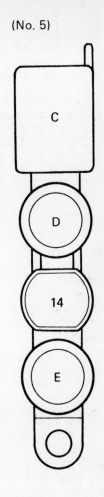

Fuses

1.	GAUGE	7.5A
2.	STOP	20A
3.	TAIL	15A
4.	CIG	15A
5.	RADIO	7.5A
6.	TURN	7.5A
7.	MIR-HTR	10A
8.	—	
9.	ENGINE	15A
10.	WIPER	20A
11.	ECU-IG	15A
12.	IGN	7.5A
13.	Circuit Breaker (Defogger)	30A
14.	Circuit Breaker (Power)	30A

Relays

A. Defogger Relay
B. Taillight Relay
C. Turn Signal Control Relay
D. Power Main Relay
E. Horn Relay

Junction block and relay block on the driver's side kick panel — 1989–90 Supra

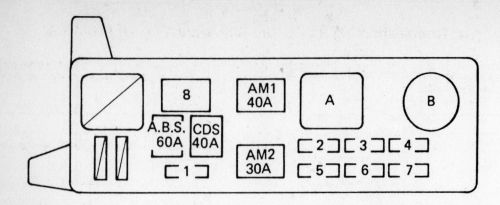

Fuses
1. RTR   30A
2. —
3. HEAD (LH)   15A
4. HEAD (RH)   15A
5. HAZ-HORN   15A
6. DOME   20A
7. EFI   15A
8. ALT   100A

Relays
A. Headlight Relay
B. EFI Main Relay

Junction block in engine compartment — 1989–90 Supra

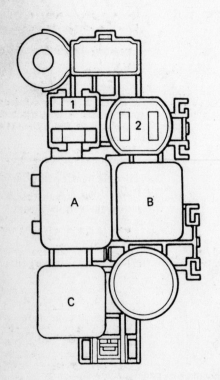

Fuses
1. A/C   10A
2. Circuit Breaker (Heater)   40A

Relays
A. Circuit Opening Relay
B. Heater Relay
C. Clutch Starter Relay

Relay block on the passenger's side of the kick panel — 1989–90 Supra

Troubleshooting Basic Turn Signal and Flasher Problems

Most problems in the turn signals or flasher system can be reduced to defective flashers or bulbs, which are easily replaced. Occasionally, problems in the turn signals are traced to the switch in the steering column, which will require professional service.

F = Front   R = Rear   ● = Lights off   ○ = Lights on

Problem		Solution
Turn signals light, but do not flash		• Replace the flasher
No turn signals light on either side		• Check the fuse. Replace if defective. • Check the flasher by substitution • Check for open circuit, short circuit or poor ground
Both turn signals on one side don't work		• Check for bad bulbs • Check for bad ground in both housings
One turn signal light on one side doesn't work		• Check and/or replace bulb • Check for corrosion in socket. Clean contacts. • Check for poor ground at socket
Turn signal flashes too fast or too slow		• Check any bulb on the side flashing too fast. A heavy-duty bulb is probably installed in place of a regular bulb. • Check the bulb flashing too slow. A standard bulb was probably installed in place of a heavy-duty bulb. • Check for loose connections or corrosion at the bulb socket
Indicator lights don't work in either direction		• Check if the turn signals are working • Check the dash indicator lights • Check the flasher by substitution
One indicator light doesn't light		• On systems with 1 dash indicator: See if the lights work on the same side. Often the filaments have been reversed in systems combining stoplights with taillights and turn signals. Check the flasher by substitution • On systems with 2 indicators: Check the bulbs on the same side Check the indicator light bulb Check the flasher by substitution

Troubleshooting Basic Lighting Problems

Problem	Cause	Solution
Lights		
One or more lights don't work, but others do	· Defective bulb(s) · Blown fuse(s) · Dirty fuse clips or light sockets · Poor ground circuit	· Replace bulb(s) · Replace fuse(s) · Clean connections · Run ground wire from light socket housing to car frame
Lights burn out quickly	· Incorrect voltage regulator setting or defective regulator · Poor battery/alternator connections	· Replace voltage regulator · Check battery/alternator connections
Lights go dim	· Low/discharged battery · Alternator not charging · Corroded sockets or connections · Low voltage output	· Check battery · Check drive belt tension; repair or replace alternator · Clean bulb and socket contacts and connections · Replace voltage regulator
Lights flicker	· Loose connection · Poor ground · Circuit breaker operating (short circuit)	· Tighten all connections · Run ground wire from light housing to car frame · Check connections and look for bare wires
Lights "flare"—Some flare is normal on acceleration—if excessive, see "Lights Burn Out Quickly"	· High voltage setting	· Replace voltage regulator
Lights glare—approaching drivers are blinded	· Lights adjusted too high · Rear springs or shocks sagging · Rear tires soft	· Have headlights aimed · Check rear springs/shocks · Check/correct rear tire pressure
Turn Signals		
Turn signals don't work in either direction	· Blown fuse · Defective flasher · Loose connection	· Replace fuse · Replace flasher · Check/tighten all connections
Right (or left) turn signal only won't work	· Bulb burned out · Right (or left) indicator bulb burned out · Short circuit	· Replace bulb · Check/replace indicator bulb · Check/repair wiring
Flasher rate too slow or too fast	· Incorrect wattage bulb · Incorrect flasher	· Flasher bulb · Replace flasher (use a variable load flasher if you pull a trailer)
Indicator lights do not flash (burn steadily)	· Burned out bulb · Defective flasher	· Replace bulb · Replace flasher
Indicator lights do not light at all	· Burned out indicator bulb · Defective flasher	· Replace indicator bulb · Replace flasher

Troubleshooting Basic Dash Gauge Problems

Problem	Cause	Solution
Coolant Temperature Gauge		
Gauge reads erratically or not at all	• Loose or dirty connections • Defective sending unit	• Clean/tighten connections • Bi-metal gauge: remove the wire from the sending unit. Ground the wire for an instant. If the gauge registers, replace the sending unit.
	• Defective gauge	• Magnetic gauge: disconnect the wire at the sending unit. With ignition ON gauge should register COLD. Ground the wire; gauge should register HOT.
Ammeter Gauge—Turn Headlights ON (do not start engine). Note reaction		
Ammeter shows charge Ammeter shows discharge Ammeter does not move	• Connections reversed on gauge • Ammeter is OK • Loose connections or faulty wiring • Defective gauge	• Reinstall connections • Nothing • Check/correct wiring • Replace gauge
Oil Pressure Gauge		
Gauge does not register or is inaccurate	• On mechanical gauge, Bourdon tube may be bent or kinked	• Check tube for kinks or bends preventing oil from reaching the gauge
	• Low oil pressure	• Remove sending unit. Idle the engine briefly. If no oil flows from sending unit hole, problem is in engine.
	• Defective gauge	• Remove the wire from the sending unit and ground it for an instant with the ignition ON. A good gauge will go to the top of the scale.
	• Defective wiring	• Check the wiring to the gauge. If it's OK and the gauge doesn't register when grounded, replace the gauge.
	• Defective sending unit	• If the wiring is OK and the gauge functions when grounded, replace the sending unit
All Gauges		
All gauges do not operate	• Blown fuse • Defective instrument regulator	• Replace fuse • Replace instrument voltage regulator
All gauges read low or erratically	• Defective or dirty instrument voltage regulator	• Clean contacts or replace
All gauges pegged	• Loss of ground between instrument voltage regulator and car • Defective instrument regulator	• Check ground • Replace regulator
Warning Lights		
Light(s) do not come on when ignition is ON, but engine is not started	• Defective bulb • Defective wire	• Replace bulb • Check wire from light to sending unit
	• Defective sending unit	• Disconnect the wire from the sending unit and ground it. Replace the sending unit if the light comes on with the ignition ON.
Light comes on with engine running	• Problem in individual system • Defective sending unit	• Check system • Check sending unit (see above)

Troubleshooting the Heater

Problem	Cause	Solution
Blower motor will not turn at any speed	• Blown fuse • Loose connection • Defective ground • Faulty switch • Faulty motor • Faulty resistor	• Replace fuse • Inspect and tighten • Clean and tighten • Replace switch • Replace motor • Replace resistor
Blower motor turns at one speed only	• Faulty switch • Faulty resistor	• Replace switch • Replace resistor
Blower motor turns but does not circulate air	• Intake blocked • Fan not secured to the motor shaft	• Clean intake • Tighten security
Heater will not heat	• Coolant does not reach proper temperature • Heater core blocked internally • Heater core air-bound • Blend-air door not in proper position	• Check and replace thermostat if necessary • Flush or replace core if necessary • Purge air from core • Adjust cable
Heater will not defrost	• Control cable adjustment incorrect • Defroster hose damaged	• Adjust control cable • Replace defroster hose

Troubleshooting Basic Windshield Wiper Problems

Problem	Cause	Solution
Electric Wipers		
Wipers do not operate— Wiper motor heats up or hums	• Internal motor defect • Bent or damaged linkage • Arms improperly installed on linking pivots	• Replace motor • Repair or replace linkage • Position linkage in park and reinstall wiper arms
Wipers do not operate— No current to motor	• Fuse or circuit breaker blown • Loose, open or broken wiring • Defective switch • Defective or corroded terminals • No ground circuit for motor or switch	• Replace fuse or circuit breaker • Repair wiring and connections • Replace switch • Replace or clean terminals • Repair ground circuits
Wipers do not operate— Motor runs	• Linkage disconnected or broken	• Connect wiper linkage or replace broken linkage
Vacuum Wipers		
Wipers do not operate	• Control switch or cable inoperative • Loss of engine vacuum to wiper motor (broken hoses, low engine vacuum, defective vacuum/fuel pump) • Linkage broken or disconnected • Defective wiper motor	• Repair or replace switch or cable • Check vacuum lines, engine vacuum and fuel pump • Repair linkage • Replace wiper motor
Wipers stop on engine acceleration	• Leaking vacuum hoses • Dry windshield • Oversize wiper blades • Defective vacuum/fuel pump	• Repair or replace hoses • Wet windshield with washers • Replace with proper size wiper blades • Replace pump

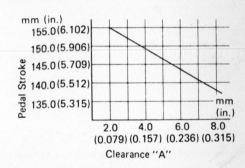

MANUAL TRANSMISSION

Identification

An identification tag is on the side of the transmission case. Included on the tag is the model number and serial number of the manual transmission.

Adjustments

LINKAGE AND SHIFTER

All Supra models utilize a floor-mounted shifter and an internally-mounted shift linkage. No external adjustments are either necessary or possible.

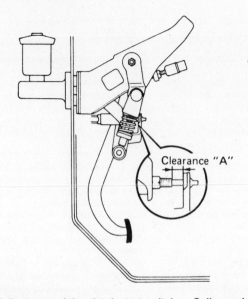

Adjustment of the clutch start switch — Celica and Supra

CLUTCH START SWITCH

Supra

1. Check that pedal height and freeplay (push rod play) are correct for the clutch start system.

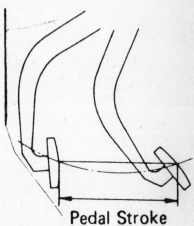

Pedal Stroke

Measuring pedal stroke — Celica and Supra

mm (in.)			
155.0 (6.102)			
150.0 (5.906)			
145.0 (5.709)			
140.0 (5.512)			
135.0 (5.315)			mm (in.)

Pedal Stroke

2.0 (0.079) 4.0 (0.157) 6.0 (0.236) 8.0 (0.315)

Clearance "A"

Clutch start clearance chart — Celica and Supra

Troubleshooting the Manual Transmission

Problem	Cause	Solution
Transmission shifts hard	• Clutch adjustment incorrect • Clutch linkage or cable binding • Shift rail binding	• Adjust clutch • Lubricate or repair as necessary • Check for mispositioned selector arm roll pin, loose cover bolts, worn shift rail bores, worn shift rail, distorted oil seal, or extension housing not aligned with case. Repair as necessary.
	• Internal bind in transmission caused by shift forks, selector plates, or synchronizer assemblies • Clutch housing misalignment • Incorrect lubricant • Block rings and/or cone seats worn	• Remove, dissemble and inspect transmission. Replace worn or damaged components as necessary. • Check runout at rear face of clutch housing • Drain and refill transmission • Blocking ring to gear clutch tooth face clearance must be 0.030 inch or greater. If clearance is correct it may still be necessary to inspect blocking rings and cone seats for excessive wear. Repair as necessary.
Gear clash when shifting from one gear to another	• Clutch adjustment incorrect • Clutch linkage or cable binding • Clutch housing misalignment • Lubricant level low or incorrect lubricant • Gearshift components, or synchronizer assemblies worn or damaged	• Adjust clutch • Lubricate or repair as necessary • Check runout at rear of clutch housing • Drain and refill transmission and check for lubricant leaks if level was low. Repair as necessary. • Remove, disassemble and inspect transmission. Replace worn or damaged components as necessary.
Transmission noisy	• Lubricant level low or incorrect lubricant • Clutch housing-to-engine, or transmission-to-clutch housing bolts loose • Dirt, chips, foreign material in transmission • Gearshift mechanism, transmission gears, or bearing components worn or damaged • Clutch housing misalignment	• Drain and refill transmission. If lubricant level was low, check for leaks and repair as necessary. • Check and correct bolt torque as necessary • Drain, flush, and refill transmission • Remove, disassemble and inspect transmission. Replace worn or damaged components as necessary. • Check runout at rear face of clutch housing
Jumps out of gear	• Clutch housing misalignment • Gearshift lever loose • Offset lever nylon insert worn or lever attaching nut loose • Gearshift mechanism, shift forks, selector plates, interlock plate, selector arm, shift rail, detent plugs, springs or shift cover worn or damaged • Clutch shaft or roller bearings worn or damaged	• Check runout at rear face of clutch housing • Check lever for worn fork. Tighten loose attaching bolts. • Remove gearshift lever and check for loose offset lever nut or worn insert. Repair or replace as necessary. • Remove, disassemble and inspect transmission cover assembly. Replace worn or damaged components as necessary. • Replace clutch shaft or roller bearings as necessary

Troubleshooting the Manual Transmission

Problem	Cause	Solution
Jumps out of gear (cont.)	• Gear teeth worn or tapered, synchronizer assemblies worn or damaged, excessive end play caused by worn thrust washers or output shaft gears • Pilot bushing worn	• Remove, disassemble, and inspect transmission. Replace worn or damaged components as necessary. • Replace pilot bushing
Will not shift into one gear	• Gearshift selector plates, interlock plate, or selector arm, worn, damaged, or incorrectly assembled • Shift rail detent plunger worn, spring broken, or plug loose • Gearshift lever worn or damaged • Synchronizer sleeves or hubs, damaged or worn	• Remove, disassemble, and inspect transmission cover assembly. Repair or replace components as necessary. • Tighten plug or replace worn or damaged components as necessary • Replace gearshift lever • Remove, disassemble and inspect transmission. Replace worn or damaged components.
Locked in one gear—cannot be shifted out	• Shift rail(s) worn or broken, shifter fork bent, setscrew loose, center detent plug missing or worn • Broken gear teeth on countershaft gear, clutch shaft, or reverse idler gear Gearshift lever broken or worn, shift mechanism in cover incorrectly assembled or broken, worn damaged gear train components	• Inspect and replace worn or damaged parts • Inspect and replace damaged part • Disassemble transmission. Replace damaged parts or assemble correctly.

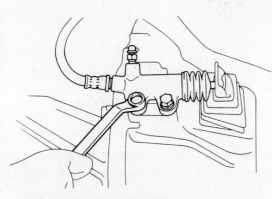

Clutch pedal adjustment points

2. Measure the pedal stroke and check the switch clearance "A" using the clutch start clearance chart as necessary.

3. Loosen and adjust the switch position as required.

4. Recheck that the engine does not start when the clutch pedal is released.

Back-Up Light Switch

REMOVAL AND INSTALLATION

Supra

1. Raise the vehicle and support safely.
2. Disconnect the electrical connection from the switch.

3. Remove the switch from the transmission housing, when removing the switch place a drain pan under the transmission to catch fluid.

4. To install reverse the removal procedures. Check and add the specified fluid as necessary to the correct level.

Transmission

REMOVAL AND INSTALLATION

Supra

1. Disconnect the negative battery cable.
2. From inside the vehicle, remove the center cluster finish panel and remove the shift lever.

3. Raise and safely support the vehicle. Drain the transmission oil.

4. On some 1986 models remove the steering gear housing but do not disconnect lines. Position and suspend housing assembly to the vehicle as necessary. Matchmark and remove the driveshaft assembly.

5. Remove the exhaust hanger/bracket and remove the front exhaust pipe.

6. Disconnect the speedometer cable, back-up light switch and rear speed sensor, if equipped with A.B.S.

7. Remove the clutch release cylinder and

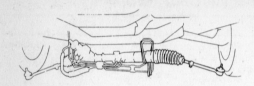

Suspend the steering rack housing; do not disconnect the fluid lines

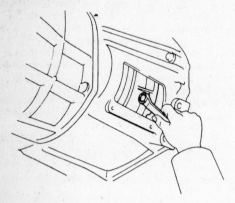

Removing clutch assembly — Supra 7M — GTE engine

move it aside. Do not disconnect hydraulic line if possible.

8. Disconnect the starter electrical connections and remove the starter assembly.

9. Using a transmission jack, secure it to the transmission and raise it slightly (do not jack to far, as fan assembly will hit) to take weight off the rear mount.

10. Remove the transmission-to-rear mount bolts, the rear mount-to-chassis bolts and rear mount crossmember.

11. Remove the flywheel undercover from the transmission.

12. On vehicles equipped with 7M-GE engine (non-turbocharged engine) remove the transmission-to-transmission housing bolts, move the transmission rearward and lower it from the vehicle.

13. On vehicles equipped with 7M-GTE engine (turbocharged engines) remove the transmission (transmission-to-engine) assembly with clutch cover and disc following the service procedure below:

a. Remove the clutch housing covers.

b. Pull out the release fork through the left clutch housing hole.

c. Place matchmark on the clutch cover and flywheel.

d. Loosen each clutch cover retaining bolt one turn at a time until spring tension is released. Rotate the engine as necessary using a tool or equivalent.

e. Remove the clutch cover and disc from the flywheel and full move them toward the transmission.

f. Remove the transmission with the clutch cover and disc assembly.

14. On vehicles equipped with 7M-GE engine (non-turbocharged engine), follow the installation service procedure below:

a. Align the input shaft spline (grease shaft) with the clutch disc (use dummy shaft tool or equivalent) and push the transmission into the correct position.

b. Install the mounting bolts and torque to 29 ft. lbs.

15. On vehicles equipped with 7M-GTE engine (turbocharged engine), follow the installation service procedure below:

a. Apply lithium base grease or equivalent to release bearing hub inside groove, input shaft spline, release fork contact surface.

b. Install the clutch cover and disc on the retainer and input shaft spline.

c. Align the input shaft tip with the pilot bearing and push the transmission fully into position. Install the mounting bolts and torque to 29 ft. lbs.

d. Align the matchmarks on the clutch cover and flywheel. Tighten the clutch cover set bolts evenly and gradually. Make several passes around the cover until the cover is snug then final torque is 14 ft. lbs.

e. Install the release fork to the release fork support through the left clutch housing hole. Install the clutch housing covers.

16. Install rear mounting assembly, starter (reconnect all electrical connections) and clutch release cylinder.

17. Reconnect back-up light switch, speedometer cable, rear speed sensor if equipped with A.B.S.

18. Install exhaust components and brackets use new exhaust clamps/brackets if necessary.

19. Install the steering gear housing as necessary. Align the matchmarks on the driveshaft flange and install driveshaft. Torque the driveshaft flange bolts to 54 ft. lbs. and center support bracket to 36 ft. lbs.

20. Install shift lever, center cluster finish panel. Reconnect the negative battery cable.

21. Fill transmission as necessary with the specified fluid to the correct level. Perform road test check for any abnormal noise and for correct operation.

Overhaul Notes

Cleanliness is an important factor in the overhaul of the manual transmission. Before opening up this unit, the entire outside of the assembly should be cleaned, preferably with a high pressure washer such as a car wash spray unit. Dirt entering the its internal parts will negate all the time and effort spent on the overhaul. During inspection and re-assembly all parts should be thoroughly cleaned with solvent then dried with compressed air. Wiping cloths and rags should not be used to dry parts.

Wheel bearing grease, long used to hold thrust washers and lube parts, should not be used. Lube seals with clean oil and use ordinary un-medicated petroleum jelly to hold the thrust washers and to ease the assembly of seals, since it will not leave a harmful residue as grease often will. Do not use solvent on neoprene seals, if they are to be reused, or thrust washers.

Before installing bolts into aluminum parts, always dip the threads into clean oil. Anti-seize compound can also be used to prevent bolts from galling the aluminum and seizing. Always use a torque wrench to keep from stripping the threads. The internal snaprings should be expanded and the external rings should be compressed, if they are to be reused. This will help ensure proper seating when installed.

W58 Transmission Overhaul

DISASSEMBLY

1. Remove the release fork and bearing.
2. Remove the back-up light switch, the speedometer driven gear, the shift lever retainer and restrict pins.
3. Remove the clutch housing-to-transmission bolts and the housing.
4. Remove the shift lever retainer-to-extension housing bolts, the retainer and oil baffle plate.
5. Using a T40 Torx® socket, remove the reverse restrict pins from both sides of the extension housing.
6. Remove the extension housing by performing the following procedures:
   a. Remove the shift lever housing set bolt.
   b. Remove the extension housing-to-transmission bolts.
   c. Using a plastic hammer, tap the extension housing.
   d. Disengage the shift and select lever from the shift head.
   e. Pull the extension housing from the transmission.
7. Remove the front bearing retainer-to-transmission bolts and remove the retainer.
8. Using snapring pliers, remove the snaprings from the input shaft and countershaft bearings.
9. Using a plastic hammer, tap the transmission case from the intermediate plate assembly.

10. Using a soft jawed vise, mount the intermediate plate assembly using 2 clutch housing bolts, washers and nuts to prevent the jaws of the vise from contacting the plate.
11. Using a detent ball plug socket, remove the 4 screw plugs from the side and top of the intermediate plate. Using a magnet finger, remove the springs and balls from the intermediate plate.
12. Remove the shift forks, the shift fork shafts and the reverse idler gear by performing the following procedures:
   a. Pry the lock washers from the No. 1 shift fork and remove the set bolt.
   b. Pry the lock washers from the No. 2 shift fork and remove the set bolt.
   c. Using 2 pry bars, tap the snapring from the No. 1 shift fork shaft.
   d. Using 2 pry bars, tap the snapring from the No. 2 shift fork shaft.
   e. Remove the stopper from the reverse idler gear shaft.
   f. Remove the reverse idler gear and shaft.
   g. Remove the No. 1 shift fork and shaft.
   h. Using a magnetic finger, remove the No. 1 and No. 2 interlock pins.
   i. Remove the No. 2 shift fork and shaft.
   j. Using a magnetic finger, remove the No. 3 interlock pin.
   k. Using a pin punch and a hammer, drive out the No. 3 fork shaft pin.
   l. Remove the No. 4 shift fork.
   m. Remove the No. 3 shift fork, the No. 3 shift fork shaft and the reverse shift arm with the pin.
13. Pry both ends of the speedometer drive gear clip and remove the gear.
14. Use a feeler gauge to measure the 5th gear thrust clearance; the standard clearance should be 0.004–0.016 in. (0.10–0.40mm) to a maximum clearance of 0.018 in. (0.46mm).
15. Remove the counter rear bearing, spacer, counter 5th gear and needle roller bearing by performing the following procedures:
   a. Using snapring pliers, remove the snapring.
   b. Using a gear puller, press the rear bearing, the spacer, the 5th gear and bearing from the countershaft; be careful not to catch the output shaft rear bearing roller on the counter 5th gear.
   c. Remove the spacer.
16. Remove the No. 3 hub sleeve assembly by performing the following procedures:
   a. Using 2 pry bars, tap the snapring from the countershaft.
   b. Using a gear puller, press the No. 3

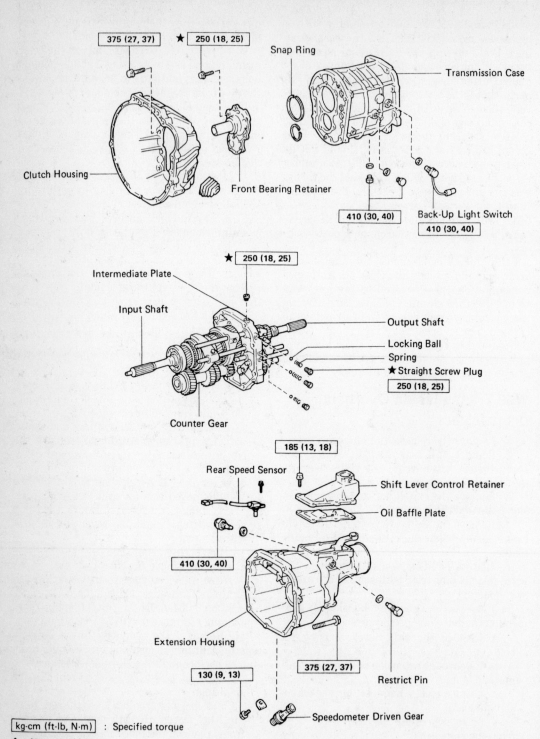

| 375 (27, 37) | ★ 250 (18, 25) |

Snap Ring

Transmission Case

Clutch Housing

Front Bearing Retainer

| 410 (30, 40) |

Back-Up Light Switch
| 410 (30, 40) |

★ | 250 (18, 25) |

Intermediate Plate

Input Shaft

Output Shaft

Locking Ball

Spring

★ Straight Screw Plug
| 250 (18, 25) |

Counter Gear

| 185 (13, 18) |

Rear Speed Sensor

Shift Lever Control Retainer

Oil Baffle Plate

| 410 (30, 40) |

Extension Housing

| 130 (9, 13) | | 375 (27, 37) |

Restrict Pin

Speedometer Driven Gear

| kg·cm (ft-lb, N·m) | : Specified torque
♦ Non-reusable part
★ Precoated part

Transmission components — Supra W58 transmission

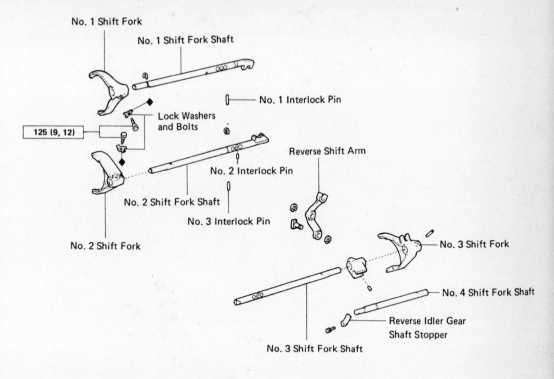

No. 1 Shift Fork

No. 1 Shift Fork Shaft

No. 1 Interlock Pin

Lock Washers
and Bolts

125 (9, 12)

Reverse Shift Arm

No. 2 Interlock Pin

No. 2 Shift Fork Shaft

No. 3 Interlock Pin

No. 2 Shift Fork

No. 3 Shift Fork

No. 4 Shift Fork Shaft

Reverse Idler Gear
Shaft Stopper

No. 3 Shift Fork Shaft

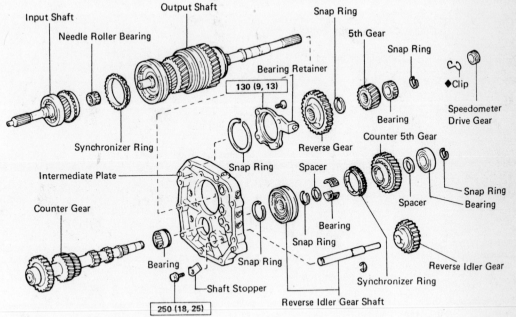

Input Shaft

Output Shaft

Snap Ring

Needle Roller Bearing

5th Gear

Snap Ring

◆Clip

Bearing Retainer

130 (9, 13)

Speedometer
Drive Gear

Bearing

Synchronizer Ring

Reverse Gear

Counter 5th Gear

Intermediate Plate

Snap Ring

Spacer

Snap Ring
Bearing

Counter Gear

Spacer

Bearing

Bearing

Snap Ring

Reverse Idler Gear

Bearing

Snap Ring

Synchronizer Ring

Shaft Stopper

Reverse Idler Gear Shaft

250 (18, 25)

kg·cm (ft·lb, N·m) : Specified torque

◆   Non-reusable part

Transmission components — Supra W58 transmission

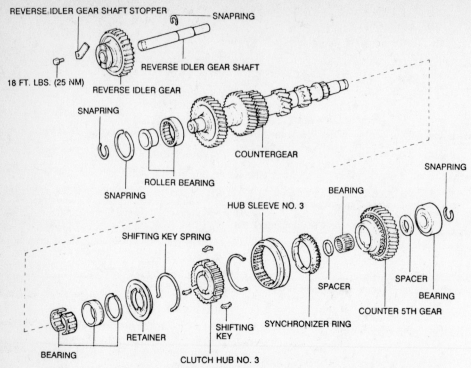

REVERSE IDLER GEAR SHAFT STOPPER — SNAPRING

REVERSE IDLER GEAR SHAFT

18 FT. LBS. (25 NM)

REVERSE IDLER GEAR

SNAPRING

COUNTERGEAR

SNAPRING

ROLLER BEARING

SNAPRING

BEARING

SNAPRING

HUB SLEEVE NO. 3

BEARING

SHIFTING KEY SPRING

SPACER

SPACER

BEARING

SPACER

BEARING

COUNTER 5TH GEAR

SHIFTING KEY

SYNCHRONIZER RING

RETAINER

CLUTCH HUB NO. 3

Exploded view of the countergear with reverse idler gear — Supra W58 transmission

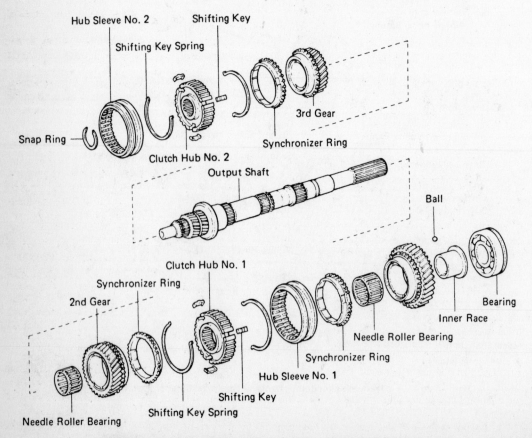

Hub Sleeve No. 2

Shifting Key

Shifting Key Spring

3rd Gear

Snap Ring

Synchronizer Ring

Clutch Hub No. 2

Output Shaft

Ball

Clutch Hub No. 1

Synchronizer Ring

2nd Gear

Bearing

Inner Race

Needle Roller Bearing

Synchronizer Ring

Hub Sleeve No. 1

Shifting Key

Shifting Key Spring

Needle Roller Bearing

Exploded view of the output shaft assembly — Supra W58 transmission

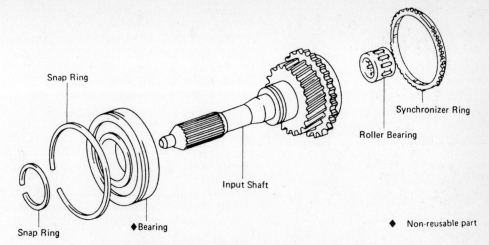

Snap Ring

Synchronizer Ring

Roller Bearing

Input Shaft

Snap Ring

◆Bearing

◆ Non-reusable part

Exploded view of the input shaft assembly — Supra W58 transmission

clutch hub from the countershaft; be sure to latch the puller claw onto the clutch hub, not the shifting key retainer.

17. Remove the output shaft rear bearing and 5th gear by performing the following procedures:

a. Using 2 pry bars, tap the snapring from the output shaft.

b. Using a gear puller, press the rear bearing and the 5th gear from the output shaft.

18. Remove the reverse gear by performing the following procedures:

a. Using 2 pry bars, tap the snapring from the countershaft.

b. Using a gear puller, press the reverse gear from the output shaft.

19. Using a T40 Torx® wrench, remove the center bearing retainer-to-intermediate plate bolts and the retainer. Using snapring pliers, remove the snapring from the center bearing.

20. Using a plastic hammer, tap the intermediate plate and remove the output shaft, the input shaft and the countershaft as an assembly. Remove the input shaft from the output shaft.

INPUT SHAFT

Disassembly

1. Check the synchronizer ring for braking action by pushing it inward and turning.

2. Using a feeler gauge, measure the clearance between the ring and the gear spline end; the standard clearance is 0.028–0.067 in. (0.70–1.70mm) and the minimum clearance is 0.020 in. (0.50mm). If the clearance is less than the limit, replace the synchronizer ring.

3. Using snapring pliers, remove the small snapring.

4. Using a shop press, press the bearing from the shaft.

Inspection

1. Inspect the synchronizer ring for wear and scoring.

2. Inspect the gear teeth and splines for chips and wear.

3. Inspect the bearings for roughness while turning.

Assembly

1. Using a shop press, press the bearing onto the shaft until it seats.

2. Select a snapring which will allow minimum axial play and install it onto the input shaft.

3. Install the needle bearing and synchronizer ring. Recheck the synchronizer ring for clearance and braking.

OUTPUT SHAFT

Pre-Disassembly Inspection

1. Using a feeler gauge, measure the thrust clearances of each gear; the standard clearance is 0.004–0.010 in. (0.10–0.25mm) and the maximum clearance is 0.012 in. (0.30mm).

2. Using a dial indicator, secure the output shaft in a vise and measure the oil clearance of each gear; the standard clearance is 0.0004–0.0024 in. (0.010–0.060mm) for 1st and 2nd gear and 0.0024–0.0041 in. (0.06–0.10mm) for 3rd gear; the maximum clearance is 0.006 in. (0.15mm) for 1st and 2nd gear and 0.008 in. (0.20mm) for 3rd gear.

Disassembly

1. Shift the No. 1 hub sleeve onto the 2nd gear. Using a shop press, press the center bearing, the 1st gear, the needle roller bearing and the synchronizer ring from the output shaft.

2. Using a magnetic finger, remove the locking ball from the shaft.

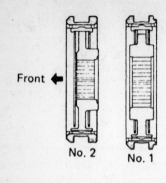

Front ←

No. 2   No. 1

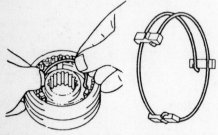

Positioning the No. 1 and No. 2 clutch hub sleeve assemblies — Supra W58 transmission

3. Using a shop press, press the No. 1 hub sleeve, the 2nd gear and the needle roller bearing from the shaft.

4. Using a pry bar, remove both shifting key springs, the shifting keys and the No. 1 hub sleeve from the No. 1 clutch hub.

5. Using snapring pliers, remove the snapring from the output shaft. Using a shop press, press the No. 2 hub sleeve, the synchronizer ring and the 3rd gear from the output shaft.

6. Using a pry bar, remove both shifting key springs, the shifting keys and the No. 2 hub sleeve from the No. 2 clutch hub.

Inspection

1. Inspect all bearings for roughness.

2. Inspect all gear teeth, splines and synchronizer parts for chipping and wear.

3. Inspect all snaprings for deformation.

4. Using calipers, measure the thickness of the output shaft flange; the minimum thickness is 0.2205 in. (5.60mm).

5. Using calipers, measure the thickness of the inner race flange; the minimum thickness is 0.1874 in. (4.76mm).

6. Using a micrometer, measure the outer diameter of the output shaft 2nd and 3rd gear journal; minimum diameter is 1.6841 in. (42.8mm) for 2nd gear and 1.4882 in. (37.80mm) for 3rd gear.

7. Using a micrometer, measure the outer diameter of the inner race; the minimum diameter is 1.687 in. (42.85mm).

8. Using a dial indicator and a set of V-

blocks, measure the runout of the output shaft; the maximum allowable runout is 0.002 in. (0.05mm). Replace the shaft, if any measurement is out of specification.

9. Push each synchronizer ring and turn it to check the braking action.

10. Measure the clearance between each synchronizer ring back and its corresponding gear spline end; the standard clearance is 0.028–0.067 in. (0.70–1.70mm), the minimum clearance is 0.020 in. (0.5mm). If the clearance is less than the limit, replace the synchronizer ring.

11. Measure the clearance between each hub sleeve and its corresponding shift fork. The maximum clearance is 0.040 in. (1.00mm).

Assembly

NOTE: *Lubricate the all of the parts before assembly.*

1. Install the No. 1 and No. 2 clutch hubs and shifting keys into the hub sleeves. Install the shifting key springs under the shifting keys so the end gaps are not aligned.

2. Place the synchronizer ring on 3rd gear and align the ring slots with the shifting keys.

3. Using a shop press, install 3rd gear and No. 2 hub sleeve onto the output shaft.

4. Select a snapring which will allow minimum axial play and install it onto the shaft.

5. Using a feeler gauge, measure the 3rd gear thrust clearance; the clearance should be 0.004–0.010 in. (0.10–0.25mm).

6. Install the 2nd gear and No. 1 clutch hub by performing the following procedures:

a. Position a synchronizer ring on the 2nd gear and align the ring slots with the shifting keys.

b. Install the needle roller bearing in the 2nd gear.

c. Using a shop press, press the 2nd gear and No. 1 clutch hub onto the shaft.

7. Using a feeler gauge, measure the 2nd gear thrust clearance; the clearance should be 0.004–0.010 in. (0.10–0.25mm).

8. Install the locking ball and the 1st gear assembly by performing the following procedures:

a. Position the locking ball into the shaft.

b. Assemble the 1st gear, the synchronizer ring, the needle bearing and the bearing inner race.

c. Install the 1st gear assembly onto the shaft; be sure to align the synchronizer ring slots with the shifting keys and turn the inner race to align it with the locking ball.

9. Using a shop press and a differential drive pinion rear bearing replacer tool, press the bearing onto the shaft with the outer race snapring groove facing rearward.

NOTE: *When pressing the rear bearing onto the shaft, be sure support the 1st gear inner race to prevent it from falling.*

10. Using a feeler gauge, measure the 1st gear thrust clearance; it should be 0.004–0.010 in. (0.10–0.25mm).

COUNTERGEAR AND REVERSE IDLER GEAR

Disassembly

1. Before disassembling the countergear, perform the following procedures:

a. Install the spacer, the counter 5th gear and the needle bearing onto the countershaft.

b. Using a dial indicator, measure the oil clearance of 5th gear; the standard clearance is 0.0004–0.0024 in. (0.01–0.06mm), the maximum clearance is 0.060 in. (1.5mm).

c. If the measurement exceeds the limit, replace the gear bearing or shaft.

2. Perform the following service procedures:

a. Remove the needle bearing, the counter 5th gear and the spacer.

b. Remove the synchronizer ring and the No. 3 clutch hub assembly.

3. Disassemble the No. 3 clutch hub assembly by performing the following procedures:

a. Using a pry bar, pry the shifting key spring from the clutch hub.

b. Remove the keys and the hub sleeve from the clutch hub.

c. Using a pry bar, remove the retainer and the front side shifting key spring.

4. Remove the front countershaft bearing and side race by performing the following procedures:

a. Using snapring pliers, remove the snapring.

b. Using a shop press and the bearing remover tool, press the bearing from the shaft.

c. Using a gear puller, press the side race from the shaft.

Inspection

1. Inspect the counter gear splines and teeth for chipping and wear.

2. Inspect the bearing for smoothness when rotating.

3. Using a feeler gauge, measure the clearance between the reverse idler gear and the shift arm shoe; the standard clearance is 0.008–0.016 in. (0.20–0.40mm), the maximum clearance is 0.0354 in. (9mm). If the clearance is beyond the limit, replace the shift arm shoe or the gear.

4. Using a dial indicator and a set of V-blocks, measure the reverse idler gear oil clearance; the standard clearance is is 0.002–0.003

in. (0.05–0.08mm), the maximum clearance is 0.0076 in. (0.19mm). If the clearance beyond the limit, replace the gear or the shaft.

5. Using a micrometer, measure the outer diameter of the countergear journal; the minimum diameter is 1.0564 in. (26.8mm) for part A or 1.1736 in. (29.8mm) for part B.

6. Push the synchronizer ring on its braking surface to check the braking action.

7. Using a feeler gauge, measure the clearance between the synchronizer ring back and the gear spline end; the standard clearance is 0.028–0.067 in. (0.70–1.70mm), the minimum clearance is 0.020 in. (0.5mm). If the clearance is less than the limit, replace the synchronizer ring.

8. Measure the clearance between the hub sleeve and its shift fork; the maximum clearance is 0.040 in. (1.00mm).

Assembly

1. Using a shop press and a socket, press the new front bearing, the side race and the inner race onto the countershaft.

2. Select a snapring which will allow minimum axial play and install it onto the shaft.

3. Install the center bearing onto the countershaft by engaging the roller cages.

4. Assemble the No. 3 clutch hub by performing the following procedures:

a. Assemble the No. 3 clutch hub and shifting keys onto the hub sleeve.

b. Install the shifting key springs under the shifting keys to the end gaps are not aligned.

c. Using a shop press and a water pump bearing replacer tool, press the shifting key retainer onto the No. 3 clutch hub assembly.

d. Position the No. 3 clutch hub assembly on the countershaft.

TRANSMISSION ASSEMBLY

NOTE: *Before installing the output shaft, use a bearing remover tool to drive the countershaft center bearing outer race from the intermediate plate.*

1. Install the output shaft into the intermediate plate by pushing on the output shaft and tapping on the intermediate plate with a plastic hammer.

2. Install the input shaft and countershaft by performing the following procedures:

a. Lubricate the the needle roller bearing.

b. Install the needle roller bearing into the input shaft.

c. Install the input shaft onto the output shaft and the countershaft into the intermediate plate, simultaneously.

d. Using a bearing installation tool and a hammer, drive the countershaft center bearing outer race into the intermediate plate; be careful not to damage the bearing rollers.

3. Using snapring pliers, install the snapring onto the output shaft bearing; be sure the snapring is flush with the intermediate plate surface.

4. Using a T40 Torx® wrench, install the bearing retainer-to-intermediate plate and torque the bolts to 9 ft. lbs.

5. Using a gear installation tool, press the reverse gear onto the output shaft.

6. Using snapring pliers, select a snapring which will allow minimum axial play and install it onto the output shaft, directly behind the reverse gear.

7. Perform the following service procedures:

a. Using a gear installation tool, press the 5th gear and rear bearing onto the output shaft.

b. Using a pry bar and a hammer, select a snapring which will allow minimum axial play and install it onto the output shaft, directly behind the rear bearing.

c. Using a driver tool and 2 hammers, drive the No. 3 clutch hub onto the countershaft.

NOTE: *When installing the clutch hub, support the front of the countershaft with a 3–5 lb. hammer.*

d. Using a pry bar and a hammer, select a snapring which will allow minimum axial play and install it onto the countershaft, directly behind the No. 3 clutch hub.

8. Install the spacer, the synchronizer ring, the needle roller bearing and the counter 5th gear by performing the following procedures:

a. Install the bearing spacer onto the countershaft.

b. Lubricate the needle roller bearing.

c. Assemble the counter 5th gear, the synchronizer ring and the needle roller bearings.

d. Install the 5th gear assembly with the synchronizer ring slots aligned with the shifting keys.

9. Install the spacer and bearing by performing the following procedures:

a. Install the spacer onto the countershaft.

b. Install the bearing with the ball shield facing rearward.

c. Using a hammer and a socket, drive the bearing onto the countershaft.

NOTE: *When installing the clutch hub, support the front of the countershaft with a 3–5 lb. hammer.*

d. Using a snapring, select a snapring which will allow minimum axial play and in-

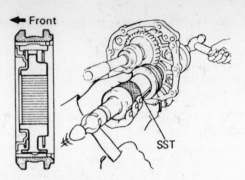

← Front

SST

Positioning and installing the No. 3 clutch hub onto the countershaft — Supra W58 transmission

stall it onto the countershaft, directly behind the bearing.

10. Position the speedometer drive gear clip into slot on the output shaft. Slide the speedometer drive gear onto the output shaft and secure it with the clip.

11. Use a feeler gauge to measure the counter 5th gear thrust clearance; it should be 0.004–0.016 in. (0.10–0.40mm).

12. Install the shift forks, the shift fork shafts and the reverse idler gear by performing the following procedures:

a. Install the reverse idler gear and shaft.

b. Grease the pin and insert it into the reverse shift head hole.

c. Align the No. 3 shift fork shaft with the No. 3 hub sleeve groove, place the reverse shift arm into the bearing arm pivot and align the reverse shift arm shoe with the reverse idler gear groove. Install the No. 3 shift fork shaft into the intermediate plate.

d. Push the pin, located in the reverse shift arm hole, into the groove of the No. 3 shift fork shaft.

e. Install the No. 4 shift fork shaft into the intermediate plate over the reverse shift arm.

f. Using a pin punch and a hammer, drive the spring pin until it is flush with the fork.

g. Grease the No. 3 interlock pin and install it into the intermediate plate hole.

h. Lubricate the No. 2 interlock pin and install it into the shaft hole.

i. Position the No. 2 shift fork into the No. 2 hub sleeve groove.

j. Install the No. 2 shift fork shaft to the shift fork through the intermediate plate.

k. Install the snapring onto the No. 2 shift fork shaft.

l. Grease the No. 1 interlock pin and install the pin into the intermediate plate.

m. Install the No. 1 shift fork into the No. 1 hub sleeve groove.

n. Insert the No. 1 shift fork shaft into

the shift fork through the intermediate plate.

o. Install the snapring onto the No. 1 shift fork shaft.

p. Install the No. 1 and No. 2 shift fork set bolts with lock washers and torque to 9 ft. lbs.

q. Using pliers, stake the bolts with the lock washers.

13. Install the locking balls and springs by performing the following procedures:

a. Install a ball and spring into each of the intermediate plate.

b. Apply sealant to the plug threads.

c. Using the detent ball plug socket, torque the plugs to 18 ft. lbs.

14. Install the reverse idler gear shaft stopper and torque the bolt to 18 ft. lbs.

15. Remove the intermediate plate assembly from the vise and remove any nuts, bolts and washers.

16. Install the transmission case to the intermediate assembly by performing the following procedures:

a. Apply sealant to the intermediate plate (transmission case side); be sure to keep the sealant on the inside of the bolt holes.

b. Install the case and align the bearing outer races with each shift fork shaft end.

c. Using a plastic hammer, tap the transmission into position.

17. Using snapring pliers, install both snaprings onto the bearing outer races.

18. Install the front bearing retainer by performing the following procedures:

a. Apply sealant to the bearing retainer; be sure to keep the sealant on the inside of the bolt holes.

b. Apply sealant to the bolt threads.

c. Install the bearing retainer-to-transmission case and torque the bolts to 18 ft. lbs.

19. Install the extension housing by performing the following procedures:

a. Insert the shift and select lever into the extension housing.

b. Apply sealant to the extension housing; be sure to keep the sealant on the inside of the bolt holes.

c. Connect the shift and select lever to the shift fork shaft.

d. Install the shift lever housing to the shift and select lever shaft, push into the extension housing.

e. Install the bolt and torque it to 29 ft. lbs.

f. Install the extension housing to intermediate plate and torque the bolts to 27 ft. lbs.

20. Make sure the input and output shafts rotate smoothly and shifting can be performed smoothly in all positions.

21. Install the restrict pins and torque to 30 ft. lbs.

NOTE: *Install the black pin on the reverse gear/5th gear side.*

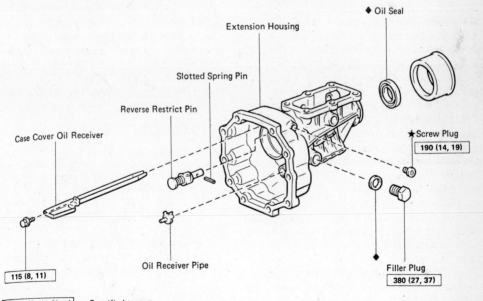

Transmission components — Supra R154 transmission

22. Install the clutch housing and torque the bolts to 27 ft. lbs.

23. Install the shift lever retainer, with the oil baffle, and torque the bolts to 13 ft. lbs.

24. Install the speedometer driven gear and the lock plate; torque the lock plate bolt to 9 ft. lbs.

25. Install the back-up light switch and torque it to 30 ft. lbs.

26. Install the release fork and bearing.

R154 Transmission Overhaul

DISASSEMBLY

1. Remove the release fork and bearing.

2. Remove the reverse light switch, speedometer driven gear, shift lever retainer and restrict pins.

3. Remove the clutch housing from the transmission.

4. Using a Torx® size T40 socket, remove the screw plug from the right side of the extension housing. Use a magnet to remove the spring and ball.

5. Remove the the shift lever housing set bolt. Remove the extension housing and shift lever.

6. Remove the screw plug from the left side of the extension housing using the Torx® size T40 socket. Drive the roll pin from the reverse restrict pin and remove the reverse restrict pin.

7. Remove the front bearing retainer and remove the seal. Remove the snaprings from the front bearings.

8. Remove the intermediate plate from the transmission case. Remove the magnet from the intermediate plate.

9. Mount the intermediate plate assembly in a vise using 2 clutch housing bolts, washers and nuts to prevent the jaws of the vise from contacting the plate.

10. Using a Torx® size T40 socket, remove the 4 straight screw plugs from the side and top of the intermediate plate. Use a magnet to remove the springs and balls.

11. Remove the shift fork set bolts.

12. Remove the snaprings from the shift fork shafts.

13. Remove the roll pins that hold the shaft in place.

14. Pull out shift fork shaft No. 5 from the intermediate plate.

15. Pull out shift fork shaft No. 2 from the intermediate plate and remove shift fork No. 2. Use a magnet to remove the interlock pin from the intermediate plate.

16. Pull out shift fork shaft No. 1 from the intermediate plate. Use a magnet to remove the interlock pins from the shaft hole and intermediate plate.

17. Pull out shift fork shaft No. 3 from the intermediate plate and remove shift fork No. 1. Use a magnet to remove the interlock pin.

18. Pull out shift fork shaft No. 4 from the intermediate plate. Remove the reverse shift head and locking ball. Remove shift fork No.3. 19. Remove the reverse shift arm from the reverse shift arm bracket and remove the bracket.

20. Remove the snapring that holds the speedometer drive gear and ball, then remove the gear and ball and the front snapring.

21. Remove the rear bearing snapring and pull the rear bearing with tool 09950–20017, or equivalent. Remove the spacer.

22. Before removing counter 5th gear, measure its thrust clearance. The specification is 0.004–0.016 in. (0.10–0.40mm).

23. Engage the gear double meshing, remove the locknut and disengage the gear double meshing.

24. Remove the gear spline piece No. 5 using puller 09213–31021, or equivalent. Remove counter 5th gear with hub sleeve No. 3. Remove the 3 shifting keys and 2 springs from the assembly.

25. Remove the thrust washer and ball from the countergear.

26. Remove the rear bearing retainer.

27. Remove the reverse idler gear and pull the shaft out toward the rear.

28. Remove the snapring from the front output shaft bearing.

29. Remove the ouput shaft, counter gear and input shaft as an assembly from the intermediate plate by pulling on the countergear and tapping on the intermediate plate with a plastic-face hammer. Remove the input shaft with needle bearing from the output shaft.

30. Using tool set 12010–35014, or equivalent, remove the counter rear bearing from the intermediate plate.

INPUT SHAFT

Disassembly

1. Check the synchronizer ring for braking action by pushing it in and trying to turn it. Measure the clearance between the ring and the gear spline end. The specification is 0.024–0.063 in. (0.60–1.60mm). Remove the ring.

2. Remove the needle bearing.

3. Remove the snapring above the bearing.

4. Remove the bearing using a press.

Inspection

1. Inspect the synchronizer ring for wear and scoring.

2. Inspect the gear teeth and splines for chips and wear.

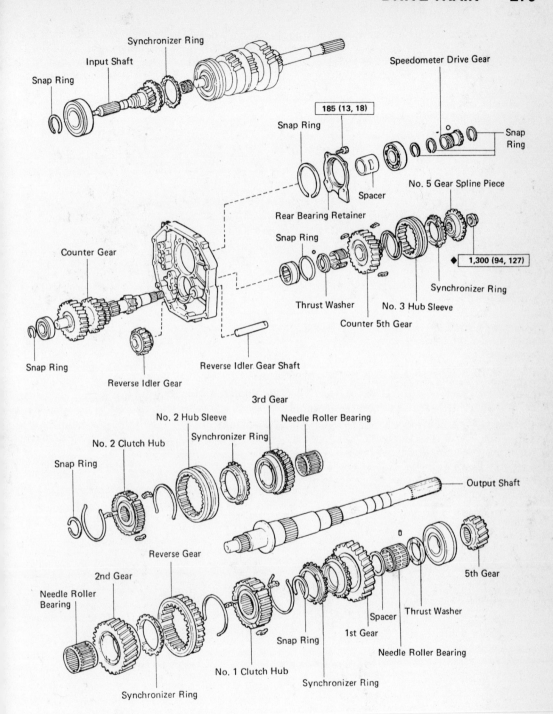

Transmission components — Supra R154 transmission

- Snap Ring
- Input Shaft
- Synchronizer Ring
- Speedometer Drive Gear
- Snap Ring
- 185 (13, 18)
- Snap Ring
- Spacer
- No. 5 Gear Spline Piece
- Rear Bearing Retainer
- Counter Gear
- Snap Ring
- 1,300 (94, 127) ◆
- Synchronizer Ring
- Thrust Washer
- No. 3 Hub Sleeve
- Counter 5th Gear
- Snap Ring
- Reverse Idler Gear Shaft
- Reverse Idler Gear
- 3rd Gear
- No. 2 Hub Sleeve
- Needle Roller Bearing
- No. 2 Clutch Hub
- Synchronizer Ring
- Snap Ring
- Output Shaft
- Reverse Gear
- 2nd Gear
- 5th Gear
- Needle Roller Bearing
- Spacer
- Thrust Washer
- Snap Ring
- 1st Gear
- No. 1 Clutch Hub
- Needle Roller Bearing
- Synchronizer Ring
- Synchronizer Ring

kg·cm (ft·lb, N·m) : Specified torque

◆ Non-reusable part

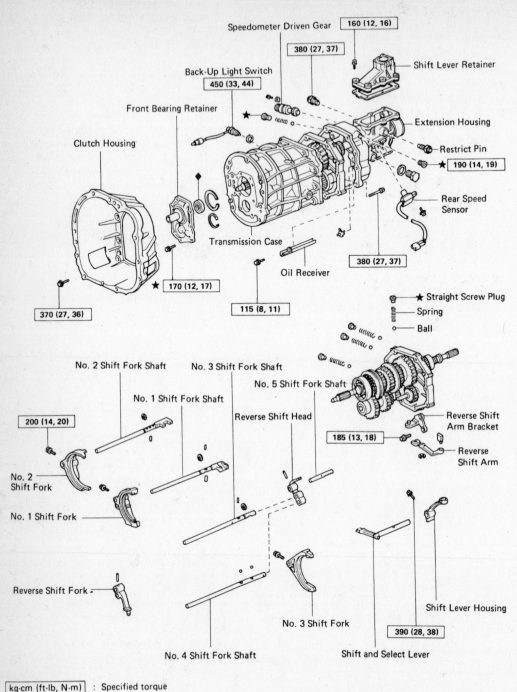

Speedometer Driven Gear

160 (12, 16)

380 (27, 37)

Shift Lever Retainer

Back-Up Light Switch

450 (33, 44)

Front Bearing Retainer

Extension Housing

Clutch Housing

Restrict Pin

190 (14, 19)

Rear Speed Sensor

Transmission Case

Straight Screw Plug

Oil Receiver

Spring

Ball

380 (27, 37)

170 (12, 17)

115 (8, 11)

370 (27, 36)

No. 2 Shift Fork Shaft

No. 3 Shift Fork Shaft

No. 1 Shift Fork Shaft

No. 5 Shift Fork Shaft

Reverse Shift Head

200 (14, 20)

Reverse Shift Arm Bracket

185 (13, 18)

Reverse Shift Arm

No. 2 Shift Fork

No. 1 Shift Fork

Reverse Shift Fork

Shift Lever Housing

No. 3 Shift Fork

390 (28, 38)

No. 4 Shift Fork Shaft

Shift and Select Lever

kg-cm (ft-lb, N·m) : Specified torque

♦ Non-reusable part

★ Precoated part

Transmission components — Supra R154 transmission

3. Inspect the bearings for roughness while turning.

Assembly

1. Install the bearing using tool 09506–35010, or equivalent and a press.

2. Install the selective snapring above the bearing that will allow the least amount of axial play. Install the snapring on the bearing.

3. Install the needle bearing and synchronizer ring. Recheck the synchronizer ring for clearance and braking.

OUTPUT SHAFT ASSEMBLY

Checking Clearances

Before disassembling the output shaft assembly, measure the following clearances. If any measurement is not within specifications, disassemble the assembly and replace selective snaprings as required.

If all measurements are within specifications and there is no visible damage to its components, there is no reason to disassemble the input shaft assembly.

1. Measure the thrust clearance of 1st and 3rd gears with a feeler gauge.

2. Measure the thrust clearance of 2nd gear with a dial indicator, moving the gear back and forth.

3. The specification for 1st gear is 0.004–0.020 in. (0.10–0.50mm). The specification for 2nd and 3rd gears is 0.004–0.012 in. (0.10–0.30mm).

4. Measure the oil clearance between each gear and the shaft with the needle bearing installed. The specification is 0.001–0.006 in. (0.025–0.150mm). If the clearance is not within specifications, disassemble the output shaft and inspect the needle roller bearing or shaft.

Disassembly

1. Using a press, remove 5th gear, the center bearing, thrust washer and 1st gear.

2. Remove the synchronizer ring.

3. Remove the straight pin and needle roller bearing.

4. Remove the spacer.

5. Remove the snapring in front of clutch hub No.1. Using a press, remove clutch hub No. 1, the synchronizer ring and 2nd gear.

6. Remove the needle roller bearing.

7. Remove the snapring behind clutch hub No. 2. Using a press, remove clutch hub No. 2, the synchronizer ring and 3rd gear.

8. Remove the needle roller bearing.

9. Remove the 3 shifting keys and 2 springs from each of the clutch hubs.

Inspection

1. Inspect all bearings for roughness.

2. Inspect all gear teeth, splines and synchronizer parts for chipping and wear.

3. Inspect all snaprings for deformation.

4. Measure the thickness of the output shaft flange. The minimum thickness is 0.185 in. (4.70mm).

5. Measure the outer diameter of the output shaft 1st gear gear journal. The minimum diameter is 1.530 in. (38.86mm).

6. Measure the outer diameter of the output shaft 2nd gear gear journal. The minimum diameter is 1.845 in. (46.86mm).

7. Measure the outer diameter of the output shaft 3rd gear gear journal. The minimum diameter is 1.491 in. (37.87mm).

8. Measure the runout of the output shaft. The maximum allowable runout is 0.002 in. (0.05mm). Replace the shaft if any measurement is out of specification.

9. Push each synchronizer ring on its braking surface to check the braking action.

10. Measure the clearance between each synchronizer ring back and its corresponding gear spline end. The specification is 0.024–0.063 in. (0.60–1.60mm). If the clearance is not within specifications, replace the synchronizer ring.

11. Measure the clearance between each hub sleeve and its corresponding shift fork. The maximum clearance is 0.040 in. (1.00mm).

Assembly

1. Install the clutch hub and shifting keys to the hub sleeve. Install the shifting key springs under the shifting keys so that their endgaps are not in line.

2. Place the synchronizer ring on 3rd gear and align the ring slots with the shifting keys.

3. Install the needle roller bearing in 3rd gear.

4. Using a press, install 3rd gear and hub sleeve No.2.

5. Install a selective snapring that will allow the least amount of axial play.

6. Remeasure the 3rd gear thrust clearance. Do not continue until the clearance specification is met.

7. Place the synchronizer ring on 2nd gear and align the ring slots with the shifting keys.

8. Install the needle roller bearing in 2nd gear.

9. Using a press, install 2nd gear and hub sleeve No. 1.

10. Install a selective snapring that will allow the least amount of axial play.

11. Install the spacer on the output shaft. Assembly 1st gear, the synchronizer ring and needle roller bearing.

12. Install the assembly on the output shaft with the ring slots aligned with the shifting keys.

13. Install the 1st gear thrust washer on the shaft with the straight pin aligned with the notch in the thrust washer.

14. Using tool 09309–35010 or equivalent, drive the bearing on with the outer race snapring groove toward the rear.

15. Remeasure the 1st and 2nd gear clearances. Do not continue until the clearance specifications are met.

16. Using tool set 09316–60010, or equivalent and a press, install 5th gear.

COUNTERGEAR

Disassembly

1. Before disassembling the countergear, measure the oil clearance of 5th gear. Reassemble the spacer, counter 5th gear and the needle roller bearing. The specification is 0.006–0.060 in. (0.15–1.5mm). If the measurement is not within specification, replace the gear bearing or shaft.

2. Remove the 3 shifting keys and 2 springs from counter 5th gear. Remove 5th gear.

3. If necessary, remove the front bearing using a press and tool 09950–00020.

Inspection

1. Inspect the counter gear splines and teeth for chipping and wear.

2. Inspect the bearing for smoothness when rotating.

3. Measure the clearance between the reverse idler gear and the shift arm shoe. The specification is 0.002–0.020 in. (0.05–0.50mm). If the clearance is not within specification, replace the shift arm shoe or the gear.

4. Measure the reverse idler gear oil clearance. The specification is 0.002–0.005 in. (0.05–0.13mm). If the clearance is not within specification, replace the gear or the shaft.

5. Measure the outer diameter of the countergear journal. If the measurement is less than 1.097 in. (27.86mm), replace the countergear.

6. Push the synchronizer ring on its braking surface to check the braking action.

7. Measure the clearance between the synchronizer ring back and the gear spline end. The specification is 0.024–0.063 in. (0.60–1.60mm). If the clearance is not within specifications, replace the synchronizer ring.

8. Measure the clearance between the hub sleeve and its shift fork. The maximum clearance is 0.040 in. (1.00mm).

Assembly

1. If it was removed, install the front bearing using a 24mm socket and a press.

2. Install a selective snapring that will give the minimum amount of axial play.

3. Install counter 5th gear and the shifting keys to the hub sleeve. Install the shifting key springs under the keys so that the endgaps are not in line.

TRANSMISSION ASSEMBLY

1. Install the output shaft to the intermediate shaft by pushing on the output shaft and tapping on the intermediate plate with a soft face hammer.

2. Install the snapring on the bearing.

3. Install the needle roller bearing to the input shaft and install the input shaft to the output shaft with the synchronizer ring slots aligned with the shifting keys.

4. Install the countergear to the intermediate plate. Install the counter rear bearing with a soft face hammer.

5. Install the reverse arm bracket. Torque the bolts to 13 ft. lbs.

6. Install the reverse shift arm to the pivot of the reverse arm bracket.

7. Align the reverse shift arm shoe to the reverse idler gear groove and insert the reverse idler gear shaft to the intermediate plate.

8. Align the rear bearing retainer to the reverse idler shaft groove. Install the retainer and torque the bolts to 13 ft. lbs.

9. Install the ball and thrust washer on the countergear.

10. Install the counter 5th gear with hub sleeve No. 3 and needle roller bearings.

11. Install the synchronizer ring on the gear spline piece No.5.

12. Drive the gear spline piece No. 5 onto the countergear using tool set 09316–60010, or equivalent. Make sure the ring slots are aligned with the shifting keys.

13. Engage the double gear meshing. Install the locknut and torque to 94 ft. lbs. Stake the locknut and disengage the double gear meshing.

14. Measure the thrust clearance of counter 5th gear. The specification is 0.004–0.014 in. (0.10–0.35mm). Do not continue until the specification is met.

15. Install the spacer on the output gear rear spacer.

16. Install the output shaft rear bearing using tool 09309–35010 or equivalent.

17. Install the selective snapring that will allow the minimum axial play behind the bearing.

18. Install the front speedometer drive gear snapring, the ball and gear and the rear snapring.

19. Place shift fork No. 3 into the groove of hub sleeve No. 3. 20. Install shift fork No. 4 to shift fork No. 3, reverse shift head and insert through the intermediate plate. Install the locking ball to the reverse head.

21. Install the locking ball into the intermediate plate. Install the interlock pin into the shaft hole.

22. Place shift fork No. 1 into the groove of hub sleeve No. 1. Install fork shaft No. 3 to the reverse shift fork and shift head through the intermediate plate.

23. Install the intermediate pin into the intermediate plate. Install the interlock pin into the shaft hole.

24. Install fork shaft No. 1 to shift fork No. 1 through the intermediate plate.

25. Install the interlock into the intermediate plate.

26. Place shift fork No. 2 into the groove of hub sleeve No. 2. 27. Install fork shaft No. 2 to shift fork Nos. 1 and 2 through the intermediate plate.

28. Install shift fork shaft No. 5 to the reverse shift head through the intermediate plate.

29. Install the roll pins to the reverse shift head and the shift fork.

30. To check the operation of the interlock, shift fork shaft No. 1 into the 1st gear position. Fork shafts Nos. 2, 3, 4 and 5 should not be free to move. If the interlock is not functioning properly, repair the problem before continuing.

31. Install the 3 snaprings on the shift shafts.

32. Install the shaft set bolts and torque to 14 ft. lbs.

33. Apply liquid sealer (Toyota part number 08833–00080, Three Bond® 1344, Loctite® 242 or equivalent) to the screw plug threads. Install the 4 locking balls and springs. Install the screw plugs and torque to 14 ft. lbs.

34. Install the magnet to the intermediate plate.

35. Thoroughly clean and dry the mating surfaces of the transmission case and the intermediate plate. Apply sealant (Toyota part number 08826–00090, Three Bond® 1281 or equivalent) to the mating surface of the transmission case.

36. Align each bearing outer race, fork shaft end and reverse idler shaft end with the case installation holes and install the case to the intermediate plate.

37. Install the snaprings to the input shaft bearing and countergear front bearing.

38. Install a new seal to the front bearing retainer using tool set 12010–35014, or equivalent. Thoroughly clean and dry the mating surfaces of the transmission case and the front bearing retainer. Apply sealant (Toyota part number 08826–00090, Three Bond® 1281 or equivalent) to the mating surface of the bearing retainer. Apply liquid sealer (Toyota part number 08833–00080, Three Bond® 1344, Loctite® 242 or equivalent) to the bolt threads and torque the bolts to 12 ft. lbs.

39. Install the reverse restrict pin into the extension housing. Drive in the roll pin. Apply liquid sealer (Toyota part number 08833–00080, Three Bond® 1344, Loctite® 242 or equivalent) to the plug threads and torque the bolts to 14 ft. lbs.

40. Thoroughly clean and dry the mating surfaces of the intermediate plate extension housing. Apply sealant (Toyota part number 08826–00090, Three Bond® 1281 or equivalent) to the mating surface of the extension housing or transfer adaptor.

41. Install the shift and select lever into the extension housing, connect the shift and select lever to the fork shaft and put into the shift lever housing. Align fork shaft No. 5 with the extension installation hole and push in the extension housing. Torque the bolts 27 ft. lbs. Torque the shift lever housing bolt to 28 ft. lbs.

42. Apply liquid sealer (Toyota part number 08833–00080, Three Bond® 1344, Loctite® 242 or equivalent) to the screw plug threads. Install the locking ball and spring to the right side of the case. Install the screw plug and torque to 14 ft. lbs.

43. At this point, check the input and output shaft for smooth rotation. Also, make sure that shifting into all gears can be accomplished smoothly. Do not continue until all items have been thoroughly checked.

44. Install the black pin on the 5th gear side of the reverse gear. Install the other pin and torque to 27 ft. lbs.

45. Install the clutch housing and torque the bolts to 27 ft. lbs.

46. Install the shift lever retainer with new gasket. Apply liquid sealer (Toyota part number 08833–00080, Three Bond® 1344, Loctite® 242 or equivalent) to the bolt threads and torque to 13 ft. lbs.

47. Install the reverse light switch with new washer.

48. Install the speedometer driven gear and lock plate. Torque the bolt to 9 ft. lbs.

49. Install the release fork and bearing.

MANUAL TRANSAXLE

Identification

The transaxle model identification number is located on the bottom of the Vehicle Identification Number (VIN) plate.

Adjustments

SHIFT LEVER FREEPLAY

1986–89 Celica And 1988–89 Celica All-Trac

Select a shim of a thickness that allow a preload 0.1–0.2 lb. at the top of lever and install it in the shift lever seat.

1990 Celica And 1990 Celica All-Trac

Select a shim of a thickness that allow a preload 0.1–0.3 lb. at the top of lever and install it in the shift lever seat.

CLUTCH START SWITCH

Celica And Celica All-Trac

1. Check that pedal height and freeplay (push rod play) are correct for the clutch start system.

2. Measure the pedal stroke and check the switch clearance "A" using the clutch start clearance chart as necessary.

3. Loosen and adjust the switch position as required.

4. Recheck that the engine does not start when the clutch pedal is released.

Back-Up Light Switch

REMOVAL AND INSTALLATION

Celica And Celica All-Trac

1. Raise the vehicle and support safely.

2. Disconnect the electrical connection from the switch.

3. Remove the switch from the transaxle housing, when removing the switch place a drain pan under the transaxle to catch fluid.

4. To install reverse the removal procedures. Check and add the specified fluid as necessary to the correct level.

Transaxle

REMOVAL AND INSTALLATION

Celica — 2 Wheel Drive

1. Disconnect the negative battery cable. On some 1987–90 vehicles it may be necessary to remove the battery. Remove the air cleaner assembly.

2. On 1987–90 vehicles remove the clutch tube bracket. Disconnect the back-up light switch at the transaxle. Disconnect the speedometer and the engine ground strap.

3. Disconnect the transaxle control cable and position them out of the way.

4. Unbolt the clutch release cylinder. It may be possible to position it out of the way with the hydraulic line still attached.

5. Remove the upper transaxle retaining

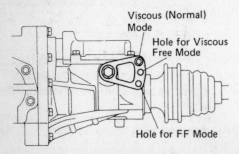

Lock mode select lever with set bolt — Celica All-Trac

bolts. Raise and support the vehicle safely. Remove the engine undercover. Drain the transaxle fluid.

6. Disconnect the exhaust pipe from the manifold. Remove the lower suspension crossmember. Remove the starter (disconnect electrical connections) assembly.

7. Properly support the engine and transaxle assembly. Remove the front and rear transaxle mounts. Remove the center engine mount.

8. Disconnect both halfshafts at the transaxle. Unbolt the steering knuckle from the suspension arm and pull it outward. Remove the left halfshaft.

9. On some vehicles, remove the No. 2 rear

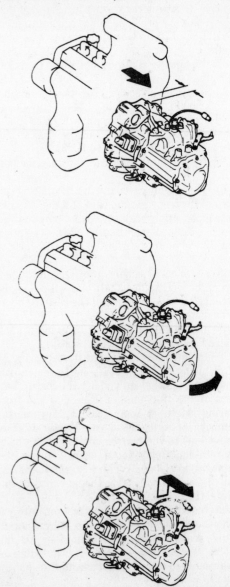

Transaxle removal procedure — Celica All-Trac

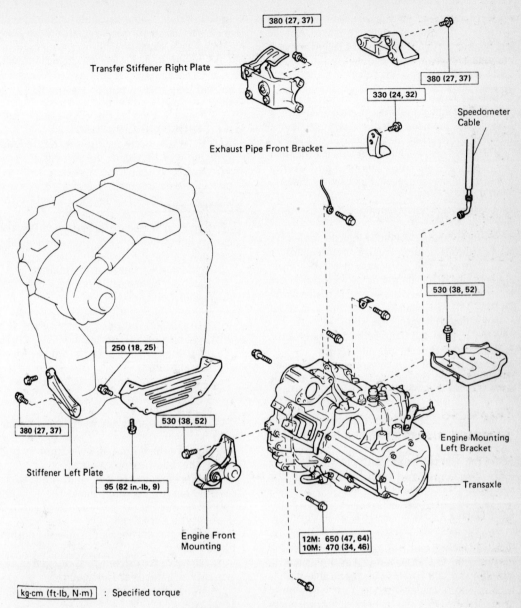

380 (27, 37)

Transfer Stiffener Right Plate

380 (27, 37)

330 (24, 32)

Speedometer
Cable

Exhaust Pipe Front Bracket

530 (38, 52)

250 (18, 25)

380 (27, 37)

Stiffener Left Plate

530 (38, 52)

95 (82 in.-lb, 9)

Engine Mounting
Left Bracket

Transaxle

Engine Front
Mounting

12M: 650 (47, 64)
10M: 470 (34, 46)

kg·cm (ft·lb, N·m) : Specified torque

Transaxle installation — Celica

engine plate. With the engine properly supported remove the left engine mount.

10. Remove the engine-to-transaxle bolts, lower the left side of the engine and carefully ease the transaxle out of the engine compartment.

11. Align the input shaft spline with the clutch disc and carefully mate the transaxle to the engine. Tighten the 12mm mounting bolts to 47 ft. lbs. and the 10mm bolts to 34 ft. lbs.

12. Install the left side engine mount and tighten the mounting bolts to 38 ft. lbs.

13. Install the starter (reconnect electrical connections).

14. Position the left halfshaft in the steering

knuckle, align it with the side gear shaft and tighten the knuckle-to-lower arm bolts to 47 ft. lbs. On 1989–90 models torque the left steering knuckle to lower arm to 94 ft. lbs.

15. Connect both halfshafts to the transaxle.

16. Install the center engine mount and tighten the bolts to 29 ft. lbs. (39 Nm). Install the front and rear mounts and tighten them to the same torque. Install the cover on the crossmember.

17. Install the lower suspension crossmember and tighten the five end bolts to 154 ft. lbs. Tighten the center bolt to 29 ft. lbs.

18. Connect the exhaust pipe to the manifold and tighten the bolts to 46 ft. lbs.

19. Installation of the remaining components is in the reverse order of removal. Fill the transaxle with ATF Dexron®II (1990 C52 type manual transaxle use SAE 75W-90 or API GL4) and then road test the vehicle.

Celica All-Trac

NOTE: *The full-time Celica 4WD is equipped with the viscous coupling type of center differential lock. DO NOT REMOVE MODE SELECT LEVER BOLT, do not move vehicle if this set bolt is removed and lever in in any other mode but VISCOUS (NORMAL) MODE.*

1. Remove the engine/transaxle assembly from the vehicle.

2. Install the engine/transaxle assembly into a suitable holding fixture or equivalent.

3. Remove the transaxle assembly from engine. Using the following service procedure since cylinder block rib contacts transfer case.

   a. Pull the transaxle assembly out about 3 in. (76mm) from the engine.

   b. Rotate the transaxle assembly in a clockwise manner while pulling out.

4. Installation is in the reverse order of removal. Tighten the 12mm engine-to-transaxle bolts to 47 ft. lbs. and the 10mm bolts to 34 ft. lbs. Tighten the left engine mount bolts to 38 ft. lbs. Tighten the center member bolts and the front and rear engine mount bolts to 29 ft. lbs.

5. Fill the transaxle with SAE 75W-90 or API GL5 to the correct level and then road test the vehicle.

Overhaul Notes

Cleanliness is an important factor in the overhaul of the manual transaxle. Before opening up this unit, the entire outside of the transaxle assembly should be cleaned, preferable with a high pressure washer such as a car wash spray unit. Dirt entering the transaxle internal parts will negate all the time and effort spent on the overhaul. During inspection and reassembly all parts should be thoroughly cleaned with solvent then dried with compressed air. Wiping cloths and rags should not be used to dry parts.

Wheel bearing grease, long used to hold thrust washers and lube parts, should not be used. Lube seals with clean transaxle oil and use ordinary un-medicated petroleum jelly to hold the thrust washers and to ease the assembly of seals, since it will not leave a harmful residue as grease often will. Do not use solvent on neoprene seals, if they are to be reused, or thrust washers.

Before installing bolts into aluminum parts, always dip the threads into clean transaxle oil. Anti-seize compound can also be used to pre-vent bolts from galling the aluminum and seizing. Always use a torque wrench to keep from stripping the threads. The internal snaprings should be expanded and the external rings should be compressed, if they are to be reused. This will help insure proper seating when installed.

S53 Transaxle Overhaul

NOTE: *When overhauling the Celica All-Trac manual transaxle, use this service procedure as a guide. Remove the transfer assembly from the transaxle as one unit.*

DISASSEMBLY

1. Remove the release fork, the bearing, the back-up light switch and the speedometer driven gear.

2. Remove the front bearing retainer.

3. Remove the transmission case cover-to-transmission bolts and the cover.

4. Remove No. 3 shift fork lock bolt.

5. Using a dial indicator, measure the 5th gear thrust clearance; it should be 0.008–0.016 in. (0.20–0.40mm) with a maximum clearance of 0.45 in. (11.5mm).

6. Loosen the locknut and remove the No. 1 and No. 2 lock ball assemblies.

7. Remove the selecting bellcrank.

8. Remove the shift and select lever assembly.

9. Remove the output shaft locknut by performing the following procedures:

   a. Working inside the shift and select lever assembly opening, move the shifting forks rearward to lock the transaxle into 2 gears at the same time.

   b. Using a cold chisel, unstake the output shaft locknut.

   c. Remove the locknut by rotating it clockwise as the threads are left hand.

   d. Move the shifting forks to unlock the transaxle.

10. Remove the No. 3 hub sleeve assembly and shift fork by performing the following procedures:

   a. Using 2 pry bars and a hammer, tap out the No. 3 hub sleeve snapring.

   b. Remove the No. 3 shift fork shifting key retainer.

   c. Using the 3 case cover set bolts, insert them into the No. 3 hub sleeve, tighten them a little at a time to remove No. 3 hub sleeve and shift fork.

11. Remove the 5th gear, the synchronizer ring, the needle roller bearing and the spacer.

12. Using a gear puller, press the 5th driven gear from the output shaft.

13. Remove the rear bearing retainer-to-transmission case bolts and the retainer.

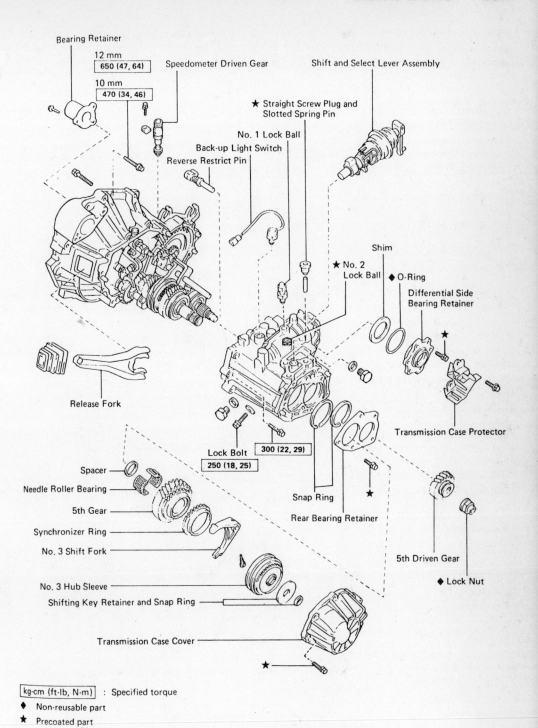

Bearing Retainer

12 mm
650 (47, 64)

10 mm
470 (34, 46)

Speedometer Driven Gear

Shift and Select Lever Assembly

★ Straight Screw Plug and
Slotted Spring Pin

No. 1 Lock Ball

Back-up Light Switch

Reverse Restrict Pin

Shim

★ No. 2
Lock Ball

◆ O-Ring

Differential Side
Bearing Retainer

Release Fork

Transmission Case Protector

Spacer

Needle Roller Bearing

5th Gear

Synchronizer Ring

No. 3 Shift Fork

Lock Bolt
250 (18, 25)

300 (22, 29)

Snap Ring

Rear Bearing Retainer

★

5th Driven Gear

◆ Lock Nut

No. 3 Hub Sleeve

Shifting Key Retainer and Snap Ring

Transmission Case Cover

★

kg·cm (ft-lb, N·m) : Specified torque

◆ Non-reusable part

★ Precoated part

Transaxle components — Celica S53 transaxle

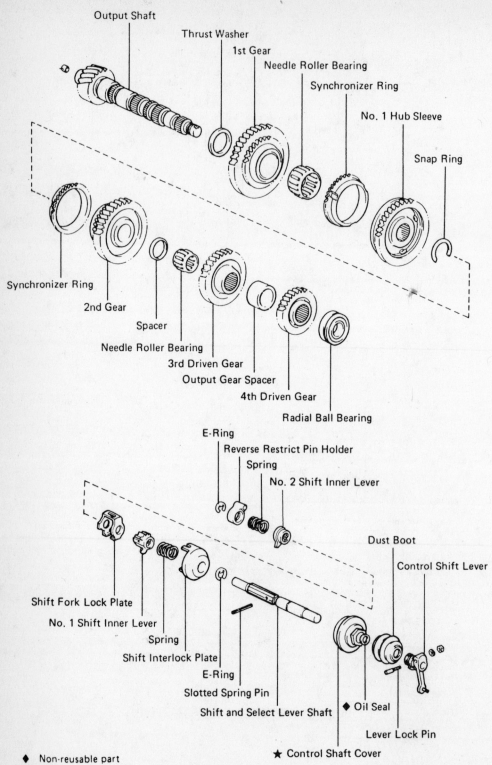

Output Shaft

Thrust Washer

1st Gear

Needle Roller Bearing

Synchronizer Ring

No. 1 Hub Sleeve

Snap Ring

Synchronizer Ring

2nd Gear

Spacer

Needle Roller Bearing

3rd Driven Gear

Output Gear Spacer

4th Driven Gear

Radial Ball Bearing

E-Ring

Reverse Restrict Pin Holder

Spring

No. 2 Shift Inner Lever

Dust Boot

Control Shift Lever

Shift Fork Lock Plate

No. 1 Shift Inner Lever

Spring

Shift Interlock Plate

E-Ring

Slotted Spring Pin

Shift and Select Lever Shaft

♦ Oil Seal

Lever Lock Pin

★ Control Shaft Cover

♦ Non-reusable part

★ Precoated part

Transaxle components — Celica S53 transaxle

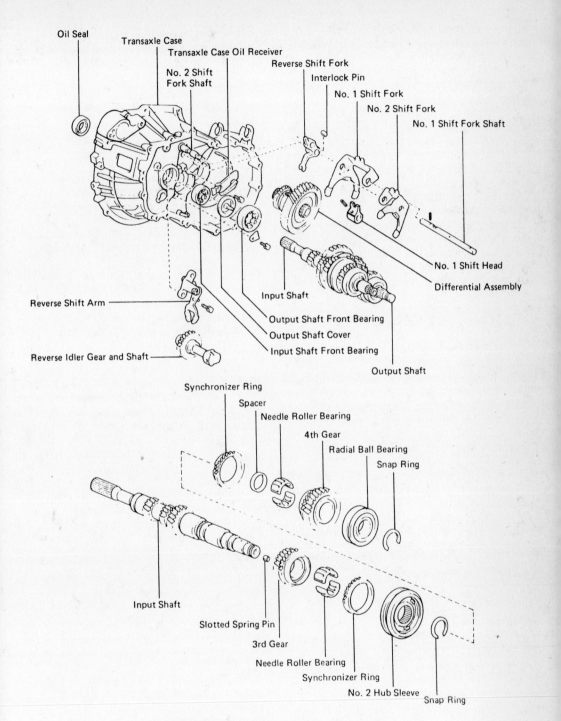

Transaxle components — Celica S53 transaxle

14. Using snapring pliers, remove the snaprings from both rear bearings.

15. From the side of the transmission case, remove reverse idler gear shaft lock bolt.

16. Remove differential side bearing retainer-to-transmission case bolts, the retainer and the shim.

17. Remove the transmission-to-transaxle case bolts. Using a plastic hammer, tap the transmission case from the transaxle.

18. Move the reverse fork shaft into reverse, remove the bolts and pull off the reverse shift arm.

19. Pull out the reverse idler shaft and remove the reverse idler gear.

20. Remove the No. 1 shift fork shaft, the No. 1 shift head and the No. 1 and No. 2 shift forks by performing the following procedures:

a. Using a pin punch and a hammer, drive the slotted spring pin from the No. 1 fork shaft.

b. Using a pin punch and a hammer, drive the slotted spring pin from the shift head.

c. Pull out the No. 1 fork shaft with the shift head and shift forks.

21. Remove the reverse shift fork and interlock pin.

22. Remove the No. 2 fork shaft by performing the following procedures:

a. Using a detent ball plug socket, remove the shaft straight screw plug from the No. 2 fork shaft.

b. Using a pin punch and hammer, drive the slotted spring pin from the No. 2 fork shaft.

c. Pull out the No. 2 fork shaft.

23. Remove input and output shafts from transaxle case, simultaneously.

24. Remove differential assembly and the magnet from the transaxle.

SHIFT AND SELECT LEVER

Disassembly

1. Remove the shift lever lock pin and nut.
2. Remove the control shift lever.
3. Remove the control shaft cover dust boot.
4. Remove the control shaft cover.
5. Remove the E-ring from the reverse restrict pin holder.
6. Remove the reverse restrict pin holder, the spring and the No. 2 shift inner lever.
7. Using a pin punch and hammer, drive out the slotted spring pin.
8. Remove the shift fork lock plate, the No. 1 shift inner lever, the spring and the shift inner lock plate.
9. Remove the E-ring from the shaft.

Inspection

1. Clean the parts in solvent.
2. Inspect the parts for wear or damage.
3. Replace the parts if necessary.

Assembly

1. Lubricate the shift lever shaft with Dexron®II.
2. Install the E-ring, the shift interlock plate and spring.
3. Install the No. 1 shift inner lever with the shift fork lock plate; align the matching portions of each part during assembly.
4. Using a pin punch and hammer, drive in the slotted spring pin.
5. Install the No. 2 shift inner lever, the spring and the reverse restrict pin holder.
6. Install the E-ring.
7. Install the control shaft cover and dust boot; position the boot's air bleed downward.
8. Install the control shift lever and insert the lever lockpin into the lever.
9. Install the washer and locknut.

INPUT SHAFT

Disassembly

1. Using a feeler gauge, measure the 3rd and 4th gear thrust clearances; they should be 0.004–0.010 in. (0.10–0.25mm) for 3rd gear and 0.008–0.018 in. (0.20–0.45mm) for 4th gear. The maximum clearance is 0.012 (0.30mm) for 3rd gear and 0.020 in. (0.50mm) for 4th gear.

2. Using 2 pry bars and a hammer, drive the snapring from the input shaft.

3. Using a shop press, press the radial ball bearing and 4th gear from the input shaft. Remove the needle roller bearings, the synchronizer ring and the spacer.

4. Using snapring pliers, remove the snapring from the input shaft.

5. Using a shop press, press the No. 2 hub sleeve, the 3rd gear, the synchronizer ring and the needle roller bearings from the input shaft.

Inspection

1. Using a micrometer, measure the input shaft journal outside diameter sections.

Minimum outer diameters:
    Section A — 1.062 in. (27.0mm)
    Section B — 1.278 in. (32.5mm)

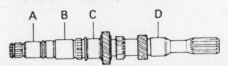

View of the input shaft journal sections — Celica S53 transaxle

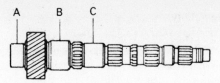

View of the output shaft journal sections — Celica S53 transaxle

Section C — 1.303 in. (33.0mm)
Section D — 1.180 in. (30.0mm)

2. Using a dial indicator, mount the input shaft on V-blocks and measure the runout. Maximum allowable runout is 0.0020 in. (0.050mm).

Assembly

1. If the input shaft was replaced, drive a slotted spring into the end of the shaft to a depth of 0.197 in. (5.0mm).

2. Assemble the No. 2 clutch hub and shifting keys onto the hub sleeve and install the shifting key springs under the shifting keys; be sure to install the key springs positioned so the end gaps are not aligned.

3. Install the 3rd gear and No. 2 hub sleeve assembly onto the input shaft by performing the following procedures:

   a. Lubricate the 3rd gear needle roller bearings with Dexron®II.

   b. Position the synchronizer ring on the 3rd gear and align ring slots with shifting keys.

   c. Using a shop press, press the input shaft into the 3rd gear and No. 2 hub sleeve.

4. Select a snapring that will allow minimum axial play and install it on the input shaft to secure the No. 2 hub assembly.

5. Using a feeler gauge, measure the 3rd gear thrust clearance; it should be 0.004–0.010 in. (0.10–0.25mm)

6. Install the 4th gear and radial ball bearing by performing the following procedures:

   a. Install the spacer.

   b. Lubricate the needle roller bearing with Dexron®II.

   c. Position the synchronizer ring on the gear and align the ring slots with the shifting keys.

   d. Using a front hub and drive pinion bearing tool set and a shop press, select the correct tool diameter and press input shaft assembly into the 4th gear and radial ball bearing.

7. Select a snapring that will allow minimum axial play and install it on the input shaft to secure the 4th gear and radial ball bearing.

8. Using a feeler gauge, measure the 4th gear thrust clearance; it should be 0.008–0.18 in. (0.20–0.45mm).

OUTPUT SHAFT

Disassembly

1. Using a feeler gauge, measure the 1st and 2nd gear thrust clearances; they should be 0.004–0.011 in. (0.10–0.28mm) for 1st gear and 0.008–0.017 in. (0.20–0.43mm) for 2nd gear. The maximum clearance is 0.014 in. (0.35mm) for 1st gear and 0.020 in. (0.50mm) for 2nd gear.

2. Using a shop press, press the radial ball bearing, the 4th driven gear and the spacer from the output shaft.

3. Remove the 3rd driven gear and the 2nd gear by performing the following procedures:

   a. Slide the No. 1 hub sleeve into 1st gear.

   b. Using a shop press, press the 3rd driven gear and 2nd gear from the output shaft.

   c. Remove the needle roller bearing, the spacer and the synchronizer ring.

4. Using 2 pry bars and a hammer, tap the snapring from the output shaft.

5. Using a shop press, press the No. 1 hub sleeve, the 1st gear and the synchronizer ring from the output shaft. Remove the needle roller bearing and the thrust washer.

Inspection

1. Using a micrometer, measure the output shaft journal outside diameter sections shown in the accompanying figure.
   Minimum outside diameters:
   Section A — 1.259 in. (32.0mm)
   Section B — 1.495 in. (38.0mm)
   Section C — 1.259 in. (32.0mm)

2. Using a dial indicator, mount the output shaft on V-blocks and measure the runout. Maximum allowable runout is 0.0020 in. (0.050mm).

Assembly

1. If the output shaft was replaced, drive a slotted spring pin into the end of the shaft to a depth of 0.197 in. (5.0mm).

2. Assemble the No. 1 clutch hub and shifting keys onto the No. 1 hub sleeve and install the shifting key springs under the shifting keys; be sure to install the key springs positioned so the end gaps are not aligned.

3. Install the 1st gear and No. 1 sleeve assembly by performing the following procedures:

   a. Lubricate the 1st gear needle roller bearing with Dexron®II.

   b. Position the 1st gear synchronizer ring on the gear and align the ring slots with the shifting keys.

   c. Using a shop press, press the output

shaft into the 1st gear and the No. 1 hub sleeve.

4. Select a snapring that will allow minimum axial play and install it on the output shaft to secure the 1st gear and No. 1 hub sleeve assembly.

5. Using a feeler gauge, measure 1st gear thrust clearance; if should be 0.004–0.011 in. (0.10–0.28mm).

6. Install the 2nd gear and 3rd driven gear assemblies by performing the following procedures:

a. Install the spacer.

b. Position the synchronizer ring on the 2nd gear and align the ring slots with the shifting keys.

c. Lubricate the the 2nd gear needle roller bearing with Dexron®II.

d. Install the 2nd gear.

e. Using a shop press, press the output shaft assembly into the 3rd driven gear.

7. Using a feeler gauge, measure the 2nd gear thrust clearance; it should be 0.008–0.017 in. (0.20–0.44mm).

8. Install the 4th driven gear and radial ball bearing by performing the following procedures:

a. Install the gear spacer.

b. Using a front hub and drive pinion bearing tool set and a shop press, select the correct diameter tool and press the output shaft assembly into the 4th driven gear and radial ball bearing.

GEAR OIL CLEARANCE

Inspection

Using a dial indicator, measure the oil clearance between the gear and the input or output shaft with the needle roller bearing installed.
Standard clearance:
1st–4th gears – 0.0004–0.0021 in. (0.01–0.05mm)
5th gear – 0.0004–0.0020 in. (0.01–0.05mm)   Maximum clearance:
All gears – 0.0028 in. (0.07mm)
If the clearance exceeds the maximum limit, replace the gear, bearing or shaft.

SYNCHRONIZER RINGS

Inspection

1. Turn the ring and push it in to check the braking action.

2. Using a feeler gauge, measure the clearance between the back of the ring and gear spline end. Minimum clearance is 0.024 in. (0.6mm).

3. If the clearance is less than the limit, replace the ring.

SHIFT FORK AND HUB SLEEVE CLEARANCE INSPECTION

1. Using a feeler gauge, measure the clearance between the hub sleeve and shift fork. Maximum clearance is 0.039 in. (1.00mm).

2. If the clearance exceeds the limit, replace the shift fork or hub sleeve.

SEALS AND BEARINGS

Inspection

Inspect all transaxle seals, bearings and races for wear and damage. Replace all damaged or worn seals, bearings and races as required.

Replacement

INPUT SHAFT FRONT BEARING

1. Unbolt and remove the transaxle case oil receiver.

2. Using an oil seal puller tool, pull out the old bearing.

3. Using a countershaft bearing replacer tool, press in the new bearing.

4. Install the oil receiver and torque the bolt to 65 inch lbs. (7.4 Nm).

OUTPUT SHAFT FRONT BEARING

1. Remove the bolt and bearing locking plate.

2. Using an oil seal puller tool, pull out the old bearing.

3. Using a countershaft bearing replacer tool, press in the new bearing.

4. Install the lock plate and torque the bolt to 13 ft. lbs. (18 Nm).

INPUT SHAFT FRONT SEAL

1. Pry out the old oil seal.

2. Using a front hub and drive pinion bearing tool set, drive in the new seal to a depth of 0.039–0.079 in. (1.00–2.00mm).

3. Once installed, coat the lip of the new seal with multi-purpose grease.

LEFT HAND SIDE OIL SEAL

1. Using a front hub and drive pinion bearing tool set, press the old seal from the retainer.

2. Using a transmission and transfer bearing replacer tool set, press in the new seal until its surface is flush with the surface of the transaxle case.

3. Coat the lip of the new seal with multi-purpose grease.

RIGHT HAND SIDE OIL SEAL

1. Drive the old seal from the retainer with a screwdriver or punch.

2. Using a transmission and transfer bearing replacer tool set, press in the new seal until

its surface is flush with the surface of the transaxle case.

3. Coat the lip of the new seal with multipurpose grease.

LEFT HAND OUTER SIDE BEARING RACE

1. Using a front hub and drive pinion bearing tool set, press out the outer race.

2. Install the bearing retainer without the O-ring.

3. Install and torque the retainer bolts to 13 ft. lbs. (18 Nm).

4. Select the thinnest shim and install it into the case.

5. Using the removal tool, press in a new outer race.

RIGHT HAND OUTER SIDE BEARING RACE

1. Using a front hub and drive pinion bearing tool set, press out the outer race with shim.

2. Place the shim into the case.

3. Using the removal tool, press in a new outer race.

CONTROL SHAFT COVER OIL SEAL

1. Pry out the old seal.

2. Using a front hub and drive pinion bearing tool set, drive in the new seal until its surface is flush with the surface of the cover.

3. Lubricate the seal lip with multi-purpose grease.

SPEEDOMETER DRIVEN GEAR OIL SEAL

1. Using a spring tension tool, pull out the old seal.

2. Using a valve guide bushing remover and replacer tool, drive in the new seal to a depth of 0.75 in. (19mm).

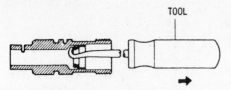

TOOL

**Removing the speedometer driven gear oil seal —
Celica**

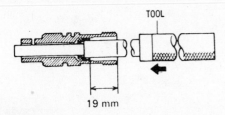

TOOL

19 mm

**Installing the speedometer driven gear oil seal —
Celica**

REVERSE RESTRICT PIN

1. Remove the screw plug.

2. Using a pin punch and hammer, drive out the slotted spring pin.

3. Remove the old reverse restrict pin and replace it with a new one.

4. Using a pin punch and hammer, drive the slotted spring pin back in.

5. Apply sealant to the screw plug threads.

6. Install the screw plug and torque to 9 ft. lbs. (13 Nm).

TRANSAXLE ASSEMBLY

1. Install the magnet into the transaxle.

2. Adjust differential side bearing preload by performing the following procedures:

   a. Install the differential into the transaxle case.

   b. Install the transmission case with gasket, if equipped, onto the transaxle case and torque the bolts to 22 ft. lbs.

   c. Install the thinnest shim into the transmission case.

   d. Install the bearing retainer without an O-ring and torque the retainer-to-transmission case bolts to 13 ft. lbs.

   e. Using a differential preload adapter and a torque wrench, measure the differential preload; it should be 8.7–13.9 inch lbs.

   f. If the preload is not within specification, remove the bearing retainer.

   g. Select another adjusting shim and re-perform the preload check.

NOTE: *The preload will change about 2.6–3.5 inch lbs. (0.3–0.4 Nm) with each shim thickness.*

3. If the preload is adjusted within specification, remove the bearing retainer, shim and transmission case; be careful not to lose the adjusted shim.

4. Mesh the input and output shaft assemblies and install them into the transaxle as an assembly.

5. Install the No. 2 fork shaft by performing the following procedures:

   a. Insert the No. 2 fork shaft into the transaxle case and align the slotted spring pin hole.

   b. Using a pin punch and hammer drive in the slotted spring pin.

   c. Apply sealant to the straight screw plug threads. Using the detent ball plug socket, install the straight screw plug and torque it to 9 ft. lbs.

6. Install the interlock pin into the reverse shift fork hole and the reverse shift fork onto the No. 2 fork shaft.

7. Install the reverse shift arm by performing the following procedures:

a. Position the reverse shift arm pivot into the reverse shift fork and install the reverse shift arm into the transaxle case.

b. Move the reverse shift arm into reverse.

c. Install and torque the retaining bolts to 13 ft. lbs.

d. Move the reverse shift arm into neutral.

8. Install reverse idler gear and shaft by aligning the transaxle case slot and slotted spring pin.

9. Install the No. 1 and No. 2 shift forks, the No. 1 shift head and the No. 1 fork shaft by performing the following procedures:

a. Position the No. 1 and No. 2 shift forks into the groove of No. 1 and No. 2 hub sleeves.

b. Support the No. 1 shift head and insert the No. 1 fork shaft into the transaxle case through the No. 1 and No. 2 shift forks, the No. 1 shift head and the reverse shift fork.

c. Using a pin punch and hammer, drive the slotted spring pin into the No. 1 shift head.

d. Move the fork shaft into reverse.

e. Using a pin punch and hammer, drive the slotted spring pin into the No. 1 fork shaft.

10. Apply sealant or gasket, if equipped, to the transmission case; keep the sealant on the inside of the bolt holes. Install the transmission case and torque the bolts 22 ft. lbs.

11. Install the side bearing retainer by performing the following procedures:

a. Using a new O-ring, install it onto the side bearing retainer.

b. Install the shim and side bearing retainer.

c. Apply sealant to the bolt threads, install and torque them bolts to 13 ft. lbs.

12. On the outside of the transmission case, install and torque reverse idler gear shaft lock bolt to 18 ft. lbs.

13. Install the both bearing snaprings.

14. Apply sealant to the rear bearing retainer bolt threads, install the retainer and torque the bolts to 13 ft. lbs.

15. Using a 5th driven gear replacer tool, press the 5th driven gear onto the output shaft.

16. Install the 5th gear onto the input shaft by performing the following procedures:

a. Install the spacer.

b. Lubricate the 5th gear needle roller bearings with Dexron®II.

c. Install the 5th gear with the needle roller bearings and synchronizer ring.

17. Assemble the No. 3 clutch hub, the shifting keys and the shifting key springs into the No. 3 hub sleeve; position the springs so the end gaps are not aligned.

18. Support the tip of the input shaft with a spacer to raise the transaxle. Using a tilt

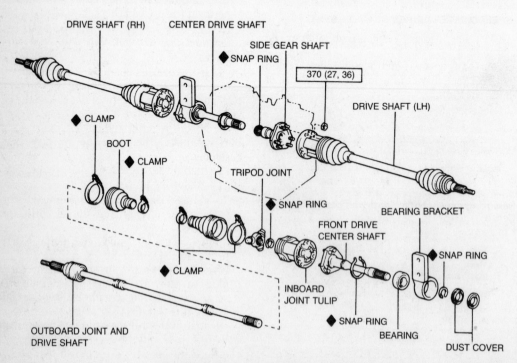

Exploded view of the halfshaft — Celica

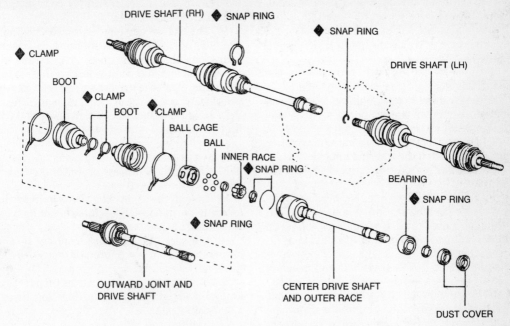

DRIVE SHAFT (RH) ◆ SNAP RING

◆ SNAP RING

DRIVE SHAFT (LH)

◆ CLAMP

BOOT

◆ CLAMP

BOOT ◆ CLAMP

BALL CAGE

BALL

INNER RACE

◆ SNAP RING

BEARING

◆ SNAP RING

◆ SNAP RING

OUTWARD JOINT AND
DRIVE SHAFT

CENTER DRIVE SHAFT
AND OUTER RACE

DUST COVER

Exploded view of the halfshaft — Celica

handle bearing replacer tool, drive the No. 3 hub sleeve assembly, with the No. 3 shift fork, onto the input shaft; align the synchronizer ring slots with the shifting keys.

19. Using a dial indicator, measure the 5th gear thrust clearance; it should be 0.008–0.016 in. (0.20–0.40mm).

20. Install the shifting key retainer.

21. Select a snapring that will allow minimum axial play and install it on the shaft.

22. Install the locknut onto the output shaft by performing the following procedures:

  a. Move the internal shifting forks to lock the transaxle into 2 gears.

  b. Rotate the locknut counterclockwise and torque it to 90 ft. lbs.

  c. Disengage the gear double meshing and stake the locknut with a small cold chisel.

23. Apply sealant to the control shaft cover. Install the shift and select lever assembly and torque the control shaft cover-to-transaxle case bolts to 27 ft. lbs.

24. Apply sealant to the lock ball assembly threads. Install the lock ball assembly and torque it to 17 ft. lbs.

25. Adjust the No. 1 lock ball assembly by performing the following procedures:

  a. Fully loosen the No. 1 locknut.

  b. Screw in the lock ball, fully.

  c. Loosen the lock ball to where the play at the shift outer lever tip is 0.004–0.020 in. (0.10–0.50mm).

  d. Hold the lock ball and torque the locknut to 27 ft. lbs.

  e. Check the shift outer level tip play; it should be 0.004–0.020 in. (0.10–0.50mm).

26. Install the selecting bellcrank.

27. Install the No. 3 shift fork locking bolt and torque it to 13 ft. lbs.

28. Apply sealant or gasket, if equipped, to the transmission case cover and the bolt threads; place the sealant on the inside of the bolt holes. Torque the transmission cover-to-transmission case bolts to 22 ft. lbs.

29. Install front release bearing retainer and torque bolts to 65 inch lbs.

30. Using molybdenum disulphide lithium base, lubricate to the following parts: release bearing hub inside groove, input shaft spline and release fork contact surface.

31. Install back-up light switch and torque to 33 ft. lbs.

32. Install speedometer driven gear.

Halfshaft

REMOVAL AND INSTALLATION

1986–89 Celica 2WD

NOTE: *The hub bearing can be damaged if it is subjected to the vehicle weight such as moving the vehicle when the driveshaft is removed. For model year 1986 with 2S-E engine use this service procedure as a guide.*

1. Raise and safely support the vehicle. Remove the wheels.

2. Remove the cotter pin, cap and locknut

(loosen locknut while depressing brake pedal) from the hub.

3. Remove the engine under covers.

4. Drain the transaxle fluid on the 3S-GE engine.

5. Remove the transaxle protector on the 3S-GE engine.

6. Loosen the 6 nuts holding front driveshaft to center driveshaft or differential side bearing shaft on the 3S-FE engine.

7. Disconnect the tie rod end (remove cotter pin and nut) from the steering knuckle.

8. Disconnect steering knuckle from the lower arm.

9. On the 3S-FE engine, remove the driveshaft from the steering knuckle using a suitable puller. Cover the driveshaft boot with shop cloth or equivalent to protect it from damage.

10. On the 3S-GE engine, mark a spot somewhere on the left side driveshaft and measure the distance between the spot and the transaxle case. Using SST 09520–32060 or equivalent pull the left side driveshaft out of the transaxle.

11. On the 3S-GE engine, use a two-armed puller and press the outer end of the right side driveshaft out of the steering knuckle. Use a pair of pliers to remove the snapring at the inner end and pull the halfshaft out of the center driveshaft (loosen the center driveshaft stopper bolt).

12. On the 3S-FE engine, drain the transaxle fluid. Loosen the center driveshaft stopper bolt. Remove the snapring on the center driveshaft with a pair of pliers and then pull the center shaft out of the transaxle case.

13. On the 3S-FE engine, install the center driveshaft using the following service procedure:

a. Apply grease to the transaxle oil seal lip.

b. Insert the center driveshaft to the transaxle through the bearing bracket.

c. Secure the center driveshaft with a new snapring. Torque the new center driveshaft stopper bolt to 24 ft. lbs.

14. On the 3S-GE engine, install the right side driveshaft with center driveshaft using the following service procedure:

a. Apply grease to the transaxle oil seal lip.

b. Insert the right side driveshaft with center driveshaft to the transaxle through the bearing bracket.

c. Secure the center driveshaft with a new snapring. Torque the new center driveshaft stopper bolt to 24 ft. lbs.

15. On the 3S-FE engine install the front driveshaft. Install the outboard joint side of the driveshaft to the axle hub. Finger tighten 6 nuts holding the driveshaft to the center driveshaft or the differential side gear.

16. On the 3S-GE engine install the front driveshaft. Install a new snapring to the inboard joint shaft. Apply grease to the transaxle oil seal and install the left side driveshaft to the transaxle. Push the driveshaft in to the correct position. Check that the measurement made in Step 10 is the same. Check that there is 0.08–0.11 in. (2–3mm) of axial play. Check also that the halfshaft will not come out by trying to pull it with your hand.

17. Install the transaxle protector on the 3S-GE engine.

18. Install the right side driveshaft to the axle hub on the 3S-GE engine. Do not damage the driveshaft boot or oil seal.

19. Connect the steering knuckle to the lower control arm and tighten the bolts to 94 ft. lbs.

20. Connect the tie rod end to the steering knuckle and tighten the nut to 36 ft. lbs. Install a new cotter pin.

21. Tighten the hub locknut to 137 ft. lbs. while depressing the brake pedal. Install the cap and use a new cotter pin.

22. Torque the 6 nuts on the inner halfshaft ends to 27 ft. lbs. while depressing the brake pedal.

23. Install the transaxle gravel shield if so equipped.

24. Fill the transaxle with gear oil or fluid.

25 Install the engine under cover.

1990 Celica — 2 Wheel Drive

NOTE: *The hub bearing can be damaged if it is subjected to the vehicle weight such as moving the vehicle when the driveshaft is removed. On vehicles with ABS after disconnecting driveshaft work carefully so as not damage the sensor rotor serrations on the driveshaft.*

1. Raise and safely support the vehicle. Remove the wheels.

2. Remove the cotter pin, cap and locknut (loosen locknut while depressing brake pedal) from the hub.

3. Remove the engine under covers.

4. Drain the transaxle fluid.

5. Remove the brake caliper and rotor disc.

6. Disconnect the tie rod end (remove cotter pin and nut) from the steering knuckle.

7. Disconnect steering knuckle from the lower arm.

8. Remove the driveshaft from the steering knuckle using a suitable puller. Cover the driveshaft boot with shop cloth or equivalent to protect it from damage.

9. Remove (tap out with brass punch) the left side driveshaft.

10. Remove the the right side driveshaft. On the 5S-FE engine remove the 2 bolts of the center bearing bracket and pull out the drive-shaft with center bearing case and center drive-shaft. On the 4A-FE engine use a brass punch tap out the right side driveshaft.

11. Install the left side driveshaft. Apply grease to the transaxle oil seal lip. Position the new snapring opening side facing downward using brass punch, tap driveshaft in until it makes contact with the pinion shaft. Install the outboard joint side of the driveshaft to the axle hub.

12. Install right side driveshaft on the 5S-FE engine using the following service proce-dure:

a. Apply grease to the transaxle oil seal lip.

b. Insert the center driveshaft with the right side to the transaxle through the bear-ing bracket. When inserting the driveshaft, insert so that the straight pin on the center bearing case aligns with the hole on the bear-ing bracket.

c. Install retaining bolts and torque to 47 ft. lbs.

d. Install the outboard joint side of the driveshaft to the axle hub.

13. Install right side driveshaft on the 4A-FE engine using the following service procedure:

a. Apply grease to the transaxle oil seal lip.

b. Position the new snapring opening side facing downward using brass punch, tap driveshaft in until it makes contact with the pinion shaft.

c. Install the outboard joint side of the driveshaft to the axle hub.

14. Check that the driveshaft will not come out by trying to pull it with your hand.

15. Connect the steering knuckle to the lower control arm and tighten the bolts to 94 ft. lbs.

16. Connect the tie rod end to the steering knuckle and tighten the nut to 36 ft. lbs. Install a new cotter pin.

17. Install all necessary brake components. Tighten the hub locknut to 137 ft. lbs. while depressing the brake pedal. Install the cap and use a new cotter pin.

18. Fill the transaxle with the specified fluid to the correct level. Install the engine under cover. Check front wheel alignment.

1988–90 Celica All-Trac

NOTE: *The hub bearing can be damaged if it is subjected to the vehicle weight such as moving the vehicle when the driveshaft is re-moved. On 1990 vehicles with ABS after dis-connecting driveshaft work carefully so as*

not damage the sensor rotor serrations on the driveshaft.

1. Raise and safely support the vehicle.

2. Remove the wheels.

3. Remove the cotter pin, cap and locknut from the hub.

4. Remove the transaxle gravel shield if so equipped. Remove the engine under cover and front fender apron seal.

5. Remove the cotter pin and nut from the tie rod end and then disconnect it from the steer-ing knuckle.

6. Remove the bolt and 2 nuts and discon-nect the steering knuckle from the lower con-trol arm.

7. Loosen the 6 nuts attaching the inner end of the driveshaft to the transaxle side gear shaft. It's a good idea to have a friend sit in the car and depress the brake pedal while removing the nuts. On the right side driveshaft remove the transaxle case protector.

8. Grasp the driveshaft (matchmark drive-shaft and side gear shaft) and push the axle car-rier outward until the shaft can be removed from the side gear shaft.

NOTE: *Wrap the exposed end of the halfshaft in an old shop cloth to prevent damage to it.*

9. Use a rubber mallet or equivalent tap the outer end of the shaft from the axle hub.

10. Install the driveshaft. Apply grease to the transaxle oil seal lip. Position the new snapring opening side facing downard using brass punch, tap driveshaft in until it makes contact with the pinion shaft. Install the out-board joint side of the driveshaft to the axle hub.

11. Tighten the 6 inner shaft mounting nuts to 48 ft. lbs.

12. Connect the steering knuckle to the lower control arm and tighten to 94 ft. lbs.

13. Connect the tie rod end to the steering knuckle and tighten the nut to 36 ft. lbs. Install a new cotter pin. If the cotter pin holes do not line up, tighten the nut until they align. Never loosen it.

14. With the brake pedal depressed, install the bearing locknut and tighten it to 137 ft. lbs. Install the cap and a new cotter pin.

15. Install the wheels. Fill transaxle with the specified fluid to the correct level. Check front wheel alignment.

CV-JOINT OVERHAUL

1. Place removed driveshaft into a suitable holding fixture.

2. Remove (cut off) inboard joint boot clamps.

3. Disassemble inboard joint tulip by follow-ing the service procedure as outlined below:

Loosen the set bolts on the clutch cover one turn at a time until the spring tension is relieved.

    a. Place matchmarks on the inboard joint tulip and tripod.

    b. Remove the inboard joint tulip from the driveshaft.

4. Disassemble tripod joint by following the service procedure as outlined below:

    a. Using snapring pliers, remove the snapring.

    b. Place matchmarks on the shaft and tripod.

    c. Using a brass punch or equivalent remove the tripod joint from the driveshaft.

5. Remove inboard joint boot.

6. Remove the outboard joint boot clamps (cut off) and boot. DO NOT DISASSEMBLE THE OUTBOARD JOINT.

7. Installation is the reverse of the removal procedures. Pack all CV-joints with suitable grease. Use new boot retaining clamps and snaprings as necessary.

CLUTCH

    The clutch is a single plate, dry disc type. All models use a diaphragm spring pressure plate. Clutch release bearings are sealed ball bearing units which need no lubrication and should

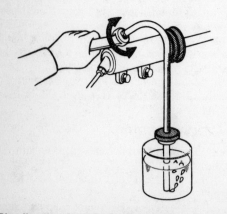

Bleeding the clutch hydraulic system

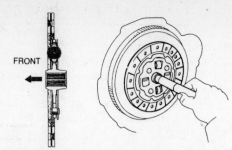

Use a clutch pilot tool to center the clutch disc on the flywheel

Remove the clip to remove the release bearing and its hub.

never be washed in any kind of solvent. All clutches are hydraulically operated.

CAUTION: *The clutch driven disc contains asbestos, which has been determined to be a cancer causing agent. Never clean clutch surfaces with compressed air! Avoid inhaling any dust from any clutch surface! When cleaning clutch surfaces, use a commercially available brake cleaning fluid.*

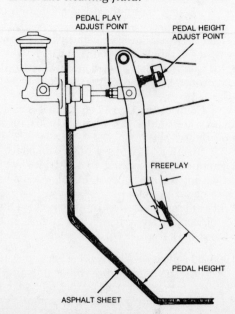

Clutch pedal adjustment points

Troubleshooting Basic Clutch Problems

Problem	Cause
Excessive clutch noise	Throwout bearing noises are more audible at the lower end of pedal travel. The usual causes are: · Riding the clutch · Too little pedal free-play · Lack of bearing lubrication A bad clutch shaft pilot bearing will make a high pitched squeal, when the clutch is disengaged and the transmission is in gear or within the first 2″ of pedal travel. The bearing must be replaced. Noise from the clutch linkage is a clicking or snapping that can be heard or felt as the pedal is moved completely up or down. This usually requires lubrication. Transmitted engine noises are amplified by the clutch housing and heard in the passenger compartment. They are usually the result of insufficient pedal free-play and can be changed by manipulating the clutch pedal.
Clutch slips (the car does not move as it should when the clutch is engaged)	This is usually most noticeable when pulling away from a standing start. A severe test is to start the engine, apply the brakes, shift into high gear and SLOWLY release the clutch pedal. A healthy clutch will stall the engine. If it slips it may be due to: · A worn pressure plate or clutch plate · Oil soaked clutch plate · Insufficient pedal free-play
Clutch drags or fails to release	The clutch disc and some transmission gears spin briefly after clutch disengagement. Under normal conditions in average temperatures, 3 seconds is maximum spin-time. Failure to release properly can be caused by: · Too light transmission lubricant or low lubricant level · Improperly adjusted clutch linkage
Low clutch life	Low clutch life is usually a result of poor driving habits or heavy duty use. Riding the clutch, pulling heavy loads, holding the car on a grade with the clutch instead of the brakes and rapid clutch engagement all contribute to low clutch life.

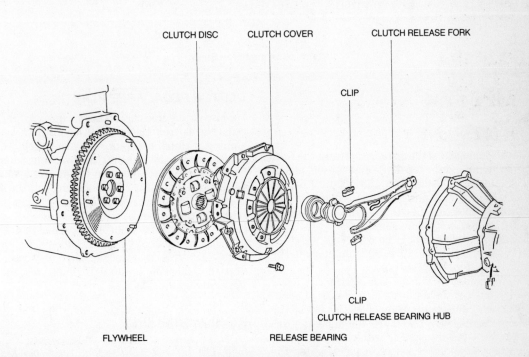

Typical clutch assembly

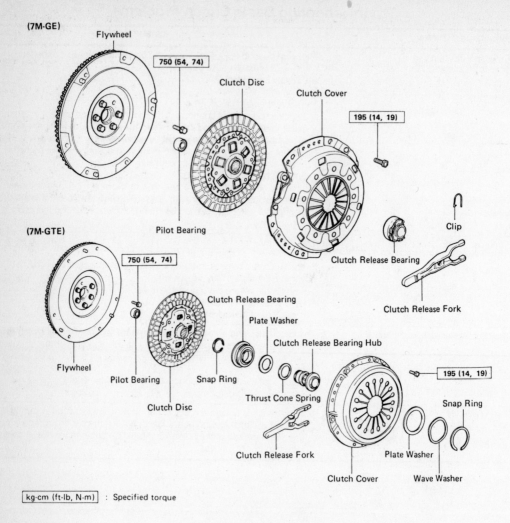

(7M-GE)
Flywheel
750 (54, 74)
Clutch Disc
Clutch Cover
195 (14, 19)
Pilot Bearing
Clip
Clutch Release Bearing
Clutch Release Fork

(7M-GTE)
750 (54, 74)
Flywheel
Pilot Bearing
Clutch Disc
Clutch Release Bearing
Plate Washer
Snap Ring
Thrust Cone Spring
Clutch Release Bearing Hub
Clutch Release Fork
195 (14, 19)
Snap Ring
Clutch Cover
Plate Washer
Wave Washer

kg·cm (ft-lb, N·m) : Specified torque

Clutch components — Supra

Adjustments

PEDAL HEIGHT

Pedal height is the distance between the floor of the car and the top of the clutch pedal pad. It should be 6.02–6.42 in. (153–163mm) on the 1986–89 Celica and Celica All-Trac. On the 1990 Celica and Celica All-Trac is should be 6.41–6.80 in. (163–173mm). On the 1986 Supra model it should be 6.02–6.42 in. (153–163mm) and on the 1987–90 Supra it should be 6.18–6.57 in. (157–167mm).

To adjust it, remove the instrument lower finish panel and air ducts as necessary. Loosen the lock nut on the stopper at the top of the clutch pedal and then turn the adjusting nut until the pedal height is within specifications. After adjusting the height, always tighten the lock nut again.

CLUTCH PEDAL FREE PLAY

Clutch pedal free play is the distance that the pedal travels from the rest position until the beginning of clutch resistance can just be felt. To adjust, loosen the lock nut (remove any trim/finish panel as necessary) on the master cylinder push rod and turn the adjusting nut until the proper free play is achieved. Don't forget to retighten the lock nut.

The clutch pedal free play specification is 0.20–0.59 in. (5.0–15.0mm) for 1986–90 Celica and Celica All-Trac. The clutch free play specification 0.20–0.59 in. (5.0–15.0mm) for the 1986–90 Supra models.

System Bleeding

NOTE: *Do not spill brake fluid on the painted surfaces of the vehicle.*

1. Fill the master cylinder reservoir with brake fluid.

2. Remove the cap and loosen the bleeder plug. Block the outlet hole with your finger.

3. Pump the clutch pedal several times, then take your finger from the hole while depressing the clutch pedal. Allow the air to flow out. Place your finger back over the hole and release the pedal.

4. After fluid pressure can be felt (with your finger), tighten the bleeder plug.

5. Fit a bleeder tube over the plug and place the other end into a clean jar half filled with brake fluid.

6. Depress the clutch pedal, loosen the bleeder plug with a wrench, and allow the fluid to flow into the jar.

7. Tighten the plug and then release the clutch pedal.

8. Repeat Steps 6–7 until no air bubbles are visible in the bleeder tube.

9. When there are no more air bubbles, tighten the plug while keeping the clutch pedal fully depressed. Replace the cap.

10. Fill the master cylinder to the specified level. (See Chapter 1).

11. Check the system for leaks.

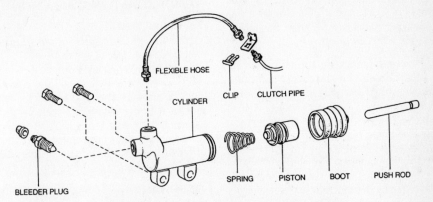

Exploded view of the typical clutch slave cylinder

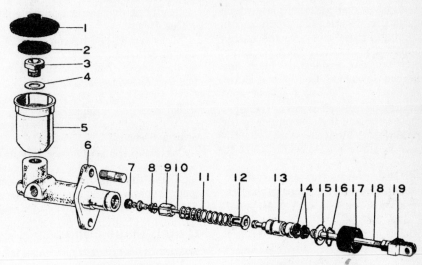

1. Reservoir filler cap
2. Reservoir float
3. Bolt
4. Washer
5. Master cylinder reservoir
6. Master cylinder body
7. Inlet valve
8. Conical spring
9. Inlet valve case
10. Inlet valve connecting rod
11. Compression spring
12. Spring retainer
13. Piston
14. Cylinder cup
15. Piston stop plate
16. Hole snap ring
17. Boot
18. Master push rod
19. Push rod clevis

An exploded view of the clutch master cylinder

Driven Disc and Pressure Plate

REMOVAL AND INSTALLATION

Celica And Supra

NOTE: *Do not allow grease or oil to get on any part of the clutch disc, pressure plate or flywheel surfaces. Do not drain transmission/transaxle oil.*

1. Remove the transmission/transaxle from the car as previously detailed.

NOTE: *On the Supra 7M-GTE (turbo-charged) engine remove the transmission with the clutch cover and disc. Remove the release bearing hub assembly from the clutch cover by removing the snapring.*

2. Place a matchmark on the clutch cover and flywheel. Loosen the clutch set bolts one turn at a time until the spring tension is relieved.

3. Remove the set bolts and then pull off the clutch assembly.

4. Remove the release bearing, fork and boot from the transmission/transaxle.

5. Inspect the parts for wear or deterioration. Replace parts as required.

6. Installation is the reverse of the removal procedures. Be sure to align the match marks on the clutch cover and pressure plate which were made during disassembly. Apply a thin coating of multipurpose grease to the release bearing hub and release fork contact points. Also, pack the groove inside the clutch hub with multipurpose grease. Center the clutch disc by using a clutch pilot tool or an old input shaft. Insert the pilot into the end of the input shaft front bearing and bolt the clutch to the flywheel. Torque the clutch assembly to the flywheel in two or three stages, evenly to 14 ft. lbs.

7. Install transmission/transaxle assembly. Road test the vehicle for proper operation.

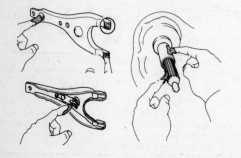

Apply grease to these areas; also pack groove of clutch hub with grease.

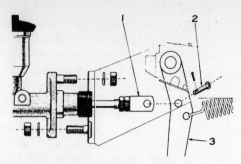

To unhook the master cylinder pushrod (1) from the clutch pedal (3), remove the clevis pin.

Clutch Master Cylinder

REMOVAL AND INSTALLATION

Celica And Supra

NOTE: *Do not spill brake fluid on the painted surfaces of the vehicle.*

1. Remove the clevis pin.
2. Detach the hydraulic line from the tube.
3. Unfasten the bolts which secure the master cylinder to the fire wall. Withdraw the assembly.
4. Installation is performed in the reverse order of removal. Bleed the system. Adjust the clutch pedal height and free play as necessary.

OVERHAUL

NOTE: *Overhaul and assemble the master cylinder only in a clean working area.*

1. Clamp the master cylinder body in a vise with soft jaws.
2. Separate the reservoir assembly from the master cylinder.
3. Remove the snapring and remove the pushrod/piston assembly.
4. Inspect all of the parts and replace nay which are worn or defective.
5. Coat all parts with clean brake fluid, prior to assembly.
6. Install the piston assembly in the cylinder bore.
7. Fit the pushrod over the washer and secure them with the snapring.
8. Install the reservoir.

Clutch Slave Cylinder

REMOVAL AND INSTALLATION

Celica And Supra

NOTE: *Do not spill brake fluid on the painted surface of the vehicle.*

1. Raise the front of the car and support it with jackstands. Be sure that it is supported securely.
2. If necessary, remove the gravel shield to gain access to the release cylinder.
3. Disconnect the hydraulic line (use a line wrench) and remove the retaining bolts.

Troubleshooting Basic Automatic Transmission Problems

Problem	Cause	Solution
Fluid leakage	· Defective pan gasket	· Replace gasket or tighten pan bolts
	· Loose filler tube	· Tighten tube nut
	· Loose extension housing to transmission case	· Tighten bolts
	· Converter housing area leakage	· Have transmission checked professionally
Fluid flows out the oil filler tube	· High fluid level	· Check and correct fluid level
	· Breather vent clogged	· Open breather vent
	· Clogged oil filter or screen	· Replace filter or clean screen (change fluid also)
	· Internal fluid leakage	· Have transmission checked professionally
Transmission overheats (this is usually accompanied by a strong burned odor to the fluid)	· Low fluid level	· Check and correct fluid level
	· Fluid cooler lines clogged	· Drain and refill transmission. If this doesn't cure the problem, have cooler lines cleared or replaced.
	· Heavy pulling or hauling with insufficient cooling	· Install a transmission oil cooler
	· Faulty oil pump, internal slippage	· Have transmission checked professionally
Buzzing or whining noise	· Low fluid level	· Check and correct fluid level
	· Defective torque converter, scored gears	· Have transmission checked professionally
No forward or reverse gears or slippage in one or more gears	· Low fluid level	· Check and correct fluid level
	· Defective vacuum or linkage controls, internal clutch or band failure	· Have unit checked professionally
Delayed or erratic shift	· Low fluid level	· Check and correct fluid level
	· Broken vacuum lines	· Repair or replace lines
	· Internal malfunction	· Have transmission checked professionally

Transmission Fluid Indications

The appearance and odor of the transmission fluid can give valuable clues to the overall condition of the transmission. Always note the appearance of the fluid when you check the fluid level or change the fluid. Rub a small amount of fluid between your fingers to feel for grit and smell the fluid on the dipstick.

If the fluid appears:	It indicates:
Clear and red colored	· Normal operation
Discolored (extremely dark red or brownish) or smells burned	· Band or clutch pack failure, usually caused by an overheated transmission. Hauling very heavy loads with insufficient power or failure to change the fluid, often result in overheating. Do not confuse this appearance with newer fluids that have a darker red color and a strong odor (though not a burned odor).
Foamy or aerated (light in color and full of bubbles)	· The level is too high (gear train is churning oil)
	· An internal air leak (air is mixing with the fluid). Have the transmission checked professionally.
Solid residue in the fluid	· Defective bands, clutch pack or bearings. Bits of band material or metal abrasives are clinging to the dipstick. Have the transmission checked professionally.
Varnish coating on the dipstick	· The transmission fluid is overheating

Lockup Torque Converter Service Diagnosis

Problem	Cause	Solution

No lockup	• Faulty oil pump
	• Sticking governor valve
	• Valve body malfunction
	  (a) Stuck switch valve
	  (b) Stuck lockup valve
	  (c) Stuck fail-safe valve
	• Failed locking clutch
	• Leaking turbine hub seal
	• Faulty input shaft or seal ring
		• Replace oil pump
		• Repair or replace as necessary
		• Repair or replace valve body or its internal components as necessary
		
		• Replace torque converter
		• Replace torque converter
		• Repair or replace as necessary

Will not unlock	• Sticking governor valve
	• Valve body malfunction
	  (a) Stuck switch valve
	  (b) Stuck lockup valve
	  (c) Stuck fail-safe valve
		• Repair or replace as necessary
		• Repair or replace valve body or its internal components as necessary

Stays locked up at too low a speed in direct	• Sticking governor valve
	• Valve body malfunction
	  (a) Stuck switch valve
	  (b) Stuck lockup valve
	  (c) Stuck fail-safe valve
		• Repair or replace as necessary
		• Repair or replace valve body or its internal components as necessary

Locks up or drags in low or second	• Faulty oil pump
	• Valve body malfunction
	  (a) Stuck switch valve
	  (b) Stuck fail-safe valve
		• Replace oil pump
		• Repair or replace valve body or its internal components as necessary

Sluggish or stalls in reverse	• Faulty oil pump
	• Plugged cooler, cooler lines or fittings
	• Valve body malfunction
	  (a) Stuck switch valve
	  (b) Faulty input shaft or seal ring
		• Replace oil pump as necessary
		• Flush or replace cooler and flush lines and fittings
		• Repair or replace valve body or its internal components as necessary

Loud chatter during lockup engagement (cold)	• Faulty torque converter • Failed locking clutch • Leaking turbine hub seal	• Replace torque converter • Replace torque converter • Replace torque converter
Vibration or shudder during lockup engagement	• Faulty oil pump • Valve body malfunction • Faulty torque converter • Engine needs tune-up	• Repair or replace oil pump as necessary • Repair or replace valve body or its internal components as necessary • Replace torque converter • Tune engine
Vibration after lockup engagement	• Faulty torque converter • Exhaust system strikes underbody • Engine needs tune-up • Throttle linkage misadjusted	• Replace torque converter • Align exhaust system • Tune engine • Adjust throttle linkage
Vibration when revved in neutral Overheating: oil blows out of dip stick tube or pump seal	• Torque converter out of balance • Plugged cooler, cooler lines or fittings • Stuck switch valve	• Replace torque converter • Flush or replace cooler and flush lines and fittings • Repair switch valve in valve body or replace valve body
Shudder after lockup engagement	• Faulty oil pump • Plugged cooler, cooler lines or fittings • Valve body malfunction • Faulty torque converter • Fail locking clutch • Exhaust system strikes underbody • Engine needs tune-up • Throttle linkage misadjusted	• Replace oil pump • Flush or replace cooler and flush lines and fittings • Repair or replace valve body or its internal components as necessary • Replace torque converter • Replace torque converter • Align exhaust system • Tune engine • Adjust throttle linkage

4. Remove the clutch slave (release) cylinder assembly with pushrod from the vehicle.

5. Installation is performed in the reverse order of removal. Bleed the hydraulic system as necessary.

OVERHAUL

NOTE: *Overhaul the slave cylinder only in a clean working area.*

1. Remove the pushrod assembly and the rubber boot.

2. Withdraw the piston, complete with its cup; don't remove the cup unless it is being replaced.

3. Wash all the parts in brake fluid.

4. Replace any worn or damaged parts.

5. Assembly is the reverse of disassembly. Coat all parts in clean brake fluid prior to assembly.

AUTOMATIC TRANSMISSION

Identification

On some models an identification tag is attached to the right rear side of the transmission case above the oil pan. Included on the tag is the model number and serial number of the unit.

Fluid Pan and Filter

REMOVAL AND INSTALLATION

1. Raise and safely support the vehicle. Clean the exterior of the transmission around the pan.

2. Remove the drain plug and drain the fluid into a suitable container.

3. Unscrew all the pan retaining bolts and carefully remove the pan assembly. Discard the gasket.

NOTE: *There will still be some fluid in the oil pan. Be careful not to damage the filler tube or the O-ring.*

4. Remove the small magnet from the bottom of the oil pan and clean it thoroughly.

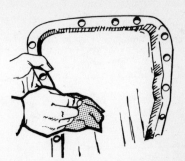

Clean the pan thoroughly and then allow it to air dry

5. Clean the transmission oil pan with a suitable solvent and allow it to air dry.

6. Remove the retaining bolts and then remove the oil strainer (filter) and gaskets.

7. Installation is the reverse of the removal procedures. Always use a new filter and gasket. Torque the oil strainer (filter) retaining bolts to 84 inch lbs. Torque the oil pan retaining bolts in (criss-cross manner) steps to 72 inch lbs. Refill with the specified fluid to the correct level (1.7 quarts).

Adjustments

THROTTLE CABLE

1. Remove the air cleaner.

2. Confirm that the accelerator linkage opens the throttle fully. Adjust the linkage as necessary.

3. Peel the rubber dust boot back from the throttle cable.

4. Loosen the adjustment nuts on the throttle cable bracket (rocker cover) just enough to allow cable housing movement.

5. Have an assistant depress the accelerator pedal fully.

6. Adjust the cable housing so that the distance between its end and the cable stop collar is 0.04 in. (1mm).

7. Tighten the adjustment nuts. Make sure that the adjustment hasn't changed. Install the dust boot and the air cleaner.

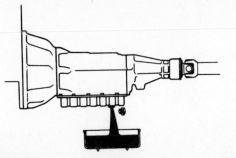

Remove the drain plug and drain transmission fluid

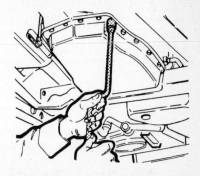

Removing the pan retaining bolts

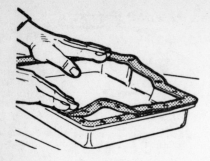

Install the new pan gasket without sealer

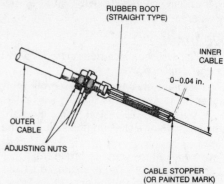

WHEN THROTTLE VALVE IS FULLY OPENED

RUBBER BOOT
(STRAIGHT TYPE)

INNER
CABLE

0–0.04 in.

OUTER
CABLE

ADJUSTING NUTS

CABLE STOPPER
(OR PAINTED MARK)

Throttle linkage adjustment — Celica and Supra

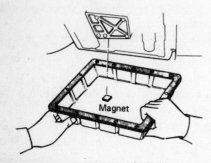

Magnet

Position the magnet so that it is directly beneath the oil strainer

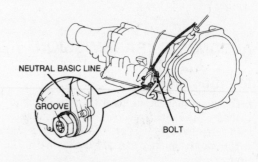

NEUTRAL BASIC LINE

GROOVE

BOLT

Neutral safety switch adjustment — Supra

SHIFT LINKAGE

1. Raise and safely support the vehicle. Loosen the adjusting nut on the shift lever.
2. Push the control shaft lever fully rearward.
3. Bring the lever (control shaft) back 2 notches to N (Neutral) position. Set the shifter lever to the N (neutral) position. Tighten the shifter lever nut.
4. Road test the vehicle for proper operation.

Neutral Safety Switch

NOTE: *On the Supra vehicles the back-up light switch is incorporated in the neutral safety switch assembly.*

REMOVAL AND INSTALLATION

1. Raise and safely support the vehicle.
2. Place vehicle in the N (neutral position). Remove the control shaft lever from the switch. Remove the neutral safety switch adjusting bolt.
3. Disconnect the electrical connections to the switch.
4. Installation is thee reverse of the removal procedures. Torque the switch adjusting bolt to 9 ft. lbs. and control shaft lever nut to 60 inch lbs. Adjust the neutral safety switch as necessary. The vehicle should start ONLY in N or P position.

ADJUSTMENT

NOTE: *If the engine will start with the selector in any range other than "N" or "P", the neutral safety switch will require adjustment.*

1. Locate the neutral safety switch on the right side of the transmission and loosen the switch bolt.
2. Move the gear selector to the "N" position.
3. Align the groove on the safety switch shaft with the basic line which is scribed on the housing.
4. With the groove and the line aligned (hold position), tighten the switch bolt to 9 ft. lbs.

Back-Up Light Switch

REMOVAL AND INSTALLATION

Supra

For back-up light removal and installation service procedure refer to the "Neutral Safety Switch".

Transmission

REMOVAL AND INSTALLATION

1. Disconnect the negative battery cable. On some 1986 vehicles drain the radiator and remove the upper radiator hose as necessary. Remove the air cleaner assembly. Disconnect the transmission throttle cable. On later models remove the engine undercover plate.

2. Raise and support the vehicle safely. Drain the transmission fluid. Disconnect the electrical connectors for the neutral safety switch and back-up lights.

3. Remove the intermediate driveshaft along with the center bearing. Disconnect the exhaust pipe from the tail pipe.

4. Disconnect the transmission oil cooler lines. Disconnect the manual shift linkage. Disconnect the speedometer cable.

5. Remove the exhaust pipe bracket and torque converter cover. Remove both stiffener brackets.

6. On some 1986 vehicles remove the power steering gear housing from the crossmember (remove yoke from gear housing) as necessary. Be sure to plug the fluid lines, as required.

7. Support the engine and transmission using the proper equipment. Remove the rear crossmember.

8. Remove the engine under cover. Remove the 6 torque converter-to-engine retaining bolts (turn the crankshaft with a suitable tool to gain access to each bolt). Remove the starter.

9. Remove the bolts retaining the transmission to the engine. Carefully remove the transmission from the vehicle. Pry on end of guide pin (a guide pin can be made by cutting off the head of a bolt) to begin moving transmission with converter assembly rearward.

10. Installation is the reverse of the removal procedure. Check torque converter installation by measuring from the installed surface of the torque converter to the front surface of the transmission housing. The correct distant is 1.039 in. (26.5mm). Adjust the throttle cable and fill the transmission with Dexron®II to the correct level.

11. Check installation for fluid leaks. Road test the vehicle for proper operation and correct shift points.

AUTOMATIC TRANSAXLE

Identification

An identification plate is normally located on the left side of the transaxle case or top front of the transaxle case with the model and serial number stamped on the plate.

Fluid Pan and Filter

REMOVAL AND INSTALLATION

1. Raise and safely support the vehicle. Clean the exterior of the transaxle around the pan.

2. Remove the drain plug and drain the fluid into a suitable container.

3. Unscrew all the pan retaining bolts and carefully remove the pan assembly. Discard the gasket.

4. Remove the small magnets from the bottom of the oil pan and clean it thoroughly.

5. Clean the transaxle oil pan with a suitable solvent and allow it to air dry.

6. Remove the retaining bolts (note location of bolts — they are different sizes) and then remove the oil strainer (filter) and gasket.

7. Installation is the reverse of the removal procedures. Always use a new filter and transaxle pan gasket. Torque the oil pan retaining bolts in (crisscross manner) steps to 48 inch lbs. Refill with the specified fluid to the correct level. Refer to the "Capacities Chart" in Chapter 1 for the correct drain and refill specification.

Adjustments

THROTTLE CABLE

1. Confirm that the accelerator linkage opens the throttle fully. Adjust the linkage as necessary.

2. Have an assistant depress the accelerator pedal fully.

3. Loosen the adjustment nuts.

4. Adjust the cable housing so that the distance between its end and the cable stop collar is 0.04 in. (1mm).

5. Tighten the adjustment nuts. Recheck the adjustments.

SHIFT CABLE

1. Raise and safely support the vehicle. Loosen the adjusting nut on the manual shift lever.

2. Push the control shaft lever fully to the right side of the vehicle.

3. Bring the lever (control shaft) back 2 notches to N (Neutral) position. Set the shifter lever to the N (neutral) position. Tighten the shifter lever nut.

4. Road test the vehicle for proper operation.

Neutral Safety Switch

NOTE: *On the Celica vehicles the back-up light switch is incorporated in the neutral safety switch assembly.*

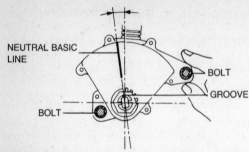

NEUTRAL BASIC LINE

BOLT

GROOVE

BOLT

Neutral safety switch adjustment — Celica

REMOVAL AND INSTALLATION

1. Raise and safely support the vehicle.

2. Place vehicle in the N (neutral position). Remove the control shaft lever from the switch. Remove the neutral safety switch retaining bolts.

3. Disconnect the electrical connections to the switch.

4. Installation is the reverse of the removal procedures. Torque the switch retaining bolts to 60 inch lbs. Adjust the neutral safety switch as necessary. The vehicle should start ONLY in N or P position.

ADJUSTMENT

NOTE: *If the engine will start with the selector in any range other than "N" or "P", the neutral safety switch will require adjustment.*

1. Loosen the neutral safety switch retaining bolts. Move the gear selector to the "N" position.

2. Align the groove on the safety switch with the basic line which is scribed on the housing.

3. With the groove and the line aligned (hold position), tighten the switch bolt to 60 inch lbs.

Back-Up Light Switch

REMOVAL AND INSTALLATION

Celica

For back-up light removal and installation service procedure refer to the "Neutral Safety Switch".

Transaxle

REMOVAL AND INSTALLATION

1. Disconnect the negative battery cable.

2. Remove the air flow meter and the air cleaner hose.

3. Raise the front of the vehicle and support it wit jackstands. Drain the transaxle fluid.

4. Disconnect the speedometer cable at the transaxle.

5. Disconnect the throttle cable from the throttle linkage and the bracket.

6. Disconnect the engine ground strap at the transaxle.

7. Tag and disconnect the starter electrical leads, remove the set bolts and then remove the starter.

8. Remove the two transaxle housing set bolts.

9. Remove the set bolt for the insulator bracket on the rear engine mount.

10. Remove the engine under covers.

11. Remove the lower suspension crossmember.

12. Remove the dust covers, remove the four bolts and then remove the front and rear mounts.

13. Remove the left side driveshaft (halfshaft). Disconnect the right side driveshaft (halfshaft) at the transaxle and wire it out of the way.

14. Disconnect the exhaust pipe at the manifold and position it out of the way.

15. Remove the stiffener plate.

16. Remove the control cable clip and retainer, disconnect the cable from the bracket and remove the bracket.

17. Disconnect the oil cooler lines. Plug the inlet holes and the ends of each line to prevent debris from entering.

18. Remove the engine rear end plate (this will provide access to the torque converter bolt).

19. Hold the crankshaft pulley bolt with a wrench and remove the six converter mounting bolts. This will require spinning the crankshaft (clockwise only) to position the different bolts.

20. Place a block of wood on an hydraulic floor jack and position the jack underneath the engine oil pan. Raise the jack just to support the engine, while at the same time easing the engine's weight on its mounts.

21. Repeat Step 20 and position the jack underneath the transaxle.

22. Remove the transaxle set bolts.

23. Disconnect the front and rear engine/transaxle mounts.

24. Lower the end of the transaxle slightly and remove the transaxle-to-engine mounting bolts.

25. Carefully slide the jack backwards slightly while lowering it and remove the transaxle. Be sure that none of the electrical wires, cables or anything else snag on the transaxle while removing it

NOTE: *Check torque converter installation by measuring from the installed surface of the torque converter to the front surface of the transaxle housing. The correct distant is 0.51 in. (13mm) except 1990 4A-FE engine is*

0.898 in. (23mm) and 5S-FE engine is 0.657 in. (16.7mm).

26. Align the two knock pins on the engine block with the converter housing to insure proper mating of the engine and transaxle. Temporarily install one bolt.

27. Install the transaxle-to-engine mounting bolts. Tighten the 12mm bolts to 47 ft. lbs. and the 10mm bolts to 34 ft. lbs.

28. Install the transmission mount set bolts and tighten them to 38 ft. lbs.

29. Install the torque converter mounting bolts. Tighten the bolts evenly to 20 ft. lbs. (on later models these bolts are coated with lock tight sealer or equivalent). Install the engine rear end plate.

30. Install the stiffener plate and tighten the mounting bolts to 27 ft. lbs.

31. Install the driveshafts (halfshafts) as outlined.

32. Install the engine mount center member cushions, install the member and tighten the bolts to 29 ft. lbs.

33. Install the front and rear mounts and tighten the bolts to 29 ft. lbs.

34. Installation of the remaining components is in the reverse order of removal. Adjust the throttle cable, fill the transaxle with the specified fluid and road test the vehicle.

Halfshaft

REMOVAL AND INSTALLATION

1986–89 Celica

NOTE: *The hub bearing can be damaged if it is subjected to the vehicle weight such as moving the vehicle when the driveshaft is removed. For model year 1986 with 2S-E engine use this service procedure as a guide.*

1. Raise and safely support the vehicle. Remove the wheels.

2. Remove the cotter pin, cap and locknut (loosen locknut while depressing brake pedal) from the hub.

3. Remove the engine under covers.

4. Drain the transaxle fluid on the 3S-GE engine.

5. Remove the transaxle protector on the 3S-GE engine.

6. Loosen the 6 nuts holding front driveshaft to center driveshaft or differential side bearing shaft on the 3S-FE engine.

7. Disconnect the tie rod end (remove cotter pin and nut) from the steering knuckle.

8. Disconnect steering knuckle from the lower arm.

9. On the 3S-FE engine, remove the driveshaft from the steering knuckle using a suitable puller. Cover the driveshaft boot with shop cloth or equivalent to protect it from damage.

10. On the 3S-GE engine, mark a spot somewhere on the left side driveshaft and measure the distance between the spot and the transaxle case. Using SST 09520–32060 or equivalent pull the left side driveshaft out of the transaxle.

11. On the 3S-GE engine, use a two-armed puller and press the outer end of the right side driveshaft out of the steering knuckle. Use a pair of pliers to remove the snapring at the inner end and pull the halfshaft out of the center driveshaft (loosen the center driveshaft stopper bolt).

12. On the 3S-FE engine, drain the transaxle fluid. Loosen the center driveshaft stopper bolt. Remove the snapring on the center driveshaft with a pair of pliers and then pull the center shaft out of the transaxle case.

13. On the 3S-FE engine, install the center driveshaft using the following service procedure:

a. Apply grease to the transaxle oil seal lip.

b. Insert the center driveshaft to the transaxle through the bearing bracket.

c. Secure the center driveshaft with a new snapring. Torque the new center driveshaft stopper bolt to 24 ft. lbs.

14. On the 3S-GE engine, install the right side driveshaft with center driveshaft using the following service procedure:

a. Apply grease to the transaxle oil seal lip.

b. Insert the right side driveshaft with center driveshaft to the transaxle through the bearing bracket.

c. Secure the center driveshaft with a new snapring. Torque the new center driveshaft stopper bolt to 24 ft. lbs.

15. On the 3S-FE engine install the front driveshaft. Install the outboard joint side of the driveshaft to the axle hub. Finger tighten 6 nuts holding the driveshaft to the center driveshaft or the differential side gear.

16. On the 3S-GE engine install the front driveshaft. Install a new snapring to the inboard joint shaft. Apply grease to the transaxle oil seal and install the left side driveshaft to the transaxle. Push the driveshaft in to the correct position. Check that the measurement made in Step 10 is the same. Check that there is 0.08–0.11 in. (2–3mm) of axial play. Check also that the halfshaft will not come out by trying to pull it with your hand.

17. Install the transaxle protector on the 3S-GE engine.

18. Install the right side driveshaft to the axle hub on the 3S-GE engine. Do not damage the driveshaft boot or oil seal.

19. Connect the steering knuckle to the

lower control arm and tighten the bolts to 94 ft. lbs.

20. Connect the tie rod end to the steering knuckle and tighten the nut to 36 ft. lbs. Install a new cotter pin.

21. Tighten the hub locknut to 137 ft. lbs. while depressing the brake pedal. Install the cap and use a new cotter pin.

22. Torque the 6 nuts on the inner halfshaft ends to 27 ft. lbs. while depressing the brake pedal.

23. Install the transaxle gravel shield if so equipped.

24. Fill the transaxle with gear oil or fluid.

25 Install the engine under cover.

1990 Celica

NOTE: *The hub bearing can be damaged if it is subjected to the vehicle weight such as moving the vehicle when the driveshaft is removed. On vehicles with ABS after disconnecting driveshaft work carefully so as not damage the sensor rotor serrations on the driveshaft.*

1. Raise and safely support the vehicle. Remove the wheels.

2. Remove the cotter pin, cap and locknut (loosen locknut while depressing brake pedal) from the hub.

3. Remove the engine under covers.

4. Drain the transaxle fluid.

5. Remove the brake caliper and rotor disc.

6. Disconnect the tie rod end (remove cotter pin and nut) from the steering knuckle.

7. Disconnect steering knuckle from the lower arm.

8. Remove the driveshaft from the steering knuckle using a suitable puller. Cover the driveshaft boot with shop cloth or equivalent to protect it from damage.

9. Remove (tap out with brass punch) the left side driveshaft.

10. Remove the the right side driveshaft. On the 5S-FE engine remove the 2 bolts of the center bearing bracket and pull out the driveshaft with center bearing case and center driveshaft. On the 4A-FE engine use a brass punch tap out the right side driveshaft.

11. Install the left side driveshaft. Apply grease to the transaxle oil seal lip. Position the new snapring opening side facing downward using brass punch, tap driveshaft in until it makes contact with the pinion shaft. Install the outboard joint side of the driveshaft to the axle hub.

12. Install right side driveshaft on the 5S-FE engine using the following service procedure:

    a. Apply grease to the transaxle oil seal lip.

    b. Insert the center driveshaft with the right side to the transaxle through the bearing bracket. When inserting the driveshaft, insert so that the straight pin on the center bearing case aligns with the hole on the bearing bracket.

    c. Install retaining bolts and torque to 47 ft. lbs.

    d. Install the outboard joint side of the driveshaft to the axle hub.

13. Install right side driveshaft on the 4A-FE engine using the following service procedure:

Troubleshooting Basic Driveshaft and Rear Axle Problems

When abnormal vibrations or noises are detected in the driveshaft area, this chart can be used to help diagnose possible causes. Remember that other components such as wheels, tires, rear axle and suspension can also produce similar conditions.

BASIC DRIVESHAFT PROBLEMS

Problem	Cause	Solution
Shudder as car accelerates from stop or low speed	• Loose U-joint • Defective center bearing	• Replace U-joint • Replace center bearing
Loud clunk in driveshaft when shifting gears	• Worn U-joints	• Replace U-joints
Roughness or vibration at any speed	• Out-of-balance, bent or dented driveshaft • Worn U-joints • U-joint clamp bolts loose	• Balance or replace driveshaft • Replace U-joints • Tighten U-joint clamp bolts
Squeaking noise at low speeds	• Lack of U-joint lubrication	• Lubricate U-joint; if problem persists, replace U-joint
Knock or clicking noise	• U-joint or driveshaft hitting frame tunnel • Worn CV joint	• Correct overloaded condition • Replace CV joint

a. Apply grease to the transaxle oil seal lip.

b. Position the new snapring opening side facing downward using brass punch, tap driveshaft in until it makes contact with the pinion shaft.

c. Install the outboard joint side of the driveshaft to the axle hub.

14. Check that the driveshaft will not come out by trying to pull it with your hand.

15. Connect the steering knuckle to the lower control arm and tighten the bolts to 94 ft. lbs.

16. Connect the tie rod end to the steering knuckle and tighten the nut to 36 ft. lbs. Install a new cotter pin.

17. Install all necessary brake components. Tighten the hub locknut to 137 ft. lbs. while depressing the brake pedal. Install the cap and use a new cotter pin.

18. Fill the transaxle with the specified fluid to the correct level. Install the engine under cover. Check front wheel alignment.

OVERHAUL

For service procedures refer to the the "Manual Transaxle CV-Joint Overhaul" section in this chapter.

TRANSFER CASE

The transfer case assembly used on the Celica All-Trac vehicles is a component of the the manual transaxle. No normal service adjustments are preformed on this unit. For removal and installation service procedures refer to the Celica All-Trac "Manual Transaxle Removal and Installation" section in this chapter.

DRIVELINE

Driveshaft, Center Bearings And U-Joints

REMOVAL AND INSTALLATION

1988–90 Celica All-Trac

1. Matchmark the front driveshaft flange and the front center bearing flange. Remove the 4 bolts, washers and nuts and disconnect the rear end of the front driveshaft from the front center bearing flange. Pull the shaft out of the transfer case and remove it. Plug the transfer case to prevent leakage.

2. With an assistant depressing the brake pedal, loosen the cross groove set bolts 1/2 turn. These bolts are at the front edge of the rear driveshaft (rear edge of the rear center bearing.

3. Matchmark the rear flange of the rear driveshaft to the differential pinion flange and then disconnect them.

4. Remove the 2 mounting bolts from the front and rear center bearings and then remove the 2 center bearings, intermediate shaft and rear driveshaft as an assembly.

5. Matchmark the universal joint and the rear center bearing flange, remove the bolts and separate the rear driveshaft from the rear center bearing.

6. Pull the front and rear center bearings from the intermediate shaft.

7. Install the 2 center bearings onto the intermediate shaft ends and then temporarily install the assembly.

8. Align the matchmarks and connect the rear driveshaft to the differential. Tighten the bolts to 54 ft. lbs.

9. Press the front driveshaft yoke into the transfer case, align the matchmarks at the rear of the shaft with those on the front center bearing flange and tighten the bolts to 54 ft. lbs.

10. With the front edge of the rear driveshaft in position, depress the brake pedal and tighten the cross groove joint set bolts to 48 ft. lbs.

11. With the car in an unladen condition, adjust the distance between the rear edge of the boot cover and the rear driveshaft to 2.85–3.05 in. (72.5–77.5mm).

12. With the car in an unladen condition, adjust the distance between the rear side of the center bearing housing and the rear side of the cushion to 0.45–0.53 in. (11.5–13.5mm).

13. Tighten the center bearing mounting bolts to 27 ft. lbs. Make sure that the center line of the bracket is at right angles to the shaft axial direction.

DRIVESHAFT AND U-JOINT OVERHAUL

NOTE: *When preforming this service operation always replace all necessary parts (snaprings, clamps, boots etc.) Always matchmark all flanges, yokes and shafts for correct installation.*

1. Loosen the staked part of the locking nut located on the rear center support bearing front flange.

2. Using a suitable tool hold the front flange and remove the nut and plate washer.

3. Matchmark the rear flange and the front shaft. Using a suitable tool remove the rear flange.

4. Remove the rear center support bearing and plate washer. Repeat Steps 1–4 remove the front center support bearing.

5. Turn the center support bearing by hand while applying force in the direction of rotation.

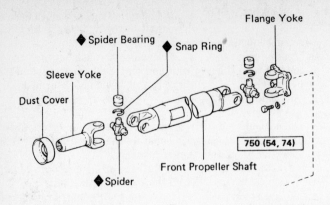

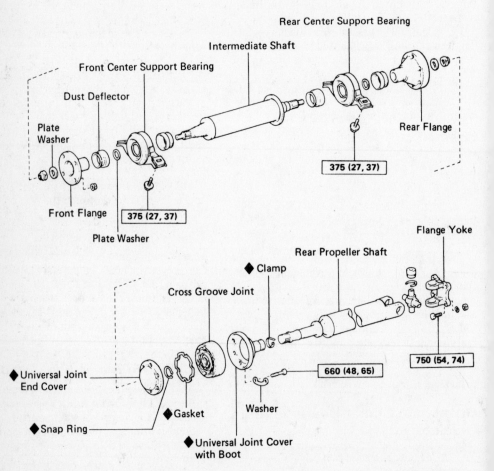

Sleeve Yoke

Spider Bearing

Snap Ring

Flange Yoke

Dust Cover

Front Propeller Shaft

Spider

750 (54, 74)

Rear Center Support Bearing

Intermediate Shaft

Front Center Support Bearing

Dust Deflector

Plate Washer

Rear Flange

Front Flange

375 (27, 37)

Plate Washer

375 (27, 37)

Flange Yoke

Rear Propeller Shaft

Clamp

Cross Groove Joint

Universal Joint End Cover

750 (54, 74)

660 (48, 65)

Gasket

Washer

Snap Ring

Universal Joint Cover with Boot

◆ Non-reusable part

kg·cm (ft-lb, N·m) : Specified torque

Propeller shaft components — Celica All-Trac

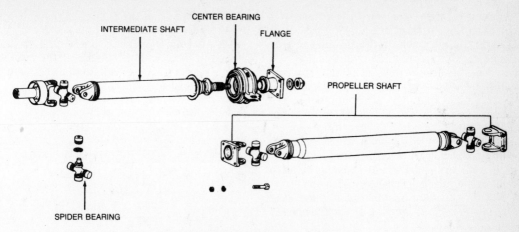

Driveshaft assembly — Supra

Check the bearing for smooth operation. Inspect both support seals for cracks and damage.

6. Remove the cross joint end cover using suitable tools. Matchmark the inner race and cross grove joint shaft.

7. Remove the snaprings using suitable tools that retain the joint to the shaft. Press out the cross joint.

8. Remove the joint end cover and gasket. Loosen the clamp and remove the universal joint cover and boot.

9. At this point of the service procedure, U-joints or spider bearings on driveshaft can be replaced/installed by following these steps:

   a. Place matchmarks on shaft and flange or yoke.

   b. Using a suitable tools remove the 4 snaprings from the grooves. Remove the U-joint or spider bearings by pressing (sometimes these bearings can be removed with a hammer and old $^3/_8$ in. or $^1/_2$ in. socket) the bearing out of the shaft.

   c. When replacing U-joint or spider bearings always use NEW snaprings. Snaprings ring are different thickness so that axial play can be adjusted. Adjust both bearings (one assembly) so that the snapring grooves are at a maximum and equal width. Axial play should be 0–0.0020 in. (0–0.05mm).

   d. Check that the U-joint or spider bearing moves smoothly.

10. After the U-joint or spider bearings are installed in the correct position. Set the front center support bearing onto the intermediate shaft. Install the plate washer and install flange (matchmarks in the correct position).

11. Using a suitable tool hold the flange, press the bearing into position by tightening down a NEW nut and washer to 134 ft. lbs. Loosen the nut. Torque the nut again to 51 ft. lbs. Stake the nut with hammer and chisel.

12. Set the rear center support bearing onto the intermediate shaft. Install the plate washer and install flange (matchmarks in the correct position).

13. Using a suitable tool hold the flange, press the bearing into position by tightening down a NEW nut and washer to 134 ft. lbs. Loosen the nut. Torque the nut again to 51 ft. lbs. Stake the nut with hammer and chisel.

14. Install the universal joint cover (apply sealant to the joint cover) with boot.

15. Install cross joint groove joint (align matchmarks) with snapring, press the universal joint cover with boot and install new boot clamp.

16. Pack the joint with suitable grease and install joint end (with new gasket) cover.

17. Reconnect the intermediate shaft with the rear driveshaft.

Driveshaft, Center Bearing And U-Joints

REMOVAL, OVERHAUL AND INSTALLATION

1986–90 Supra

NOTE: *When preforming this service operation always replace all necessary parts. Always matchmark all flanges, yokes and shafts for correct installation.*

1. Raise the rear of the car and support the rear axle housing with jackstands. Be sure that

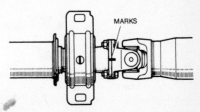

Removing the propeller shaft from the intermediate; the arrow indicates the matchmarks

the car is securely supported. Remember, you will be working underneath it.

2. Scribe alignment marks on the two rear flanges (one comes out of the differential and one is attached to the propeller shaft, they are both attached to each other).

3. Loosen the four attaching bolts and remove the U-joint flange from the differential flange.

4. Remove the two bolts which hold the center support bearing to the body.

5. Pull on the driveshaft assembly so as to remove the yoke from the transmission.

NOTE: *Quickly insert a transmission plug or an old rag into the transmission to prevent fluid leakage.*

6. Scribe alignment marks across the two forward flanges of the propeller (rear) shaft.

7. Unscrew the four bolts and remove the propeller shaft form the intermediate (front) shaft.

8. Put alignment marks on the flange (attached to the center support bearing) and the intermediate shaft and then unscrew the retaining nut.

9. Slide the flange and the center support bearing off the intermediate shaft.

10. At this point of the service procedure, U-joints or spider bearings on driveshaft can be replaced/installed by following these steps:

a. Place matchmarks on shaft and flange or yoke.

b. Using a suitable tools remove the 4 snaprings from the grooves. Remove the U-joint or spider bearings by pressing (sometimes these bearings can be removed with a hammer and old $3/8$ in. or $1/2$ in. socket) the bearing out of the shaft.

c. When replacing U-joint or spider bearings always use NEW snaprings. Snapring ring are different thickness so that axial play can be adjusted. Adjust both bearings (one assembly) so that the snapring grooves are at a maximum and equal width. Axial play should be 0–0.0020 in. (0–0.05mm).

d. Check that the U-joint or spider bearing moves smoothly.

10. After the U-joint or spider bearings are installed in the correct position coat the splines on the rear of the intermediate shaft with multipurpose grease.

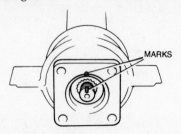

After removing the retaining nut, slide the center support bearing and the flange off the intermediate shaft (note matchmarks).

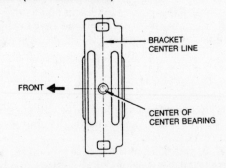

Positioning of the center support bearing is crucial

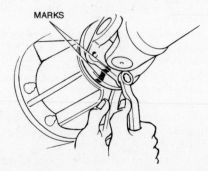

Scribe alignment marks on the two rear flanges before removal

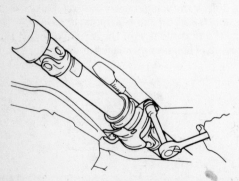

Removing the center support bearing mounting bolts

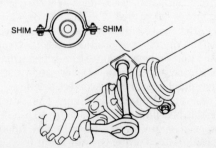

Attaching the center support bearing to the body of the car

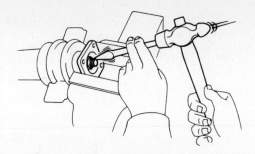

Once installed, use a hammer and a punch to stake the center support bearing retaining nut.

11. Slide the center support bearing and the flange onto the shaft and align the marks.

12. Place the flange in a soft jawed vise and install a new nut to press the bearing into position. Tighten the nut to 134 ft. lbs. Loosen the nut and then tighten it again, this time to 51 ft. lbs.

13. Using a hammer and a punch, stake the nut.

14. Align the marks on the bearing flange and the propeller shaft flange and insert the bolts. Tighten the bolts to 54 ft. lbs.

15. Insert the yoke on the intermediate shaft into the transmission.

16. Align the marks on the propeller shaft flange and the differential flange and insert the bolts. Tighten the bolts to 54 ft. lbs.

17. Place a height spacer if so equipped, between the body and the center support bearing and install the two mounting bolts finger tight.

18. Check that the bearing bracket is at right angles to the propeller shaft. Adjust if necessary.

19. Check that the center line of the bearing is set to the center line of the bracket when the car is in the no-load condition. Adjust if necessary.

20. Tighten the center support bearing mounting bolts to 36 ft. lbs.

REAR AXLE

Determining Axle Ratio

The drive axle of a car is said to have a certain axle ratio. This number (usually a whole number and a decimal fraction) is actually a comparison of the number of gear teeth on the ring gear and the pinion gear. For example, a 4.11 rear means that theoretically, there are 4.11 teeth on the ring gear and one tooth on the pinion gear or, put another way, the driveshaft must turn 4.11 times to turn the wheels once. Actually, on a 4.11 rear, there might be 37 teeth on the ring gear and 9 teeth on the pinion

gear. By dividing the number of teeth on the ring gear, the numerical axle ratio (4.11) is obtained. This also provides a good method of ascertaining exactly which axle ratio one is dealing with.

Another method of determining gear ratio is to jack up and support the car so that both rear wheels are off the ground. Make a chalk mark on the rear wheel and the driveshaft. Put the transmission in neutral. Turn the rear wheel one complete turn and count the number of turns that the driveshaft makes. The number of turns that the driveshaft makes in one complete revolution of the rear wheel is an approximation of the rear axle ratio.

Halfshaft (Rear Driveshaft)
REMOVAL AND INSTALLATION
1988–90 Celica All-Trac

NOTE: *The hub bearing can be damaged if it is subjected to the vehicle weight such as moving the vehicle when the driveshaft is removed.*

1. Raise the rear of the car and support it with safety stands. Remove the wheels.

2. Remove the cotter pin and locknut cap. Have a friend depress the brake pedal and then remove the bearing lock nut.

3. Scribe matchmarks on the inner joint tulip and the side gear shaft flange. Loosen and remove the 4 nuts.

NOTE: *To remove the left driveshaft disconnect strut rod and suspension arms from carrier.*

4. Disconnect the inner end of the shaft by pushing it upward and then pull the outer end from the axle carrier. Remove the halfshaft.

5. Position the halfshaft into the axle carrier and pull the inner end down until the matchmarks are aligned.

6. Connect the halfshaft to the side gear shaft and tighten the nuts to 51 ft. lbs. Torque the strut rod to axle carrier 83 ft. lbs. and suspension arm to axle carrier to 90 ft. lbs.

7. Install the bearing nut and tighten it to 137 ft. lbs. with the brake pedal depressed. Install the cap and a new cotter pin.

8. Check rear wheel alignment. Install the wheels and lower the car.

1986 Supra

1. Raise and support the rear of the vehicle on jackstands.

2. Place matchmarks on the driveshaft (halfshaft) and flanges.

3. Remove the 4 nuts retaining the driveshaft (halfshaft) to the differential and disconnect the driveshaft from the differential.

4. Remove the 4 nuts retaining the driveshaft to the axle shaft and disconnect the driveshaft from the axle shaft. Remove the driveshaft (halfshaft) from the under the vehicle.

5. Installation is the reverse order of the removal procedure. Be sure to line up the matchmarks on the driveshaft (halfshaft) and torque the retaining nuts to 51 ft. lbs.

1987–90 Supra

1. Raise and support the rear of the vehicle safely. Remove the rear wheels.

2. Using a suitable jack, raise the No. 2 suspension arm until it is horizontal. Place matchmarks to the rear driveshaft (halfshaft) and side gear shaft flange.

3. Remove the 6 retaining nuts (while and assistant is depressing the brake pedal) and disconnect the rear driveshaft from the differential.

4. Remove the cotter pin and lock nut cap. Loosen and remove the bearing lock nut.

5. Using a suitable plastic hammer, tap out the rear halfshaft.

6. Installation is the reverse order of the removal procedure. Tighten the bearing lock nut to 203 ft. lbs. and the 6 driveshaft (halfshaft) retaining bolts to 51 ft. lbs.

CV-JOINT OVERHAUL

1. Place removed driveshaft into a suitable holding fixture.

2. Remove (cut off) inboard joint boot clamps.

3. Disassemble inboard joint tulip by following the service procedure as outlined below:

    a. Place matchmarks on the inboard joint tulip and tripod.

    b. Remove the inboard joint tulip from the driveshaft.

4. Disassemble tripod joint by following the service procedure as outlined below:

    a. Using snapring pliers, remove the snapring.

    b. Place matchmarks on the shaft and tripod.

    c. Using a brass punch or equivalent remove the tripod joint from the driveshaft.

5. Remove inboard joint boot.

6. Remove the outboard joint boot clamps (cut off) and boot. DO NOT DISASSEMBLE THE OUTBOARD JOINT!

7. Installation is the reverse of the removal procedures. Pack all CV-joints with suitable grease. Use new boot retaining clamps and snaprings as necessary.

Rear Axle Hub, Carrier And Bearing

REMOVAL AND INSTALLATION

1986–90 Celica — 2 Wheel Drive

1. Raise and safely support the vehicle.

2. Remove the brake drum or disc rotor. Disconnect the hydraulic brake line.

3. Remove the 4 axle hub and carrier mounting bolts. Remove the axle hub and brake assembly.

NOTE: *The bearing assembly can be replaced by removing staked nut, bearing races, seal and pressing bearing in and out. Torque the bearing assembly retaining nut to 90 ft. lbs.*

4. At this point of the service remove the rear axle carrier by following this procedure:

    a. Remove the strut rod mounting bolt from the axle carrier.

    b. Remove all rear suspension arm mounting bolts from the axle carrier.

    c. Remove the 2 axle carrier mounting bolts from the shock absorber. Remove the rear axle carrier assembly from vehicle.

5. Installation is the reverse of the removal procedure. Install new O-ring in axle carrier. Torque the rear axle carrier to shock absorber to 166 ft. lbs. and the 4 axle hub retaining bolts to 59 ft. lbs. Torque strut rod to 83 ft. lbs. and suspension arm to 134 ft. lbs. with vehicle weight on suspension. Check rear wheel alignment as necessary.

1988–90 Celica All-Trac 4 Wheel Drive

1. Raise the rear of the vehicle and support it with jackstands.

2. Remove the rear wheel. Remove the disc brake caliper from the rear axle carrier and suspend it with wire. Remove the rotor disc.

3. Disconnect the parking brake cable assembly and remove the cable.

4. Remove the 2 axle carrier set nuts and the 2 bolts and then remove the camber adjusting cam.

5. Disconnect the strut rod at the axle carrier. Disconnect the No. 1 and No. 2 suspension arms at the axle carrier. Remove the axle carrier and hub.

NOTE: *The bearing assembly can be replaced by removing bearing races, seals and snaprings and pressing bearing in and out.*

6. Installation is in the reverse order of removal. Please observe the following notes:

    a. Tighten the axle carrier-to-shock bolts to 188 ft. lbs.

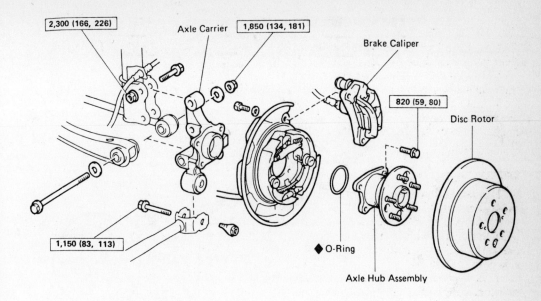

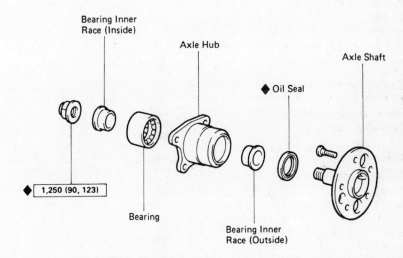

kg·cm (ft·lb, N·m) : Specified torque

◆ Non-reusable part

Rear axle hub and carrier — Celica 2WD

b. Tighten the brake caliper mounting bolts to 34 ft. lbs.

c. Tighten the bearing locknut to 137 ft. lbs. (use new cotter pin).

d. With the wheels resting on the ground, tighten the strut rod bolt to 83 ft. lbs. and tighten the 2 suspension arms to 90 ft. lbs.

e. Check the rear wheel alignment as necessary.

1986 Supra

1. Raise the rear of the vehicle and support it safely with jackstands.

2. Disconnect the axle driveshaft from the axle flange and lower the axle driveshaft out of the way.

3. Apply the parking brake completely (pulled up as far as possible).

4. Remove the axle flange nut.

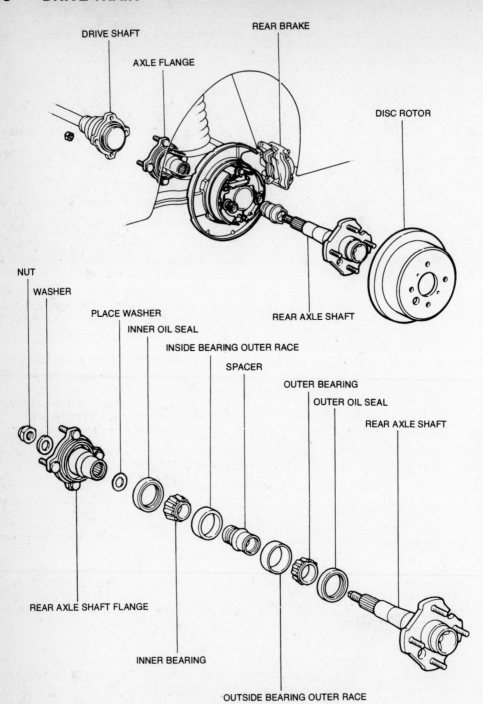

DRIVE SHAFT

AXLE FLANGE

REAR BRAKE

DISC ROTOR

NUT

WASHER

PLACE WASHER

INNER OIL SEAL

INSIDE BEARING OUTER RACE

SPACER

OUTER BEARING

OUTER OIL SEAL

REAR AXLE SHAFT

REAR AXLE SHAFT

REAR AXLE SHAFT FLANGE

INNER BEARING

OUTSIDE BEARING OUTER RACE

Rear axle assembly — 1986 Supra

NOTE: *The axle flange nut is staked in place. It will be necessary to loosen the staked part of the nut with a hammer and chisel, prior to loosening the nut.*

5. Using Toyota special service tool No. SST 09557–22022 (or its equivalent), disconnect the axle flange from the axle shaft. Be care-ful not to lose the plate washer from the bearing side of the flange.

6. Remove the rear brake caliper and disc rotor.

7. Using Toyota special service tool No. SST 09520–00031 (or its equivalent), pull out the rear axle shaft, along with the oil seal and outer bearing.

8. Inspect the components. Clean and inspect the bearings, races, and seal. If these parts are in good condition, repack the bearings with MP grease No. 2 and proceed to Step 15 to install the axle shaft.

9. To replace the bearings and seals use a hammer and chisel, increase the clearance between the axle shaft hub and the outer bearing.

10. Using a puller installed with the jaws in the gap made in Step 9, pull the outer bearing from the axle shaft and remove the oil seal.

11. Drive the outer bearing race out of the hub with a brass drift and a hammer.

NOTE: *Bearing and races must be replaced in matched sets. NEVER use a new bearing with an old race, or vice-versa.*

12. Drive the new outer bearing race into the axle shaft hub until it is completely seated.

NOTE: *The inner bearing race is replaced in the same manner as Steps 11 and 12.*

13. Repack and install both bearings into the hub, being careful not to damage the bearings.

NOTE: *The bearings should be packed with No.2 multipurpose grease.*

14. Drive the seals into place. The inner seal should be driven to a depth of 1.22 in. (30mm); the outer to 0.236 in. (60mm).

15. To install the rear axle shaft apply a thin coat of grease to the axle shaft flange. Install the rear axle shaft into the housing and install the flange with the plate washer.

16. Using Toyota special service tool No. SST 09557–22022 (or its equivalent), draw the axle shaft into the flange.

17. Remove the special service tool and install a new axle shaft flange nut. Torque the nut to 29 ft. lbs. There should be no horizontal play evident at the axle shaft.

18. Turn the axle shaft back and forth and retorque the nut to 58 ft. lbs.

19. Using a torque wrench, check the amount of torque required to turn the axle shaft. The correct rotational torque is 0.9–3.5 inch lbs.

NOTE: *The shaft should be turned at a rate of six seconds per turn to attain a true rotational torque reading.*

20. If the rotational torque is less than specified, tighten the nut 5–10 degrees at a time until the proper rotational torque is reached. DO NOT tighten the nut to more than 145 ft. lbs.

21. If the rotational torque is greater than specified, replace the bearing spacer and repeat Steps 18–20 (if necessary).

22. After the proper rotational torque is reached, restake the nut into position.

23. Install the brake components.

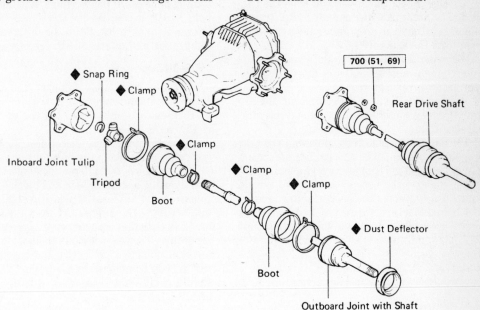

700 (51, 69)

Snap Ring
Clamp
Clamp
Rear Drive Shaft
Inboard Joint Tulip
Tripod
Boot
Clamp
Clamp
Dust Deflector
Boot
Outboard Joint with Shaft

kg·cm (ft-lb, N·m) : Specified torque

◆ Non-reusable part

Differential assembly — Supra

24. Connect the axle driveshaft to the flange and torque the nuts to 51 ft. lbs.

NOTE: *If the maximum torque is exceeded while retightening the nut, replace the bearing spacer and repeat Steps 18–20. DO NOT back off the axle shaft nut to reduce the rotational torque.*

25. Install the rear wheel and lower the vehicle.

1987–90 Supra

1. Raise the rear of the vehicle and support it with jackstands.

2. Remove the rear wheel and tire assembly. Remove the disc brake caliper from the rear axle carrier and suspend it with wire. Remove the rotor disc (check the axle shaft flange runout — 0.0020 in. (0.05mm).

3. Remove the rear driveshaft. Disconnect the parking brake cable assembly.

4. Remove the bolt and nut attaching the carrier to the No. 1 suspension arm. Using a suitable tool, disconnect the No.1 suspension arm from the axle carrier.

5. Remove the bolt and nut attaching the carrier to the No. 2 suspension arm.

6. Disconnect the strut rod from the axle carrier. Disconnect the strut assembly from the axle carrier.

7. Disconnect the upper arm from the body and remove the axle hub assembly. Remove the upper arm mounting nut and remove the upper arm from the axle carrier.

8. Separate the backing plate and axle carrier. Using a suitable puller, remove the upper arm from the axle carrier.

9. Remove the dust deflector from the axle hub. Using a suitable puller remove the inner oil seal. Remove the hole snapring.

10. Using a suitable press, press out the bearing outer race from the axle carrier. Be sure to always replace the bearing as an assembly.

11. Remove the bearing inner race (inside) and 2 bearings from the bearing outer race.

12. Installation is the reverse order of the removal procedure. Torque the suspension mounting bolts and nuts with the vehicle weight on the suspension.

Observe the following torques:

    a. Backing plate to axle carrier nuts — 43 ft. lbs.

    b. Backing plate to axle carrier bolts — 19 ft. lbs.

    c. No. 1 suspension arm nut — 43 ft. lbs.

    d. Upper arm mounting nut — 80 ft. lbs.

    e. Strut assembly nut — 101 ft. lbs. (137 Nm).

    f. Upper arm to body bolt — 121 ft. lbs.

    g. No. 2 suspension arm to axle carrier — 121 ft. lbs.

    h. Strut rod to axle carrier — 121 ft. lbs.

Differential Carrier
REMOVAL AND INSTALLATION
1988–90 Celica All-Trac

1. Raise and safely support the vehicle. Drain the the differential oil.

2. Remove both rear halfshafts (driveshafts) as outlined.

3. Matchmark and disconnect driveshaft (propeller shaft) from the differential.

4. To remove the differential assembly using a suitable jack and block of wood lift the assembly up slightly and remove the retaining bolts and nuts. Remove the rear crossmeber and lower the carrier assembly away from the vehicle.

5. Installation is the reverse of the removal procedure. Torque the 4 bottom differential retaining bolts to 70 ft. lbs. and 2 side mounting bolts to 108 ft. lbs. Torque the rear crossmember bolts to 53 ft. lbs. Refill the differential assembly with 1.2 quarts of API GL-5 gear oil.

1986–90 Supra

1. Raise and safely support the vehicle. Drain the the differential oil.

2. Remove both rear halfshafts (driveshafts) as outlined.

3. Matchmark and disconnect driveshaft (propeller shaft) from the differential.

4. To remove the differential support the assembly using a suitable jack and block of wood. Remove the 4 differential mounting bolts and 2 nuts. Remove the differential from the body.

5. Installation is the reverse of the removal procedure. Torque stud bolts to 58 ft. lbs., rear nuts and bolts to 67 ft. lbs. Torque the differential to body front retaining bolts to 122 ft. lbs. Refill the differential assembly with 1.4 quarts of API GL-5 gear oil.

Suspension and Steering

8

FRONT SUSPENSION

The front suspension system for Celica and Supra is of the MacPherson strut design. The struts used on either side are a combination spring and shock absorber with the outer casing of the shock actually supporting the spring at the bottom and thus forming a major structural component of the suspension.

NOTE: *Exercise extreme caution when working with the front suspension. Coil spring and other suspension components are under extreme tension and result in severe injury if released unexpectedly.*

Shock Absorbers

TESTING

The function of the shock absorber is to dampen harsh spring movement and provide a means of controlling the motion of the wheels so that the bumps encountered by the wheels are not totally transmitted to the body of the car and, therefore, to you and your passengers. As the wheel moves up and down, the shock absorber shortens and lengthens, thereby imposing a restraint on excessive movement by its hydraulic action.

A good way to see if your shock absorbers are working properly is to push on one corner of the car until it is moving up and down for almost the full suspension travel, then release it and watch its recovery. If the car bounces slightly about one more time and then comes to a rest, you can be fairly certain that the shock is OK. If the car continues to bounce excessively, the shocks will probably require replacement.

NOTE: *On MacPherson strut shock absorbers if oil is leaking from the cylinder portion of the assembly the shock absorber must be replaced.*

MacPherson Struts

The struts retain the springs under tremendous pressure, even when removed from the car. For this reason, several expensive special tools and substantial specialized knowledge are required to safely and effectively work on these components. If spring and shock absorber work is required, it is a good idea to remove the strut involved yourself and then take it to a repair facility which is fully equipped and familiar with MacPherson struts.

REMOVAL AND INSTALLATION

1986–90 Celica And Celica All-Trac

1. Raise and safely support the vehicle.
2. Remove the brake hose from the caliper.
3. Disconnect the steering knuckle from the shock absorber assembly.
4. Disconnect the shock absorber (3 top retaining nuts) from the body.
5. Installation is the reverse of removal procedure. Torque the 3 upper shock retaining nuts to 47 ft. lbs. and the shock absorber to steering knuckle to 188 ft. lbs. Bleed brakes and check front end alignment.

1986 Supra

1. Remove the hub cap and loosen the lug nuts.
2. Raise the front of the car and support it on the chassis jacking plates provided, with jackstands.

NOTE: *Do not support the weight of the car on the suspension arm; the arm will deform under its weight.*

3. Unfasten the lug nuts and remove the wheel.
4. Detach the front brake line from its clamp.
5. Remove the caliper and wire it out of the way.
6. Unfasten the three nuts which secure

Troubleshooting Basic Steering and Suspension Problems

Problem	Cause	Solution
Hard steering (steering wheel is hard to turn)	• Low or uneven tire pressure	• Inflate tires to correct pressure
	• Loose power steering pump drive belt	• Adjust belt
	• Low or incorrect power steering fluid	• Add fluid as necessary
	• Incorrect front end alignment	• Have front end alignment checked/adjusted
	• Defective power steering pump	• Check pump
	• Bent or poorly lubricated front end parts	• Lubricate and/or replace defective parts
Loose steering (too much play in the steering wheel)	• Loose wheel bearings	• Adjust wheel bearings
	• Loose or worn steering linkage	• Replace worn parts
	• Faulty shocks	• Replace shocks
	• Worn ball joints	• Replace ball joints
Car veers or wanders (car pulls to one side with hands off the steering wheel)	• Incorrect tire pressure	• Inflate tires to correct pressure
	• Improper front end alignment	• Have front end alignment checked/adjusted
	• Loose wheel bearings	• Adjust wheel bearings
	• Loose or bent front end components	• Replace worn components
	• Faulty shocks	• Replace shocks
Wheel oscillation or vibration transmitted through steering wheel	• Improper tire pressures	• Inflate tires to correct pressure
	• Tires out of balance	• Have tires balanced
	• Loose wheel bearings	• Adjust wheel bearings
	• Improper front end alignment	• Have front end alignment checked/adjusted
	• Worn or bent front end components	• Replace worn parts
Uneven tire wear	• Incorrect tire pressure	• Inflate tires to correct pressure
	• Front end out of alignment	• Have front end alignment checked/adjusted
	• Tires out of balance	• Have tires balanced

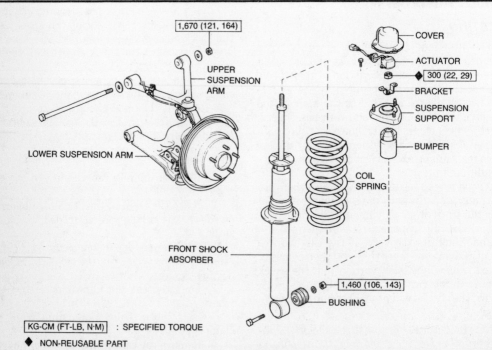

KG-CM (FT-LB, N·M) : SPECIFIED TORQUE

◆ NON-REUSABLE PART

Components of the MacPherson strut assembly — 1987–90 Supra

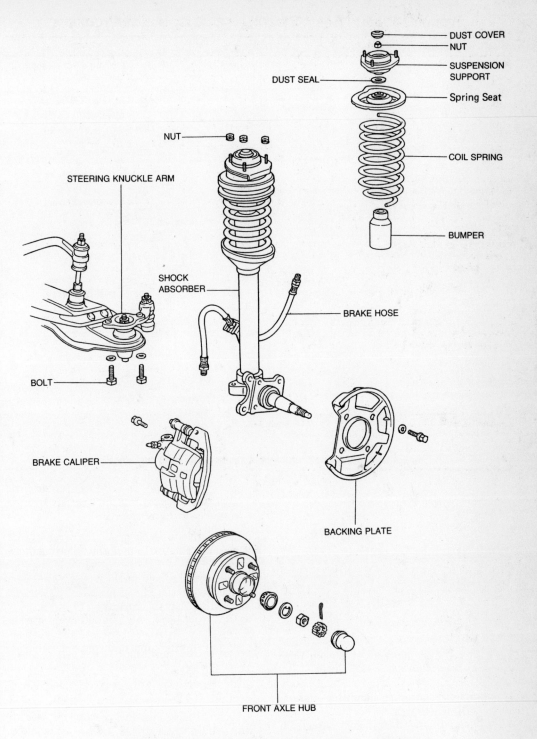

DUST COVER
NUT
SUSPENSION
SUPPORT
DUST SEAL
Spring Seat
NUT
COIL SPRING
STEERING KNUCKLE ARM
SHOCK
ABSORBER
BUMPER
BRAKE HOSE
BOLT
BRAKE CALIPER
BACKING PLATE
FRONT AXLE HUB

Components of the MacPherson strut assembly — 1986 Supra

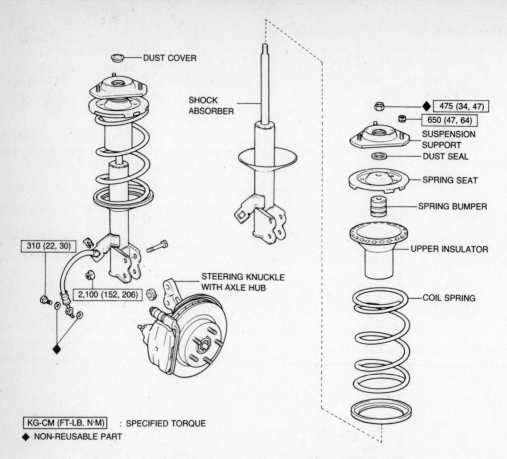

DUST COVER

SHOCK ABSORBER

310 (22, 30)

2,100 (152, 206)

STEERING KNUCKLE WITH AXLE HUB

475 (34, 47)

650 (47, 64)

SUSPENSION SUPPORT

DUST SEAL

SPRING SEAT

SPRING BUMPER

UPPER INSULATOR

COIL SPRING

KG-CM (FT-LB, N·M) : SPECIFIED TORQUE

◆ NON-REUSABLE PART

Components of the MacPherson strut assembly — 1986–90 Celica

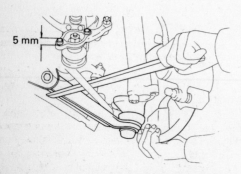

5 mm

Make sure you clear the knuckle collars when prying down the control arm — 1986 Supra

the upper shock absorber mounting plate to the top of the wheel arch.

7. Remove the two bolts which attach the shock absorber lower end to the steering knuckle lower arm.

NOTE: *Press down on the suspension lower arm, in order to remove the strut assembly. This must be done to clear the collars on the steering knuckle arm bolt holes when removing the shock/spring assembly. The steering knuckle bolt holes have collars that extend*

about 5mm (0.20 in.). Be careful to clear them when separating the steering knuckle from the strut assembly.

Installation is performed in the reverse order of removal. Be sure to note the following, however:

8. Align the hole in the upper suspension support with the shock absorber piston rod end, so that they fit properly.

9. Always use a new nut and nylon washer on the shock absorber piston rod end when securing it to the upper suspension support. Torque the nut to 34 ft. lbs.

NOTE: *Do not use an impact wrench to tighten the nut.*

10. Coat the suspension support bearing with multipurpose grease prior to installation. Pack the space in the upper support with multipurpose grease, also, after installation.

11. Tighten the suspension support-to-wheel arch bolts to 27 ft. lbs.

12. Tighten the shock absorber-to-steering knuckle arm bolts to 72 ft. lbs.

13. Adjust the front wheel bearing pre-load as outlined. Bleed the brake system.

1987-90 Supra

1. Raise and safely support the vehicle.
2. Remove the disc brake caliper and suspend it out of the way.
3. Remove the TEMS actuator if so equipped.
4. Loosen (till it can be turn by hand) the piston locknut on top of the shock assembly.
5. Remove upper suspension arm retaining long bolt.
6. Disconnect the shock absorber (3 top retaining nuts) from the body.
7. Disconnect the shock absorber from the lower suspension arm.
8. Installation is the reverse of removal procedure. Torque the 3 upper shock retaining nuts to 26 ft. lbs. (piston rod locknut to 22 ft. lbs.) and the shock absorber to lower suspension arm to 106 ft. lbs. Torque the upper suspension arm retaining long bolt, with the weight of the vehicle on the front suspension to 121 ft. lbs.

OVERHAUL

CAUTION: *The springs are retained under considerable pressure. They can exert enough force when released to cause serious injury. Exercise extreme caution when disassembling the strut.*

This procedure requires the use of a spring compressor; it cannot be performed without one. If you do not have access to this special tool, DO NOT attempt to disassemble the strut.

1. Remove the strut assembly as outlined.
2. Fabricate a strut assembly mounting stand as necessary. Bolt the assembly to the stand and then mount the stand in a vise. On later models install a bolt and 2 nuts to the bracket at the lower portion of the shock absorber shell and secure it in a vise. Do not attempt to clamp the strut assembly in a vise without the mounting stand as this will result in damage to the strut tube.

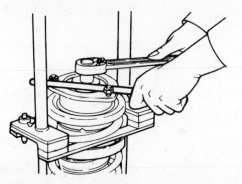

Hold the upper mount with a rod to unscrew the piston rod nut

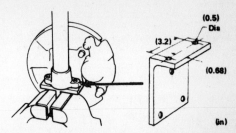

Fabricate a shock absorber stand (arrow) and mount it with the shock in the vise as shown

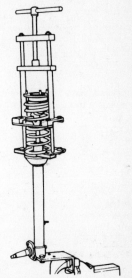

Spring compressor installed on the coil spring for removal

3. Attach a spring compressor and compress the spring until the upper spring retainer is free of any spring tension.
4. Use a spring seat holder to hold the support and then remove the nut on the strut bearing plate.
5. Remove the bearing plate, the support, (dust seal and spring bumper if so equipped) the upper spring retainer and then slowly and cautiously unscrew the spring compressor until all spring tension is relieved. Remove the spring and the dust cover.

NOTE: *Do not allow the piston rod to retract into the shock absorber (if you are going to replace shock absorber lower bushing or spring). If it falls, screw a nut onto the rod and pull the rod out by the nut. Do not use pliers or the like to grip the rod as they will damage its surface, resulting in leaks, uneven operation or seal damage. Be extremely careful not to stress or contact the rod.*

6. Replace the shock absorber assembly and install the compressed spring. Installation is in the reverse order of removal. Align the coil

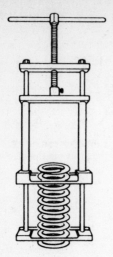

Spring compressor installed on the coil spring for installation — leave the upper coils free

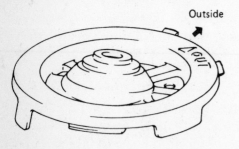

Upper spring seat assembly in correct position

spring end with the lower seat end. Position the OUT marking on the upper spring seat toward the outside of the vehicle. Install and torque a new suspension support nut to 34 ft. lbs. (22 ft. lbs. on Supra vehicles).

Upper Ball Joint

INSPECTION

1987–90 Supra

Remove the front wheels (safely support the vehicle). Move the upper suspension arm up and down. Check the upper ball joint for excessive play. No upper ball joint vertical play is permitted.

REMOVAL AND INSTALLATION

On these models the upper ball joint is an integral component of the upper control arm. Upper ball joint replacement requires that the entire upper arm assembly be replaced. Please refer to "Upper Control Arm" removal and installation service procedures.

Lower Ball Joint

INSPECTION

Celica

1. Jack up the vehicle and place wooden blocks under the front wheels. The block height should be 180.0–200.0mm (7.09–7.87 in.).
2. Use jack stands for additional safety.
3. Make sure the front wheels are in a straight forward position.
4. Check the wheels.
5. Lower the jack until there is approximately half a load on the front springs.
6. Move the lower control arm up and down to check that there is no ball joint play. No ball joint vertical play is permitted.

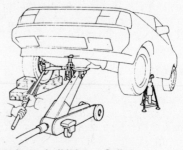

Checking lower ball joint — Celica

1986 Supra

1. Jack up the vehicle and place wooden blocks under the front wheels. The block height should be 180.0–200.0mm (7.09–7.87 in.).
2. Use jack stands for additional safety.
3. Make sure the front wheels are in a straight forward position.
4. Check the wheels.
5. Lower the jack until there is approximately half a load on the front springs.
6. Move the lower control arm up and down to check that the ball joint has no excessive play. The ball joint vertical play specification is 2.5mm (0.098 in.).

1987–90 Supra

1. Jack up the vehicle and safely support.
2. Make sure the front wheels are in a straight forward position.
3. Jack up the lower suspension arm until there is approximately half a load on the front springs.
4. Move the lower control arm up and down to check that the ball joint has no excessive play. The ball joint vertical play specification is 0.3mm (0.012 in.).

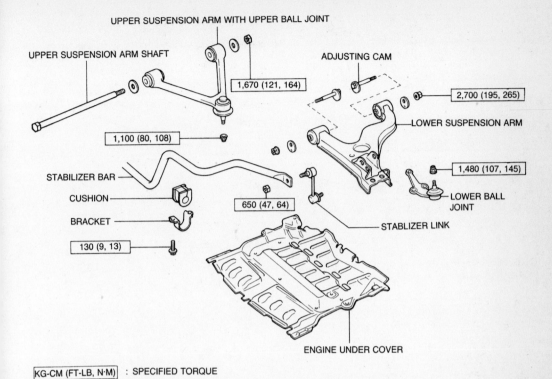

UPPER SUSPENSION ARM WITH UPPER BALL JOINT

UPPER SUSPENSION ARM SHAFT

ADJUSTING CAM

1,670 (121, 164)

2,700 (195, 265)

LOWER SUSPENSION ARM

1,100 (80, 108)

1,480 (107, 145)

STABILIZER BAR

CUSHION

LOWER BALL JOINT

BRACKET

650 (47, 64)

STABLIZER LINK

130 (9, 13)

ENGINE UNDER COVER

KG-CM (FT-LB, N·M) : SPECIFIED TORQUE

◆ NON-REUSABLE PART

Components of the front suspension — 1987–90 Supra

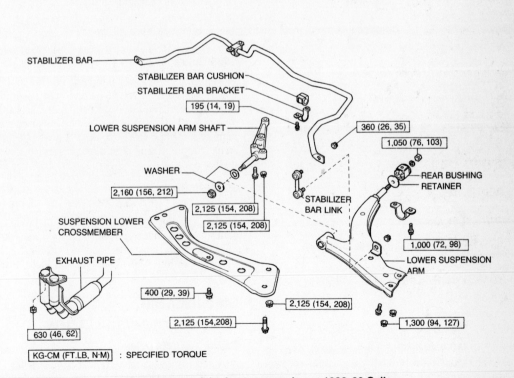

STABILIZER BAR

STABILIZER BAR CUSHION

STABILIZER BAR BRACKET

195 (14, 19)

LOWER SUSPENSION ARM SHAFT

360 (26, 35)

1,050 (76, 103)

WASHER

REAR BUSHING RETAINER

2,160 (156, 212)

2,125 (154, 208)

STABILIZER BAR LINK

SUSPENSION LOWER CROSSMEMBER

2,125 (154, 208)

1,000 (72, 98)

EXHAUST PIPE

LOWER SUSPENSION ARM

400 (29, 39)

2,125 (154, 208)

630 (46, 62)

2,125 (154,208)

1,300 (94, 127)

KG-CM (FT.LB, N·M) : SPECIFIED TORQUE

Components of the front suspension — 1986–90 Celica

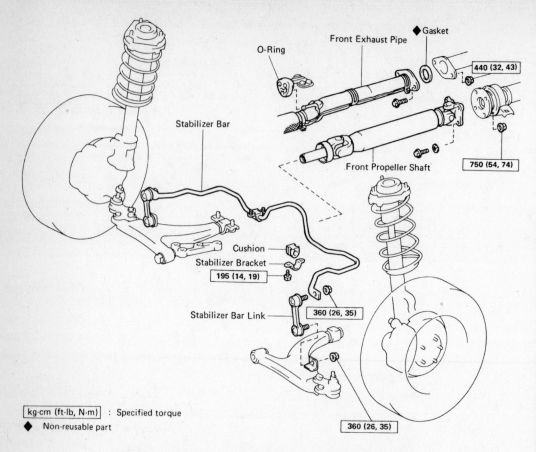

kg-cm (ft-lb, N·m) : Specified torque

◆ Non-reusable part

Components of the front suspension — 1988–90 Celica All-Trac

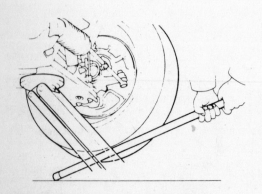

Checking lower ball joint — 1987–90 Supra

REMOVAL AND INSTALLATION

1986–90 Celica

To replace the lower ball joint on these models the lower control (suspension) arm assembly must be removed (then remove cotter pin, retaining nut and ball joint assembly from the steering knuckle). Refer to the "Lower Control Arm" removal and installation service procedures.

1986 Supra

To replace the lower ball joint on this models the lower control (suspension) arm assembly must be removed and replaced as an assembly. The lower ball joint is part of the lower control arm assembly. Refer to the "Lower Control Arm" removal and installation service procedures.

1987–90 Supra

To replace the lower ball joint on these models the lower control (suspension) arm assembly must be removed (then remove ball joint from the suspension arm). Refer to the "Lower Control Arm" removal and installation service procedures.

Stabilizer Bar
REMOVAL AND INSTALLATION

Celica 2-Wheel Drive

1. Raise and safely support the vehicle.
2. Remove the stabilizer bar link assembly (joint stud).
3. Remove both stabilizer bar brackets and cushion from the body of the vehicle.

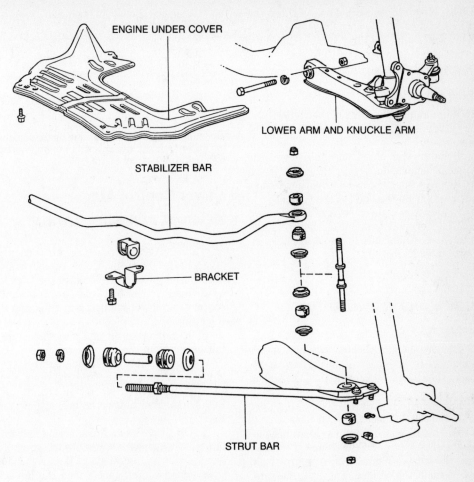

ENGINE UNDER COVER

LOWER ARM AND KNUCKLE ARM

STABILIZER BAR

BRACKET

STRUT BAR

Components of the front suspension — 1986 Supra 1986

4. Disconnect the exhaust pipe from the exhaust manifold and tailpipe exhaust bracket or rubber ring (to gain access for removal of stabilizer bar).

5. Remove the stabilizer bar from the vehicle.

6. Installation is the reverse of the removal procedure. Torque stabilizer bar brackets to 14 ft. lbs. and stabilizer bar link to 26 ft. lbs.

Celica 4-Wheel Drive

1. Raise and safely support the vehicle.

2. Disconnect (matchmarks on flanges) the front propeller shaft from the intermediate propeller shaft.

3. Remove the front propeller shaft from the transaxle. Insert a tool or equivalent into the transaxle extension housing to prevent oil leakage.

4. Disconnect the front exhaust pipe from the tailpipe.

5. Remove the stabilizer bar link assembly (joint stud).

6. Remove both stabilizer bar brackets and

cushion from the body of the vehicle. Remove the stabilizer bar from the vehicle.

7. Installation is the reverse of the removal procedure. Torque stabilizer bar brackets to 14 ft. lbs. and stabilizer bar link to 26 ft. lbs. Refill transaxle as necessary.

1986 Supra

1. Remove the engine under cover.

2. Disconnect each side of the stabilizer bar at the control arms.

3. Remove both stabilizer bar brackets from the strut bar brackets.

4. Remove the two nuts and disconnect the strut bar from the lower arm.

5. Remove the stabilizer bar by pulling it through the strut bar bracket hole.

6. Reinsert the stabilizer bar through the strut bar bracket hole. Install the strut bar bracket and tighten the bolts to 34 ft. lbs.

7. Install the strut bar and tighten the nuts to 48 ft. lbs.

8. Position the stabilizer bar and then in-

stall both bushings and brackets. Tighten the bolts to 9 ft. lbs.

9. Connect the stabilizer bar to the lower arms and tighten the bolts to 13 ft. lbs.

10. Install the engine under cover.

1987–90 Supra

1. Raise and safely support the vehicle.

2. Disconnect the stabilizer link from the stabilizer bar.

3. Remove the stabilizer link from the lower suspension arm.

4. Remove the stabilizer bar with cushions and brackets from the body of the vehicle.

5. Installation is the reverse of the removal procedure. Torque the stabilizer link to stabilizer bar to 47 ft. lbs. and link to lower suspension arm to 47 ft. lbs.

Strut Bar

REMOVAL AND INSTALLATION

1986 Supra

1. Remove the nut, washer, retainer, spacer and cushion from the strut bar where it attaches to the chassis. Do not remove the staked nut.

2. Raise the lower control arm with a floor jack and then disconnect the strut bar.

3. To install check that the distance between the staked nut and the center of the bolt hole on the bar is 369mm (14.531 in.) for 1986 Supra. Adjust the staked nut as necessary. Never adjust the staked nut unless required.

4. Raise the lower arm and connect the strut bar. Tighten to 49 ft. lbs.

5. Reconnect the bar and all the hardware to the chassis bracket. Tighten the bolt to 76 ft. lbs. Check front end alignment.

Upper Control Arm

REMOVAL AND INSTALLATION

1987–90 Supra

1. Raise the front of the vehicle and support it with safety stands. Remove the wheels.

2. Unclip the brake hose bracket at the steering knuckle, remove the retaining nut and press the upper arm out of the knuckle.

3. Remove the upper mounting bolt and nut and lift out the upper control arm.

4. Connect the upper arm to the body. Connect the arm to the steering knuckle.

5. Install the wheels and lower the car. Bounce it several times to set the suspension and then tighten the arm-to-knuckle nut to 76 ft. lbs. Tighten the arm-to-body bolt to 121 ft. lbs.

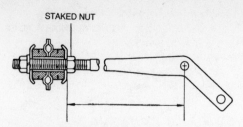

STAKED NUT

When installing the strut bar, the distance between the staked nut and the center of the bolt hole must be measured — 1986 Supra

Lower Control Arm

REMOVAL AND INSTALLATION

1986–90 Celica

1. Raise the front of the vehicle and support it with jackstands. Remove the wheel.

2. Remove the bolt and two nuts and disconnect the lower control arm from the steering knuckle.

3. Remove the nut and disconnect the stabilizer bar from the control arm.

4. On all but the left side control arm on models with automatic transmissions, remove the control arm front set nut and washer. Remove the rear bracket bolts and then remove the arm.

5. On the left side arm on models with automatic transmissions, remove the control arm front set nut and washer. Remove the four bolts and two nuts that attach the lower suspension crossmember to the frame and remove the crossmember. Remove the bolt and nut and lift out the lower arm with the lower arm shaft.

6. On all but the left side control arm on models with automatic transmissions, install the lower control arm shaft washer with the tapered side toward the body. Install the lower arm with the bracket and then temporarily install the washer and nut to the lower arm shaft and bracket bolts.

7. On the left side arm on models with automatic transmissions, position the washer on the lower arm shaft and then install them to the lower arm. Temporarily install the washer and nut to the shaft with the tapered side toward the body. Install the lower arm with the shaft to the body and temporarily install the rear brackets. Install the bolt and nut to the lower arm shaft and tighten them to 154 ft. lbs. Install the crossmember to the body and tighten the four bolts to 154 ft. lbs. Tighten the two nuts to 29 ft. lbs.

8. Connect the lower arm to the steering knuckle and tighten the bolt and two nuts to 94 ft. lbs.

9. Connect the stabilizer bar to the control

arm and tighten the nut to 26 ft. lbs.

10. Install the wheel, lower the vehicle and bounce it several times to set the suspension.

11. Tighten the front set nut to 156 ft. lbs. Tighten the rear bracket bolts to 72 ft. lbs. Check front wheel alignment.

1986 Supra

1. Raise and safely support the vehicle as necessary.

2. Disconnect the knuckle arm from the shock assembly.

3. Push the lower arm down and disconnect the shock from the arm assembly.

4. Disconnect the tie rod end (remove the cotter pin) from the knuckle arm.

5. Disconnect the stabilizer bar and strut bar from the lower arm.

6. Remove the lower arm (rack boot protector) from the crossmember.

7. At this point of the service procedure, remove the cotter pin and nut holding the knuckle arm to the ball joint. Press off the knuckle arm from the lower arm.

8. Installation is the reverse of the removal procedure. Lower car to ground, rock it from side-to-side several times and torque control arm mounting bolts to 80 ft. lbs, stabilizer bar to 13 ft. lbs., strut bar to 48 ft. lbs., and shock absorber to 72 ft. lbs. Check front wheel alignment.

1987–90 Supra

1. Raise the front of the vehicle and support it with safety stands. Remove the wheels.

2. Disconnect the stabilizer bar link from the lower control arm. Remove the locknut and press the ball joint out of the steering knuckle.

3. Disconnect the lower control arm at the strut. Matchmark the front and rear adjusting cams to the body. Remove the nuts and cams and then remove the lower arm.

4. Unbolt the ball joint from the control arm.

5. Install the ball joint to the arm and tighten the nuts to 94 ft. lbs.

6. Position the lower control arm and install the adjusting cams and nuts (finger tight).

7. Connect the ball joint to the steering knuckle and tighten locknut to 92 ft. lbs. (use a new cotter pin).

8. Tighten the arm-to-strut bolt to 106 ft. lbs. Tighten the stabilizer bar link nut to 47 ft. lbs.

9. Install the wheels and lower the vehicle. Bounce the car several times to set the suspension. Align the matchmarks on the adjusting cams and the body and tighten them to 177 ft. lbs. Check the front alignment.

Front Axle Hub and Bearing
REMOVAL AND INSTALLATION

1986 Supra

1. Raise the front of the vehicle and support it with jackstands. Remove the wheel.

NOTE: *To adjust the front wheel bearings on the 1986 Supra (1987–90 do not require adjustment) go to Step 6b.*

2. Remove the front disc brake caliper mounting bolts and position it safely out of the way.

3. Pry off the bearing cap and then remove the cotter pin, lock cap and the adjusting nut.

4. Remove the axle hub and disc together with the outer bearing and thrust washer.

NOTE: *Be careful not to drop the outer bearing during removal.*

5. Using a small pry bar, pry out the oil seal from the back of the hub and then remove the inner bearing. At this point of the service procedure, remove as necessary the bearing races (if bearing is replaced the race must be replaced) using a brass drift pin and hammer drive out the race.

6. Installation is in the reverse order of removal. Please not the following:

a. Place some axle grease into the palm of your hand and then take the bearing and work the grease into it until it begins to ooze out the other side. Coat the inside of the axle hub and bearing cap with the same grease.

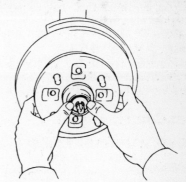

Slide the axle hub and disc off the wheel spindle

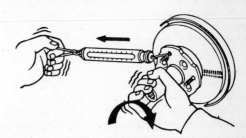

Use a spring scale to measure the wheel bearing preload

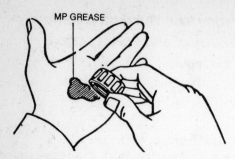

Packing the wheel bearing with grease

b. Install the bearing adjusting nut and tighten it to 22 ft. lbs. Snug down the bearing by turning the hub (back and forth) several times. Loosen the nut until it can be turned by hand and then, using a spring scale, retighten it until the pre-load measures 0–2.3 lbs. Use a new cotter pin when installing the lock cap.

1987–90 Supra

1. Raise and safely support the vehicle.

NOTE: *When removing the axle hub with anti-lock brake system, be careful not to apply excessive force to the hub. Do not let the hub fall.*

2. Remove the speed sensor from the steering knuckle if so equipped.
3. Remove the brake hose bracket from the steering knuckle. Remove the brake caliper and position it out of the way.
4. Remove the rotor disc (matchmark the rotor disc to the axle hub).
5. Disconnect the tie rod end from the steering knuckle.
6. Disconnect the steering knuckle from the upper suspension arm. Remove the steering knuckle.

7. At this point of the service the front axle hub can be disassembled by following this service procedure:

    a. Remove the hub bearing cap from the steering knuckle. Loosen the staked part of axle hub nut and remove the nut.

    b. Use a two armed puller or equivalent to remove the axle hub from the axle bearing.

    c. Remove the hub bearing inner race.

    d. Remove the dust cover from the steering knuckle, outer seal, snapring and hub bearing.

8. Follow this service procedure to reassemble the axle hub:

    a. Install hub bearing and snapring.

    b. Install outer seal and dust cover.

    c. Install the hub bearing inner race to the hub. Install the axle hub to the steering knuckle.

    d. Install and torque a NEW axle hub lock nut to 147 ft. lbs. then stake nut. Install the hub bearing cap.

9. Install the steering knuckle to the upper joint, torque the nut to 76 ft. lbs. (use new cotter pin).

10. Install the steering knuckle to the lower ball joint, torque the nut to 92 ft. lbs. (use a new cotter pin).

11. Install the tie rod to the steering knuckle torque the nut to 36 ft. lbs. secure it with a new cotter pin.

12. Install all remaining components in the reverse of the removal procedure. Check front wheel alignment.

NOTE: *To grease a bearing place some axle grease into the palm of your hand and then take the bearing and work the grease into it*

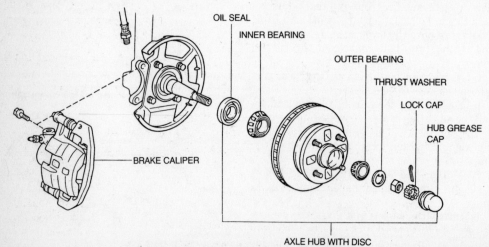

Front axle hub and wheel bearing — 1986 Supra

until it begins to ooze out the other side. Coat the inside of the axle hub and bearing cap with the same grease.

1986–90 Celica

1. Raise the front of the vehicle and support it with jackstands. Remove the wheel.

2. Remove the cotter pin from the bearing locknut cap and then remove the cap.

3. Have a friend depress the brake pedal and loosen the bearing locknut.

4. Remove the brake caliper mounting nuts, position the caliper out of the way with the hydraulic line still attached and suspend it with a wire.

5. Remove the disc rotor assembly. If vehicle is equipped with ABS remove the speed sensor.

6. Remove the cotter pin and nut from the tie rod end and then, using a tie rod end removal tool, remove the tie rod.

7. Place matchmarks on the shock absorber lower mounting bracket and the camber adjustment cam, remove the bolts and separate the steering knuckle from the strut.

8. Remove the two ball joint attaching nuts

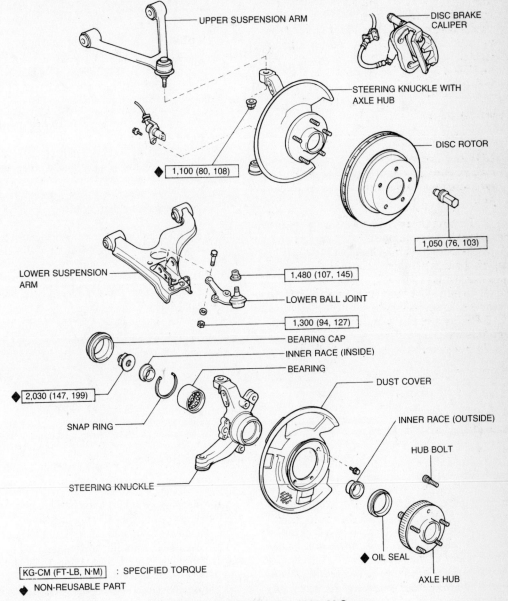

UPPER SUSPENSION ARM

DISC BRAKE CALIPER

STEERING KNUCKLE WITH AXLE HUB

DISC ROTOR

◆ 1,100 (80, 108)

1,050 (76, 103)

LOWER SUSPENSION ARM

1,480 (107, 145)

LOWER BALL JOINT

1,300 (94, 127)

BEARING CAP

INNER RACE (INSIDE)

BEARING

DUST COVER

◆ 2,030 (147, 199)

SNAP RING

STEERING KNUCKLE

INNER RACE (OUTSIDE)

HUB BOLT

◆ OIL SEAL

AXLE HUB

KG-CM (FT-LB, N·M) : SPECIFIED TORQUE

◆ NON-REUSABLE PART

Front axle hub and bearing — 1987–90 Supra

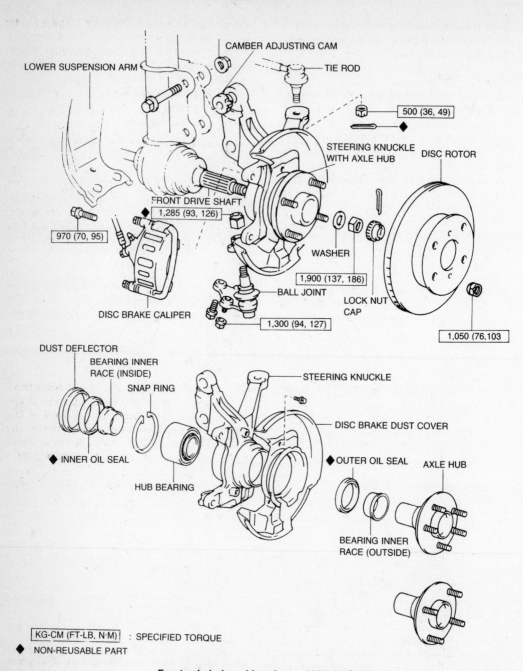

LOWER SUSPENSION ARM

CAMBER ADJUSTING CAM

TIE ROD

500 (36, 49)

STEERING KNUCKLE WITH AXLE HUB

DISC ROTOR

FRONT DRIVE SHAFT

1,285 (93, 126)

970 (70, 95)

WASHER

1,900 (137, 186)

BALL JOINT

LOCK NUT CAP

DISC BRAKE CALIPER

1,300 (94, 127)

1,050 (76,103

DUST DEFLECTOR

BEARING INNER RACE (INSIDE)

SNAP RING

STEERING KNUCKLE

DISC BRAKE DUST COVER

INNER OIL SEAL

OUTER OIL SEAL

AXLE HUB

HUB BEARING

BEARING INNER RACE (OUTSIDE)

KG-CM (FT-LB, N·M) : SPECIFIED TORQUE

◆ NON-REUSABLE PART

Front axle hub and bearing — 1986-90 Celica

and disconnect the lower control arm from the steering knuckle.

9. Carefully grasp the axle hub and pull it out from the halfshaft. This may require a two armed puller or the like.

NOTE: *Be sure to cover the halfshaft boot with a shop rag to protect it from any damage.*

10. Clamp the steering knuckle in a vise. Remove the dust deflector. Remove the nut hold-

ing the steering knuckle to the ball joint. Press the ball joint out of the steering knuckle.

11. Remove the dust deflector from the hub.

12. Use a slide hammer to remove the bearing inner oil seal and then remove the hole snaping with needle nose pliers.

13. Remove the three bolts attaching the steering knuckle to the disc brake dust cover.

14. Use a two armed puller to remove the axle hub from the steering knuckle.

15. Remove the bearing inner race (inside).

16. Remove the bearing inner race (outside).

17. Remove the oil seal from the knuckle.

18. Position an old bearing inner race (outside) on the bearing and then use a hammer and a drift to carefully knock the bearing out of the knuckle.

19. To assembly the front axle hub, press a new bearing into the steering knuckle.

NOTE: *To grease a bearing place some axle grease into the palm of your hand and then take the bearing and work the grease into it until it begins to ooze out the other side. Coat the inside of the axle hub and bearing cap with the same grease.*

20. Using an oil seal installation tool, drive a new oil seal into the knuckle.

21. Install the disc brake dust cover onto the knuckle using liquid sealant.

22. Apply grease between the oil seal lip, oil seal and the bearing and then press the axle hub into the steering knuckle.

23. Install a new hole snapring into the knuckle with pliers.

24. Press a new oil seal onto the knuckle and coat the contact surface of the seal and the halfshaft with grease. Press a new duct deflector into the knuckle.

25. Position the ball joint on the steering knuckle and tighten the nut to 14 ft. lbs. Remove the nut, install a new one and tighten it to 93 ft. lbs.

26. Connect the knuckle assembly to the lower strut bracket. Insert the mounting bolts from the rear and make sure the matchmarks made earlier are in alignment. Tighten the nuts to 188 ft. lbs.

27. Connect the tie rod end to the knuckle, tighten the nut to 36 ft. lbs. and install a new cotter pin.

28. Connect the ball joint to the lower control arm and tighten the bolt to 47 ft. lbs.

29. Install the brake disc and the caliper and tighten caliper mounting bolts. Install the ABS speed sensor if so equipped.

30. Install the bearing locknut while having

someone depress the brake pedal. Tighten it to 137 ft. lbs. Install the adjusting nut cap and insert a new cotter pin. Check the front wheel alignment.

Front End Alignment

Alignment should only be performed after it has been verified that all parts of the steering and suspension systems are in good operating condition. The car gas tank must be empty. The tires must be cold and inflated to the correct pressure and the test surface must be level and horizontal. Because special, elaborate equipment is required for proper front end alignment, it is recommended that the car be taken to a reputable alignment

CASTER

Caster is the tilt of the front steering axis either forward or backward away from the front of the vehicle. If the caster cannot be adjusted within the limits, inspect or replace any damaged or worn suspension parts.

CAMBER

Camber is the slope of the front wheels from the vertical when viewed from the front of the vehicle. When the wheels tile outward at the top, the camber is positive (+). When the wheels tile inward at the top, camber is negative (–). The amount of positive and negative camber is measured in degrees from the vertical and the measurement is called camber

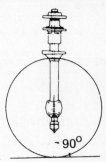

Caster is the forward or backward tilt of the steering axis

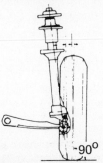

Camber is the slope of the front wheels when viewed from the front of the car

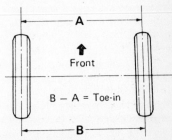

When the front of the tires are closer together then the rear, you have toe-in

Front Wheel Alignment Specifications

Years	Model	Caster		Camber		Toe (in.)	Steering Axis Inclination (deg.)
		Range (deg.)	Preferred Setting (deg.)	Range (deg.)	Preferred Setting (deg.)		
1986–90	Celica	7/16P–1 15/16P	1 3/16P	15/16N–9/16P	3/16N	0.08 out–0.08 in	13 1/2
1986	Supra	3 7/16P–4 15/16P	4 3/16P	1/16P–1 9/16P	1 3/16P	0.04–0.020	10 1/4
1987–90	Supra	6 3/4P–8 1/4P	7 1/2P	13/16N–1 1/16P	1/16N	0.08 out–0.08 in	11

Rear Wheel Alignment Specifications

Years	Model	Caster		Camber		Toe-In (in.)
		Range (deg.)	Preferred Setting (deg.)	Range (deg.)	Preferred Setting (deg.)	
1986–90	Celica	—	—	1 1/4N–1/4N	3/4N	13/64
1986	Supra	—	—	11/16N–5/16P	3/16N	0
1987–90	Supra	—	—	3/4N–1/4P	1/4N	1/8

angle. Camber is preset at the factory, therefore it is not adjustable. If the camber angle is out of tolerance, inspect or replace worn or damaged suspension parts.

TOE

Toe is the amount measured in a fraction of an inch that the front wheels are closer together at one end than the other. Toe-in means that the front wheels are closer together at the front of the tire than at the rear; toe-out means that the rear of the tires are closer together than the front.

REAR SUSPENSION

Coil Springs And Shock Absorber
REMOVAL AND INSTALLATION

1986 Supra
CAUTION: *The coil springs are retained under extreme pressure. They can release enough energy to cause serious injury. Exercise extreme caution when working with the coil springs.*

1. Jack up the rear end of the car, keeping the pad of the hydraulic floor jack underneath the differential housing. Support the suspension control arms with safety stands.
2. Remove the brake hose clips. Disconnect the stabilizer bar end.
3. Disconnect the drive halfshaft at the CV-joint on the wheel side.
4. With a jackstand underneath the suspen-

Correct lower insulator installation

sion control arm, unbolt the shock absorber at its lower end. Using a screwdriver to keep the shaft from turning, remove the nut holding the shock absorber to its upper mounting. Remove the shock.

5. Lower the rear suspension arm (do not pull the brake line or brake cable out). While lowering the rear suspension arm, remove the coil spring, upper and lower spring insulators.

6. Installation is in the reverse order of removal. Check that the lower insulator is installed correctly. Torque the halfshaft nuts to 44–57 ft. lbs.; torque the upper shock mounting nut to 14–22 ft. lbs., and the lower shock mounting nut to 22–32 ft. lbs.

TESTING

Shock absorbers require replacement if the car fails to recover quickly after hitting a large bump or if it sways excessively following a directional change.

A good way to test the shock absorbers is to intermittently apply downward pressure to the side of the car until it is moving up and down for almost its full suspension travel. Release it

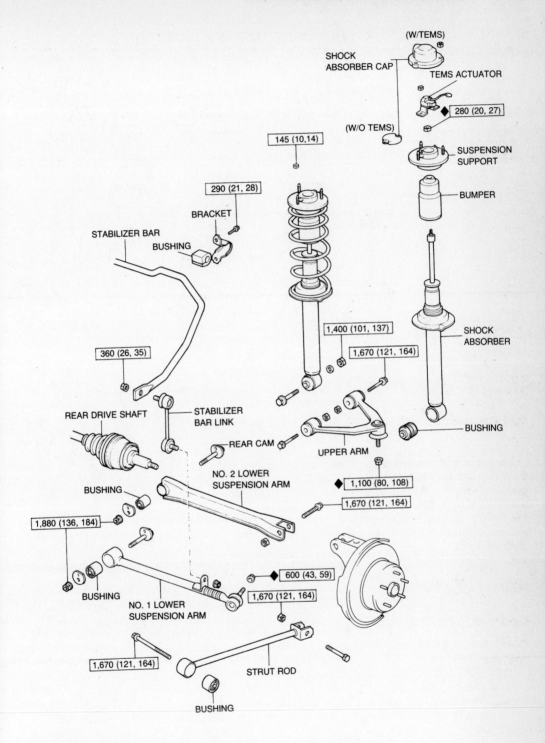

(W/TEMS)

SHOCK
ABSORBER CAP

TEMS ACTUATOR

◆ 280 (20, 27)

145 (10,14)

(W/O TEMS)

SUSPENSION
SUPPORT

290 (21, 28)

BRACKET

BUMPER

STABILIZER BAR

BUSHING

1,400 (101, 137)

SHOCK
ABSORBER

1,670 (121, 164)

360 (26, 35)

REAR DRIVE SHAFT

STABILIZER
BAR LINK

BUSHING

REAR CAM

UPPER ARM

NO. 2 LOWER
SUSPENSION ARM

◆ 1,100 (80, 108)

BUSHING

1,670 (121, 164)

1,880 (136, 184)

◆ 600 (43, 59)

BUSHING

1,670 (121, 164)

NO. 1 LOWER
SUSPENSION ARM

1,670 (121, 164)

STRUT ROD

BUSHING

| KG-CM (FT-LB, N·M) | : SPECIFIED TORQUE

◆ NON-REUSABLE PART

Rear suspension components — 1987–90 Supra

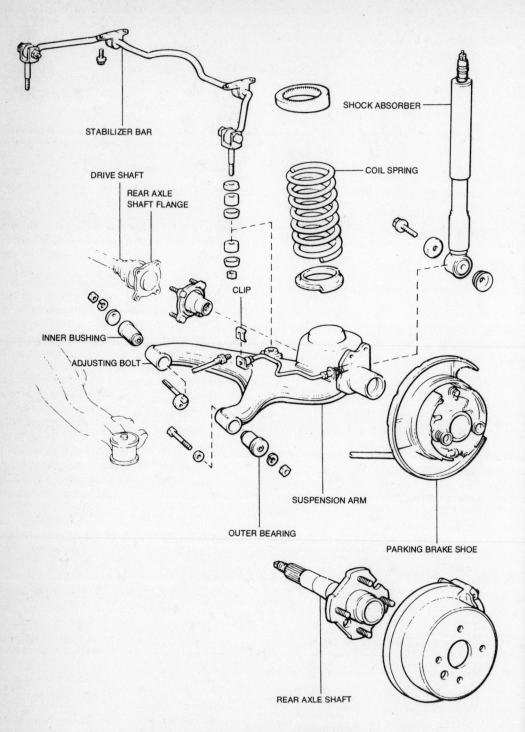

STABILIZER BAR

SHOCK ABSORBER

DRIVE SHAFT

REAR AXLE
SHAFT FLANGE

COIL SPRING

CLIP

INNER BUSHING

ADJUSTING BOLT

SUSPENSION ARM

OUTER BEARING

PARKING BRAKE SHOE

REAR AXLE SHAFT

Rear suspension components -- 1986 Supra

and observe its recovery. If the car bounces once or twice after having been released and then comes to a rest, the shocks are alright. If the car continues to bounce, the shocks will probably require replacement

MacPherson Struts
REMOVAL AND INSTALLATION
1986–90 Celica And Celica All-Trac

1. Raise the rear of the vehicle and support it with jackstands. Position an hydraulic jack underneath the rear hub assembly; raise it just enough to support the assembly.
2. On the liftback, remove the rear speaker grilles.
3. On the coupe, remove the suspension service hole cover.
4. Disconnect and plug the brake line at the backing plate. Remove the clip and E-ring and then disconnect the brake hose and tube from the strut housing.
5. if equipped with rear disc brakes, remove the union bolts and gaskets and disconnect the brake line from the brake cylinder. Remove the clip and E-ring from the strut and then disconnect the brake hose from the strut housing.
6. Loosen, but do not remove, the nut attaching the suspension support to the strut.
7. Disconnect the stabilizer bar at the lower end of the strut housing.
8. Disconnect the strut at the axle carrier.
9. Remove the three strut-to-body bolts and then remove the strut.
10. Tighten the upper strut-to-body nuts to 23 ft. lbs.
11. Tighten the lower strut-to-carrier bolts to 119 ft. lbs.
12. Connect the stabilizer bar to the strut and tighten the bolts to 26 ft. lbs.
13. Tighten the strut holding nut to 36 ft. lbs. Install the dust cover onto the suspension support.
14. Reconnect the brake line and hose. Install all other components that were removed. Bleed the system, lower the car and check the rear wheel alignment.

1987–90 Supra

1. Raise and support the rear of the vehicle safely. Remove the wheel assemblies.
2. Remove the speaker grill and interior quarter panel trim (if equipped with TEMS).
3. Disconnect the strut from the axle carrier.
4. Remove the strut cap. Remove the TEMS (Toyota electronic modulated suspension) actuator.
5. Remove the 3 strut mounting nuts from the body and remove the strut assembly.

6. To install connect the strut assembly with the 3 retaining nuts and torque them to 10 ft. lbs.
7. Connect the strut assembly to the axle carrier and torque it to 101 ft. lbs.
8. Install the TEMS actuator and strut cap. Install the quarter panel trim panel and speaker grille.

OVERHAUL

CAUTION: *The springs are retained under considerable pressure. They can exert enough force when released to cause serious injury. Exercise extreme caution when disassembling the strut.*

This procedure requires the use of a spring compressor; it cannot be performed without one. If you do not have access to this special tool, DO NOT attempt to disassemble the strut.

1. Remove the strut assembly as outlined.
2. Mount the strut assembly in a suitable vise. Using a suitable spring compressor, compress the coil spring.
3. Remove the strut suspension support nut. Remove the strut suspension support, remove the coil spring and bumper.
4. Install the bumper to the strut, align the coil spring end with the lower seat hollow and install the coil spring.
5. Align the strut suspension support hole and piston rod and install it. Align the suspension support with the strut lower bushing.
6. Install the strut suspension support nut and torque it to 36 ft. lbs on Celica and 20 ft. lbs. on Supra.

Control Arm/Suspension Arm
REMOVAL AND INSTALLATION
Celica And Celica All-Trac
LOWER ARM ASSEMBLY

1. Raise and safely support the vehicle.
2. If equipped with ABS disconnect the speed sensor wire from the suspension arm.
3. Disconnect suspension arm from the axle carrier (disconnect long assist suspension arm from axle carrier).
4. Matchmark the adjusting cam bolts to the body of the vehicle. Remove the cam and bolt assemblies.
5. Remove the suspension (mark suspension arm for direction-front to back) arm from the vehicle.
6. Install the arm (in the correct position) so that the complete mark is in the position that it was at removal. Tighten, but do not torque the mounting bolts.
7. Installation of the remaining components is in the reverse order of removal. Lower

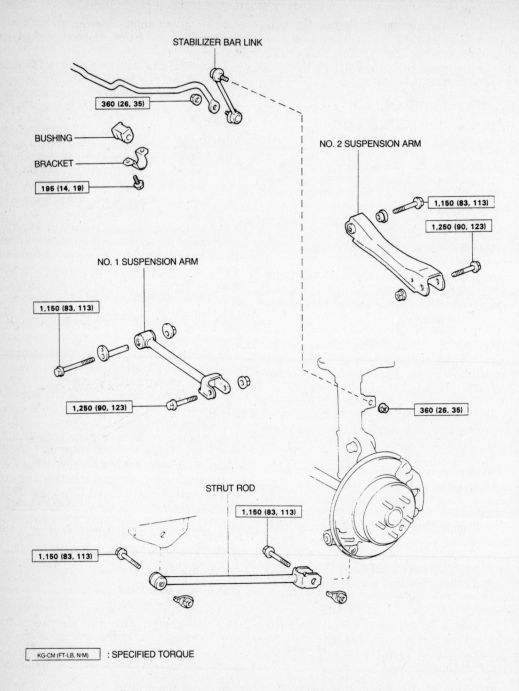

STABILIZER BAR LINK

360 (26, 35)

BUSHING

BRACKET

195 (14, 19)

NO. 2 SUSPENSION ARM

1,150 (83, 113)

1,250 (90, 123)

NO. 1 SUSPENSION ARM

1,150 (83, 113)

1,250 (90, 123)

360 (26, 35)

STRUT ROD

1,150 (83, 113)

1,150 (83, 113)

KG-CM (FT-LB, N·M) : SPECIFIED TORQUE

Rear suspension components — 1988–90 Celica All-Trac

the vehicle and bounce it up and down several times. Torque suspension arm mounting bolts to 134 ft. lbs. Check the rear wheel alignment.

1986 Supra

LOWER ARM ASSEMBLY

1. Disconnect the stabilizer bar at the lower arm.

2. Disconnect the rear halfshaft.
3. Remove the rear axle shaft flange.
4. Remove the disc rotor and then remove the rear axle shaft.
5. Remove the brake backing plate or dust cover. Disconnect and plug the brake line.
6. Disconnect the rear shock absorber at the lower arm.
7. Remove the coil spring.

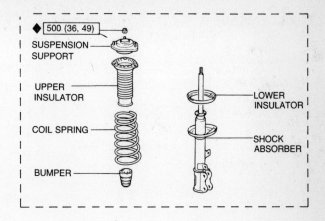

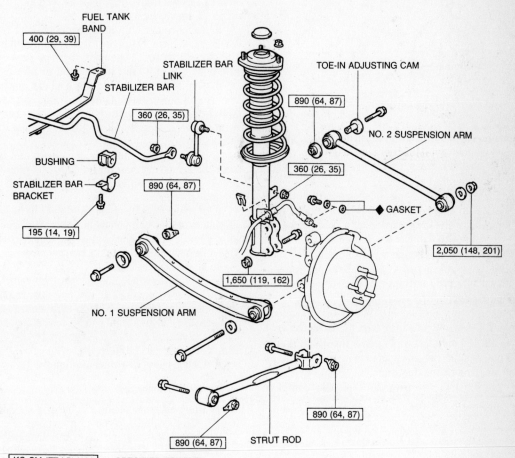

KG-CM (FT-LB, N·M) : SPECIFIED TORQUE

Rear suspension components — 1986–90 Celica 2WD

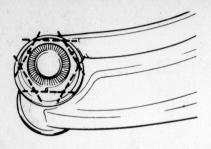

Cut off the flange tip of the bushing — 1986 Supra

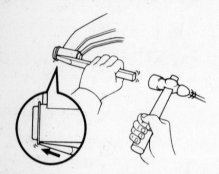

Bend the remaining portion inward — 1986 Supra

8. Remove the two mounting bolts, remove the camber adjusting cam and then remove the rear suspension arm and the lower control bushing.

9. To replace the bushings cut off the flange tip of the bushing and then bend the remaining portion inward with a cold chisel. Be careful not to damage the flange itself.

10. Bend the flange tips in and then pull off the flange with a pair of pliers. Bend the remaining portion of the flange so that the puller can be installed.

11. Using SST 09710–22040 or its equivalent, press out the outer bushing from the arm.

12. To install, simply press the bushing into the arm. Do not allow grease or oil to come in contact with the bushing.

13. Install the arm so that the complete

Use pliers to pull off the flange — 1986 Supra

mark is in the position that it was at removal. Tighten, but do not torque the mounting bolts.

14. Installation of the remaining components is in the reverse order of removal.

15. Lower the vehicle and bounce it up and down several times.

16. Torque the inside suspension arm mounting bolts to 96 ft. lbs.; the outer ones to 85 ft. lbs.

16. Check the rear wheel alignment as detailed previously, adjust if necessary. Bleed the brakes.

1987–90 Supra

LOWER ARM ASSEMBLY

1. Raise the rear of the vehicle and support it with safety stands. Remove the wheels.

2. Remove the halfshaft.

3. Remove the nut and disconnect the No. 1 lower arm from the axle carrier. Matchmark the adjusting cam to the body, remove the cam and bolt and then lift out the No. 1 arm.

4. Remove the bolt and nut and disconnect the No. 2 lower arm from the axle carrier. Matchmark the adjusting cam to the body, remove the cam and bolt and then lift out the No. 2 arm.

5. To install position the No. 2 arm and install the adjusting cam and bolt so the matchmarks are in alignment. Connect the arm to the axle carrier.

6. Position the No. 1 arm and install the adjusting cam and bolt so the matchmarks are in alignment. Connect the arm to the axle carrier. Use a new nut and tighten it to 43 ft. lbs.

7. Install the halfshaft.

8. Install the wheels and lower the vehicle. Bounce it several times to set the suspension and then tighten the body-to-arm bolts and nuts to 136 ft. lbs. Tighten the No. 2 arm-to-carrier bolt to 121 ft. lbs. Tighten the No. 1 arm-to-carrier nut to 36 ft. lbs.

9. Check the rear wheel alignment.

UPPER ARM ASSEMBLY

1. Raise the rear of the vehicle and support it with safety stands. Remove the wheels.

2. Unbolt the brake caliper and suspend it with wire so it is out of the way. Remove the halfshaft.

3. Disconnect the parking brake cable at the equalizer. Remove the 2 cable brackets from the body and then pull the cable through the suspension member.

4. Disconnect the 2 lower arms and the strut rod at the axle carrier. Disconnect the lower strut mount.

5. Disconnect the upper arm at the body and remove the axle hub assembly.

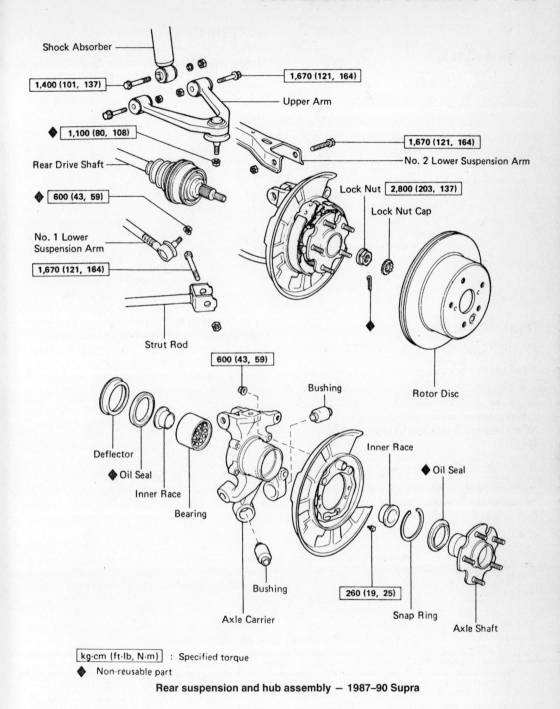

Shock Absorber

1,400 (101, 137)

1,670 (121, 164)

Upper Arm

1,100 (80, 108)

1,670 (121, 164)

No. 2 Lower Suspension Arm

Rear Drive Shaft

Lock Nut   2,800 (203, 137)

Lock Nut Cap

600 (43, 59)

No. 1 Lower
Suspension Arm

1,670 (121, 164)

Strut Rod

600 (43, 59)

Bushing

Rotor Disc

Deflector

Inner Race

Oil Seal

Oil Seal

Inner Race

Bearing

Bushing

260 (19, 25)

Axle Carrier

Snap Ring

Axle Shaft

kg-cm (ft-lb, N·m) : Specified torque

◆ Non-reusable part

Rear suspension and hub assembly — 1987–90 Supra

6. Remove the upper arm mounting nut. Remove the backing plate mounting nuts and separate the plate from the carrier. Press the upper arm out of the axle carrier.

7. To install connect the upper arm to the body.

8. Connect the axle hub assembly to the arm with a new nut.

9. Connect the No. 1 lower control arm with a new nut and tighten it to 43 ft. lbs. Connect the No. 2 lower arm and the strut rod.

10. Tighten the upper arm mounting nut to 80 ft. lbs. Tighten the strut to 101 ft. lbs.

11. Reconnect the parking brake cable and install the halfshaft. Install the brake caliper and tighten the bolts to 34 ft. lbs.

12. Install the wheels and lower the car. Bounce it several times to set the suspension

and then tighten the upper arm-to-body bolt, the No. 2 lower arm-to-carrier and the strut rod to 121 ft. lbs.

Rear Stabilizer Bar

REMOVAL AND INSTALLATION

1. Remove all necessary components to gain access for removal and installation of stabilizer bar. Remove the stabilizer bar brackets.

2. Remove the nuts, cushions and links holding both sides of the stabilizer bar from the suspension arms. Remove the stabilizer bar.

3. To install assemble the stabilizer link sub-assembly and install the link to the arm.

4. Install the stabilizer bar to the link.

5. Install the stabilizer bar bracket to the differential support member.

6. Install all necessary components that were removed for removal access of stabilizer bar.

Rear Wheel Bearings

REMOVAL AND INSTALLATION

All Models

There are no conventional rear wheel bearings that are used on the Celica and Supra models. For more service information please refer to "Rear Axle Hub, Carrier And Bearing" in Chapter 7.

Rear Wheel Alignment

Rear wheel alignment should be performed at a reputable wheel alignment shop or authorized Toyota service facility. Before proper alignment can be performed, check the tires for unusual wear/correct inflation, tire rim (wheel) condition and rear suspension parts. Rear wheel toe in and rear wheel camber can be adjusted on the Celica and Supra vehicles.

STEERING

Steering Wheel

REMOVAL AND INSTALLATION

Two Spoke Wheel Assembly

NOTE: *Do not attempt to remove or install the steering wheel by hammering on it. Damage to the energy absorbing steering column could result.*

1. Position the front wheels in the straight ahead position.

2. Carefully pry off the steering wheel center pad. Some models utilize a mounting screw at the bottom of the pad. Remove the screw and pull the pad out upward.

3. Disconnect all electrical connections at horn pad or steering wheel center pad.

4. Remove the steering wheel center nut.

5. Scribe match marks on the hub and the steering shaft to aid in proper installation.

6. Using a steering wheel puller, remove the wheel.

7. Installation is in the reverse order of removal. Torque the retaining nut to 22–28 ft. lbs.

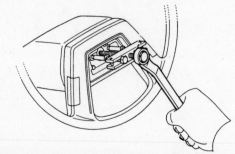

Use a steering wheel puller to remove the wheel

Troubleshooting the Ignition Switch

Problem	Cause	Solution
Ignition switch electrically inoperative	• Loose or defective switch connector • Feed wire open (fusible link) • Defective ignition switch	• Tighten or replace connector • Repair or replace • Replace ignition switch
Engine will not crank	• Ignition switch not adjusted properly	• Adjust switch
Ignition switch wil not actuate mechanically	• Defective ignition switch • Defective lock sector • Defective remote rod	• Replace switch • Replace lock sector • Replace remote rod
Ignition switch cannot be adjusted correctly	• Remote rod deformed	• Repair, straighten or replace

Troubleshooting the Steering Column

Problem	Cause	Solution
Will not lock	• Lockbolt spring broken or defective	• Replace lock bolt spring
High effort (required to turn ignition key and lock cylinder)	• Lock cylinder defective • Ignition switch defective • Rack preload spring broken or deformed • Burr on lock sector, lock rack, housing, support or remote rod coupling • Bent sector shaft • Defective lock rack • Remote rod bent, deformed • Ignition switch mounting bracket bent • Distorted coupling slot in lock rack (tilt column)	• Replace lock cylinder • Replace ignition switch • Replace preload spring • Remove burr • Replace shaft • Replace lock rack • Replace rod • Straighten or replace • Replace lock rack
Will stick in "start"	• Remote rod deformed • Ignition switch mounting bracket bent	• Straighten or replace • Straighten or replace
Key cannot be removed in "off-lock"	• Ignition switch is not adjusted correctly • Defective lock cylinder	• Adjust switch • Replace lock cylinder
Lock cylinder can be removed without depressing retainer	• Lock cylinder with defective retainer • Burr over retainer slot in housing cover or on cylinder retainer	• Replace lock cylinder • Remove burr
High effort on lock cylinder between "off" and "off-lock"	• Distorted lock rack • Burr on tang of shift gate (automatic column) • Gearshift linkage not adjusted	• Replace lock rack • Remove burr • Adjust linkage
Noise in column	• One click when in "off-lock" position and the steering wheel is moved (all except automatic column) • Coupling bolts not tightened • Lack of grease on bearings or bearing surfaces • Upper shaft bearing worn or broken • Lower shaft bearing worn or broken • Column not correctly aligned • Coupling pulled apart • Broken coupling lower joint • Steering shaft snap ring not seated • Shroud loose on shift bowl. Housing loose on jacket—will be noticed with ignition in "off-lock" and when torque is applied to steering wheel.	• Normal—lock bolt is seating • Tighten pinch bolts • Lubricate with chassis grease • Replace bearing assembly • Replace bearing. Check shaft and replace if scored. • Align column • Replace coupling • Repair or replace joint and align column • Replace ring. Check for proper seating in groove. • Position shroud over lugs on shift bowl. Tighten mounting screws.
High steering shaft effort	• Column misaligned • Defective upper or lower bearing • Tight steering shaft universal joint • Flash on I.D. of shift tube at plastic joint (tilt column only) • Upper or lower bearing seized	• Align column • Replace as required • Repair or replace • Replace shift tube • Replace bearings
Lash in mounted column assembly	• Column mounting bracket bolts loose • Broken weld nuts on column jacket • Column capsule bracket sheared	• Tighten bolts • Replace column jacket • Replace bracket assembly

Troubleshooting the Steering Column (cont.)

Problem	Cause	Solution
Lash in mounted column assembly (cont.)	• Column bracket to column jacket mounting bolts loose	• Tighten to specified torque
	• Loose lock shoes in housing (tilt column only)	• Replace shoes
	• Loose pivot pins (tilt column only)	• Replace pivot pins and support
	• Loose lock shoe pin (tilt column only)	• Replace pin and housing
	• Loose support screws (tilt column only)	• Tighten screws
Housing loose (tilt column only)	• Excessive clearance between holes in support or housing and pivot pin diameters	• Replace pivot pins and support
	• Housing support-screws loose	• Tighten screws
Steering wheel loose—every other tilt position (tilt column only)	• Loose fit between lock shoe and lock shoe pivot pin	• Replace lock shoes and pivot pin
Steering column not locking in any tilt position (tilt column only)	• Lock shoe seized on pivot pin	• Replace lock shoes and pin
	• Lock shoe grooves have burrs or are filled with foreign material	• Clean or replace lock shoes
	• Lock shoe springs weak or broken	• Replace springs
Noise when tilting column (tilt column only)	• Upper tilt bumpers worn	• Replace tilt bumper
	• Tilt spring rubbing in housing	• Lubricate with chassis grease
One click when in "off-lock" position and the steering wheel is moved	• Seating of lock bolt	• None. Click is normal characteristic sound produced by lock bolt as it seats.
High shift effort (automatic and tilt column only)	• Column not correctly aligned	• Align column
	• Lower bearing not aligned correctly	• Assemble correctly
	• Lack of grease on seal or lower bearing areas	• Lubricate with chassis grease
Improper transmission shifting— automatic and tilt column only	• Sheared shift tube joint	• Replace shift tube
	• Improper transmission gearshift linkage adjustment	• Adjust linkage
	• Loose lower shift lever	• Replace shift tube

Three Spoke Wheel Assembly

NOTE: *Do not attempt to remove or install the steering wheel by hammering on it. Damage to the energy absorbing steering column could result.*

1. Disconnect the negative battery cable. Position the wheels in the straight ahead position.

NOTE: *On 1990 SRS vehicles, you must wait AT LEAST 30 seconds after disconnecting the battery before doing any work. The SRS has a built-in backup which will allow the system to remain energized for a period of time after the power is disconnected.*

2. Loosen the trim pad retaining screws from the back of the steering wheel.

3. Lift the trim pad and horn button assembly from the wheel.

4. Disconnect all electrical connections at steering wheel trim pad.

5. Remove the steering wheel hub retaining nut.

6. Scribe match marks on the hub and the steering shaft to aid in proper installation.

7. Using a steering wheel puller, remove the wheel.

8. Installation is in the reverse order of removal. Tighten the steering wheel hub retaining nut to 25 ft. lbs.

Combination Switch
REMOVAL AND INSTALLATION
Celica And Supra

1. Disconnect the negative battery cable.

NOTE: *On 1990 SRS vehicles, you must wait AT LEAST 30 seconds after disconnecting the battery before doing any work. The SRS has a built-in backup which will allow the system to remain energized for a period of time after the power is disconnected.*

2. Unscrew the two retaining bolts and remove the steering column garnish.

Troubleshooting the Turn Signal Switch

Problem	Cause	Solution
Turn signal will not cancel	• Loose switch mounting screws • Switch or anchor bosses broken • Broken, missing or out of position detent, or cancelling spring	• Tighten screws • Replace switch • Reposition springs or replace switch as required
Turn signal difficult to operate	• Turn signal lever loose • Switch yoke broken or distorted • Loose or misplaced springs • Foreign parts and/or materials in switch • Switch mounted loosely	• Tighten mounting screws • Replace switch • Reposition springs or replace switch • Remove foreign parts and/or material • Tighten mounting screws
Turn signal will not indicate lane change	• Broken lane change pressure pad or spring hanger • Broken, missing or misplaced lane change spring • Jammed wires	• Replace switch • Replace or reposition as required • Loosen mounting screws, reposition wires and retighten screws
Turn signal will not stay in turn position	• Foreign material or loose parts impeding movement of switch yoke • Defective switch	• Remove material and/or parts • Replace switch
Hazard switch cannot be pulled out	• Foreign material between hazard support cancelling leg and yoke	• Remove foreign material. No foreign material impeding function of hazard switch—replace turn signal switch.
No turn signal lights	• Inoperative turn signal flasher • Defective or blown fuse • Loose chassis to column harness connector • Disconnect column to chassis connector. Connect new switch to chassis and operate switch by hand. If vehicle lights now operate normally, signal switch is inoperative • If vehicle lights do not operate, check chassis wiring for opens, grounds, etc.	• Replace turn signal flasher • Replace fuse • Connect securely • Replace signal switch • Repair chassis wiring as required
Instrument panel turn indicator lights on but not flashing	• Burned out or damaged front or rear turn signal bulb • If vehicle lights do not operate, check light sockets for high resistance connections, the chassis wiring for opens, grounds, etc. • Inoperative flasher • Loose chassis to column harness connection • Inoperative turn signal switch • To determine if turn signal switch is defective, substitute new switch into circuit and operate switch by hand. If the vehicle's lights operate normally, signal switch is inoperative.	• Replace bulb • Repair chassis wiring as required • Replace flasher • Connect securely • Replace turn signal switch • Replace turn signal switch
Stop light not on when turn indicated	• Loose column to chassis connection • Disconnect column to chassis connector. Connect new switch into system without removing old.	• Connect securely • Replace signal switch

Troubleshooting the Turn Signal Switch (cont.)

Problem	Cause	Solution
Stop light not on when turn indicated (cont.)	Operate switch by hand. If brake lights work with switch in the turn position, signal switch is defective.	
	• If brake lights do not work, check connector to stop light sockets for grounds, opens, etc.	• Repair connector to stop light circuits using service manual as guide
Turn indicator panel lights not flashing	• Burned out bulbs • High resistance to ground at bulb socket • Opens, ground in wiring harness from front turn signal bulb socket to indicator lights	• Replace bulbs • Replace socket • Locate and repair as required
Turn signal lights flash very slowly	• High resistance ground at light sockets • Incorrect capacity turn signal flasher or bulb • If flashing rate is still extremely slow, check chassis wiring harness from the connector to light sockets for high resistance • Loose chassis to column harness connection • Disconnect column to chassis connector. Connect new switch into system without removing old. Operate switch by hand. If flashing occurs at normal rate, the signal switch is defective.	• Repair high resistance grounds at light sockets • Replace turn signal flasher or bulb • Locate and repair as required • Connect securely • Replace turn signal switch
Hazard signal lights will not flash—turn signal functions normally	• Blow fuse • Inoperative hazard warning flasher • Loose chassis-to-column harness connection • Disconnect column to chassis connector. Connect new switch into system without removing old. Depress the hazard warning lights. If they now work normally, turn signal switch is defective. • If lights do not flash, check wiring harness "K" lead for open between hazard flasher and connector. If open, fuse block is defective	• Replace fuse • Replace hazard warning flasher in fuse panel • Conect securely • Replace turn signal switch • Repair or replace brown wire or connector as required

3. Remove the upper and lower steering column covers.

4. Remove the steering wheel as detailed previously.

5. Trace the switch wiring harness to the multi-connector. Push in the lock levers and pull apart the connector.

6. On models equipped with electronic modulated suspension (TEMS) remove the steering sensor as necessary. Unscrew the 4 mounting screws and remove the switch.

7. Installation is in the reverse order of removal procedure.

Ignition Lock/Switch

REMOVAL AND INSTALLATION

Celica And Supra

1. Disconnect the negative battery cable.

NOTE: *On 1990 SRS vehicles, you must wait AT LEAST 30 seconds after disconnecting the battery before doing any work. The SRS has a built-in backup which will allow the system to remain energized for a period of time after the power is disconnected.*

2. Unfasten the ignition switch connector underneath the instrument panel.

Troubleshooting the Power Steering Gear

Problem	Cause	Solution
Hissing noise in steering gear	• There is some noise in all power steering systems. One of the most common is a hissing sound most evident at standstill parking. There is no relationship between this noise and performance of the steering. Hiss may be expected when steering wheel is at end of travel or when slowly turning at standstill.	• Slight hiss is normal and in no way affects steering. Do not replace valve unless hiss is extremely objectionable. A replacement valve will also exhibit slight noise and is not always a cure. Investigate clearance around flexible coupling rivets. Be sure steering shaft and gear are aligned so flexible coupling rotates in a flat plane and is not distorted as shaft rotates. Any metal-to-metal contacts through flexible coupling will transmit valve hiss into passenger compartment through the steering column.
Rattle or chuckle noise in steering gear	• Gear loose on frame	• Check gear-to-frame mounting screws. Tighten screws to 88 N·m (65 foot pounds) torque.
	• Steering linkage looseness	• Check linkage pivot points for wear. Replace if necessary.
	• Pressure hose touching other parts of car	• Adjust hose position. Do not bend tubing by hand.
	• Loose pitman shaft over center adjustment **NOTE:** A slight rattle may occur on turns because of increased clearance off the "high point." This is normal and clearance must not be reduced below specified limits to eliminate this slight rattle.	• Adjust to specifications
	• Loose pitman arm	• Tighten pitman arm nut to specifications
Squawk noise in steering gear when turning or recovering from a turn	• Damper O-ring on valve spool cut	• Replace damper O-ring
Poor return of steering wheel to center	• Tires not properly inflated	• Inflate to specified pressure
	• Lack of lubrication in linkage and ball joints	• Lube linkage and ball joints
	• Lower coupling flange rubbing against steering gear adjuster plug	• Loosen pinch bolt and assemble properly
	• Steering gear to column misalignment	• Align steering column
	• Improper front wheel alignment	• Check and adjust as necessary
	• Steering linkage binding	• Replace pivots
	• Ball joints binding	• Replace ball joints
	• Steering wheel rubbing against housing	• Align housing
	• Tight or frozen steering shaft bearings	• Replace bearings
	• Sticking or plugged valve spool	• Remove and clean or replace valve
	• Steering gear adjustments over specifications	• Check adjustment with gear out of car. Adjust as required.
	• Kink in return hose	• Replace hose
Car leads to one side or the other (keep in mind road condition and wind. Test car in both directions on flat road)	• Front end misaligned	• Adjust to specifications
	• Unbalanced steering gear valve **NOTE:** If this is cause, steering effort will be very light in direction of lead and normal or heavier in opposite direction	• Replace valve

Troubleshooting the Power Steering Gear (cont.)

Problem	Cause	Solution
Momentary increase in effort when turning wheel fast to right or left	• Low oil level • Pump belt slipping • High internal leakage	• Add power steering fluid as required • Tighten or replace belt • Check pump pressure. (See pressure test)
Steering wheel surges or jerks when turning with engine running especially during parking	• Low oil level • Loose pump belt • Steering linkage hitting engine oil pan at full turn • Insufficient pump pressure • Pump flow control valve sticking	• Fill as required • Adjust tension to specification • Correct clearance • Check pump pressure. (See pressure test). Replace relief valve if defective. • Inspect for varnish or damage, replace if necessary
Excessive wheel kickback or loose steering	• Air in system • Steering gear loose on frame • Steering linkage joints worn enough to be loose • Worn poppet valve • Loose thrust bearing preload adjustment • Excessive overcenter lash	• Add oil to pump reservoir and bleed by operating steering. Check hose connectors for proper torque and adjust as required. • Tighten attaching screws to specified torque • Replace loose pivots • Replace poppet valve • Adjust to specification with gear out of vehicle • Adjust to specification with gear out of car
Hard steering or lack of assist	• Loose pump belt • Low oil level **NOTE:** Low oil level will also result in excessive pump noise • Steering gear to column misalignment • Lower coupling flange rubbing against steering gear adjuster plug • Tires not properly inflated	• Adjust belt tension to specification • Fill to proper level. If excessively low, check all lines and joints for evidence of external leakage. Tighten loose connectors. • Align steering column • Loosen pinch bolt and assemble properly • Inflate to recommended pressure
Foamy milky power steering fluid, low fluid level and possible low pressure	• Air in the fluid, and loss of fluid due to internal pump leakage causing overflow	• Check for leak and correct. Bleed system. Extremely cold temperatures will cause system aeriation should the oil level be low. If oil level is correct and pump still foams, remove pump from vehicle and separate reservoir from housing. Check welsh plug and housing for cracks. If plug is loose or housing is cracked, replace housing.
Low pressure due to steering pump	• Flow control valve stuck or inoperative • Pressure plate not flat against cam ring	• Remove burrs or dirt or replace. Flush system. • Correct
Low pressure due to steering gear	• Pressure loss in cylinder due to worn piston ring or badly worn housing bore • Leakage at valve rings, valve body-to-worm seal	• Remove gear from car for disassembly and inspection of ring and housing bore • Remove gear from car for disassembly and replace seals

Troubleshooting the Power Steering Pump

Problem	Cause	Solution
Chirp noise in steering pump	• Loose belt	• Adjust belt tension to specification
Belt squeal (particularly noticeable at full wheel travel and stand still parking)	• Loose belt	• Adjust belt tension to specification
Growl noise in steering pump	• Excessive back pressure in hoses or steering gear caused by restriction	• Locate restriction and correct. Replace part if necessary.
Growl noise in steering pump (particularly noticeable at stand still parking)	• Scored pressure plates, thrust plate or rotor • Extreme wear of cam ring	• Replace parts and flush system • Replace parts
Groan noise in steering pump	• Low oil level • Air in the oil. Poor pressure hose connection.	• Fill reservoir to proper level • Tighten connector to specified torque. Bleed system by operating steering from right to left—full turn.
Rattle noise in steering pump	• Vanes not installed properly • Vanes sticking in rotor slots	• Install properly • Free up by removing burrs, varnish, or dirt
Swish noise in steering pump	• Defective flow control valve	• Replace part
Whine noise in steering pump	• Pump shaft bearing scored	• Replace housing and shaft. Flush system.
Hard steering or lack of assist	• Loose pump belt • Low oil level in reservoir **NOTE:** Low oil level will also result in excessive pump noise • Steering gear to column misalignment • Lower coupling flange rubbing against steering gear adjuster plug • Tires not properly inflated	• Adjust belt tension to specification • Fill to proper level. If excessively low, check all lines and joints for evidence of external leakage. Tighten loose connectors. • Align steering column • Loosen pinch bolt and assemble properly • Inflate to recommended pressure
Foaming milky power steering fluid, low fluid level and possible low pressure	• Air in the fluid, and loss of fluid due to internal pump leakage causing overflow	• Check for leaks and correct. Bleed system. Extremely cold temperatures will cause system aeriation should the oil level be low. If oil level is correct and pump still foams, remove pump from vehicle and separate reservoir from body. Check welsh plug and body for cracks. If plug is loose or body is cracked, replace body.
Low pump pressure	• Flow control valve stuck or inoperative • Pressure plate not flat against cam ring	• Remove burrs or dirt or replace. Flush system. • Correct
Momentary increase in effort when turning wheel fast to right or left	• Low oil level in pump • Pump belt slipping • High internal leakage	• Add power steering fluid as required • Tighten or replace belt • Check pump pressure. (See pressure test)
Steering wheel surges or jerks when turning with engine running especially during parking	• Low oil level • Loose pump belt • Steering linkage hitting engine oil pan at full turn • Insufficient pump pressure	• Fill as required • Adjust tension to specification • Correct clearance • Check pump pressure. (See pressure test). Replace flow control valve if defective.

Troubleshooting the Power Steering Pump (cont.)

Problem	Cause	Solution
Steering wheel surges or jerks when turning with engine running especially during parking (cont.)	• Sticking flow control valve	• Inspect for varnish or damage, replace if necessary
Excessive wheel kickback or loose steering	• Air in system	• Add oil to pump reservoir and bleed by operating steering. Check hose connectors for proper torque and adjust as required.
Low pump pressure	• Extreme wear of cam ring • Scored pressure plate, thrust plate, or rotor • Vanes not installed properly • Vanes sticking in rotor slots • Cracked or broken thrust or pressure plate	• Replace parts. Flush system. • Replace parts. Flush system. • Install properly • Freeup by removing burrs, varnish, or dirt • Replace part

3. Remove the screws which secure the upper and lower halves of the steering column cover.

4. Turn the lock cylinder to the **ACC** position with the ignition key.

5. Push the lock cylinder stop in with a small, round object (cotter pin, punch, etc.). It may be necessary to remove the steering wheel and combination switch first for easier removal.

6. Withdraw the lock cylinder from the lock housing while depressing the stop tab.

7. To remove the ignition switch, remove its securing screws (on the column tube non-tilt wheel) and withdraw the switch from the lock housing.

8. To install align the locking cam with the hole in the ignition switch and insert the switch into the lock housing.

9. Secure the switch with its screw(s).

10. Make sure that both the lock cylinder and column lock are in the **ACC** position. Slide the cylinder into the lock housing until the stop tab engages the hole in the lock.

11. The remainder of the installation in the reverse order of removal.

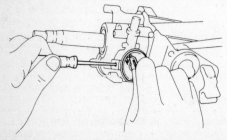

Push the lock cylinder stop in to remove the cylinder

Steering Column

REMOVAL AND INSTALLATION

Celica And Supra

1. Disconnect the negative battery cable.

NOTE: *On 1990 SRS vehicles, you must wait AT LEAST 30 seconds after disconnecting the battery before doing any work. The SRS has a built-in backup which will allow the system to remain energized for a period of time after the power is disconnected.*

2. On Celica models, remove the universal joint at the steering gear (under the car-remove the front wheel as necessary) and at the main shaft of the steering column assembly.

3. On Supra models, disconnect upper (joint that is on the column assembly) universal joint from the intermediate shaft.

4. Remove the steering wheel as outlined. Remove the instrument lower finish panels, air ducts and column covers.

5. Disconnect all electrical connections for ignition switch and combination switch. Remove the combination switch as necessary.

6. On Celica models, loosen column hole cover clamp bolt. Remove the support mounting bolt. Remove the 4 column tube mounting bolts. Pull out steering column.

7. On Supra models, remove the 2 (3 bolts used on the 1987–90 models/some models have one bolt to the hole cover that must be removed from the engine compartment) mounting bolts from the column hole cover plate. Remove 2 column bracket mounting nuts. Turn the steering column assembly clockwise and remove it from the vehicle as necessary.

8. Place the steering column assembly in the installed position. Tighten all necessary

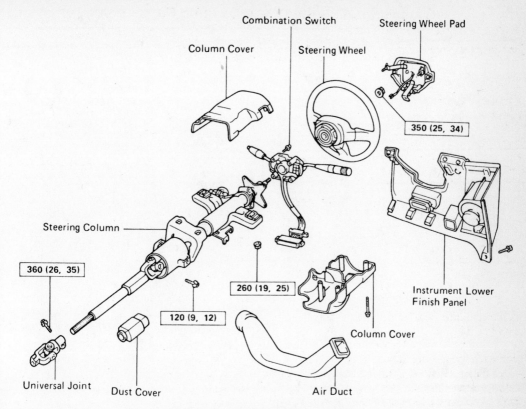

Steering column assembly — Celica

mounting nuts (torque evenly). Install and tighten all column cover bolts. Tighten column hole cover clamp bolt as necessary.

9. Install combination switch. Reconnect all electrical connectors.

10. Install instrument lower finish panels, air duct and column covers.

11. Install or connect the universal joint. Insure that the retaining bolts are installed through both shaft grooves. Torque the retaining bolts to 26 ft. lbs.

12. Install steering wheel and connect the negative battery cable.

Steering Linkage
REMOVAL AND INSTALLATION
Tie Rod

1. Raise and safely support the vehicle.
2. Scribe alignment marks on the tie rod and rack end.
3. Working at the steering knuckle arm, pull out the cotter pin and then remove the castellated nut.
4. Using a tie rod end puller, disconnect the tie rod from the steering knuckle arm.
5. To install, align the alignment marks on the tie rod and rack end. Install the tie rod end.

6. Tighten the nuts to 19 ft. lbs. Check wheel alignment.

Power Steering Gear
ADJUSTMENTS
Celica And Supra

Adjustments to the power steering gear are not necessary during normal service. Adjustments are performed only as part of overhaul.

REMOVAL AND INSTALLATION
1986–90 Celica And Celica All-Trac

1. Raise and safely support the vehicle as necessary. Remove the right front wheel.
2. Remove the both engine under covers.
3. Remove the two bolts that connect the steering column U-joint to the rack and then disconnect the column from the rack.
4. Remove the cotter pin and nut and then using a tie rod end removal tool, disconnect the tie rod ends from the steering knuckle.

NOTE: *On Celica All-Trac models, remove (matchmark propeller shaft flange to intermediate shaft flange) the front propeller shaft. Disconnect the stabilizer bar on the right side by removing stabilizer bar bracket*

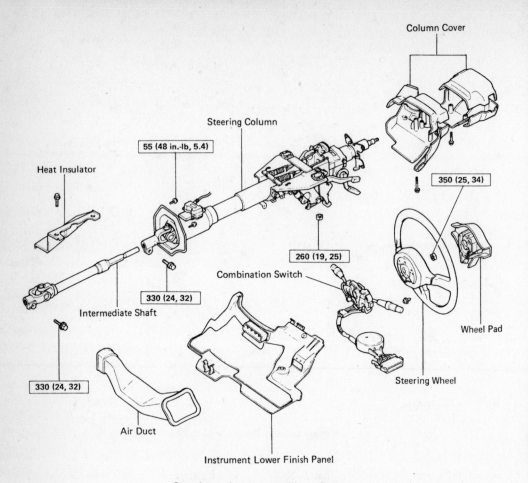

Column Cover

Steering Column

55 (48 in.-lb, 5.4)

Heat Insulator

350 (25, 34)

260 (19, 25)

Combination Switch

330 (24, 32)

Intermediate Shaft

Wheel Pad

330 (24, 32)

Steering Wheel

Air Duct

Instrument Lower Finish Panel

Steering column assembly — Supra

(right side) and disconnecting stabilizer link from the lower arm. Remove all necessary undercarriage crossmembers or support members.

5. Remove the lower suspension crossmember.

6. Remove the mounting bolts and remove the center engine mount member.

7. Disconnect the exhaust pipe from the manifold. Position it out of the way.

8. Tag and disconnect the two hydraulic lines. Position them out of the way and suspend them with a wire.

9. Remove the rear engine mount bracket.

10. Remove the mounting bolts and brackets and lower steering rack from the vehicle.

11. To install position the rack assembly, install the grommets and brackets and then tighten the two bolts and two nuts to 43 ft. lbs.

12. Install the rear engine mount bracket and tighten the two bolts to 38 ft. lbs.

13. Connect the hydraulic lines and tighten the union nuts to 29 ft. lbs.

NOTE: *On Celica All-Trac models, install the front propeller shaft. Reconnect the stabilizer bar on the right side. Install all neces-*

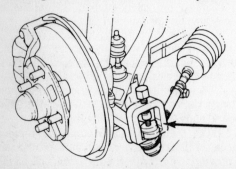

Remove the tie rod ends with a tie rod puller (arrow)

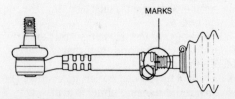

MARKS

Scribe alignment marks on the tie rod and rack

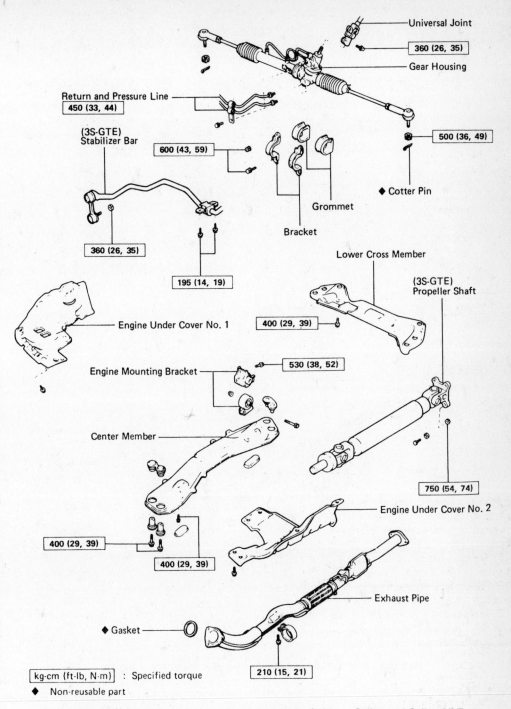

Universal Joint

360 (26, 35)

Gear Housing

Return and Pressure Line

450 (33, 44)

(3S-GTE) Stabilizer Bar

600 (43, 59)

500 (36, 49)

◆ Cotter Pin

Grommet

Bracket

360 (26, 35)

195 (14, 19)

Lower Cross Member

(3S-GTE) Propeller Shaft

Engine Under Cover No. 1

400 (29, 39)

Engine Mounting Bracket

530 (38, 52)

Center Member

750 (54, 74)

Engine Under Cover No. 2

400 (29, 39)

400 (29, 39)

Exhaust Pipe

◆ Gasket

kg-cm (ft-lb, N·m) : Specified torque

◆ Non-reusable part

210 (15, 21)

Removal and installation power steering gear assembly — Celica and Celica All-Trac

sary undercarriage crossmembers or support members.

14. Connect the exhaust pipe to the manifold.

15. Install the center engine mount member and tighten bolts to 29 ft. lbs.

16. Install the lower crossmember and tighten the five outer bolts to 154 ft. lbs. Tighten the center bolts to 29 ft. lbs.

17. Installation of the remaining components is in the reverse order of removal. Tighten the tie rod end nuts to 36 ft. lbs. and use a new cotter pin. Tighten the steering column U-joint bolts to 26 ft. lbs. Fill the power

w/o PPS

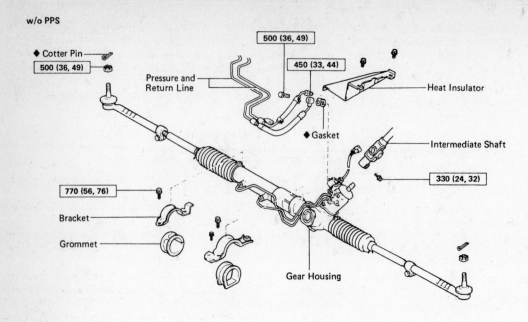

w/ PPS

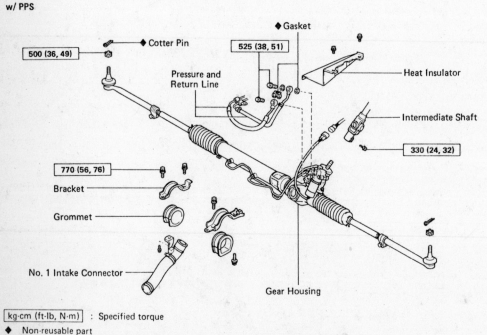

| kg·cm (ft-lb, N·m) | : Specified torque
◆ Non-reusable part

Removal and installation power steering gear assembly — Supra

steering pump with the specified fluid, bleed the system and check the wheel alignment.

1986–90 Supra

1. Raise and safely support the vehicle as necessary. Remove the engine under cover. Remove the front wheels.

NOTE: *On the 7M-GTE engine (turbo-charged engine) remove the air intake connector and air hose.*

2. Disconnect (matchmark) lower universal joint from the intermediate shaft.

3. Remove the cotter pins and nuts holding the knuckle arms to the tie rod ends. Using a tie rod puller, disconnect the tie rod ends from the knuckle arms.

4. Remove the steering damper and tube clamp brackets if so equipped.

5. Tag and disconnect the power steering lines. Remove the steering housing brackets and remove the housing.

6. Installation is the reverse of removal. Torque the rack housing mounting bolts to 56 ft. lbs., and the tie rod set nuts to 36 ft. lbs. Use a new cotter pins. Torque the universal joint assembly to 24 ft. lbs. Refill with the specified fluid, bleed the power steering system and check for fluid leaks. Check front wheel alignment.

Power Steering Pump

REMOVAL AND INSTALLATION

1986–90 Celica And Celica All-Trac

1. Raise and safely support the vehicle as necessary.
2. Disconnect the pressure line and return line (place drain pan under pump assembly) and position lines out of the way.
3. Remove the front right side wheel and engine under cover.
4. Remove the lower crossmember. Disconnect vacuum hose from air control valve.

NOTE: *On some models it is necessary to remove the right side tie rod end from the steering knuckle and remove the pump through tie rod end hole.*

5. Loosen adjusting bolts and remove the drive belt. Remove all retaining bolts from the power steering pump assembly. Remove the power steering pump from the vehicle.

6. Installation is the reverse of the removal procedure. Adjust drive belt and refill with the specified fluid. Bleed system and check for leaks. Check front wheel alignment as necessary.

1986–90 Supra

5M-GE AND 7M-GE ENGINES

NOTE: *On the 1986 Supra vehicle equipped with the 5M-GE engine modify this service procedure as necessary.*

1. Raise and support the vehicle safely. Drain the fluid from the reservoir tank.
2. Disconnect the air hose from the air control tank. Disconnect the return hose from the reservoir tank.
3. Remove the engine under cover. Disconnect and plug the pressure hose from the power steering pump.
4. Holding the power steering pump pulley, remove the pulley set nut. Remove the drive belt adjusting nut.
5. Remove the power steering pump set bolt. Remove the drive belt, pulley and woodruff key.
6. Disconnect the oil cooler hose bracket

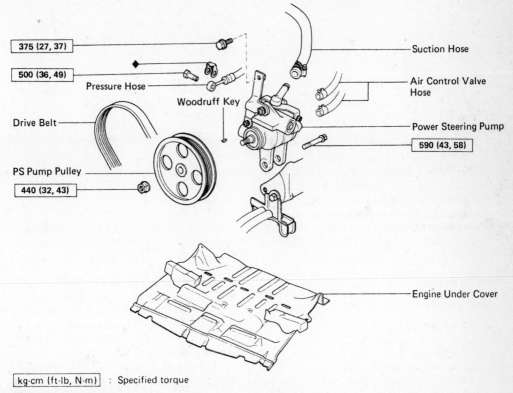

375 (27, 37)

500 (36, 49)

Pressure Hose

Woodruff Key

Drive Belt

PS Pump Pulley

440 (32, 43)

Suction Hose

Air Control Valve Hose

Power Steering Pump

590 (43, 58)

Engine Under Cover

kg·cm (ft-lb, N·m) : Specified torque

◆ Non-reusable part

Removal and installation power steering pump — Supra 7M-GE engine

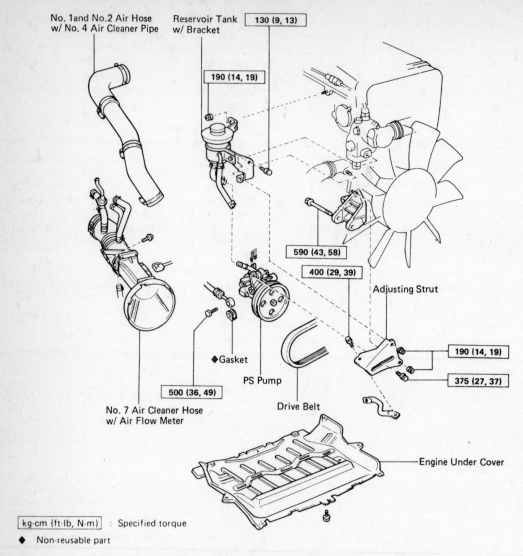

No. 1and No.2 Air Hose w/ No. 4 Air Cleaner Pipe

Reservoir Tank w/ Bracket

130 (9, 13)

190 (14, 19)

590 (43, 58)

400 (29, 39)

Adjusting Strut

190 (14, 19)

375 (27, 37)

◆Gasket

PS Pump

Drive Belt

500 (36, 49)

No. 7 Air Cleaner Hose w/ Air Flow Meter

Engine Under Cover

kg·cm (ft·lb, N·m) : Specified torque

◆ Non-reusable part

Removal and installation power steering pump — Supra 7M-GTE engine

from the power steering pump. Remove the drive belt adjust bolt and remove the power steering set bolt and power steering pump.

7. Installation is the reverse order of the removal procedure. Adjust drive belt and refill with the specified fluid. Bleed system and check for leaks.

1987–90 Supra

7M-GTE ENGINE

1. Raise and support the vehicle safely. Drain the fluid from the reservoir tank.

2. Remove the No. 1 and No. 2 air hoses with the No. 4 air cleaner pipe.

3. Disconnect the connector from the air flow meter. Remove the air flow meter installation bolt. Loosen the 5 clamps and disconnect the air hoses, release the 3 clips on the air

cleaner case. Loosen the No. 7 air hose clamp and remove the No. 7 air cleaner hose with the air flow meter.

4. Remove the oil reservoir tank with bracket. Disconnect the 2 air hoses from the air control valve on the power steering pump.

5. Remove the adjusting strut. Remove the engine under cover.

6. Holding the power steering pump pulley, remove the pulley set nut. Remove the drive belt adjusting nut.

7. Remove the power steering pump set bolt. Remove the drive belt, pulley and woodruff key.

8. Disconnect and plug the pressure hose from the power steering pump.

9. Remove the power steering set bolt and power steering pump.

10. Installation is the reverse order of the re-

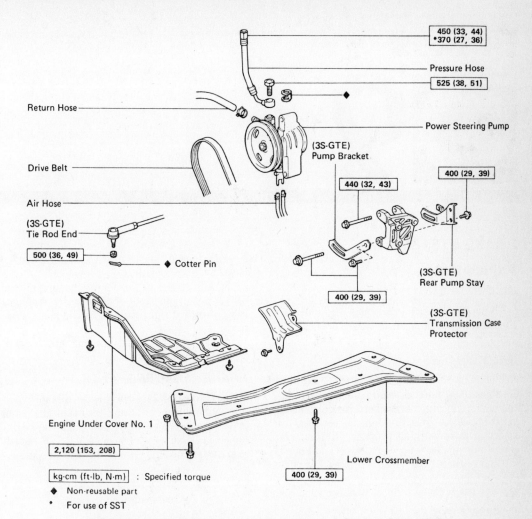

450 (33, 44)
*370 (27, 36)

Pressure Hose

525 (38, 51)

Return Hose

Power Steering Pump

(3S-GTE)
Pump Bracket

Drive Belt

440 (32, 43)

400 (29, 39)

Air Hose

(3S-GTE)
Tie Rod End

500 (36, 49)

Cotter Pin

(3S-GTE)
Rear Pump Stay

400 (29, 39)

(3S-GTE)
Transmission Case
Protector

Engine Under Cover No. 1

2,120 (153, 208)

kg-cm (ft-lb, N·m) : Specified torque

Lower Crossmember

400 (29, 39)

◆ Non-reusable part

* For use of SST

Removal and installation power steering pump — Celica and Celica All-Trac

moval procedure. Adjust drive belt and refill with the specified fluid. Bleed system and check for leaks.

BLEEDING

NOTE: *When preforming this service procedure always keep a watch on the power steering fluid level. Never run the power steering system dry.*

1. Jack up the front end of the car and safely support it with jackstands.

2. Check that the steering fluid is topped up to within the COLD LEVEL if cold, or the HOT LEVEL if the car has been running. Add fluid if necessary.

3. Start the engine and turn the steering wheel from lock to lock fully three or four times with the engine at idle.

4. Recheck the power steering fluid level. Check that the fluid is not foamy or cloudy and does not rise over the maximum when the engine is stopped.

5. Start the engine and let it idle. Turn the steering wheel from lock to lock two or three times.

6. Lower the car to the ground. With the engine idling, turn the steering wheel from lock to lock several times. Center the steering wheel.

7. The bleeding is complete if the oil level in the reservoir has not risen excessively and there is no foaming or clouding of the fluid. If excessive rise and/or foaming is noticed, repeat Step 6 until the fluid level and condition is correct.

Brakes

BRAKE SYSTEM

Adjustments

DISC BRAKES

All disc brakes are inherently self-adjusting. No periodic adjustment is either necessary or possible.

DRUM BRAKES

The rear drum brakes used on Celicas are equipped with automatic adjusters actuated by the parking brake mechanism. No periodic adjustment of the drum brakes is necessary if this mechanism is working properly. If the brake shoe-to-drum clearance is incorrect, and applying and releasing the parking brake a few times does not adjust it properly, then further service work to the brake system, is necessary.

PARKING BRAKE

Refer to the Parking Brake section in this chapter for adjustment procedure.

BRAKE PEDAL HEIGHT

The brake pedal height is the distance between the floor of the car and the top of the brake pedal pad. The brake pedal height specification is 153–163mm (6.02–6.42 in.) for the 1986–89 Celica and Celica All-Trac. For the 1990 Celica and Celica All-Trac, the brake pedal height specification is 168.5–178.5mm (6.638–7.031 in.) for manual transaxle and 168–178mm (6.614–7.008 in.) for the automatic transaxle equipped vehicles.

The 1986 Supra brake pedal height specification is 154–164mm (6.06–6.46 in.) and 151.5–161.5mm (5.96–6.36 in.) for the 1987–90 Supra.

To adjust brake pedal height use the following service procedure:

1. Remove the instrument lower finish panel and air duct as necessary.

2. Loosen the stop light switch locknut. Sufficiently loosen the stop light switch and brake pedal pushrod locknut.

3. Adjust the pedal height by turning the brake pedal pushrod. Position the stoplight switch until it lightly contacts the pedal stopper.

4. Tighten the locknuts and check stoplights for proper operation.

BRAKE PEDAL FREE PLAY

The brake pedal free play is the distance (due to play between clevis and pin) that the pedal travels from the rest position until the beginning of resistance can just be felt. To adjust, stop the engine and depress the brake pedal sev-

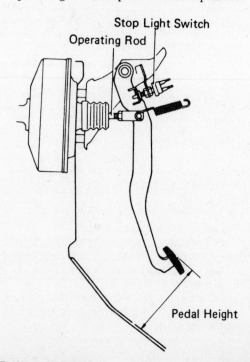

Brake pedal height

Troubleshooting the Brake System

Problem	Cause	Solution
Low brake pedal (excessive pedal travel required for braking action.)	• Excessive clearance between rear linings and drums caused by in-operative automatic adjusters	• Make 10 to 15 alternate forward and reverse brake stops to adjust brakes. If brake pedal does not come up, repair or replace adjuster parts as necessary.
	• Worn rear brakelining	• Inspect and replace lining if worn beyond minimum thickness specification
	• Bent, distorted brakeshoes, front or rear	• Replace brakeshoes in axle sets
	• Air in hydraulic system	• Remove air from system. Refer to Brake Bleeding.
Low brake pedal (pedal may go to floor with steady pressure applied.)	• Fluid leak in hydraulic system	• Fill master cylinder to fill line; have helper apply brakes and check calipers, wheel cylinders, differential valve tubes, hoses and fittings for leaks. Repair or replace as necessary.
	• Air in hydraulic system	• Remove air from system. Refer to Brake Bleeding.
	• Incorrect or non-recommended brake fluid (fluid evaporates at below normal temp).	• Flush hydraulic system with clean brake fluid. Refill with correct-type fluid.
	• Master cylinder piston seals worn, or master cylinder bore is scored, worn or corroded	• Repair or replace master cylinder
Low brake pedal (pedal goes to floor on first application—o.k. on subsequent applications.)	• Disc brake pads sticking on abutment surfaces of anchor plate. Caused by a build-up of dirt, rust, or corrosion on abutment surfaces	• Clean abutment surfaces
Fading brake pedal (pedal height decreases with steady pressure applied.)	• Fluid leak in hydraulic system	• Fill master cylinder reservoirs to fill mark, have helper apply brakes, check calipers, wheel cylinders, differential valve, tubes, hoses, and fittings for fluid leaks. Repair or replace parts as necessary.
	• Master cylinder piston seals worn, or master cylinder bore is scored, worn or corroded	• Repair or replace master cylinder
Decreasing brake pedal travel (pedal travel required for braking action decreases and may be accompanied by a hard pedal.)	• Caliper or wheel cylinder pistons sticking or seized	• Repair or replace the calipers, or wheel cylinders
	• Master cylinder compensator ports blocked (preventing fluid return to reservoirs) or pistons sticking or seized in master cylinder bore	• Repair or replace the master cylinder
	• Power brake unit binding internally	• Test unit according to the following procedure: (a) Shift transmission into neutral and start engine (b) Increase engine speed to 1500 rpm, close throttle and fully depress brake pedal (c) Slow release brake pedal and stop engine (d) Have helper remove vacuum check valve and hose from power unit. Observe for backward movement of brake pedal. (e) If the pedal moves backward, the power unit has an internal bind—replace power unit

Troubleshooting the Brake System (cont.)

Problem	Cause	Solution
Spongy brake pedal (pedal has abnormally soft, springy, spongy feel when depressed.)	• Air in hydraulic system • Brakeshoes bent or distorted • Brakelining not yet seated with drums and rotors • Rear drum brakes not properly adjusted	• Remove air from system. Refer to Brake Bleeding. • Replace brakeshoes • Burnish brakes • Adjust brakes
Hard brake pedal (excessive pedal pressure required to stop vehicle. May be accompanied by brake fade.)	• Loose or leaking power brake unit vacuum hose • Incorrect or poor quality brakelining • Bent, broken, distorted brakeshoes • Calipers binding or dragging on mounting pins. Rear brakeshoes dragging on support plate. • Caliper, wheel cylinder, or master cylinder pistons sticking or seized • Power brake unit vacuum check valve malfunction • Power brake unit has internal bind • Master cylinder compensator ports (at bottom of reservoirs) blocked by dirt, scale, rust, or have small burrs (blocked ports prevent fluid return to reservoirs). • Brake hoses, tubes, fittings clogged or restricted • Brake fluid contaminated with improper fluids (motor oil, transmission fluid, causing rubber components to swell and stick in bores • Low engine vacuum	• Tighten connections or replace leaking hose • Replace with lining in axle sets • Replace brakeshoes • Replace mounting pins and bushings. Clean rust or burrs from rear brake support plate ledges and lubricate ledges with molydisulfide grease. **NOTE:** If ledges are deeply grooved or scored, do not attempt to sand or grind them smooth—replace support plate. • Repair or replace parts as necessary • Test valve according to the following procedure: (a) Start engine, increase engine speed to 1500 rpm, close throttle and immediately stop engine (b) Wait at least 90 seconds then depress brake pedal (c) If brakes are not vacuum assisted for 2 or more applications, check valve is faulty • Test unit according to the following procedure: (a) With engine stopped, apply brakes several times to exhaust all vacuum in system (b) Shift transmission into neutral, depress brake pedal and start engine (c) If pedal height decreases with foot pressure and less pressure is required to hold pedal in applied position, power unit vacuum system is operating normally. Test power unit. If power unit exhibits a bind condition, replace the power unit. • Repair or replace master cylinder **CAUTION:** Do not attempt to clean blocked ports with wire, pencils, or similar implements. Use compressed air only. • Use compressed air to check or unclog parts. Replace any damaged parts. • Replace all rubber components, combination valve and hoses. Flush entire brake system with DOT 3 brake fluid or equivalent. • Adjust or repair engine

Troubleshooting the Brake System (cont.)

Problem	Cause	Solution
Grabbing brakes (severe reaction to brake pedal pressure.)	• Brakelining(s) contaminated by grease or brake fluid	• Determine and correct cause of contamination and replace brakeshoes in axle sets
	• Parking brake cables incorrectly adjusted or seized	• Adjust cables. Replace seized cables.
	• Incorrect brakelining or lining loose on brakeshoes	• Replace brakeshoes in axle sets
	• Caliper anchor plate bolts loose	• Tighten bolts
	• Rear brakeshoes binding on support plate ledges	• Clean and lubricate ledges. Replace support plate(s) if ledges are deeply grooved. Do not attempt to smooth ledges by grinding.
	• Incorrect or missing power brake reaction disc	• Install correct disc
	• Rear brake support plates loose	• Tighten mounting bolts
Dragging brakes (slow or incomplete release of brakes)	• Brake pedal binding at pivot	• Loosen and lubricate
	• Power brake unit has internal bind	• Inspect for internal bind. Replace unit if internal bind exists.
	• Parking brake cables incorrrectly adjusted or seized	• Adjust cables. Replace seized cables.
	• Rear brakeshoe return springs weak or broken	• Replace return springs. Replace brakeshoe if necessary in axle sets.
	• Automatic adjusters malfunctioning	• Repair or replace adjuster parts as required
	• Caliper, wheel cylinder or master cylinder pistons sticking or seized	• Repair or replace parts as necessary
	• Master cylinder compensating ports blocked (fluid does not return to reservoirs).	• Use compressed air to clear ports. Do not use wire, pencils, or similar objects to open blocked ports.
Vehicle moves to one side when brakes are applied	• Incorrect front tire pressure	• Inflate to recommended cold (reduced load) inflation pressure
	• Worn or damaged wheel bearings	• Replace worn or damaged bearings
	• Brakelining on one side contaminated	• Determine and correct cause of contamination and replace brakelining in axle sets
	• Brakeshoes on one side bent, distorted, or lining loose on shoe	• Replace brakeshoes in axle sets
	• Support plate bent or loose on one side	• Tighten or replace support plate
	• Brakelining not yet seated with drums or rotors	• Burnish brakelining
	• Caliper anchor plate loose on one side	• Tighten anchor plate bolts
	• Caliper piston sticking or seized	• Repair or replace caliper
	• Brakelinings water soaked	• Drive vehicle with brakes lightly applied to dry linings
	• Loose suspension component attaching or mounting bolts	• Tighten suspension bolts. Replace worn suspension components.
	• Brake combination valve failure	• Replace combination valve
Chatter or shudder when brakes are applied (pedal pulsation and roughness may also occur.)	• Brakeshoes distorted, bent, contaminated, or worn	• Replace brakeshoes in axle sets
	• Caliper anchor plate or support plate loose	• Tighten mounting bolts
	• Excessive thickness variation of rotor(s)	• Refinish or replace rotors in axle sets
Noisy brakes (squealing, clicking, scraping sound when brakes are applied.)	• Bent, broken, distorted brakeshoes	• Replace brakeshoes in axle sets
	• Excessive rust on outer edge of rotor braking surface	• Remove rust

Troubleshooting the Brake System (cont.)

Problem	Cause	Solution
Noisy brakes (squealing, clicking, scraping sound when brakes are applied.) (cont.)	• Brakelining worn out—shoes contacting drum of rotor	• Replace brakeshoes and lining in axle sets. Refinish or replace drums or rotors.
	• Broken or loose holddown or return springs	• Replace parts as necessary
	• Rough or dry drum brake support plate ledges	• Lubricate support plate ledges
	• Cracked, grooved, or scored rotor(s) or drum(s)	• Replace rotor(s) or drum(s). Replace brakeshoes and lining in axle sets if necessary.
	• Incorrect brakelining and/or shoes (front or rear).	• Install specified shoe and lining assemblies
Pulsating brake pedal	• Out of round drums or excessive lateral runout in disc brake rotor(s)	• Refinish or replace drums, re-index rotors or replace

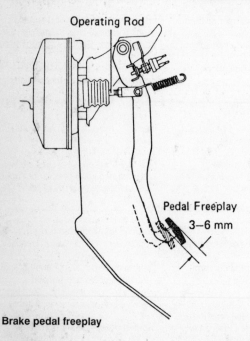

Brake pedal freeplay

eral times until there is no more vacuum left in the booster. Loosen the lock nut (remove any trim/finish panel as necessary) on the brake master cylinder pushrod and turn the adjusting nut until the proper free play is achieved. Don't forget to retighten the lock nut. Check the pedal height as necessary.

The brake pedal free play service specification for all 1986–90 Celica, Celica All-Trac and Supra vehicles is 3.0–6.0mm (0.12–0.24 in.).

Brake Light Switch

REMOVAL AND INSTALLATION

Celica and Supra

1. Disconnect the negative battery cable.
2. Disconnect the wiring connector at the brake light switch.

3. Remove the switch locknuts. Remove the brake light switch.
4. To install the brake light switch position the stoplight switch until it lightly contacts the pedal stopper. Tighten the locknuts and check stoplights for proper operation.

Master Cylinder

REMOVAL AND INSTALLATION

Celica And Supra

NOTE: *Be careful not to spill brake fluid on the painted surfaces of the vehicle is it will damage the paint.*

1. Remove the air cleaner assembly (remove connections for air flow meter) and the upper suspension brace if necessary to gain access for removal and installation.
2. Disconnect the fluid level warning switch connector.
3. Remove the brake fluid from cylinder as necessary (cylinder can be removed with the old brake fluid still inside).
4. Disconnect all brake lines (hydraulic tubes) to the master cylinder, use a line wrench or equivalent.
5. Remove the brake master cylinder retaining bolt from the brake booster and remove the gasket. Remove the master cylinder.
6. Installation is the reverse of the removal procedures. Some models have an **UP** mark on the cylinder boot, make sure this is in the correct position. Before tightening the master cylinder mounting nuts or bolts, screw the hydraulic line into the cylinder body a few turns. After installation is completed, bleed the master cylinder and the brake system, as required.

When replacing the master cylinder it is best to BENCH BLEED the master cylinder before installing it to the vehicle. Mount the master cylinder into a vise or suitable equivalent (do not damage the cylinder). Fill the cylinder to the correct level with the specified fluid. Block off all the outer brake line holes but one-then using a long tool such as rod position it in the cylinder to actuate the brake master cylinder. Pump (push tool in and out) the brake master cylinder 3 or 4 times till brake fluid is release out and no air is in the brake fluid. Repeat this procedure until all brake fluid is released out of every hole and no air is expelled.

OVERHAUL

NOTE: *Use this service procedure and exploded view diagrams as a guide for overhaul of the master cylinder assembly. If in doubt about overhaul condition or service procedure replace the complete assembly with a new master cylinder assembly.*

1. Place the cylinder securely in a vise. Remove the reservoir caps and floats. Unscrew the bolts which secure the reservoir(s) to the main body.

2. Remove the pressure differential warning switch assembly. Then, working from the rear of the cylinder, remove the boot, snapring, stop washer, piston No. 1, spacer, cylinder cup, spring retainer, and spring, in that order.

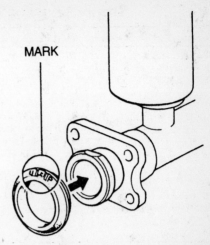

MARK

Always be sure that the UP mark on the master cylinder boot is in the correct position.

3. Remove the end plug and gasket from the front of the cylinder, then remove the front piston stop bolt from underneath. Pull out the spring, retainer, piston No. 2, spacer, and the cylinder cup.

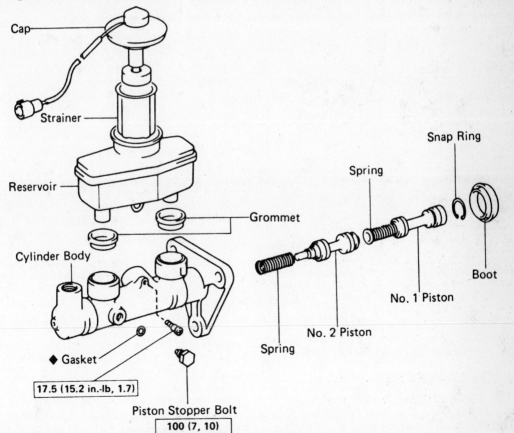

Cap
Strainer
Reservoir
Cylinder Body
◆ Gasket
17.5 (15.2 in.-lb, 1.7)
Grommet
Spring
No. 2 Piston
No. 1 Piston
Spring
Snap Ring
Boot
Piston Stopper Bolt
100 (7, 10)

Exploded view master cylinder/without anti-lock brake system

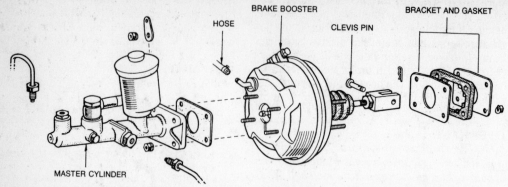

Exploded installation view of the master cylinder and vacuum booster assembly

4. Remove the two outlet fittings, washers, check valves and springs.

5. Remove the piston cups from their seats only if they are to be replaced.

After washing all parts in clean brake fluid, dry them with compressed air (if available). Drying parts with a shop rag can deposit lint and dirt particles inside the assembled master cylinder. Inspect the cylinder bore for wear, scuff marks, or nicks. In view of the importance of the master cylinder, it is recommended that it is replaced rather than overhauled if worn or damaged.

6. Assembly is performed in the reverse order of disassembly. Absolute cleanliness is essential. Coat all parts with clean brake fluid prior to assembly.

7. Bleed the complete hydraulic system as required.

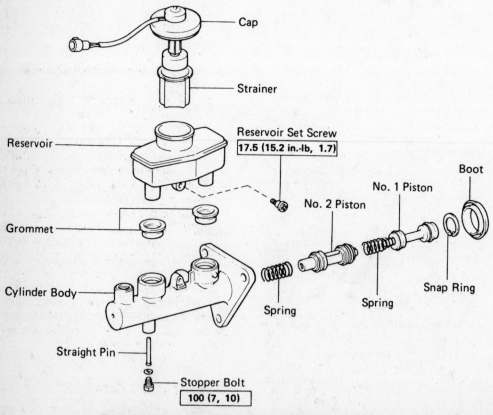

Exploded view master cylinder/with anti-lock brake system

Vacuum Booster

REMOVAL AND INSTALLATION

Celica And Supra

1. Remove the master cylinder as previously detailed.
2. On some models, remove the upper suspension upper brace, related components and engine wire bracket as necessary. Disconnect the brake vacuum hose from the brake booster.
3. Remove the instrument lower finish panel. Locate the clevis rod where it attaches to the brake pedal. Pull out the clip and then remove the clevis pin.
4. Loosen the four nuts and then pull out the vacuum booster, the bracket and the gasket from out the engine compartment.
5. Installation is in the reverse order of removal procedure. Fill brake reservoir and bleed the complete hydraulic system.

Proportioning Valve

Some models may use a proportioning valve to reduce the hydraulic pressure to the rear brakes because of weight transfer during high speed stops. This helps to keep the rear brakes from locking up by improving front-to-rear balance. The proportioning valve can be found in the engine compartment, near the master cylinder.

REMOVAL AND INSTALLATION

1. Disconnect the brake lines from the valve unions.
2. Unfasten the valve mounting bolt, if used.
3. Remove the proportioning valve assembly.
NOTE: *If the proportioning valve is defective, it must be replaced as an assembly; it cannot be rebuilt.*
4. Installation is the reverse of removal. Bleed the brake system after it is completed.

Brake Hoses

REMOVAL AND INSTALLATION

Celica And Supra

1. Raise and safely support the vehicle as necessary.
2. Remove the retaining clip and E-ring from the brake hose mounting clip.
3. Using a back-up wrench to hold the hose fitting and a line wrench to hold the brake line fitting. Remove the brake hose from the vehicle.
4. Installation is the reverse of the removal procedure. Inspect the hose for damage, cracks or swelling always REPLACE the brake hose never try to repair the brake hose. Always start brake line hose threads by hand than tighten with a back-up wrench (hose fitting) and line wrench (hydraulic brake line fitting).

Bleeding

NOTE: *Do not reuse hydraulic brake fluid which has been bled from the brake system. Refer to Master Cylinder Removal and Installation for bench bleeding procedures for the master cylinder assembly.*

1. Insert a clear vinyl tube into the bleeder plug on the master cylinder or the wheel cylinders.

NOTE: *If the master cylinder has been overhauled or if air is present in it, start the bleeding procedure with the master cylinder. Otherwise (and after bleeding the master cylinder), start with the wheel cylinder which is farthest from the master cylinder.*

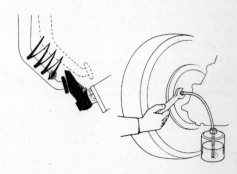

Bleed the brake into a half filled jar of brake fluid

2. Insert the other end of the tube into a jar which is half filled with brake fluid.
3. Have an assistant slowly pump the brake pedal several times. On the last pump, have the assistant hold the pedal to the floor (fully depressed). While the pedal is depressed, open the bleeder plug until fluid starts to run out, then close the plug.

NOTE: *If the brake pedal is depressed too fast, small air bubbles will form in the brake fluid which will be very difficult to remove.*

4. Bleed the cylinder before hydraulic pressure decreases in the cylinder.
5. Repeat this procedure until the air bubbles are removed and then go on to the next wheel cylinder. Replenish the brake fluid in the master cylinder reservoir, so that it does not run out during bleeding.

FRONT DISC BRAKES

CAUTION: *Brake pads contain asbestos, which has been determined to be a cancer causing agent. Never clean the brake sur-*

faces with compressed air! Avoid inhaling any dust from any brake surface! When cleaning brake surfaces, use a commercially available brake cleaning fluid.

Disc Brake Pads

INSPECTION

For proper inspection, the front disc brake cylinder (caliper) and the brake pads themselves must be removed. See following section for details.

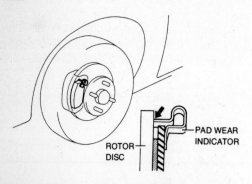

When the front or rear brakes squeal, check the wear indicators on disc brake system

NOTE: *If a squealing noise occurs from the front disc brakes while driving check the pad wear indicator. If there are traces of the indicator contacting the rotor (disc), the brake pads must be replaced.*

REMOVAL AND INSTALLATION

All Models

NOTE: *Do not allow oil or grease to contact the surface face of the disc brake pads. Always change the pads on one wheel at a time, as there is a possibility of the opposite brake caliper (brake cylinder) piston flying out. Note location of all brake hardware and wear indicator(s) before starting service procedure.*

1. Raise and safely support the vehicle as necessary. Remove the front wheels. Temporarily fasten the rotor disc with 2 wheel lug nuts.

2. Siphon a sufficient quantity of brake fluid from the master cylinder reservoir to prevent any brake fluid from overflowing the master cylinder when removing or installing the new disc brake pads.

3. At this point of the service procedure check the pad thickness through the brake cylinder (brake caliper) inspection hole. The mini-

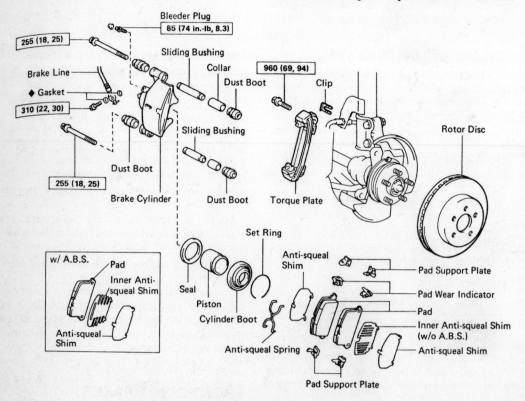

Exploded view front brake assembly — Celica 2WD

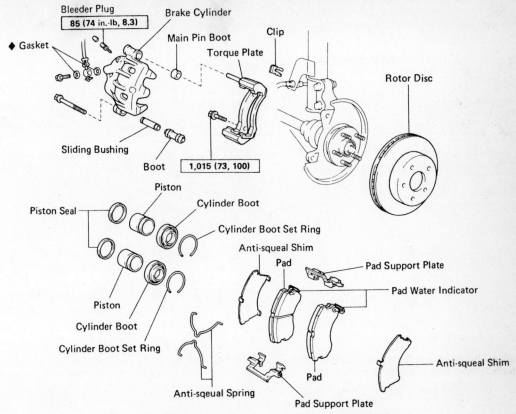

Exploded view front brake assembly — Celica All-Trac

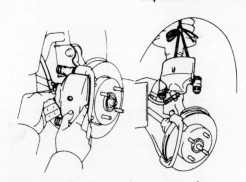

Suspend brake caliper to front suspension

mum thickness is 1mm (0.039 in.). Refer to the Brake Specifications Chart in this Chapter.

NOTE: *Minimum lining thickness is as recommended by the manufacturer. Because of variations in state inspection regulations, the minimum allowable thickness may be different than recommended by the manufacturer.*

3. Remove the brake hose bracket if so equipped. Remove the two installation bolts from the torque plate.

4. Remove the caliper assembly (brake cylinder) and suspend it (do not allow the brake caliper assembly to hang by the brake hose)

from the suspension with a wire or rope without disconnecting the brake hose.

5. Remove the following parts:
• Two anti-squeal springs
• Two brake pads
• Two, three or four anti-squeal shims
• Two pad wear indicator plates (note location as some models vary)
• Four pad support plates

6. Install the pad wear indicator plate to the pad with the arrow pointing in the rotating direction of the disc (the wear indicator must face the brake rotor). Install the anti-squeal shims to the pad.

7. Install the pads onto each support plate.

8. Install the anti-squeal springs in position.

9. Press the piston in the caliper (brake cylinder) assembly in with a hammer handle or equivalent and install the caliper assembly. Insert the caliper onto the rotor carefully so that the boot is not wedged. Torque the two installation bolts for caliper mounting to 18 ft. lbs. Celica 2-Wheel Drive and 27 ft. lbs. on Celica All-Trac and Supra vehicles. Refill the brake fluid to the proper level. Roadtest the vehicle for proper operation.

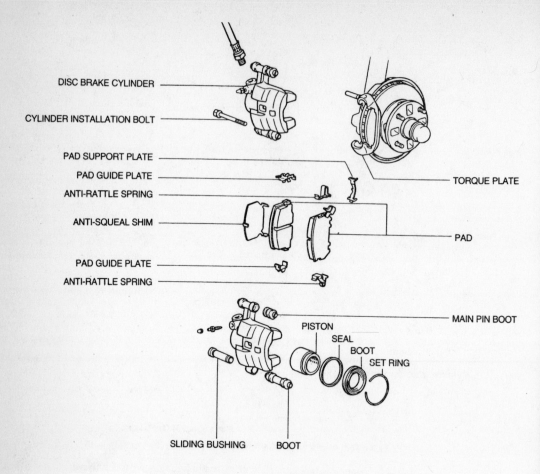

DISC BRAKE CYLINDER

CYLINDER INSTALLATION BOLT

PAD SUPPORT PLATE
PAD GUIDE PLATE
ANTI-RATTLE SPRING

ANTI-SQUEAL SHIM

PAD GUIDE PLATE
ANTI-RATTLE SPRING

TORQUE PLATE

PAD

MAIN PIN BOOT

PISTON
SEAL
BOOT
SET RING

SLIDING BUSHING   BOOT

Exploded view front brake assembly — 1986 Supra

Brake Caliper

REMOVAL AND INSTALLATION

All Models

1. Raise and safely support the vehicle as necessary. Remove the front wheels.
2. Remove the brake hose bracket if so equipped.
3. Disconnect brake hose by removing the union bolt on the brake caliper (brake cylinder). Use a suitable container to catch the brake fluid.
4. Remove the brake caliper (brake cylinder) from the torque plate by removing the 2 installation bolts. Slide out the brake caliper (brake cylinder) from the vehicle.
5. Installation is the reverse of the removal procedure. Torque the two installation bolts for brake caliper (brake cylinder) to 18 ft. lbs. Celica 2-Wheel Drive and 1986 Supra and 27 ft. lbs. on Celica All-Trac and 1987–90 Supra vehicles. Refill the brake fluid to the proper level and bleed brake system.

OVERHAUL

1. Remove the brake caliper (brake cylinder) assembly from the vehicle. Position the brake caliper assembly onto a suitable work bench or vise.
2. Remove the sliding bushing and boot.
3. Carefully remove the main pin boot with a chisel tool.
4. Remove the cylinder boot(s) and set ring(s) from the cylinder.
5. Apply compressed air to the brake line union to force the piston(s) out of its bore. Be careful! The piston may come out forcefully.
6. Carefully pry the piston seal(s) out of the cylinder bore(s). Check the piston(s) and cylinder bore(s) for wear and/or corrosion. Clean all metal components in clean brake fluid; replace any rubber part that is visibly worn or damaged.
7. Install the seal(s) and piston(s) in the cylinder bore(s), after coating them with the rubber lubricant supplied in the rebuilding kit. Seat the piston in the bore with your fingers.
8. Install the cylinder boot(s) and set

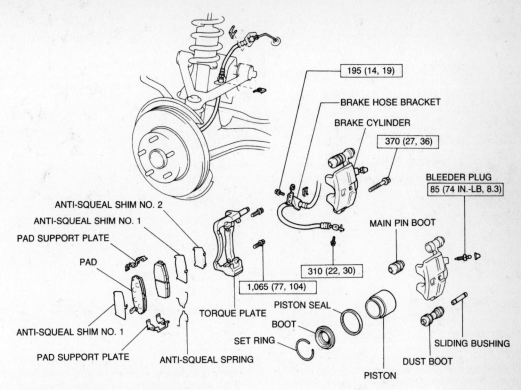

195 (14, 19)

BRAKE HOSE BRACKET

BRAKE CYLINDER

370 (27, 36)

BLEEDER PLUG
85 (74 IN.-LB, 8.3)

ANTI-SQUEAL SHIM NO. 2

ANTI-SQUEAL SHIM NO. 1

PAD SUPPORT PLATE

PAD

MAIN PIN BOOT

310 (22, 30)

1,065 (77, 104)

ANTI-SQUEAL SHIM NO. 1

PAD SUPPORT PLATE

TORQUE PLATE

ANTI-SQUEAL SPRING

PISTON SEAL

BOOT

SET RING

PISTON

SLIDING BUSHING

DUST BOOT

KG-CM (FT-LB, N·M) : SPECIFIED TORQUE

Exploded view front brake assembly — 1987–90 Supra

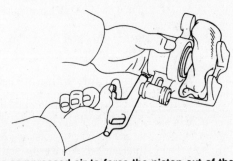

Use compressed air to force the piston out of the cylinder

ring(s) in the correct position.

9. Install the main pin boot in place. Install dust boot and sliding bushing.

Brake Disc (Rotor)

REMOVAL AND INSTALLATION

1986–90 Celica And Celica All-Trac 1987–90 Supra

1. Raise and safely support the vehicle as necessary. Remove the front wheels.

2. Remove the complete front brake caliper assembly (brake cylinder) or position the front brake caliper assembly to the suspension with a wire or rope without disconnecting the brake hose.

3. Remove the torque plate as required. Remove the brake disc (rotor) from the vehicle.

4. Installation is the reverse of the removal procedures. Bleed brakes as necessary. The torque plate mounting bolts are torque to 69 ft. lbs. Celica 2-Wheel Drive and 73 ft. lbs. Celica 4-Wheel Drive. The torque plate mounting bolts are torque to 77 ft. lbs. for Supra vehicles.

1986 Supra

NOTE: *Refer to Chapter 8 "Front Axle Hub and Bearing" removal and installation procedure for wheel bearing adjustment information.*

1. Raise and safely support the vehicle as necessary. Remove the front wheels.

2. Remove the front brake caliper assembly (brake cylinder) or position the front brake caliper assembly to the suspension with a wire or rope without disconnecting the brake hose.

3. Remove the torque plate as required. Remove the grease cap from the hub. Remove the cotter pin and the castellated nut.

4. Remove the wheel hub and brake disc assembly from the vehicle.

5. Installation is the reverse of the removal procedures. Always use a new cotter pin and

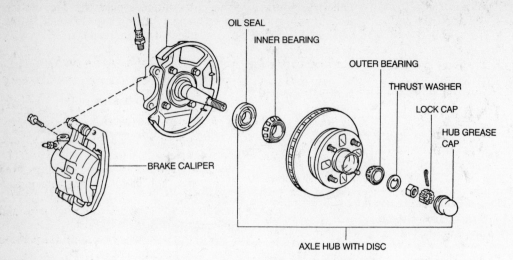

OIL SEAL

INNER BEARING

OUTER BEARING

THRUST WASHER

LOCK CAP

HUB GREASE CAP

BRAKE CALIPER

AXLE HUB WITH DISC

Front axle hub and wheel bearing — 1986 Supra

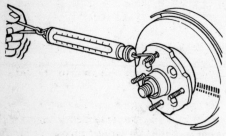

Tighten the nut, then measure preload with spring scale

adjust the front wheel bearings as outlined. Bleed the brake system as necessary.

INSPECTION

Examine the disc. If it is worn, warped or scored, it must be replaced. Check the thickness of the disc against the specifications given in the "Brake Specifications Chart". If it is below specifications, replace it. Use a micrometer to measure the thickness.

The disc run-out should be measured before the disc is removed and again, after the disc is installed. Use a dial indicator mounted on a stand to determine run-out. If run-out exceeds specifications, replace the disc. Refer to the "Brake Specifications Chart".

REAR DRUM BRAKES

CAUTION: *Brake shoes contain asbestos, which has been determined to be a cancer causing agent. Never clean the brake surfaces with compressed air! Avoid inhaling any dust from any brake surface! When cleaning brake surfaces, use a commercially available brake cleaning fluid.*

Brake Drums

REMOVAL AND INSTALLATION

Celica

NOTE: *The 1986–90 Supra vehicles use a rear disc brakes, refer to the necessary service procedure. The parking brake must be fully released in order for brake drum removal.*

1. Remove the hub cap (if used) and loosen the lug nuts. Release the parking brake.
2. Block the front wheels, raise the rear of the car, and support it with jackstands. Support the car securely.
3. Remove the lug nuts and the wheel.
4. Unfasten the brake drum retaining screws.
5. Tap the drum lightly with a mallet in order to free it. If the drum cannot be removed easily, insert a screwdriver or equivalent into the hole in the backing plate and hold the automatic adjusting lever away from the star adjusting bolt. Using another screwdriver or equivalent, relieve the brake shoe tension by turning the star adjusting bolt clockwise. If the drum

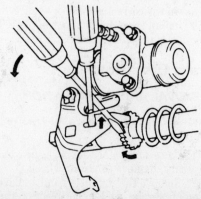

Backing off self-adjuster to remove brake drum

still will not come off, use a puller; but first make sure that the parking brake is released.

NOTE: *DO NOT depress the brake pedal once the brake drum has been removed.*

6. Inspect the brake drum as detailed in the following section.

7. Installation is in the reverse order of removal.

INSPECTION

1. Clean the drum.

2. Inspect the drum for scoring, cracks, grooves and out-of-roundness. Replace the drum or have it "turned" at a machine or brake specialist shop, as required.

NOTE: *If the brake drum is scored or worn, the brake drum may be machined to the maximum inside diameter.*

3. Light scoring may be removed by dressing the drum with fine emery cloth.

4. Heavy scoring will require the use of a brake drum lathe to turn the drum.

Brake Shoes

INSPECTION

Inspect all parts (springs) for wear, rust or damage. Using a feeler gauge, measure clearance between brake shoe and parking lever assembly. The standard clearance is less than 0.35mm (0.0138 in.). If the clearance is not within specification, replace the shim between brake shoe and parking lever assembly (shims are available in different sizes).

REMOVAL AND INSTALLATION

NOTE: *Record location of all brake hardware (springs etc.) before starting this service procedure. Do one side at a time, so that the other side may be used as a guide.*

1. Perform the "Brake Drum Removal" procedure as previously detailed.

2. Unhook the shoe tension springs from the shoes with the aid of a brake spring removing tool.

3. Remove the holddown spring, cups and pins.

4. On the rear shoe, disconnect the parking brake cable from the anchor plate.

5. On the rear shoe, using pliers, disconnect the parking brake cable from the lever and remove the rear shoe together with the adjuster.

6. Remove the adjuster lever spring and the adjuster from the rear shoe.

Installation is performed in the following order.

NOTE: *Grease (use suitable white grease) the point of the shoe which slides against the backing plate. Do not get grease on the linings.*

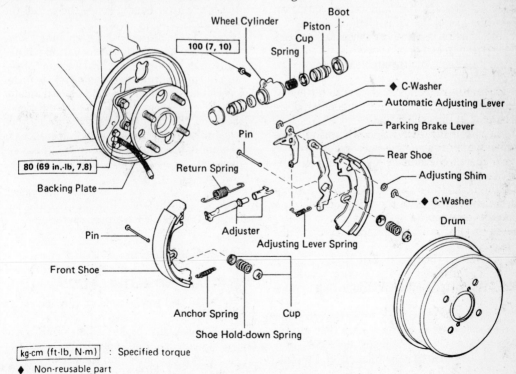

Exploded view rear brake assembly — Celica

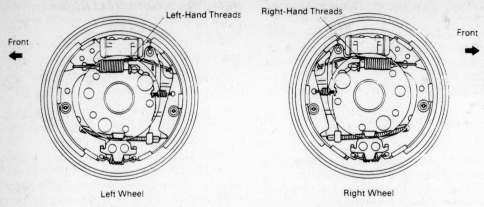

The rear brakes must be assembled in the proper direction — Celica

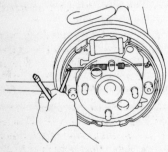

Use a brake spring tool to remove the tension spring

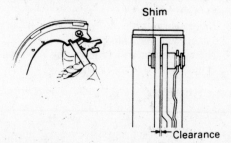

Measuring brake shoe and parking brake lever clearance — Celica

7. Set the adjuster and return spring in place and install the adjusting lever spring.

8. Using pliers, connect the parking brake cable to the lever.

9. Pass the cable through the notch in the anchor plate.

10. Set the rear shoe in place with the end of the shoe inserted in the wheel cylinder and the other end in the anchor plate.

11. Install the shoe holddown spring, cups and pin.

12. Install the anchor spring between the front and rear shoes.

13. Set the front shoe in place with the end of the shoe inserted in the wheel cylinder and the adjuster in place.

14. Install the shoe holddown spring, cups and pin.

15. Connect the return spring.

16. At this point of the service procedure check operation of automatic adjusting mechanism as follows:

   a. Move the parking brake lever of the rear shoe back and forth. Check that the adjuster turns. If the adjuster does not turn, check for incorrect installation of the rear brake shoes.

   b. Adjust the adjuster length assembly to the shortest possible amount.

   c. Install the brake drum. Pull the parking brake lever handle inside the car all the way up.

   d. Check clearance between brake shoe and drum by releasing the parking brake fully, and removing the brake drum. Measure the brake drum inside diameter (requires special brake gauge tool) and outer diameter of the brake shoes. Check that the difference between the diameters is the correct shoe clearance. The brake shoe clearance is 0.6mm (0.024 in.) for all 1986–90 Celica vehicles. If incorrect, check the parking brake system.

17. Install the brake drum and rear wheel. Check or refill the brake fluid in the reservoir. Roadtest the vehicle for proper operation.

Wheel Cylinders

REMOVAL AND INSTALLATION

1. Raise and safely support the vehicle as necessary.

2. Remove the brake drums and brake shoes as detailed in the appropriate sections.

3. Working from behind the backing plate, disconnect the hydraulic line (use a line wrench) from the wheel cylinder.

4. Unfasten the bolts retaining the wheel cyl-

inder to backing plate and withdraw the cylinder.

5. Installation is performed in the reverse order of removal. Remember to bleed the brake system after completing wheel cylinder, brake shoe and drum installation.

REAR DISC BRAKES

CAUTION: *Brake pads contain asbestos, which has been determined to be a cancer causing agent. Never clean the brake surfaces with compressed air! Avoid inhaling any dust from any brake surface! When cleaning brake surfaces, use a commercially available brake cleaning fluid.*

Disc Brake Pads

INSPECTION

For proper inspection, the rear disc brake cylinder (caliper) and the brake pads themselves must be removed. See following section for details.

NOTE: *If a squealing noise occurs from the rear disc brakes while driving check the pad wear indicator. If there are traces of the indicator contacting the rotor (disc), the brake pads must be replaced.*

REMOVAL AND INSTALLATION

All Models

NOTE: *Do not allow oil or grease to contact the surface face of the disc brake pads. Always change the pads on one wheel at a time, as there is a possibility of the opposite brake caliper (brake cylinder) piston flying out. Note location of all brake hardware and wear indicator(s) before starting service procedure.*

1. Raise and safely support the vehicle as necessary. Remove the rear wheels. Temporarily fasten the rotor disc with 2 wheel lug nuts.

2. Siphon a sufficient quantity of brake fluid from the master cylinder reservoir to prevent any brake fluid from overflowing the master cylinder when removing or installing the new rear disc brake pads.

3. At this point of the service procedure check the pad thickness through the brake cylinder (brake caliper) inspection hole. The minimum thickness is 1mm (0.039 in.). Refer to the Brake Specifications Chart in this Chapter.

NOTE: *Minimum lining thickness is as recommended by the manufacturer. Because of variations in state inspection regulations, the minimum allowable thickness may be different than recommended by the manufacturer.*

4. Remove the two rear caliper installation bolts from the torque plate.

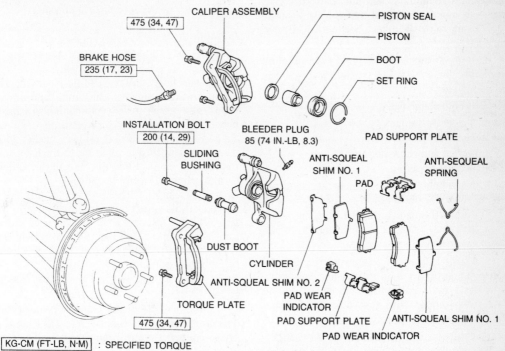

KG-CM (FT-LB, N·M) : SPECIFIED TORQUE

Exploded view of the rear disc brake assembly — Supra

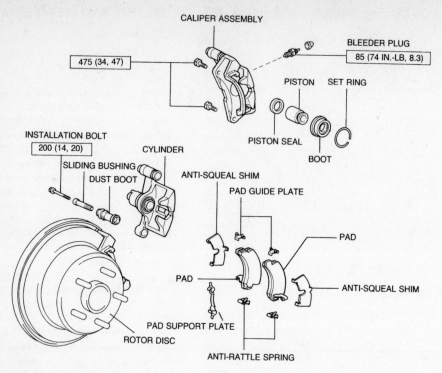

CALIPER ASSEMBLY

BLEEDER PLUG
85 (74 IN.-LB, 8.3)

475 (34, 47)

PISTON   SET RING

INSTALLATION BOLT
200 (14, 20)

PISTON SEAL

BOOT

CYLINDER

SLIDING BUSHING

DUST BOOT

ANTI-SQUEAL SHIM

PAD GUIDE PLATE

PAD

PAD

ANTI-SQUEAL SHIM

PAD SUPPORT PLATE

ROTOR DISC

ANTI-RATTLE SPRING

KG-CM (FT-LB, N·M) : SPECIFIED TORQUE

Exploded view of the rear disc brake assembly — Celica

5. Remove the caliper assembly (brake cylinder) and suspend it (do not allow the rear brake caliper assembly to hang by the brake hose) from the rear suspension with a wire or rope without disconnecting the brake hose.

6. Remove (note position and location of all hardware-some models may slightly differ) the following parts:

- anti-squeal springs
- brake pads
- anti-squeal shims
- pad wear indicator plates
- pad support plates

7. Install the pad wear in correct location. Install the anti-squeal shims to the pad.

8. Install the pads onto each support plate.

9. Install the anti-squeal springs in position.

10. Press the piston in the caliper (brake cylinder) assembly in with a hammer handle or equivalent and install the caliper assembly. Insert the caliper onto the rotor carefully so that the boot is not wedged. Torque the two installation bolts for rear caliper mounting to 14 ft. lbs. for Celica 2-Wheel Drive, Celica All-Trac and Supra vehicles. Refill the brake fluid to the proper level. Roadtest the vehicle for proper operation.

Brake Caliper

REMOVAL AND INSTALLATION

All Models

1. Raise and safely support the vehicle as necessary. Remove the rear wheels.

2. Disconnect brake hose by removing the union bolt or removing the brake line on the rear brake caliper (brake cylinder). Use a suitable container to catch the brake fluid.

3. Remove the brake caliper (brake cylinder) from the torque plate by removing the 2 installation bolts. Slide out the brake caliper (brake cylinder) from the vehicle.

4. Installation is the reverse of the removal procedure. Torque the two installation bolts for rear brake caliper (brake cylinder) to 14 ft. lbs. for Celica, Celica All-Trac and Supra vehicles. Refill the brake fluid to the proper level and bleed brake system.

OVERHAUL

1. Remove the brake caliper (brake cylinder) assembly from the vehicle. Position the brake caliper assembly onto a suitable work bench or vise.

2. Remove the sliding bushing and boot.

3. Carefully remove the main pin boot with a chisel tool.

4. Remove the cylinder boot and set ring from the cylinder.

5. Apply compressed air to the brake line union to force the piston out of its bore. Be careful! The piston may come out forcefully.

6. Carefully pry the piston seal out of the cylinder bore. Check the piston and cylinder bore for wear and/or corrosion. Clean all metal components in clean brake fluid; replace any rubber part that is visibly worn or damaged.

7. Install the seal and piston in the cylinder bore, after coating them with the rubber lubricant supplied in the rebuilding kit. Seat the piston in the bore with your fingers.

8. Install the cylinder boot and set ring in the correct position.

9. Install the main pin boot in place. Install dust boot and sliding bushing.

Brake Disc (Rotor)

REMOVAL AND INSTALLATION

All Models

NOTE: *The parking brake on rear disc brake equipped vehicles are actually small drum brakes. Their design and construction is virtually identical to the rear drum service brakes. If the brake rotor/hub cannot be removed easily, return (remove drum plug-turn star adjuster upwards) the shoe adjuster until the wheel turns free.*

1. Raise and safely support the vehicle as necessary. Remove the rear wheels.

2. Remove the complete rear brake caliper assembly (brake cylinder) or position the rear brake caliper assembly to the rear suspension with a wire or rope without disconnecting the brake hose.

3. Remove the torque plate as required. Remove (matchmark disc) the brake disc (rotor) from the vehicle.

4. Installation is the reverse of the removal procedures. Bleed brakes as necessary. The torque plate mounting bolts are torque to 34 ft. lbs. on all vehicles.

INSPECTION

Examine the disc. If it is worn, warped or scored, it must be replaced. Check the thickness of the disc against the specifications given in the "Brake Specifications Chart". If it is below specifications, replace it. Use a micrometer to measure the thickness.

The disc run-out should be measured before the disc is removed and again, after the disc is installed. Use a dial indicator mounted on a stand to determine run-out. If run-out exceeds specifications, replace the disc. Refer to the "Brake Specifications Chart".

PARKING BRAKE

Cable

REMOVAL AND INSTALLATION

All Models

NOTE: *On the 1986–90 Celica and Supra models no factory removal and installation procedures are given use this procedure as a guide.*

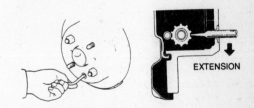

Adjusting parking brake shoe clearance

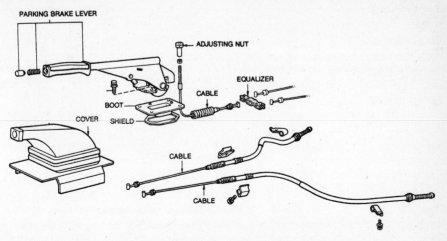

Parking brake cables and lever assembly

1. Raise and safely support the vehicle. Remove the rear console box.

2. Remove the cable adjusting nut.

3. Unscrew the four mounting bolts and remove the parking brake lever.

4. Working under the car, disconnect the parking brake cable equalizer.

5. Remove the two cable clamps from each side of the driveshaft tunnel.

6. Remove the rear brakes and then disconnect the parking brake cable from the lever.

7. Remove the cable from the brake backing plate.

8. Installation is in the reverse order of removal.

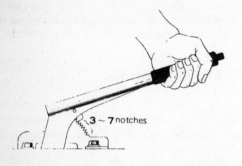

There should be 3–7 notches (5–8 on models with rear disc brakes) visible when the parking brake lever is all the way up.

ADJUSTMENT

NOTE: *For correct adjustment of the parking brake make sure that the rear service brake shoe clearance has been adjusted. If vehicle is equipped with rear disc brakes make sure that the parking brake shoe clearance is adjusted.*

1. Pull the parking brake lever all the way up, count the number of clicks.

2. The parking brake lever travel should be 3–7 clicks for all Celica vehicles and 5–8 clicks for Supra vehicles.

3. Adjust the parking brake as follows:

   a. Remove the console box.

   b. Loosen the locknut and turn the adjusting nut until the lever travel is correct.

   c. Tighten the locknut to 4 ft. lbs. Install the console box.

Parking Brake Shoes

REMOVAL, INSTALLATION AND ADJUSTMENT

The parking brakes on rear disc brake equipped models are actually small drum brakes which work inside the brake rotor/disc. Their design and construction is virtually identical to the rear drum service brakes found on other models. Also, replacement shoes/linings are usually bought on an exchange basis, as are most drum type service brake shoes. Note the

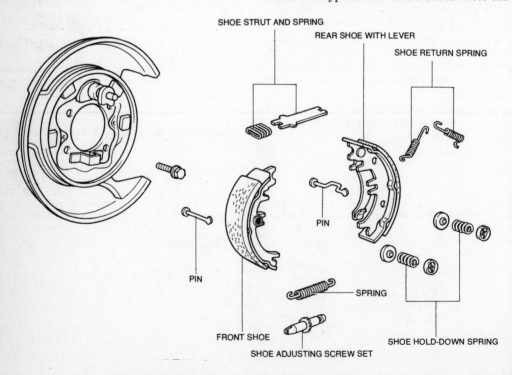

SHOE STRUT AND SPRING

REAR SHOE WITH LEVER

SHOE RETURN SPRING

PIN

PIN

SPRING

FRONT SHOE

SHOE ADJUSTING SCREW SET

SHOE HOLD-DOWN SPRING

Parking brake assembly — disc brake system models

location of all brake hardware (springs etc.) before starting this service procedure.

1. Raise and safely support the vehicle. Remove the rear disc brake caliper and rotor/disc assembly.

2. Remove the shoe return springs.

3. Remove the shoe strut with spring.

4. Disconnect the tension spring and remove the front shoe. Slide out the front shoe and remove the shoe adjuster. Remove the front shoe, adjuster and tension spring.

5. Remove the shoe hold down spring cups, springs and pins. Disconnect the parking brake cable from the parking brake shoe lever. Remove the tension spring from the rear shoe. Slide out the rear shoe.

6. To reassemble the parking brake assembly, apply non-melting type grease to the sliding surfaces on the back plate. Apply the same grease to the adjusting screw threads.

7. Compress the cable spring and connect the parking brake lever to the cable. Install the shoe hold down springs, cups and pins.

8. Slide the rear brake shoe between the holddown spring seat and the backing plate.

NOTE: *Do not allow oil or grease to contact the faces of the brake linings.*

9. Install the tension spring to the rear shoe, and connect the front shoe to the tension spring. Install the shoe adjusting screw set between the front and rear shoes. Slide in the front shoe between the shoe holddown spring seat and the backing plate.

10. Install the front shoe return spring, and also the strut with the spring forward.

11. Install the brake rotor/disc assembly. Temporarily install the rotor/disc hub nuts. From the front side of the hub, turn the adjuster star wheel and expand the shoes until the rotor/disc assembly cannot be turned by hand. Back off the adjuster wheel about 8 notches.

12. Install the rear brake caliper (brake cylinder) assembly as outlined.

13. Recheck and adjust the parking brake lever travel.

Brake Specifications

All measurements given are inches unless noted

Years	Model	Lug Nut Torque (ft. lbs.)	Master Cylinder Bore	Brake Disc		Brake Drum		Minimum Lining Thickness	
				Minimum Thickness	Maximum Run-out	Diameter	Max. Wear Limit	Front	Rear
1986	Celica	76	N.A.	①	0.006	7.874	7.913	0.040	0.040
	Supra	76	N.A.	②	0.006	—	—	0.118	0.118
1987	Celica	76	N.A.	①	0.006	7.874	7.913	0.040	0.040
	Supra	76	N.A.	③	0.006	—	—	0.040	0.040
1988	Celica	76	N.A.	④	0.006	7.874	7.913	0.040	0.040
	Supra	76	N.A.	③	0.006	—	—	0.040	0.040
1989	Celica	76	N.A.	④	0.006	7.874	7.913	0.040	0.040
	Supra	76	N.A.	③	0.006	—	—	0.040	0.040
1990	Celica	76	N.A.	⑤	0.003	7.874	7.913	0.040	0.040
	Supra	76	N.A.	③	0.006	—	—	0.040	0.040

NOTE: Minimum lining thickness is as recommended by the manufacturer. Because of variations in state inspection regulations, the minimum allowable thickness may be different than recommended by the manufacturer.

N.A. Not available

① Front 0.827
　Rear 0.354
② Front 0.750
　Rear 0.670
③ Front 0.827
　Rear 0.669
④ 0.827 except 3S-GE engine
　with A.B.S. and 3S-GTE engine—0.945
⑤ 0.787 except 3S-GTE engine—0.945

Body

10

EXTERIOR

Doors

REMOVAL AND INSTALLATION

1. Pull the door stopper pin upward while pushing in on the claw. Leave the claw raised after removing the pin.

2. Place a wooden block or equivalent under the door for protection and support it with a floor jack.

3. Remove the door mounting bolts (special box wrenchs are available to remove the door hinge mounting bolts) and remove the door.

4. Installation is the reverse of removal. Adjust the door as necessary.

ADJUSTMENT

1. To adjust the door in the forward/rearward and vertical directions, loosen the body

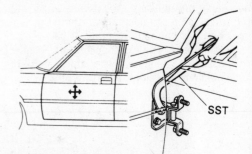

Front door forward/rearward adjustment

side hinge bolts and move the door to the desired position.

2. To adjust the door in the left/right and vertical direction, loosen the door side hinge bolts and move the door to the desired position.

3. Adjust the door lock striker as necessary by slightly loosening the striker mounting

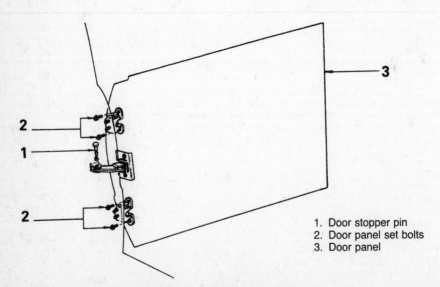

1. Door stopper pin
2. Door panel set bolts
3. Door panel

Typical front door hinge assemblies

CHILTON'S
AUTO BODY
REPAIR TIPS

Tools and Materials • Step-by-Step Illustrated Procedures
How To Repair Dents, Scratches and Rust Holes
Spray Painting and Refinishing Tips

With a little practice, basic body repair procedures can be mastered by any do-it-yourself mechanic. The step-by-step repairs shown here can be applied to almost any type of auto body repair.

TOOLS & MATERIALS

You may already have basic tools, such as hammers and electric drills. Other tools unique to body repair — body hammers, grinding attachments, sanding blocks, dent puller, half-round plastic file and plastic spreaders — are relatively inexpensive and can be obtained wherever auto parts or auto body repair parts are sold. Portable air compressors and paint spray guns can be purchased or rented.

Auto Body Repair Kits

The best and most often used products are available to the do-it-yourselfer in kit form, from major manufacturers of auto body repair products. The same manufacturers also merchandise the individual products for use by pros.

Kits are available to make a wide variety of repairs, including holes, dents and scratches and fiberglass, and offer the advantage of buying the materials you'll need for the job. There is little waste or chance of materials going bad from not being used. Many kits may also contain basic body-working tools such as body files, sanding blocks and spreaders. Check the contents of the kit before buying your tools.

BODY REPAIR TIPS

Safety

Many of the products associated with auto body repair and refinishing contain toxic chemicals. Read all labels before opening containers and store them in a safe place and manner.
• Wear eye protection (safety goggles) when using power tools or when performing any operation that involves the removal of any type of material.
• Wear lung protection (disposable mask or respirator) when grinding, sanding or painting.

Sanding

1 Sand off paint before using a dent puller. When using a non-adhesive sanding disc, cover the back of the disc with an overlapping layer or two of masking tape and trim the edges. The disc will last considerably longer.

2 Use the circular motion of the sanding disc to grind *into* the edge of the repair. Grinding or sanding away from the jagged edge will only tear the sandpaper.

3 Use the palm of your hand flat on the panel to detect high and low spots. Do not use your fingertips. Slide your hand slowly back and forth.

WORKING WITH BODY FILLER

Mixing The Filler

Cleanliness and proper mixing and application are extremely important. Use a clean piece of plastic or glass or a disposable artist's palette to mix body filler.

1 Allow plenty of time and follow directions. No useful purpose will be served by adding more hardener to make it cure (set-up) faster. Less hardener means more curing time, but the mixture dries harder; more hardener means less curing time but a softer mixture.

2 Both the hardener and the filler should be thoroughly kneaded or stirred before mixing. Hardener should be a solid paste and dispense like thin toothpaste. Body filler should be smooth, and free of lumps or thick spots.

Getting the proper amount of hardener in the filler is the trickiest part of preparing the filler. Use the same amount of hardener in cold or warm weather. For contour filler (thick coats), a bead of hardener twice the diameter of the filler is about right. There's about a 15% margin on either side, but, if in doubt use less hardener.

3 Mix the body filler and hardener by wiping across the mixing surface, picking the mixture up and wiping it again. Colder weather requires longer mixing times. Do not mix in a circular motion; this will trap air bubbles which will become holes in the cured filler.

Applying The Filler

1 For best results, filler should not be applied over ¼" thick.

Apply the filler in several coats. Build it up to above the level of the repair surface so that it can be sanded or grated down.

The first coat of filler must be pressed on with a firm wiping motion.

Apply the filler in one direction only. Working the filler back and forth will either pull it off the metal or trap air bubbles.

REPAIRING DENTS

Before you start, take a few minutes to study the damaged area. Try to visualize the shape of the panel before it was damaged. If the damage is on the left fender, look at the right fender and use it as a guide. If there is access to the panel from behind, you can reshape it with a body hammer. If not, you'll have to use a dent puller. Go slowly and work the metal a little at a time. Get the panel as straight as possible before applying filler.

1 This dent is typical of one that can be pulled out or hammered out from behind. Remove the headlight cover, headlight assembly and turn signal housing.

2 Drill a series of holes ½ the size of the end of the dent puller along the stress line. Make some trial pulls and assess the results. If necessary, drill more holes and try again. Do not hurry.

3 If possible, use a body hammer and block to shape the metal back to its original contours. Get the metal back as close to its original shape as possible. Don't depend on body filler to fill dents.

4 Using an 80-grit grinding disc on an electric drill, grind the paint from the surrounding area down to bare metal. Use a new grinding pad to prevent heat buildup that will warp metal.

5 The area should look like this when you're finished grinding. Knock the drill holes in and tape over small openings to keep plastic filler out.

6 Mix the body filler (see Body Repair Tips). Spread the body filler evenly over the entire area (see Body Repair Tips). Be sure to cover the area completely.

7 Let the body filler dry until the surface can just be scratched with your fingernail. Knock the high spots from the body filler with a body file ("Cheesegrater"). Check frequently with the palm of your hand for high and low spots.

8 Check to be sure that trim pieces that will be installed later will fit exactly. Sand the area with 40-grit paper.

9 If you wind up with low spots, you may have to apply another layer of filler.

10 Knock the high spots off with 40-grit paper. When you are satisfied with the contours of the repair, apply a thin coat of filler to cover pin holes and scratches.

11 Block sand the area with 40-grit paper to a smooth finish. Pay particular attention to body lines and ridges that must be well-defined.

12 Sand the area with 400 paper and then finish with a scuff pad. The finished repair is ready for priming and painting (see Painting Tips).

Materials and photos courtesy of Ritt Jones Auto Body, Prospect Park, PA.

REPAIRING RUST HOLES

There are many ways to repair rust holes. The fiberglass cloth kit shown here is one of the most cost efficient for the owner because it provides a strong repair that resists cracking and moisture and is relatively easy to use. It can be used on large and small holes (with or without backing) and can be applied over contoured areas. Remember, however, that short of replacing an entire panel, no repair is a guarantee that the rust will not return.

1 Remove any trim that will be in the way. Clean away all loose debris. Cut away all the rusted metal. But be sure to leave enough metal to retain the contour or body shape.

2 Grind away all traces of rust with a 24-grit grinding disc. Be sure to grind back 3-4 inches from the edge of the hole down to bare metal and be sure all traces of paint, primer and rust are removed.

3 Block sand the area with 80 or 100 grit sandpaper to get a clear, shiny surface and feathered paint edge. Tap the edges of the hole inward with a ball peen hammer.

4 If you are going to use release film, cut a piece about 2-3" larger than the area you have sanded. Place the film over the repair and mark the sanded area on the film. Avoid any unnecessary wrinkling of the film.

5 Cut 2 pieces of fiberglass matte to match the shape of the repair. One piece should be about 1" smaller than the sanded area and the second piece should be 1" smaller than the first. Mix enough filler and hardener to saturate the fiberglass material (see Body Repair Tips).

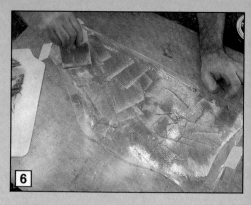

6 Lay the release sheet on a flat surface and spread an even layer of filler, large enough to cover the repair. Lay the smaller piece of fiberglass cloth in the center of the sheet and spread another layer of filler over the fiberglass cloth. Repeat the operation for the larger piece of cloth.

7 Place the repair material over the repair area, with the release film facing outward. Use a spreader and work from the center outward to smooth the material, following the body contours. Be sure to remove all air bubbles.

8 Wait until the repair has dried tack-free and peel off the release sheet. The ideal working temperature is 60°-90° F. Cooler or warmer temperatures or high humidity may require additional curing time. Wait longer, if in doubt.

9 Sand and feather-edge the entire area. The initial sanding can be done with a sanding disc on an electric drill if care is used. Finish the sanding with a block sander. Low spots can be filled with body filler; this may require several applications.

10 When the filler can just be scratched with a fingernail, knock the high spots down with a body file and smooth the entire area with 80-grit. Feather the filled areas into the surrounding areas.

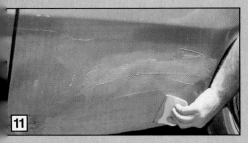

11 When the area is sanded smooth, mix some topcoat and hardener and apply it directly with a spreader. This will give a smooth finish and prevent the glass matte from showing through the paint.

12 Block sand the topcoat smooth with finishing sandpaper (200 grit), and 400 grit. The repair is ready for masking, priming and painting (see Painting Tips).

Materials and photos courtesy Marson Corporation, Chelsea, Massachusetts

PAINTING TIPS

Preparation

1 SANDING — Use a 400 or 600 grit wet or dry sandpaper. Wet-sand the area with a 1/4 sheet of sandpaper soaked in clean water. Keep the paper wet while sanding. Sand the area until the repaired area tapers into the original finish.

2 CLEANING — Wash the area to be painted thoroughly with water and a clean rag. Rinse it thoroughly and wipe the surface dry until you're sure it's completely free of dirt, dust, fingerprints, wax, detergent or other foreign matter.

3 MASKING — Protect any areas you don't want to overspray by covering them with masking tape and newspaper. Be careful not get fingerprints on the area to be painted.

4 PRIMING — All exposed metal should be primed before painting. Primer protects the metal and provides an excellent surface for paint adhesion. When the primer is dry, wet-sand the area again with 600 grit wet-sandpaper. Clean the area again after sanding.

Painting Techniques

Paint applied from either a spray gun or a spray can (for small areas) will provide good results. Experiment on an old piece of metal to get the right combination before you begin painting.

SPRAYING VISCOSITY (SPRAY GUN ONLY) — Paint should be thinned to spraying viscosity according to the directions on the can. Use only the recommended thinner or reducer and the same amount of reduction regardless of temperature.

AIR PRESSURE (SPRAY GUN ONLY) — This is extremely important. Be sure you are using the proper recommended pressure.

TEMPERATURE — The surface to be painted should be approximately the same temperature as the surrounding air. Applying warm paint to a cold surface, or vice versa, will completely upset the paint characteristics.

THICKNESS — Spray with smooth strokes. In general, the thicker the coat of paint, the longer the drying time. Apply several thin coats about 30 seconds apart. The paint should remain wet long enough to flow out and no longer; heavier coats will only produce sags or wrinkles. Spray a light (fog) coat, followed by heavier color coats.

DISTANCE — The ideal spraying distance is 8″-12″ from the gun or can to the surface. Shorter distances will produce ripples, while greater distances will result in orange peel, dry film and poor color match and loss of material due to overspray.

OVERLAPPING — The gun or can should be kept at right angles to the surface at all times. Work to a wet edge at an even speed, using a 50% overlap and direct the center of the spray at the lower or nearest edge of the previous stroke.

RUBBING OUT (BLENDING) FRESH PAINT — Let the paint dry thoroughly. Runs or imperfections can be sanded out, primed and repainted.

Don't be in too big a hurry to remove the masking. This only produces paint ridges. When the finish has dried for at least a week, apply a small amount of fine grade rubbing compound with a clean, wet cloth. Use lots of water and blend the new paint with the surrounding area.

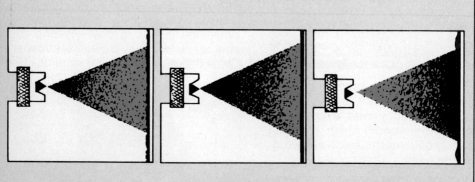

WRONG	CORRECT	WRONG
Thin coat. Stroke too fast, not enough overlap, gun too far away.	*Medium coat. Proper distance, good stroke, proper overlap.*	*Heavy coat. Stroke too slow, too much overlap, gun too close.*

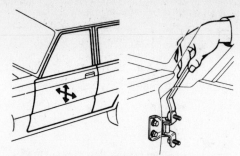

Front door up and down adjustment

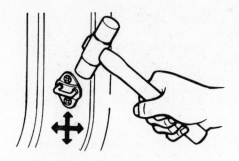

Front door striker adjustment

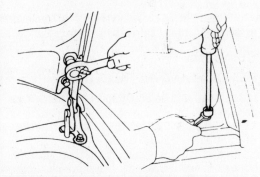

Adjust hood hinge (all directions)

screws, and hitting the striker lightly with a hammer or equivalent. Tighten the striker mounting screws.

Hood

REMOVAL AND INSTALLATION

1. Protect the painted areas such as the fenders with a protective cover.
2. Matchmark the hood hinges to the body. Loosen the hinge to body retaining bolts.
3. With the aid of an assistant remove the retaining bolts and lift the hood away from the car.
4. Installation is the reverse of removal. Align the hood to the proper position.

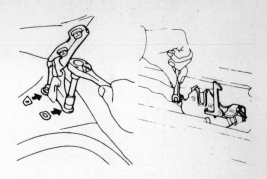

Adjust hood (vertical direction) and hood lock

Alignment

1. For forward/rearward and left/right adjustments, loosen the bolts and move the hood the desired position.
2. For vertical adjustment of the hoods front edge, turn the cushion.
3. For vertical adjustment of the rear end of the hood, increase or decrease the number of washers.
4. Adjust the hood lock if necessary by loosening the bolts.

Luggage Compartment Lid

REMOVAL AND INSTALLATION

Coupe

1. Remove the hinge mounting bolts.
2. It may be necessary to remove the torsion bar.
3. Installation is the reverse of removal. Adjust as necessary.

Liftback

1. Disconnect the lift cylinder from the body.
2. Remove the hinge bolts and remove the lid.
3. Installation is the reverse of removal. Adjust as necessary.

ADJUSTMENT

1. For forward/rearward and left/right adjustments, loosen the bolts and move the hood the desired position.
2. For vertical adjustment of the front end of the lid, increase or decrease the number of washers.

Lift Cylinder

REMOVAL AND INSTALLATION

NOTE: *Do not disassemble the cylinder because it is filled with pressurized gas.*

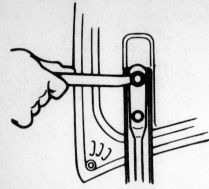

Adjust the luggage compartment lid — Coupe

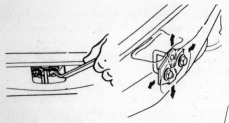

Adjust the luggage compartment lock and strike — Coupe

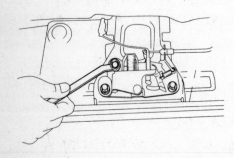

Adjust the luggage compartment lock and strike — Liftback

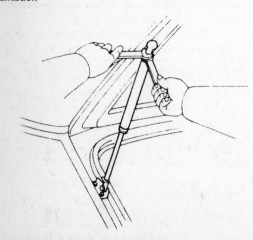

Removal of damper stay — Liftback

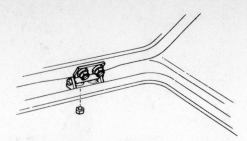

Adjust the luggage compartment lid — Liftback

Coupe

1. Remove the lift cylinder upper end from the lid.
2. Remove the lift cylinder lower end from hinge.
3. Install lift cylinder lower end to hinge.
4. Install lift cylinder upper end to lid. Adjust the lid as neceeary.

Liftback

1. Remove the roof side inner garnish.
2. Remove the lift cylinder lower end from the body.
3. Remove the lift cylinder upper end from the backdoor.
4. Installation is the reverse of the removal procedures. Adjust the liftback as necessary.

Bumpers

REMOVAL AND INSTALLATION

1. Raise and safely support the vehicle as necessary.
2. Disconnect all electrical connections at the bumper assembly.
3. Remove the bumper mounting bolts and bumper assembly. Remove the shock absorbers from the bumper as necessary.
   NOTE: *The shock absorber is filled with a high pressure gas and should not be disassembled.*
4. Install shock absorber and bumper assemble in the reverse order of the removal.

Fog Lights

REMOVAL AND INSTALLATION

Refer to Chapter 6 for the necessary service procedure.

Outside Mirror

REMOVAL AND INSTALLTION

Manual And Electric

1. On manual mirrors, remove the setting screw and knob. Tape the end of a thin screwdriver or equivalent and pry retainer loose to remove the cover.

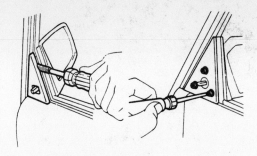

Removal of the outside mirror

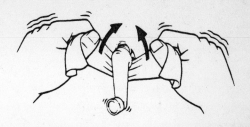

Removing the door regulator handle with a soft cloth

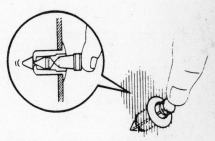

Locking the trim panel with locking clip

2. Remove the 3 retaining screws and reomve the mirror assembly.

3. On electric mirrors (follow service procedure as outlined-remove cover and mounting screws) disconnect electrical connector to mirror then remove the mirror asembly.

4. Installation is the reverse of the removal prcocedure. Cycle the mirror several times to make sure thatr it works properly.

Antenna

REPLACEMENT

Fender Mount Type

1. Remove the antenna mounting nut.

2. Disconnect the antenna lead at the radio (refer to radio removal and installation if necessary in Chapter 6).

3. Remove the antenna assembly from the vehicle.

4. Installation is the reverse of the removal procedure.

Windshield
Rear Window Glass (Coupe)
Back Door Glass (Liftback)

REMOVAL AND INSTALLATION

The windshield and rear glass assemblies are installed with a urethane bonding agent and installation has to conform to Federal Motor Vehicle Safety Standards. Special tools and service procedures are necessary to perform this kind of repair. Therefore all glass replacement work should be performed by a qualified technician at a professional glass shop.

INTERIOR

Door Panels

REMOVAL AND INSTALLATION

1. Remove the door inside handle (pull handle) and arm rest, if so equipped.

2. Remove the regulator handle snap ring

with a tool or pull off the snap ring with a cloth.

3. Remove the door lock lever bezel, inside handle bezel and door courtesy light, if so equipped.

4. Remove the door trim retaining screws.

5. Loosen the door trim by prying between the retainers (tape the screwdriver before use) and the door trim then disconnect the power window switch, if so equipped.

6. Installation is the reverse of removal procedure. Handle the door trim panel with care after removal.

Door Locks

REMOVAL AND INSTALLATION

1. Remove the inside door trim panel and access cover.

2. Disconnect the links from the outside handle and door lock cylinder.

3. On models with power door locks it will be necessary to disconnect the connectors from the door lock solenoid and key unlock switch.

4. Remove the door lock retaining bolts or screws and remove the door lock.

5. Installation is the reverse of removal procedure.

Door Glass

REMOVAL AND INSTALLATION

1. Remove the door inner trim panel.

2. Remove the service hole cover.

3. Remove the rear view mirror.

4. Remove the top of the weatherstrip on both sides of the door, remove the two screws and remove the belt moulding.

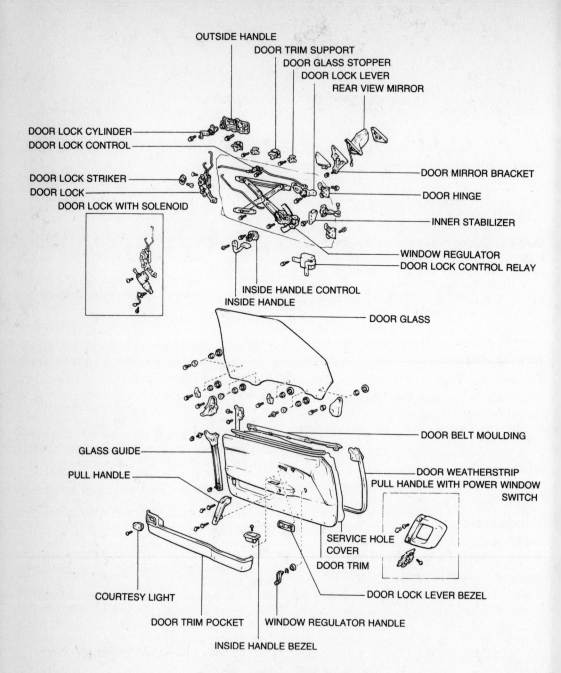

OUTSIDE HANDLE
DOOR TRIM SUPPORT
DOOR GLASS STOPPER
DOOR LOCK LEVER
REAR VIEW MIRROR

DOOR LOCK CYLINDER
DOOR LOCK CONTROL

DOOR MIRROR BRACKET

DOOR LOCK STRIKER
DOOR LOCK
DOOR LOCK WITH SOLENOID

DOOR HINGE

INNER STABILIZER

WINDOW REGULATOR
DOOR LOCK CONTROL RELAY

INSIDE HANDLE CONTROL
INSIDE HANDLE

DOOR GLASS

DOOR BELT MOULDING

GLASS GUIDE

PULL HANDLE

DOOR WEATHERSTRIP
PULL HANDLE WITH POWER WINDOW
SWITCH

SERVICE HOLE
COVER

DOOR TRIM

COURTESY LIGHT

DOOR LOCK LEVER BEZEL

DOOR TRIM POCKET
WINDOW REGULATOR HANDLE

INSIDE HANDLE BEZEL

Front door components — Celica

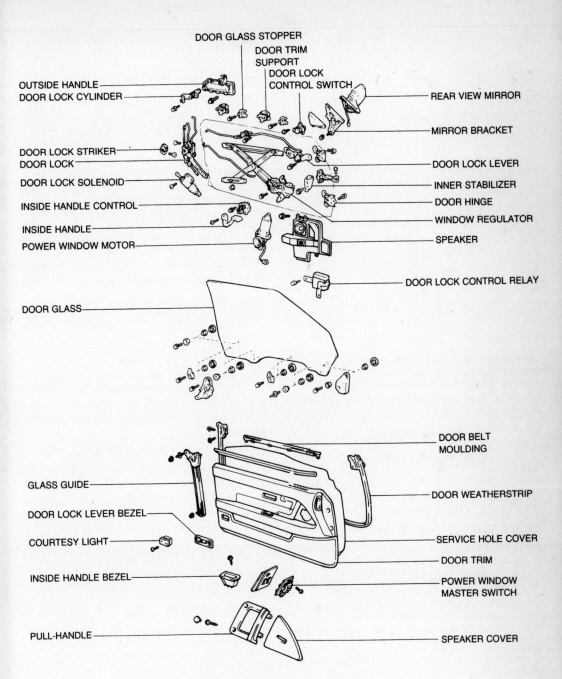

DOOR GLASS STOPPER

DOOR TRIM
SUPPORT

DOOR LOCK
CONTROL SWITCH

OUTSIDE HANDLE
DOOR LOCK CYLINDER

REAR VIEW MIRROR

MIRROR BRACKET

DOOR LOCK STRIKER
DOOR LOCK

DOOR LOCK LEVER

DOOR LOCK SOLENOID

INNER STABILIZER

INSIDE HANDLE CONTROL

DOOR HINGE

WINDOW REGULATOR

INSIDE HANDLE
POWER WINDOW MOTOR

SPEAKER

DOOR LOCK CONTROL RELAY

DOOR GLASS

DOOR BELT
MOULDING

GLASS GUIDE

DOOR WEATHERSTRIP

DOOR LOCK LEVER BEZEL

COURTESY LIGHT

SERVICE HOLE COVER

DOOR TRIM

INSIDE HANDLE BEZEL

POWER WINDOW
MASTER SWITCH

PULL-HANDLE

SPEAKER COVER

Front door components — Supra

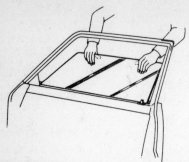

Pull the front door glass out in this manner

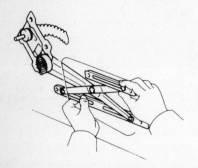

Removing the regulator assembly through the access hole

5. Remove the upper stopper trim support and inner stabilizer.

6. Raise the window approx. one inch and remove the two guide set bolts.

7. Remove the door glass by pulling it upward.

8. Installation is the reverse of removal.

Window Regulator

REMOVAL AND INSTALLATION

1. Remove the door trim panel and service hole.

2. Raise the window and secure the glass.

3. Disconnect the wiring connector, if equipped with power windows.

4. Remove the regulator mounting bolts.

5. Remove the regulator through the service hole.

6. Installation is the reverse of removal procedures.

Power Window Motor

REMOVAL AND INSTALLATION

1. Remove the door trim panel and service hole.

2. Raise the window and secure the glass.

3. Disconnect the wiring connector. Remove the regulator/power window motor mounting bolts.

5. Remove the regulator/power window

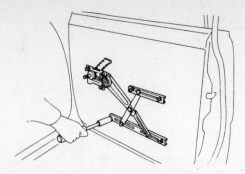

Removing the front door glass regulator bolts

motor through the service hole.

6. Remove the power window motor from the regulator assembly.

7. Installation is the reverse of removal procedures.

Inside Rear View Mirror

REMOVAL AND INSTALLATION

1. Remove the rear view mirror mounting bolt cover.

2. Remove the rear view mirror mounting bolt.

3. Remover the mirror.

4. Installation is the reverse order of removal.

Seats

REMOVAL AND INSTALLATION

Front

NOTE: *On power seat models remove the seat then remove the power seat motor assembly and drive cable.*

1. Remove the front seat mounting bolts.

2. Remove the front seat assembly.

3. Installation is in the reverse order of removal procedure.

Rear (Fixed Type)

1. Remove the rear seat cushion mounting bolts and disengage lower seat from the retaining clip.

2. Remove the rear seat back by tilting forward and pulling straight up.

3. Installation is in the revese of the removal procedure.

Rear (Split Foldable Type)

1. Disengage the rear seat back lock.

2. Remove the rear seat center hinge mounting bolts.

3. Disengage lower seat cushion assembly from the retaining clip.

4. Installation is the reverse of the removal procedure.

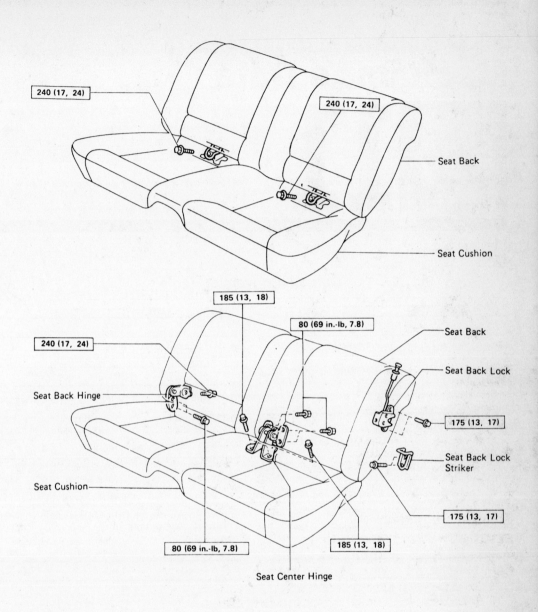

240 (17, 24)

240 (17, 24)

Seat Back

Seat Cushion

185 (13, 18)

80 (69 in.-lb, 7.8)

Seat Back

240 (17, 24)

Seat Back Lock

Seat Back Hinge

175 (13, 17)

Seat Back Lock
Striker

Seat Cushion

175 (13, 17)

80 (69 in.-lb, 7.8)

185 (13, 18)

Seat Center Hinge

kg·cm (ft·lb, N·m) : Specified torque

Rear seat assembly — Celica and Supra

General Conversion Table

Multiply By	To Convert	To	
	LENGTH		
2.54	Inches	Centimeters	.3937
25.4	Inches	Millimeters	.03937
30.48	Feet	Centimeters	.0328
.304	Feet	Meters	3.28
.914	Yards	Meters	1.094
1.609	Miles	Kilometers	.621
	VOLUME		
.473	Pints	Liters	2.11
.946	Quarts	Liters	1.06
3.785	Gallons	Liters	.264
.164	Cubic inches	Liters	61.02
16.39	Cubic inches	Cubic cms.	.061
28.32	Cubic feet	Liters	.0353
	MASS (Weight)		
28.35	Ounces	Grams	.035
.4536	Pounds	Kilograms	2.20
—	To obtain	From	Multiply by

Multiply By	To Convert	To	
	AREA		
6.45	Square inches	Square cms.	.155
.836	Square yds.	Square meters	1.196
	FORCE		
4.448	Pounds	Newtons	.225
.138	Ft. lbs.	Kilogram/meters	7.23
1.356	Ft. lbs.	Newton-meters	.737
.113	In. lbs.	Newton-meters	8.844
	PRESSURE		
.068	Psi	Atmospheres	14.7
6.89	Psi	Kilopascals	.145
	OTHER		
1.104	Horsepower (DIN)	Horsepower (SAE)	.9861
.746	Horsepower (SAE)	Kilowatts (KW)	1.34
1.609	Mph	Km/h	.621
.425	Mpg	Km/L	2.35
—	To obtain	From	Multiply by

Tap Drill Sizes

National Coarse or U.S.S.

Screw & Tap Size	Threads Per Inch	Use Drill Number
No. 5	.40	.39
No. 6	.32	.36
No. 8	.32	.29
No. 10	.24	.25
No. 12	.24	.17
1/4	.20	8
5/16	.18	F
3/8	.16	5/16
7/16	.14	U
1/2	.13	27/64
9/16	.12	31/64
5/8	.11	17/32
3/4	.10	21/32
7/8	9	49/64

National Coarse or U.S.S.

Screw & Tap Size	Threads Per Inch	Use Drill Number
1	8	7/8
1 1/8	7	63/64
1 1/4	7	1 7/64
1 1/2	6	1 11/32

National Fine or S.A.E.

Screw & Tap Size	Threads Per Inch	Use Drill Number
No. 5	.44	.37
No. 6	.40	.33
No. 8	.36	.29
No. 10	.32	.21

National Fine or S.A.E.

Screw & Tap Size	Threads Per Inch	Use Drill Number
No. 12	.28	.15
1/4	.28	3
6/16	.24	1
3/8	.28	Q
7/16	.20	W
1/2	.20	29/64
9/16	.18	33/64
5/8	.18	37/64
3/4	.16	11/16
7/8	.14	13/16
1 1/8	.12	1 3/64
1 1/4	.12	1 11/64
1 1/2	.12	1 27/64

Drill Sizes In Decimal Equivalents

Inch	Decimal	Wire	mm	Inch	Decimal	Wire	mm	Inch	Decimal	Wire & Letter	mm	Inch	Decimal	Letter	mm	Inch	Decimal	mm
1/64	.0156		.39		.0730	49			.1614		4.1		.2717		6.9		.4331	11.0
	.0157		.4		.0748		1.9		.1654		4.2		.2720	I		7/16	.4375	11.11
	.0160	78			.0760	48			.1660	19			.2756		7.0		.4528	11.5
	.0165		.42		.0768		1.95		.1673		4.25		.2770	J		29/64	.4531	11.51
	.0173		.44	5/64	.0781		1.98		.1693		4.3		.2795		7.1	15/32	.4688	11.90
	.0177		.45		.0785	47			.1695	18			.2810	K			.4724	12.0
	.0180	77			.0787		2.0	11/64	.1719		4.36	9/32	.2812		7.14	31/64	.4844	12.30
	.0181		.46		.0807		2.05		.1730	17			.2835		7.2		.4921	12.5
	.0189		.48		.0810	46			.1732		4.4		.2854		7.25	1/2	.5000	12.70
	.0197		.5		.0820	45			.1770	16			.2874		7.3		.5118	13.0
	.0200	76			.0827		2.1		.1772		4.5		.2900	L		33/64	.5156	13.09
	.0210	75			.0846		2.15		.1800	15			.2913		7.4	17/32	.5312	13.49
	.0217		.55		.0860	44			.1811		4.6		.2950	M			.5315	13.5
	.0225	74			.0866		2.2		.1820	14			.2953		7.5	35/64	.5469	13.89
	.0236		.6		.0886		2.25		.1850	13		19/64	.2969		7.54		.5512	14.0
	.0240	73			.0890	43			.1850		4.7		.2992		7.6	9/16	.5625	14.28
	.0250	72			.0906		2.3		.1870		4.75		.3020	N			.5709	14.5
	.0256		.65		.0925		2.35	3/16	.1875		4.76		.3031		7.7	37/64	.5781	14.68
	.0260	71			.0935	42			.1890		4.8		.3051		7.75		.5906	15.0
	.0276		.7	3/32	.0938		2.38		.1890	12			.3071		7.8	19/32	.5938	15.08
	.0280	70			.0945		2.4		.1910	11			.3110		7.9	39/64	.6094	15.47
	.0292	69			.0960	41			.1929		4.9	5/16	.3125		7.93		.6102	15.5
	.0295		.75		.0965		2.45		.1935	10			.3150		8.0	5/8	.6250	15.87
	.0310	68			.0980	40			.1960	9			.3160	O			.6299	16.0
1/32	.0312		.79		.0981		2.5		.1969		5.0		.3189		8.1	41/64	.6406	16.27
	.0315		.8		.0995	39			.1990	8			.3228		8.2		.6496	16.5
	.0320	67			.1015	38			.2008		5.1		.3230	P		21/32	.6562	16.66
	.0330	66			.1024		2.6		.2010	7			.3248		8.25		.6693	17.0
	.0335		.85		.1040	37		13/64	.2031		5.16		.3268		8.3	43/64	.6719	17.06
	.0350	65			.1063		2.7		.2040	6		21/64	.3281		8.33	11/16	.6875	17.46
	.0354		.9		.1065	36			.2047		5.2		.3307		8.4		.6890	17.5
	.0360	64			.1083		2.75		.2055	5			.3320	Q		45/64	.7031	17.85
	.0370	63		7/64	.1094		2.77		.2067		5.25		.3346		8.5		.7087	18.0
	.0374		.95		.1100	35			.2087		5.3		.3386		8.6	23/32	.7188	18.25
	.0380	62			.1102		2.8		.2090	4			.3390	R			.7283	18.5
	.0390	61			.1110	34			.2126		5.4		.3425		8.7	47/64	.7344	18.65
	.0394		1.0		.1130	33			.2130	3		11/32	.3438		8.73		.7480	19.0
	.0400	60			.1142		2.9		.2165		5.5		.3445		8.75	3/4	.7500	19.05
	.0410	59			.1160	32		7/32	.2188		5.55		.3465		8.8	49/64	.7656	19.44
	.0413		1.05		.1181		3.0		.2205		5.6		.3480	S			.7677	19.5
	.0420	58			.1200	31			.2210	2			.3504		8.9	25/32	.7812	19.84
	.0430	57			.1220		3.1		.2244		5.7		.3543		9.0		.7874	20.0
	.0433		1.1	1/8	.1250		3.17		.2264		5.75		.3580	T		51/64	.7969	20.24
	.0453		1.15		.1260		3.2		.2280	1			.3583		9.1		.8071	20.5
	.0465	56			.1280		3.25		.2283		5.8	23/64	.3594		9.12	13/16	.8125	20.63
3/64	.0469		1.19		.1285	30			.2323		5.9		.3622		9.2		.8268	21.0
	.0472		1.2		.1299		3.3		.2340	A			.3642		9.25	53/64	.8281	21.03
	.0492		1.25		.1339		3.4	15/64	.2344		5.95		.3661		9.3	27/32	.8438	21.43
	.0512		1.3		.1360	29			.2362		6.0		.3680	U			.8465	21.5
	.0520	55			.1378		3.5		.2380	B			.3701		9.4	55/64	.8594	21.82
	.0531		1.35		.1405	28			.2402		6.1		.3740		9.5		.8661	22.0
	.0550	54		9/64	.1406		3.57		.2420	C		3/8	.3750		9.52	7/8	.8750	22.22
	.0551		1.4		.1417		3.6		.2441		6.2		.3770	V			.8858	22.5
	.0571		1.45		.1440	27			.2460	D			.3780		9.6	57/64	.8906	22.62
	.0591		1.5		.1457		3.7		.2461		6.25		.3819		9.7		.9055	23.0
	.0595	53			.1470	26			.2480		6.3		.3839		9.75	29/32	.9062	23.01
1/16	.0610		1.55		.1476		3.75	1/4	.2500		6.35		.3858		9.8	59/64	.9219	23.41
	.0625		1.59		.1495	25			.2520		6.		.3860	W			.9252	23.5
	.0630		1.6		.1496		3.8		.2559		6.5		.3898		9.9	15/16	.9375	23.81
	.0635	52			.1520	24			.2570	F		25/64	.3906		9.92		.9449	24.0
	.0650		1.65		.1535		3.9		.2598		6.6		.3937		10.0	61/64	.9531	24.2
	.0669		1.7		.1540	23			.2610	G			.3970	X			.9646	24.5
	.0670	51		5/32	.1562		3.96		.2638		6.7		.4040	Y		31/32	.9688	24.6
	.0689		1.75		.1570	22		17/64	.2656		6.74	13/32	.4062		10.31		.9843	25.0
	.0700	50			.1575		4.0		.2657		6.75		.4130	Z		63/64	.9844	25.0
	.0709		1.8		.1590	21			.2660	H			.4134		10.5	1	1.0000	25.4
	.0728		1.85		.1610	20			.2677		6.8	27/64	.4219		10.71			

AIR/FUEL RATIO: The ratio of air to gasoline by weight in the fuel mixture drawn into the engine.

AIR INJECTION: One method of reducing harmful exhaust emissions by injecting air into each of the exhaust ports of an engine. The fresh air entering the hot exhaust manifold causes any remaining fuel to be burned before it can exit the tailpipe.

ALTERNATOR: A device used for converting mechanical energy into electrical energy.

AMMETER: An instrument, calibrated in amperes, used to measure the flow of an electrical current in a circuit. Ammeters are always connected in series with the circuit being tested.

AMPERE: The rate of flow of electrical current present when one volt of electrical pressure is applied against one ohm of electrical resistance.

ANALOG COMPUTER: Any microprocessor that uses similar (analogous) electrical signals to make its calculations.

ARMATURE: A laminated, soft iron core wrapped by a wire that converts electrical energy to mechanical energy as in a motor or relay. When rotated in a magnetic field, it changes mechanical energy into electrical energy as in a generator.

ATMOSPHERIC PRESSURE: The pressure on the Earth's surface caused by the weight of the air in the atmosphere. At sea level, this pressure is 14.7 psi at 32°F (101 kPa at 0°C).

ATOMIZATION: The breaking down of a liquid into a fine mist that can be suspended in air.

AXIAL PLAY: Movement parallel to a shaft or bearing bore.

BACKFIRE: The sudden combustion of gases in the intake or exhaust system that results in a loud explosion.

BACKLASH: The clearance or play between two parts, such as meshed gears.

BACKPRESSURE: Restrictions in the exhaust system that slow the exit of exhaust gases from the combustion chamber.

BAKELITE: A heat resistant, plastic insulator material commonly used in printed circuit boards and transistorized components.

BALL BEARING: A bearing made up of hardened inner and outer races between which hardened steel balls roll.

BALLAST RESISTOR: A resistor in the primary ignition circuit that lowers voltage after the engine is started to reduce wear on ignition components.

BEARING: A friction reducing, supportive device usually located between a stationary part and a moving part.

BIMETAL TEMPERATURE SENSOR: Any sensor or switch made of two dissimilar types of metal that bend when heated or cooled due to the different expansion rates of the alloys. These types of sensors usually function as an on/off switch.

BLOWBY: Combustion gases, composed of water vapor and unburned fuel, that leak past the piston rings into the crankcase during normal engine operation. These gases are removed by the PCV system to prevent the buildup of harmful acids in the crankcase.

BRAKE PAD: A brake shoe and lining assembly used with disc brakes.

BRAKE SHOE: The backing for the brake lining. The term is, however, usually applied to the assembly of the brake backing and lining.

BUSHING: A liner, usually removable, for a bearing; an anti-friction liner used in place of a bearing.

BYPASS: System used to bypass ballast resistor during engine cranking to increase voltage supplied to the coil.

CALIPER: A hydraulically activated device in a disc brake system, which is mounted straddling the brake rotor (disc). The caliper contains at least one piston and two brake pads. Hydraulic pressure on the piston(s) forces the pads against the rotor.

CAMSHAFT: A shaft in the engine on which are the lobes (cams) which operate the valves. The camshaft is driven by the crankshaft, via a belt, chain or gears, at one half the crankshaft speed.

CAPACITOR: A device which stores an electrical charge.

CARBON MONOXIDE (CO): A colorless, odorless gas given off as a normal byproduct of combustion. It is poisonous and extremely dangerous in confined areas, building up slowly to toxic levels without warning if adequate ventilation is not available.

CARBURETOR: A device, usually mounted on the intake manifold of an engine, which mixes the air and fuel in the proper proportion to allow even combustion.

CATALYTIC CONVERTER: A device installed in the exhaust system, like a muffler, that converts harmful byproducts of combustion into carbon dioxide and water vapor by means of a heat-producing chemical reaction.

CENTRIFUGAL ADVANCE: A mechanical method of advancing the spark timing by using fly weights in the distributor that react to centrifugal force generated by the distributor shaft rotation.

CHECK VALVE: Any one-way valve installed to permit the flow of air, fuel or vacuum in one direction only.

CHOKE: A device, usually a movable valve, placed in the intake path of a carburetor to restrict the flow of air.

CIRCUIT: Any unbroken path through which an electrical current can flow. Also used to describe fuel flow in some instances.

CIRCUIT BREAKER: A switch which protects an electrical circuit from overload by opening the circuit when the current flow exceeds a predetermined level. Some circuit breakers must be reset manually, while most reset automatically

COIL (IGNITION): A transformer in the ignition circuit which steps up the voltage provided to the spark plugs.

COMBINATION MANIFOLD: An assembly which includes both the intake and exhaust manifolds in one casting.

COMBINATION VALVE: A device used in some fuel systems that routes fuel vapors to a charcoal storage canister instead of venting them into the atmosphere. The valve relieves fuel tank pressure and allows fresh air into the tank as the fuel level drops to prevent a vapor lock situation.

COMPRESSION RATIO: The comparison of the total volume of the cylinder and combustion chamber with the piston at BDC and the piston at TDC.

CONDENSER: 1. An electrical device which acts to store an electrical charge, preventing voltage surges.
2. A radiator-like device in the air conditioning system in which refrigerant gas condenses into a liquid, giving off heat.

CONDUCTOR: Any material through which an electrical current can be transmitted easily.

CONTINUITY: Continuous or complete circuit. Can be checked with an ohmmeter.

COUNTERSHAFT: An intermediate shaft which is rotated by a mainshaft and transmits, in turn, that rotation to a working part.

CRANKCASE: The lower part of an engine in which the crankshaft and related parts operate.

CRANKSHAFT: The main driving shaft of an engine which receives reciprocating motion from the pistons and converts it to rotary motion.

CYLINDER: In an engine, the round hole in the engine block in which the piston(s) ride.

CYLINDER BLOCK: The main structural member of an engine in which is found the cylinders, crankshaft and other principal parts.

CYLINDER HEAD: The detachable portion of the engine, fastened, usually, to the top of the cylinder block, containing all or most of the combustion chambers. On overhead valve engines, it contains the valves and their operating parts. On overhead cam engines, it contains the camshaft as well.

DEAD CENTER: The extreme top or bottom of the piston stroke.

DETONATION: An unwanted explosion of the air/fuel mixture in the combustion chamber caused by excess heat and compression, advanced timing, or an overly lean mixture. Also referred to as "ping".

DIAPHRAGM: A thin, flexible wall separating two cavities, such as in a vacuum advance unit.

DIESELING: A condition in which hot spots in the combustion chamber cause the engine to run on after the key is turned off.

DIFFERENTIAL: A geared assembly which allows the transmission of motion between drive axles, giving one axle the ability to turn faster than the other.

DIODE: An electrical device that will allow current to flow in one direction only.

DISC BRAKE: A hydraulic braking assembly consisting of a brake disc, or rotor, mounted on an axle, and a caliper assembly containing, usually two brake pads which are activated by hydraulic pressure. The pads are forced against the sides of the disc, creating friction which slows the vehicle.

DISTRIBUTOR: A mechanically driven device on an engine which is responsible for electrically firing the spark plug at a predetermined point of the piston stroke.

DOWEL PIN: A pin, inserted in mating holes in two different parts allowing those parts to maintain a fixed relationship.

DRUM BRAKE: A braking system which consists of two brake shoes and one or two wheel cylinders, mounted on a fixed backing plate, and a brake drum, mounted on an axle, which revolves around the assembly. Hydraulic action applied to the wheel cylinders forces the shoes outward against the drum, creating friction, slowing the vehicle.

DWELL: The rate, measured in degrees of shaft rotation, at which an electrical circuit cycles on and off.

ELECTRONIC CONTROL UNIT (ECU): Ignition module, amplifier or igniter. See Module for definition.

ELECTRONIC IGNITION: A system in which the timing and firing of the spark plugs is controlled by an electronic control unit, usually called a module. These systems have no points or condenser.

ENDPLAY: The measured amount of axial movement in a shaft.

ENGINE: A device that converts heat into mechanical energy.

EXHAUST MANIFOLD: A set of cast passages or pipes which conduct exhaust gases from the engine.

FEELER GAUGE: A blade, usually metal, of precisely predetermined thickness, used to measure the clearance between two parts. These blades usually are available in sets of assorted thicknesses.

F-HEAD: An engine configuration in which the intake valves are in the cylinder head, while the camshaft and exhaust valves are located in the cylinder block. The camshaft operates the intake valves via lifters and pushrods, while it operates the exhaust valves directly.

FIRING ORDER: The order in which combustion occurs in the cylinders of an engine. Also the order in which spark is distributed to the plugs by the distributor.

FLATHEAD: An engine configuration in which the camshaft and all the valves are located in the cylinder block.

FLOODING: The presence of too much fuel in the intake manifold and combustion chamber which prevents the air/fuel mixture from firing, thereby causing a no-start situation.

FLYWHEEL: A disc shaped part bolted to the rear end of the crankshaft. Around the outer perimeter is affixed the ring gear. The starter drive engages the ring gear, turning the flywheel, which rotates the crankshaft, imparting the initial starting motion to the engine.

FOOT POUND (ft.lb. or sometimes, ft. lbs.): The amount of energy or work needed to raise an item weighing one pound, a distance of one foot.

FUSE: A protective device in a circuit which prevents circuit overload by breaking the circuit when a specific amperage is present. The device is constructed around a strip or wire of a lower amperage rating than the circuit it is designed to protect. When an amperage higher than that stamped on the fuse is present in the circuit, the strip or wire melts, opening the circuit.

GEAR RATIO: The ratio between the number of teeth on meshing gears.

GENERATOR: A device which converts mechanical energy into electrical energy.

HEAT RANGE: The measure of a spark plug's ability to dissipate heat from its firing end. The higher the heat range, the hotter the plug fires. **HUB:** The center part of a wheel or gear.

HYDROCARBON (HC): Any chemical compound made up of hydrogen and carbon. A major pollutant formed by the engine as a byproduct of combustion.

HYDROMETER: An instrument used to measure the specific gravity of a solution.

INCH POUND (in.lb. or sometimes, in. lbs.): One twelfth of a foot pound.

INDUCTION: A means of transferring electrical energy in the form of a magnetic field. Principle used in the ignition coil to increase voltage.

INJECTION PUMP: A device, usually mechanically operated, which meters and delivers fuel under pressure to the fuel injector.

INJECTOR: A device which receives metered fuel under relatively low pressure and is activated to inject the fuel into the engine under relatively high pressure at a predetermined time.

INPUT SHAFT: The shaft to which torque is applied, usually carrying the driving gear or gears.

INTAKE MANIFOLD: A casting of passages or pipes used to conduct air or a fuel/air mixture to the cylinders.

JOURNAL: The bearing surface within which a shaft operates.

KEY: A small block usually fitted in a notch between a shaft and a hub to prevent slippage of the two parts.

MANIFOLD: A casting of passages or set of pipes which connect the cylinders to an inlet or outlet source.

MANIFOLD VACUUM: Low pressure in an engine intake manifold formed just below the throttle plates. Manifold vacuum is highest at idle and drops under acceleration.

MASTER CYLINDER: The primary fluid pressurizing device in a hydraulic system. In automotive use, it is found in brake and hydraulic clutch systems and is pedal activated, either directly or, in a power brake system, through the power booster.

MODULE: Electronic control unit, amplifier or igniter of solid state or integrated design which controls the current flow in the ignition primary circuit based on input from the pickup coil. When the module opens the primary circuit, the high secondary voltage is induced in the coil.

NEEDLE BEARING: A bearing which consists of a number (usually a large number) of long, thin rollers.

OHM:(Ω) The unit used to measure the resistance of conductor to electrical flow. One ohm is the amount of resistance that limits current flow to one ampere in a circuit with one volt of pressure.

OHMMETER: An instrument used for measuring the resistance, in ohms, in an electrical circuit.

OUTPUT SHAFT: The shaft which transmits torque from a device, such as a transmission.

OVERDRIVE: A gear assembly which produces more shaft revolutions than that transmitted to it.

OVERHEAD CAMSHAFT (OHC): An engine configuration in which the camshaft is mounted on top of the cylinder head and operates the valves either directly or by means of rocker arms.

OVERHEAD VALVE (OHV): An engine configuration in which all of the valves are located in the cylinder head and the camshaft is located in the cylinder block. The camshaft operates the valves via lifters and pushrods.

OXIDES OF NITROGEN (NOx): Chemical compounds of nitrogen produced as a byproduct of combustion. They combine with hydrocarbons to produce smog.

OXYGEN SENSOR: Used with the feedback system to sense the presence of oxygen in the exhaust gas and signal the computer which can reference the voltage signal to an air/fuel ratio.

PINION: The smaller of two meshing gears.

PISTON RING: An open ended ring which fits into a groove on the outer diameter of the piston. Its chief function is to form a seal between the piston and cylinder wall. Most automotive pistons have three rings: two for compression sealing; one for oil sealing.

PRELOAD: A predetermined load placed on a bearing during assembly or by adjustment.

PRIMARY CIRCUIT: Is the low voltage side of the ignition system which consists of the ignition switch, ballast resistor or resistance wire, bypass, coil, electronic control unit and pick-up coil as well as the connecting wires and harnesses.

PRESS FIT: The mating of two parts under pressure, due to the inner diameter of one being smaller than the outer diameter of the other, or vice versa; an interference fit.

RACE: The surface on the inner or outer ring of a bearing on which the balls, needles or rollers move.

REGULATOR: A device which maintains the amperage and/or voltage levels of a circuit at predetermined values.

RELAY: A switch which automatically opens and/or closes a circuit.

RESISTANCE: The opposition to the flow of current through a circuit or electrical device, and is measured in ohms. Resistance is equal to the voltage divided by the amperage.

RESISTOR: A device, usually made of wire, which offers a preset amount of resistance in an electrical circuit.

RING GEAR: The name given to a ring-shaped gear attached to a differential case, or affixed to a flywheel or as part a planetary gear set.

ROLLER BEARING: A bearing made up of hardened inner and outer races between which hardened steel rollers move.

ROTOR: 1. The disc-shaped part of a disc brake assembly, upon which the brake pads bear; also called, brake disc.
2. The device mounted atop the distributor shaft, which passes current to the distributor cap tower contacts.

SECONDARY CIRCUIT: The high voltage side of the ignition system, usually above 20,000 volts. The secondary includes the ignition coil, coil wire, distributor cap and rotor, spark plug wires and spark plugs.

SENDING UNIT: A mechanical, electrical, hydraulic or electromagnetic device which transmits information to a gauge.

SENSOR: Any device designed to measure engine operating conditions or ambient pressures and temperatures. Usually electronic in nature and designed to send a voltage signal to an on-board computer, some sensors may operate as a simple on/off switch or they may provide a variable voltage signal (like a potentiometer) as conditions or measured parameters change.

SHIM: Spacers of precise, predetermined thickness used between parts to establish a proper working relationship.

SLAVE CYLINDER: In automotive use, a device in the hydraulic clutch system which is activated by hydraulic force, disengaging the clutch.

SOLENOID: A coil used to produce a magnetic field, the effect of which is to produce work.

SPARK PLUG: A device screwed into the combustion chamber of a spark ignition engine. The basic construction is a conductive core inside of a ceramic insulator, mounted in an outer conductive base. An electrical charge from the spark plug wire travels along the conductive core and jumps a preset air gap to a grounding point or points at the end of the conductive base. The resultant spark ignites the fuel/air mixture in the combustion chamber.

SPLINES: Ridges machined or cast onto the outer diameter of a shaft or inner diameter of a bore to enable parts to mate without rotation.

TACHOMETER: A device used to measure the rotary speed of an engine, shaft, gear, etc., usually in rotations per minute.

THERMOSTAT: A valve, located in the cooling system of an engine, which is closed when cold and opens gradually in response to engine heating, controlling the temperature of the coolant and rate of coolant flow.

TOP DEAD CENTER (TDC): The point at which the piston reaches the top of its travel on the compression stroke.

TORQUE: The twisting force applied to an object.

TORQUE CONVERTER: A turbine used to transmit power from a driving member to a driven member via hydraulic action, providing changes in drive ratio and torque. In automotive use, it links the driveplate at the rear of the engine to the automatic transmission.

TRANSDUCER: A device used to change a force into an electrical signal.

TRANSISTOR: A semi-conductor component which can be actuated by a small voltage to perform an electrical switching function.

TUNE-UP: A regular maintenance function, usually associated with the replacement and adjustment of parts and components in the electrical and fuel systems of a vehicle for the purpose of attaining optimum performance.

TURBOCHARGER: An exhaust driven pump which compresses intake air and forces it into the combustion chambers at higher than atmospheric pressures. The increased air pressure allows more fuel to be burned and results in increased horsepower being produced.

VACUUM ADVANCE: A device which advances the ignition timing in response to increased engine vacuum.

VACUUM GAUGE: An instrument used to measure the presence of vacuum in a chamber.

VALVE: A device which control the pressure, direction of flow or rate of flow of a liquid or gas.

VALVE CLEARANCE: The measured gap between the end of the valve stem and the rocker arm, cam lobe or follower that activates the valve.

VISCOSITY: The rating of a liquid's internal resistance to flow.

VOLTMETER: An instrument used for measuring electrical force in units called volts. Voltmeters are always connected parallel with the circuit being tested.

WHEEL CYLINDER: Found in the automotive drum brake assembly, it is a device, actuated by hydraulic pressure, which, through internal pistons, pushes the brake shoes outward against the drums.

A: Ampere

AC: Alternating current

A/C: Air conditioning

A–h: Amper hour

AT: Automatic transmission

ATDC: After top dead center

μA: Microampere

bbl: Barrel

BDC: Bottom dead center

bhp: Brake horsepower

BTDC: Before top dead center

BTU: British thermal unit

C: Celsius (Centigrade)

CCA: Cold cranking amps

cd: Candela

cm^2: Square centimeter

cm^3, cc: Cubic centimeter

CO: Carbon monoxide

CO_2: Carbon dioxide

cu.in., in^3: Cubic inch

CV: Constant velocity

Cyl.: Cylinder

DC: Direct current

ECM: Electronic control module

EFE: Early fuel evaporation

EFI: Electronic fuel injection

EGR: Exhaust gas recirculation

Exh.: Exhaust

F: Farenheit

F: Farad

pF: Picofarad

μF: Microfarad

FI: Fuel injection

ft.lb., ft. lb., ft. lbs.: foot pound(s)

gal: Gallon

g: Gram

HC: Hydrocarbon

HEI: High energy ignition

HO: High output

hp: Horsepower

Hyd: Hydraulic

Hz: Hertz

ID: Inside diameter

in.lb; in. lbs.; in. lbs.: inch pound(s)

Int: Intake

K: Kelvin

kg: Kilogram

kHz: Kilohertz

km: Kilometer

km/h: Kilometers per hour

kΩ: Kilohm

kPa: Kilopascal

kV: Kilovolt

kW: Kilowatt

l: Liter

l/s: Liters per second

m: Meter

mA: Milliampere

mg: Milligram

mHz: Megahertz

mm: Millimeter

mm^2: Square millimeter

m^3: Cubic meter

MΩ: Megohm

m/s: Meters per second

MT: Manual transmission

mV: Millivolt

μm: Micrometer

N: Newton

N–m: Newton meter

NOx: Nitrous oxide

OD: Outside diameter

OHC: Over head camshaft

OHV: Over head valve

Ω: Ohm

PCV: Positive crankcase ventilation

psi: Pounds per square inch

pts: Pints

qts: Quarts

rpm: Rotations per minute

rps: Rotations per second

R–12: refrigerant gas (Freon)

SAE: Society of Automotive Engineers

SO$_2$: Sulfur dioxide

T: Ton

t: Megagram

TBI: Throttle Body Injection

TPS: Throttle Position Sensor

V: 1. Volt; 2. Venturi

μV: Microvolt

W: Watt

∞: Infinity

<: Less than

>: Greater than

A

Abbreviations and Symbols   389
Air cleaner   10
Air conditioning
  Blower   241
  Charging   29
  Compressor   133
  Condenser   135
  Control panel   245
  Discharging   27
  Evacuating   29
  Evaporator   243
  Gauge sets   26
  General service   22
  Inspection 24
  Operation   25
  Preventive maintenance   29
  Safety precautions   22
  Sight glass check   22
  System capacities   30
  Troubleshooting   28
Air flow meter   214
Alternator
  Alternator precautions   92
  Operation   92
  Removal and installation   93
  Specifications   95
  Troubleshooting   96
Alignment, wheel
  Camber   335
  Caster   335
  Toe   336
Ammeter   236
Antenna   383
Antifreeze   45
Automatic transaxle
  Adjustments   307
  Back-up light switch   307
  Neutral safety switch   307
  Pan removal   307
  Removal and installation   308
Automatic transmission
  Adjustments   305
  Back-up light switch   306
  Filter change   305
  Fluid change   305
  Linkage adjustments   305
  Neutral safety switch   306
  Pan removal   305
  Removal and installation   307
  Troubleshooting   303
Auxiliary oil cooler   54
Axle
  Front   331
  Rear   315

B

Back-up light switch
  Automatic transmission   306
  Manual transmission   267
Ball joints
  Inspection   326
  Removal and installation   326, 328
Battery
  Fluid level and maintenance   16
  Jump starting   55
  Removal and installation   93
Bearings
  Axle   316, 331
  Differential   316
  Driveline   311
  Engine   180, 182
  Wheel   49
Belts   17, 18
Boot (CV-Joint)   297
Brakes
  Bleeding   367
  Brake light switch   364
  Disc brakes (Front)
    Caliper   370
    Operating principals   361
    Pads   368
    Rotor (Disc)   371
  Disc brakes (Rear)
    Caliper   376
    Pads   375
    Rotor (Disc)   377
  Drum brakes
    Drum   372
    Shoes   373
    Wheel cylinder   374
  Fluid level   48
  Hoses and lines   367
  Master cylinder   364
  Parking brake
    Adjustment   378
    Removal and installation   377
  Power booster
    Removal and installation   367
  Proportioning valve   367
  Specifications   379
  Troubleshooting   361
Bulbs   249
Bumpers   382

C

Calipers   370
Camber   335

Camshaft and bearings
  Service   175
  Specifications   110
Camshaft cover   122
Camshaft sprocket   174
Capacities Chart   56
Caster   335
Catalytic converter   189
Charging system   92
Chassis electrical system
  Circuit protection   249
  Heater and air conditioning   241
  Instrument panel   245
  Troubleshooting   262
  Windshield wipers   244
Chassis lubrication   49
Circuit breakers   249
Circuit protection   249
Clutch
  Adjustment   300
  Hydraulic system bleeding   300
  Master cylinder   302
  Operation   298
  Removal and installation   298
  Slave cylinder   302
  Start switch   265, 284
  Troubleshooting   299
Coil (ignition)   85
Combination switch   346
Compression testing   104
Compressor
  Removal and installation   133
Condenser
  Air conditioning   135
Connecting rods and bearings
  Service   176
  Specifications   112
Console   247
Control arm
  Lower   330
  Upper   330
Cooling system   45
Crankcase ventilation valve   191
Crankshaft
  Service   182
  Specifications   112
Cylinder head   139
Cylinders
  Inspection   180
  Reboring   181
  Refinishing   181

D

Differential carrier   320
Disc brakes   369
Distributor
  Removal and installation   87
Door glass   383

Door locks   383
Doors
  Glass   373
  Locks   373
  Removal and installation   371
  Striker plate   371
Door trim panel   383
Drive axle (front)
  Axle shaft and bearing   331
  Fluid recommendations   44
  Front hub and wheel bearings   331
  Removal and installation   331
Drive axle (rear)
  Axle shaft   315
  Axle shaft bearing   316
  Fluid recommendations   44
  Lubricant level   44
  Ratios   315
  Removal and installation   320
  Troubleshooting   310
Driveshaft
  Front   311
  Rear   311
Drive Train   265
Drum brakes   372

E

EGR valve   193
Electrical
  Chassis
    Battery   93
    Bulbs   249
    Circuit breakers   249
    Fuses   251
    Fusible links   250
    Heater and air conditioning   241
    Jump starting   55
    Spark plug wires   62
  Engine
    Alternator   92
    Coil   86
    Distributor   87
    Electronic engine controls   64
    Ignition module   64
    Starter   95
Electronic engine controls   64
Electronic Ignition   64, 85
Emission controls
  Application   194
  Catalytic Converter   193
  Dash pot   193
  Evaporative canister   191
  Exhaust Gas Recirculation
    (EGR) system   193
  Fuel Tank Vapor Control system   191
  Oxygen (O_2) sensor   192
  PCV valve   191
  Service reminder lights   193

Engine
  Application chart 8
  Camshaft 175
  Camshaft cover 122
  Compression testing 104
  Connecting rods and bearings 176
  Crankshaft 182
  Cylinder head 139
  Cylinders 180
  Cylinder sleeves 180
  Electronic controls 64
  Exhaust manifold 129
  Fluids and lubricants 39
  Flywheel 189
  Front (timing) cover 165
  Front seal 176
  Identification 7, 8
  Intake manifold 126
  Main bearings 183
  Oil pan 162
  Oil pump 164
  Overhaul 102
  Piston pin 179
  Pistons 176
  Rear main seal 181
  Removal and installation 106
  Rings 178
  Rocker cover 122
  Rocker shafts 123
  Spark plug wires 62
  Specifications 109
  Thermostat 125
  Tools 2
  Troubleshooting 107
  Turbocharger 130
  Valve guides 160
  Valve seats 161
  Valve springs 161
  Valve stem oil seals 159
  Valve timing 70
  Water pump 136
Evaporative canister 15
Evaporator 243
Exhaust Manifold 129
Exhaust pipe 189
Exhaust system 189
Extension housing seal
  Manual transmission 269

F

Filters
  Air 10
  Fuel 13
  Oil 40
Firing orders 63
Flashers 251
Flexplate 189
Fluids and lubricants

Automatic transmission 43
Battery 48
Chassis greasing 49
Coolant 45
Drive axle 44
Engine oil 39
Fuel 39
Manual transmission 42
Master cylinder
  Brake 48
  Clutch 48
  Power steering pump 48
Flywheel and ring gear 189
Fog lights 249
Front bumper 382
Front suspension
  Ball joints 326
  Description 321
  Knuckles 331
  Lower control arm 330
  Shock absorbers 321
  Spindles 331
  Stabilizer bar 328
  Struts 321
  Troubleshooting 322
  Upper control arm 330
  Wheel alignment 335
Front wheel bearings 331
Fuel gauge 213
Fuel injection
  Cold start valve 218
  Fuel pressure regulator 213
  Fuel pump 211
  Idle speed actuator motor 218
  Injectors 219
  Operation 204
  Relieving fuel system pressure 203
  Throttle body 215
  Throttle position sensor 215
  Troubleshooting 203
Fuel filter 13
Fuel pump 211
Fuel tank 223
Fuses and circuit breakers 251
Fusible links 250

G

Gauges 245
Gearshift linkage
  Adjustment
    Automatic 305
    Manual 265
Glass
  Door 383
  Liftgate 383
  Rear side window 383
  Windshield 383
Glossary 392

H

Halfshaft 295
Hazard flasher 251
Headlights 249
Heater
　Blower 241
　Control panel 243
　Core 243
Hinges 380
Hoisting 35
Hood 331
Hoses
　Brake 367
　Coolant 22
How to Use This Book 1

I

Identification
　Engine 7
　Model 6
　Serial number 6
　Transmission
　　Automatic 9
　　Manual 9
　Vehicle 6
Idle speed and mixture
　adjustment 68
Ignition
　Coil 85
　Electronic 85
　Lock cylinder 348
　Module 64
　Switch 348
　Timing 65
Injectors fuel 219
Instrument cluster 245
Instrument panel
　Cluster 245
　Console 247
　Radio 244
　Speedometer cable 248
Intake manifold 126

J

Jacking points 35
Jump starting 55

K

Knuckles 331
Knuckle oil seal 331

L

Lighting
　Fog/driving lights 249
　Headlights 249
　Signal and marker lights 249
Liftgate 381
Liftgate cylinder 381
Liftgate glass 383
Lower ball joint 326
Lubrication
　Chassis 49

M

MacPherson struts 321
Main bearings 183
Maintenance intervals 57
Manifolds
　Intake 126
　Exhaust 129
Manual transmission
　Linkage adjustment 265
　Overhaul 268
　Removal and installation 267
　Troubleshooting 266
Marker lights 249
Master cylinder
　Brake 364
　Clutch 302
Mechanic's data 393
Mirrors 302
Model identification 6
Module (ignition) 64
Muffler 190
Multi-function switch 346

N

Neutral safety switch 306, 307

O

Oil and fuel recommendations 39
Oil and filter change (engine) 40
Oil level check
　Differential 44
　Engine 39
　Transmission
　　Automatic 43
　　Manual 42
Oil pan 162
Oil pump 164
Oxygen (O_2) sensor 194

P

Parking brake 378
Pilot bearing 300
Piston pin 179
Pistons 176
PCV valve 14
Power brake booster 367
Power seat motor 386
Power steering gear
  Adjustments 353
  Removal and installation 353
  Troubleshooting 349
Power steering pump
  Fluid level 48
  Removal and installation 357
  Troubleshooting 351
Power windows 386
Preventive maintenance charts 57
Printed circuit board 245
Pushing 51

R

Radiator 134
Radiator cap 45
Radio 244
Rear axle
  Axle shaft 315
  Axle shaft bearing 315
  Fluid recommendations 44
  Lubricant level 44
  Operation 315
  Ratios 315
  Removal and installation 320
Rear brakes 375
Rear bumper 382
Rear main oil seal 181
Rear suspension
  Control arms 339
  Shock absorbers 336, 339
  Springs 339
  Sway bar 344
Rear wheel bearings 344
Regulator 93
Rings 176
Rocker arms or shaft 123
Rotor (brake disc) 371
Routine maintenance 10

S

Safety notice 1
Seats 386
Serial number location 6
Shock absorbers 321
Slave cylinder 302
Solenoid 100

Spark plugs 59
Spark plug wires 62
Special tools 2, 189
Specifications Charts
  Alternator and regulator 95
  Brakes 379
  Camshaft 110
  Capacities 56
  Crankshaft and connecting rod 112
  General engine 109
  Piston and ring 113
  Preventive Maintenance 57
  Starter 102
  Torque 111
  Tune-up 60
  Valves 110
  Wheel alignment 336
Speedometer cable 248
Spindles 331
Stabilizer bar 328
Stain removal 388
Starter
  Drive replacement 100
  Overhaul 100
  Removal and installation 95
  Solenoid or relay replacement 100
  Specifications 102
Steering column 352
Steering gear 353
Steering knuckles 331
Steering linkage 353
Steering lock 348
Steering wheel 344
Stripped threads 104
Suspension 321
Switches
  Back-up light 248
  Headlight 248
  Ignition switch 248, 348
  Multi-function switch 346
  Windshield wiper 248

T

Tailgate 381
Tailpipe 190
Thermostat 128
Throttle body 215
Tie rod ends 353
Timing (ignition) 64
Timing belt 165
Timing gear cover 165
Tires
  Description 31
  Rotation 31
  Troubleshooting 32
  Wear problems 34
Tire Size Chart 32

Toe-in 336
Tools 2
Torque specifications 111
Towing 52
Trailer towing 53
Transmission
  Application charts 9
  Automatic 305
  Manual 269
  Routine maintenance 43
Troubleshooting Charts
  Air conditioning 28
  Automatic transmission 303
  Brakes 361
  Charging system 96
  Clutch 299
  Cooling system 109
  Drive belts 20
  Driveshaft 310
  Engine mechanical 107
  Gauges 263
  Heater 264
  Ignition switch 344
  Lights 262
  Lockup torque converter 304
  Manual transmission 266
  Power steering gear 349
  Power steering pump 351
  Rear axle 310
  Starting system 103
  Steering and suspension 322
  Steering column 345
  Tires 32
  Turn signals and flashers 261
  Turn signal switch 347
  Wheels 33
  Windshield wipers 264
Trunk lid 381
Tune-up
  Distributor 87
  Idle speed 68
  Ignition timing 65
  Procedures 59
  Spark plugs and wires 62
  Specifications 60
  Turbocharger 130

Turn signal flasher 251
Turn signal switch 346

U
U-joints 311

V
Vacuum diagrams 195
Valve guides 160
Valve lash adjustment 70
Valve seats 161
Valve service 158
Valve specifications 110
Valve springs 161
Vehicle identification 6
Voltmeter 234

W
Water pump 136
Wheel alignment 336
Wheel bearings
  Front axle 331
  Front wheel 49
  Rear wheel 315
Wheel cylinders 374
Wheels 34
Window glass 383
Window regulator 386
Windshield wipers
  Arm 244
  Blade 30, 244
  Linkage 245
  Motor 245
  Windshield wiper switch 248
Wiring
  Spark plug 62
  Trailer 53
Wiring harnesses 237
Wiring repair 238

CHILTON'S REPAIR MANUAL MODEL INDEX
Car and truck model names are listed in alphabetical and numerical order

Part No.	Model	Repair Manual Title
6980	Accord	Honda 1973-88
7747	Aerostar	Ford Aerostar 1986-90
7165	Alliance	Renault 1975-85
7199	AMX	AMC 1975-86
7163	Aries	Chrysler Front Wheel Drive 1981-88
7041	Arrow	Champ/Arrow/Sapporo 1978-83
7032	Arrow Pick-Ups	D-50/Arrow Pick-Up 1979-81
6637	Aspen	Aspen/Volare 1976-80
6935	Astre	GM Subcompact 1971-80
7750	Astro	Chevrolet Astro/GMC Safari 1985-90
6934	A100, 200, 300	Dodge/Plymouth Vans 1967-88
5807	Barracuda	Barracuda/Challenger 1965-72
6844	Bavaria	BMW 1970-88
5796	Beetle	Volkswagen 1949-71
6837	Beetle	Volkswagen 1970-81
7135	Bel Air	Chevrolet 1968-88
5821	Belvedere	Roadrunner/Satellite/Belvedere/GTX 1968-73
7849	Beretta	Chevrolet Corsica and Beretta 1988
7317	Berlinetta	Camaro 1982-88
7135	Biscayne	Chevrolet 1968-88
6931	Blazer	Blazer/Jimmy 1969-82
7383	Blazer	Chevy S-10 Blazer/GMC S-15 Jimmy 1982-87
7027	Bobcat	Pinto/Bobcat 1971-80
7308	Bonneville	Buick/Olds/Pontiac 1975-87
6982	BRAT	Subaru 1970-88
7042	Brava	Fiat 1969-81
7140	Bronco	Ford Bronco 1966-86
7829	Bronco	Ford Pick-Ups and Bronco 1987-88
7408	Bronco II	Ford Ranger/Bronco II 1983-88
7135	Brookwood	Chevrolet 1968-88
6326	Brougham 1975-75	Valiant/Duster 1968-76
6934	B100, 150, 200, 250, 300, 350	Dodge/Plymouth Vans 1967-88
7197	B210	Datsun 1200/210/Nissan Sentra 1973-88
7659	B1600, 1800, 2000, 2200, 2600	Mazda Trucks 1971-89
6840	Caballero	Chevrolet Mid-Size 1964-88
7657	Calais	Calais, Grand Am, Skylark, Somerset 1985-86
6735	Camaro	Camaro 1967-81
7317	Camaro	Camaro 1982-88
7740	Camry	Toyota Camry 1983-88
6695	Capri, Capri II	Capri 1970-77
6963	Capri	Mustang/Capri/Merkur 1979-88
7135	Caprice	Chevrolet 1968-88
7482	Caravan	Dodge Caravan/Plymouth Voyager 1984-89
7163	Caravelle	Chrysler Front Wheel Drive 1981-88
7036	Carina	Toyota Corolla/Carina/Tercel/Starlet 1970-87
7308	Catalina	Buick/Olds/Pontiac 1975-90
7059	Cavalier	Cavalier, Skyhawk, Cimarron, 2000 1982-88
7309	Celebrity	Celebrity, Century, Ciera, 6000 1982-88
7043	Celica	Toyota Celica/Supra 1971-87
8058	Celica	Toyota Celica/Supra 1986-90
7309	Century FWD	Celebrity, Century, Ciera, 6000 1982-88
7307	Century RWD	Century/Regal 1975-87
5807	Challenger 1965-72	Barracuda/Challenger 1965-72
7037	Challenger 1977-83	Colt/Challenger/Vista/Conquest 1971-88
7041	Champ	Champ/Arrow/Sapporo 1978-83
6486	Charger	Dodge Charger 1967-70
6845	Charger 2.2	Omni/Horizon/Rampage 1978-88
6739	Cherokee 1974-83	Jeep Wagoneer, Commando, Cherokee, Truck 1957-86
7939	Cherokee 1984-89	Jeep Wagoneer, Comanche, Cherokee 1984-89
6840	Chevelle	Chevrolet Mid-Size 1964-88
6836	Chevette	Chevette/T-1000 1976-88
6841	Chevy II	Chevy II/Nova 1962-79
7309	Ciera	Celebrity, Century, Ciera, 6000 1982-88
7059	Cimarron	Cavalier, Skyhawk, Cimarron, 2000 1982-88
7049	Citation	GM X-Body 1980-85
6980	Civic	Honda 1973-88
6817	CJ-2A, 3A, 3B, 5, 6, 7	Jeep 1945-87
8034	CJ-5, 6, 7	Jeep 1971-90
6842	Colony Park	Ford/Mercury/Lincoln 1968-88
7037	Colt	Colt/Challenger/Vista/Conquest 1971-88
6634	Comet	Maverick/Comet 1971-77
7939	Comanche	Jeep Wagoneer, Comanche, Cherokee 1984-89
6739	Commando	Jeep Wagoneer, Commando, Cherokee, Truck 1957-86
6842	Commuter	Ford/Mercury/Lincoln 1968-88
7199	Concord	AMC 1975-86
7037	Conquest	Colt/Challenger/Vista/Conquest 1971-88
6696	Continental 1982-85	Ford/Mercury/Lincoln Mid-Size 1971-85
7814	Continental 1982-87	Thunderbird, Cougar, Continental 1980-87
7830	Continental 1988-89	Taurus/Sable/Continental 1986-89
7583	Cordia	Mitsubishi 1983-89
5795	Corolla 1968-70	Toyota 1966-70
7036	Corolla	Toyota Corolla/Carina/Tercel/Starlet 1970-87
5795	Corona	Toyota 1966-70
7004	Corona	Toyota Corona/Crown/Cressida/Mk.II/Van 1970-87
6962	Corrado	VW Front Wheel Drive 1974-90
7849	Corsica	Chevrolet Corsica and Beretta 1988
6576	Corvette	Corvette 1953-62
6843	Corvette	Corvette 1963-86
6542	Cougar	Mustang/Cougar 1965-73
6696	Cougar	Ford/Mercury/Lincoln Mid-Size 1971-85
7814	Cougar	Thunderbird, Cougar, Continental 1980-87
6842	Country Sedan	Ford/Mercury/Lincoln 1968-88
6842	Country Squire	Ford/Mercury/Lincoln 1968-88
6983	Courier	Ford Courier 1972-82
7004	Cressida	Toyota Corona/Crown/Cressida/Mk.II/Van 1970-87
5795	Crown	Toyota 1966-70
7004	Crown	Toyota Corona/Crown/Cressida/Mk.II/Van 1970-87
6842	Crown Victoria	Ford/Mercury/Lincoln 1968-88
6980	CRX	Honda 1973-88
6842	Custom	Ford/Mercury/Lincoln 1968-88
6326	Custom	Valiant/Duster 1968-76
6842	Custom 500	Ford/Mercury/Lincoln 1968-88
7950	Cutlass FWD	Lumina/Grand Prix/Cutlass/Regal 1988-90
6933	Cutlass RWD	Cutlass 1970-87
7309	Cutlass Ciera	Celebrity, Century, Ciera, 6000 1982-88
6936	C-10, 20, 30	Chevrolet/GMC Pick-Ups & Suburban 1970-87

Chilton's Repair Manuals are available at your local retailer or by mailing a check or money order for **$14.95** per book plus **$3.50** for 1st book and **$.50** for each additional book to cover postage and handling to:

Chilton Book Company
Dept. DM
Radnor, PA 19089

NOTE: When ordering be sure to include your name & address, book part No. & title.

CHILTON'S REPAIR MANUAL MODEL INDEX
Car and truck model names are listed in alphabetical and numerical order

Part No.	Model	Repair Manual Title	Part No.	Model	Repair Manual Title
8055	C-15, 25, 35	Chevrolet/GMC Pick-Ups & Suburban 1988-90	7593	Golf	VW Front Wheel Drive 1974-90
6324	Dart	Dart/Demon 1968-76	7165	Gordini	Renault 1975-85
6962	Dasher	VW Front Wheel Drive 1974-90	6937	Granada	Granada/Monarch 1975-82
5790	Datsun Pickups	Datsun 1961-72	6552	Gran Coupe	Plymouth 1968-76
6816	Datsun Pickups	Datsun Pick-Ups and Pathfinder 1970-89	6552	Gran Fury	Plymouth 1968-76
			6842	Gran Marquis	Ford/Mercury/Lincoln 1968-88
7163	Daytona	Chrysler Front Wheel Drive 1981-88	6552	Gran Sedan	Plymouth 1968-76
6486	Daytona Charger	Dodge Charger 1967-70	6696	Gran Torino 1972-76	Ford/Mercury/Lincoln Mid-Size 1971-85
6324	Demon	Dart/Demon 1968-76			
7462	deVille	Cadillac 1967-89	7346	Grand Am	Pontiac Mid-Size 1974-83
7587	deVille	GM C-Body 1985	7657	Grand Am	Calais, Grand Am, Skylark, Somerset 1985-86
6817	DJ-3B	Jeep 1945-87			
7040	DL	Volvo 1970-88	7346	Grand LeMans	Pontiac Mid-Size 1974-83
6326	Duster	Valiant/Duster 1968-76	7346	Grand Prix	Pontiac Mid-Size 1974-83
7032	D-50	D-50/Arrow Pick-Ups 1979-81	7950	Grand Prix FWD	Lumina/Grand Prix/Cutlass/Regal 1988-90
7459	D100, 150, 200, 250, 300, 350	Dodge/Plymouth Trucks 1967-88	7308	Grand Safari	Buick/Olds/Pontiac 1975-87
			7308	Grand Ville	Buick/Olds/Pontiac 1975-87
7199	Eagle	AMC 1975-86	6739	Grand Wagoneer	Jeep Wagoneer, Commando, Cherokee, Truck 1957-86
7163	E-Class	Chrysler Front Wheel Drive 1981-88			
6840	El Camino	Chevrolet Mid-Size 1964-88	7199	Gremlin	AMC 1975-86
7462	Eldorado	Cadillac 1967-89	6575	GT	Opel 1971-75
7308	Electra	Buick/Olds/Pontiac 1975-90	7593	GTI	VW Front Wheel Drive 1974-90
7587	Electra	GM C-Body 1985	5905	GTO 1968-73	Tempest/GTO/LeMans 1968-73
6696	Elite	Ford/Mercury/Lincoln Mid-Size 1971-85	7346	GTO 1974	Pontiac Mid-Size 1974-83
			5821	GTX	Roadrunner/Satellite/Belvedere/GTX 1968-73
7165	Encore	Renault 1975-85			
7055	Escort	Ford/Mercury Front Wheel Drive 1981-87	5910	GT6	Triumph 1969-73
			6542	G.T.350, 500	Mustang/Cougar 1965-73
7059	Eurosport	Cavalier, Skyhawk, Cimarron, 2000 1982-88	6930	G-10, 20, 30	Chevy/GMC Vans 1967-86
			6930	G-1500, 2500, 3500	Chevy/GMC Vans 1967-86
7760	Excel	Hyundai 1986-90	8040	G-10, 20, 30	Chevy/GMC Vans 1987-90
7163	Executive Sedan	Chrysler Front Wheel Drive 1981-88	8040	G-1500, 2500, 3500	Chevy/GMC Vans 1987-90
7055	EXP	Ford/Mercury Front Wheel Drive 1981-87	5795	Hi-Lux	Toyota 1966-70
			6845	Horizon	Omni/Horizon/Rampage 1978-88
6849	E-100, 150, 200, 250, 300, 350	Ford Vans 1961-88	7199	Hornet	AMC 1975-86
			7135	Impala	Chevrolet 1968-88
6320	Fairlane	Fairlane/Torino 1962-75	7317	IROC-Z	Camaro 1982-88
6965	Fairmont	Fairmont/Zephyr 1978-83	6739	Jeepster	Jeep Wagoneer, Commando, Cherokee, Truck 1957-86
5796	Fastback	Volkswagen 1949-71			
6837	Fastback	Volkswagen 1970-81	7593	Jetta	VW Front Wheel Drive 1974-90
6739	FC-150, 170	Jeep Wagoneer, Commando, Cherokee, Truck 1957-86	6931	Jimmy	Blazer/Jimmy 1969-82
			7383	Jimmy	Chevy S-10 Blazer/GMC S-15 Jimmy 1982-87
6982	FF-1	Subaru 1970-88	6739	J-10, 20	Jeep Wagoneer, Commando, Cherokee, Truck 1957-86
7571	Fiero	Pontiac Fiero 1984-88			
6846	Fiesta	Fiesta 1978-80	6739	J-100, 200, 300	Jeep Wagoneer, Commando, Cherokee, Truck 1957-86
5996	Firebird	Firebird 1967-81			
7345	Firebird	Firebird 1982-90	6575	Kadett	Opel 1971-75
7059	Firenza	Cavalier, Skyhawk, Cimarron, 2000 1982-88	7199	Kammback	AMC 1975-86
			5796	Karmann Ghia	Volkswagen 1949-71
7462	Fleetwood	Cadillac 1967-89	6837	Karmann Ghia	Volkswagen 1970-81
7587	Fleetwood	GM C-Body 1985	7135	Kingswood	Chevrolet 1968-88
7829	F-Super Duty	Ford Pick-Ups and Bronco 1987-88	6931	K-5	Blazer/Jimmy 1969-82
7165	Fuego	Renault 1975-85	6936	K-10, 20, 30	Chevy/GMC Pick-Ups & Suburban 1970-87
6552	Fury	Plymouth 1968-76			
7196	F-10	Datsun/Nissan F-10, 310, Stanza, Pulsar 1976-88	6936	K-1500, 2500, 3500	Chevy/GMC Pick-Ups & Suburban 1970-87
6933	F-85	Cutlass 1970-87	8055	K-10, 20, 30	Chevy/GMC Pick-Ups & Suburban 1988-90
6913	F-100, 150, 200, 250, 300, 350	Ford Pick-Ups 1965-86	8055	K-1500, 2500, 3500	Chevy/GMC Pick-Ups & Suburban 1988-90
7829	F-150, 250, 350	Ford Pick-Ups and Bronco 1987-88			
7583	Galant	Mitsubishi 1983-89	6840	Laguna	Chevrolet Mid-Size 1964-88
6842	Galaxie	Ford/Mercury/Lincoln 1968-88	7041	Lancer	Champ/Arrow/Sapporo 1977-83
7040	GL	Volvo 1970-88	5795	Land Cruiser	Toyota 1966-70
6739	Gladiator	Jeep Wagoneer, Commando, Cherokee, Truck 1962-86	7035	Land Cruiser	Toyota Trucks 1970-88
			7163	Laser	Chrysler Front Wheel Drive 1981-88
6981	GLC	Mazda 1978-89	7163	LeBaron	Chrysler Front Wheel Drive 1981-88
7040	GLE	Volvo 1970-88	7165	LeCar	Renault 1975-85
7040	GLT	Volvo 1970-88			

Chilton's Repair Manuals are available at your local retailer or by mailing a check or money order for **$14.95** per book plus **$3.50** for 1st book and **$.50** for each additional book to cover postage and handling to:

Chilton Book Company
Dept. DM
Radnor, PA 19089

NOTE: When ordering be sure to include your name & address, book part No. & title.

CHILTON'S REPAIR MANUAL MODEL INDEX
Car and truck model names are listed in alphabetical and numerical order

Part No.	Model	Repair Manual Title
5905	LeMans	Tempest/GTO/LeMans 1968-73
7346	LeMans	Pontiac Mid-Size 1974-83
7308	LeSabre	Buick/Olds/Pontiac 1975-87
6842	Lincoln	Ford/Mercury/Lincoln 1968-88
7055	LN-7	Ford/Mercury Front Wheel Drive 1981-87
6842	LTD	Ford/Mercury/Lincoln 1968-88
6696	LTD II	Ford/Mercury/Lincoln Mid-Size 1971-85
7950	Lumina	Lumina/Grand Prix/Cutlass/Regal 1988-90
6815	LUV	Chevrolet LUV 1972-81
6575	Luxus	Opel 1971-75
7055	Lynx	Ford/Mercury Front Wheel Drive 1981-87
6844	L6	BMW 1970-88
6844	L7	BMW 1970-88
6542	Mach I	Mustang/Cougar 1965-73
6812	Mach I Ghia	Mustang II 1974-78
6840	Malibu	Chevrolet Mid-Size 1964-88
6575	Manta	Opel 1971-75
6696	Mark IV, V, VI, VII	Ford/Mercury/Lincoln Mid-Size 1971-85
7814	Mark VII	Thunderbird, Cougar, Continental 1980-87
6842	Marquis	Ford/Mercury/Lincoln 1968-88
6696	Marquis	Ford/Mercury/Lincoln Mid-Size 1971-85
7199	Matador	AMC 1975-86
6634	Maverick	Maverick/Comet 1970-77
6817	Maverick	Jeep 1945-87
7170	Maxima	Nissan 200SX, 240SX, 510, 610, 710, 810, Maxima 1973-88
6842	Mercury	Ford/Mercury/Lincoln 1968-88
6963	Merkur	Mustang/Capri/Merkur 1979-88
6780	MGB, MGB-GT, MGC-GT	MG 1961-81
6780	Midget	MG 1961-81
7583	Mighty Max	Mitsubishi 1983-89
7583	Mirage	Mitsubishi 1983-89
5795	Mk.II 1969-70	Toyota 1966-70
7004	Mk.II 1970-76	Toyota Corona/Crown/Cressida/Mk.II/Van 1970-87
6554	Monaco	Dodge 1968-77
6937	Monarch	Granada/Monarch 1975-82
6840	Monte Carlo	Chevrolet Mid-Size 1964-88
6696	Montego	Ford/Mercury/Lincoln Mid-Size 1971-85
6842	Monterey	Ford/Mercury/Lincoln 1968-88
7583	Montero	Mitsubishi 1983-89
6935	Monza 1975-80	GM Subcompact 1971-80
6981	MPV	Mazda 1978-89
6542	Mustang	Mustang/Cougar 1965-73
6963	Mustang	Mustang/Capri/Merkur 1979-88
6812	Mustang II	Mustang II 1974-78
6981	MX6	Mazda 1978-89
6844	M3, M6	BMW 1970-88
7163	New Yorker	Chrysler Front Wheel Drive 1981-88
6841	Nova	Chevy II/Nova 1962-79
7658	Nova	Chevrolet Nova/GEO Prizm 1985-89
7049	Omega	GM X-Body 1980-85
6845	Omni	Omni/Horizon/Rampage 1978-88
6575	Opel	Opel 1971-75
7199	Pacer	AMC 1975-86
7587	Park Avenue	GM C-Body 1985
6842	Park Lane	Ford/Mercury/Lincoln 1968-88
6962	Passat	VW Front Wheel Drive 1974-90
6816	Pathfinder	Datsun/Nissan Pick-Ups and Pathfinder 1970-89
5790	Patrol	Datsun 1961-72
6934	PB100, 150, 200, 250, 300, 350	Dodge/Plymouth Vans 1967-88
5982	Peugeot	Peugeot 1970-74
7049	Phoenix	GM X-Body 1980-85
7027	Pinto	Pinto/Bobcat 1971-80
6554	Polara	Dodge 1968-77
7583	Precis	Mitsubishi 1983-89
6980	Prelude	Honda 1973-88
7658	Prizm	Chevrolet Nova/GEO Prizm 1985-89
8012	Probe	Ford Probe 1989
7660	Pulsar	Datsun/Nissan F-10, 310, Stanza, Pulsar 1976-88
6529	PV-444	Volvo 1956-69
6529	PV-544	Volvo 1956-69
6529	P-1800	Volvo 1956-69
7593	Quantum	VW Front Wheel Drive 1974-87
7593	Rabbit	VW Front Wheel Drive 1974-87
7593	Rabbit Pickup	VW Front Wheel Drive 1974-87
6575	Rallye	Opel 1971-75
7459	Ramcharger	Dodge/Plymouth Trucks 1967-88
6845	Rampage	Omni/Horizon/Rampage 1978-88
6320	Ranchero	Fairlane/Torino 1962-70
6696	Ranchero	Ford/Mercury/Lincoln Mid-Size 1971-85
6842	Ranch Wagon	Ford/Mercury/Lincoln 1968-88
7338	Ranger Pickup	Ford Ranger/Bronco II 1983-88
7307	Regal RWD	Century/Regal 1975-87
7950	Regal FWD 1988-90	Lumina/Grand Prix/Cutlass/Regal 1988-90
7163	Reliant	Chrysler Front Wheel Drive 1981-88
5821	Roadrunner	Roadrunner/Satellite/Belvedere/GTX 1968-73
7659	Rotary Pick-Up	Mazda Trucks 1971-89
6981	RX-7	Mazda 1978-89
7165	R-12, 15, 17, 18, 18i	Renault 1975-85
7830	Sable	Taurus/Sable/Continental 1986-89
7750	Safari	Chevrolet Astro/GMC Safari 1985-90
7041	Sapporo	Champ/Arrow/Sapporo 1978-83
5821	Satellite	Roadrunner/Satellite/Belvedere/GTX 1968-73
6326	Scamp	Valiant/Duster 1968-76
6845	Scamp	Omni/Horizon/Rampage 1978-88
6962	Scirocco	VW Front Wheel Drive 1974-90
6936	Scottsdale	Chevrolet/GMC Pick-Ups & Suburban 1970-87
8055	Scottsdale	Chevrolet/GMC Pick-Ups & Suburban 1988-90
5912	Scout	International Scout 1967-73
8034	Scrambler	Jeep 1971-90
7197	Sentra	Datsun 1200, 210, Nissan Sentra 1973-88
7462	Seville	Cadillac 1967-89
7163	Shadow	Chrysler Front Wheel Drive 1981-88
6936	Siera	Chevrolet/GMC Pick-Ups & Suburban 1970-87
8055	Siera	Chevrolet/GMC Pick-Ups & Suburban 1988-90
7583	Sigma	Mitsubishi 1983-89
6326	Signet	Valiant/Duster 1968-76
6936	Silverado	Chevrolet/GMC Pick-Ups & Suburban 1970-87
8055	Silverado	Chevrolet/GMC Pick-Ups & Suburban 1988-90
6935	Skyhawk	GM Subcompact 1971-80
7059	Skyhawk	Cavalier, Skyhawk, Cimarron, 2000 1982-88
7049	Skylark	GM X-Body 1980-85

Chilton's Repair Manuals are available at your local retailer or by mailing a check or money order for **$14.95** per book plus **$3.50** for 1st book and **$.50** for each additional book to cover postage and handling to:

Chilton Book Company
Dept. DM
Radnor, PA 19089

NOTE: When ordering be sure to include your name & address, book part No. & title.

CHILTON'S REPAIR MANUAL MODEL INDEX
Car and truck model names are listed in alphabetical and numerical order

Part No.	Model	Repair Manual Title	Part No.	Model	Repair Manual Title
7675	Skylark	Calais, Grand Am, Skylark, Somerset 1985-86	7040	Turbo	Volvo 1970-88
7657	Somerset	Calais, Grand Am, Skylark, Somerset 1985-86	5796	Type 1 Sedan 1949-71	Volkswagen 1949-71
7042	Spider 2000	Fiat 1969-81	6837	Type 1 Sedan 1970-80	Volkswagen 1970-81
7199	Spirit	AMC 1975-86	5796	Type 1 Karmann Ghia 1960-71.	Volkswagen 1949-71
6552	Sport Fury	Plymouth 1968–76	6837	Type 1 Karmann Ghia 1970-74	Volkswagen 1970-81
7165	Sport Wagon	Renault 1975-85	5796	Type 1 Convertible 1964-71	Volkswagen 1949-71
5796	Squareback	Volkswagen 1949-71	6837	Type 1 Convertible 1970-80	Volkswagen 1970-81
6837	Squareback	Volkswagen 1970-81	5796	Type 1 Super Beetle 1971	Volkswagen 1949-71
7196	Stanza	Datsun/Nissan F-10, 310, Stanza, Pulsar 1976-88	6837	Type 1 Super Beetle 1971-75	Volkswagen 1970-81
6935	Starfire	GM Subcompact 1971-80	5796	Type 2 Bus 1953-71	Volkswagen 1949-71
7583	Starion	Mitsubishi 1983-89	6837	Type 2 Bus 1970-80	Volkswagen 1970-81
7036	Starlet	Toyota Corolla/Carina/Tercel/Starlet 1970-87	5796	Type 2 Kombi 1954-71	Volkswagen 1949-71
7059	STE	Cavalier, Skyhawk, Cimarron, 2000 1982-88	6837	Type 2 Kombi 1970-73	Volkswagen 1970-81
5795	Stout	Toyota 1966-70	6837	Type 2 Vanagon 1981	Volkswagen 1970-81
7042	Strada	Fiat 1969-81	5796	Type 3 Fastback & Squareback 1961-71	Volkswagen 1949-71
6552	Suburban	Plymouth 1968-76	7081	Type 3 Fastback & Squareback 1970-73	Volkswagen 1970-70
6936	Suburban	Chevy/GMC Pick-Ups & Suburban 1970-87	5796	Type 4 411 1971	Volkswagen 1949-71
8055	Suburban	Chevy/GMC Pick-Ups & Suburban 1988-90	6837	Type 4 411 1971-72	Volkswagen 1970-81
6935	Sunbird	GM Subcompact 1971-80	5796	Type 4 412 1971	Volkswagen 1949-71
7059	Sunbird	Cavalier, Skyhawk, Cimarron, 2000, 1982-88	6845	Turismo	Omni/Horizon/Rampage 1978-88
7163	Sundance	Chrysler Front Wheel Drive 1981-88	5905	T-37	Tempest/GTO/LeMans 1968-73
7043	Supra	Toyota Celica/Supra 1971-87	6836	T-1000	Chevette/T-1000 1976-88
8058	Supra	Toyota Celica/Supra 1986-90	6935	Vega	GM Subcompact 1971-80
6837	Super Beetle	Volkswagen 1970-81	7346	Ventura	Pontiac Mid-Size 1974-83
7199	SX-4	AMC 1975-86	6696	Versailles	Ford/Mercury/Lincoln Mid-Size 1971-85
7383	S-10 Blazer	Chevy S-10 Blazer/GMC S-15 Jimmy 1982-87	6552	VIP	Plymouth 1968-76
7310	S-10 Pick-Up	Chevy S-10/GMC S-15 Pick-Ups 1982-87	7037	Vista	Colt/Challenger/Vista/Conquest 1971-88
7383	S-15 Jimmy	Chevy S-10 Blazer/GMC S-15 Jimmy 1982-87	6933	Vista Cruiser	Cutlass 1970-87
7310	S-15 Pick-Up	Chevy S-10/GMC S-15 Pick-Ups 1982-87	6637	Volare	Aspen/Volare 1976-80
7830	Taurus	Taurus/Sable/Continental 1986-89	7482	Voyager	Dodge Caravan/Plymouth Voyager 1984-88
6845	TC-3	Omni/Horizon/Rampage 1978-88	6326	V-100	Valiant/Duster 1968-76
5905	Tempest	Tempest/GTO/LeMans 1968-73	6739	Wagoneer 1962-83	Jeep Wagoneer, Commando, Cherokee, Truck 1957-86
7055	Tempo	Ford/Mercury Front Wheel Drive 1981-87	7939	Wagoneer 1984-89	Jeep Wagoneer, Comanche, Cherokee 1984-89
7036	Tercel	Toyota Corolla/Carina/Tercel/Starlet 1970-87	8034	Wrangler	Jeep 1971-90
7081	Thing	Volkswagen 1970-81	7459	W100, 150, 200, 250, 300, 350	Dodge/Plymouth Trucks 1967-88
6696	Thunderbird	Ford/Mercury/Lincoln Mid-Size 1971-85	7459	WM300	Dodge/Plymouth Trucks 1967-88
7814	Thunderbird	Thunderbird, Cougar, Continental 1980-87	6842	XL	Ford/Mercury/Lincoln 1968-88
7055	Topaz	Ford/Mercury Front Wheel Drive 1981-87	6963	XR4Ti	Mustang/Capri/Merkur 1979-88
6320	Torino	Fairlane/Torino 1962-75	6696	XR-7	Ford/Mercury/Lincoln Mid-Size 1971-85
6696	Torino	Ford/Mercury/Lincoln Mid-Size 1971-85	6982	XT Coupe	Subaru 1970-88
7163	Town & Country	Chrysler Front Wheel Drive 1981-88	7042	X1/9	Fiat 1969-81
6842	Town Car	Ford/Mercury/Lincoln 1968-88	6965	Zephyr	Fairmont/Zephyr 1978-83
7135	Townsman	Chevrolet 1968-88	7059	Z-24	Cavalier, Skyhawk, Cimarron, 2000 1982-88
5795	Toyota Pickups	Toyota 1966-70			
7035	Toyota Pickups	Toyota Trucks 1970-88	6735	Z-28	Camaro 1967-81
7004	Toyota Van	Toyota Corona/Crown/Cressida/Mk.II/Van 1970-87	7318	Z-28	Camaro 1982-88
7459	Trail Duster	Dodge/Plymouth Trucks 1967-88	6845	024	Omni/Horizon/Rampage 1978-88
7046	Trans Am	Firebird 1967-81	6844	3.0S, 3.0Si, 3.0CS	BMW 1970-88
7345	Trans Am	Firebird 1982-90	6817	4-63	Jeep 1981-87
7583	Tredia	Mitsubishi 1983-89			

Chilton's Repair Manuals are available at your local retailer or by mailing a check or money order for **$14.95** per book plus **$3.50** for 1st book and **$.50** for each additional book to cover postage and handling to:

Chilton Book Company
Dept. DM
Radnor, PA 19089

NOTE: When ordering be sure to include your name & address, book part No. & title.

CHILTON'S REPAIR MANUAL MODEL INDEX
Car and truck model names are listed in alphabetical and numerical order

Part No.	Model	Repair Manual Title
6817	4 × 4-63	Jeep 1981-87
6817	4-73	Jeep 1981-87
6817	4 × 4-73	Jeep 1981-87
6817	4-75	Jeep 1981-87
7035	4Runner	Toyota Trucks 1970-88
6982	4wd Wagon	Subaru 1970-88
6982	4wd Coupe	Subaru 1970-88
6933	4-4-2 1970-80	Cutlass 1970-87
6817	6-63	Jeep 1981-87
6809	6.9	Mercedes-Benz 1974-84
7308	88	Buick/Olds/Pontiac 1975-90
7308	98	Buick/Olds/Pontiac 1975-90
7587	98 Regency	GM C-Body 1985
5902	100LS, 100GL	Audi 1970-73
6529	122, 122S	Volvo 1956-69
7042	124	Fiat 1969-81
7042	128	Fiat 1969-81
7042	131	Fiat 1969-81
6529	142	Volvo 1956-69
7040	142	Volvo 1970-88
6529	144	Volvo 1956-69
7040	144	Volvo 1970-88
6529	145	Volvo 1956-69
7040	145	Volvo 1970-88
6529	164	Volvo 1956-69
7040	164	Volvo 1970-88
6065	190C	Mercedes-Benz 1959-70
6809	190D	Mercedes-Benz 1974-84
6065	190DC	Mercedes-Benz 1959-70
6809	190E	Mercedes-Benz 1974-84
6065	200, 200D	Mercedes-Benz 1959-70
7170	200SX	Nissan 200SX, 240SX, 510, 610, 710, 810, Maxima 1973-88
7197	210	Datsun 1200, 210, Nissan Sentra 1971-88
6065	220B, 220D, 220Sb, 220SEb	Mercedes-Benz 1959-70
5907	220/8 1968-73	Mercedes-Benz 1968-73
6809	230 1974-78	Mercedes-Benz 1974-84
6065	230S, 230SL	Mercedes-Benz 1959-70
5907	230/8	Mercedes-Benz 1968-73
6809	240D	Mercedes-Benz 1974-84
7170	240SX	Nissan 200SX, 240SX, 510, 610, 710, 810, Maxima 1973-88
6932	240Z	Datsun Z & ZX 1970-87
7040	242, 244, 245	Volvo 1970-88
5907	250C	Mercedes-Benz 1968-73
6065	250S, 250SE, 250SL	Mercedes-Benz 1959-70
5907	250/8	Mercedes-Benz 1968-73
6932	260Z	Datsun Z & ZX 1970-87
7040	262, 264, 265	Volvo 1970-88
5907	280	Mercedes-Benz 1968-73
6809	280	Mercedes-Benz 1974-84
5907	280C	Mercedes-Benz 1968-73
6809	280C, 280CE, 280E	Mercedes-Benz 1974-84
6065	280S, 280SE	Mercedes-Benz 1959-70
5907	280SE, 280S/8, 280SE/8	Mercedes-Benz 1968-73
6809	280SEL, 280SEL/8, 280SL	Mercedes-Benz 1974-84
6932	280Z, 280ZX	Datsun Z & ZX 1970-87
6065	300CD, 300D, 300SD, 300SE	Mercedes-Benz 1959-70
5907	300SEL 3.5, 300SEL 4.5	Mercedes-Benz 1968-73
5907	300SEL 6.3, 300SEL/8	Mercedes-Benz 1968-73
6809	300TD	Mercedes-Benz 1974-84

Part No.	Model	Repair Manual Title
6932	300ZX	Datsun Z & ZX 1970-87
5982	304	Peugeot 1970-74
5790	310	Datsun 1961-72
7196	310	Datsun/Nissan F-10, 310, Stanza, Pulsar 1977-88
5790	311	Datsun 1961-72
6844	318i, 320i	BMW 1970-88
6981	323	Mazda 1978-89
6844	325E, 325ES, 325i, 325iS, 325iX	BMW 1970-88
6809	380SEC, 380SEL, 380SL, 380SLC	Mercedes-Benz 1974-84
5907	350SL	Mercedes-Benz 1968-73
7163	400	Chrysler Front Wheel Drive 1981-88
5790	410	Datsun 1961-72
5790	411	Datsun 1961-72
7081	411, 412	Volkswagen 1970-81
6809	450SE, 450SEL, 450 SEL 6.9	Mercedes-Benz 1974-84
6809	450SL, 450SLC	Mercedes-Benz 1974-84
5907	450SLC	Mercedes-Benz 1968-73
6809	500SEC, 500SEL	Mercedes-Benz 1974-84
5982	504	Peugeot 1970-74
5790	510	Datsun 1961-72
7170	510	Nissan 200SX, 240SX, 510, 610, 710, 810, Maxima 1973-88
6816	520	Datsun/Nissan Pick-Ups and Pathfinder 1970-89
6844	524TD	BMW 1970-88
6844	525i	BMW 1970-88
6844	528e	BMW 1970-88
6844	528i	BMW 1970-88
6844	530i	BMW 1970-88
6844	533i	BMW 1970-88
6844	535i, 535iS	BMW 1970-88
6980	600	Honda 1973-88
7163	600	Chrysler Front Wheel Drive 1981-88
7170	610	Nissan 200SX, 240SX, 510, 610, 710, 810, Maxima 1973-88
6816	620	Datsun/Nissan Pick-Ups and Pathfinder 1970-89
6981	626	Mazda 1978-89
6844	630 CSi	BMW 1970-88
6844	633 CSi	BMW 1970-88
6844	635CSi	BMW 1970-88
7170	710	Nissan 200SX, 240SX, 510, 610, 710, 810, Maxima 1973-88
6816	720	Datsun/Nissan Pick-Ups and Pathfinder 1970-89
6844	733i	BMW 1970-88
6844	735i	BMW 1970-88
7040	760, 760GLE	Volvo 1970-88
7040	780	Volvo 1970-88
6981	808	Mazda 1978-89
7170	810	Nissan 200SX, 240SX, 510, 610, 710, 810, Maxima 1973-88
7042	850	Fiat 1969-81
7572	900, 900 Turbo	SAAB 900 1976-85
7048	924	Porsche 924/928 1976-81
7048	928	Porsche 924/928 1976-81
6981	929	Mazda 1978-89
6836	1000	Chevette/1000 1976-88
6780	1100	MG 1961-81
5790	1200	Datsun 1961-72
7197	1200	Datsun 1200, 210, Nissan Sentra 1973-88
6982	1400GL, 1400DL, 1400GF	Subaru 1970-88
5790	1500	Datsun 1961-72

Chilton's Repair Manuals are available at your local retailer or by mailing a check or money order for **$14.95** per book plus **$3.50** for 1st book and **$.50** for each additional book to cover postage and handling to:

Chilton Book Company
Dept. DM
Radnor, PA 19089

NOTE: When ordering be sure to include your name & address, book part No. & title.

CHILTON'S REPAIR MANUAL MODEL INDEX
Car and truck model names are listed in alphabetical and numerical order

Part No.	Model	Repair Manual Title	Part No.	Model	Repair Manual Title
6844	1500	DMW 1970-88	6844	2000	BMW 1970-88
6936	1500	Chevy/GMC Pick-Ups & Suburban 1970-87	6844	2002, 2002Ti, 2002Tii	BMW 1970-88
8055	1500	Chevy/GMC Pick-Ups & Suburban 1988-90	6936	2500	Chevy/GMC Pick-Ups & Suburban 1970-87
6844	1600	BMW 1970-88	8055	2500	Chevy/GMC Pick-Ups & Suburban 1988-90
5790	1600	Datsun 1961-72	6844	2500	BMW 1970-88
6982	1600DL, 1600GL, 1600GLF	Subaru 1970-88	6844	2800	BMW 1970-88
6844	1600-2	BMW 1970-88	6936	3500	Chevy/GMC Pick-Ups & Suburban 1970-87
6844	1800	BMW 1970-88	8055	3500	Chevy/GMC Pick-Ups & Suburban 1988-90
6982	1800DL, 1800GL, 1800GLF	Subaru 1970-88			
6529	1800, 1800S	Volvo 1956-69	7028	4000	Audi 4000/5000 1978-81
7040	1800E, 1800ES	Volvo 1970-88	7028	5000	Audi 4000/5000 1978-81
5790	2000	Datsun 1961-72	7309	6000	Celebrity, Century, Ciera, 6000 1982-88
7059	2000	Cavalier, Skyhawk, Cimarron, 2000 1982-88			